Contemporary Criminol

This book offers a critical introduction to trends and developments in contemporary criminological theory. Designed both as a companion to *An Introduction to Criminological Theory* – also by Roger Hopkins Burke and published by Routledge – and as a standalone advanced textbook, it develops themes introduced previously in more detail, incorporates new critical and radical concepts and explores cutting-edge advances in theory. Key topics include the following:

- Constitutive, anarchist, green and species, bio-critical, cultural, abolitionist and convict criminologies
- Globalization and organized crime
- Southern theory
- Critical race theory
- Terrorism and state violence
- Gender, feminism and masculinity
- Ultra-realism
- Radical moral communitarianism

These key issues are discussed in the context of debates about the fragmentation of modernity and the postmodern condition; the rise of political populism, risk, surveillance and social control, and speculation about living in post-COVID-19 society and the future of neoliberalism.

Written in a clear and direct style, this book will appeal to both undergraduate and postgraduate students of criminology, sociology and politics and is essential reading for advanced students of criminology looking for a way to engage with contemporary themes and concepts in theory.

Roger Hopkins Burke is Visiting Professor of Criminology at the University of Derby and an independent consultant. He is the author of numerous books and articles in the areas of criminology, criminal justice and social philosophy with vast teaching and research experience.

Contemporary Criminological Theory

Crime and Criminal Behaviour in the Age of Moral Uncertainty

Roger Hopkins Burke

Routledge
Taylor & Francis Group

LONDON AND NEW YORK

First published 2021
by Routledge
2 Park Square, Milton Park, Abingdon, Oxon OX14 4RN

and by Routledge
52 Vanderbilt Avenue, New York, NY 10017

Routledge is an imprint of the Taylor & Francis Group, an informa business

British Library Cataloguing-in-Publication Data
A catalogue record for this book is available from the British Library

Library of Congress Cataloging-in-Publication Data
A catalog record for this book has been requested

ISBN: 978-0-8153-7447-3 (hbk)
ISBN: 978-0-8153-7448-0 (pbk)
ISBN: 978-1-351-24209-7 (ebk)

Typeset in Bembo
by Apex CoVantage, LLC

For all my family. Past, present and future.

Contents

Acknowledgements

I would like to thank everyone who has helped keep me physically and mentally fit during the writing of this book over the past two years. You know who you are and I am very grateful for what you have done. Bless you all.

Chapter 1

Introduction and structure of the book

Key issues

1 Contemporary debates in criminological theory in political and socio-economic context
2 Rise and fall of modern societies and criminological theories conceptualized in that context
3 Response of society and the criminal justice system to crime in the modern era
4 Contradictions and failings of the postmodern world
5 Inadequacies of modernist criminal justice systems in the postmodern condition

Introduction

This book is a companion to *An Introduction to Criminological Theory* which is currently in its fifth edition written by this author and published by Routledge. During the review process for that book, reviewers expressed interest in developing the themes and theories discussed in the final section and agreed with my proposition that these should be located in an expanded discussion of the contemporary socio-political context. This new book does just that.

Contemporary Criminological Theory is thus – as the name suggests – a very current text which both develops those previous themes in more detail and one which introduces new critical and radical themes/theoretical approaches which have arisen in recent years in the context of a fragmented even chaotic socio-political environment in post-industrial societies. In short, this is a critical discussion of the criminological and socio-economic responses to a contemporary social condition which has had a differential but negative impact on the lives of most social groups in society. The outcome has been widespread pessimism and anger indicated in the various and varied recent electoral results to have occurred throughout the liberal democratic Western world and which appear to have in common a rejection of the usual political elites. This book seeks out to show that forms of crime and criminal behaviour plus the nature of the criminal justice response are of necessity very distinctive in different epochs and forms of society.

Crime is a feature of all societies at all times. Nevertheless, certain trends and patterns appear consistently at different times and places. In general, traditional or premodern societies, that is rural and agricultural societies which lack significant economic development, tend to have more violent crime and less property crime than economically developed societies. In traditional societies, violent crimes such as murder, rape and assault may be fairly common and often are accepted and tolerated as an unavoidable part of ordinary, everyday life. As these societies modernize and become economically developed, violent acts become increasingly unacceptable and they also become increasingly rare. At the same time, while valuable property exists in traditional societies, it is generally not very portable – the most valuable property may include such things as land and animals – and thus, there is little property crime. Ownership of valuable, portable goods expands rapidly with economic development, and with that expansion comes a vast increase in the stealing of those goods, along with a vast increase in the ways in which those goods can be stolen (e.g. stealing with a pen rather than with a gun). This is a book about explaining crime and criminality in a contemporary criminogenic neoliberal society.

The structure of the book

The book is divided into three parts. The first tells the story of the rise and fall of modern societies and locates within this narrative a brief résumé of the theories of crime and criminal behaviour which have prevailed during an epoch epitomized largely by political confidence and moral certainty. That story concludes with the fragmentation of modernity, the rise of the postmodern condition and a transition to an era of moral uncertainty.

Chapter 2 considers the rise of modern societies and how these were very different from those which had existed previously. During the relatively unchallenged confident modern years, there were different often competing perspectives and these theories – ideologies and 'isms' – sought to explain in their own terms the nature and purpose of society, how it worked and in whose interest this all occurred. People understood that by following their particular perspective or *grand theory* – whether it be liberal democracy, conservatism, fascism, socialism, communism or other – things would *eventually* get better. All you needed to do was follow and have faith in the sacred texts prescribed by your particular grand theory which was usually supported by some form of research and scholarship which you could claim to be neutral and objective. Social engineering, welfarism and the manipulation and/or even the changing of 'the system' would bring about a better world. People were confident that this would happen. It was just necessary to follow the tenets of the sacred texts and the subsequent action they proposed, and all would be well. This was the age of moral certainty.

Chapter 3 considers how crime was explained and dealt with by the criminal justice system in the undisputable modern age. The theories that came to the fore during that period can be broadly conceptualized in terms of one of three models of crime and criminal behaviour with each becoming incrementally more sophisticated over time. The chapter provides a relatively brief, selective resume of these models and the theories contained within them, but all can be located in an unambiguously modernist context.

First, the rational actor model – with its origins in the late eighteenth-century European Enlightenment – proposes that human beings enjoy free will and can thus freely choose to offend in very much the same way that they can decide to engage in other activities. But choices nevertheless entail responsibilities and inevitably consequences. The recommended solution to the crime problem from this perspective is the introduction of punishments designed with the appropriate level of severity to deter people from committing crime. Crime therefore becomes an unattractive choice of action to the rational actor – in theory at least. Clearly, reality has been rather different.

Second, the predestined actor model denies the possibility of human free will and proposes that human behaviour (including criminality) is determined by forces – either internal or external to the individual – to which they have little or no control. There are three formulations of this positivist model – biological, psychological and sociological – and these were to become the dominant orthodoxy throughout much of the twentieth century.

Third, the victimized actor model proposes that it is the offender who is the victim of an unjust and unequal society. It is the behaviour and activities of the poor and power-less which are targeted and criminalized while those of the rich and powerful are either ignored or not even defined as criminal. The victimized actor model encourages neither punishment nor the treatment of offenders, instead proposing non-criminalization and measures to reduce unequal power relations and improve the life chances of the individual.

The three models are very much part of the modern tradition. Proponents usually believe in what they are doing and acknowledge that by rectifying perceived and proven errors often in response to 'neutral' objective research findings they can revitalize the whole theory or even the broader contextual model. Some researchers and scholars have gone further and sought to show that the integration of theories from different tra-ditions can produce an even stronger explanatory model. Again, these can be easily conceptualized as part of the modernist tradition. They are very much underpinned by a fundamental moral certainty and as such are discussed much more thoroughly in the companion text.

Chapter 4 concludes the first part and discusses the fragmentation of the modernity that has provided the socio-economic foundations underpinning the criminological the-ories discussed in the previous chapter. This fragmentation consists of an ever-increasing succession of economic and political developments that were to increasingly indicate a retreat from the post–Second World War settlement between governments and the people. These agreements were primarily based on the full-employment, subsidized housing, free education and 'cradle to grave' welfare policies which were to provide socio-economic orthodoxy throughout the Western world until at least the mid-1970s. This period – little more than 30 years in total – arguably marks the highpoint of modernism. The world was often (sometimes cruelly) unequal but things were on balance getting better and there was still widespread confidence in the capacity of social democratic institutions and the relevant grand theories to deliver the good life. Eventually. With a little encouragement. At the ballot box or picket line. An age of moral certainty.

Cracks within the modernist project were nevertheless becoming increasingly apparent with the old certainties being questioned right across the political spectrum. For example should groups of workers – such as the powerful National Union of Mineworkers – be able to hold the government and the country to ransom in pursuit of higher pay and bet-ter conditions of employment? Increasingly more and more people asked this and similar questions. With the passing of time, these and other contradictions become ever more apparent with the consequence that modernist societies were becoming increasingly unmanageable during the first two decades of the twenty-first century. They have now reached a virtual crisis point. At the same time, there has been a serious decline in the confidence of the old trusted grand theories to take us to the promised land. The sacred texts have been found increasingly inadequate or simply wrong. Yet, ironically, they have managed to find credibility amongst previously fringe political groups who have actually gained in popularity among whole groups of the previously politically unrepresented.

The second part of this book provides a substantive discussion of crime and criminal behaviour, the response of society, criminal justice professionals, criminologists and other 'moral entrepreneurs' during this era of a fragmented modernity or postmodern condition. The nature of crime and what is considered to be crime is ever changing as society becomes more diverse and the old traditional modernist criminal justice responses increasingly appear to be inadequate and inappropriate.

Chapter 5 thus discusses the morally ambiguous nature of crime and criminal behaviour in what some social scientists have called the postmodern condition. Postmodernism nevertheless provides an extremely negative and nihilistic vision, for, if, as it is proposed, there is no such thing as the 'truth of the human condition', it is clearly difficult to formulate an argument in support of basic human rights or to locate legitimate foundations for law. The relativism implied by postmodernism simply denies the possibility of objective truth and hence of justice in anything other than a purely subjective form, which inevitably consigns us to the prospect of conflict and confusion. The essential problem for the development of legislation and explanations of crime and criminal behaviour in the fragmented modernity or postmodern condition remains the crucial difficulty of making any objective claims for truth, goodness and morality. Postmodernism advocates giving a voice to the oppressed and less powerful – and may celebrate diversity – but it could be argued that, in practice, power relations and political decisions are fundamentally important and may restrict this ideal.

Chapter 6 considers constitutive criminology which is the only well-developed attempt to rethink the central issues and themes of criminology in terms of postmodernism. Proponents have defined crime as the power to deny others and have argued that the conventional crime control strategies, in the form of the fast-expanding criminal justice industry with which we are familiar – the police and prisons, in particular – or as political rhetoric rehearsed in the media, actually fuels the engine of crime.

Chapter 7 considers anarchist criminology, which, in contrast to most modernist intellectual orientations that we encountered in the previous part of this book, seeks not to incorporate reasoned or reasonable critiques of law and legal authority but, in contrast, argues that progressive social change requires the pursuit of the 'unreasonable' and the 'unthinkable'. Thinking outside the traditional modernist correctional box. Anarchist criminology thus advocates the abolition of criminal justice systems and considers the state to be an inherently oppressive entity. Anarchist justice advocates not only social justice (equal access to all resources) but also the protection of diversity and differences among people.

Chapter 8 discusses cultural criminology and its key proposition that the various crime control agencies are simply cultural products which can only be understood in terms of the meanings they carry for those involved. Everyday existences, life histories, music, dance and performance have been used by cultural criminologists to discover how and why it is that certain cultural forms become criminalized and others do not. Jack Katz has written about the 'seductions of crime' in which disorder is itself a 'delight' to be sought and savoured with the causes of crime constructed by the offenders themselves in ways which are compellingly seductive – getting satisfaction from a job well done.

Mike Presdee (2000) has developed this sense of the interrelationship between pleasure and pain with his notion of 'crime as carnival' where the pleasures of playing at the boundaries of illegality are temporarily legitimated at the time of 'carnival'. Think Christmas and the office party. This author takes this proposition further and uses the phrase 'the schizophrenia of crime' to refer to the apparently contradictory contemporary duality of attitude to criminal behaviour whereby there is both a widespread public demand for a rigorous intervention against criminality, while, at the same time, lawbreaking is widespread to the virtual point of universality with most people having committed criminal offences and/or indulged in deviant activities at some point in their life. These issues are developed with the new 'deviant leisure' perspective which discusses activities that – through their adherence to cultural values celebrated by consumer capitalism – have the potential to result in harm. Using the ideological primacy of consumer capitalism as a point of departure, the proponents of this perspective discuss the harm potential that exists beneath the surface of even the most embedded and culturally accepted forms of leisure.

Chapter 9 considers the relationship between crime and the ever-increasing globalization. There is thus reflection on the globalization of a range of criminal activities with the observation that dealing in illicit drugs, illegal trafficking in weapons and human beings, money laundering, corruption and violence, including terrorism and war crimes, are all characteristic developments. The growing influence of global organized crime is seen as a significant rival to legitimate multinational corporations as an economic power, with globalization having greatly facilitated the growth of international terrorism.

Chapter 10 discusses Southern theory which has emerged as an antidote to what scholars from Australasia and parts of the developing world have seen to be the intellectual and explanatory hegemony of the Northern Hemisphere not least in the area of crime and criminal behaviour. The perspective can be loosely defined as a conversation which questions universalism in criminological and social theory. The dominance of Western models is challenged, identifying alternative thinkers and particular issues which have been overlooked in the traditional academy. It is a perspective that has sought to empower thinkers beyond the transatlantic metropolitan centres to focus on experiences specific to their geographical location.

Chapter 11 considers critical race theory which refers to a historical and contemporary body of scholarship that aims to interrogate the discourses, ideologies and social structures which have produced and maintained conditions of racial injustice. Thus, in the post–civil rights era, critical race theorists have exposed and criticized the ways that the myths of US democracy, meritocracy and progress and the ideology of individualism all function to justify changing forms of racial domination. In particular, critical race theorists have analysed new forms of colour-blind racism that enable and conceal the reproduction of racial inequality without direct reference to the social constructions of race. A major trajectory in this analysis of colour-blind racism has been the analysis of the law and legal institutions as crucial sites for the production of colour-blind policies and practices.

Chapter 12 examines the major explanations of 'terrorism', itself an emotive term, which emphasizes the extreme fear caused by apparently indiscriminate violent actions of individuals claiming to be operating on behalf of some particular cause in a complex, fragmented, modern international context. Sometimes terrorist activities are funded by states (state-sponsored terrorism), and the West has been keen to accuse countries such as Libya, Iran, (previously) Iraq and Syria of doing so, yet Western states have also supported terrorism when it has been in their political interests to do so. Most of the major theories which have sought to explain terrorism have been derived from theories of collective violence developed in the field of political science and in a criminological sense can be conceptualized in the context of the rational actor model. It is noted that about a quarter of all terrorist groups – with about half of the most dangerous ones – primarily motivated by religious concerns believing that God demands action. Religious terrorism is nevertheless not about extremism, fanaticism, sects or cults but about a fundamentalist or militant interpretation of the basic tenets of their religion. Martha Crenshaw (1995) has this argued that terrorism is not a pathological phenomenon and proposes that the focus of study should be on why it is that some groups find terrorism useful while other groups do not. Thus, Nassar has argued that the processes of globalization have contributed to dreams, fantasies and rising expectations which leads to dashed hopes, broken dreams and unfulfilled achievements. Terrorism breeds in the gap between expectations and achievements.

Whether terrorist activities can be considered 'just' wars has been widely debated but it does seem that they can be considered perfectly normal activities which make perfect sense to the participants. The events of 11 September 2001 nevertheless – it is argued – marked the end for any positive notion of a postmodern society which can only function successfully if there is a reciprocal acceptance of diverse values from all participant groups. This is clearly not the case. The US-led response to these events, the subsequent 'war on terror' alerts us to the reality that sovereign states have a perceived monopoly on the legitimate use of violence, but this legitimacy is seriously questioned by others, thus the adage that 'one person's terrorist is another person's freedom fighter'.

Chapter 13 considers contemporary issues surrounding gender, feminism and masculinity. Feminists, of course, argue that men are the dominant group in society, and it is thus privileged males who make and enforce the rules to the detriment of women. Feminism is nevertheless not a unitary body of thought, and we start with a discussion of the development of feminism and its different contemporary manifestations in societies permeated with the postmodern condition. There follows an examination of the notion of masculinity where feminism has encouraged a small but growing group of male writers to take the issue seriously and where it is recognized that men have differences and are thus not a generic group. This is followed by a discussion of queer criminology and the contradictions that have occurred in this perspective recently, not least the sometimes-rancorous debate between radical feminism and the transgender community. The chapter concludes with reflections on the notion of patriarchy in fragmented modernity, considering contemporary debates on misogyny and misandry in terms of postmodern power relations.

Chapter 14 considers the contemporary ecological issues addressed by green and species criminology. The former is the analysis of environmental harms from a criminological perspective, or the application of criminological theory to environmental issues. It is a perspective which requires us to think about offences (what crimes or harms are inflicted on the environment, and how), offenders (who commits crime against the environment, and why) and victims (who suffers as a result of environmental damage, and how) but, at the same time, about responses to environmental crimes: policing, punishment and crime prevention. On a more theoretical level, green criminology is interested in the social, economic and political conditions which have led to environmental crimes. On a philosophical level, it is concerned with what types of harms should be considered 'crimes' and therefore come within the remit of a green criminology.

Species criminology is a non-human or biocentric discourse which emphasizes the importance of non-human rights. Thus, human beings are not the only creatures with rights, nor are humans superior to other beings. In other words, there is no hierarchy of existence with human beings at the pinnacle. All living things share an equal status of importance and to prohibit or disregard non-human creatures as not of equal standing within the natural environment denies the value and worth of those species. On the other hand, it may be argued that existence or survival (and indeed evolution itself) is dependent upon one species consuming another. An analysis from this perspective aids a critique of how rights are constructed. Thus, if rights are about ensuring health and well-being while minimizing pain and suffering, then humans are not the only species to experience such emotions.

Chapter 15 introduces debates critical of the new biosocial criminology which is itself presented as an 'integrated' and 'modern' approach which attempts to synthesize the sciences of life, of the psyche and of the social. In the eyes of its proponents, this biosocial approach is revolutionizing criminology; it is a total paradigm shift rather arrogantly assumed to be unavoidable, while the social sciences in general are blamed for impeding the speed and magnitude of the revolution by discounting the bios for ideological reasons. Biocritical criminologists respond by arguing that biosocial criminology represents a 'Ptolemization' or fortifying of the Lombrosian paradigm rather than a 'Copernican' revolutionizing of criminology.

Chapter 16 considers contemporary proposals to abolish the prison – that great punishment institution of modernism – and considers convict criminology or voices from the consumers of modernist criminal justice. The prison abolition movement is a loose network of groups and activists which seek to reduce or eliminate prisons and the prison system and replace them with systems of rehabilitation that do not place a focus on punishment and government institutionalization. Convict criminology is a relatively new and controversial perspective which provides an alternative view to the way crime and criminal justice problems are usually seen by researchers, policymakers and politicians. Many of whom have had minimal contact with jails, prisons and convicts.

The first part of the book told the story of the rise and fall of modern societies: an era of self-confidence and moral certainty which was to become subverted over time by doubt, fragmentation and the postmodern condition and where we were to enter a period of moral uncertainty. There was thus a constant decline in confidence in the potential of the old certainties to deliver the good life. This was the fragmentation of modernity or the postmodern condition. The third part of the book considers the contradictions and failings of a postmodern world and its foundations in moral ambiguity and the impossibility of objective truth – multiple truths and a post-truth society – and discusses the possibilities and problematics of rebuilding a revitalized modernity and a new moral certainty, one where ultimately involvement in crime and criminal behaviour makes less sense to increasingly more people but at the same as more activities are criminalized and definitions of criminality seemingly forever widen.

Chapter 17 considers the rise of political populism which has been underpinned greatly by the contradictions and failings of neoliberalism, the dominant worldwide economic and political perspective since the late 1970s. The term *philosophy* would appear to be an inappropriate nomenclature for a series of disparate strategies, with many denying any connection between them and this is certainly avoided here. This denial is certainly the case in the US, where ironically there is also widespread repudiation of the existence of the postmodern condition. This is ironic because in no other nation on earth is both the postmodern condition and neoliberalism and its contradictions more apparent. Challenges from across the political spectrum, the enfranchisement of the previously unenfranchised, support for a range of previously barely supported fringe individuals, groups and political entities have further threatened stability and has brought about a period of political confusion throughout the post-industrial Western world.

Chapter 18 discusses the notion that in a complex post-industrial world permeated with inherent risk and problematic disenfranchised 'risky' groups with at best a vague commitment to society and considered by some to be in desperate need of some form of social control. Central to such strategies has been the increasing use of surveillance techniques which have become a pervasive part of our lives (Hopkins Burke, 2004a).

Surveillance societies are those which function, in part, because of the extensive collection, recording, storage, analysis and application of information collated on individuals and groups throughout society. Surveillance enables corporations and governments to manage or govern resources, activities and populations. The example cited here is one relevant to academics and their students: that of the changes instigated by neoliberalism in – what has become – the higher education industry.

It is observed that the societal relevance of the universities previously demanded by critical students has been turned on its head in neoliberal society to become economically relevant to business and industry. The development of new public management and the rise of pro-entrepreneurial government has sought to reform the public sector by implementing serious cuts in public spending and by the introduction of private sector management techniques and strategies. The withdrawal of trust, via processes instigated by the government, has forced universities to create bureaucratic machinery and formulas to steer and manage the institutions from outside the system.

Chris Lorenz (2012) observes that new public managerialism is remarkably reminiscent of state communism. Both are totalitarian because it leaves no institutionalized room for criticism which is always seen as subversive. It is an organizational discourse which promotes and legitimizes the takeover of power by managers in public organizations that were previously run by professionals in accordance with their standards. In the now-orthodox economic view students do not pay to be taught a discipline by professionals who have proven expertise and subject knowledge but for the end product of education: a degree or other qualification, the investment of which will bring them profits in the labour market.

Chapter 19 discusses the revitalizing criminology agenda presented by Steve Hall and Simon Winlow (2018) where they argue that the mistakes, weaknesses and cul-de-sacs of traditional liberal criminology are to be resolved in a new paradigm of *ultra-realism* which draws heavily on the work of significant contemporary critical realist social theorists, where it is argued that the context of criminological reality is provided by a global capitalism and neoliberalism which is in a condition of permanent intensifying crisis and insecurity. The scholars fundamentally follow the philosopher Slavoj Žižek, whose work is infamously idiosyncratic and features striking reversals of received common sense while challenging many of the crucial assumptions of the contemporary left-liberal academy, including the elevation of difference or otherness to ends in themselves, the reading of the Western Enlightenment as implicitly totalitarian and the pervasive scepticism towards any context-transcendent notions of truth or the good which have underpinned postmodern thought. It is proposed that only radical social change will overcome the confusions of contemporary politics and the failings of the liberal left. Ripping it all up and starting again – revolution – is the only way that the weaknesses and contradictions of the previous liberal modern state and the contemporary state of confusion can be overcome.

Wood *et al.* (2020) nevertheless articulate a series of reservations about ultra-realist crime causation theory whereby they (1) question the ability of the breakdown of the pseudo-pacification process to account for gender-related disparities in criminal behaviour; (2) critically consider the explanation of violence offered by ultra-realism through reference to drives, libidinal energy and sublimation; and (3) outline reservations about special liberty with regard to its explanation of crime as an expression of capitalist values.

Chapter 20 discusses the political philosophy of radical moral communitarianism, devised by this author, which, while accepting much of the revitalizing modernity agenda proposed by ultra-realism – certainly the determining context of the economy – is nevertheless concerned at the failings of most previous attempts at radical social change, via revolution and the invariably subsequent disastrous one-party political state. It thus provides an alternative political agenda which can be conceptualized in the context of liberal democratic politics. It takes as its starting point the work of Emile Durkheim (1933, originally 1893) and his observations on the moral component of the division of labour in society, and it is proposed that this perspective provides the theoretical foundations of a 'new' social democratic egalitarianism: a radical moral communitarianism which actively promotes the rights and responsibilities of both individuals and communities in the context of an equal division of labour. The latter is a highly significant element which deviates significantly from the orthodox version of communitarianism promoted in the US since the 1980s and which was to be embraced but distorted in the UK by New Labour, with its enthusiasm for a strong dictatorial central state apparatus with which to enforce its agenda. Radical moral communitarianism proposes the introduction of policies which promote a fine balance between the rights and responsibilities of individuals and the communities in which they live.

Chapter 21 concludes the book by providing a summary of the story so far as outlined and discussed and then considers and speculates on the possibilities for a future world changed beyond all comprehension by the COVID-19 pandemic which was to push the state and public sector into the foreground. We now found that the experts were back in fashion. Every pandemic generates conspiracy theories. Thus, the coronavirus has been seen as a bioweapon created by China or Big Pharma or American scientists, or it is caused by 5G technology, or it does not exist, just a 'hoax' made up by the enemies of Donald Trump. The key issue in challenging these potentially dangerous conspiracy theories would seem to be communicating with target groups in non-patronizing language.

Suppressing the virus was to necessitate an unprecedented economic shutdown but one which could only be temporary, but when the economy was to restart, there was likely to be a world different previously, one where governments would act to curb the global market. There is a recognition that economic expansion is not indefinitely sustainable. It can only worsen climate change and turn the planet into a garbage dump. But with highly uneven living standards, still rising human numbers and intensifying geopolitical rivalries, zero growth is also unsustainable. This is possibly the greatest conundrum facing post-pandemic society. But will there be such a society?

The notion persists that pandemics are blips rather than an integral part of history. There is a belief that humans are no longer part of the natural world and can create an autonomous ecosystem, separate from the rest of the biosphere. We are superior beings and can control the world in our interests. COVID-19 is telling us we cannot. Technology will help us adapt in our present extremity. Physical mobility can be reduced by shifting many of our activities into cyberspace. Offices, schools, universities, general practitioner surgeries and other work centres are most likely to change permanently. So, what about crime possibilities in this new world order? Well, at the time of significant economic recession when legitimate jobs become few and far between, you can usually rely on the illegitimate market to provide new crime opportunities. The pandemic COVID-19 has to date provided crime opportunities in the EU in the areas of cybercrime, fraud, counterfeit and substandard goods, organized and property crime.

In May 2020, the leading free-market thinktanks, which had backed the tax-cutting and privatization agenda of Margaret Thatcher – thus helping to introduce neoliberalism to the world – were to lend their support to the plans of the Conservative government for unprecedented and sustained increases in public spending. With COVID-19 – as in 2008 – politicians were forced to implement policies which seemed to contradict their adherence to market supremacy, but it could be argued that it would again be the intention to do so to swiftly return to 'normal' and wean the public off their 'addiction' to state support.

Summary of main points

1   This book is a companion to An *Introduction to Criminological Theory* which introduces new critical and radical themes and locates them in a political and a socio-economic context.
2   Forms of crime and criminal behaviour, plus the nature of the criminal justice response, are of necessity very distinctive in different epochs.
3   The first part tells the story of the rise and fall of modern societies and locates within this narrative a brief résumé of the theories of crime and criminal behaviour which dominated that era.
4   Modernity was an age of confidence and moral certainty.
5   Three different competing models of crime and criminal behaviour can be identified during that period with each becoming incrementally more sophisticated over the years.
6   Later modern theorists have sought to show that the integration of theories from different traditions can produce an even stronger explanatory model.
7   Cracks within the modernist project became increasingly apparent with the old moral certainties being questioned right across the political spectrum.
8   The second part provides a substantive discussion of crime, the response of the criminal justice system and 'moral entrepreneurs' during this era of moral uncertainty, fragmented modernity or the postmodern condition.
9   The nature of crime and what is considered to be crime is ever changing as society becomes more diverse and the old traditional modernist criminal justice responses increasingly appear inadequate and inappropriate.
10 The third part considers the contradictions and failings of a world permeated by the postmodern condition and its foundations in moral ambiguity and discusses the possibilities and problematics of rebuilding a revitalized modernity and new moral certainty.

Discussion questions

1   Why do you think that forms of crime and societal response are different in distinctive epochs?
2   How would you describe moral certainty and uncertainty?

3   What is fragmented modernity and give examples.
4   Why do you think the old methods of responding to and dealing with crime have become problematic during the contemporary era?
5   How would you explain moral ambiguity?

Further reading

Hopkins Burke (2018) provides a comprehensive introduction to 'traditional' modernist criminological theory, including some very contemporary theories not deemed appropriate for this text.

References

Crenshaw, M. (ed.) (1995) *Terrorism in Context*. University Park, PA: Pennsylvania State University Press.
Durkheim, E. (1933, originally 1893) *The Division of Labour in Society*. Glencoe, IL: Free Press.
Hall, S. and Winlow, S. (2018) 'Ultra Realism', in *Routledge Handbook of Critical Criminology*. London: Routledge.
Hopkins Burke, R.D. (ed.) (2004a) *'Hard Cop/Soft Cop': Dilemmas and Debates in Contemporary Policing*. Cullompton: Willan Publishing.
Hopkins Burke, R.D. (2018) *An Introduction to Criminological Theory Fifth Edition*. Abingdon: Routledge.
Lorenz, C. (2012) 'If You're So Smart, Why Are You under Surveillance? Universities, Neoliberalism, and New Public Management', *Critical Enquiry*, 38(3): 599–629.
Presdee, M. (2000) *Cultural Criminology and the Carnival of Crime*. London: Routledge.
Wood, M.A., Anderson, B. and Richards, I. (2020) 'Breaking Down the Pseudo-Pacification Process: Eight Critiques of Ultra-Realist Crime Causation Theory', *The British Journal of Criminology*, 60(3): 642–61.

Part I

From the modern to the postmodern condition

Chapter 2

The rise and triumph of the modern

Key issues

1   Three philosophical epochs
2   From the premodern to the modern
3   Crime and policing: from the premodern to the modern
4   The fragmentation of modernity
5   Policing the fragmentation of modernity

This chapter considers the rise of modern societies and how these were very different from those which had existed in the premodern era or epoch. During the relatively unchallenged confident modern years, there were to be different often competing perspectives and these theories – ideologies and 'isms' – sought to explain in their own terms the nature and purpose of society, how it worked and in whose interest this all occurred. People understood that by following their particular perspective or *grand theory* – whether it be liberal democracy, conservatism, fascism, socialism communism or others – things would *eventually* get better. All you needed to do was follow and have faith in the sacred texts prescribed by your particular grand theory, while these tended to be supported by some form of research and scholarship which you could claim to be neutral and objective. Social engineering, welfarism and the manipulation and/or even the changing of 'the system' would bring about a better world. People were confident that this would happen. It was just necessary to follow the tenets of the sacred texts and the subsequent action they proposed, and all would be well. This was the age of moral certainty.

Three philosophical epochs

Modernism has its most notable origins in the sixteenth century which was a period of vigorous economic expansion and this was to play a major, indeed crucial, role in the many other transformations – social, political and cultural – that occurred during the early modern age. Understanding the three major philosophical epochs discussed in this book – premodernism, modernism and postmodernism (or the preferred postmodern condition) – requires us to understand how these terms are used. Thus, each of these can be considered as periods of time and as philosophical systems. When discussing them as philosophies, it is probably best to view them as 'isms' in the sense that within each epoch there were many different invariably competing approaches or (some of them *grand*) theories.

Philosophical epochs are time periods defined by the dominant explanatory or theoretical orthodoxy of the time. Thus, from the beginnings of history until the mid-seventeenth century, the dominant way of viewing the world was largely consistent with the premodern philosophical system. This is not to say there were not ideas in existence that we would now consider to be modern or even postmodern, but premodernism was the dominant world view. Then from around the middle of the seventeenth-century premodernism began to lose its authority and came to be replaced by the modern era, and this was to become the dominant and virtually unquestioned philosophical system in Western culture. The 1950s are considered to be the time when the transition from modernism to postmodernism evidenced by the increasing fragmentation of modernity started to become apparent. But in many ways, modernism remains dominant within much of Western culture, although the cracks in that edifice are increasingly showing, and that process is clearly accelerating.

Premodernism, modernism and postmodernism are three very different ways of looking at the world, but the differences between these philosophies should not be reduced simply to matters of epistemology or ways of knowing. There are many differences between the philosophical epochs we will encounter throughout this book, but it is important to remember that each of these major 'isms' has many different philosophical approaches or theories which can be categorized within them. There is thus no unified premodern, modern or postmodernism philosophical systems.

The primary epistemology of the premodern period was based on the notion of revealed knowledge from authoritative sources. It was thus believed that *ultimate truth* could be known and the way to access this knowledge is through direct revelation which was generally assumed to come from God or a god. Those in the Christian Church were the holders and interpreters of revealed knowledge in Europe and the primary authoritative source in premodern times.

Two new approaches to knowing were to become dominant during the later modern period. The first epistemology was empiricism (knowing through the senses) which gradually evolved into scientific empiricism or modern science with the development of modernist methodology. The second was reason or logic which was often used in collaboration or conjunction with science. With a significant shift in the possession of power during the modern era, there was inevitably a change in the accepted sources of authority, by way of a transference from the church towards politics, governments and universities, although a religious perspective was invariably integrated into these modern authority sources. The church nevertheless no longer enjoyed the privileged power position.

Postmodernism – or the postmodern condition – brought with it a fundamental questioning of the previous approaches to knowing. Thus, instead of relying on one dominant approach we now encounter the encouragement of epistemological pluralism, which utilizes multiple ways of knowing. These can include the premodern ways (revelation) and modern ways (science and reason), along with many other ways of knowing such as intuition, relational and spiritual. Postmodern approaches seek to deconstruct previous authority sources and power and because it is distrusted, they attempt to establish less hierarchical approaches in which authority sources are more diffuse.

From the premodern to the modern

By 1500, the population in most areas of Europe was increasing after two centuries of decline or stagnation. The bonds of commerce within Europe now tightened, and the 'wheels of commerce' (in the phrase of the twentieth-century French historian Fernand Braudel) spun ever faster. The great geographic discoveries then in process were integrating Europe into a world economic system. New commodities, many of them imported from recently discovered lands, enriched material life. Not only trade but also the production of goods increased as a result of new ways of organizing production. Merchants, entrepreneurs and bankers accumulated and manipulated capital in an unprecedented volume. Most historians locate in the sixteenth century the beginning – or at least the maturation of Western capitalism. Capital now came to assume a pivotal role not only in economic organization but also in political life and international relations. Culturally, new values – many of them associated with the Renaissance and Reformation – were disseminated throughout Europe and were to crucially change the ways in which people acted and the perspectives or theories by which they viewed themselves and the world.

The world of early capitalism was nonetheless neither stable nor uniformly prosperous. Financial crashes were common: thus, for example, the Spanish crown, the biggest borrower in Europe, suffered repeated bankruptcies (in 1557, 1575–77, 1596, 1607, 1627, and 1647). The poor and destitute in society became, if not more numerous at least more visible. Even as capitalism advanced in the West, the once-free peasants of central and eastern Europe slipped into serfdom. The apparent prosperity of the sixteenth century was, moreover, to give way in the middle and late periods of the seventeenth century to a 'general crisis' in many European regions. Politically, the new centralized states insisted on new levels of cultural conformity on the part of their subjects, with several expelling Jews and almost all of them refusing to tolerate religious dissent. Culturally, in spite of the revival of ancient learning and the reform of the churches, a hysterical fear of witches grasped large segments of the population, even among the educated.

The rise of modern society

The idea of the modern thus originated as a description of the forms of thought and action that had begun to emerge with the decline of the medieval societies in Western Europe which had provided the foundations of the late premodern. The authority of the old aristocracies was being seriously questioned, both because of their claims to natural superiority and their corrupt political practices. A new and increasingly powerful middle class (or bourgeoisie) was emerging and benefitting from the profits of trade, industry and agricultural rationalization in early capitalist society. In the interests of the latter, the enclosure movement dispossessed many of the rural poor from access to common lands and smallholding tenancies, which had been theirs by customary right, thus causing great hardship to those involved yet, at the same time, producing a convenient readily available pool of cheap labour to satisfy the demands of the Industrial Revolution. The aggregate outcome of these fundamental social changes was that societies were becoming increasingly industrialized and urbanized, causing previous standard forms of human relationships based on familiarity, reputation and localism to give way to more fluid, often anonymous interactions, which significantly posed problems for existing forms of social control.

The notion of the modern essentially involved a secular rational tradition with the following origins. First, there was the emergence of humanist ideas and Protestantism in the sixteenth century. Previously, the common people had been encouraged by the established church to unquestioningly accept their position in life and look for salvation in the afterlife. It was with the rise of the 'Protestant ethic' that people came to expect success in return for hard work in *this* world. At the same time, assumptions about the natural superiority – or the divine right – of the powerful aristocracy came to be questioned. Second, there was the scientific revolution of the seventeenth century when our understanding of the world around us was first explained by reference to natural laws. Third, the eighteenth-century philosophical Enlightenment proposed that the social world could similarly be explained and regulated by natural laws and political systems should be developed which embraced new ideas of individual rationality and free will. Indeed, inspired by such ideas and responding to dramatically changing economic and political circumstances, revolutions occurred in the American colonies and in France. These were widely influential and ideas concerning human rights were championed in many European countries by the emergent bourgeoisie, merchant, professional and middle classes. Subsequently, there were significant changes in the nature of systems of government, administration and law. Fourth, the increasingly evident power of industrial society and the prestige afforded to scientific explanation in the nineteenth and twentieth centuries seemed to confirm the superiority of the modernist intellectual tradition over all others (Harvey, 1989).

The principal features that characterize the idea of modern society can be identified in three main areas. First, in the area of economics, there was the development of a market economy involving the growth of production for profit, rather than immediate local use, the development of industrial technology with a considerable extension of the division of labour, while wage labour became the principal form of employment. Second, in the area of politics, there was the growth and consolidation of the centralized nation state and the extension of bureaucratic forms of administration, systematic forms of surveillance and control and the development of representative democracy and political party systems. Third, in the area of culture, there was a challenge to tradition in the name of rationality with the emphasis on scientific and technical knowledge.

Prior to the modern age, crime and criminal behaviour in Europe was mainly explained for over a thousand years by spiritualist notions (Vold *et al.*, 1998). The influential theologian St Thomas Aquinas (1225–74) had argued that there is a God-given 'natural law' revealed by observing – through the eyes of faith – the natural tendency of people to do good rather than evil. Those who violate the criminal law are therefore not only criminals but also 'sinners', and thus, crime harms not only victims but also the offender because it damages their essential 'humanness' or natural tendency to do good (Bernard, 1983). Central to spiritualist thought was demonology, where it was proposed that criminals were possessed by demons which forced them to do wicked things beyond their control. These days, criminal activity is not usually attributed to the influence of devils from hell – well, at least not by criminologists and criminal justice system practitioners – but the logic underlying this idea that criminals are driven by forces beyond their control is still with us. What can arguably be regarded as a modified variant of this form of thought – but where the explanatory power of spirituality has been replaced by science.

Premodern European legal systems were founded on spiritualist explanations of crime, and what little written law that did exist was applied through judicial interpretation and caprice and, in the main, utilized against those who were not of the aristocracy. In a world where human beings were believed to be born in the image of God, criminality was clearly a sin, a retreat from godliness, contamination. The criminal who had no free will or choice in the matter consequently had to be unequivocally possessed by demons, and this appreciation gave the state the moral authority to use horrible tortures and punishments. Those accused of crime often faced secret accusations, torture and closed trials, with arbitrary and harsh sanctions applied to the convicted. The emphasis of punishment was thus on the physical body of the accused, for the bulk of the population possessed little else on which the power to punish could be usefully exercised (Foucault, 1977).

Little use was made of imprisonment as a punishment in the premodern era. Prisons were most commonly places for holding suspects and offenders prior to trial or punishment. It would appear that those who framed and administrated the law enacted and exercised the criminal codes on the premise that it was only the threat of savage and cruel punishments, delivered in public and with theatrical emphasis, that would deter the dangerous materially dispossessed classes who constituted 'the mob'.

The administration of criminal justice in the premodern era was chaotic, predominantly non-codified, irrational and irregular and at the whim of individual judgement. It was the emergence and establishment of the modern era and the subsequent new ways of seeing and responding to the world which provided the preconditions for a major break in the way in which crime and criminal behaviour was both conceptualized and came to be dealt with. Explanations of crime and criminality during the modern era is the focus of the following chapter. We here consider the societal response to crime.

Crime and policing: from the premodern to the modern

All modern societies use some form of state-sponsored professionalized police force to control crime and to contribute to public order. This is an essential element of modern societies which disconnects them from the premodern and in which we can identify three essential components of a legitimate police force. First, it is subject to the rule of law which embodies values respectful of human dignity, rather than the wishes of a powerful leader or political party. Second, it can intervene in the life of citizens only under limited and carefully controlled circumstances. Third, it is accountable to the public for its actions.

The meaning of the word *police* has changed considerably from its origins in premodern society and the term *polity* which means the form of government of a political body. Thus, in the fifteenth century, policing was done intermittently by the military with society largely 'un-policed' accept at a very local community level. It was with the formation of modern states with clear national borders, beginning in the eighteenth century, that the term *police* began to refer to the specific functions of crime prevention and order maintenance. It was then only a small step to identify the word *police* with the *personnel* (Johnson, 1992). With the expansion of the law over the next several centuries, policing also came to be increasingly concerned with the prevention of public dangers such as crime and disorder and the prevention, or redress of breaches of law. The police also themselves came to be more controlled by the law (Lane, 1967; Critchley, 1972; Fogelson, 1977).

Crowther (2007) observes that the emergence of the modern professional police service in England in the early nineteenth century can only be understood with reference to the system in place before that time. Moreover, it should be noted that early government institutions and the philosophies on which they are founded throughout the 'new world' (including the US and Australasia) invariably have their roots in Britain and this is particularly the case with law enforcement. Thus, this premodern history is for many in modern societies worldwide a shared history.

A rather simplistic account suggests that before the Industrial Revolution – that occurred in Britain approximately between 1750 and 1830 – society was predominantly constituted of relatively small rural homogeneous communities which were largely self-policing. The fourteenth-century system of policing based on justices of the peace, constables and the watch – which placed an onus on all citizens to assist constables and help maintain the peace – had remained in place for 500 years. But from the mid-eighteenth century, the series of fundamental changes that were to occur in society – and from which emerged the beginnings of the modern era – was to lead to the eventual breakdown of the traditional system of policing which had served society well.

The effectiveness of the premodern policing system was based and dependent on the existence of stable, homogeneous and largely rural communities characterized by high levels of mechanical solidarity (Durkheim, 1933, originally 1893), whereby people knew one another by name, sight and/or reputation. During the eighteenth century, such communities began to break down in the face of the rapid transition to an industrial urban economy, based increasingly on organic solidarity, whereby there is a more developed division of labour, less reliance on maintaining uniformity between individuals and more on the management of the diverse functions of different groups with different occupations and increasingly worldviews (ibid). At the same time, the unpaid and frequently reluctant holders of posts, such as the parish constable and the watch, failed to carry out their duties with great diligence.

The fast-expanding towns and cities were increasingly becoming a haven for the poor and those dispossessed of their land as a result of the land enclosures.[1] The rookeries, slum areas and improvised shelters for the poor grew rapidly in the eighteenth century as the urban areas expanded to serve the labour needs of the growing industrial machine. These areas were extremely overcrowded, lacked elementary sanitation and were characterized by disease, grinding poverty, excessive drinking and casual violence. Prostitution and thieving were invariably the only realistic means of survival (Emsley, 2002).

In addition to the increasingly serious problem of ordinary crime and lawlessness – thieving, violence and vice – the urban poor constituted a serious threat to public order. The example of the French Revolution had led to the ruling classes becoming extremely wary of the impoverished mob on their doorstep. This fear was accentuated by the recognition of the English tradition whereby the crowd exercised a degree of power by protesting or rioting – often in a non-political fashion – against local grievances to restore traditional rights eroded by economic and social change. In this way, the poor posed a threat to the seats of both local and national power and which were often close to where they lived. In the eyes of the propertied and the powerful something had to be done for the protection of individual lives and property and for collective security (Emsley, 1996).

In the sixteenth century, during a period of widespread social disruption and poverty, savage penalties had been imposed on the perpetrators of what would now be regarded as fairly minor property crimes. By the early eighteenth century, penalties such as hanging, mutilation or transportation to the colonies were being imposed for an extensive list of petty crimes. It was a strategy pursued with the intention of protecting life and property from the depredations of the poor, who were at the time being herded into locally run workhouses.

The continuing rise in property crimes demonstrated that such a harsh penal code was not merely unjust but clearly inadequate, while the traditional agents of authority were failing to achieve their goals of protecting life and property. The growth of the teeming and anonymous urban environment dissipated the individualistic, charismatic exercise of power by judges and powerful individuals, compromising the exercise of local power which had typified the face-to-face relationships of smaller, less complex societies. The injustice of severe penalties for minor crimes also discouraged juries from reaching guilty verdicts in an increasing number of cases where guilt was clearly obvious. The culmination of all these changes led to increasing pressure for reform of 'the old system'.

The first influential advocates of reform were the Fielding brothers. The older brother, Henry Fielding, was appointed chief magistrate of Bow Street in 1748 and from this position attempted to address the corrupt state of justice and influence the level of crime. He wrote a series of pamphlets on these issues and established himself as a leading thinker on crime and penal policy, with perhaps his most important initiative being the establishment of a small body of thief takers who evolved into the famous 'Bow Street Runners'. He died in 1754 and was succeeded by his brother John, who carried on his work.

In the summer of 1780, London was abandoned to mob violence during the Gordon Riots,[2] and William Pitt, influenced by the work of the Fieldings, attempted to introduce legislation to establish a police force in London. The bill was bitterly opposed and failed (Critchley, 1978), but a similar bill was successfully introduced to establish a police force in Dublin, and in 1786, the first modern police force in the British Isles began patrolling that city.[3]

The next major advocate for reform was Patrick Colquhoun, a self-made entrepreneur and a former provost of Glasgow, who spent much of his 25 years as a London magistrate promoting reform of the police. Colquhoun used techniques which are very common today, but which were rare at the time, such as employing statistics to illustrate arguments. He also wrote lengthy treatises arguing for a well-regulated police force and publicly supported the activities of the French police, who were generally seen as the antithesis of what was needed in England and Wales. Colquhoun advocated the separation of police and judicial powers, the creation of a central board to consist of five commissioners under the control of the home secretary, and in every parish, a nucleus of professional police headed by a high constable assisted by a parochial chief constable (Rawlings, 2001).

Colquhoun's most influential contribution to the debates of the time was his *Treatise on the Commerce and Police of the River Thames* published in 1800. The Port of London docks had become the centre of international trade and they had also become the centre of very large losses resulting from criminal activity. In 1798, Colquhoun estimated the docks were plundered to the extent of £506,000, a huge sum in those days. This finding encouraged the West India Merchants to introduce a Marine Police Establishment which was to have such a dramatic impact on the level of crime that the force became a model for preventative policing (Radzinowicz, 1956).

Despite the efforts of Colquhoun, other advocates of reform such as Jeremy Bentham and Luke Chadwick and three successive parliamentary committees (1816, 1818 and 1822) there was still strong opposition to reform. A further Select Committee in 1828 nevertheless recommended the establishment of an Office of Police under the direction of the home secretary and that it be funded partly from public funds and partly by a local rate. Significantly, the City of London which had been a fierce opponent of the 'old system' of policing was to be exempt from the provisions of the legislation.

The Metropolitan Police Act 1829 established two commissioners of police who were to be responsible for the administration of the force and to be appointed by the Home

Secretary. The force was to be composed of a 'significant number of fit and able men'. The constables would be sworn in by local justices and have the powers of a constable at common law. The legislation was successfully passed without any significant opposition and was to remain the governing statute of the Metropolitan Police until the Police Act 1964.

Most of the police officers were recruited from among the upper end of the working class and were commanded by middle-class officers. The new body was soon established as a semi-professional occupational group and was rigidly disciplined, and many recruits were dismissed for improper behaviour in the formative years. At first, the 'New Police' were very unpopular among *all* sections of society and they were referred to by a range of derogatory terms. Within a year, there were calls for their abolition, and early crowd control techniques merely fuelled the hostility. There is nevertheless evidence to suggest that the force had a considerable impact on the level of crime and perceptions of public safety in some areas of London and this encouraged the increasingly influential middle classes to come to accept the police. The latter also began to realize that the middle classes were their principal allies and focused on protecting them from victimization from the poorer sections of society, the 'dangerous classes', those with little stake in society (Bunyan, 1978).

Following the establishment of the London Metropolitan Police Force in 1829, and its gradual acceptance by the upper and middle classes there ensued 140 years of expansion and rationalization in accordance with the now-dominant modernist philosophy. In the rest of the country, the old systems were slow to be replaced, but the increasing possibility of crime displacement from the capital was the basis for the establishment of police forces outside the metropolis.

The 1830s witnessed public order problems associated with the Chartist movement, and these events provided considerable motivation towards further expansion of the police throughout the country. The County Police Act 1839 was passed which permitted counties to form police forces, but again, it was left to the discretion of the individual county council as to whether they adopted the legislation. Twenty-eight of the 56 counties in England and Wales had established police forces by 1856, with the City of London finally succumbing to political and public pressure in 1839 (Critchley, 1978).

There were now two forms of policing in existence in England and Wales. First, there were the Metropolitan Police in London and outside the capital hundreds of small forces controlled by local magistrates. Second, there were large rural areas where the old premodern system of policing was still in existence. The new forces established outside London were nevertheless insufficiently integrated or controlled to meet the challenges proffered by a growing industrialized economy, for the general population in urban areas was increasing rapidly and becoming increasingly refined in terms of reading and writing and political sophistication. The Chartist movement for political reform grew rapidly from 1837 to 1848, causing considerable unease among the established economic and political interests.

To contain what many considered potentially revolutionary activity, the police had to be rationalized and made accountable to some kind of central control and coordination. The Metropolitan Police from its inception was responsible to the home secretary, but other forces were subject to the control of local magistrates. The next important legislative initiatives tackled these issues and introduced a degree of rationalization and centralization. The County and Borough Police Act 1856 made the establishment of full-time police forces compulsory throughout the country. Many of the new local forces were too small and inefficient to adequately perform their designated roles but the second half of the nineteenth century was characterized by the consolidation of the police throughout the country. The Local Government Act 1888 abolished independent police forces in towns with a population under 10,000 with the outcome of this reform being a reduction in the number of forces from 231 in 1880 to 183 nine years later (Critchley, 1978).

During this period, we can identify three significant changes to the police which were in accordance with modernist philosophy. First, there was an increasing extension of police activity in working-class areas. Second, there were internal reforms such as the introduction of record keeping and improvements in pay and conditions. Third, the detection of crimes was initiated with the establishment of the Criminal Investigations Department.

Identified and defined criminal activity appeared to be the preserve of certain sections of the working class, and it was claimed that the detection of crime would only be possible through a thorough understanding of the culture of this group. It was therefore necessary to patrol the areas in which these people lived. Not surprisingly, this strategy led to a hostile reaction from some of those under surveillance and there were many reports of policemen being physically attacked by disgruntled residents. It can nevertheless be argued that by patrolling these areas the police came to protect 'respectable' working-class people from the ravages of society and in particular the rougher elements in their midst at the time.

During this period there were improvements in the quality of record keeping, a degree of managerial rationalization and the introduction of science. The Criminal Records Office at Scotland Yard was established in 1871, with the use of fingerprinting introduced in 1894. In 1917, the first women police officers were appointed in the face of much male police and indeed public hostility. Moreover, there was considerable internal dissent about poor pay and conditions, with police officers receiving on average the wage of an unskilled labourer, and for this remuneration, they were expected to work a seven-day week, for an average day of 10 to 12 hours and they would often patrol 20 miles plus in a day. They were expected to wear their uniform at all times, not associate with civilians and attend church (Critchley, 1978).

There was extensive initial public resistance to the criminal investigation branch because the image of police officers operating out of uniform to many revived fears of 'state spies' on the continental model. The need for a policing initiative dedicated to the tracking down of criminals – building on the private investigative tradition – was nevertheless recognized within the service. As early as 1842, the Metropolitan Police had established a detective force consisting of two inspectors and six sergeants, and this slowly expanded to a complement of 15 officers by 1867.

The period from 1920 saw a succession of attempted and successful initiatives by the Home Office to further centralize and rationalize the number of police forces. By 1939, a House of Commons Select Committee recommended that there should be no non-county borough forces in areas with a population under 30,000, but on the eve of the Second World War, in 1939, there were still a total of 183 police forces in England and Wales. The home secretary was nevertheless given increasingly more powers during the war years, and a number of amalgamations were forced through in military-sensitive areas. After the war, the Police Act 1946 forced the pace of amalgamations, abolished non-county borough forces and gave executive powers to the home secretary to enable him or her to require amalgamations if he or she considered it to be in the public interest. When the legislation was implemented on 1 April 1947, 45 non-county borough forces were immediately abolished, and by the end of this series of amalgamations completed by 1960, there were a total of 125 forces in England and Wales (Critchley, 1978).

From the 1930s, there was an increasing expansion in the use of technology and more sophisticated forms of training by the police. During the 1930s and 1940s, cars and motorcycles were increasingly used partly as a result of their increased role in policing road traffic. In addition, forensic laboratories were introduced to help in the detection of crimes. The first police dogs were deployed in 1934 and their numbers grew rapidly throughout the 1940s and 1950s. During this period, a National Police College was established as well as recruitment training centres for new recruits. In addition, central promotion exams were introduced and negotiating machinery for pay bargaining.

There was also the establishment of specialist police squads during this period. In the 1950s, a number of specialist detective branches were established to combat specific crime problems such as vice, murder and organized crime. This period also saw the first specialist traffic squads.

By the end of the 1950s, the police were facing a crisis. They were under-staffed and unable to retain trained personnel, while there were increasing cases of malpractice coming to public notice at a time of a constant increase in the crime figures. It was in response to these problems that the Home Secretary established a Royal Commission under the auspices of Henry Willink which reported in 1962 and culminated in the Police Act 1964.

The outcome of the Police Act was to strengthen and increase central government control over the police service, strengthen the powers and operational discretion of individual chief constables, seriously weaken local control over policing and produce a higher degree of rationalization and uniformity over the force. By the early 1970s, the number of police forces in England and Wales had been reduced to 43.

The period following the Second World War has been described as a 'golden age of British Policing' (Emsley, 2009). Thus, by the 1950s, a police officer was regarded as a semi-skilled working-class job and one whose terms and conditions had gradually improved, although the force always had vacancies. Following the war, their role had nonetheless changed. The arrival of mass-produced motor cars created new crimes to investigate and 'traffic offences' brought the police into conflict with the respectable middle classes, often for the first time. The police too had cars which meant a steady decline in foot patrols but, in general, relations with the wider public were harmonious, certainly more so than in the period of social turmoil before the war.

Wider social, political and economic changes were responsible for creating the 'golden age of British Policing'. In the 1950s, Britain had seemingly entered an era of progress and prosperity for all, an era that would have been unthinkable to those who had lived through the 1930s, or to those who had experienced the savage butchery of the Second World War. The political truce between capital and labour in the post-war era was to produce social stability and cohesion, which consequently improved the relationship between working-class communities and the police. The fear of the pre-war 'red menace' or communist threat had dissipated and by the 1960s few people took seriously the idea that the British working classes were the agents of proletarian revolution. Instead of revolution – which had been genuinely feared by the ruling elites during the 1920s and 1930s – the working class were now en masse participants in the new consumer society.

Modern market economies had now appeared for the first time to deliver satisfaction and security for the majority of citizens. The average British house was equipped with refrigerators, washing machines, telephones and television sets. Young people, or 'teenagers', occupied their time buying pop records and devouring a steady diet of popular culture invariably originating from the US. By the late 1960s, most people owned a car and new markets in tourism meant that ordinary working-class people could, for the first time, travel beyond the British Isles. The workers of the modernist Western world appeared to have far more to lose than just their chains. This was also the golden age of modernity and moral certainty was arguably at its zenith.

From golden age to fragmentation

Those of us born and raised in the UK during the mid-twentieth century were familiar with apocryphal stories of how in the 'good old days' – or 'before the (Second World) War' – people left their doors open and neighbours entered unannounced to borrow a cup of sugar. These accounts of community and working-class solidarity were also a staple of classical sociological texts (see Dennis et al., 1956). But the truth was probably rather different: thus, in all probability, there was little else to borrow or for that matter steal. The defining characteristic of the lives of the great majority of people in those days was poverty and that was the case whether in work or not. The extent of ambition for most people was to earn sufficient money to feed, clothe and keep a roof over the heads of their families. There was no television, limited radio, no videos or DVDs, no motor cars for the vast majority of the population and certainly no overseas holidays, let alone the social media and computer use that has permeated the lives of all but the poorest and most disadvantaged people in contemporary society. Most people were poor and had limited ambitions and aspirations beyond basic survival, and in reality, most were rather unsophisticated in comparison with (in particular young) people in a similar social position today. Significantly, there was a relatively high level of social consensus and group solidarity because people had very similar life experiences.

In the language of the French sociologist Emile Durkheim over a century ago, the lives of ordinary working people – regardless of whether they lived in the great mass industrial areas or the rural countryside – were characterized by high levels of mechanical solidarity. They had similar beliefs, understandings and life experiences which encouraged feelings of group solidarity and community which discouraged widespread involvement in criminal activity (Durkheim, 1964). Crime was quantitatively and qualitatively different in a society characterized by relative poverty and very limited aspirations. Poor people undoubtedly did steal from each other, but the level of economic gain would have been small. Theft from a neighbour would have been relatively unlikely in the areas with the greatest group solidarity and the least money.

But we should not really be surprised that crime levels rose so much – and so regularly – from 1955, because the nature of British society was itself to change radically in the intervening years. Wartime rationing finally ended in 1955 and the bright, brash consumer society that was to produce an educated, relatively sophisticated, affluent population of people with diverse knowledge, skills and experiences of life was born. In the language of Durkheim, the lives of people were to become increasingly characterized by high levels of organic solidarity where there is less dependence on the maintenance of uniformity between individuals and more emphasis on the management of the diverse functions of different groups (Durkheim, 1964).

Perhaps the most important development in the 60-plus years following the emergence of the consumer society is the reality that the UK is considerably more prosperous than at any time in its history. The annual gross domestic product (GDP) figures show that the output of the economy has risen by a colossal 377% since 1955 allowing for inflation (The Guardian Online, 2015), but significantly, this growth in prosperity has not been equally shared with more inequality in our society than at any time since the 1930s.

The skilled industrial worker – largely male – has virtually disappeared and been replaced by casualized, low-paid, temporary, part-time workers ('McJobs')[4] many on 'zero-hours' contracts,[5] a substantial proportion of them female. Increased material affluence in the past sixty years was invariably the outcome of a shift towards dual-income families, where both parents work and spend less time with their children, and lone parenthood, with its associated significant social consequences (Rowntree Foundation, 1995). Perhaps, most significant, the qualitative experience of poverty and unemployment today is rather different than in the past.

Life pre–World War 11 was characterized by a generalized, shared working-class experience of poverty, whether in work or not. Today, the level of home ownership is substantially higher than in the past, and car ownership and holidays in increasingly more exotic overseas locations are becoming a widespread norm. The workless and increasingly homeless, nevertheless, live alongside, or at least not far from, the relatively affluent. The wonders and delights of the consumer society are aggressively advertised during the low-budget television programmes churned out 24 hours a day to entertain the 'new leisure classes' and on the World Wide Web in more recent years. Moreover, the contemporary economically dispossessed have very different aspirations than their predecessors 60 years ago. Many aspire to the products they see widely advertised in television commercials and the social media world beyond and they are not easily distracted from these ambitions. They do not accept poverty in the same stoic fashion as their predecessors. They have legitimate aspirations to a share in the 'good life'. It is these socio-economic changes that have provided the cultural context for the huge explosion in recorded crime which has occurred since the beginning of consumer society and the golden age of modernity. Four closely interconnected explanations have been offered from various sources – some more contested than others – to explain this huge increase in crime post-1955 (Hopkins Burke, 1998a).

First, relatively non-contentiously, there has been a huge increase in opportunity provided by the growth of the consumer society, and it is instructive that 94% of all notifiable offences recorded by the police are against property (Barclay, 1995), and of course, ownership of consumer durables is very widespread.[6] In contemporary society, most people have something worth stealing even if it is only their welfare benefits.

Second, a further, more contested, explanation points to the 'breakdown in informal social controls' that has occurred in society, with commentators drawing attention to the decline in the traditional nuclear family, increases in number of the single-parent families and the 'parenting deficit' (Dennis and Erdos, 1992).

Third, a less widely voiced explanation observes the disintegration of the traditional collective working-class culture and the triumph of competitiveness and entrepreneurialism.[7] The 'go for it' philosophy of the enterprise culture came to permeate the whole social structure, from the boardrooms of big business to youths carrying out robberies on the street or committing burglaries, and your entrepreneurial local drug dealer is seen to be more akin to a social worker than a criminal in their local communities. Everyone is an entrepreneur now and the boundaries between many legitimate and illegitimate business activities are becoming increasingly blurred (see Hobbs, 1994, 1988) and morality is indeed ambiguous (Hopkins Burke, 2007). Moreover, few now subjectively claim to be working class, beyond a few ageing academics, although many clearly are in any objective sense.

Fourth, the mass working-class culture of modernity was based on the similarity of existence described earlier. In contrast, the increasingly diverse and fragmented consumer society has brought spending power and opportunities and with it new and diverse groups with subjective and varied interests which have often set them against the traditions of their parent communities and increasingly themselves. Young people, of course, have been in the vanguard of this change and the development of a group identity through an association with others who share a particular taste in music and clothes has been an important part of the transition to adulthood for many young people since the beginnings of the consumer society. It was against this background that crime levels were to increase substantially over much of the past 60 years with parallel concerns as to how the authorities should respond to an apparently growing and unstoppable problem although the official statistics suggest to the more gullible that there has been something of a 'crime drop' in more recent times, a point to which we will return shortly.

Policing fragmented modernity

The golden age of policing did not last long. New challenges and problems were to emerge which had been, in reality, apparent even during the good times. The police, who were an inherently conservative institution, were slow to respond to the challenges of change, particularly the social and cultural changes of the 1960s (Emsley, 2009). Sexist and homophobic attitudes were common amongst 1960s' British police officers whilst racism was endemic. The police did not welcome the era of 'multiculturalism' which transformed British social and cultural life, for many 'immigrant' meant 'criminal', and while a tiny fraction of the 'minority ethnic' community may have joined the service, they were often subjected to systematic racist taunts from fellow officers (Reiner, 2000).

Cultural attitudes towards young people changed in the 1960s, particularly amongst those who had benefited from the expansion of higher education. Britain had adopted the welfare/treatment model as an intervention strategy in youth justice, and it was an approach that had given credence and opportunities to social workers and other public sector professionals who were proud of their liberal attitudes towards young people. The police were hostile to 'welfarism' with many rank-and-file police officers dismissive of 'social workers' 'as 'do-gooders' and the Children and Young Person's Act 1969 was a pivotal piece of legislation which was strongly opposed by the police (Hopkins Burke, 2016).

By the end of the 1970s, crime rates were rising dramatically, and crime was now a political issue for the first time in many years. The spectre of poverty had returned – or was 'rediscovered' – and a crisis in the international financial markets brought with it the return of (mass) unemployment, while the disastrous and architecturally ugly public housing projects of the 1960s had re-created the modern equivalent of the slum, or 'inner-city' areas. The age of prosperity was coming to an end, and so, too, was the age of welfarism (Hopkins Burke, 1998b).

Margaret Thatcher fought the British General Election in 1979 on a strong law-and-order platform with authoritarian political discourse dominating the Conservative Party campaign with reference made to a 'moral crisis' which appeared to engulf the nation. According to a narrative, which was well received by people from all social classes, welfarism was seen not as a solution to social problems but as an unmistakeable part of the problem. The discourse had shifted from 'blaming society' towards personal responsibility, law and order and punishment. Most police officers welcomed this shift, and the Police Federation began to relish a Conservative victory in the 1979 election. On her first day in office, Margaret Thatcher increased the pay of police officers and the service was nicknamed by the press, 'Maggie's Boys'. Nevertheless, despite generous pay increases and other entitlements, the police were to pay another price. The era of harmonious community relations was now over and the 'golden age of British policing' was little more than a distant memory. Class war was to return to the streets of Britain as 'Maggie's Boys' were called on to defeat the National Union of Minerworkers (NUM).

The Miners' Strike 1984–1985 seemed to be a return to the pre-war years of social chaos and instability. The police were central to government plans to defeat the miners and officers began to look increasingly like a strong-arm instrument of an authoritarian state. Enormous numbers of police officers were moved around the country in what effectively became a national force while the security services undoubtedly played a significant part in the operations (Emsley, 2009). The purpose of what was to become a very successful policing strategy was to disrupt the pickets and to guarantee that imported coal made its way through the picket lines. Moreover, the police ensured that strike breakers were escorted into work to maintain production. Police officers, now equipped with riot shields and fitted in flameproof overalls with a vestured helmet and usually on horseback, went to war against the very communities they were sworn to protect. In what effectively became scenes resembling a civil war, the police were willed on by a ruthless government determined to succeed at any cost. When the strike ended in 1985 it was evident that the police had played a definitive role in defeating the NUM. The scars of the strike would last a generation and for some people, a lifetime. The defeat of the miners opened up a whole new era in politics and policing (Emsley, 2009) and significantly helped to destroy effective organized labour in the UK.

In the aftermath of the miners' strike, the reputation of the police had been damaged in working-class communities, particularly in the former heartlands of industrial labour. At the turn of the twentieth century, they had been called 'the blue drones' or 'blue locusts' (Storch, 1975); by the 1980s, they were known in some working-class communities as the 'pigs' or the 'scum' (Emsley, 2009). The miners' strike had shattered the social consensus which had existed in the post-war decades. Social life in Britain was dramatically altered, and by the end of the decade, it was obvious to most political commentators, that the era when organized industrial labour could be a significant force in British politics was finished. There was to be an irretrievable fragmentation within the former working class, resulting in deep social division (Hopkins Burke, 1999).

Traditional political loyalties were transformed as elements of the working classes bought their way into the new meritocracy and took an 'upward strategy', whilst others languished on the scrap heap and joined the swelling ranks of the 'underclass' ostensibly following a 'downward' strategy (Hopkins Burke, 1998b). Those who prospered were thus referred to as the 'upwardly mobile' as they could look forward to owning their own homes, living in private estates and buying shares in the privatized utilities. Political consciousness in some sections of the working class drifted to the right, and this was linked to the emergence of the 'underclass' which was characterized as a dangerous sub-group of amoral wasters who lived off the welfare state and were habitually criminal.

The issue of policing the 'underclass' became one of the dominant themes in British policing in the 1990s, with the force receiving support and sympathy from both the public and politicians alike (Crowther, 1998, 2000a, 2000b). The police were to spend much of their time dealing with the everyday affairs of those living on the margins of society whose lifestyles were labelled 'dysfunctional' and 'chaotic', and high levels of crime were to become commonplace, a taken-for-granted part of life in the inner-city

In the 1990s, the British public accepted a tradeoff between the provision of security and the loss of certain civil liberties. As a consequence, more powers were given to the police, and certain communities experienced an almost permanent police presence, alongside with closed-circuit television and other crime-fighting measures. Whilst intellectuals on the left talked about the 'occupation of poor communities by the police', the measures adopted by New Labour often had popular support, with 'more police on the street' becoming a repeated slogan stemming from working-class communities.

The establishment of the state-sponsored police at the outset in the nineteenth century had appeared inevitable but the question remained as to whether it necessarily had to take the form that it did. It can thus be argued that the emergence of a police bureaucracy in Britain was not inevitable but dependent on the vision of the political elite as to what an orderly disciplined society should be like (Hopkins Burke, 2004b). In many parts of the UK, this vision of social order and authority was contested, and from the outset, each new policing service had to struggle to establish the legitimacy to exist. At the same time, a wide range of other individuals and groups – the old parish constables, gamekeepers and private watchmen, the docks and railway police and the increasingly expanding private security industry – continued to operate (Emsley, 2001).

Thus, from their inception, the new public police service was never the only organization undertaking police work in British society; new forms were negotiated with different audiences and multiple versions were produced. What differentiated the new police from their predecessors and competitors was that they were, from the outset, an instrument of government. Political opposition obliged the nineteenth-century policing reformers to drop all hopes of creating a national service on the continental model and consequently, an assortment of forces gradually took to the streets alongside those other individuals and groups performing policing functions. A progressive rationalization took place throughout the twentieth century and to the present day, in response to the increasing threats posed by public order (including terrorism) and crime, invariably appearing inadequate to the task. Moreover, the extensive expansion in demands placed on the police service increasingly stretched their resources. At the same time, it was regularly and roundly criticized for its apparent failure to produce value for money with the level of recorded crime consistently increasing, while police clear-up rates decreased dramatically.

While there has been a considerable decrease in police effectiveness during the past half century this reality has coincided in a huge and indeed constantly growing increase in public expectations and demands for the wide range of services they provide. Five broad and closely interlinked developments can be detected that have accelerated the growth in these expectations on which the police cannot realistically be expected to deliver.

First, there has been the enormous *increase in criminal opportunities* that have occurred as a result of the increasing affluence in British society since the end of war-time rationing and the beginning of the consumer society which we encountered earlier. Felson (1998) observed that huge increases in the number of high-value portable domestic products attractive to criminals were to occur at the very same time there was to be a considerable *decrease* in informal capable guardians – such as ourselves – with the great expansion in dual-income households which invariably leave homes unoccupied for long periods.

Second, there was an *increase in motivated offenders* which had been notably ignored in earlier variants of opportunity theories. Mike Sutton (1995, 1998) argued persuasively that it is the existence of stolen goods markets that provides the crucial stimulus for theft; much of the motivation for seeking out those markets invariably provided by the large increase in drug addiction in recent years that it is discussed elsewhere in this book.

Third, there has been the increasing embourgeoisement or *civilizing process* whereupon standards of acceptable behaviour have changed over time. Elias (1978, 1982) – in what constitutes a sociological history of manners – observed a progressive moderation and discipline of personal behaviour which centres on a restraint in emotions and the possibilities for embarrassment and shame. This has become increasingly persuasive in view of changes in acceptable behaviour particularly those – popularly termed 'political correctness' – endemic in the extensive public sector.

Fourth, there has been an ever-increasing *social construction of crime* and the *criminalization* of a whole range of new offences, many associated with technological innovations, for example, consider the number of criminal offences associated with the motor car, and there are many more than the simple theft of the vehicle. Computer crime was unknown until relatively recently but now provides widespread and very varied criminal opportunities. There are offences where computers are the *objects of crime*, for example they can be damaged or stolen; they provide a *criminal environment*, for the illegal downloading or unauthorized copying of programmes or films; and they can be the *instrument of the criminal act* in the case of downloading or distributing pornography.

Other recently defined offences are closely linked with the notion of the civilizing process and include domestic violence, stalking and date rape. Thirty years ago, the then Metropolitan Police Commissioner, Sir Kenneth Newman, dismissed domestic violence as 'rubbish work' akin to dealing with stray dogs and not worthy of police time (Hopkins Burke, 2004a). Following a concerted campaign by feminists to put the issue firmly at the top of the policing agenda, it is now almost universally taken seriously by the service,

Fifth, there is the *increasing complexity of society* that has occurred with the fragmentation of modernity and the arrival of the postmodern condition. The public police service is very much the product of modern mass societies characterized by moral certainty and confidence in the capacity of grand social and political theories we have noted earlier. Modern societies had sought to develop social and economic programmes which satisfied the different and often antagonistic class interests in society, and they were for at least the first 30 years following the Second World War. The role of the church, education system and mass media were all cited at various times as helping to develop and maintain an invariably conservative social consensus (see Althusser, 1969; Anderson, 1968). Others have – as we saw earlier – noted the disciplinary role of the public police service in the pursuit of those goals (see e.g. Bunyan, 1976; Cohen, 1979; Scraton, 1985; Storch, 1975). Essential to that disciplinary and missionary project had long been the nature and – often unintended – outcomes of recruitment policies.

Sir Robert Peel had decided from the outset of the Metropolitan Police in 1829 that his officers should come from the unskilled and semi-skilled working class, and this policy became the orthodoxy with the other 'new police' forces (Emsley, 2001). This tough working-class police culture – 'canteen culture' as it has been subsequently termed (see Holdaway, 1983; Fielding, 1988; Reiner, 2000) – transmitted and adapted to changing circumstances across the generations was undoubtedly *relatively* non-problematic during a reasonably consensual modern era. The disciplinary missionary intervention against the rougher elements of the working class had undoubted support from most elements of society including essentially the socially aspiring respectable elements of that class who lived cheek by jowl with the roughs and sought protection from them.

It was with the fragmentation of modernity that this macho-police occupational culture was to become increasingly problematic in a society composed of myriad interest groups, and it was to become increasingly the role of the contemporary police service to intervene and arbitrate in the disputes and conflicts which inevitably occur in such societies. Crucially, the moral certainties of the dominant mono-cultural occupational police culture were now unacceptable in this greatly changed world.

These five broad societal developments – the increase in criminal opportunities and motivated offenders, the increasing embourgeoisement and lower tolerance of criminal activities and social disorder, alongside the great expansion in the number of criminal offences on the statute book at a time of increasingly complex social relations – has increased public expectations of the police service to an extent that they have been unable to meet during the era of fragmented modernity or the postmodern condition.

Crime in fragmented modernity

Crime includes many different activities such as theft, fraud, robbery, corruption, assault, rape and murder. The simplest way of defining crime is that it is an act which contravenes the criminal law but that is nevertheless a problematic definition, for many people break the criminal law but are not considered 'criminals'. In English law, for example, some offences such as murder, theft or serious assaults are described as *mala in se* or wrong in themselves. These are often seen as 'real' crimes in contrast to acts that are *mala prohibita*, prohibited not because they are morally wrong but for the protection of the public (Lacey *et al.*, 1990). Thus, the criminal law is used to enforce regulations concerning public health or pollution not because they are morally wrong but because it is considered to be the most effective way of ensuring that regulations are enforced.

Legal definitions also change over time and vary across cultures. Thus, for example, in some countries, the sale and consumption of alcohol is a crime, while, in others, the sale and consumption of opium, heroin or cannabis are perfectly legal. For some years now, there have been arguments in Britain for the use of some soft drugs such as cannabis to be legalized, and in 2004, the latter was downgraded from Class B to Class C, which meant that the police could no longer automatically arrest those caught in possession, although it remained illegal (Crowther, 2007). The government subsequently reclassified cannabis from Class C to Class B in January 2009. They did this to reflect the fact that skunk, a much stronger version of the drug, now accounted for more than 80% of the cannabis available, compared to just 30% in 2002 (Home Office, 2009).

The situation in North America is very different from the UK. Thus, in November 2018, Michigan became the 10th US state to legalize recreational marijuana, and two others, Utah and Missouri, voted to legalize medical marijuana. In June 2018, Oklahoma voted to legalize medical marijuana, joining numerous other states that have passed such legislation. Earlier, in January 2018, Vermont became the first state to legalize marijuana through its legislature rather than a popular-ballot initiative. Ten States and Washington, D.C., have legalized marijuana for recreational use for adults over 21. Thirty-three states have legalized medical marijuana.

Marijuana prohibition in the US began 80 years ago when the federal government banned the sale, cultivation and use of the cannabis plant. It remains illegal at the federal level in the US. Overturning prohibition is nevertheless one of the few relatively non-contentious topics with widespread support in a politically fragmented society. A recent poll by the Pew Research Center (2018) found that 62% of Americans, including 74% of millennials, said they supported legalizing marijuana. And 2018 was a headline year for marijuana legalization in North America. In October, the federal government of Canada legalized marijuana becoming the first G7 country to do so. In the same month, Mexico's Supreme Court ruled that marijuana prohibition is unconstitutional, thus giving the new leader of the country, Andrés Manuel López Obrador, the opportunity to follow the lead of Canada.

At the same time, in contrast to demands for the decriminalization of some activities, there has been a call for other activities to be criminalized, and in recent years, these have included 'stalking', 'hate' crime, knowingly passing on the AIDS virus and abortion, which has an ambiguous status, legal in some places and illegal in others. The way that crime is defined is therefore a social construction.

Crime is usually associated with particular groups such as young men or the unemployed, some of whom become 'folk devils', and are identified with certain kinds of offences. This social construction of crime is reflected in media discussions and portrayals of what constitutes the 'crime problem'. Thus, for example, rising crime rates or policies are introduced to 'crack down' on crimes such as burglary or violent street crime rather than on environmental crimes such as pollution, corporate crimes or major frauds, although the situation has changed rather in recent years and with the fragmentation of modernity and the arrival of the postmodern condition a plethora of new offences have come to the fore, as we have seen.

The vast majority of criminological research has targeted the poorer sections of society because concerns about this apparently 'dangerous class' have dominated criminological thought since at least the beginning of modern society. The substitution of determinate prison sentences for those of capital punishment and transportation came to mean in reality the existence of a growing population of convicted criminals that frightened many in 'respectable society'. It is therefore perhaps not surprising that both the law and criminology have subsequently targeted this group.

The problem of 'white-collar', business or corporate crime has been recognized since at least the beginning of the twentieth century, although it continued to be neglected and under-researched. This criminological neglect does appear at first sight surprising. For examples, it has been estimated that in the US, the economic losses from various white-collar crimes are about ten times those from 'ordinary' economic crime, with corporate crime killing and maiming more than any violence committed by the poor. In the same country, 100,000 people have died each year from occupationally related diseases which have mostly been contracted as a result of wilful violation of laws designed to protect workers (Swartz, 1975), defective products have killed another 30,000 US citizens annually (Kramer, 1984), while US manufacturers have been observed to dump drugs and medical equipment in developing countries after they have been banned from the home market (Braithwaite, 1984). Croall (1992, 2001) observes that the activities of the corporate criminal have not only a greater impact than those committed by the 'ordinary' offender but that they are also longer lasting in effect.

White-collar crime has nevertheless been taken increasingly more seriously by the authorities in recent years in both the US and latterly the UK, for example, not least following the Great Crash of 2008 that devasted the economies of the world. Moreover, it is a category which now includes the fast-growing criminological area of cybercrime. Prosecutions for the latter rose by a third during 2015 with a small rise in white-collar cases.

Cybercrime is growing fast as we observed earlier, and we are all at risk of victimization. The Crime Survey for England and Wales 2015 reported that about 3.8 million adults in England and Wales had been victims of some form of online fraud in the span of a year. The survey, which included statistics on internet crime for the first time, found an estimated 5.1 million incidents of online fraud and an estimated 2.5 million incidents categorized under the Computer Misuse Act, whereby the computer or other device of the victim was infected by a virus or where their email or social media account had been hacked. During 2015, 617,618 fraud offences were recorded in England and Wales, up 4% on the previous year (Croft, 2016).

There were 34,504 computer software service fraud reports made to the UK's national fraud and cyber-reporting centre, Action Fraud, over the financial year 2014–15. The 'scammers' usually declare that they have detected a fault with their target's PC and fool victims into giving them remote access to it. They then often install images that appear to show the computer is infected or install malware themselves. Finally, they demand a fee to fix the issue or otherwise convince the victim to share their bank account details. Sometimes the target is then contacted again at a later date from someone claiming to work for the same service, who says they are due a refund. If they hand over their bank details again, further money is taken from their account. Action Fraud says the average age of victims is 62 years of age, and they typically pay out £600 (BBC News, 2017).

What is clear is that the nature of crime has changed over time invariably because of technological and social factors. Crime fashions come and go and are replaced by others as factors change. Common criminal types of the past which are now either extinct or their numbers significantly depleted include highway men, poachers, pick pockets, sheep rustlers and 'Peterman' (safe-blowers), while a number of crimes common during my lifetime are also virtually non-existent or at least far less common and these include 'wages snatches', theft from a utility meter, cheque fraud and even bank robbery

Most advanced countries have experienced a significant decline in 'traditional' street crime from at least the 1990s (Farrell, 2013). This 'crime drop' not surprisingly first became big news in the US, where total violent crime fell over 70% between 1993 and 2011 (Truman and Planty, 2012), but this decline was not entirely new, with some property crimes falling since the early 1970s. In the mid-1990s, the UK began to experience dramatic falls across a wide range of property, personal and violent crimes, falling by over 50% in some cases (Office of National Statistics, 2013) a pattern similar to that in other advanced societies. Thus, in Canada, falls in homicide and other crime were very similar to the US (Ouimet, 2002), New Zealand experienced similar declines in property crime (burglary, motor vehicle theft and other theft) but not all personal crimes (Mayhew, 2012), with the Australian 'crime drop' starting a little later, around 2001, when reductions in motor vehicle theft preceded steep falls in burglary, theft and robbery but not some personal crimes (Mayhew, 2012). Furthermore, there is considerable evidence, from the International Crime Victims Survey in particular, that most European countries experienced significant crime drops (Van Dijk *et al.*, 2008; Van Dijk, 2008; Van Dijk and Tseloni, 2012). Tseloni *et al.* (2010) go further and suggest that the crime drop is more widespread than advanced countries and could perhaps be labelled as global.

Whether crime in general has decreased or whether criminal endeavour has been channelled into other less visible activities is another matter and one which we can neither prove nor disapprove. The problem with crime is that it is illegal. This means it is secret especially when it does not occur on the visible 'street' in front of neutral witnesses. This clearly provides serious problems for the police and those who collate statistics and seek to discover the extent of crime. For that is the problem. Much crime in fragmented modernity is invisible and thus exactly how much there is we simply do not know (Davies, 2003).

Let us reconsider the 'crime drop' thesis and two significant issues which help illuminate the invisibility thesis. First, the fall has occurred right across the developed world. Second, it has happened at the same time that every developed country in the world reports more black-market drug use. The British Home Office proposed that there are at least 250,000 problematic users of Class A drugs, such as heroin, in the country, and it is these users who are statistically the prolific offenders, responsible for more than 50% of crime. It would appear incomprehensible that there can be a growing number of prolific offenders while, at the same time, there is less crime. There is nevertheless one explanation which fits the facts: the drug users who drive the crime figures are committing a mass of offences which are statistically invisible. Specifically, repeated surveys of drug users in custody show that easily their most common property crime is shoplifting (50% of their offences in most surveys), and beyond that, most drug users fund their habit by selling drugs, whether to friends or strangers. And, in both cases, these offences are almost entirely invisible to police records (they are recorded only when they are detected) and completely invisible to the British Crime Survey (they have no adult victims). It is one of the enduring problems of criminal justice systems that they can change the pattern of crime but struggle to change its scale. The one explanation which applies to all the developed countries which have seen their crime figures fall is that they have shifted their expanding population of black-market drug users into committing a surge of invisible offences. We cannot prove that is what has happened because this crime is hidden. But it is fair to say that the great crime fall is at best unproven and at worst a politically useful myth which has helped governments make massive cuts in police officer numbers during the current long recession (The Economist, 2016).

If we really want to understand the reality of crime in this country, the figures that matter are those which show that just 1% of the population suffers 59% of all violent crime; that just 2% of the population suffers 41% of all property crime. And where are these victims? Most criminals commit their offences within 1.8 miles of their front door. In other words, they rob their neighbours. And overwhelmingly, those offenders live in the shabby tower blocks and council estates which have been consumed by poverty and criminalized by the war against drugs. That is where crime is booming, where, as a single example, an 18-year-old lone woman with a child is more than five times more likely than the average to be a crime victim, far away from the statisticians and the politicians and their celebrations of the 'crime drop' – real crime which is almost invisible (The Economist, 2016).

The illegal drug trade is a global black market dedicated to the cultivation, manufacture, distribution and sale of drugs subject to drug prohibition laws. The UN Office on Drugs and Crime's *World Drug Report 2005* estimated the size of the global illicit drug market at US$321.6 billion in 2003 the latest comprehensive figures available. With a world GDP of US$36 trillion in the same year, the illegal drug trade may be estimated as nearly 1% of the total global trade, one of the biggest industries in the world and one of the largest employers. The distribution and consumption of illegal drugs are widespread globally.

Online drug markets are part of the 'dark web': sites only accessible through browsers such as Tor, which route communications via several computers and layers of encryption, making them almost impossible for law enforcement officers to track. Buyers and sellers make contact using e-mail providers such as Sigaint, a secure dark-web service, and encryption software, such as Pretty Good Priva. Almost all sales are via 'cryptomarkets': dark websites which act as shop fronts. These provide an escrow service, holding payments until customers agree to the Bitcoin being released. Feedback systems like those on legitimate sites such as Amazon and eBay allow buyers to rate their purchases and to leave comments, helping other customers to choose a trustworthy supplier. The administrators take a 5% to 10% cut of each sale and set broad policy (e.g. whether to allow the sale of guns). They pay moderators in Bitcoin to run customer forums and handle complaints.

The powerful 'cartels' which have long dominated the drugs trade seem to have taken little interest in the dark web. One reason is that they have established supply chains which they are not keen to disrupt. Their special skills – smuggling, intimidation and violence – are useless online. And their comparative advantage is in shifting drugs in tonnes, not kilograms. The drug trade may be experiencing the equivalent of the online retail boom of the 1990s, when department stores played down the threat posed by insurgent e-tailers. Those department stores have since built websites of their own or simply gone out of business. Old-style drug lords may well want to think about investing in cryptomarkets or risk being disrupted out of existence.

Whether there is less or more crime, we thus simply do not know. Much crime is invisible. The 'crime drop' research shows quite clearly that there has been a worldwide decline in certain 'street' offences because of security initiatives which have significantly reduced their popularity. What appears to have happened is a 'retreat from the street' and a growth in newer forms of criminality which are invisible and much harder for the authorities to detect and measure. Then the 'traditional' crime figures apparently rose again.

The total number of crimes reported to and recorded by the police rose by 10% between April 2016 and March 2017 to almost 5 million. Significantly, violent crime increased by 18%, robbery by 16% and sex offences by 14%. Crimes of violence are very difficult to conceal, and in the case of homicide, this is very much the case. At the same time the Crime Survey of England and Wales showed a 7% drop (BBC, 2017). The two sets of figures clearly are measuring different offences as our earlier discussion demonstrates.

Policing fragmented modernity revisited

The nature of crime in fragmented modernity – or the postmodern condition has been rapidly changing and the state-sponsored policing strategies of modernity seem poorly equipped to challenge this apparent crime boom. Those with criminal intent have come to realize that there is money to be made, with less risk of getting caught, and smaller penalties if you are apprehended, by using technology. Thus, why rob a convenience store, or someone in the street, if you can get on a computer, steal someone's identity (or create an entirely new, fictitious identity of a person who does not exist) and steal large sums from major banks or credit card companies. It is a much 'cleaner' way of profiting from crime, with no potentially dangerous confrontations with victims. The risk is substantially lower and the rewards higher, with criminal penalties in some cases being essentially non-existent. Crime statistics thus do not reflect most of these changes.

According to the Federal Bureau of Investigation, there were 4,251 bank robberies in the US in 2016, which was a 45% decrease when compared to 2004. At the same time, there were nearly 300,000 reports of people being victimized on the internet. In one famous incident, thieves working with computer experts in more than 20 countries stole $45 million from thousands of automated teller machines over a 10-hour period, which was more than the total losses from 'traditional' physical robberies of banks over an entire year (*New York Times*, 2016). Internet-based crimes are clearly rising, but the existing systems for measuring crime are a product of old-style modernist policing methods and totally inadequate for measuring new crimes. Apparently only an estimated 15% of fraud victims report their crimes to law enforcement, according to the FBI. This means that for every crime that is reported to the police, there are about six more crimes that are not reported. While the exact totals are not known, it is clear that millions of people in the US are victims of internet crimes each year (Federal Bureau of Investigation, 2016).

Even when technologies are invented to prevent crime, criminals adapt. For example the electronic chips in car keys have made it almost impossible for a thief to start the engine and steal a car. So criminals developed key-fob jamming devices. As a car owner walks away from their car and clicks the key to lock the doors, the criminal uses an electronic device to disrupt the signal, so the car is not really locked. The criminal waits until the owner disappears from sight and then gets in the car, usually not to steal it but to look for the registration, insurance cards or other paperwork such as credit card statements that can be used to commit identity theft (Federal Bureau of Investigation, 2016).

In the complex societies of fragmented modernity, the work of criminal investigators is also becoming more complex. Wexler (2018) observes that not long ago, detectives responding to a homicide or other serious crime had a clear focus: quickly get to the scene, collect physical evidence and interview any witnesses. Today, investigators must retrieve smartphones from victims and suspects and scour their social media accounts for clues; access nearby security camera feeds, automated license plate readers and traffic enforcement cameras; and try to obtain data from other devices such as Fitbits, GPS devices, and video cameras in the victims' or suspects' cars. Moreover, investigators must do all this work quickly before the digital trail gets cold.

Police are not getting a lot of help from the technology sector. As we have seen, criminals are using the 'dark web' to make themselves anonymous online. Even when police obtain court orders allowing them to get into a cell phone to find out who a victim or suspect was communicating with, they often find that there is no way to get past the passcode of the user. Smartphone manufacturers argue that they cannot build a special 'backdoor' for police to access the data in these devices, because criminals inevitably would hack into the backdoor, making the use of all phones less safe.

Wexler (2018) observes that technology is changing the environment every day, and most police agencies are far behind. Policing in the US is decentralized; there are thousands of small and medium-sized agencies that lack the resources to respond to the changes cited earlier. Even large, well-funded agencies have a lot of work to do: finding and hiring technology experts; training officers to understand the basics of crime-related technologies; and rethinking the traditional structure of a police agency in modernist society. The old 'silos', such as special units for organized crime, gangs and narcotics, are becoming less relevant as cybercrime becomes a part of all these traditional categories. Crime data systems have simply not kept pace with changes in crime, and we do not know how much crime there is.

Wexler (2018) observes that in many cases, it not clear how, or even if, local police are prepared to take reports and investigate offences like identity theft and credit card fraud. In 2000, the FBI created the Internet Crime Complaint Center (IC3), whose mission is 'to provide the public with a reliable and convenient reporting mechanism to submit information to the FBI concerning suspected internet-facilitated criminal activity' (Federal Bureau of Investigation, 2016: 2). However, 17 years later, it was found that only an estimated 15% of US fraud victims report their crime to law enforcement. In many cases, there is little incentive to report internet crime. Banks and credit card companies routinely cancel fraudulent charges made against a victim's account, so there is no need to report the crime to be reimbursed. By contrast, victims of 'traditional' crimes such as burglary often must obtain a police report – or a crime number – to file insurance claims, so there is more reporting of such crimes although we might observe these are unlikely to be investigated. So the true extent of this problem is hidden. But we do know that the total financial losses due to just one type of internet crime – identity theft –amounted to more than $15 billion in 2014, according to a crime victimization survey conducted by the Bureau of Justice Statistics (Federal Bureau of Investigation, 2016). Wexler observes that data collection is more than just an academic undertaking to support research. Data help drive policy, resources and operations. Without accurate data, we have no idea what resources are required to respond to what is invariably an invisible crime problem. The extent of which appears much bigger than anyone might have expected and is not confined to the US.

A very similar situation exists in the UK with organized crime being bigger than ever and a resource-starved police service struggling to keep up with developments. Lynne Owens, the country's most senior police officer as head of the National Crime Agency (NCA) notes the extent of the problem. Major resource-intensive crimes in recent times have included the attempt by Russia to kill former spy Sergei Skripal, a North Korean cyber-attack that brought the National Health Service virtually to a halt for four days, Eastern European slave traffickers who invariably provide the staff for the mail bars and car washes near you, Albanian cocaine smugglers who control the London drugs trade, hundreds of billions of pounds being laundered through London every year, a dramatic rise in the murder rate in the capital in four years, historic child abuse in Rotherham and fentanyl manufacturers in Merseyside and Manchester (Perry, 2018). All the cases Owens cites are examples of organized crime, illicit national and transnational networks that have multiplied since the 1980s and now make an annual £1.5 trillion around the world and £37 billion, or 1.8% of GDP, in Britain. It was to tackle this threat that the NCA was established five years ago as a national intelligence and police force – inevitably described in the press as the closest thing Britain has to an FBI. Its caseload has expanded again to include investigations into the origins of Brexiter Arron Banks campaign cash and how an Azerbaijani banker's wife, Zamira Hajiyeva, sustained a lifestyle that ran to spending £16 million in Harrods in a decade. The latest figures provided by the NCA show that there are 4,629 criminal gangs and syndicates in Britain employing 33,598 professional gangsters (Perry, 2018).

Popular perception of organized crime in Britain is anchored in fictional portrayals such as *The Godfather* or historic villains like the Great Train Robbers – and there was once some truth to these legends. In the first decades of the twentieth century, the gangs that held sway over parts of London or Birmingham, including the real-life Peaky Blinder, tended to be hierarchies based around family or ethnicity, making money from robbery, protection, casinos and war-time black markets.

In the 1980s and 1990s, gangland transformed. An explosion in counterfeit goods and drugs – particularly cocaine – and an eased flow of money, communications, commodities and people propelled the rise of flexible, horizontal criminal networks that displaced small family operations. While these new forms of crime defy old stereotypes, for those who know where to look, signs of it are all around. Every year, Britons unwittingly drink millions of bottles of untaxed Italian wine, smuggled in by the Calabrian mafia, the 'Ndrangheta'. Farmers and owners of empty factories who wake up one morning to find their land buried under tonnes of rubbish are victims of an illegal waste disposal industry worth billions a year. Many of the workers picking fruit and vegetables on farms across the UK are also indentured labour. The NCA registered a 35% rise in reports of slavery in the UK from 2016 to 2017 (Perry, 2018). Such is the changed nature of crime in fragmented modernity and the issue of organized crime and globalization is discussed further and In greater detail in the second part of this book.

Summary of main points

1   The idea of the modern originated as a description of the forms of thought and action which emerged with the decline of medieval societies in Western Europe.

2   The administration of criminal justice in the premodern era had been chaotic, predominantly non-codified, irrational and irregular and at the whim of individual judgement.

3   All modern societies use some form of state-sponsored professionalized police force to control crime and to contribute to public order.

4   Following the establishment of the London Metropolitan Police Force in 1829, there were to be 140 years of expansion and rationalization in accordance with modernist philosophy.

5   Wider social, political and economic changes were responsible for creating the 'golden age of British policing'. Modern market economies had now appeared for the first time to deliver satisfaction and security for the majority of citizens.

6   The golden age did not last long. New challenges and problems were to emerge and the police, who were an inherently conservative institution, were slow to respond to the challenges posed by social and cultural changes in the 1960s.

7   By the end of the 1970s, crime rates were rising dramatically, and crime was now a political issue for the first time in many years. The spectre of poverty had returned, and a crisis in the international financial markets brought with it the return of (mass) unemployment.

8 Traditional political loyalties were transformed as elements of the working classes bought their way into the new meritocracy and took an 'upward strategy', whilst others languished on the scrap heap and joined the swelling ranks of the 'underclass'.

9 The nature of crime has changed over time invariably because of technological and social factors. Crime fashions come and go and are replaced by others as factors change.

10 The nature of crime in fragmented modernity – or the postmodern condition has been rapidly changing and the state-sponsored policing strategies of modernity seem poorly equipped to challenge this apparent crime boom.

Discussion questions

1 Why do you think that forms of crime and societal response are different in distinctive epochs?

2 What were the main problems facing the police service in the modern era?

3 Why was there a big increase in crime following the Second World War?

4 What are the new crimes to have emerged with the fragmentation of modernity, and why do we not know the extent of the problem?

5 What are the problems facing the police service in contemporary society?

Further reading

For some contrasting accounts from very different perspectives of premodern criminal justice and attempts to explain the causes of crime, see Foucault (1977), Hay (1981) and Thompson (1975). Garland (1997) provides something of a pragmatic antidote to those who seek to identify distinct ruptures between premodern and modern thinking. For an introduction to the notion of modern society and modernity, albeit in the context of his discussion of postmodernity, see Harvey (1989).

Notes

1 Enclosure was the legal process in England of consolidating (enclosing) small landholdings into larger farms since the 13th century. Once enclosed, use of the land became restricted and available only to the owner, and it ceased to be common land for communal use.

2 The Gordon Riots of 1780 were several days of rioting in London motivated by anti-Catholic sentiment. They began with a large and orderly protest against the Papists Act of 1778, which was intended to reduce official discrimination against British Catholics enacted by the Popery Act 1698.

3 The Civil Patrolmen (nicknamed the 'Charlies') 1723–1786; formed as armed constables to patrol Dublin City. They were reformed as an unarmed force in 1786 as the Dublin Police. The Dublin Police 1786–1836; replaced the Civil Patrolmen and included a mounted troop.

4 McJob is slang for a low-paying, low-prestige dead-end job that requires few skills and offers very little chance of intracompany advancement.

5 Zero-hours contracts are also known as casual contracts. Zero-hours contracts are usually for 'piece work' or 'on call' work, for example for interpreters. This means: a) they are on call to work when you need them, b) you do not have to give them work, and c) they do not have to do work when asked.

6 Durables, also known as durable goods or consumer durables, is a category of consumer goods that do not wear out quickly, and therefore do not have to be purchased frequently. They are known as "durable goods" because they tend to last for at least three years.

7 Entrepreneurialism is defined as starting new businesses, or getting involved with new ventures or ideas. An example of entrepreneurialism is starting new businesses and always being involved in investing in the latest ventures.

References

Althusser, L. (1969) *For Marx*. London: Allen Lane.

Anderson, P. (1968) 'Components of the National Culture', *New Left Review*, 161, January.

Barclay, G.C. (1995) *The Criminal Justice System in England and Wales 1995*. London: Home Office, Research and Statistics Department.

BBC News (2017) *Arrests in UK over Microsoft Scam Calls*, 28 June 2017. [Online] Available from: www.bbc.co.uk/news/technology-40430048 [Accessed 15 May 2020].

Bernard, T.J. (1983) *The Consensus – Conflict Debate*. New York: Columbia University Press.

Braithwaite, J. (1984) *Corporate Crime in the Pharmaceutical Industry*. London: Routledge.

Bunyan, T. (1976) *The Political Police in Britain*. London: Julian Friedmann Publishers.

Bunyan, T. (1978) *The History and Practice of the Political Police in Britain*. London: Quartet.

Cohen, P. (1979) 'Policing the Working Class City', in B. Fine, R. Kinsey, J. Lea, S. Picciotto and J. Young (eds.) *Capitalism and the Rule of Law*. London: Hutchinson.

Critchley, T.A. (1972) *A History of Police in England and Wales*, 2nd ed. Montclair, NJ: Patterson.

Critchley, T.A. (1978) *A History of Police in England and Wales*. London: Constable.

Croall, H. (1992) *White-Collar Crime*. Buckingham: Open University Press.

Croall, H. (2001) *Understanding White-Collar Crime, Crime and Justice Series*. Buckingham: Open University Press.

Croft, J. (2016) 'Prosecutions Rise for Cyber and White Collar Crime', *Financial Times*, May 23.

Crowther, C. (1998) 'Policing the Excluded Society', in R.D. Hopkins Burke (ed.) *Zero Tolerance Policing*. Leicester: Perpetuity Press.

Crowther, C. (2000a) *Policing Urban Poverty*. Basingstoke: Macmillan.

Crowther, C. (2000b) 'Thinking About the "Underclass": Towards a Political Economy of Policing', *Theoretical Criminology*, 4(2): 149–67.

Crowther, C. (2007) *An Introduction to Criminology and Criminal Justice*. Basingstoke: Palgrave Macmillan.

Davies, N. (2003) 'Exploding the Myth of the Falling Crime Rate', *The Guardian*, July 10.

Dennis, N. and Erdos, G. (1992) *Families without Fatherhood*. London: Institute for Economic Affairs.

Dennis, N., Henriques, F. and Slaughter, C. (1956) *Coal Is Our Life*. London: Eyre & Spottiswoode.

Durkheim, E. (1933 originally 1893) *The Division of Labour in Society*. Glencoe, IL: Free Press.

Durkheim, E. (1964 originally 1915) *The Elementary Forms of Religious Life*. Glencoe, IL: Free Press.

The Economist (2016) 'Buying Drugs Online: Shedding Light on the Dark Web', *The Economist*, July 16.

Elias, N. (1978) *The Civilising Process, Vol. 1: The History of Manners*. Oxford: Blackwell.

Elias, N. (1982) *The Civilising Process, Vol. 2: State-Formation and Civilisation*. Oxford: Blackwell.

Emsley, C. (1996) *The English Police: A Political and Social History*. Harlow: Longman.

Emsley, C. (2001) 'The Origins and Development of the Police', in E. McLaughlin and J. Muncie (eds.) *Controlling Crime*. London: Sage with the Open University.

Emsley, C. (2002) 'The History of Crime and Crime Control Institutions', in M. Maguire, R. Morgan and R. Reiner (eds.) *The Oxford Handbook of Criminology*, 3rd ed. Oxford: Oxford University Press.

Emsley, C. (2009) *The Great British Bobby*. London: Queraus Books.

Farrell, G. (2013) 'Five Tests for a Theory of the Crime Drop', *Crime Science*, 2(5): 1–8.

Federal Bureau of Investigation (2016) *2016 Internet Crime Report*. Washington, DC: Federal Bureau of Investigation.

Felson, M. (1998) *Crime and Everyday Life*, 2nd ed. Thousand Oaks, CA: Pine Forge.

Fielding, N. (1988) *Joining Forces*. London: Routledge.

Fogelson, R. (1977) *Big City Police*. Cambridge, MA: Harvard University. Press.

Foucault, M. (1977) *Discipline and Punish – the Birth of the Prison*. London: Allen Lane.

Garland, D. (1997) 'The Development of British Criminology', in M. Maguire, R. Morgan and R. Reiner (eds.) *The Oxford Handbook of Criminology*. Oxford: Clarendon Press.

Guardian Online (2015) 'UK GDP since 1955', *Data Blog*. Available from: www.theguardian.com/news/datablog/2009/nov/25/gdp-uk-1948-growth-economy.

Harvey, D. (1989) *The Condition of Postmodernity: An Enquiry into the Origins of Cultural Change*. Oxford: Blackwell.

Hay, D. (1981) 'Property, Authority and the Criminal Law', in M. Fitzgerald, G. McLennan and J. Pawson (eds.) *Crime and Society: Readings in History and Theory*. London: Open University Press/Routledge.

Hobbs, D. (1988) *Doing the Business: Entrepreneurship, the Working Class and Detectives in East London*. Oxford: Clarendon Press.

Hobbs, D. (1994) 'Professional and Organised Crime in Britain', in M. Maguire, R. Morgan, and R. Reiner (eds.) *The Oxford Handbook of Criminology*. Oxford: Clarendon Press.

Holdaway, S. (1983) *Inside the British Police: A Force at Work*. Oxford: Blackwell.

Home Office (2009) *Controlled Drugs: Reclassification of Cannabis*. London: HMSO.

Hopkins Burke, R.D. (ed.) (1998a) *Zero Tolerance Policing*. Leicester: Perpetuity Press.

Hopkins Burke, R.D. (1998b) 'The Contextualisation of Zero Tolerance Policing Strategies', in R.D. Hopkins Burke (ed.) *Zero Tolerance Policing*. Leicester: Perpetuity Press.

Hopkins Burke, R.D. (1999) 'The Socio-Political Context of Zero Tolerance Policing Strategies', *Policing: An International Journal of Police Strategies & Management*, 21(4): 666–82.

Hopkins Burke, R.D. (ed.) (2004a) *'Hard Cop/Soft Cop': Dilemmas and Debates in Contemporary Policing*. Cullompton: Willan Publishing.

Hopkins Burke, R.D. (2004b) 'Policing Contemporary Society', in R.D. Hopkins Burke (ed.) *'Hard Cop/Soft Cop': Dilemmas and Debates in Contemporary Policing*. Cullompton: Willan Publishing.

Hopkins Burke, R.D. (2007) 'Moral Ambiguity, the Schizophrenia of Crime and Community Justice', *British Journal of Community Justice*, 5(1): 43–64.

Hopkins Burke, R.D. (2016) *Young People, Crime and Justice*, 2nd ed. Cullompton: Willan Publishing.

Johnson, L. (1992) *The Rebirth of Private Policing*. London: Routledge.

Lacey, N., Wells, C. and Meure, D. (1990) *Reconstructing Criminal Law: Critical Social Perspectives on Crime and the Criminal Process*. London: Weidenfeld & Nicolson.

Lane, R. (1967) *Policing the City*. Cambridge: Harvard University Press.

Mayhew, P. (2012) 'The Case of Australia and New Zealand', in J.J.M van Dijk, A Tseloni and G. Farrell (eds.), *The International Crime Drop: New Directions in Research*. Basingstoke: Palgrave Macmillan.

New York Times (2016) 'In Hours, Thieves Took $45 Million in A.T.M. Scheme', *New York Times*, May 9.

Office of National Statistics (2013) *Crime in England and Wales, Year Ending December 2012*. Newport: ONS.

Ouimet, M. (2002) 'Explaining the American and Canadian Crime "Drop" in the 1990s', *Canadian Journal of Criminology and Criminal Justice*, 44(1): 33–50.

Perry, A. (2018) *Organised Crime in the UK is Bigger Than Ever Before: Can the Police Catch Up?* [Online] Available from: www.alex-perry.com/organised-crime-uk-bigger-ever-can-police-catch/ [Accessed 7 May 2019].

Pew Research Center (2018) *Support for Marijuana Legalization Continues to Rise*. Washington, DC: Pew Research Center.

Radzinowicz, L. (1948–1986) *A History of English Criminal Law and its Administration from 1750*, 5 volumes: i) (1948) The Movement for Reform; ii) (1956) The Clash Between Private Initiative and Public Interest in the Enforcement of the Law; iii) (1956) Cross Currents in the Movement of the Reform of the Police; iv) (1968) Grappling for Control; v) (with R. Hood, 1986) The Emergence of Penal Policy in Victorian and Edwardian England, London: Stevens & Sons.

Rawlings, P. (2001) *Policing: A Short History*. Cullompton: Willan.

Reiner, R. (2000) *The Politics of the Police*, 3rd ed. Oxford: Oxford University Press.

Rowntree Foundation (1995) *Income and Wealth: Report of the JRF Inquiry Group, Summary*. York: Joseph Rowntree.

Scraton, P. (1985) *The State of the Police*. London: Pluto.

Storch, R. (1975) 'The Plague of the Blue Locusts: Police Reform and Popular Resistance in Northern England 1840–57', *International Review of Social History*, 20: 61–90.

Sutton, M. (1995) 'Supply by Theft: Does the Market for Second-Hand Goods Play a Role in Keeping Crime Figures High?', *British Journal of Criminology*, 38(3): 352–65.

Sutton, M. (1998) *Handling Stolen Goods and Theft: A Market Reduction Approach*, Home Office Research Study 178. London: Home Office.

Swartz, J. (1975) 'Silent Killers at Work', *Crime and Social Justice*, 3: 15–20.

Thompson, E.P. (1975) *Whigs and Hunters*. London: Allen Lane.

Truman, J.L. and Planty, M. (2012) *Criminal Victimization, 2011*. Washington, DC: U.S. Department of Justice, Office of Justice Programs, Bureau of Justice Statistics.

Tseloni, A., Farrell, G., Tilley, N., Grove, L. Thompson, R. and Garius, L. (2010) 'Towards a Comprehensive Research Plan on Opportunity Theory and the Crime Falls', in J.J.M. Van Dijk *et al.* (eds.) *The International Crime Drop: New Directions in Research*. New York: Palgrave Macmillan.

Van Dijk, J.J.M. (2008) *The World of Crime*. London: Sage.

Van Dijk, J.J.M., Manchin, R., Van Kesteren, J., Nevala, S. and Hideg, G. (2008) *The Burden of Crime in the EU*. Research Report: A Comparative Analysis of the European Survey of Crime and Safety (EU ICS) 2005.

Van Dijk, J.J.M. and Tseloni, A. (2012) 'Global Overview: International Trends in Victimization and Recorded Crime', in J.J.M. Van Dijk, A. Tseloni and G. Farrell (eds.) *The International Crime Drop: New Directions in Research*. London: Palgrave Macmillan.

Vold, G.B., Bernard, T.J. and Snipes, J.B. (1998) *Theoretical Criminology*, 4th ed. Oxford: Oxford University Press.

Wexler, C. (2018) 'Crime Has Been Changing and Police Agencies Need to Catch Up', in Police Executive Research Forum, *The Changing Nature of Crime and Criminal Investigation*, Critical Issues in Policing Series. Washington, DC: Police Executive Research Forum.

Chapter 3

Explaining crime in the modern era

Key issues

1 Three models of crime and criminal behaviour
2 The rational actor model
3 The predestined actor model
4 The victimized actor model
5 The centrality of modernist models in criminological explanation

This chapter considers how crime was explained by what might be loosely termed 'criminologists' and other closely linked, primarily social science disciplines and subsequently dealt with by the diverse criminal justice system, in a predominantly unequivocal modern age. The theories – or explanations – that came to the fore during that epoch can be broadly conceptualized in one of three different competing models of crime and criminal behaviour – the rational actor, the predestined actor and the victimized actor models – with each becoming incrementally more sophisticated over the years. This chapter provides a relatively brief, selective résumé of these competing, but ultimately compatible, explanatory models, which can all be conceptualized in the modernist world of moral certainty, where it is proposed that given time, reflection and revision, they can solve the crime problem.

The rational actor model

The rational actor model has its origins in the ideas of the late eighteenth- and early nineteenth-century modernist philosophers Cesare Beccaria in Italy and Jeremy Bentham in Britain. This model proposes that criminal behaviour is simply the outcome of rational, calculating individuals who enjoy and exercise free will and hence choose to commit crime in preference to law-abiding activities. The recommended criminal justice response is that the individual should be held fully responsible for their transgressions and punished accordingly. Since the calculation for choosing to offend involves the acquisition of a benefit (pleasure), society must thus develop policies to increase the cost of this benefit (pain). Punishment should become incrementally harsher as the extent and impact of criminal behaviour become greater and more serious, while the costs of engaging in crime must always outweigh the possible benefits that might be obtained. Crucially punishment should fit the crime and not the characteristics and/or circumstances of the individual. All are equal in the eyes of law and they are to be dealt with accordingly (see Table 3.1).

Table 3.1 Rational actor model

- People enjoy free will and have freedom of action.
- They choose to engage in criminal activity.
- Society should deter offending by the punishment of those who have offended and others at risk of offending.
- Punishment should be proportional to the offence committed.
- Punishment be guaranteed and delivered quickly.

The purist rational actor model proposition of equal treatment for all people regardless of status has an intuitive appeal but is nevertheless problematic. Children, the 'feeble-minded' and the insane were all dealt with by the early modernist criminal justice system as if they were fully rational and competent people capable of making decisions for which they could legitimately be held fully responsible. It nonetheless became increasingly apparent that this was not the case. The outcome was a compromise where ordinary, sane adults were considered to be fully responsible for their actions but others – children and the insane, in particular – were considered less responsible for their actions.

Subsequent revisions to the penal code were to subsequently admit into the courts for the first time non-legal 'experts', including doctors, psychiatrists and later social workers, to determine the extent to which offenders were to be considered responsible for their actions. The outcome was that sentences became more individualized and dependent on the supposed degree of culpability of the offender.

Furthermore, it was recognized that different punishments would have different effects on different people. Consequently, punishment became increasingly expressed in terms of the individual characteristics of the person and their potential for rehabilitation. The purist rational actor was now breached. Increasingly, there would be disparities in the punishments handed out to offenders who had committed similar offences. Punishment came to fit the person, not the crime.

The rational actor model went into increasing decline as an explanation of offending behaviour but was to return to favour with a vengeance during the last quarter of the twentieth century and the emergence of the populist conservatives (political) and the 'right realists' (criminological) where the ever-increasing crime levels came to be blamed on weakening sources of social authority, the family, schools religion and other key institutions and on the corrosive influence of the surrounding legitimating liberal socialist culture, with its emphasis on rights rather than responsibilities. It was now once again proposed that offenders should take full responsibility for their actions and that punishment was to be about devising penalties to fit the crime and ensuring they were carried out.

There are three categories of contemporary theories which can be considered in the context of the rational actor model: (a) contemporary variants on traditional deterrence theories, (b) rational choice theories and (c) routine activity theories.

Contemporary deterrence theories

These are founded on the twin rational actor principles that punishment must occur quickly after the offence has been committed and on the certainty that it will be carried out. If the punishment is sufficiently severe, certain to occur and be swiftly carried out, the rational individual, it is argued, will conclude that there is more to be lost than gained and hence desist from offending (Wright, 1993).

There are two variants of the deterrence doctrine and these operate in different but closely connected ways. With the notion of general deterrence, the capture and punishment of offenders demonstrate clearly to *all* what will happen if they break the law, while specific deterrence demonstrates to the apprehended and punished *individual* the futility of further criminal involvement. However, the high rate of recidivism challenges the effectiveness of deterrence with reoffending rates historically high.

Contemporary rational choice theories

Rational choice theories had originally compared the decision-making process of offenders with straightforward economic choice. The person thus chooses the activity – either legal or illegal – that offers the best return and, it is argued, could be deterred from making 'the wrong' decision by a more effective and rigorous criminal justice system (Becker, 1968). Not surprisingly, this early version was accused of implying too high a degree of rationality.

Clarke and Cornish were to nevertheless produce an influential modified variant of rational choice theory where crime is defined as 'the outcome of the offender's choices or decisions, however hasty or ill-considered these might be' (Clarke, 1987: 118). It was now recognized that offenders will not always be able to obtain all the facts needed to make a wise decision, and the information available will not necessarily be weighed carefully or appropriately, but the individual will make a decision that is rational to them in the context of their lives, experiences, cultural background and knowledge base. Thus, a juvenile brought up in a location where criminality is common, with their family and friends actively involved in illicit activities, which appear to bring them easily obtained material rewards and where access to legitimate opportunities appear both limited and implausible, could well consider involvement in criminal activities a very rational choice. This is a key observation for proponents of the contemporary rational actor model.

Routine activities theory

Routine activities theory observes that, for a crime to occur, there must be at the same time and place a perpetrator, a victim and/or an object of property (Felson, 1998). The offence can take place if there are persons or circumstances that encourage it to happen, but it can be prevented if the potential victim or another person present take action to deter it. Cohen and Felson (1979) argued that fundamental changes in daily activities related to work, school and leisure which have increasingly occurred since the 1950s, have placed more people in particular localities at certain times and increased their accessibility as crime targets, while they were away from home and unable to guard their property and possessions.

It is often juveniles and children who are found wandering the streets when adults are at work and who are prepared to take advantage of crime opportunities when they arise – and indeed, they may be actively looking for these in the first place. Moreover, these transgressions are most likely to occur when the child is in the company of like-minded others, in particular when they are truanting or excluded from school or in subsequent years when, having left school with inadequate educational qualifications and no marketable skills, they find themselves excluded from legitimate economic opportunities.

Rational actor model: conclusions and policy implications

The rational actor model proposes that individuals choose to offend because it makes rational sense to them in the context of their lives. Offending choices are more attractive than legitimate activities, which are usually unavailable to them or of limited value. Deterrence theory suggests that people can be deterred from criminality by the threat or imposition of rigorous penalties, but recidivism rates suggest that this strategy has not been very successful.

The other strategy implication of the rational actor model is to improve the life chances of individuals, so they have access to good quality, legitimate opportunities which make offending a less rational choice. Offenders will desist from criminal behaviour when they are provided with such rational alternatives.

The other two models of criminal behaviour elaborate on the individual and social circumstances that impact significantly on choices that they might make and encourage involvement in criminality.

The predestined actor model

The predestined actor model replaces the rational actor notion of free will with the doctrine of determinism. Offending behaviour is now explained in terms of factors, internal (biological or psychological) or external (sociological or environmental) to the individual, which cause or determine them to act in ways over which they have little or no control. In short, something is making them behave in this way, they have little or no choice. There are three basic formulations of the predestined actor model – biological, psychological and sociological – but all incorporate the same fundamental assumptions, and with these factors in place, the person is predestined to be a criminal (see Table 3.2).

Biological theories

These have their origins in the work of the Italian School at the end of the nineteenth century. Lombroso (1875) famously – indeed, notoriously – argued that criminals are a physical type distinct from non-criminals and they can be recognized by their physical appearance: low foreheads, big ears, misshaped noses, for example. While his work is considered simplistic by the standards of today, he later importantly recognized the need for

Table 3.2 Predestined actor model

- The rational actor emphasis on free will is replaced with the doctrine of determinism.
- Criminal behaviour is explained in terms of factors, internal or external to the individual, that cause people to act in ways over which they have little or no control.
- The individual is thus in some way predestined to be a criminal.
- There are three basic formulations – biological, psychological and sociological – but all incorporate the same fundamental determinist assumptions.
- Treatment of the offender is proposed rather than punishment.

multifactor accounts that include hereditary, social, cultural and economic factors. Ferri (1895) also argued that criminal behaviour could be explained by studying the interaction between physical, individual and social factors, proposing that crime could be controlled by improving the living conditions of the poor. It is thus a key tenet of predestined actor model thinking that some form of 'treatment' should be used to correct the behaviour of the offender or their environment.

Biological theories were to become increasingly more sophisticated but invariably remained problematic in explaining criminal behaviour. The notion of inherited criminal characteristics was, for example, a central theme, although research ultimately failed to distinguish between biological and environmental factors. In short, was the young person an offender because they had inherited the relevant biological characteristics from their parents or simply because they were growing up in an enabling criminal environment where criminality appears to be normal behaviour?

Genetic structure explanations have considered abnormalities in the genetic structure of the offender. Thus, some men were found to have an extra female chromosome (with supposedly more female characteristics) while others had an extra male chromosome (supra-male characteristics). Nevertheless, these theories were flawed, not least because it was 'found' that there were thousands of perfectly normal and harmless people in the general population with an extra chromosome. We might nevertheless question exactly what characteristics constitute a 'normal' and 'harmless' person. Is it simply a matter of never having been convicted of a criminal offence or are there other unpleasant manifestations of antisocial behaviour which are not technically against the law but in which such people regularly engage? We do not know because the research has not been conducted.

The more recent discovery that some traits of personality can be explained by a genetic component (Jones, 1993) certainly strengthens the possibility that at least some criminal behaviour can be explained by an inherited genetic propensity, which is triggered by environmental factors, for example, being in an aggressive situation while having drunk more than a little alcohol. More recent socio-biological theories develop this argument further and these are considered below.

Criminal body type theories are part of a long-established tradition – with their origins in the work of Lombroso – which propose that offenders are organically inferior people. Thus, Sheldon (1949) linked different types of physique to temperament, intelligence and criminality and Glueck and Glueck (1950) also proposed that offenders have different shaped bodies than non-offenders. Problematically, all these researchers failed to establish whether their research subjects were offenders because of their build and disposition, because their physique and dispositions were socially conceived as associated with offenders, or whether poverty and deprivation affected both their body build and offending behaviour.

Biochemical theories link criminality with substances that are either already present in the body or are created by some internal physiological process. Thus, it has long been recognized that most male animals are more aggressive than females, and this has been linked to the male sex hormone, testosterone, although the relationship between the two in human beings appears to be more ambiguous. Olwens (1987), nevertheless, found a clear link between testosterone and verbal and physical aggression in young males, with a further distinction being between provoked and unprovoked aggressive behaviour. Schalling (1987) found high testosterone levels in young males to be associated with verbal but not actual physical aggression, which suggests a concern to protect their status by threats. Ellis and Crontz (1990) observed that testosterone levels peak during puberty and the early 20s, which correlates with the highest crime rates, although they produced no real evidence of a causal relationship. There is nevertheless a long-established widespread recognition of the need to control the physical exuberance of young males going back at least to the public school system and the development of team sports which became a template for state schools with the dreaded cross-country run followed by a cold shower. Regular physical exercise is clearly considered to be positive.

Hypoglycaemia, or low blood sugar levels, has been found to result in irritable, aggressive reactions and may culminate in sexual offences, assaults and motiveless murder. Felson (1998) discovered that by lowering the daily sucrose intake of incarcerated juveniles it is possible to reduce the level of their antisocial behaviour and aggression, while Virkkunen (1987) went further and linked hypoglycaemia with truancy, low verbal IQ, tattooing and stealing from home during childhood. Diet can clearly impact on the propensity of the young person to offend and when radically changed may even help in encouraging them to desist.

Baldwin (1990) proposed that the significant link between (young) age and crime rates – which has long been established – can be partially explained by arousal rates, observing that young people quickly become used to stimuli that had previously excited them, become bored with more of the same and thus seek ever more thrilling inputs. The stimulus (or buzz) received from offending was moreover found to decline with age, as did the level of physical fitness, strength and agility required to perform many of these activities. In this scenario, desistance is simply a part of getting old in the same way as the capacity to engage in competitive team games declines with age.

Altered biological state theories associate behavioural changes in the individual with the introduction of an external chemical agent and establish links between irritability and aggression which may lead individuals to commit criminal assault. Research on the criminological implications of allergies to such things as pollen, inhalants, drugs and food suggests two main reactions: emotional immaturity, characterized by temper tantrums, screaming episodes, whining and impatience and antisocial behaviour characterized by sulkiness and cruelty (Virkkunen, 1987).

Substance abuse occurs through the intake of drugs, some of which are legal and freely available, such as alcohol, glues and lighter fluids, others prescribed by the medical profession, such as barbiturates, and those only available illegally, such as cannabis, amphetamines, LSD, MDA or ecstasy, and opiates (usually cocaine or heroin). Alcohol is extremely significant because it is legal, readily available and long been associated with antisocial behaviour and crime.

Alcohol and young people are closely linked in the public mind, but this has not always been the case. In the interwar period, young people were the lightest drinkers in the adult population, and alcohol did not play a significant part in the youth culture that emerged during the 1950s. It was not until the 1960s that pubs and drinking became an integral part of the youth scene; by the 1980s, those aged 18 to 24 years had become the heaviest drinkers in the population. Hazardous drinking is now most prevalent in teenagers and young adults: 32% of females between 16 and 19 years of age and 62% of males between 20 and 24 have a hazardous drinking pattern. These changes have been accompanied by a decline in the age of regular drinking, with many drinking regularly by the age of 14 or 15 (Institute of Alcohol Studies, 2005). There has also been a growing trend of drinking for effect and intoxication, which is partly related to the merging of the alcohol and drug scenes in youth culture. Alcohol is now one of a range of psychoactive products available on the recreational drug market in the UK. A large survey of teenagers found that, by the age of 15 or 16, binge drinking was common, as was being 'seriously drunk' (Jefferis et al., 2005).

Recent evidence nevertheless shows that alcohol consumption among juveniles and young people is in decline. An Office of National Statistics report (ONS, 2015) shows that less than 50% of young people actually drink alcohol now with equally large numbers desisting from binge drinking. It was found that the proportion of young adults' binge drinking has fallen more than a third since 2005, from 29% to 18%. Juveniles and young people interviewed in the study observed that the shame of appearing on social media drunk, scantily dressed and in very embarrassing poses has deterred many from participating in the binge-drinking culture.

The term *alcohol-related crime* usually refers to offences involving (a) a combination of criminal damage, drunk and disorderly and other public disorder offences; (b) young males, typically 18 to 30; and (c) the entertainment areas of town and city centres invariably closely linked to involvement in the binge drinking culture. Research, moreover, shows that a high proportion of victims of violent crime are drinking or under the influence of alcohol at the time of their assault and a minimum of one in five people arrested by the police test positive for alcohol (Bennett, 2000). Clearly the significant decline in the numbers of young people drinking alcohol and in particular binge drinking has had a large impact of the numbers involved in alcohol-related crime.

Different measures have been introduced in the last few years seeking to curtail the dangerous and anti-social consequences of youthful alcohol consumption – increasing prices to breathalysing would be entrants to night clubs – but it seems that the biggest impact on this age group has been the pressures of peer group shaming. Binge drinking is not so cool now.

Widespread illegal drug use emerged in the UK during the late 1960s. Drugs are chemicals which alter the biochemical balance of the body and brain and can affect behaviour in different ways depending on the type and quantity of the drug taken. The biological effects of cannabis and opiates such as heroin tend to reduce aggressive hostile tendencies, while cocaine and its derivative crack are more closely associated with violence. The most commonly used drug by young people is cannabis, which has been used by 33% of young men and 22% of young women. Ecstasy is the most commonly used class A drug, with higher use among 16- to 24-year-olds, while in recent years, there has been an increase in the use of cocaine among young people, especially among males. By contrast, the use of amphetamines and LSD has declined (Institute of Alcohol Studies, 2005). Drug use has been found to be widespread among school pupils, although there has been a decrease in prevalence in recent years (Department of Health, 2005) although young people 16 to 24 continue to be the demographic group with the largest use in the UK.

In summary, a number of biological studies suggest that some individuals are born with a physiological condition which predisposes them to commit crime, but closer investigation suggests that social and environmental background are at least equally important. Evidence nevertheless suggests that, in cases where the biology of the individual has been altered through the introduction of a foreign chemical agent such as diet, alcohol and/or illegal drugs, behaviour can be substantially changed and significant increases in criminal involvement may follow.

There have been attempts in recent years to rehabilitate biological explanations by incorporating social and environmental factors into a 'multifactor' approach. These sociobiologists argue that the presence of certain biological predispositions – and the introduction of foreign chemical agents – may increase the likelihood, but not determine absolutely, that an individual will offend (Mednick *et al.*, 1987). Jeffery (1977) observed that offenders are more likely to experience an inferior-quality diet and be exposed to pollutants, with the resulting nutrients and chemicals transformed by the biochemical system into neurochemical compounds in the brain. Poverty thus leads to behavioural differences, which occur through the interaction of the individual and environment.

Wilson and Herrnstein (1985) argued that an amalgam of gender, age, intelligence, body type and personality factors constitute the individual, who is projected into a social world where they learn what kind of behaviour is rewarded in what circumstances. Heavily influenced by the psychological behaviourism we will encounter later, the authors argued that individuals learn to respond to situations according to how their behaviour has been previously rewarded and punished, and their environment should therefore be changed to produce the desired conduct desired and hence discourage involvement in criminality. Thus, to understand the propensity to commit crime, it is important to identify the ways in which the environment might operate on particular individuals to produce this response. Within this general learning framework, the influence of the family, school and wider community is identified as being crucial.

Psychological theories

Psychological theories direct our intention to notions of the 'criminal mind' or 'personality', where it is proposed that there are patterns of reasoning and behaviour specific to offenders and that these remain constant regardless of the different social experiences encountered by the individual.

There are three broad categories of psychological theories: the first two – psychodynamic and behavioural learning theories – have firm roots in the predestined actor tradition, the third – cognitive learning theories – reject much of the positivist tradition and, in incorporating notions of creative thinking and choice, are in many ways more akin to the rational actor model. Each tradition nonetheless proposes that the personality is developed during the early formative childhood years through a process of learning. Psychodynamic and behavioural learning involve a process of subconscious non-reflective learning when we are very young and which we will not remember, cognitive learning involves reflection and some choice and is more likely to occur when we are a little older.

Psychodynamic theories

Psychodynamic theories have their origins in the work of Sigmund Freud (1856–1939) and his ideas about how our personalities develop as an outcome of our intimate relationships with our parents, in particular, the mother. His assertion that sexuality is present from birth – and has a subsequent course of development – is the fundamental basis of psychoanalysis.

In the psychoanalytical model, the human personality has three sets of interacting forces: (1) the id, or primitive biological drives; (2) the superego – or conscience – that operates in the unconsciousness but which is composed of values internalized through the early interactions of the child, in particular those with their parents; and (3) the ego, or the conscious personality, which has the important task of balancing the demands of the id against the inhibitions imposed by the superego, as the child responds to external influences (Freud, 1927).

Freud proposed two different explanations of offending behaviour. First, some crimes are the product of mental disturbance or illness. His theory of psychosexual development proposes a number of complex stages of psychic development in early childhood which may easily be disrupted, leading to neuroses or severe difficulties when we get older. Crucially, a disturbance at one or more of these stages can lead to criminal behaviour in later life. Of central importance is the nature of the relationship the child has with its parents and significantly, many influences are unconscious, with neither the child nor its parents are aware of the impact they are having on each other.

Second, it was argued that offenders possess a 'weak conscience', the development of which is of fundamental importance in the upbringing of the child. A sense of morality is closely linked to guilt, and those possessing the greatest degree of unconscious 'guilt' are likely to be those with the strictest consciences and are the most unlikely to offend. Guilt results not from committing crimes but from a deeply embedded feeling which develops in childhood, the outcome of the way in which the parents respond to transgressions. It is a theory which has led to a proliferation of tests attempting to measure conscience or levels of guilt, in the belief that this will allow a prediction of later offending behaviour.

The Freudian approach is firmly embedded in the predestined actor model: unconscious conflicts or tensions determine all actions and it is the purpose of the conscious (ego) to resolve these tensions by finding ways to satisfy the basic inner urges by engaging in activities sanctioned by society such as playing organized sport or involvement in drama or artistic activities.

The Freudian theory on which psychoanalysis is based is contentious and widely challenged, and it is virtually untestable by researchers. It was nevertheless extremely influential throughout the twentieth century not least because the central propositions of psychoanalytic theory – children need close loving relationships with parents, develop positive and negative attitudes during socialization and repress unpleasant experiences – have been testable with the outcomes invariably explainable without recourse to the general theory.

Later Freudians were concerned with elaborating the development of the ego more specifically. Aichhorn (1925) argued that at birth a child is unaware of the norms of society but has certain instinctive drives that demand satisfaction. The child is then considered to be in an 'asocial state'. The task is to bring it into a social state but when the development process is ineffective, he or she remains asocial. Thus, if the instinctive drives are not acted out, the child becomes suppressed and is in a state of 'latent delinquency'. Given outside provocative stimuli, this can be transformed into actual offending behaviour. If you bring up your child instilled with positive attitudes and values, they are likely to turn out to be law-abiding citizens. If you do not, then future criminality is highly likely.

Healy and Bronner (1936) sought to explain why siblings exposed to similar unfavourable circumstances might react differently, with one becoming an offender and the others not. Offenders were found to be more emotionally disturbed, needing to express their frustrations through deviant activities, while non-offenders channelled their frustrated needs into socially accepted activities. Kate Friedlander (1947) later argued that some children simply develop an antisocial behaviour or a faulty character which leaves them susceptible to deviant behaviour. Redl and Wineman (1951) argued that some children develop a delinquent ego and a subsequent hostile attitude towards authority because they have not developed a good ego and superego.

John Bowlby (1952) influentially argued that offending takes place when a child has not enjoyed a close and continuous relationship with its mother during its formative years. His maternal deprivation theory had a major and lasting influence on the training of social workers, while a plethora of researchers have sought to test it empirically. Rutter (1981) conducted a comprehensive review of these studies and concluded that the stability of the child/mother relationship is more important than the absence of breaks and proposed that a small number of substitutes can successfully carry out mothering functions provided such care is of good quality. The crucial issue is the quality of child-rearing practices.

Glueck and Glueck (1950) had found that the fathers of offenders generally provide lax and inconsistent discipline, with the use of physical punishment common and the giving of praise rare. McCord *et al.* (1959) agreed that the consistency of discipline is more important than the degree of strictness, while Bandura and Walters (1959) found fathers of aggressive boys more likely to punish such behaviour in the home while approving of it outside.

Hoffman and Saltzstein (1967) identified three types of child-rearing techniques: First, power assertion, involves the parental use of physical punishment and/or the withdrawal of material privileges; second, love withdrawal, where the parent withdraws affection from the child, for example by paying no attention to it; and, third, induction, which entails letting the child know how its actions have affected the parent, thus encouraging a sympathetic or empathetic response. The first technique primarily relies on the instillation of fear, while the other two depend on the fostering of guilt feelings in the child. The researchers were to conclude that children who have been nurtured through the use of love withdrawal or induction techniques develop greater internalized controls and are less likely to offend than those raised through power assertion techniques.

Research has suggested that a 'broken home', where one of the birth parents is not present, may be a factor in the development of offending. Glueck and Glueck (1950) thus found that 60% of the offenders in their sample came from such a home, a finding supported in Britain by Burt (1945) and Mannheim (1948). Others have observed that the 'broken home' is not a homogenous category and a range of different factors need to be considered (Tappan, 1960). Nye (1958) and Gibbens (1963) thus found that offending behaviour is more likely to occur among children from intact but unhappy homes. West and Farrington (1973) found that about twice as many offenders as non–offenders came from homes broken by parental separation before the child was ten years old. Monahan (1957) suggested that broken homes were far more common among black than white offenders, while Chilton and Markle (1972) found that the rate of family breakdown was much higher in black than in white families and suggested that this may explain why more black young offenders come from broken homes. Pitts (1986) later claimed a link between criminality and homelessness and found that black youths were more likely to become homeless than whites. Significantly, studies have found that broken homes and early separation predict convictions up to the age of 33 where the separation occurred before the age of 5 (Farrington, 1992).

All of the studies reported earlier nevertheless tell stories that intuitively make sense without any recourse whatsoever to psychoanalytical theory which may or may not be correct. We simply do not know.

Behavioural learning theories

Behavioural theories have their origins in the work of Ivan Pavlov, who famously studied the processes involved in very simple, automatic animal behaviours where the dog came to associate a ringing bell with food, and B.F. Skinner, who extended the behaviourist conditioning principle to active learning, whereby the animal has to do something to obtain a reward or avoid punishment. These theories propose that the behaviours we learn in our childhood are caused, strengthened or weakened by external stimuli in our environment and are an automatic response without thought or reflection.

Operant conditioning is thus a method of learning that occurs through rewards and punishments, which become associated with certain behaviours. Children thus might complete homework to earn a reward from a parent or teacher. In this example, the promise or possibility of a reward causes a qualitative improvement in behaviour. But operant conditioning can also be used to reduce less desirable activities. For example a child may be told they will have privileges withdrawn if they misbehave or talk in class and it is this potential for punishment which may lead to a decrease in disruptive behaviour.

Cognitive learning theories

Cognitive learning theories have their foundations in a fundamental critique of the pre-destined actor model and explain human behaviour in terms of a three-way dynamic exchange, in which personal factors, external influences and behaviour continually inter-act. Cognitivists share the view of the operant conditioning perspective that the child must actively respond to stimuli if they are to learn but shift the emphasis to mental rather than physical activity. This social learning theory emphasizes that behaviour may be rein-forced not only through actual rewards and punishments but also through expectations which are learned by watching what happens to other children. Ultimately, the person will make a choice as to what they will learn and how. If the other (perhaps older) child appears to get a positive response from adults or other children the observed 'cool' behav-iour might be considered worth imitating.

An early proponent of the notion that crime is simply a normal learned behaviour was Gabriel Tarde (1843–1904), who argued that offenders are primarily normal people who by accident of birth are brought up in a situation where they learn crime as a way of life. His laws of imitation thus propose that people imitate and copy each other in proportion to the amount of contact they have. First, the law of close contact proposes that if a per-son is regularly in the company of offenders, they are more likely to imitate this behav-iour than that of non-offenders with whom they have little association. Second, the law of imitation of superiors by inferiors proposes that youngsters imitate older individuals. Children hanging out on the street thus tend to take their cues and are heavily influenced by older children. Third, the law of insertion proposes that new activities and behaviours are superimposed on old ones and subsequently either reinforce or discourage previous customs. This law refers to the power said to be inherent in newness or novelty, where new fashions replace old 'customs'. Thus, illicit drug taking may become popular among a group of juveniles who have previously favoured alcohol.

The imitation thesis has been very influential. Social psychologists propose that pat-terns of illicit drug use may have their origins in the observation of parental drug use, which begins to have a damaging effect on children as young as two years old (Wills *et al.*, 1996). However, children respond to peer group influences more readily than adults because of the crucial role these relationships play in identity formation. Their greater desire for acceptance and approval from their peers makes them more susceptible to peer influences as they adjust their behaviour and attitudes to conform to those of their contemporaries. Significantly, young people 'commit crimes, as they live their lives, in groups' (Morse, 1997a: 108) an important concept which is explored further later. More indirectly, the desire of juveniles for peer approval can affect the choices they make without any direct coercion. Morse (1997b) observed that peers may provide models for behaviour that juveniles believe will assist them in accomplishing their own ends.

Sutherland (1937) used the term *differential association* when influentially arguing that it is the frequency and consistency of contacts that individuals have with criminality that significantly impacts on the likelihood that they will regularly participate in criminal behaviour. The basic cause of such behaviour is the existence of different cultural groups with different attitudes and values within the same society that has produced a situation of differential social organization. He was to later argue that criminal behaviour occurs when individuals acquire sufficient attitudes in favour of criminality to outweigh their association with non-criminal tendencies (Sutherland, 1947). The associations or contacts that have the greatest impact are those which are frequent, early in point of origin or the most intense. Thus, hanging around with children who are involved in deviant and offending is much more likely to lead to criminal behaviour than if you spend your time with the law-abiding. For the latter, criminal behaviour is simply not cool and probably inconceivable.

Akers (1985) later restated dissociation theory and focused on four central concepts. First, differential association refers to the patterns of interactions with others that are the source of social learning and which can be either favourable or unfavourable to offending. He updates the theory to include more distant reference groups such as the media, including, more recently internet access, which can bring like-minded people together from all around the world (Hopkins Burke and Pollock, 2004). Second, definitions reflect the meanings that a person applies to their own behaviour; for example the wider peer group might not define recreational drug use as deviant, and the individual does not consider their behaviour to be criminal. Third, differential reinforcement refers to the actual or anticipated consequences of a particular behaviour: thus, children will do things they think will result in rewards and avoid activities they think will result in punishment. Fourth, imitation involves observing what others do, but whether a decision is made to imitate that behaviour will depend on the characteristics of the person being observed, the actual behaviour the person engages in and the observed consequences of that behaviour for others. If the observed young person appears to be 'cool', is engaged in activities which appear to be 'cool', rewarding and/or pleasurable, it is likely that the behaviour will be imitated. The converse is also true. Behaviour perceived to be 'uncool', engaged in by those seen as 'uncool', is unlikely to be imitated by those with aspirations to being 'cool'.

Sociological theories

Sociologists have broadly rejected the individualist explanations favoured by biological and psychological perspectives and in contrast have examined the environmental factors which are considered the most important in the creation of crime. It is an enduring tradition, informed by the influential social theory of Emile Durkheim and his concerns at the end of the nineteenth/early twentieth century with the social problems created by the rapid social change brought about by the great European Industrial Revolution and its aftermath. It is an approach which clearly remains highly significant in the present day as we continue to undergo unprecedented rapid social change and repeated increasingly unfathomable economic crises

Social disorganization thesis

Durkheim (1933, originally 1893) provides us with two alternative arguments to explain the rise in crime in fast changing modern industrial societies. First, such societies encourage a state of unbridled 'egoism' – the notion that in a free-market economy, individuals should pursue their own rational self-interest without reference to the collective interest of society – which, it is observed, is contrary to the maintenance of social solidarity and conformity to the law. Second, the likelihood of inefficient regulation is greater at a time of rapid modernization because new forms of control have evolved insufficiently to replace the older and now less appropriate means of maintaining solidarity. In such a period, society is in a state of normlessness or 'anomie', a condition characterized by a breakdown in norms and common understandings. The old ways of doing things are challenged, not least today by the unparalleled growth in social media.

Durkheim claimed that without adequate external controls human beings have unlimited aspirations; it is thus appropriate for society to indicate what are acceptable rewards. This it is argued works reasonably well in times of social stability, but at times of major economic upheaval, society comes adrift from its 'realistic' moorings and is unable to control the ambitions of individuals. Thus, during an economic depression, people are forced to lower their sights, a situation which some will find intolerable, particularly when for many there appears no way out of the economic impasse and, at that point, start to look around for other ways of making a rewarding living. On the other hand, when there is an improvement in economic conditions the social equilibrium will break down, with uncontrollable desires released. Both situations lead to increased criminality, the first through need and the second through greed.

This social disorganization thesis was later developed by sociologists based at the University of Chicago who introduced us to the idea that criminality is not so much about the individuals involved but rather something about the socially disorganized neighbourhoods where the offenders live.

Ernest Burgess (1928) argued that as modern industrial cities expand in size their development is patterned socially. He observed that commercial enterprises were located in the central business district, with the most expensive residential areas in the outer suburbs, away from the bustle of the city centre and the homes of the poor. It was the 'zone in transition' – what we might term the inner city in the contemporary British context – which contained rows of deteriorating tenements, often built in the shadow of ageing factories, that were the centre of attention. The outward expansion of the business district led to the constant displacement of residents and, as the least desirable living area, the zone was the focus for the influx of waves of immigrants who were too poor to reside elsewhere. Burgess observed that these social patterns weakened family and community ties, with the outcome being social disorganization and criminal behaviour.

Clifford Shaw and Henry McKay (1972, originally 1931) found that crime levels were highest in the slum neighbourhoods of the zone of transition regardless of which ethnic group resided there and, significantly, as these groups moved to other zones, their offending rates correspondingly decreased. It was this observation that led them to the conclusion that it is the nature of the neighbourhood that regulates involvement in crime not the characteristics of particular individuals. The researchers emphasized the importance of neighbourhood organization in allowing or preventing juvenile offending. In the more affluent communities, parents fulfilled the needs of their offspring and carefully supervised their activities; in the zone of transition, families and other conventional institutions were strained, if not destroyed, by rapid urban growth, migration and poverty. Left to their own devices, juveniles were not subject to the social constraints placed on those in more affluent areas, not least because of the very limited family living space available and were more likely to seek excitement and friends on 'the street'. The street which was to take on an almost mythical status among groups of young people and an increasingly iconic space immortalized in popular culture.

Shaw and McKay (1972: 174) thus concluded that disorganized neighbourhoods help produce and sustain 'criminal traditions' which compete with conventional values and can be 'transmitted down through successive generations of juveniles, in much the same way that language and other social forms are transmitted'. Thus, children growing up in socially disorganized inner-city slum areas, characterized by the existence of a value system which condones criminal behaviour, can readily learn these values in their daily interactions with older adolescents.

The Chicago school tradition emphasized criminal behaviour in the inner city while, at the same time, a natural process whereby slum-dwellers appear to 'make good', escape social disorganization and inherently criminal neighbourhoods and join the socially aspirational flight to the suburbs. In the UK, in particular, this has been a far from natural process with housing policy relocating large numbers of social housing tenants often to the vast outer estates built on the outskirts of every town and city in the in the immediate post–Second World War period. At a time of full employment, these new estates housed the workers, with the onset of mass unemployment and the big expansion in the number of non-working single-parent families from the late 1970s onwards, these localities became increasingly socially disorganized and criminogenic. Shifting social problems from the centre of town to the outskirts in the British context.

The US variant of social disorganization theory – epitomized by the Chicago school – called for efforts to reorganize communities with treatment programmes that attempted to reverse the criminal learning of offenders. Juvenile offenders, it is argued, should be placed in settings where they receive pro-social reinforcement, for example, through the use of positive peer counselling and mentoring. With this form of intervention, the juvenile offender can be persuaded to desist from offending.

Durkheim had proposed that human needs or aspirations were 'natural' in the sense that they are socially constructed through reference to other individuals and groups. His US successor Robert Merton, by contrast, argued that needs are usually socially learned while – and this is the central component of his argument – there are social structural limitations imposed on access to the means to achieve these goals. Merton (1938) observed that it is possible to overemphasize either the goals or the means, with the outcome being social strains or his version of 'anomie'. Deviant, especially criminal, behaviour results when cultural goals are accepted – and, for example, people would like to be materially successful – but where access to the means to achieve that goal is limited by the position of the individual in the social structure. In some cases, where the individual has limited access to the legitimate means of material success, they will adopt innovative strategies for attaining their objective, which will include criminality.

Deviant subculture theories

Deviant subculture theories originated in the US during the 1950s and, while there are different versions, all propose that some social groups have values and attitudes which encourage members to offend. Children and juveniles thus come together – invariably on the mythical street – to engage in activities that may or may not be criminal because, in the language of today, they appear to be 'cool' and the individual can gain 'respect' from their peers.

Albert Cohen (1955) proposed that offending was commonplace among lower-class males, with the most popular form being the juvenile gang who were said to have values in opposition to those of the dominant culture. Delinquent boys came together to define status, with offending behaviour serving no real purpose and participants often discarding or destroying what they had stolen. They were simply a short-term hedonistic subculture: offending tended to be random and directed at people and property; stealing served as a form of achieving peer status within the group. There was no other motive. It was simply cool.

Miller (1958) argued that working-class morality emerged as a response to living in the brutalized conditions of the slums, which encouraged offending. His concept of focal concerns describes important aspects of participation in this working-class subculture. First, there is a concern over trouble: both getting into trouble and staying out of it are important daily preoccupations. Second, toughness represents commitment to breaking the law and being a problem to others, with machismo and daring emphasized. Third, smartness is the ability to gain some advantage by outsmarting or conning others. Fourth, excitement is living on the edge and doing dangerous things for 'the buzz' and which are 'cool'. Fifth, fate is of crucial concern, with many believing their lives to be subject to forces outside their control. Sixth, autonomy signifies being independent, not relying on others and a rejection of authority.

Cloward and Ohlin (1960) argued that delinquent subcultures flourish among the lower classes but take different forms, with the means to achieve illegitimate success no more equally distributed than it is for legitimate success. Three different variants of subculture were proposed, and it was argued that the capacity for each to flourish is dependent on the locality in which they develop and the availability of deviant opportunities.

First, criminal gangs emerge in localities where conventional as well as non-conventional values are integrated through the close connection of illegitimate and legitimate businesses. Older criminals serve as role models in established criminal groups or gangs, teach the necessary criminal skills and provide available opportunities and a career structure. Second, the conflict or violent gang is a non-stable and non-integrated grouping, which exists where there is an absence of a stable criminal organization, and its members seek a reputation and respect for toughness and destructive violence. Third, the retreatist gang is equally unsuccessful in the pursuit of illegitimate or legitimate opportunities and members are seen to be double failures, retreating into a world of sex, drugs and alcohol, although these elements can also be elements of the other subcultural variations.

Spergel (1964) identified an 'anomie gap' between the aspirations that young people have, their expected occupations and income, finding that the extent of this gap differed significantly between offenders, non-offenders and young people in different subcultures. He thus introduced his own three-part subculture typology. First, a racket subculture develops in areas where organized adult criminality is already in existence and highly visible; second, a theft subculture, involving offences such as burglary, shoplifting and taking and driving away cars, develops where a criminal subculture already exists but is not very well established; and, third, conflict subcultures involve gang fighting and the pursuit of reputation where there is limited or no access to either criminal or conventional activities. Drug misuse was found to be common to all subcultures as part of the transition from juvenile delinquent activity to conventional or fully developed criminal activity.

These early US deviant subcultural theories were widely accused of being overly determinist, with offenders seen to be not only different from non-offenders – a key component of predestined actor model thinking – but in some way committed to an alternative 'ethical' code which made criminal involvement virtually compulsory and from which they could not escape. Now, while it is likely that some young people are so strongly socialized into the mores of a particular worldview through membership of a particular ethnic group, their upbringing and/or the reinforcing influences of neighbourhood groups or gangs that they do not challenge this heritage in any way, it is likely that many others have less consistent socialization experiences and a far more tangential relationship to deviant behaviour.

The most comprehensive critique of the overly determinist, early deviant subcultural tradition – where young people appear destined to a life of crime because of their early offending in the company of likeminded others – is provided by the classic work of Sykes and Matza (1957), who crucially observed that these studies simply fail to explain why it is that mostly young people 'grow out' of their criminality. Their drift theory proposes that juveniles sense a moral obligation to be bound to the law, and if that bond remains in place, they will remain law abiding most of the time. It is when that bond is not in place that they will drift between involvement in legitimate and illegitimate activities.

Sykes and Matza proposed that young offenders actually hold values, beliefs and attitudes which are very similar to those of law-abiding citizens. This being the case, the issue is how they can justify their involvement in criminality to themselves. What we might call the 'how do you sleep at night conundrum', The answer is that they learn 'techniques' which enable them to 'neutralize' their law-abiding values and attitudes temporarily and thus drift back and forth between legitimate and illegitimate behaviours. Much of the time such young people participate in conventional activities but shun these while offending. In such situations, the individual disregards the controlling influences of rules and values and utilizes 'techniques of neutralization' to weaken the hold society has over them. In other words, these techniques act as defence mechanisms that release the young person from the constraints associated with the moral order.

Matza (1964) later rejected the notion that young people maintain a set of values which are independent of the dominant culture, proposing that they appreciate the culturally held goals and expectations of the middle class but feel the pursuit of such aspirations would be frowned on by their peers as they are not 'cool'. Moreover, such beliefs remain almost unconscious – or subterranean – because young people fear expressing them to their peers. It is when they reach a situation where they can admit these feelings to a close friend that they will simply grow out of offending. Of course, some never do, and it is these young offenders who develop adult criminal careers.

Early British deviant subcultural studies followed the lead of the US theories. Mays (1954) thus argued that, in some working-class areas, the residents share a number of attitudes and ways of behaving that predispose them to activities which just happen to be criminal. Working-class culture is not intentionally criminal; it is just a different socialization, which, at times, happens to be contrary to the law. Criminal behaviour is not a conscious rebellion against middle-class values but is part of an alternative subculture which has developed over the years in a random sort of way. Morris (1957) observed that the family controls middle-class socialization, is very ordered and almost all activities are centred on the home and the family. By contrast, the socialization of the working class tends to be divided between family, peer group and street acquaintances, with the latter likely to have a less ordered and regulated upbringing. The peer group is a much stronger influence from a much earlier age among the working classes, who encounter controls only after they have transgressed and are processed by the criminal justice system. The whole ethos of the working class is oriented towards antisocial activities which happen to be criminal.

Downes (1966) found that a large amount of offending happened in street corner groups rather than organized gangs. Status frustration did not occur to a significant degree, but the typical response to a lack of success at school or work was one of dissociation: 'What is the point of school?' There was an emphasis on leisure activities, with a dominant interest in commercial forms of entertainment, rather than youth clubs with their middle-class orientation, but access was nevertheless restricted by a lack of money, and juveniles would participate in petty criminality to find excitement. Peter Wilmott (1966) also found that offending was simply part of a general lower working-class subculture. Teenagers became involved in petty crime simply for the fun and togetherness of a shared activity.

Parker (1974) conducted a survey of unskilled adolescents in an area of Liverpool with a high rate of youth offending and found a pattern of loosely knit peer groups with criminality a central activity. Young males shared common problems such as unemployment, while leisure opportunities were limited and consequently some of their number developed a solution in the form of stealing car radios. The community largely condoned this behaviour as long as the victims were from outside the area and not part of their own.

These British subcultural studies are important because they identify specific historical factors, in particular the level of economic activity and the importance of a structural class analysis in helping to explain involvement in offending (Hopkins Burke and Sunley, 1998). The subculture concept was subsequently revised and revitalized by radical sociologists based at the Birmingham Centre for Contemporary Cultural Studies (CCCS) in the 1970s. They pertinently observed that subcultures arise at particular historical 'moments' as cultural solutions to the same structural economic problems created by rapid social change. The focus was on two broad areas: (1) mainstream youth and delinquency and (2) expressive or spectacular youth subcultures.

The two major studies of mainstream youth subcultures were those of Willis (1977) and Corrigan (1979), with both concerned with the transition from school to work among urban lower working-class boys. Their 'problem' was found to be an alien or seemingly irrelevant education system followed by the prospect of a boring and dead-end job. The 'solution' was a 'culture of resistance' manifested in truancy and petty offending notably during a period of relatively full employment during the early 1970s.

Willis calls his book *Learning to Labour: How Working-Class Kids Get Working Class Jobs*. He found that the 'lads' he followed during a two-year ethnographic study in the West Midlands – their final year at the local comprehensive school and the following one in the local factory – were completely uninterested in school; they saw the whole point as 'having a laff' rather than trying to get qualifications. Their approach to school was to survive it, do as little work as possible and have as much fun as possible by pushing the boundaries of authority and playing truant as much as they could. They did not value education because they knew their inevitable destiny was getting a job in the local factory and this did not require any formal qualifications. They saw school as a 'bit cissy' and for middle-class kids, while at the same time, they acquired the transferrable skills necessary to survive the mind-numbing boredom of working-class factory life.

Crucially, such predominantly unskilled factory jobs were to fast disappear from the late 1970s onwards, with the consequences significantly contributing to the creation of a socially excluded 'underclass' of, in particular, young males without the education, skills or training necessary to be employed in this completely restructured labour market, or put more simply, what happened when working-class kids ceased getting working-class jobs. The tacit skills acquired in surviving and indeed avoiding school would need to be utilized in rather different ways in 'post-work' society.

'Spectacular' youth subcultures – such as teddy boys, mods, skinheads, punks, rude boys – involved the adoption, at different times, by young people of both sexes, a distinctive style of dress combined with particular lifestyles, behaviour patterns and musical preferences. The Birmingham CCCS studies represent an important development of the subcultural tradition because they recognize that these groupings emerge in response to the distinctive economic problems encountered by different groups of young people in particular historical moments.

Hopkins Burke and Sunley (1998) observed that these studies presume a linear development of history where different subcultures arise, coalesce, fade and are replaced as economic circumstances change; for example the Mods were a product of the upwardly mobile working classes during the optimistic 1960s whereas the punks were a product of the 'dole queue', 'no future' despondency of the late 1970s. The researchers noted, in contrast, the subsequent coexistence of different subcultures and observed that these were a product of a fragmented modernity where different groups of young people were to coalesce to create solutions to their socio-economic problems specific to their group. Central to this account is the possibility of choice. The simultaneous existence of different subcultures enables some young people to choose the solution to their problem from the various subcultures available, although that choice will be crucially and significantly constrained by structural factors, not least those of (often multiple) social exclusion where choice is very much limited or even realistically non-existent.

Earlier subcultural studies had suggested that young people have limited choices, if any, between the deviant subculture available at a particular time and its location and a life of conventionality. A more contemporary interpretation of youth subcultures enables us to recognize that different groups of young people, have had very different experiences of the radical economic change that has occurred in Britain since the late 1970s, very much like the differential experience of social classes in the parental culture with the contemporary term *the left-behinds* accurately describing very large numbers of people – going well beyond the ranks of the socially excluded underclass – who have had an extremely negative experience of economic change during the past 40 years. This will all be discussed further later in this book.

Social control theories

The theories (or explanations) of criminal behaviour we have encountered so far consistently view conformity and law-abiding behaviour to be the almost natural state of being with any deviations from that normality considered abnormal or pathological. Social control theories usefully challenge that orthodoxy and turn the usual criminological question on its head and ask not 'Why do some people commit crime?' but 'Why is it that most of us conform?' The unifying factor in the different versions of control theories is that criminality can be expected when social and personal controls fail to restrain the individual from criminal involvement. Conversely, desistance can clearly occur when these controls or bonds are strengthened.

Early theories in this tradition emphasized personal psychological factors. Reiss (1951) thus distinguished between the effects of personal control, where individuals internalize the norms and rules of non-deviant primary groups, to the extent that they become their own, and social controls, where external social groups or institutions make rules or norms which we accept and are effective. Personal controls were considered to be far more important in preventing deviance than external social controls.

Nye (1958) subsequently identified four modes of social control which were said to encourage conformity in juveniles. First, direct control is imposed through external forces such as parents, teachers and the police, who use direct restraint and punishment. Second, individuals themselves, in the absence of external regulation, exercise internalized control. Third, indirect control is dependent on the degree of affection an individual has for conventional significant others. Thus, developing an affection or admiration for a non-conventional or an offending significant other is problematic. Fourth, control through alternative means of needs satisfaction works by reducing the temptation for individuals to resort to illegitimate means. Although independent of each other, these four modes of control are mutually reinforcing and work effectively together.

Reckless (1967) sought to explain why it is that despite the various encouragements and enticements which may tempt or encourage individuals to break the law, most people resist such possibilities and remain law abiding. He argued that a combination of control factors, both internal and external to the individual, serve as insulators or 'containments' attaching much more importance to the former, arguing that these tend to control the individual irrespective of external change of environment. First, individuals with a strong and favourable self-concept are better insulated against factors that encourage offending. Second, goal orientation is the extent to which the person has a clear direction in life, oriented towards the achievement of legitimate goals such as education and career. Third, frustration tolerance is where contemporary society with its emphasis on individualism and immediate gratification might generate considerable frustration. Fourth, norm retention is the extent to which individuals accept, internalize and are committed to conventional laws, norms, values and rules and the institutions which represent and uphold these.

Travis Hirschi (1969) made arguably the most significant contribution to social control theory, and his work was to be very influential within the criminal justice system not least in working with young people. Hirschi observes that, at their simplest level, all social control theories share the same core assumption that criminality occurs when the individual bond to legitimate society is weak or broken and identifies four crucial variables. First, attachment refers to the capacity of individuals to form effective relationships with other people and institutions: in the case of children, with their parents, peers and school. Second, commitment refers to the social investments made by the individual to conventional activities that could be put at risk by engaging in criminal behaviour. Third, involvement refers to the simple reality that a person may be too busy or tired from doing conventional things to find time to engage in deviant activities. Fourth, beliefs are a set of impressions and convictions which require constant reinforcement, and this component is closely connected to the pattern and strength of attachments an individual has to other people and institutions.

Hirschi (1969) proposes that these variables, although independent, are highly interrelated and help to prevent law-breaking activities in most people. Again, of course, the converse is clearly true. Those who come from backgrounds where family and friends are involved in offending and where positive attitudes to schooling and other legitimate activities are non-existent or negative are very likely to be offenders themselves as the research evidence suggests. Thus, the aspects of the social bond most consistently related to offending behaviour are those of the family and the school and there is substantial evidence that juveniles with strong attachments to their law-abiding family are less likely to offend. The evidence on the association between attachment and commitment to school, particularly poor school performance, not liking school and low educational and occupational aspirations and delinquency, is even stronger (Hopkins Burke, 2016).

Researchers have subsequently sought to strengthen control theory by integration with other theoretical perspectives and this has invariably meant the incorporation of a structural element which considers the extent of legitimate opportunities available – or increasingly not available – in wider society. Elliot *et al.* (1979) thus expand and synthesize anomie theories, social learning and social control perspectives, with their starting point being that individuals have different early socialization experiences which lead to variable degrees of commitment to the conventional social order. These initial social bonds can be reinforced by positive experiences at school and in the wider community. The structural dimension is explicit in their analysis of the factors which serve to loosen social bonds, such as limited or blocked opportunities, including the highly significant impact of (later long-term) economic recession and unemployment.

Stephen Box (1981) combined control theory with a labelling/conflict victimized actor model perspective (see the following discussion), arguing that differences in policing practices and institutional biases at different stages of the criminal justice system operate very much to the disadvantage of the underprivileged. Stigma and a sense of injustice can be likewise provoked by the criminalization process, which provides further impetus towards criminal behaviour. Box (1987) later showed how the impact of economic recession can fuel an increase in criminal activity. First, by further reducing legitimate opportunities and increasing deprivation, it produces more 'strain' and more individuals have a motive to offend. Commitment to society is thus undermined because access to conventional modes of activity have been reduced. Second, by undermining the family and conventional employment prospects, the ability and motivation of an individual to develop an attachment to other human beings, who might introduce a controlling influence in their life, is substantially reduced.

John Braithwaite (1989) integrated elements of control, labelling, strain and subcultural theories and proposed that the way to reduce crime is to have a commitment to reintegrative forms of shaming. A crucial distinction is made here between first, the negative shaming (or labelling) which is a fundamental characteristic of contemporary criminal justice systems worldwide, which he observes leads to the stigmatizing, outcasting and exclusion of the individual, and, second, shaming which is reintegrative and seeks to restore the individual to legitimate society. The former orthodox approach simply pushes offenders towards criminal subcultures, which become increasingly attractive to the stigmatized individual seeking emotional and social support. Participation in these illegitimate groups can also supply criminal role models, knowledge on how to offend and techniques of neutralization, which, taken together, can make the choice to engage in crime even more rational.

Gottfredson and Hirschi (1990) were to combine rational actor and predestined actor principles and produce a theoretical perspective which defines crime as acts of force or fraud undertaken in pursuit of self-interest. They propose that the vast bulk of criminal acts are trivial and mundane affairs which result in little gain and require little in the way of effort, planning, preparation or skill. Their 'versatility construct' considers crime to be essentially interchangeable: the characteristics of ordinary criminal events are simply inconsistent with notions of specialization or the criminal career. The likelihood of criminal behaviour is closely linked to the availability of opportunity, the characteristics of situations and the personal properties of individuals and their level of self-control. This latter concept is not only confined to criminal acts but also implicated in many analogous undertakings, such as promiscuity, alcohol use and smoking, where such behaviour is portrayed as the impulsive actions of disorganized individuals seeking quick gratification.

Gottfredson and Hirschi turned to the predestined actor model to account for variations in self-control and argue that the main cause of low self-control is ineffective parenting, which they identified as a failing which cannot easily be remedied in later life. According to this 'stability postulate', levels of self-control will remain stable throughout the life course. By asserting that crime is essentially interchangeable, while the propensity to become involved in criminality remains stable, the theory has no need to provide different explanations for different types of crime, nor for primary or persistent secondary deviation.

Hirschi (1995) later concluded that policies designed to deter (the rational actor model) or rehabilitate (the predestined actor model) will continue to have little success in reducing crime, influentially (and controversially in some liberal quarters) proposing that effective policies will be those which support and enhance socialization in the family by improving the quality of child-rearing practices, with the core focus on the form, size and stability of the family unit. Thus, there should always be two parents for every child, no more than three children in a family, with the relationship between parents and children strong and durable. Furthermore, it is not young teenage mothers who are a problem; it is having a mother without a father. Effective policies are those which focus not on preventing teenage pregnancies but on maintaining the involvement of the father in the life of the child. Hirschi proposed that these polices would strengthen family bonds, increase positive socialization and create greater self-control in the child.

Predestined actor model: conclusion and policy implications

The predestined actor model proposes that juveniles become offenders because of individual or social factors in their lives which cause or determine them to behave in ways over which they have little or no control. The solution is to remove or restrict the influence of these factors, for example, genetic predisposition to aggression can be countered by the provision of sporting or artistic diversionary activities, altered biological state factors can be reduced or eradicated by challenging alcohol or drug use, psychological factors can be countered by behavioural programmes to unlearn previously damaging behaviour, and environmental/sociological factors can be addressed by removing the juvenile from negative social environments. Offenders are most likely to desist from offending when these biological, psychological or sociological factors are addressed.

The victimized actor model

The victimized actor model of crime and criminal behaviour proposes that the offender is the product of an unjust and unequal society where it is the behaviour and activities of the poor and socially excluded which are invariably targeted and criminalized by criminal justice agencies (see Table 3.3).

Labelling theories

The central proposition of the long-established but incredibly enduring labelling theory tradition is that it is the reactions of other people, or an audience, that is the most important variable in the ongoing process of action. Thus, Albert Cohen (1955) had emphasized how the negative and malicious characteristics of young offender activities can encourage a strong societal reaction, which leads to them being categorized as abnormal and unacceptable. The outcome is the denial of legitimate opportunities for young people labelled as deviant and this encourages them to pursue illegitimate activities.

Stan Cohen (1973) instigated an interest in the activities of prominent agents of social reaction, using the term 'moral panic'. His account of how the media amplified the initially rather innocuous mods and rocker 'riots' that occurred at Clacton during Easter 1964 is now staple fare for criminology students. The media stereotyped and polarized the contending groups (not only mods and rockers but juveniles in general and the police) and increased the sensitivity of the participants, which encouraged further delinquent behaviour. The following Spring Bank Holiday – six weeks later – saw clashes between mods and rockers in many English seaside towns.

Table 3.3 Victimized actor model

- The offender is the victim of an unjust and unequal society.
- The behaviour and activities of the poor and powerless sections of society are targeted and criminalized.
- Neither punishment nor treatment of offenders is proposed, but non-criminalization and measures are introduced to reduce unequal power relations and improve the life chances of the individual.

Social reactions have also been studied at the micro-level, and this brings us to the classic work of Howard Becker (1963), who argued that, since social groups create rules, they also create deviants or outsiders. Deviancy is not about the quality of the act itself but about the social process of recognition and rule enforcement, and our attention is here directed to the rule-makers and those who enforce the rules – the 'moral entrepreneurs' – as much as to the deviants. Morality is an enterprise, not just a simple natural social process, and our attention is directed to the values of those who have the power to label or define an activity as immoral or deviant (Becker, 1967).

The work of Becker is the usual source of radical variants of labelling theory. He implies that there is no need to explain deviance in the first place, it is simply a very common social activity, a normal one, which only becomes abnormal when it is so labelled by an outside audience. The application of the label confirms the initial diagnosis and becomes a self-fulfilling prophecy, launching juveniles on a deviant career from which they will have increasing difficulty leaving, not least because they have acquired the criminal record which makes them virtually unemployable and often ostracized from polite society.

Conflict and radical theories

Conflict and radical theories take the labelling and social reaction thesis further and seek to explain criminality in terms of the unequal nature of society thus incorporating a significant structural component to their explanation of crime and criminal behaviour. Conflict theories take a more liberal pluralist stance observing that society consists of different groups with very different levels of economic power, all involved in a very competitive struggle to promote their material interests in a very unequal market place, while the radical variants are heavily influenced by Marxist political economy which identifies the power of the state to criminalize, make laws and prosecute offenders (Taylor et al., 1973).

There are two current variants of the radical tradition, but only critical criminology has undeniable foundations in the victimized actor model. From this perspective, crime is defined in terms of the concept of oppression and it is observed that some groups in society – the working class, women and minority ethnic groups, in particular – are the most likely to suffer oppressive social relations based on class division, sexism and racism. Criminal behaviour among such groups is seen to be the rational outcome of the interaction between the marginalization or exclusion from access to mainstream institutions and that of criminalization by the state authorities. The latter involves a process in which the law, agencies of social control and the media associate crime with particular groups who are subsequently identified and targeted as a threat (Scraton and Chadwick, 1996, originally 1992).

Left realism is the other contemporary radical criminological perspective. Although it has its roots in the radical tradition, there is very much a recognition that crime is a real problem for ordinary people and their victimization must be taken seriously. Central to this perspective is the proposition that crime requires a comprehensive solution that is both 'tough on crime' and 'tough on the causes of crime'. The first part of this equation proposes that offenders should accept and take responsibility for their actions and has its theoretical foundations in the rational actor model. The second part proposes a tough stance on the causes of crime by targeting the individual and, in particular, structural factors, such as poor education, lack of training and skills, poverty and lack of legitimate employment opportunities, which encourage criminality. It is therefore in accordance not only with the predestined actor model but also with the victimized actor model.

Victimized actor model: conclusions and policy implications

The victimized actor model proposes that offenders are the product of a highly competitive but unequal neoliberal society. Statistically, these offenders are significantly overrepresented among the ranks of the socially excluded, with invariably very limited life chances. The clear policy implication of this model is to significantly improve access to education, training and skills and thus enhance legitimate career prospects making illicit opportunities significantly less attractive. Offenders are likely to desist from criminal involvement when these exclusion needs are met and the individual has available legitimate opportunities.

Discussion and conclusion

This chapter has considered how different criminological theories have sought to explain crime and offending behaviour during the modern epoch. Three different models of offending behaviour have been identified as belonging unequivocally to this explanatory tradition. First, the rational actor model proposes that human beings enjoy free will and they can choose to offend in very much the same way as they elect to engage in any other activity available to them. But with choice comes responsibility an – having made the choice to offend – the individual can be legitimately held accountable for their actions. Thus, accepting the punishment that society considers appropriate. Second, the predestined actor model, proposes that criminal behaviour is determined by factors, either internal or external to the individual, which leads them to behave in ways over which they have little or no control and which will thus mitigate the extent of their culpability, while treatment is the preferred intervention rather than punishment. Third, the victimized actor model, asserts that offenders are themselves the victims of an unequal and unjust society, where the choices they make are invariably significantly restricted by the socially excluded circumstances in which they live their lives. It is thus becoming apparent that all three models of criminal behaviour can be legitimately used in order to address different components of offending behaviour and that ultimately these models are both competitive and compatible. This well-travelled author of criminological theory texts has reached the conclusion that people commit criminal offences when it simply makes sense to them in the circumstances in which they find themselves. There can clearly be a multitude of possible circumstances – biological, psychological, sociological and not least socio-economic – and at least theoretically, the person can be dissuaded from (further) criminal involvement if and when they are provided with adequate grounds for non-involvement in such activities. An exciting, interesting and ultimately economically rewarding crime substitute can be very much central to such initiatives. Nevertheless, in the context of contemporary fragmented modernity and increasingly unrestrained rampant neoliberalism, adequate legitimate economic reward is likely to prove the most challenging goal to achieve, as this book will proceed to establish. In the meantime, we should note that the three models of criminal behaviour outlined here remain the most effective means of explaining criminal behaviour in the postmodern condition. What is missing is the previous moral certainty.

Summary of main points

1 Criminological theories which have come to the fore during the modern era can be broadly conceptualized in one of three different competing models of crime and criminal behaviour.
2 The rational actor model proposes that criminal behaviour is simply the outcome of rational, calculating individuals who enjoy and exercise free will and choose to commit crime in preference to law-abiding activities.
3 Since the calculation for choosing to offend involves the acquisition of a benefit (pleasure), society must thus develop policies to increase the cost of this benefit (punishment).
4 Deterrence theory suggests that people can be deterred from criminality by the threat or imposition of rigorous penalties, but recidivism rates suggest that this strategy has not been very successful.
5 The predestined actor model explains criminal behaviour in terms of factors, internal or external to the individual, that cause people to act in ways over which they have little or no control.
6 There are three basic formulations – biological, psychological and sociological positivism – but all three incorporate the same fundamental determinist assumptions.
7 Treatment of the offender is proposed rather than punishment.
8 The victimized actor model proposes that the offender is the product of an unjust and unequal society.
9 It is the behaviour and activities of the poor and socially excluded that are targeted and criminalized by criminal justice agencies.
10 Neither punishment nor treatment of offenders is proposed, but non-criminalization and measures are introduced to reduce unequal power relations and improve the life chances of the individual.

Discussion questions

1 What are the main points and policy implications of the rational actor model?
2 What are the main points and policy implications of the predestined actor model?
3 What are the main points and policy implications of the victimized actor model?
4 Which of three models of criminal behaviour do you consider best explains criminality in contemporary society, and why?

Further reading

There are a few readily available books that provide an introduction to most of the criminological theories introduced in this chapter. Those wanting a full and comprehensive discussion of the three models of criminal behaviour and the theories contained within them are nevertheless directed to the companion to this text *An Introduction to Criminological Theory – Fifth Edition* written by this author and published by Routledge in 2018.

References

Aichhorn, A. (1925) *Wayward Youth*. New York: Meridian Books.

Akers, R.L. (1985) *Deviant Behaviour: A Social Learning Approach*, 3rd ed. Belmont, CA: Wadsworth.

Baldwin, J.D. (1990) 'The Role of Sensory Stimulation in Criminal Behaviour, with Special Attention to the Age Peak in Crime', in L. Ellis and H. Hoffman (eds.) *Crime in Biological, Social and Moral Contexts*. New York: Praeger.

Bandura, A. and Walters, R.H. (1959) *Adolescent Aggression*. New York: Ronald Press.

Becker, G.S. (1968) 'Crime and Punishment: An Economic Approach', *Journal of Political Economy*, 76(2): 169–217.

Becker, H. (1963) *Outsiders: Studies in the Sociology of Deviance*. New York: Free Press.

Becker, H. (1967) 'Whose Side Are We On?', *Social Problems*, 14(3): 239–47.

Bennett, T. (2000) *Drugs and Crime: The Results of the Second Developmental Stage of the New-Adam Programme, Home Office Research Study 2005*. London: Home Office.

Bowlby, J. (1952) *Maternal Care and Mental Health*, 2nd ed. Geneva: World Health Organization.

Box, S. (1981) *Deviance, Reality and Society*, 2nd ed. London: Rinehart and Winston.

Box, S. (1987) *Recession, Crime and Punishment*. London: Macmillan.

Braithwaite, J. (1989) *Crime, Shame and Reintegration*. Cambridge: Cambridge University Press.

Burgess, E.W. (1928) 'The Growth of the City', in R. Park, E.W. Burgess and R.D. McKenzie (eds.) *The City*. Chicago, IL: University of Chicago Press.

Burt, C. (1945) *The Young Delinquent*. London: University of London Press.

Chilton, R.J. and Markle, G.E. (1972) 'Family Disruption, Delinquent Conduct, and the Effect of Sub-classification', *American Sociological Review*, 37: 93–108.

Clarke, R.V.G. (1987) 'Rational Choice Theory and Prison Psychology', in B.J. McGurk, D. Thornton and M. Williams (eds.) *Applying Psychology to Imprisonment: Theory and Practice*. London: HMSO.

Cloward, R.A. and Ohlin, L.E. (1960) *Delinquency and Opportunity: A Theory of Delinquent Gangs*. New York: Free Press.

Cohen, A.K. (1955) *Delinquent Boys: The Culture of the Gang*. New York: Free Press.

Cohen, L.E. and Felson, M. (1979) 'Social Inequality and Predatory Criminal Victimization: An Exposition and Test of a Formal Theory', *American Sociological Review*, 44: 588–608.

Cohen, S. (1973) *Folk Devils and Moral Panics: The Creation of the Mods and Rockers*. London: Paladin.

Corrigan, P. (1979) *The Smash Street Kids*. London: Paladin.

Department of Health (2005) *Smoking, Drinking and Drug Use Among Young People in England in 2004*. London: Department of Health.

Downes, D. (1966) *The Delinquent Solution*. London: Routledge & Kegan Paul.

Durkheim, E. (1933 originally 1893) *The Division of Labour in Society*. Glencoe, IL: Free Press.

Elliot, D.S., Ageton, S.S. and Canter, J. (1979) 'An Integrated Theoretical Perspective on Delinquent Behaviour', *Journal of Research in Crime and Delinquency*, 16: 126–49.

Ellis, L. and Crontz, P.D. (1990) 'Androgens, Brain Functioning, and Criminality: The Neurohormonal Foundations of Antisociality', in L. Ellis and H. Hoffman (eds.) *Crime in Biological, Social, and Moral Contexts*. New York: Praeger.

Farrington, D. (1992) 'Explaining the Beginning, Progress, and Ending of Antisocial Behaviour from Birth to Adulthood', in J. McCord (ed.) *Facts, Frameworks, and Forecasts: Advances in Criminological Theory*, Vol. 3. New Brunswick, NJ: Transaction Publishers.

Felson, M. (1998) *Crime and Everyday Life*, 2nd ed. Thousand Oaks, CA: Pine Forge.

Ferri, E. (1895) *Criminal Sociology*. London: Unwin.

Friedlander, K. (1947) *The Psychoanalytic Approach to Juvenile Delinquency*. London: Kegan Paul.

Freud, S. (1927) *The Ego and the Id*. London: Hogarth.

Gibbens, T.C.N. (1963) *Psychiatric Studies of Borstal Lads*. Oxford: Oxford University Press.

Glueck, S. and Glueck, E. (1950) *Unravelling Juvenile Delinquency*. Oxford: Oxford University Press.

Gottfredson, M.R. and Hirschi, T. (1990) *A General Theory of Crime*. Stanford, CA: Stanford University Press.

Healy, W. and Bronner, A.F. (1936) *New Light on Delinquency and Its Treatment*. New Haven, CT: Yale University Press.

Hirschi, T. (1969) *Causes of Delinquency*. Berkeley, CA: University of California Press.

Hirschi, T. (1995) 'The Family', in J.Q. Wilson and J. Petersilia (eds.) *Crime*. San Francisco, CA: ICS Press.

Hoffman, M.L. and Saltzstein, H.D. (1967) 'Parent Discipline and the Child's Moral Development', *Journal of Personality and Social Psychology*, 5: 45.

Hopkins Burke, R.D. (2016) *Young People, Crime and Justice*, 2nd ed. Cullompton: Willan Publishing.

Hopkins Burke, R.D. and Pollock, E. (2004) 'A Tale of Two Anomies: Some Observations on the Contribution of (Sociological) Criminological Theory to Explaining Hate Crime Motivation', *Internet Journal of Criminology*, November.

Hopkins Burke, R.D. and Sunley, R. (1998) 'Youth Subcultures in Contemporary Britain', in K. Hazlehurst and C. Hazlehurst (eds.) *Gangs and Youth Subcultures: International Explorations*. New Brunswick, NJ: Transaction Press.

Institute of Alcohol Studies (2005) *Adolescents and Alcohol*. St Ives, Cambridgeshire: IAS.

Jefferis, B.J.M.H., Power, C. and Manor, O. (2005) 'Adolescent Drinking Level and Adult Binge Drinking in a National Cohort', *Addiction*, 100(4): 543–9.

Jeffery, C.R. (1977) *Crime Prevention Through Environmental Design*. Beverly Hills, CA: Sage.

Jones, S. (1993) *The Language of the Genes*. London: Harper Collins.

Lombroso, C. (1875) *L'uomo delinquente (The Criminal Man)*. Milan: Hoepli.

Mannheim, H. (1948) *Juvenile Delinquency in an English Middletown*. London: Kegan Paul, Turner, Trubner and Co. Ltd.

Matza, D.M. (1964) *Delinquency and Drift*. New York: Wiley.

Mays, J.B. (1954) *Growing Up in the City: A Study of Juvenile Delinquency in an Urban Neighbourhood*. Liverpool: Liverpool University Press.

McCord, W., McCord, J. and Zola, I.K. (1959) *Origins of Crime: A New Evaluation of the Cambridge-Somerville Youth Study*. New York: Columbia University Press.

Mednick, S.A., Moffitt, T.E. and Stack, S. (eds.) (1987) *The Causes of Crime: New Biological Approaches*. Cambridge: Cambridge University Press.

Merton, R.K. (1938) 'Social Structure and Anomie', *American Sociological Review*, 3: 672–82.

Miller, W.B. (1958) 'Lower Class Culture as a Generalising Milieu of Gang Delinquency', *Journal of Social Issues*, 14: 5–19.

Monahan, T.P. (1957) 'Family Status and the Delinquent Child: A Reappraisal and Some New Findings', *New Forces*, 35: 250–66.

Morris, T. (1957) *The Criminal Area: A Study in Social Ecology*. London: Routledge & Kegan Paul.

Morse, S.M. (1997a) 'Immaturity and Irresponsibility', *Journal of Criminal Law and Criminology*, 88.

Morse, S.M. (1997b) 'Delinquency and Desert', *The ANNALS of the American Academy of Political and Social Science*, 564(1): 56–80.

Nye, F.I. (1958) *Family Relationships and Delinquent Behaviour*. New York: Wiley.

Office of National Statistics (ONS) (2015) *How Much Do People Binge Drink in Great Britain?* London: ONS.

Olwens, D. (1987) 'Testosterone and Adrenaline: Aggressive and Antisocial Behaviour in Normal Adolescent Males', in S.A. Mednick, T.E. Moffitt and S. Stack (eds.) *The Causes of Crime: New Biological Approaches*. Cambridge: Cambridge University Press.

Parker, H. (1974) *View From the Boys*. Newton Abbot: David and Charles.

Pitts, J. (1986) 'Black Young People and Juvenile Crime: Some Unanswered Questions', in R. Matthews and J. Young (eds.) *Confronting Crime*. London: Sage.

Reckless, W. (1967) *The Crime Problem*, 4th ed. New York: Appleton Century Crofts.

Redl, F. and Wineman, D. (1951) *Children Who Hate*. New York: Free Press.

Reiss, A.J. (1951) 'Delinquency as the Failure of Personal and Social Controls', *American Sociological Review*, 16: 213–39.

Rutter, M. (1981) *Maternal Deprivation Reassessed*. Harmondsworth: Penguin.

Schalling, D. (1987) 'Personality Correlates of Plasma Testosterone Levels in Young Delinquents: An Example of Person–Situation Interaction', in S.A. Mednick, T.E. Moffitt and S.A. Stack (eds.) *The Causes of Crime: New Biological Approaches*. Cambridge: Cambridge University Press.

Scraton, P. and Chadwick, K. (1996, originally 1992) 'The Theoretical Priorities of Critical Criminology', in J. Muncie, E. McLaughlin, and M. Langan (eds.) *Criminological Perspectives: A Reader*. London: Sage.

Shaw, C.R. and McKay, H.D. (1972 originally 1931) *Juvenile Delinquency and Urban Areas*. Chicago, IL: University of Chicago Press.

Sheldon, W.H. (1949) *Varieties of Delinquent Youth*. London: Harper.

Spergel, I.A. (1964) *Racketsville, Slumtown, Haulburg*. Chicago, IL: University of Chicago Press.

Sutherland, E.H. (1937) *The Professional Thief: By a Professional Thief*. Chicago, IL: University of Chicago Press.

Sutherland, E.H. (1947) *Principles of Criminology*, 4th ed. Philadelphia, PA: Lippincott.

Sykes, G. and Matza, D. (1957) 'Techniques of Neutralization: A Theory of Delinquency', *American Sociological Review*, 22(6): 664–70.

Tappan, P.W. (1960) *Crime, Justice and Correction*. New York: McGraw-Hill.

Taylor, I., Walton, P. and Young, J. (1973) *The New Criminology: For a Social Theory of Deviance*. London: Routledge & Kegan Paul.

Virkkunen, M. (1987) 'Metabolic Dysfunctions Amongst Habitually Violent Offenders: Reactive Hypoglycaemia and Cholesterol Levels', in S.A. Mednick, T.E. Moffitt, and S.A. Stack (eds.) *The Causes of Crime: New Biological Approaches*. Cambridge: Cambridge University Press.

West, D.J. and Farrington, D.P. (1973) *Who Becomes Delinquent?* London: Heinemann.

Willis, P. (1977) *Learning to Labour*. London: Saxon House.

Wills, T.A., Vaccaro, D., McNamara, G. and Hirky, E.A. (1996) 'Escalated Substance Use: A Longitudinal Grouping Analysis from Early to Middle Adolescence', *Journal of Abnormal Psychology*, April: 166–80.

Wilmott, P. (1966) *Adolescent Boys in East London*. London: Routledge & Kegan Paul.

Wilson, J.Q. and Herrnstein, R.J. (1985) *Crime and Human Nature*. New York: Simon and Schuster.

Wright, R.A. (1993) 'A Socially Sensitive Criminal Justice System', in J.W. Murphy and D.L. Peck (eds.) *Open Institutions: The Hope for Democracy*. Westport, CT: Praeger.

Chapter 4

The crisis of modernity

Key issues

1   The age of moral uncertainty
2   The retreat from welfarism
3   The rise of neoliberalism
4   Neoconservatism
5   The rise and fall of 'New' Labour

An age of moral uncertainty

This chapter concludes the first part of the book. It introduces us to the notion of the fragmentation of the modernity which had provided the socio-economic foundations underpinning the criminological theories we encountered in the previous chapter. This fragmentation was to consist of an ever-increasing succession of economic and political developments that were to increasingly indicate a retreat from the post-Second World War settlement between governments and its people. These agreements had been primarily based on the full-employment, subsidized housing, free education and 'cradle to grave' welfare policies that had provided the socio-economic orthodoxy throughout the Western world until at least the mid-1970s. This period – little more than 30 years in total – arguably marks the highpoint of modernism. The world was often (sometimes cruelly) unequal, but things were on balance getting better and there was still widespread confidence in the capacity of social democratic institutions and the grand theories to deliver the good life – eventually. With a little encouragement most people believed that, at the ballot box or picket line, things would get better. It was an age of moral certainty.

Cracks within the modernist project were nevertheless becoming increasingly apparent and the old certainties were being questioned right across the political spectrum. For example it was asked, should groups of workers – such as the powerful National Union of Mineworkers – be able to hold the government and the country to ransom in pursuit of higher pay and better conditions? Increasingly more and more people asked this and similar questions. With the passing of time these and other contradictions become ever more apparent with the consequence that modernist societies became increasingly unmanageable. The discussion starts with the end of the Second World War.

The rise of neoliberalism

Britain emerged from the 1939–45 war military victorious but economically exhausted. It was one of the top three post-war superpowers, but in reality, it was a distant third behind the US and the Soviet Union. Nevertheless, its political system and the British state had been vindicated by success in war, and over the next few years emerged as what many considered to be a model social democracy which combined planning and collectivism with civil liberties (Kavanagh, 1987). The is the highpoint of modernity. The Labour government elected in 1945 was largely responsible for what became known as the 'post-war consensus' although some of the key elements can trace their origins to the war-time coalition government and the influence of Liberals like William Beveridge (who devised the welfare state) and the economist John Maynard Keynes (who had a whole school of economics named after him).

Essentially, there was a belief that government could play a positive role in promoting greater equality through social engineering, and we can identify five major features of this strategy. First, all governments accepted a commitment to maintain full employment by Keynesian techniques of economic management. Ministers used levers, such as cutting taxes and boosting state spending, to increase the level of economic activity. Second, there was an acceptance and indeed some encouragement of the role of the trade unions. In contrast to the pre-war years, governments recognized and consulted them regularly on workplace relations and economic policy. Their access to government was increased partly by full employment and partly by governments turning post-1961 to income policies as a way of curbing inflation. Third, there was a mixed economy, with a large role for state ownership of the utilities (such as gas, electricity, coal and rail), some wealth creation (steel and the car industry) and intervention and planning in the economy. Fourth, there was the creation of the welfare state. The object of the national insurance system and the National Health Service (NHS) was to provide an adequate income and free health care when the income of a family was hit by, for example, sickness, old age, unemployment or death of the main breadwinner. The services were funded through general taxation, or insurance and were seen as a key component of social citizenship. Fifth, there was a belief that government could play a positive role in promoting greater equality through social engineering, for example, by progressive taxation, redistributive welfare spending, comprehensive education and regional policies.

These policies were pursued by both Labour and Conservative governments, the latter because they thought it was necessary to gain working-class support to win general elections and gain the consent of the major interest groups. Consensus is nevertheless not an ideal term because it might suggest that there were no differences between the two main political parties. In fact, the previously mentioned ideas and policies were often challenged by the left of the Labour Party and by the free market or right wing of the Conservatives. But much of the political elite – the media, civil service and the leaderships of the parties, particularly when they were in government – shared many of these ideas (Kavanagh, 1987).

Throughout the 1960s and 1970s, the two main political parties – the Conservatives and Labour – competed to reverse the relative economic decline of Britain. There was a growing awareness that the economic league tables showed the country to be at the wrong end for figures regarding industrial strikes, productivity, inflation, economic growth and rising living standards. Virtually all European countries, with the exception of Britain, had so-called post-war economic miracles, with the latter often described as the 'sick man of Europe'. The targets for blame included a failure to invest in new plant and machinery, restrictive working practices and outdated attitudes on the shop floor ('us and them'), amateurish and incompetent management, the incremental loss of overseas markets and the rise of competition increasingly from the developing world with its far lower wage costs. In short, Britain appeared to be the weak link in the international liberal-capitalist economic system, plagued by high inflation, low growth and irresponsible trade union power.

It seemed to many that the UK was ungovernable and that no government had an answer to inflation. Consequently, governments of both parties turned their attention to incomes policies as an answer to inflation seeking to agree a 'norm' for annual wage rises with the unions. This was always difficult for the unions, for their purpose is collective bargaining and while this policy managed to keep prices down for a time, it would collapse when powerful groups broke the 'norm'. Such policies failed dramatically with the Conservative government in 1973–74 (miners' strikes and the 'three-day week' and again with the Labour government in 1979, 'the Winter of Discontent').

Measures introduced to boost economic activity and reduce unemployment tended to have the unintended consequences of pulling in extra imports from overseas, thereby worsening the trade balance, and which again seemed to lead to unacceptable rises in inflation. The consequential loss of confidence of the financial markets meant a sharp slide in the value of sterling, which, in turn, led to the necessity of a humiliating International Monetary Fund (IMF) 'rescue' package in 1976 where a loan was granted to the British government in return for spending cuts and continued anti-inflation policies. That this happened at a time of high unemployment seemed to signal the end of the era of Keynesian economic policies.

The Winter of Discontent of 1978–79 was a key event. The rash of strikes in crucial public services against the income policies of the Labour government seemed to show that the country was ungovernable and that no government had an answer to inflation. Moreover, it destroyed the reputation of the government for prudent economic management and its ability to gain the cooperation of the unions. Just as the Heath government had fallen following the miners' damaging strike against its incomes policy and subsequently lost the February 1974 general election, so the Labour government lost office in 1979, in very similar circumstances. There were two responses to this failure. From the political right, the new ideas of economists Friedrich Hayek and Milton Friedman – advocating monetarism, a greater scope for markets and limited government spending – won out over the ideas of the left for more state ownership and the protection of industry following a withdrawal from the European Community.

The Conservative Party – under the leadership of Margaret Thatcher – won the 1979 election, and much of so-called Thatcherism (which along with 'Reaganomics' named after President Ronald Reagan in the US, provided the origins of what is now called neoliberalism) actually evolved pragmatically as circumstances allowed but was crucially helped by the failures of the opposition. For example the privatization of public-owned utilities, which was to become a flagship policy, was not mentioned in the 1979 manifesto. At the following general election in 1983 and in spite of unemployment doubling to some 3 million, the government won a landslide victory thanks in large part to divisions in the Labour Party and its left-wing policies. Significantly, the

Thatcher government insisted that it could no longer be a universal provider of benefits and the post-war socio-economic political consensus between the main political parties was over, with major changes to the fabric of society arising. First, trade unions were now be required to operate within an increasingly tighter legal framework, including the requirement for pre-strike ballots before taking industrial action, the end of the 'closed shop' (where union membership had been a precondition of employment in a specific industry) and making unions liable for damages incurred in illegal strikes. The unions were hardly consulted by the government during the course of these incremental changes and their influence waned in part because of the abandonment of income policies and rising unemployment. Second, the spread of privatization of the major utilities altered the balance of the mixed economy. Gas, electricity, telecommunications, British Airways and later British Rail were all privatized. There was also a huge sale to tenants of council housing. Third, the government abandoned its commitment to full employment, stating this was the responsibility of employers and employees, and accorded priority instead to keeping inflation low. Fourth, welfare state benefits were increasingly subject to means-testing with entitlement restricted. Sixth, the government insisted that it could no longer be a universal provider with more left to the market, the voluntary sector and self-help.

There was nonetheless far from universal endorsement of Thatcherism in 1979 (Kavanagh, 1987). As late as October 1978, Labour was still ahead in some opinion polls, but the Winter of Discontent turned the public against Labour and the unions. The election was nevertheless more of a rejection of Labour than an endorsement of Thatcherism. It was the recapture of the Falkland Islands from Argentina in 1982 that was important for the success of the Thatcher project, coinciding with an improvement in the public standing of the government and of Margaret Thatcher herself. The victory seemed to vindicate her claims in domestic politics that she could provide strong leadership and stand up for the nation. The war rhetoric could now be turned against the perceived enemies within – particularly the trade unions.

There are academic disputes about the extent to which military success boosted Conservative chances in the 1983 election for there were signs of a revival in the polls and greater economic optimism even before the capture. But the big unanswerable question is whether the government would have survived if the Falklands had not been recaptured. Crucially, Labour could not exploit widespread dissatisfaction in the country, because it was seen as weak and divided (Kavanagh, 1987). Thatcher was respected but she was not liked by the British public. For all the talk of sweeping election successes, her government only gained an average of 42% of the vote at general elections but the peculiarities of the British electoral system and the split of the non-Conservative vote between the Labour and Liberal-Alliance Parties meant that the government was able to win over 60% of seats in the House of Commons.

Surveys at the time showed limited support for many of Thatcher's values. Ivor Crewe (1989) noted the lack of support for her policies on 'tax-and-spend' and replacing the dependency culture with an enterprise culture. Moreover, there was greater approval for a more equal society and for social and collective provision of welfare as against her vision of people looking after themselves. But Labour could not exploit this dissatisfaction, because it was not trusted on the economy or defence and was consigned to the electoral backwoods for 18 years. The post-war socio-economic consensus that provided the crucial foundations of high modernity was now over.

The fragmentation of modernity

Modern societies at their most confident had been fundamentally mass societies with a very high demand for workers and military personnel (Harvey, 1989; Hopkins Burke, 1999). In such societies, people were an important commodity, with not least children and young people perceived to be economic assets worthy of nurture and protection to be productive workers of the future. There were frequent concerns about the quality of that population and their fitness for work and war, with the outcome being increasing state intervention in the socialization of children and young people and especially their re-socialization when their behaviour became problematic or indeed criminal (Hopkins Burke, 2016). People nevertheless continued to be at least potential societal assets regardless of the level and extent of any bad behaviour and were always worthy of reintegration into mainstream society. Jock Young (1999) observes this process of societal reintegration to be the overriding welfare strategy of modernity. The situation was to change significantly with the fragmentation of that modernity (Hopkins Burke, 1999) and the arrival of what some have termed the postmodern condition (Lyotard, 1984).

From at least the last three decades of the twentieth century, substantial doubts were beginning to emerge – and again from disparate sources – about the sustainability of the modernist project in an increasingly fragmented social world. The collapse of the post-war socio-political consensus and an intensifying lack of enthusiasm for large-scale state intervention in the socio-economic sphere coincided with a decreasing enthusiasm for grand theoretical explanations in the social sciences. Underlying this disintegration of confidence was the beginning of an economic and political transformation accelerated by the oil crisis of the early 1970s, the abandonment of full employment policies with a decline in economic competitiveness and a restructuring of the world economy with the rise in the productive capacity of the nations of the Pacific Rim. At the same time, increasingly diverse and fragmented social structures began to emerge in the economic, political and cultural spheres. In the economic sphere, there was a rejection of mass production-line technology in favour of flexible working patterns and a flexible labour force. This involved a weakening of trade unions, greater reliance on peripheral and secondary labour markets, the development of a low-paid and part-time, often female, labour force, and the shift towards a service, rather than manufacturing, economy. Politically, there was the dismantling of elaborate state planning and provision in the fields of welfare. Meanwhile, most conventional representative democratic systems were proving increasingly inadequate to the task of representing myriad interest groups as diverse as major industrialists and financiers, small business proprietors, the unemployed and dispossessed, wide-ranging gender and sexual preference interests, environmentalists and the homeless (Giddens, 1994), a situation that has become increasingly problematic in recent years, reaching virtual crisis point at the time of writing in early 2019, with the UK appearing ungovernable (the battle for Brexit) and in the US the business of government having been brought to a halt (Donald Trump and his 'wall').

It had thus been with the emergence of modernity and the needs of a mass industrial economy that a sustainable growing population had become for the first time in history an asset rather than a liability to society. The modern epoch was thus epitomized by strategies to control the activities of children and young people in particular via education and discipline with the implicit objective of integration into an inclusive and productive, albeit unequal, society. As we have seen, the period of high modernity – circa 1945–75 – was distinguished by an unwritten social contract secured between government and the people based on full employment and a relatively generous welfare state. Working-class youth, moreover, came to accept and reproduce their role within that economically and socially unequal industrial modernity with very little criticism (Willis, 1977).

It was with the fragmentation of that modernity that whole tracts of the former industrial working class now appeared superfluous to the requirements of society and the consequences – either intended or unintended – of subsequent government policies were to lead to growing social exclusion for this group. The unwritten social contact of high modernity had collapsed. The total transformation of the UK economy that occurred during the 1980s brought with it perhaps the last chance for a now far from confident modern mass society. Mass unemployment had now arrived:

> On official figures . . . unemployment increased from 4.1 percent of the labour force in 1972 to 10.3 percent in 1981. Official figures suggest that the highest level of unemployment in the 1980s in Britain was 12.4 percent in 1983, declining to 6.8 in 1990, returning to 11 percent (three million) in 1992, and declining again to 8 percent in 1996.
>
> (Taylor, 1997: 281)

The end of full employment as a social and political project led to increasing social exclusion for whole groups of low-skilled workers with many being absorbed into a poorly educated 'underclass' with little value or use to contemporary society. An ever-increasing group of people who were to become more and more 'left behind' by any form of 'progressive' socio-economic developments in a highly disputed political terrain exacerbated by the changing nature of 'conservatism' as we shall see.

At the same time collective political opposition to the ever-increasing neoliberalism was often undermined by the development of identity politics – a political approach with its origins in the US during the late 1970s – which was based on identifying the simultaneity of experiences such as sexism, racism, heterosexist and classism. The original aim was to support and focus the concerns, agendas and projects of particular oppressed groups usually ignored or marginalized in left-leaning movements for social justice and political liberation. In academic usage, the term *identity politics* has been used to refer to a wide range of political activities and theoretical analyses rooted in experiences of injustice shared by different, often excluded social groups. In this usage, identity politics typically aims to reclaim greater self-determination and political freedom for marginalized groups through understanding the distinctive interests of each group and challenging externally imposed characterizations and limitations, instead of organizing solely around status quo belief systems or traditional party affiliations. Neofotistos (2013: 174) defines identity in this context as

> as a tool to frame political claims, promote political ideologies, or stimulate and orient social and political action, usually in a larger context of inequality or injustice and with the aim of asserting group distinctiveness and belonging and gaining power and recognition.

The term *identity politics* has been in use in various forms since the early 1980s but has been applied, at times, with radically different meanings by different populations. It has gained currency with the emergence of social movements such as the feminist movement, the civil rights movement in the US and the LGBTQ (lesbian, gay, bisexual, transgender, queer) movement, as well as nationalist and postcolonial movements. Contemporary categories of identity politics are race, ethnicity, sex, gender identity, sexual orientation, age, economic class, disability status, education, religion, language and geographic location. Gaining a progressive coalition between these groups as an organized political collective is nevertheless often fraught with difficulty and when other 'less progressive' groups enter the mix then difficulties become readily more apparent. Identity politics can thus be left-wing or right-wing, with examples of the latter being Ulster Loyalism, Islamism and Christian Identity movements with contemporary examples including such luminaries as white supremacists, nationalists and incels. Most of these groups get further mention later in this book. Now for the changing nature of conservatism.

Neoconservatism

Conservatism is a political and social philosophy, with its origins in eighteenth-century Britain and was given significant direction by the conservative philosopher Edmund Burke (1729–97). It promotes the maintenance of traditional institutions and opposes rapid change in society. Some conservatives seek to preserve things as they are, emphasizing stability and continuity, while others oppose modernism in its entirety and seek a return to 'the way things were' or a (mythical) 'golden age before' before industrialization and the 'dark satanic mills'. The term *conservative* itself derives from the Latin *conservare* (conserve), meaning to keep, guard, observe. To a conservative, the goal of change is nevertheless less important than the insistence that change be brought about with a respect for the rule of law and traditions of society. Change is clearly necessary and to be welcomed on occasion but needs to be introduced with thought and reflection on the impact on social structure and order.

Neoliberalism is often associated with supposed conservatives through implementation. It is a policy model with its origins in the 'Thatcherism' and 'Regeanomics' referred to above and which enthusiastically pursues the transfer of economic control from the public sector to the private sector. It is a perspective founded on the basic principles of neoclassical liberal economics (hence the name 'neoliberalism') and which promotes the sovereignty of the free market. Governments should thus provide support for the market where at all possible by reducing constraints and restrictions such as subsidies, make reforms to tax law in order to expand the tax base, reduce deficit spending (which has been a major issue in the UK since at least 2010 and the introduction of austerity measures as a means of dealing with this), limit trade protectionism, and open markets up to trade which is the economic thinking behind Brexit and demands to leave the EU (which is seen by Brexit proponents as a huge restriction on free trade). Neoliberalism also seeks to abolish fixed exchange rates, support deregulation, encourage and promotes private property and privatize businesses run by the state and cutback significantly on welfare expenditure. Liberalism, in economics, thus refers to a freeing of the economy by eliminating regulations and barriers which place restrictions on the activities of entrepreneurial economic actors. Neoliberal policies aim for a laissez-faire (or hands-off) approach to economic development and its proponents cannot be conceived as conservatives in the traditional sense.

Neoconservatism (commonly shortened to neocon) is a political movement with its origins in the US during the 1960s and emerged among conservative-leaning Democrats who had become disenchanted with the party's foreign policy and many of its adherents became politically famous during the Republican presidential administrations of the 1970s, 1980s, 1990s and 2000s. Neoconservatives peaked in influence during the administration of George W. Bush, when they played a major role in promoting and planning the invasion of Iraq in 2003. Prominent neoconservatives in the Bush administration included Paul Wolfowitz, Elliott Abrams, Richard Perle and Paul Bremer. Senior officials Vice President Dick Cheney and Secretary of Defense Donald Rumsfeld, while not identifying as neoconservatives, listened closely to neoconservative advisers regarding foreign policy, especially the defence of Israel and the promotion of democracy in the Middle East.

The term *neoconservative* thus refers to those who made the ideological journey from the anti-Stalinist Left to the camp of US conservatism. Neoconservatives typically advocate the promotion of democracy and the US national interest in international affairs, including by means of military force and are known for their contempt for communism and political radicalism. The movement had its intellectual roots in the Jewish monthly review magazine *Commentary*, published by the American Jewish Committee. They spoke out against and challenged the New Left and in that way helped define the movement. C. Bradley Thompson, a professor at Clemson University, claims that most influential neoconservatives refer explicitly to the theoretical ideas in the philosophy of Leo Strauss (1899–1973), in which he argues that political things are, by their nature, subject to approval and disapproval, praise and blame, choice and rejection – that is they are not neutral, nor are they objective – although it is widely thought that they interrelated this sophisticated political philosophy in way that Strauss himself would not endorse. Clearly conservatives – but not in the traditional sense – they have been supporters, enablers and promoters of neoliberal economic policies.

British neoconservatism is more socially liberal than its US counterpart but shares a worldview of threats and opportunities. British neoconservatives are rigorous proponents of foreign intervention in the Arab world and beyond, to rebuild these societies in the image of Western-style liberal democracies, while promoting the role of the private sector in military contracts and maintaining an alliance with Israel. Neoconservatism is also attractive to members of the Christian right based on shared values. Factions in the British Conservative Party refer to themselves as being liberal conservative rather than neoconservative but nevertheless share a similar worldview.

Traditional conservatism – also known as Toryism – is a political philosophy which emphasizes the need for the principles of natural law and transcendent moral order, tradition, hierarchy and organic unity, agrarianism, classicism and high culture and the intersecting spheres of loyalty. Some traditionalists have even embraced the labels 'reactionary' and 'counterrevolutionary', happily flouting the stigma that has attached to these terms since the Enlightenment. Neoliberalism and neoconservatism embrace key ideas and values from traditional conservatism but differ in many crucial ways. Prime Minister Margaret Thatcher, a major player in the creation of neoliberalism and a supposed conservative talking to *Women's Own* magazine, October 31, 1987, famously said:

> I think we've been through a period where too many people have been given to understand that if they have a problem, it's the government's job to cope with it. 'I have a problem, I'll get a grant.' 'I'm homeless, the government must house me.' They're casting their problem on society. And, you know, there is no such thing as

society. There are individual men and women, and there are families. And no government can do anything except through people, and people must look to themselves first. It's our duty to look after ourselves and then, also to look after our neighbour. People have got the entitlements too much in mind, without the obligations. There's no such thing as entitlement, unless someone has first met an obligation.

This viewpoint is a long way from traditional paternalistic Conservatism and Toryism with its concerns for a strong secure society where the strong look after the weak and disadvantaged. From this perspective, what passes as conservativism is no such thing. We will return to these notions later in this book, not least when we discuss radical moral communitarianism. We next consider the electoral 'left' response to the rise of neoliberalism and neoconservatism. The ultimately unsuccessful attempt by 'New' Labour to reach an accommodation with these philosophies.

'The Third Way': the rise and fall of 'New' Labour

The Labour Party was founded in 1900, having grown out of the trade union movement and socialist parties of the nineteenth century. It overtook the Liberal Party to become the main opposition to the Conservatives in the early 1920s, forming minority governments under Ramsey MacDonald in 1924 and from 1929 to 1931. Labour later served in the war-time coalition from 1940 to 1945, after which it formed a majority government under Clement Attlee until 1951. Labour next formed governments from 1964 to 1970 under Harold Wilson and from 1974 to 1979, first under Wilson and then James Callaghan.

The General Election held in 1983 marked a low point for the Labour Party. Led by Michael Foot, it suffered a landslide defeat, taking just 27.6% of the vote and giving the Conservative Party led by Margaret Thatcher a 144-seat Commons majority. The party's manifesto, with its pledges of unilateral nuclear disarmament and withdrawal from the European Common Market, was memorably described as the 'longest suicide note in history'.

Memories of the last Labour government, which had ended in economic paralysis and the Winter of Discontent, were strong. The Social Democratic Party (SDP), founded by breakaway Labour moderates, was also draining support. The situation looked hopeless. Yet, amid the carnage of 1983, two ambitious young members of Parliament (MPs) entered Parliament – Gordon Brown and Tony Blair. Sharing a Commons office, they began discussing how Labour might become electable again.

Neil Kinnock is widely seen as having done much of the groundwork to make the New Labour project possible. As Labour leader, he fought hard to remove the left-wing militant tendency from the party and attempted to modernize its image and policies. He hired TV producer Peter Mandelson to oversee Labour's next election campaign, and under his leadership the red rose symbol – rather than the red flag – was adopted.

The election held in 1987 saw another big loss, with the Conservatives achieving a 102-seat majority. Brown and Blair, on the modernizing wing of the party, concluded that much of Labour's traditional dogma had to be abandoned if they were to win an election. Both rose through the ranks under the Kinnock leadership, with Brown becoming shadow trade and industry secretary and Blair shadow home secretary. Labour had expected to lose to the Tories in 1983 and 1987, but 1992 was its biggest disappointment, with a third defeat in a row. Much of the blame was placed on Labour's 'shadow budget', including shadow chancellor John Smith's proposal to raise the top rate of income tax from 40p to 50p. The Tories were thus able to lampoon Labour's 'tax bombshell'.

Kinnock resigned after the election and Smith took over the leadership, with Brown as shadow chancellor and Blair keeping the home affairs brief. Blair and Brown now decided to fight the Tories on their own traditional territory, making Labour appear an obvious, safe, reliable party of government. The phrase 'tough on crime, tough on the causes of crime' provides a key example of the strategy. It differed from Tory Home Secretary Michael Howard's 'tough on crime' in appearing to offer a more fundamental solution to the problem of law-breaking, while still being hard line, rather than soft.

Blair, Brown and Mandelson, now an MP, became convinced that Labour must drop some of its old orthodoxies – such as being seen as a high-tax party – to convince the public it was ready for power. When Smith died of a heart attack in May 1994, the modernizers knew their time had come. The question was, who would run for leader: Blair or Brown? Mandelson, previously seen as closer to the early front-runner Brown, switched to back Blair. The outcome was a huge rift in 'The Project', as the modernizing scheme became known, which would last more than a decade. Brown, widely considered to be the senior figure in the partnership, stood aside for the more telegenic Blair after the two met to hammer out a deal at an Islington restaurant.

Blair, now Labour leader, extended the party's lead over the tired John Major–led Conservative government. The *Daily Mirror* journalist Alastair Campbell became spokesman for Blair, adding extra media nous to the team as they sought to win over previously anti-Labour newspapers. The message was that Labour had changed. Mantra-like, at that year's autumn conference, Blair closed his speech with the words: 'Our Party – New Labour. Our mission – New Britain. New Labour – New Britain'. There followed a great battle against the party's traditionalists, eventually abandoning the historic and highly symbolic Clause IV of the party constitution, which called for the 'common ownership of the means of production', and for many critics within its ranks, there was the accusation that it had abandoned socialism.

New Labour now claimed that it had changed sufficiently to challenge the Tories on the economy, erasing voters' painful memories of the late 1970s, and began the 'prawn cocktail offensive' to win over a sceptical city, convincing many financiers that the party had learned the importance of financial responsibility.

Eighteen years in opposition came to an end on 1 May 1997. Labour won a 179-seat majority – the biggest in its history on a manifesto which not only promised no income tax rise, but also a pledge to stick to Conservative spending plans. Blair quickly became the global focus for centre-left politicians and a close friend of US president Bill Clinton. The 'Third Way', described as the ideological underpinning of the New Labour project and bringing market models to some government-run services, aroused interest across the Western world. An improving economy moreover boosted the credibility of the party and their ambition of being in government for a generation.

New Labour was now unassailable in the Commons. The huge majority meant that backbench rebellions from the 'traditional left' could be simply ignored. There was one significant casualty for The Project during the first New Labour government. Mandelson, who had moved from the background to the frontline, was sacked – twice – from the cabinet. He and Brown had long since stopped being close, but he continued to advise

Blair. The Tories nevertheless appeared to be completely out of touch with the electorate and continued to struggle in the polls under the leadership of William Hague.

In an election dubbed the 'quiet landslide' by some commentators, Labour won again in 2001 with another huge Commons majority, of 167. Moreover, with the first-term pledge to match the Conservatives on public finances now expired, Brown could start spending. The NHS, schools and other public services saw large infusions of cash.

Stories about the leadership 'deal' made between Blair and Brown in 1994 were to become more widespread, with speculation about when the chancellor would become prime minister. Some commentators nevertheless regarded the pair as joint prime ministers anyway, with Brown having primacy over vast areas of domestic policy. Increased spending on hospitals and medical staff was popular among all sections of Labour. The leadership nevertheless used up much of its goodwill within the party with the Iraq war – opposed by 139 Labour MPs – and by introducing 'top-up' university fees for higher education students in England – opposed by 71 of their MPs. The latter measure was passed by just five votes, after the intervention of Brown to ensure his backers supported the government.

The World Trade Center bombings on 11 September 2001 shocked the world with the prime minister immediately pledging his support for President Bush's 'war on terror'. Later that year, the UK joined the United Nations–backed invasion of Taliban-ruled Afghanistan, and this was supported by most Labour supporters. The alliance with Bush nevertheless drew Blair and the UK into New Labour's largest foreign affairs crisis, the invasion of Iraq.

Despite hundreds of thousands of protesters massing on the streets of London in 2003 and a parliamentary rebellion by Labour MPs following a bitter debate, the war went ahead. The defeat of Saddam Hussein was swift, but the situation in Iraq was volatile with frequent suicide bombings and 179 UK service personnel and Ministry of Defence staff dying as UK and US (non)planning for the aftermath of war became highly criticized. The war became more unpopular throughout New Labour's second term, undermining Blair's authority and leading to ever-increasing questions about whether he was planning to step down.

Under pressure from Brown's supporters, frustrated that their man had still not risen to the Labour leadership, Blair finally gave way. He announced in late 2004, that he would fight the next election and then serve a 'full term' in office but leave without contesting a fourth election. Critics were to claim that this fundamentally undermined the authority of the prime minister, knowing that he had set himself a timetable, however vague, for his time in office. Blair nevertheless won an unprecedented third term in power for Labour in 2005, with a reduced, but still sizeable, Commons majority of 66.

Conservative leader Michael Howard resigned, and the government now faced a tougher challenge from David Cameron, a man who, like Blair and Brown more than a decade earlier, was determined to make his party electable once more. A young man, he had even described himself during his leadership campaign as the 'heir to Blair'. The threat was real. In his first prime minister's questions session Cameron looked at Blair and proclaimed that 'he was the future once'. The lustre of New Labour and Blair was fading.

Finally, in 2006, following an attempted backbench coup against him led by Brown supporters, Blair announced he would leave office within a year and did so in June 2007, after more than ten years in power. Brown easily beat off his rivals, who did not gain enough support among the party's MPs to ensure a vote among the full membership. Despite lacking the charisma of his predecessor, Brown enjoyed a 'honeymoon period', with some saying a less showy leader was what the country needed – 'Not Flash, Just Gordon'.

Leading Cameron in the polls, many thought the prime minister would call a general election for autumn 2007. Media speculation was allowed to continue, if not actively encouraged. But with election fever at a peak, the BBC's Andrew Marr was called in to interview the prime minister and came out of Downing Street to announce Brown had decided against going to the country. The Conservatives, whose post-conference poll boost was seen as prompting the decision to abandon plans for an election, called Mr Brown a 'bottler'. His poll ratings slumped and never recovered.

A key basis of New Labour's electability – economic soundness – was undermined when the credit crunch hit. This struck directly at Brown, who had been chancellor for a decade before entering 10 Downing Street and had taken the plaudits for UK economic success. As the financial contagion became widespread, the government acted to bail out the banks, nationalizing and part-nationalizing some of the biggest names on the High Street. Brown, moreover, gained praise for leading a global effort to stem the worst of the crisis, and he and Chancellor Alistair Darling raised the rate of income tax for top earners – something Labour had pledged not to do in their 2005 manifesto.

Despite earning considerable respect abroad for his role in apparently helping the world avoid financial collapse, his popularity domestically continued to fall. Electorally, the party did disastrously in local and European elections, also losing the London mayoralty and being beaten by the Scottish Nationalist Party in Scotland. In what with hindsight can be seen as New Labour's offensive to reverse their catastrophic decline in public support, Lord Mandelson was brought back in late 2008 from his job as a European commissioner and swiftly became the de facto deputy prime minister and front man for the government. By the time the general election was called for May 2010 the economy was out of recession. But Labour seemed to know it was heading out of office.

At the subsequent 2010 election, Labour gained just 29% of the vote – little more than Michael Foot had achieved 27 years earlier. The party came second to the Conservatives, with no one gaining a majority. After a flurry of talks a Conservative–Lib Dem government, the first Westminster coalition since the war-time coalition in the 1940s, was formed. David Cameron and his allies had captured much of the coveted centre ground of politics, so hard won by Blair, Brown and Mandelson in the 1990s.

Brown left to set up a leadership contest, saying the election result had been 'my fault and my fault alone'. Anthony Giddens the eminent social theorist, the political thinker behind the Third Way, declared: 'New Labour as such is dead and it is time to abandon the term'. The five candidates to succeed Brown as leader of the party seemed keen to abandon their previous commitment to New Labour. The flirtation of the 'electoral' left with neoliberalism was over.

An assessment of 'New' Labour

Giddens (2010) noted that it was now conventional to disparage the record of New Labour in government. Even sympathetic observers argued that little of substance has been achieved, but for the more determined critics, their period in power had been a disaster. New Labour had led an onslaught on civil liberties, betrayed leftist ideals, failed to make any impact on inequality and, worst of all, embarked on a calamitous war in Iraq. They had promised a 'new dawn', and many felt betrayed.

Giddens (2010) nevertheless argued that a realistic starting point for mounting a rigorous defence of New Labour was to compare their period in government with those of social democratic parties in other countries over roughly the same period – Bill Clinton and the Democrats in the US, Lionel Jospin's Socialists in France and the SDP in Germany, led by Gerhard Schröder – who had all reached accommodations with and indeed helped facilitate the growth of neoliberalism worldwide. Labour managed to remain in government longer than any of these – longer, indeed, than any other left-of-centre party in recent times, including those in Scandinavia.

Giddens moreover observes that the ideological changes associated with the invention of the term 'New' Labour had played a large part in this electoral success. 'New' Labour had not simply been an empty soundbite designed to disguise a vacuum where policies should have been. From the outset, the architects of 'the project' offered a compelling diagnosis of why innovation in left-of-centre politics was necessary, coupled with a clear policy agenda. In outline, this diagnosis was as follows: the values of the left – solidarity, a commitment to reducing inequality and protecting the vulnerable, and a belief in the role of active government – remained intact, but it had been recognized that the policies designed to pursue these ends had to shift radically because of profound changes going on in the wider world. Such changes included intensifying globalization, the development of a post-industrial or service economy and, in an information age, the emergence of a more articulate and combative citizenry, less deference to authority figures than in the past (a process that was to intensify considerably with the advent of the internet).

Most of Labour's policy prescriptions followed from this analysis. The era of Keynesian demand management, linked to the state direction of economic enterprise, was considered over. A different enabling relationship of government to business had to be established, with a recognition of the vital role of enterprise in wealth creation and the limits of state power. No country, however large and powerful, it was argued, could control that marketplace. Neoliberalism had to be dealt with on its own terms. There was no realistic alternative was the prognosis.

The expansion of the service economy went hand in hand with the shrinking of the working class, once the bastion of Labour support. Henceforth, to win elections, a left-of-centre party would need to reach a much wider set of voters, including those who had never endorsed it in the past. Labour could no longer represent sectional class interests alone. In Tony Blair the party seemed to have found the perfect leader to help it further this aim.

Labour policies did evolve during its years in government, but some core ideas nevertheless remained the same. Giddens observes that economic prosperity – albeit in a globalized marketplace – had to take primacy as the precondition of effective social policy. An increasingly prosperous economy would generate the resources needed to fund public investment, dispensing with the need to raise taxes. Labour thus sought to break away from its previous predilection for tax-and-spend. 'Prudence' was Gordon Brown's watchword as chancellor. Prudent economic management was essential if welfare spending was to rise and social justice to be enhanced.

Labour also had to struggle with the disastrous legacy of the Thatcher years. Inequality had increased more steeply in the UK during those years than in any industrial country except for New Zealand (which had also followed Thatcher-style policies). The welfare system was run–down, so investment in public services, coupled with reforms designed to make them more flexible and more responsive to the needs of their users, became a guiding principle. Labour was to be the party not of the big state but of the intelligent state.

A further important strand of New Labour policy was its refusal to allow any issues to be 'owned' by the political right. The task, rather, was to provide left–of–centre solutions to them. This strategy became the focus of attacks by critics worried about its implications for civil liberties but was vital to Labour's longevity in power. Social democrats fell from power in other countries because of their failure to do the same. In the past, the left had tried to explain away, rather than confront directly, questions having to do with crime, social disorder, migration and cultural identity – as if the concerns citizens had about such issues were misplaced or irrelevant. It was assumed, for example, that most crime resulted from inequality and that once inequality was reduced, crime would inevitably decline. Without denying the connection, New Labour took a different view. Tony Blair's 1997 manifesto pledge 'tough on crime and tough on the causes of crime' was not just a slogan, it was adopted as a principle of policy.

Giddens (2010) observes that while it might seem a long way from these concerns to the New Labour emphasis on the need for an activist foreign policy. But it was not. Because of globalization, domestic and foreign policy now overlapped each other far more than previously. Britain faced no visible threat of invasion but would need to assume an active role in the wider world. Interventionism became necessary doctrine when national sovereignty lost much of its meaning and where there were universal humanitarian concerns that had come to override local interests. Transnational terrorism, itself a creature of globalization, was perceived as a threat far greater than the more localized forms of terrorism prevalent in the past.

Giddens observes that New Labour's record is distinctly patchy but notes that it did have far more impact than did any of the other centre-left governments mentioned earlier. The UK enjoyed ten years of unbroken economic growth, not to be dismissed as simply based on a housing and credit bubble. That growth took place alongside the introduction of a national minimum wage. Large-scale investment was made in public services and significant reform was achieved in the areas of health and education.

Wage and income inequality were contained, although not significantly reduced. But, the position of the poor improved substantially. Targets to reduce child poverty were not met, but before the recession, 600,000 children were raised out of relative poverty; measured against an absolute standard, the number is about twice that figure. The New Deal, Sure Start and tax credit policies all had their difficulties but mostly proved their worth. Even the much-derided private finance incentive worked, at least when measured against public procurement. Devolution of power to Scotland and Wales was to be largely successful, and what looks like a lasting peace has been achieved in Northern Ireland. Crime rates came down substantially in the UK as a whole, while Britain made a more fruitful adaptation to increasing cultural diversity than most other European countries.

From a party so often seen as illiberal and authoritarian, there were substantial achievements in the opposite direction. Labour thus signed up to the EU Social Chapter, together with the European Convention on Human Rights, introduced a Freedom of Information Act and endorsed civil partnerships for same-sex couples. Britain became a more liberal and tolerant society than it was, and Labour's policies played a part in this change. In foreign policy, overseas aid was increased well beyond anything preceding Tory governments had managed.

The military interventions in Bosnia, Kosovo – where Blair played a crucial role in persuading the Americans to contemplate deploying ground forces – and Sierra Leone were widely regarded as successes. If only it had stopped there, notes Giddens. For nothing corroded Blair's reputation more than his ill-starred decision to become George Bush's main partner in the invasion of Iraq.

Other far-reaching mistakes were made. The experiment with spin and media management during Labour's early years in power backfired and helped create the impression that New Labour was about presentation rather than policy. Blair did not succeed in integrating Britain more closely into the EU, and some of his closest relationships with other European leaders – notably with the Italian premier, Silvio Berlusconi – were puzzling.

It was right to argue that Labour should become more business–friendly, and it was also right to recognize the importance of the City to the British economy. But it was a fundamental error to allow the prawn cocktail offensive to evolve into fawning dependence, with the result that the UK was transformed into a kind of gigantic tax haven. The idea that Labour should be 'intensely relaxed about people getting filthy rich' not only exacerbated inequalities but also helped create a culture of irresponsibility. Bosses protected themselves from the risks they asked their employees to bear.

Giddens (2010) nevertheless observes that New Labour was not just a continuation of Thatcherism. Its policies involved extensive government intervention in economic life, although mainly on the supply side. And there was a genuine preoccupation with increasing social justice – a notion alien to Margaret Thatcher, Keith Joseph and their guru Milton Friedman. Yet, he observes, Blair and Brown should have made it much clearer than they did that recognizing the virtues of markets is quite different from prostrating oneself before them. Market fundamentalism should have been more explicitly criticized and its limitations exposed. As for proportional representation and wider constitutional reform – surely Labour should have endorsed these as a matter of principle, not as a result of political expediency.

The global financial crisis, foreseen by very few, seems to have put an end to the world that helped to shape New Labour. Suddenly, everything has gone into juddering reverse: Keynesianism and government economic intervention were back. No one was now to deny that we should seek to regulate the financial markets that once seemed so omnipotent. A tax on world financial transactions, previously dismissed as unrealistic, was now on the cards. It is, after all, possible to increase the tax rates of the rich. But ultimately, New Labour failed to halt the growth and expansion of neoliberalism, and this was to be the crucial problem. The socio-economic context may have changed but could a New Labour government in power have done more to stem the ever-increasing global expansion of neoliberalism before it was to become apparently unstoppable.

Policy implications of the crisis of modernity

The crisis of modernity is epitomized by the rise of neoliberalism which is a policy model that transfers control of economic factors to the private sector from the public sector. Its central doctrine is economic growth through increasing competition by deregulation of social, welfare, health, labour and environmental laws, opening domestic markets to foreign competition, limiting the role of the state by the privatization of state assets and the liberalization of economic policies and increasing corporate influence and involvement in governance. This agenda of economic reform was institutionalized by the IMF starting in the 1980s and was accepted worldwide because it profited the governing elite politician–corporate nexus in all countries.

Development through neoliberalism is based on personal profit-at-any-cost from capital- and energy-intensive industrialization. Through economic reform, governments maintain the interests of the ultra-rich, who gradually take over public assets by restricting governance to creating and defending markets and protecting private property. Neoliberal economic growth promotes global trade, consumerism and debt. It thus subordinates democracy, equity, social justice and freedom and wreaks economic violence on the majority poor.

Neoliberalism also nurtures inequality. Today, the wealthiest 62 people on earth own as much wealth as the bottom half 3.5 billion, and the top 1% are wealthier than the remaining 99%. Over decades, the third-world governments have been encouraged to introduce neoliberal economic reform. This has been done via global training and outreach programmes in World Bank institutes and reputed Western universities, of thousands of central and state legislators, bureaucrats, technical specialists, journalists, teachers and civil society leaders, in subjects related to economic development.

The effects of neoliberal policies have been debt crises, severe environmental degradation and crashing economies, currency collapse, rising unemployment, rising food and fuel prices and falling wages. The social ill effects have been exacerbated by the imposition of 'austerity measures' of cutting subsidies for the poor and reducing public spending on health, welfare and education.

Summary of main points

1 Following the Second World War, there was a belief in the UK that government could play a positive role in promoting greater equality through social engineering.
2 Such policies were pursued by both Labour and Conservative governments, the latter because they thought it was necessary to gain working-class support to win general elections and gain the consent of the major interest groups.
3 Throughout the 1960s and 1970s, these two main political parties competed to reverse the relative economic decline of Britain. But it seemed to many that the UK was ungovernable.
4 Consequently, governments of both parties turned their attention to incomes policies which failed dramatically with the Conservative Government in 1973–74 (Miner's strikes and the 'three-day week' and again with the Labour Government in 1979 (the Winter of Discontent).
5 The Conservative Party – under the leadership of Margaret Thatcher – won the 1979 election, and much of so-called Thatcherism (which along with 'Reaganomics' named after President Ronald Reagan in the US) provided the origins of what is now called neoliberalism.
6 The Thatcher government insisted that it could no longer be a universal provider of benefits and the post-war socio-economic political consensus between the main political parties was over.
7 From at least the last three decades of the twentieth century, substantial doubts were beginning to emerge – and again from disparate sources – about the sustainability of the modernist project in an increasingly fragmented social world.

8   The collapse of the post-war socio-political consensus and an intensifying lack of enthusiasm for large-scale state intervention in the socio-economic sphere coincided with a decreasing enthusiasm for grand theoretical explanations in the social sciences.

9   The 'Third Way', described as the ideological underpinning of the New Labour brought market models to government-run services and it was a strategy that aroused interest across the Western world by reaching an accommodation with neoliberalism.

10   A key basis of New Labour's electability – economic soundness – was undermined by the credit crunch.

Discussion questions

1   What were the main features of the socio-economic policies introduced post-war and enjoyed consensus from the main political parties?
2   Why did the post-war social consensus come to end?
3   What is the fragmentation of modernity?
4   Explain neoliberal socio-economic policies.
5   In what ways did New Labour reach an accommodation with neoliberalism, and what brought about is demise?

Suggested further reading

There are numerous accessible books available on the post–Second War political and economy of Britain from which you can take your pick. For anyone interested in the intellectual underpinnings of New Labour should consult Anthony Giddens (1994, 1998).

References

Crewe, I. (1989) *The Thatcher Effect*. London: Wiley.

Giddens, A. (1994) *Beyond Left and Right: The Future of Radical Politics*. Cambridge: Polity Press.

Giddens, A. (1998) *The Third Way: The Renewal of Social Democracy*. Cambridge: Polity Press.

Giddens, A. (2010) 'The Rise and Fall of New Labour', *The New Statesman*, 17 May 2010.

Harvey, D. (1989) *The Condition of Postmodernity: An Enquiry into the Origins of Cultural Change*. Oxford: Blackwell.

Hopkins Burke, R.D. (1999) Youth Justice and the Fragmentation of Modernity. Scarman Centre for the Study of Public Order Occasional Paper Series, The University of Leicester.

Hopkins Burke, R.D. (2016) *Young People, Crime and Justice*, 2nd ed. Cullompton: Willan Publishing.

Kavanagh, D. (1987) *Thatcherism and British Politics: The End of Consensus?* Oxford: Oxford University Press.

Lyotard, J.-F. (1984) *The Post-Modern Condition: A Report on Knowledge*. Manchester: Manchester University Press.

Neofotistos, V. (2013) *Identity Politics*. Oxford: Oxford University Press.

Taylor, I. (1997) 'Crime and Social Insecurity in Europe', *Criminal Justice Matters*, 27(Spring): 3–5.

Willis, P. (1977) *Learning to Labour*. London: Saxon House.

Young, J. (1999) *The Exclusive Society: Social Exclusion, Crime and Difference in Late Modernity*. London: Sage.

Part II

Crime and criminal behaviour in the era of fragmented modernity

Chapter 5

Fragmentation of modernity and the postmodern condition

Key issues

1   The emergence of the postmodern
2   Crime and criminal justice in the postmodern condition
3   Crime and the risk society
4   The clash of civilizations
5   An age of moral ambiguity; post-truth society

This chapter discusses the morally ambiguous nature of crime and criminal behaviour in what some social scientists have called the postmodern condition. Postmodernism stands accused of being an extremely negative and nihilistic vision, for, if, as it is proposed, there is no such thing as the 'truth of the human condition', it becomes clearly difficult to formulate an argument in support of basic human rights or to locate legitimate foundations for law. Postmodernism implies a relativism which denies the possibility of objective truth and hence of justice in anything other than a purely subjective form, which inevitably consigns us to the prospect of conflict and confusion. The essential problem for the development of legislation and explanations of crime and criminal behaviour in fragmented modernity or the postmodern condition remains the crucial difficulty of making any objective claims for truth, goodness and morality. Postmodernism advocates giving a voice to the oppressed and less powerful – and celebrates diversity – but in practice, power relations and political decisions are fundamentally important and place significant restrictions on this ideal not least in the context of neoliberalism

The emergence of the postmodern

Chapter 3 provided us with an overview of the ways in which crime and criminal behaviour have been explained during the relatively uncontested modern epoch, approximately the past 250 years. It was shown that explanations – or theories – have been proposed at various times by among others legal philosophers, biologists, psychologists, sociologists, political scientists and geographers, but it was observed that these many and varied criminological theories can all be explained in the context of one of three models. The first – the rational actor model – proposes that human beings enjoy free will which enables them to choose whether or not to engage in criminal activities. Crime can be controlled by making the costs of offending – that is punishment – sufficient to discourage the pursuit of criminal rewards. The second – the predestined actor model and in complete contrast to the rational actor – proposes that criminal behaviour is explained in terms of factors which exist either within the individual or their environment which *causes* them to act in ways over which they have little or no control. From this perspective, crime can be controlled by identifying and eradicating these factors through some form of treatment. Thus, biological and psychological variants of the model propose that the individual should be changed, while sociological versions have advocated the transformation of the criminogenic environment. The third tradition – the victimized actor model – denies neither entirely the prescriptions of the other two models but recognizes that people make decisions to behave in ways which may well be perfectly rational for them in the circumstances in which they find themselves. It is invariably the activities of the economically poor and politically powerless which are criminalized, a process which is conducted in the interests of those with power and wealth. From this perspective, crime is a social construction which can be controlled or reduced by not criminalizing dispossessed unfortunates and by abolishing legislation which proscribes their activities. In more recent years attempts have been made to produce a synthesis of different perspectives with the aim of providing a bigger, better, all-encompassing theory which explains as much criminality as possible and preferably all. All of these theories and their host model nevertheless enjoy a common principal characteristic. Each is a product of the modern age.

But, in the last decades of the twentieth century, there were increasing doubts about the sustainability of the modernist project in an increasingly fragmented and diverse social world, a situation that some social scientists have referred to as the postmodern condition (see Lyotard, 1984; but also, Baudrillard, 1988; Bauman, 1989, 1991, 1993).

Three main sources for the idea of the postmodern can be identified. First, there was the emergence and consolidation of an intellectual current articulated by the publication of two books by Daniel Bell, *The End of Ideology* (1960) and *The Coming of Post-Industrial Society* (1973). It was an emerging world view with two sub-currents: first, there was the ideological exhaustion of the post-war world with the retreat from the pre-war ideologies of communism and national socialism which had seemed to lead to only totalitarianism, world war and holocaust; second, there was a growing interest in the idea of a post-industrial – or later 'post-Fordist' – society where manufacturing was giving way to the service industry, primary production was being displaced by secondary exploitation – especially of science and technology – and consumers were coming to outperform producers in the economy. In this changed context, the old radical class analyses seemed to make little sense and the intellectual categories around which modernism had been built appeared to have lost their explanatory power.

The second source is poststructuralism, a movement which had flourished mainly in France during the late 1960s and 1970s and, as its name suggests, succeeded structuralism, which had flourished a decade or so earlier, most notably in the work of Claude Levi-Strauss, but which could be traced back to the nineteenth century. While structuralists had been preoccupied with the 'deep structures' of language and society, poststructuralists were sceptical of efforts to attach meanings to words. Michel Foucault significantly contributed to the wider popular influence of poststructuralism by arguing that knowledge and language – and so the categories derived from them – cannot be regarded as anything other than subjective and relative (Foucault, 1980). Thus, by emphasizing the subjectivity of language, poststructuralism contributed to the central belief of postmodernism, that no intellectual tradition can have privileged authority over another.

The third source was an aesthetic movement with its foundations in an architectural controversy centred on the rejection of the so-called international style of austere unadorned modernism epitomized by 1960s' tower blocks and multi-storey car parks.

In summary, there are three significant characteristics which distinguish postmodernism from modernism. First, there is an aversion to 'metadiscourses' – or grand self-legitimating theories – 'isms' or ideologies – which it is argued can lead to intellectual sterility and political oppression. Second, there is an awareness of the indeterminacy of knowledge and the impossibility of absolute truth which has been inherited from poststructuralism. Third, there is an enthusiasm for eclecticism and variety derived from art, architecture and literature but which has come to have much stronger intellectual reverberations.

The idea of the postmodern thus involves claims that modernist features of society are under serious challenge. This can be seen in the realm of culture, where self-proclaimed modern thinkers and artists were challenged from the mid-1960s by anti-modernist ideas which attacked the dehumanization of modern society, questioned the authority of technical experts and celebrated human diversity in place of the pressure to encourage rationalized, standardized human conformity to systems developed by 'experts' and technicians (see Marcuse, 1964). These concerns were reflected in the social sciences by the emergence of radical efforts to challenge orthodox, positivist forms of thought, whose claims to objective scientific status were questioned and rejected.

Underlying these changes were the beginning of the economic and political transformations evident in the breakdown of the Keynesian and Fordist practices of the post-war world in the industrial West. This had been prompted by the oil crisis of the early 1970s, an abandonment of full-employment policies with a decline in economic competitiveness and a restructuring of the world economy with the rise in the productive capacity of the nations of the Pacific Rim. Thus, in all three areas, the economy, the political system and culture, there began to emerge increasingly diverse and fragmented social structures that heralded the beginning of postmodernism or the postmodern condition.

Economically, postmodernity is often described as post-Fordism, which involves the rejection of mass production-line technology in favour of both flexible working patterns and labour force. This in turn involves a weakening of trade unions, greater reliance on peripheral and secondary labour markets, the development of a low-paid and part-time, often female, labour force, and the shift towards a service, rather than manufacturing, economy. On the side of capital owning and controlling interests, there is a greater stress on enterprise and entrepreneurialism, corporate restructuring and the growth of small businesses acting as subcontractors to larger firms. These trends are often seen as evidence of deindustrialization and the disorganization of capitalism.

Politically, postmodernity is complex and is difficult to categorize in traditional invariably class-based terms. An interesting development was Michel Foucault's (1980) poststructuralist conceptualization of power, which he argued is not simply the prerogative of the state. Strategies of power are pervasive throughout society, with the state only one location of the points of control and resistance. From this perspective, there should be a move away from a restricted chain of criminological references – 'state–law–crime–criminals' – to a wider chain of associations that need to be addressed. Thus, for Foucault (1971, 1976) particular areas of social life – for example medicine, law, sexuality – are colonized and defined by the norms and control strategies which are devised and implemented by a variety of institutions and experts. These networks of power and control are governed as much by the *knowledge* and concepts that define them as by the definite intentions of individuals and groups.

The state, for its part, is implicated in this matrix of power and knowledge, but it is only part of it and, in this vein, it has been argued that within civil society there are numerous 'semi-autonomous' realms and relations – such as communities, occupations, organizations, families – where certain kinds of 'policing' and 'order' are indeed present but where the state administration and police force are technically absent. These semi-autonomous arenas are often appropriately negotiated and resisted by their participants in ways over which even now the state has little jurisdiction. To some, it might seem ironic that this emphasis was to come at a time when many of the traditional coercive and regulatory roles of the state were being *enhanced* politically and technologically, and it is a point to which we return later, for in more recent years, many of these previously autonomous locations have been incorporated into multi-agency partnerships delivering the interests of the state from a distance.

Postmodernity has been expressed in neoconservative ideas, such as those promoted by the British prime minister Margaret Thatcher and her contemporary US President Ronald Reagan (and subsequently in the US by George Bush, father and son), and termed *Thatcherism* and *Reaganomics* and which were to metamorphize into the *neoliberalism* which provides the socio-economic context of much of this text. These ideologies included the offering of tax cuts as a means of facilitating consumer choice and the dismantling of elaborate state planning and provision in the fields of welfare. At the same time, the ever-increasing diversity of interests – some of which we will encounter later in this second part of the book – were placing considerable pressure on conventional representative democratic systems, a situation which appeared to have reached crisis point with the intense fragmented political debates surrounding Brexit. Should we stay or should we go.

Modernity was essentially an era characterized by moral certainty. There was a confidence and belief in the superiority and infallibility of natural science that had filtered through into the social sciences, in particular social and political theory. There was a confidence in the explanatory power of the grand theories – or sacred texts – to solve the problems of humanity. Thus, there may well have been competing theories but the devotees of each of these had confidence in the fundamental capacity of their doctrine to solve the crime problem. This might well entail revisions to the theory, the incorporation of concepts from other theoretical perspectives and indeed other models of criminal behaviour, but in the final analysis, the intention was the same as was observed earlier, the creation of a criminological theory which explains most – if not all – criminal activity.

Postmodern societies are – in contrast to modern societies – characterized by moral ambiguity. Now this condition should not be confused with a period of moral uncertainty where the reconsideration and rebuilding of theoretical perspectives can rekindle the moral certainty of old. It is a condition characterized by a terminal loss of certainty with absolutely no expectation that it will ever return.

Postmodern social scientists were thus to recognize the complexity of society and the moral ambiguities which are inherent within it; while, there is an appreciation of a range of different discourses which can be legitimate and hence right for different people, at different times, in different contexts. It is a perspective founded on cultural relativism, the notion that there are a series of legitimate discourses on a particular issue and that it is difficult, if not impossible, to objectively choose between them. Essentially, the objective truth – or the competing objective realities – of modernity is now replaced by recognition of the multiple realities or moral ambiguities of the postmodern condition. These realities are invariably complex, are highly susceptible to inconsistent interpretation and are contested by individuals – politicians and members of the public – who often make short-term, pragmatic and inconsistent judgements without reference to any coherent body of knowledge, hence the many and varied arguments, discourses and interests surrounding the protracted and apparently unsolvable Brexit negotiations. There are simply good reasons for going and for staying.

Whereas modernists had attempted to develop large-scale theories to explain society in terms of enduring, identifiable social structures, postmodernists have followed in the poststructuralist tradition emphasizing the redundancy and futility of such efforts and contested the entire concept of truth. The social sciences – since their very inception in the modern era – had made efforts to transcend the relativity of social situations and identify 'what is going on' systematically and objectively, while philosophers had, in contrast, attempted to establish some rational standpoint from which reality could be described.

Postmodern writers have celebrated the failure of the modernist project to establish rational foundations for knowledge and have embraced the trend towards human diversity and social fragmentation, arguing that there is no objective reality behind the plethora of social meanings. Accounts and definitions have no objective or external reference but are merely elements in a free-floating system of images which are produced and reproduced through the medium of popular mass communication and come to define reality to consumers.

To some, postmodernism is – not surprisingly – a nightmare vision, but others have embraced and celebrated its implications. The fragmentation of social institutions such as social class and status may have increased our uncertainty in how we understand society but – on the other hand – the same trends allow the expression of the diversity of human needs, interests and sensitivities. By challenging the validity of modern claims to privileged forms of knowledge for the powerful, postmodernism gives a voice to the less powerful and oppressed, and it is thus not surprising that some branches of feminism have embraced this approach. Indeed, this is very much the case with the contemporary fourth wave we will encounter in Chapter 13.

Postmodernists came to celebrate the development of new social movements such as travelling communities as these groups sought to live a lifestyle outside of the constraints and dictates of the modern world. In the Western world, gay and what were formerly regarded as other unconventional sexual interest groups were to be celebrated for their efforts to break down restrictive stereotypes and 'expert' knowledge surrounding the pursuit of sexual pleasure (see Chapter 13). The ideas and interests of animal rights groups and environmental concerns were also very much welcomed (see Chapter 14). These have all challenged the adequacy of representation in long-established representative democracies in which party systems commonly only represent the interests of people as members of a social class and, hence, give rise to a restricted form of political agenda, which fails to address other interests. The celebration and acceptance of diversity were therefore seen as a positive thing.

Lyotard reflects on some of the horrors of the past two centuries of modernist society when people have controlled and killed others in their pursuit of a rational, scientific world order that he argues – in the criminological context – has led us logically from the biological notions of Lombroso via Goring to Auschwitz:

The nineteenth and twentieth centuries have given us as much terror as we can take. We have paid a high enough price for the nostalgia of the whole and the one, for the reconciliation of the concept and the sensible, of the transparent and the communicable experience. Under the general demand for slackening and for appeasement, we can hear the mutterings of the desire for a return to terror, for the realisation of the fantasy to seize reality. The answer is: let us wage war on totality; let us be witness to the unrepresentable; let us activate the differences and save the honour of the name.

(1984: 81–82)

The philosopher of the social sciences Paul Feyerabend had also celebrated a non-rationalist – even anarchistic – approach to the manner in which we study the world. Highly critical of efforts to unify and control the limits of science and the potential for knowledge as authoritarian and inhumane, he argues that 'science is an essentially anarchistic enterprise: theoretical anarchism is more humanitarian and more likely to encourage progress than its "law and order" alternatives' (Feyerabend, 1975: 17).

Problematically, given this general approach, we might legitimately ask how Feyerabend can legitimately judge what is 'more humanitarian' and more 'progressive'. What exactly is progressive, and why is this so? The Feyerabend legacy is nevertheless significant because it alerts us not to be slaves to dominant paradigms of how we see the world but be prepared to take risks – perhaps even be prepared to consider the previously unthinkable at least in terms of contemporary orthodoxy – and be prepared to consider the potential of a whole range of often neglected theoretical perspectives.

Criminal justice and the postmodern condition

Postmodernism is for many an extremely negative and nihilistic vision. If there is no such thing as the 'truth of the human condition', it is clearly difficult to formulate an argument in support of basic human rights or to locate legitimate foundations for law, if the human experience is merely reflexive and relative. The relativism implied by postmodernism thus denies the possibility of truth and hence of justice in anything other than a purely subjective form, which inevitably consigns us to the prospect of conflict.

Politically, postmodernism can carry us right the way across the traditional political spectrum from the libertarian right-wing assumption of a war of all against all, resonant of the work of Thomas Hobbes, to a libertarianism of the left or even anarchism, which celebrates and tolerates all human diversity and activity. It thus appears contemptuous of the possibility of developing an objective normative – moral – order that human beings can translate into enforceable norms or laws. Hence, while intellectually challenging and providing a possible explanation for the nature of social change in contemporary Western societies, postmodernism would seem to be extremely problematic for developing a plausible criminological strategy.

By regarding postmodernism in two distinct ways, it is nevertheless possible that we can accept some of its power to explain the enormous diversity in contemporary society without accepting some of the baggage of philosophical relativism. Pauline-Marie Rosenau identifies two different interpretations, what she terms *sceptical* and *affirmative* postmodernism:

The sceptical postmodernism (or merely sceptic), offering a pessimistic, negative, gloomy assessment, argues that the postmodern age is one of fragmentation, disintegration, malaise, meaninglessness, a vagueness, or even absence of moral parameters and societal chaos. . . . This is the dark side of postmodernism, the postmodernism of despair, the postmodernism that speaks of the immediacy of death, the demise of the subject, the end of the author, the impossibility of truth. They argue that the destructive nature of modernity makes the postmodern age one of 'radical, unsuppressible uncertainty' . . . characterised by all that is grim, cruel, alienating, hopeless, tired and ambiguous. In this period no social or political project is worthy of commitment. If, as the sceptics claim, there is no truth, then all that is left is play, the play of words and meaning.

(1992: 15)

Acknowledging that there is no clear-cut divide between the approaches, Rosenau identifies an alternative and altogether more positive tendency in the postmodern movement:

Although the affirmative postmodernists . . . agree with the sceptical postmodern critique of modernity, they have a more hopeful, optimistic view of the postmodern age. More indigenous to Anglo–North American culture than to the [European] Continent, the generally optimistic affirmatives are oriented towards process. They are either open to positive political action (struggle and resistance) or content with the recognition of visionary, celebratory, personal, non-dogmatic projects that range from New Age religion to New Wave lifestyles and include a whole spectrum of postmodern social movements. Most affirmatives seek a philosophical and intellectual practice that is non-dogmatic, tentative and non-ideological. These postmodernists do not, however, shy away from affirming an ethic, making normative choices, and striving to build issue-specific political coalitions. Many affirmatives argue that certain value choices are superior to others, a line of reasoning that would incur the disapproval of the sceptical postmodernists.

(1992: 15–16)

The essential problem for the development of legislation and explanations of crime and criminal behaviour in the postmodern condition nevertheless remains the difficulty of making any objective claims for truth, goodness and morality. This is, of course, less the case for the affirmatives than for the sceptics. On the issue of the foundations of knowledge (epistemology), Rosenau notes:

Postmodern social science . . . announces the end of all paradigms. Only an absence of knowledge claims, an affirmation of multiple realities, and an acceptance of divergent interpretations remain. We can convince those who agree with us, but we have no basis for convincing those who dissent and no criteria to employ in arguing for the superiority of any particular view. Those who disagree with us can always argue that different interpretations must be accepted and that in a postmodern world one interpretation is as good as another. Postmodernists have no interest in convincing others that their view is best – the most just, appropriate, or true. In the end the problem with most postmodern social science is that you can say anything you want, but so can everyone else. Some of what is said will be interesting and fascinating, but some will also be ridiculous and absurd. Postmodernism provides no means to distinguish between the two.

(1992: 137)

There are clearly some fundamental logical intellectual difficulties posed for those seeking to research and explain criminal behaviour. First, there is little available empirical evidence to support the assumption that we have already reached a post-ideological climate. To argue that we can achieve the position that no intellectual tradition can be considered to have privileged authority over another is seriously problematic, as the only too obvious reality is that particular traditions are usually seen to be more authoritative. We should, moreover, note at this juncture that many influential social scientists and theorists deny the notion of postmodern society – which for such a social formation to exist would require some substantive rupture with the modernist social formation – and thus emphasizing the continuities and following the then influential social theorist Anthony Giddens (1990, 1991) use the term 'late modernity'. The term *postmodern condition* has been favoured by this author and is thus used in this book, although he also favours the analogous phrase 'the fragmentation of modernity', while we might note that another very distinguished social theorist Norbert Elias (1978, 1982) has previously proposed that we live in a period of late barbarism, and at times, it is very difficult to dissent from that viewpoint.

Second, while postmodernism may advocate giving a voice to the oppressed and less powerful (and may celebrate diversity), it could be argued that, in practice, power relations and political decisions are fundamentally important and may restrict this ideal. Indeed, it could be argued that recent criminal justice policy (in both the UK and the US and beyond) and the politics that have informed it have tended to encourage less tolerance of difference rather than more. Problematically, society has become complex, fragmented and thus very difficult to control, not least in liberal democratic societies.

Crime and the risk society

In a complex world permeated with the morally ambiguous postmodern condition, where the boundaries between criminals and non-criminals and legal and illegal activities have become increasingly difficult to distinguish, the classic crime control methods of modernity were to become increasingly problematic. Some criminologists were to draw on the 'governmentality' literature to explore the links between contemporary neoliberal political policy and the growing use of 'actuarial' or 'risk-based' strategies of crime control (Stenson and Sullivan, 2001). This new governmentality thesis thus refers to 'the new means to render populations thinkable and measurable through categorization, differentiation, and sorting into hierarchies, for the purpose of government' (Stenson, 2001: 22–23). This section considers these new modes of governance, the wider notion of the risk society and the threats contained within it, which seem to be a significant outcome of the postmodern condition.

The principal feature of the concept of governance is a rupture with traditional perceptions that place the state at the centre of the exercise of political power. In this new Foucauldian conceptualization, power is not simply possessed by the state to be wielded over civil society but is tenuous, unresolved and the outcome of struggles between coalitions of public and private, formal and informal, actors. These struggles are rooted in the central paradox of power: thus, when actors possess the potential to govern, they are not powerful because they are not actually governing, but neither are they powerful when they govern because they are dependent on others to carry out their commands (Clegg, 1989).

This all implies a new complex and fragile process of governing through negotiation, bargaining and other relationships of exchange rather than through command, coercion or normative appeals for support. It is altogether more subtle. Thus, to accomplish and sustain political authority, would-be political leaders have to appreciate their 'power-dependence' on others and recruit and retain sufficient supporters to maintain a governing coalition (Rhodes, 1997). A criminological example – from the New Labour era, in particular – was to control crime through partnerships of statutory, commercial and voluntary organizations (Crawford, 1997). It was a multi-agency approach brought about by an official recognition of the limits of state capacity to reduce crime, in particular the insufficiency of criminal justice, and the consequent need to enrol expertise and resources from non-state actors, including the 'responsibilization' of private citizens for their own security (Garland, 2001).

This idea of 'joined-up' government to attack multifaceted and complex problems such as, for example, youth offending, through multi-agency partnerships employing a broad spectrum of social policy interventions, was to represent a definite break with the methods of modern public administration. It was to challenge the specialization of government into discrete areas of functional expertise and, in so doing, defined new objects of governance. Youth offending, for example, ceased to be defined only in terms of 'criminality' (and thus subject to the expertise of criminal justice professionals) but was to become a problem of education, health and one of 'social exclusion' and 'antisocial behaviour' (Hopkins Burke, 2008).

For most of the twentieth century, crime control had been dominated by the 'treatment model' prescribed by the predestined actor model of crime and criminal behaviour and was closely aligned to a powerful and benevolent state: one which was obliged to intervene in the lives of individual offenders and seek to diagnose and cure their criminal behaviour. It was the apparent failure of that interventionist modernist project epitomized by chronically high crime rates and the apparent failure of criminal justice intervention which was to lead to a rediscovery of the rational actor model and an increased emphasis on preventive responses.

Garland (1996) argued that this new governmental style was organized around 'economic forms of reasoning', and this is reflected in those contemporary rational actor theories which view crime as simply a matter of opportunity and which require no special disposition or abnormality to offend. The subsequent outcome was to be a shift in policies from those directed at the individual offender to those directed at 'criminogenic situations' which were to include 'unsupervised car parks, town squares late at night, deserted neighbourhoods, poorly lit streets, shopping malls, football games, bus stops, subway stations and so on' (Garland, 1999: 19).

Feeley and Simon (1994: 180) had previously influentially argued that these changes should be seen as part of a paradigm shift in the criminal justice process from the 'old penology' (penal welfarism) to the 'new penology' (risk management). The former was concerned with the identification of the individual criminal for the purpose of ascribing guilt and blame, the imposition of punishment and treatment, while the latter is 'concerned with techniques for identifying, classifying and managing groups assorted by levels of dangerousness' based not on individualized suspicion but on the probability that an individual may be an offender. Justice is thus becoming 'actuarial', its interventions increasingly based on risk assessment, rather than on the identification of specific criminal behaviour, and we are therefore witnessing an increase in, and the legal sanction of, such practices as preventive detention, offender profiling, mass surveillance (Norris and Armstrong, 1999) and indeed – when that fails – mass incarceration.

McCahill and Norris (2002) observed that the previous 30 years had witnessed an ever-increasing use of surveillance technologies designed to regulate groups as part of a strategy of managing danger and these had included the ubiquitous city-centre surveillance systems referred to earlier, the testing of employees for the use of drugs (Gilliom, 1994) and the introduction of the blanket DNA testing of entire communities (Nelken and Andrews, 1999). The introduction of these new technologies was apt to be justified in terms of their capacity to monitor 'risk' groups who pose a serious threat to society, but, once introduced, the concept of dangerousness is broadened to include a much wider range of offenders and suspects (see Pratt, 1999). Thus, the National DNA Database was originally established in the UK as a forensic source to help identify those involved in serious crimes, such as murder and rape, but an amendment to the Criminal Justice and Public Order Act 1994 allowed samples to be taken without consent from any person convicted or *suspected* of a recordable offence (Home Office, 1999).

For some, these trends were symptomatic of a broader transition in structural formation from an industrial society towards that of a risk society (Beck, 1992). Now this concept was not intended to imply any increase in the levels of risk that exist in society but rather refers to a social formation organized in order to respond to risks. As Anthony Giddens (1998: 3) observed, 'it is a society increasingly preoccupied with the future (and also with safety), which generates the notion of risk'. Beck (1992: 21) had himself defined risk in such a social formation as 'a systematic way of dealing with hazards and insecurities induced and introduced by modernisation itself'.

Human beings have always been exposed to certain levels of risk, but modern societies have created a particular type, and these are the outcome of the modernization process itself and this can be seen in changes in the very nature of social organization itself. Thus, there are risks such as natural disasters which have always had negative effects on human populations, but these are produced by non-human forces. Modern risks, in contrast, are the product of human activity, and Giddens (1998) refers to these two different categories as *external* and *manufactured* risks. Risk society is predominantly concerned with the latter.

Because manufactured risks are the product of human agents, there is the potential to assess the level of risk that is being – or about to be – produced. The outcome is that risks have transformed the very process of modernization. Thus, with the introduction of human-caused disasters, such as Chernobyl (in Ukraine)[1] and the Love Canal Crisis (in New York City),[2] public faith in the modernist project declined, leaving only variable trust in industry, government and experts (Giddens, 1990). The increased critique of modern industrial practices was to result in a state of reflexive modernization with widespread consideration given to issues of sustainability and the precautionary principle, which focuses on preventative measures to reduce risk levels. Contemporary debates about global warming and the future of the planet should be seen in the context of debates about the risk society.

Social relations have changed significantly with the introduction of manufactured risks and reflexive modernization. Risks, much like wealth, are distributed unevenly in a population and, thus, differentially, influence the quality of life. People will occupy social risk positions they achieve through aversion strategies and these differ from wealth positions which are gained through accumulation. Beck (1992) proposes that widespread risks contain a 'boomerang effect', whereby individual producers of risk will at the same time be exposed to them, which suggests, for example, that wealthy individuals whose capital is largely responsible for creating pollution will suffer when, for example, contaminants seep into the water supply. This argument might appear to be oversimplified, as wealthy people may have the ability to mitigate risk more easily, but the argument is that the distribution of the risk originates from knowledge as opposed to wealth.

Ericson and Haggerty argued that, in the area of criminal justice, we have witnessed a transformation of legal forms and policing strategies that have reflected the transition to the risk society:

> Risk society is fuelled by surveillance, by the routine production of knowledge of populations useful for their administration. Surveillance provides biopower, the power to make biographical profiles of human populations to determine what is probable and possible for them. Surveillance fabricates people around institutionally established norms – risk is always somewhere on the continuum of imprecise normality.
>
> (1997: 450)

McCahill and Norris (2002) later observed that, in these circumstances, policing, for example, becomes increasingly proactive rather than reactive and – given that risk assessment is probabilistic rather than determinist – it requires the assignment of individuals and events to classificatory schemes, which a provide differentiated assessment of risk and calls for management strategies. Returning to the predestined actor tradition, offenders are now classified as 'prolific' rather than merely opportunistic and, having been designated as such, the individual becomes a candidate for targeting by more intensive forms of technical or human surveillance. The emphasis on risk makes everyone a legitimate target for surveillance,

McCahill and Norris (2002) noted that many of the programmes of practical action which flow from strategies of 'risk management' in the criminal justice system are increasingly addressed not just by central-state agencies such as the police 'but beyond the state apparatus, to the organisations, institutions and individuals in civil society' (O'Malley, 1992; Fyfe, 1995; Garland, 1996: 451). Following the demise of the Keynesian welfare state which had epitomized for many the high point in modernity in advanced capitalist nations (Hopkins Burke, 1999), the emphasis on individuals managing their own risk finds converts from all parts of the political spectrum (Barry et al., 1996). Thus, Pat O'Malley (1992) writes of the emergence of a new form of 'prudentialism' where insurance against future risks becomes a private obligation of the active citizen. Responsibilization strategies are therefore designed to offload the responsibility for risk management from central government on to the local state and non-state agencies, hence the increasing emphasis on public/private partnerships, inter-agency cooperation, inter-governmental forums and the rapid growth of non-elected government agencies. The composition of such networks was to allow the state to 'govern-at-a-distance' – to utilize the norms and control strategies of those formerly autonomous institutions identified by Foucault (1971, 1976) – while leaving 'the centralised state machine more powerful than before, with an extended capacity for action and influence' (Garland, 1996: 454).

It is in this context that this author has directed our attention not just to the increasing pervasiveness of policing in its various disguises in society (Hopkins Burke, 2004) but also significantly to our own contribution in the legitimization of this state of affairs, and his neo–Foucauldian left realist variation on the carceral surveillance society proposes that, in a complex fragmented dangerous global risk society, it is *we* the public – regardless of class location, gender or ethnic origin – which have a significant material interest in the development of that surveillance matrix, not least at an international level where the fragmentation of modernity and the postmodern condition have produced a whole range of new threats to worldwide peace and harmony.

The clash of civilizations

The clash of civilizations thesis involves a contentious proposition that it is the cultural and religious identities of people that will be the primary source of conflict following the collapse of communism in the Soviet Union and the ending of the Cold War (Huntington, 1993). Samuel P. Huntington developed his argument in response to that of his former student Francis Fukuyama, who had influentially argued that liberal democracy and market capitalism had now triumphed over the socialist or communist opposition and were now unassailable. The highest state of political and economic being had now been achieved. Huntington simply rejects this argument. The age of ideology had ended but the world had only reverted to a normal state of affairs characterized by cultural conflict.

Huntington (1993) observes that the trends of global conflict following the Cold War are increasingly materializing as divisions between civilizations. Wars such as those following the break-up of Yugoslavia, in Chechnya, and between India and Pakistan were cited as evidence of inter–civilizational conflict. He, moreover, argues that the widespread Western belief in the universality of their post–Enlightenment values and political systems is simply naïve, while continued insistence on democratization and such 'universal' norms will only further antagonize other civilizations. The West is seen as reluctant to accept this state of affairs because it built the international system, wrote its laws and gave it substance in the form of the United Nations.

Huntington (1993), moreover, identifies a major shift of economic, military and political power from the West to the other civilizations of the world, most significantly to what he refers to as the two 'challenger civilizations', Sinic and Islam. East Asian Sinic civilization is seen to be culturally asserting itself and its values relative to the West due to its rapid economic growth. It is the intention of China to reassert itself as the regional hegemon and other countries in the region will 'bandwagon' with that country due to the history of hierarchical command structures implicit in the Confucian Sinic civilization: a culture fundamentally opposed to the individualism and pluralism valued in the West. Huntington proposes that regional powers such as the two Koreas and Vietnam will acquiesce to Chinese demands and become more supportive of China rather than attempting to oppose it. The rise of China thus poses the most powerful long–term threat to the West, as Chinese cultural assertion clashes with the desire of the US for a lack of a regional hegemony in East Asia.

Huntington (1993) argues that the Islamic civilization has experienced a massive population explosion which is fuelling instability both on the borders of Islam and in its interior, where fundamentalist movements are becoming increasingly popular. Manifestations of what he terms the 'Islamic Resurgence' include the Iranian Revolution in 1979 and the first Gulf War. Perhaps the most controversial statement that Huntington made was that 'Islam has bloody borders' which he considers to be a real consequence of several factors, including a Muslim youth bulge and population growth and Islamic proximity to many civilizations including Sinic, Orthodox, Western and African.

Huntington offers six explanations for why there will inevitably a clash of civilizations. First, differences among civilizations are fundamental because they are differentiated from each other by history, language, culture, tradition and, most important, religion. These fundamental differences are the product of centuries and provide the foundations of different civilizations, meaning they will not be gone soon. Second, the world is becoming a smaller place with the outcome that interactions across the world are increasing, which intensifies 'civilization consciousness' and the awareness of differences and commonalities between and within civilizations, because of economic development. Third, because of economic development and social change, people are separated from long-standing local identities. Instead, religion has filled this gap, which provides a basis for identity and commitment which transcends national boundaries and unites civilizations. Fourth, the growth of civilization-consciousness is enhanced by the dual role of the West. On one hand, the West is at a peak of its power, but, at the same time, there is a return-to-the-roots phenomenon occurring among non-Western civilizations. Thus, a West at the peak of its power confronts non-Western countries which increasingly have the desire, the will and the resources to shape the world in non-Western ways. Fifth, cultural characteristics and differences are less changeable and hence less easily compromised and resolved than political and economic ones. Sixth, economic regionalism is increasing which will reinforce civilization-consciousness: economic regionalism may succeed only when it is rooted in a common civilization.

Huntington (1993) suggests that the future central axis of world politics will be the conflict between Western and non-Western civilizations. There are three proposed forms of general actions that non-Western civilization can take in response to the Western countries. First, they can attempt to achieve isolation to preserve their own values and protect themselves from Western invasion. The costs of this action are nevertheless high, and only a few states can afford to follow this strategy. Second, according to the theory of 'band-waggoning', non-Western countries can join and accept Western values. Third, they can make an effort to balance Western power through modernization. They can develop economic and military power and cooperate with other non-Western countries against the West, while still preserving their own values and institutions. Huntington believes that the increasing power of non-Western civilizations in international society will make the West begin to develop a better understanding of the cultural fundamentals underlying other civilizations. Western civilization will thus no longer be regarded as 'universal', but different civilizations will learn to coexist and join together to shape the future world in a state of interdependency.

Huntington argues that inter-civilizational conflict manifests itself in two forms: fault-line conflicts and core-state conflicts. First, *fault-line conflicts* occur on a local level and between adjacent states belonging to different civilizations or within states that are home to populations from different civilizations. Second, *core-state conflicts* occur on a global level between the major states of different civilizations. Core state conflicts can arise out of fault line conflicts when core states become involved. These conflicts may result for a number of reasons, such as relative influence or power (military or economic), discrimination against people from a different civilization, intervention to protect kinsmen in a different civilization, or different values and culture, particularly when one civilization attempts to impose its values on people of a different civilization.

Japan, China and the Four Asian Tigers have modernized in many respects while maintaining traditional or authoritarian societies which distinguish them from the West. Some of these countries have clashed with the West and some have not. Perhaps the ultimate example of non-Western modernization is Russia, the core state of the Ortho-dox Christian civilization. Russia is primarily a non-Western state, although it shares a considerable amount of cultural ancestry with the modern West. But the West is distin-guished from Orthodox Christian countries by its experience of the Renaissance, Ref-ormation, the Enlightenment and overseas colonialism rather than adjacent expansion and by the infusion of Classical culture through ancient Greece rather than through the continuous trajectory of the Byzantine Empire.

Huntington (1993) refers to countries that are seeking to affiliate with another civilization as 'torn countries'. Thus, Turkey, whose political leadership has systematically tried to Westernize the country since the 1920s, provides his chief example. Turkey's history, culture and traditions are derived from Islamic civilization, but its elite – beginning with Mustafa Kemal Ataturk who was its first president in 1923 – have imposed Western insti-tutions and dress, embraced the Latin alphabet, joined the North Atlantic Treaty Organi-zation and sought to join the EU. Mexico and Russia are also considered torn countries. Australia is seen to be a country torn between its Western civilizational heritage and its growing economic engagement with Asia.

Huntington argues that a torn country must meet three requirements to redefine its civilizational identity. First, its political and economic elite must support the move. Second, the public must be willing to accept the redefinition. Third, the elites of the civilization that the torn country is trying to join must accept the country. It is observed that to date, no torn country has successfully redefined its civilizational identity which is mostly due to the elites of the 'host' civilization refusing to accept the torn country, although if Turkey gained membership in the EU, it has been noted that many of its people would support Westernization.

Criticisms of the clash of civilizations thesis

The clash of civilizations thesis has been widely criticized by various by various left-leaning academic writers who have either empirically, historically, logically or ideologically challenged its claims (Fox, 2005; Mungiu-Pippidi and Mindruta, 2002; Henderson and Tucker, 2001; Russett et al., 2000). Amartya Sen (1999: 10) argues:

> Diversity is a feature of most cultures in the world. Western civilization is no excep-tion. The practice of democracy that has won out in the modern West is largely a result of a consensus that has emerged since the Enlightenment and the Industrial Revolution, and particularly in the last century or so. To read in this a historical commitment of the West – over the millennia – to democracy, and then to contrast it with non-Western traditions (treating each as monolithic) would be a great mistake.

Paul Berman (2003) argues that distinct cultural boundaries do not exist in the present day. He contends that there is no 'Islamic civilization' or 'Western civilization' and that the evidence for a civilization clash is not convincing, especially when considering rela-tionships such as that between the US and Saudi Arabia. In addition, he cites the fact that many Islamic extremists have spent a significant amount of time living or studying in the Western world. Bergman argues that conflict arises because of philosophical beliefs vari-ous groups share (or do not share), regardless of cultural or religious identity. Timothy Garton Ash (2000: 95) objects to the 'extreme cultural determinism . . . crude to the point of parody' of the idea that Catholic and Protestant Europe is headed for democracy but that Orthodox Christian and Islamic Europe must accept dictatorship. Edward Said (2001) argues that the categorization of the world's fixed 'civilizations' omits the dynamic interdependency and interaction of culture. A long-time critic of the Huntingtonian paradigm, and an outspoken proponent of Arab issues, Said (2004: 292) also argues that the clash of civilizations thesis is an example of 'the purest invidious racism, a sort of parody of Hitlerian science directed today against Arabs and Muslims'. Noam Chomsky has criticized the concept of the clash of civilizations as just being a new justification for the US 'for any atrocities that they wanted to carry out', which was required after the Cold War as the Soviet Union was no longer a viable threat.

We next consider a very recent and problematic consequence of the postmodern condition and a moral ambiguity which has abandoned any legitimate notion of objective truth, post-truth society.

An age of moral ambiguity: post-truth society

Post-truth (PT) is a periodizing concept (Green, 1995; Besserman, 1998) which refers to a historically particular anxiety about who has the authority to be a legitimate public truth-teller. The term is itself problematic for at least two reasons. First, it refers to two different but related forms of truth: honesty, on one hand, and factuality and knowledge (justified belief), on the other. Second, there are problems similar to other grand periodizing concepts we have encountered in this book, and it is thus sometimes interpreted as a time beyond, after or without truth, which is not the case.

PT is primarily recognizable by a constant obsession with accusations of dishonesty and by the simultaneous public anxiety and distrust it generates. At the same time, a significant increase in human resources has been necessary to produce and attempt to refute or clarify inaccurate or deceptive statements. Thus, the proliferation of 'fact-checking' and rumour or hoax de-bunking schema. It is essentially part of a culture saturated in deception and promotionalism: with the material impact of false or intentionally misleading claims and emotive public opinion which is consequently generated. It can be found in the documents of politics and business built around the deception of artificial intelligence (bots) and in the political consulting industry, which is now heavily informed by cognitive science and big data analytics, corresponding to emotionally pinpointed, demographically micro-targeted influence strategies and practices. It is nevertheless nothing new, but part of a long-established tradition which has been simply accentuated and hastened by the fragmentation of modernity and the emergence of the postmodern condition.

Modernism has long produced critiques of powerful traditional institutions of truth-telling, which were viewed as highly superstitious but which had a monopoly on the means in which to enforce their theories and (rationally indefensible) truth claims. Their targets of critique ranged from, first, the relationship of religious truth to theories of human behaviour and thought and, second, political practice associated with critiques of monarchy and aristocratic class systems (Bristow, 2017; Israel, 2001).

Despite some claims that PT politics and society is the product of postmodernism (McIntyre, 2018), they only share a general concern about knowledge, truth and reality. The PT condition is thus not simply about the fragmentation of justifying stories for truth claims but one beset by suspicion of truth-tellers as dishonest. PT especially refers to a socio-political condition perceived as endemic with dishonesty and distrust, inaccuracies or false knowledge, all corresponding to a crisis of shared trusted adjudicating authorities. Systematic deception and lack of authority are furthermore reproduced by and contribute to a problem of distrust (Stoker, 2017). The public problems for which PT is symptomatic are epistemic (false knowledge, competing truth claims), fiduciary (distrust of society-wide authoritative truth-tellers, trust in micro-truth-tellers) and ethical-moral (conscious disregard for factual evidence – bullshitting – or intentional, strategic falsehoods/lying – dishonesty), the latter of which is often seen as a key part of political strategy (Harding, 2008).

Napoli (2011) observes that audiences have become increasingly divided in contemporary liberal democracies, where thanks to competing truths and truth-tellers or prevalent non-dialogue between them, political polarization ensues. Such liberal democracies basically lack common authorities, discourses, and institutions which are capable of effectively bringing together these competing knowledges and authorities. It is therefore perfectly reasonable to refer to PT as signifying the end of the road for the stable liberal democratic nation state and institutions which held it together. This partly explains the heightened discourse of panic from some quarters of popular politics and academia (Bennett and Livingston, 2018) and which was epitomized by the multiplicity of malevolent discourses surrounding Brexit and the complete failure to reach any sort of consensus agreement.

The concept of PT appears to have been first used in academic and public discourse in the early 1990s but was to increase enormously over the next two decades. Two popular books from 2004 drew attention to the anxiety about public trust and knowledge to which the concept now commonly refers. In *The Post-Truth Era*, Ralph Keyes argued mass dishonesty had arrived. The same year, in his book *When Presidents Lie* (2004), Eric Alterman devised the term 'post-truth presidency' with reference to the George W. Bush presidency. The following year, the Princeton philosopher Harry Frankfurt published a best-selling book, *On Bullshit*, the latter of which, unlike lying, he said, demonstrated a simple disregard for the factuality of the truth claims one was making. Farhad Manjoo (2008) later announced the arrival of 'post-fact society'. All of these popular works emphasized rampant lying as the primary driver of PT politics and society.

Critical scholarly attention to shifts in public knowledge or belief and trust were developing before the turn of the millennium. John Hartley (1992) thus proposed the idea of journalism as a 'truth regime', although he refers to a specific mass broadcast era, in the main pre-internet. He nonetheless anticipated later PT theory by focusing on the blurring of fact/fiction boundaries in television. While a regime generates and polices boundaries between fact and fiction – not the least in journalistic professional codes – hierarchies of truth and regimes are contested. Publishing and TV are 'incommensurate regimes of truth' (1992: 46).

The propaganda apparatus of the George W. Bush administration and the confusion surrounding Iraq – al-Qaeda links and Saddam Hussein's weapons of mass destruction was a turning point for early PT scholarship. Jones (2009) considered 'truthiness' to be characteristic of a shift from a journalistic regime of truth, based on 'truth in fact', to one where a mix of groups (citizens, politicians, journalists, satirists) creates 'believable fictions'. The privileged institutional role of journalism as truth-teller or mediator was now diminished. Its role was now contested and shared with others, which resulted in liberal democratic panic, in journalism, the political establishment and academia.

PT is not simply about lies and false beliefs but also about confusion amidst a surfeit of information and influential appeals, the difficulty in discerning one from the other, the constant selective use and presentation of information and appeals for strategic political (and business) ends and the incessant public disputes about what is (in)accurate and (dis)honest. Some inaccurate statements of fact are made innocently, if unethically and cavalierly (i.e. what is called bullshit, without regard for knowledge of true or false; Frankfurt, 2005). But a great deal of it is deliberate, strategically aimed at disinformation as a way to manage opponents and/or govern by capturing attention.

Misinformation is the spreading of inaccurate or false information while *mistakenly* thinking that one is sharing accurate information: *disinformation*, on the other hand, is *deliberately* spreading false or inaccurate information. The two are nevertheless closely linked. One can spread a false statement that one took to be true, which was originally produced to misinform. Disinformers may produce misinformers. In terms of ethics, intention and effect, misinform corresponds to inaccuracy, a false statement but not a falsehood. If the recipient of misinformation believes it, takes it as fact or true, then they are misinformed but not manipulated for the strategic ends of the misinformer. Disinformation, however, is closer to lying, as both are dishonest. The producer of disinformation knowingly utters falsehoods, not just false statements. Somewhere in between is the bullshitter, who makes statements that may be false. The point is that he or she does not care (Frankfurt, 2005).

Deliberate rumours (just like lying) in politics is again nothing new but it has now become a core issue. No US president before Barak Obama felt it necessary to release his long-form birth certificate in response to constantly weaponized rumours that he was not born in the US. The rumour was used to 'bomb' the news agenda and preoccupy his communication professionals to respond defensively. The fact that majorities do not believe it is all the more proof of its usefulness (Dimock, 2008). Shibutani (1966) had argued that rumours are 'improvised news', a non-professional form of news-telling in conditions of information scarcity. Yet, in twenty-first-century media and politics, rumours flourish in the opposite condition of information overload (Andrejevic, 2013), fragmentation of attention and decline of culture-wide authorities or truth-tellers (Harsin, 2006, 2014, 2015).

Rumour bombs correspond to fake news and strategic political communication developments, which have helped distinguish them from simple rumours and as a counterpart to other contemporary communication bombs (Google bombs and Twitter bombs, for example, which were various ways of 'bombing' the field of attention). Rumour bombs referred to the core definition of *rumour* as a statement whose veracity is unknown or unprovable and to communication bombs as long-time forms of information warfare migrating from military to politics as 'war by other means' (Caplow, 1947): Iraq–al-Qaeda links, John Kerry lied about Vietnam, Obama is a Muslim, and former French president François Hollande was supported by over 700 mosques are all are rumour bombs professionally operationalized in popular political struggles (Kessler, 2014; Harsin, 2018).

Rumour bombs normally differ from fake news in the sense that rumours may turn out to be true. Fake news is false news, although its core propositions may be contextualized by facts. Moreover, rumour bombs tend to use deliberately ambiguous claims to generate not just belief but conflict and disagreement or debate as well. For example what does *links* mean in the claim that there were Iraq–al-Qaeda 'links'? The claim may be more influential when the word is not defined and left to the imagination of the audience. A rumour bomb may be accompanied by a story, attempting to provide evidence for the core claim. That evidence usually is not fake, just an example of poor reasoning.

Fake news is usually the presentation of new events where the event is presented as a discovery of something hitherto hidden. Thus, fake birth certificate allegations aimed at

Obama and accusations that Clinton had sold weapons to ISIS (the Islamic State of Iraq and Syria). Moreover, in the era of citizen journalism, fake news could appear rather unadorned, thanks to easily accessible photo-editing software and web page templates, it may also appear in the style of news organizations with high production values. Imitating the style of professional journalism is the way fake news produces its credibility for some audiences.

All these forms of PT misinformation can contain lies. Yet there is a difference between them. PT is perhaps most significantly discernible by an emphasis on lying, constant accusations of lying (without proof) and revelations of lying (with convincing proof). While it is nearly impossible to prove definitively that there are more lies or liars today than in the past, there is clearly an observable discourse about lying, which claims that there are more, that people perceive or feel there must be more, because there is also so much empirically verifiable distrust and documentable dishonesty. Fake news provides the quintessential example.

Political communication and news practices and values have shifted in recent years in a way which favours even facile lying, whereby 'honesty is a novelty' (Corner and Pels, 2003: 11). The very conditions for being considered honest and truthful have been reconfigured thanks to processes of mediatization and celebrification in politics, the internalizing of entertainment genre expectations and values in their political performances as a perceived requirement for gaining attention. Yet, while claims of increased lying appear constantly, it would be almost impossible to prove such claims convincingly.

Changes in journalism, such as downsizing staff while accelerating the publication pace (Kovach and Rosenstiel, 1999, 2010), have invited inaccuracies and vulnerabilities to hoaxes (later fake news) and partly arising from 'citizen journalism' whereupon everyone is now a journalist and which brings with it not just hordes of watchdogs but also armies of rumour bombers and fake news purveyors. The latter was partly explained by market pressures to grab the attention of readers and viewers which partly resulted in trends of infotainment, tabloidization and politainment which allowed for the repetition of rumours and disinformation as agenda-setting topics themselves (Thussu, 2009; Riegert and Collins, 2015). Market pressures are also blamed for significant amounts of public relations material that appear unidentified in news products (Bennett, 2003; Lewis et al., 2008). Finally, new apps allow quick posting of citizen journalist content, while critics have warned about a 'high potential for abuse', not least for producing 'fake news'.

If journalism has lost its authority to tell and distinguish truth, while news has a proliferating and competing cast of truth-tellers, promotional culture applies cultural pressure to journalism, politics and everyday social relations. The relationship of promotionalism to truth has always been more like Harry Frankfurt's (2005) notion of bullshit. It is cynical about truth in its strategies to promote attention and consumption. Promotional culture scholars view bullshit-friendly communication as having become accepted in a wider and wider array of human practices, not in the least politics. Professional bullshitters are essential to contemporary consumer economies and politics.

Several PT commentators point to the post-9/11 Bush regime's sophisticated propaganda as a turning point in contemporary state communication. Karl Rove, George W. Bush's legendary spin doctor and strategist, bragged that journalists naively belonged to a 'reality-based community' while strategists like himself 'create our own reality' which journalists are free to 'study'. Journalists will be simply left to just study what strategists do (Suskind, 2004). Communication strategists are sometimes forced to respond to journalist-produced events and, perhaps more often, to events opponents publicize with the assistance of news organizations. They nonetheless lead by misleading. Frank Rich (2005) observed that the Bush strategy team used 'fake reporters' and fake broadcast segments (video news releases dutifully broadcast by local newscasts) over a decade prior to the term becoming a 'word of the year'. Rich was explicit: 'The White House Stages Its "Daily Show"', he wrote.

Hannah Arendt (1972) had, 30 years previously, foreseen that organized, systematic lying or, more easily proven, deceptions, the bread and butter of consumer capitalism and the communications wing of the state security apparatus, were going to become the organizing force of political life. Both consumer capitalism, deeply embedded in everyday life, and elite liberal democracy, as its communication apparatus, demand deceptive communication. It is systematic, strategic and highly organized.

The foundations of popular truth were often taken for granted in the heyday of mass communication and the monopoly of journalism on authoritative truth (re)telling. The PT world is in contrast epitomized by (dis)trust. The sociologist Georg Simmel (1900: 179) had, a century previously, argued that trust is actually a 'weak form of inductive knowledge' and 'very few relationships would endure if trust were not as strong as, or stronger than, rational proof or personal observation'. The evidence suggests a great increase in public distrust.

Consider, for example, the declining numbers of voters in presidential and parliamentary elections across the Western liberal democratic world, where similar techniques of strategic political communication, among other things, are imitated. Countries such as the US, the UK and France have seen electoral participation decrease by 30 percentage points over the past 50 years. On the other hand, compare the decline in voter turnout with the rise of self-identified disenfranchised movements and new parties in the very same countries. On the right, one sees the Front National in France, the UK Independence Party (UKIP) and latterly the Brexit Party, Germany's AFD (Alternative for Germany), and even the insurgent democratic socialist challenge to the US Democratic Party by Bernie Sanders and the virtual takeover of the British Labour Party by the 'hard' left epitomized by Jeremy Corbyn and his cohorts. Meanwhile, left 'prefigurative' social-political movements such as *les Indignados* in Spain, Occupy in the US and *Nuit Debout* in France have stressed their alienation from the lack of real choices and opportunities offered by liberal democracy.

Anthony Giddens (1994) had argued that modern and traditional societies differ importantly in terms of trust-granting and that late modern societies underwent a shift from 'passive trust' toward social institutions and their experts to general distrust and fleeting, 'active trust' today. Trust-granting appears to have taken even more intensely restricted roles, based much of the time on performativity (rhetorical devices to produce credibility) and ongoing 'facework'.

If trust in PT society is short term and if maintained and constantly renewed, how is active public trust to be earned today in a state of fragmented modernity permeated with the postmodern condition? One argument is that the collaborative agencies of PT society favour highly emotional communication and that this is partly the way many subjects identify with truthful communication. This resort to emotion and affect is nevertheless not based on a traditional rational/irrational, reason/emotion dualism. On the contrary, it builds on revolutions in cognitive science and neurophilosophy over the last 30 years, which proposes that there is no actual separation between emotion and reason. They, moreover, insist that the conceptual distinction be maintained since there are different degrees of emotion in reasoning, even shown to be located in different parts of the brain (Damasio, 1994). While promotional industries and political communication have for some time used this research to produce strategies (hoping especially for quick manageable affective responses), journalism is now visiting this research in order to manage visitor attention online (and probably in what remains of print and broadcast).

Here, resource-rich political and economic actors using big data analytics and sentiment analysis target audiences emotionally, hoping not simply to produce beliefs (ideological effects) but also to modulate cognition, emotion and attention, via quick likes/dislikes and shares, before moving on. In a culture of speed and simultaneous attention deficit, demands and expectations of faking or exaggeration (promotionalism), slower, perhaps 'quieter' forms of communication are suspicious to some audiences. These audiences are attracted to what appears to be 'authentic', which seems to periodically escape the demands of promotional culture (Banet-Weiser, 2012). These fleeting moments have been described as emotional truth and 'emo-truth' (Harsin, 2017, 2018).

Emotional/emo-truth theory proposes that there are parallels in reality TV and popular politics regarding the way truth and trust is performed and granted. The theory is based on insights from audience studies of melodrama genres and 'fact-based' programmes (i.e. reality TV) audiences (Hill, 2007; Grindstaff, 2008). Emo-truth is truth where emotion serves as inference (prime or indexical sign, emotional or unconscious affective response and hey presto: truth). It is felt (although not necessarily consciously), not accompanied by long temporal reasoning. It is akin to what reality TV audience scholarship has documented as trust in perceived authenticity (i.e. truth) of moments where participants lose control, get angry and aggressive, bully or, conversely, cry (Harsin, 2018).

With such pervasive, systematic, strategic deception in PT society and politics, it is these transient moments of emo-truth that connect with some audiences, which helps to explain the success of aggressive emo-truth masculinities, fond of insulting, spectacular claims, of attacking political correctness and of figures such as Donald Trump and Boris Johnson, among others, in varying degrees of the style (Harsin, 2017). Not all PT political performance is, of course, emo-truth, and not all its performers do it as effectively or constantly. The key is that the connection of trust, the lack of concern with the falsity of some truth claims, is explained by an emotional, not rational, connection, and perhaps for the angriest most distrustful citizens, the anger and aggression of emo-truth are most appealing. Emotional truth and emo-truth political communication also show signs of the normalization of celebrity politics and its games of authenticity and appeal (Street, 2004).

Policy implications of the postmodern condition

The fundamental policy implication confronting us in fragmented modernity is how will it be possible to stop investing in structures of oppression whose appearance channels and sustains the very use of the power to harm, without at the same time actually exercising power. A related problem is how, given the nature of power and social structure, is it possible to change the reified products of discourse that we take to be structure, culture and nature? This is the major – some suggest insurmountable – problem facing the criminological project in the postmodern condition. We consider these issues further in the following chapter that discusses constitutive criminology.

In recent years, the theory of 'dialogue among civilizations' – in contrast to the 'clash of civilizations' thesis – has become the centre of some international attention. The concept was originally devised by Austrian philosopher Hans Köchler (1972) in an essay on cultural identity. Thirty years later, in 2001, Iranian president Mohammad Khatam introduced the concept at the global level and the following year the United Nations proclaimed the year 2001 as the 'United Nations Year of Dialogue among Civilizations'.

The Alliance of Civilizations initiative was proposed at the 59th General Assembly of the United Nations in 2005 by the Spanish prime minister, Jose Luis Rodriguez Zapatero and co-sponsored by the Turkish prime minister, Recep Tayyip Erdogan. The initiative was intended to galvanize collective action across diverse societies to combat extremism, to overcome cultural and social barriers between mainly the Western and predominantly Muslim worlds and to reduce the tensions and polarization between societies which differ in religious and cultural values. An attempt to bring together diverse cultures in a neo-Durkheimian state of international independency as a response to the divisions between countries worldwide brought about in no small measure by the apparently irreversible spread of globalization and neoliberalism. We return to these themes later in this book in the discussion of radical moral communitarianism found in Chapter 20.

A recent report by academics and journalists, sponsored by the EU, touches upon what have become common policy recommendations for providing solutions to the problems raised by PT society. First, it is proposed that there is a need to enhance the transparency of online news, involving an adequate and privacy-compliant sharing of data about the systems which enable their circulation online. Second, there should be programmes to promote media and information literacy to counter disinformation and help users navigate the digital media environment. Third, tools should be developed for empowering users and journalists to tackle disinformation and foster a positive engagement with fast-evolving information technologies. Fourth, there is a need to safeguard the diversity and sustainability of the European news media ecosystem.

Harsin (2018) nevertheless proposes more radical alternative solutions which follow logically from critical post-truth theory. He observes the need to bear in mind the fact that the majority of people in many countries report that they distrust news media, corporations, government, democracy, capitalism and other major institutions and traditionally accepted sacred organizing discourses of social life. Thus, at the most fundamental level of 'fixing' PT society would, first of all, mean recovering social trust by a radical transformation of various significant aspects of that culture. First, consumer capitalism (propelled by PT communication strategies and tactics – promotional culture) and its deep mediatization in an attention economy, since the latter must be made to serve ends beyond attention capture and data harvesting for marketing, that is corporate profit and state surveillance. Second, the slide of journalism into PT infotainment must be contained and reversed with a debate about how it should be financed and what it can and should do under current conditions of communication and culture. Third, dealing with the unequal resources of professional political communication used to study, quantify, construct and control pseudo-publics, instead of turning such communication channels by providing more tools to more democratic actors with a strong emphasis on ethics. Fourth, there should a programme of education teaching the history of anti-democratic elite forces that from the onset of mass communication commandeered scientific knowledges, immense communication resources and strategic skills to manipulate and control the political agenda, with varying degrees of success.

Summary of main points

1   Postmodernism implies a relativism which denies the possibility of objective truth and hence of justice in anything other than a purely subjective form.
2   The problem for the development of legislation and explanations of crime and criminal behaviour in fragmented modernity or the postmodern condition remains the crucial difficulty of making any objective claims for truth, goodness and morality.
3   The idea of the postmodern involves claims that modernist features of society are under serious challenge. Underlying these changes was the beginning of the economic and political transformations evident in the breakdown of the Keynesian and Fordist practices of the post-war world in the industrial West.
4   Strategies of power are pervasive throughout society with the state only one location of the points of control and resistance. The state, for its part, is implicated in this matrix of power and knowledge, but it is only part of it.
5   Postmodern societies are characterized by moral ambiguity whereby there is no objective truth.
6   Postmodernism provides for many an extremely negative and nihilistic vision. If there is no such thing as the 'truth of the human condition', it is clearly difficult to formulate an argument in support of basic human rights or to locate legitimate foundations for law.
7   In a complex world permeated with the morally ambiguous postmodern condition, where the boundaries between criminals and non-criminals and legal and illegal activities have become increasingly difficult to distinguish, the classic crime control methods of modernity have become increasingly problematic.
8   Feeley and Simon (1994: 180) have influentially argued that these changes should be seen as part of a paradigm shift in the criminal justice process from the 'old penology' to the 'new penology'. These trends were for some symptomatic of a broader transition from an industrial society towards that of a risk society (Beck, 1992).
9   The clash of civilizations thesis is a proposition that it is the cultural and religious identities of people that will be the primary source of conflict following the collapse of communism in the Soviet Union and the ending of the Cold War (Huntington, 1993).
10   Post-truth is a periodizing concept (Green, 1995; Besserman, 1998) which refers to a historically particular anxiety about who has the authority to be a legitimate public truth-teller.

Discussion questions

1   What were the factors that brought about the postmodern condition?
2   How does postmodernism explain power relations in contemporary society?
3   Differentiate between the 'old penology' and the 'new penology'?
4   Explain the clash of civilizations thesis.
5   What is post-truth, and what is its connection to the postmodern condition?

Suggested further reading

The following texts are recommended for those seeking an introduction to the notion of the postmodern condition: Baudrillard (1988), Bauman (1991, 1993), Harvey (1989) and Lyotard (1984). Rosenau (1992) is essential reading on the relationship of postmodernity to the social sciences. Both Davis (1990) and Young (1999) provide rather different accounts of contemporary post-industrial societies and the significance for criminology.

The notion of risk society in general is discussed by Beck (1992) and the significance of this analysis for controlling crime and the notion of governance with the decline of the sovereign state by Garland (1996). For an excellent discussion of 'actuarial justice' and 'risk society' as applied to criminal justice, see O'Malley (1992), Feeley and Simon (1994) and Ericson and Haggerty (1997). Giddens (1994, 1998) attempts to square the circle between the postmodern condition (for him, late modernity), left realism and the 'Third Way' political strategy of New Labour. Hopkins Burke (2004) discusses the pervasiveness of multi-agency 'policing' in contemporary societies and apparently contradictory demands for security and human rights.

The essential reading for the clash of civilization thesis is of course Samuel P. Huntington (1993), and Fox (2005) offers an excellent riposte. There are numerous discussions of post-truth society and Harry H. Frankfurt's (2005) treatise on 'bullshit' is a must-read, while Keyes (2014), Harsin (2015) and McIntyre (2018) are also recommended.

References

Alterman, E. (2004) *When Presidents Lie: A History of Official Deception and its Consequences*. New York, NY: Viking.

Andrejevic, M. (2013) *InfoGlut: How Too Much Information is Changing the Way We Think and Know*. New York, NY: Routledge.

Arendt, H. (1972) *Crises of the Republic: Lying in Politics; Civil Disobedience; On Violence; Thoughts on Politics and Revolution*. New York, NY: Harcourt Brace Jovanovich.

Banet-Weiser, S. (2012) *Authentic TM: The Politics and Ambivalence in a Brand Culture*. New York, NY: New York University Press.

Barry, A., Osborne, T. and Rose, N. (1996) *Foucault and Political Reason: Liberalism, Neo-Liberalism and Rationalities of Government*. London: UCL Press.

Baudrillard, J. (1988) *Selected Writings*. Stanford, CA: Stanford University Press.

Bauman, Z. (1989) *Modernity and the Holocaust*. Cambridge: Polity Press.

Bauman, Z. (1991) *Modernity and Ambivalence*. Cambridge: Polity Press.

Bauman, Z. (1993) *Postmodern Ethics*. Oxford: Blackwell.

Beck, U. (1992) *Risk Society*. London: Sage.

Bennett, W.L. (2003) *News: The Politics of Illusion*. New York: Longman.

Bennett, W.L. and Livingston, S. (2018) 'The Disinfornation Order: Disruptive Communication', *European Journal of Communication*, 33(2): 122–39.

Berman, P. (2003) *Terror and Liberalism*. London: W W Norton & Company.

Besserman, L. (1998) 'The Challenge of Periodization: Old Paradigms and new Perspetives', *Speculum*, 73(3): 915–23.

Bristow, W. (2017) 'Enlightenment', in E.N. Zalta (ed.) *The Stanford Encyclopedia of Philosophy (Fall)*. Metaphysics Research Lab, Stanford, CA: Stanford University.

Caplow, T. (1947) 'Rumors in War', *Social Forces*, 25: 298–302.

Clegg, S. (1989) *Frameworks of Power*. London: Sage.

Corner, J. and Pels, D. (2003) *Media and the Restyling of Politics: Consumerism, Celebrity and Cynicism*. London: Sage.

Crawford, A. (1997) *The Local Governance of Crime: Appeals to Community and Partnerships*. Oxford: Clarendon Press.

Damasio, A.R. (1994) *Descartes' Error: Emotion, Reason, and the Human Brain*. New York, NY: Putnam.

Davis, M. (1990) *The City of Quartz: Evacuating the Future in Los Angeles*. London: Verso.

Dimock, M. (2008) 'Belief that Obama Is Muslim Is Durable, Bi-Partisan – But Most Likely to Sway Democratic Votes', Pew Research Center (July 15).

Elias, N. (1978) *The Civilising Process, Vol. 1: The History of Manners*. Oxford: Blackwell.

Elias, N. (1982) *The Civilising Process, Vol. 2: State-Formation and Civilisation*. Oxford: Blackwell.

Ericson, R.V. and Haggerty, D. (1997) *Policing the Risk Society*. Oxford: Clarendon Press.

Feeley, M. and Simon, J. (1994) 'Actuarial Justice: The Emerging New Criminal Law', in D. Nelken (ed.) *The Futures of Criminology*. London: Sage.

Feyerabend, P. (1975) *Against Method: Outline of an Anarchistic Theory of Knowledge*. London: New Left Books.

Foucault, M. (1971) *Madness and Civilisation: A History of Insanity in the Age of Reason*. London: Tavistock.

Foucault, M. (1976) *The History of Sexuality*. London: Allen Lane.

Foucault, M. (1980) *Power/Knowledge: Selected Interviews and Other Writings 1972–77*, edited by C. Gordon. Brighton: Harvester Press.

Fox, J. (2005) 'Paradigm Lost: Huntington's Unfulfilled Clash of Civilizations Prediction into the 21st Century', *International Politics*, 42: 428–57.

Frankfurt, H.G. (2005) *On Bullshit*. Princeton, NJ: Princeton University Press.

Fyfe, N.R. (1995) 'Law and Order Policy and the Spaces of Citizenship in Contemporary Britain', *Political Geography*, 14(2): 177–89.

Garland, D. (1996) 'The Limits of the Sovereign State: Strategies of Crime Control in Contemporary Society', *British Journal of Criminology*, 34(4): 445–71.

Garland, D. (1999) '"Governmentality" and the Problem of Crime', in R. Smandych (ed.) *Governable Places: Readings on Governmentality and Crime Control*. Aldershot: Ashgate.

Garland, D. (2001) *The Culture of Control*. Oxford: Oxford University Press.

Garton Ash, T. (2000) *History of the Present*. London: Penguin.

Giddens, A. (1990) *The Consequences of Modernity*. Cambridge: Polity Press.

Giddens, A. (1991) *Modernity and Self-Identity*. Cambridge: Polity Press.

Giddens, A. (1994) *Beyond Left and Right: The Future of Radical Politics*. Cambridge: Polity Press.

Giddens, A. (1998) *The Third Way: The Renewal of Social Democracy*. Cambridge: Polity Press.

Gilliom, J. (1994) *Surveillance, Privacy and the Law: Employee Drug Testing and the Politics of Social Control*. Ann Arbor, MI: University of Michigan Press.

Green, W.A. (1995) 'Periodizing World History', *History and Theory*, 34(2): 99–111.

Grindstaff, L. (2008) *The Money Shot: Trash, Class, and the Making of TV Talk Shows*. London: University of Chicago Press.

Harding, J. (2008) *Alpha Dogs: The Americans Who Turned Political Spin Into a Global Business*. New York, NY: Farrar, Straus and Giroux.

Harsin, J. (2006) 'The Rumour Bomb: Theorising the Convergence of New and Old Trends in Mediated US Politics', *Southern Review: Communication, Politics & Culture*, 39(1): 76–93.

Harsin, J. (2014) 'Public Argument in the New Media Ecology: Implications of Temporality, Spatiality, and Cognition', *JAIC Journal of Argumentation in Context*, 3(1): 7–34.

Harsin, J. (2015) 'Regimes of Posttruth, Postpolitics, and Attention Economies', *Communication, Culture & Critique*, 8(2): 327–33.

Harsin, J. (2017) 'Trump L'oeil: Is Trump's Post-truth Communication Translatable?', *Contemporary French and Francophone Studies*, 21(5): 512–22.

Harsin, J. (2018) 'Post-truth Populism: The French Anti-gender Theory Movement and Cross-Cultural Similarities', *Communication, Culture and Critique*, 11(1): 35–52.

Hartley, J. (1992) *The Politics of Pictures: The Creation of the Public in the Age of Popular Media*. London: New York, NY: Routledge, Chapman & Hall.

Harvey, D. (1989) *The Condition of Postmodernity: An Enquiry into the Origins of Cultural Change*. Oxford: Blackwell.

Henderson, E.A. and Tucker, R. (2001) 'Clear and Present Strangers: The Clash of Civilizations and International Conflict', *International Studies Quarterly*, 45: 317–38.

Hill, A. (2007) *Restyling Factual TV Audiences and News, Documentary and Reality Genres*. New York, NY: Routledge.

Home Office (1999) *Proposals for Revising Legislative Measures on Fingerprints, Footprints and DNA Samples.* London: Home Office.

Hopkins Burke, R.D. (1999) Youth Justice and the Fragmentation of Modernity. Scarman Centre for the Study of Public Order Occasional Paper Series, The University of Leicester.

Hopkins Burke, R.D. (ed.) (2004) *'Hard Cop/Soft Cop': Dilemmas and Debates in Contemporary Policing.* Cullompton: Willan Publishing.

Hopkins Burke, R.D. (2008) *Young People, Crime and Justice.* Cullompton: Willan Publishing.

Huntington, S.F. (1993) 'The Clash of Civilisations', *Foreign Affairs,* Summer.

Israel, J.I. (2001) *Radical Enlightenment: Philosophy and the Making of Modernity 1650–1750.* Oxford: Oxford University Press.

Jones, J.P. (2009) *Entertaining Political Television and Civic Culture.* Lanham, MD: Rowman & Littlefield.

Kessler, G. (2014) 'The Cheneys's Claim of a "Deep, Longstanding, Far-reaching Relationship" Between Al-Qaeda and Saddam', *The Washington Post,* July 17.

Keyes, R. (2014) *The Post-truth Era: Dishonesty and Deception in Contemporary Life.* New York, NY: St. Martin's Press.

Köchler, H. (1972) 'Die Europaische Aufgabe Der Alphen region', Leitartikel/Editorial, in *Tiroler Bauernzeitung,* 66(29): 1.

Kovach, B. and Rosenstiel, T. (1999) *Warp Speed: America in the Age of Mixed Media.* New York, NY: Century Foundation Press.

Kovach, B. and Rosenstiel, T. (2010) *Blur: How to Know What's True in the Age of Information Overload.* New York, NY: Bloomsbury.

Lewis, J., Williams, A. and Franklin, B. (2008) 'Four Rumours and an Explanation', *Journalism Practice,* 2(1): 27–45.

Lyotard, J.-F. (1984) *The Post-Modern Condition: A Report on Knowledge.* Manchester: Manchester University Press.

Manjoo, F. (2008) *True Enough: Learning to Live in a Post-Fact Society.* Hoboken, NJ: Wiley.

Marcuse, H. (1964) *One-Dimensional Man.* Boston, MA: Beacon.

McCahill, M. and Norris, C. (2002) *Literature Review: Working Paper Number Two.* [Online]. Available from: www.urbaneye.net/results/ue_wp2.pdf [Accessed 15 September 2008].

McIntyre, L.C. (2018) *Post-Truth.* Cambridge, MA: MIT Press.

Mungiu-Pippidi, A. and Mindruta, D. (2002) 'Was Huntington Right? Testing Cultural Legacies and the Civilization Border', *International Politics,* 39(2): 193–213.

Napoli, P.M. (2011) *Audience Evolution: New Technologies and the Transformation of Media Audiences.* New York: Columbia University Press.

Nelken, D. and Andrews, L. (1999) 'DNA Identification and Surveillance Creep', *Sociology of Health and Illness,* 21(5): 689–706.

Norris, C. and Armstrong, G. (1999) *The Maximum Surveillance Society: The Rise of CCTV.* Oxford: Berg.

O'Malley, P. (1992) 'Risk, Power and Crime Prevention', *Economy and Society,* 21(3): 252–75.

Pratt, J. (1999) 'Governmentality, Neo-Liberalism and Dangerousness', in R. Smandych (ed.) *Governable Places: Readings on Governmentality and Crime Control.* Dartmouth: Ashgate.

Rhodes, R.A.W. (1997) *Understanding Governance: Policy Networks, Governance, Reflexivity and Accountability.* Buckingham: Open University Press.

Rich, F. (2005) 'The White House Stages Its Daily Show', *The New York Times,* February 17.

Riegert, K. and Collins, S. (2015) 'Politainment', in *The International Encyclopedia of Political Communication.* Hoboken, NJ: John Wiley & Sons.

Rosenau, P.-M. (1992) *Post-Modernism and the Social Sciences: Insights, Inroads and Intrusions.* Princeton, NJ: Princeton University Press.

Russett, B.M., Oneal, J.R. and Cox, M. (2000) 'Clash of Civilizations, or Realism and Liberalism Déjà Vu? Some Evidence', *Journal of Peace Research,* 37(5): 583–608.

Said, E.W. (2001) 'The Clash of Ignorance', *The Nation,* October.

Said, E.W. (2004) *From Oslo to Iraq and the Road Map.* New York: Pantheon.

Sen, A. (1999) 'Democracy as a Universal Value', *Journal of Democracy,* 10(3): 3–17.

Shibutani, T. (1966) *Improvised News: A Sociological Study of Rumor*. Indianapolis: Bobbs-Merrill.

Simmel, G. (1900) *The Philosophy of Money*. London: Routledge & Kegan Paul.

Stenson, K. (2001) 'The New Politics of Crime Control', in K. Stenson and R.R. Sullivan (eds.) *Crime, Risk and Justice: The Politics of Crime Control in Liberal Democracies*. Cullompton: Willan Publishing.

Stenson, K. and Sullivan, R.R. (2001) *Crime, Risk and Justice: The Politics of Crime Control in Liberal Democracies*. Cullompton: Willan Publishing.

Street, J. (2004) 'Celebrity Politicians: Popular Culture and Political Representation', *The British Journal of Politics & International Relations*, 6(4): 435–52.

Stoker, G. (2017) *Why Politics Matters: Making Democracy Work*. London: Palgrave Macmillan.

Suskind, R. (2004) 'Faith, Certainty and the Presidency of George W. Bush', *New York Times*, October 17.

Thussu, D.K. (2009) *News as Entertainment: The Rise of Global Infotainment*. Thousand Oaks, CA: Sage.

Young, J. (1999) *The Exclusive Society: Social Exclusion, Crime and Difference in Late Modernity*. London: Sage.

Chapter 6

Constitutive criminology

Key issues

1 Jacques Lacan and constitutive criminology
2 Chaos theory and constitutive criminology
3 Constitutive criminology and the 'war on terror'
4 The UK and the 'war on terror'
5 Constitutive penology

Introduction

Constitutive criminology is an important attempt to consider the central principles of criminology in the context of postmodernism, but we should nevertheless note that its original proponents – Stuart Henry and Dragan Milovanovic (1996, 1999, 2000, 2001) – deny that they are postmodernists. Regardless of their protestations, they have produced a fairly orthodox account of postmodernism. It is an interpretation which recognizes no privileged knowledges, everyone or anyone is an expert, with a celebration of diversity, plurality and the subjugated. Aspects of modernism are nonetheless still used to identify the marginalized and oppressed. The two key contributions to this theory are (1) an interpretation of the post-Freudian Jacques Lacan and (2) chaos theory, which, in its original manifestation, describes the behaviour of certain dynamic systems. We consider each in turn.

Jacques Lacan and constitutive criminology

The ideas of Lacan centre on key Freudian concepts such as the unconscious, the castration complex and the ego, with the focus being on the importance of language to subjectivity. Lacan has been extremely influential in critical theory, literary studies and twentieth-century French philosophy, but it is his interpretation of clinical psychoanalysis which has influenced constitutive criminologists.

Lacan essentially understands psychoanalysis to be a process involving four major discourses: (1) the discourse of the master, (2) the university, (3) the hysteric and (4) the analyst. It is invariably the role of the discourse of the analyst to help develop the discourse of the hysteric, to assist him or her through a process to articulate their desire. In the criminological context, this can be a prisoner, an oppressed community or group who are being helped by an expert activist. Williams and Arrigo (2004) cite the example of young offenders involved in restorative justice.

Constitutive criminologists argue that people who are repressed by the criminal justice system are very likely to be suffering oppression in other forms and would as a result benefit from assistance in articulating their needs. Yet, at the same time, these same people might well have desires which are not socially acceptable in their present form and which could well get them into trouble with the law. This notion is thus clearly problematic because of the difficulty of reconciling individual needs with those of the group. Henry and Milovanovic acknowledge this conundrum to some extent and note that 'satisfying positions of desire can occur at another's expense' (2001: 168).

Constitutive criminologists have a strong commitment to social justice rather than merely criminal justice, and thus, Henry and Milovanovic (1996: 64) aim for a 'constitutive theorizing [which] is a contingently and provisionally based humanistic vision of what could be a radical super-liberalism', where justice is considered to be specific to particular sites and which cannot be linked to a desire for consensus or universally suggested agreement. Tracy Young (1999) adopts a similar approach observing that modernist criminal justice systems are concerned with the rationality, uniformity and consistency of treatment before the law, whereas the postmodern alternative is founded on the concepts of chaos theory, which allows room for creativity. Variation and creativity are thus considered desirable, and some of this thinking is linked to the idea that different local justice systems can coexist with each other. Young (1999) uses the examples of a Native American system – or one within a professional body – which she observes can coexist within the wider state justice system.

Chaos theory and constitutive criminology

Henry and Milovanovic (1996) observe that chaos theory is a central component of much postmodern analysis and it is thus worthwhile exploring this notion a little further. Chaos theory began as a field of physics and mathematics dealing with the structures of turbulence and self-similar forms of fractal geometry. As it is popularly understood, chaos deals with unpredictable complex systems, and the theory originates, in part, from the work of Edward Lorenz, a meteorologist, who simulated weather patterns on a computer. Working with a computer that had limited memory and after viewing a particular pattern, he wanted to recover the data and started the program again, except he put in the values rounded off to three places instead of the original six. He was astonished to find a completely different result on his computer than previously which looked like Figure 6.1 when it was printed out.

This has become known as the 'butterfly effect' and is often used to refer to complexity and unpredictability and in chaos theory refers to the discovery that, in a chaotic system such as the global weather, tiny perturbations – or slight disturbances of a system by a secondary influence within the system – may sometimes lead to major changes in the overall system. It is thus theoretically possible that a slight rise in temperature in the ocean off the coast of Peru will create tiny changes in the airflow that will eventually lead to different weather in North America and Europe. In most cases, the slight change would make no difference whatsoever, but, when the system is unpredictable at a certain stage, the future may unfold quite differently, depending upon what little difference occurred. Chaos theory has been subsequently applied to the study of management and organizations – including those within the criminal justice system – and where the constituents of a system are observed to be complex and unpredictable. Some observe clear

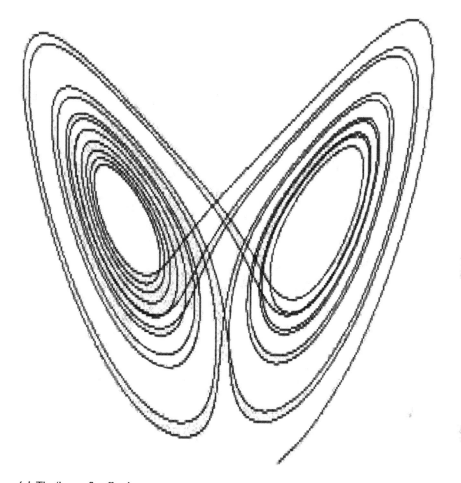

Figure 6.1 The 'butterfly effect'

parallels between chaos theory and postmodernism even to the extent of proposing that the former is postmodern science (Hayles, 1990, 1991; Brennan, 1995; Bloland, 1995; Markus, 2000), but there has also been significant opposition to that notion.

The application of the mathematics of chaos theory to society and not least the operation of the criminal justice system is inherently problematic (Cowling, 2006). Chaos theory tends to be seen as applicable to physical phenomena governed by deterministic laws, which are predictable in principle but unpredictable in practice because they are so sensitive to initial conditions. This is famously expressed in the idea that a butterfly flapping its wings in Brazil might cause a hurricane in Florida three weeks from that date and that this is why, although it is possible to predict roughly the sort of weather that can be expected in a particular place in three weeks' time, it is not possible to produce an accurate weather forecast. Human societies, in contrast, are complicated systems involving vast numbers of variables, for which it is impossible – at least currently – to develop any legitimate equations, and thus to speak of systems in terms of chaos takes us no further than the intuition already contained in popular wisdom (Sokal and Bricmont, 1999). Thus, the sort of situation in society where a small cause can produce a large effect will also be a highly unpredictable situation and where it is not at all clear what will eventually emerge. Thus, for example, the assassination of Archduke Franz Ferdinand of Austria in Sarajevo in 1914 precipitated a complex chain of events that was to lead to the First World War and a multitude of subsequent momentous linked events, which have changed the history of the world. Few, if any, of these events could have been predicted at the time. Some of those involved in the constitutive criminology project thus use chaos theory simply as a metaphor (Simons and Stroup, 1997; Arrigo, 1997a, 1997b; Williams and Arrigo, 2004), but in the main, the authors see themselves as applying chaos theory (Cowling, 2006).

Constitutive criminologists adopt three main concepts from chaos theory: (1) the notion of undecidability or uncertainty, (2) the idea that one individual can make a significant difference and (3) the analysis of conditions being far from equilibrium. The first two outcomes flow from the crucial idea that a very small initial difference (or input) can have a massive causal effect, but the problem with this is that, given the very many possible initial variables, the very idea of undecidability means that social science becomes impossible. We simply cannot know what outcome we might expect from an initial set of variables. The constitutive response to this conundrum is simply to celebrate the unexpected, surprise, ironic, contradictory and emergent (Milovanovic, 1997a), but this does all seem to occur in a context where there is no background of regularity against which to contrast the unexpected.

Cowling (2006) observes that the idea that one individual can make a difference is found repeatedly in constitutive criminology and the best way of assessing the idea is to consider some ways in which it might be recognized in practice. The examples provided by the constitutive criminologists concern things such as a crossing guard who takes an interest in one particular young person, thus helping him avoid becoming delinquent when his circumstances would make this likely, or going to a demonstration, signing a petition, engaging in civil disobedience or simply voting (Milovanovic, 1997b).

A further use of chaos theory concerns situations where, following a great deal of replication, far from equilibrium conditions result, and the system itself may thus change dramatically. Young (1999) provides an example by proposing that white-collar crime may be instigated by four or more unmanageable parameters. Thus, for example, a doctor might cope with a general drop in his or her income, the failure of investment portfolios and the reduction in rent payments from tenants if a major corporation was to move from the city, but any further losses such as patients defaulting on bills could well drive them to crime. We might call this the 'straw that broke the camel's back' argument.

A rather different use of chaos theory is the claim that truth values are 'fractal': thus, matters of right or wrong, good or bad, just or unjust are simply matters of degree (Arrigo, 1997a). This claim is nevertheless overly optimistic for the practical consequence of the unpredictability that follows from chaos theory is that standard moral judgements become impossible. Cowling (2006) observes that we commend acts of charity because they help people in need, while we condemn random unpremeditated violence because it harms people who do not deserve to be harmed. The adoption of chaos theory simply undermines any confidence we might have in typical consequences and thus we have no legitimate basis for making moral judgements.

Henry and Milovanovic (1996) define crime as the power to deny others and argue that conventional crime control strategies, in the form of fast-expanding criminal justice institutions – the police and prisons – or as political rhetoric rehearsed in the media, merely fuels the engine of crime. What they seek is the development of 'replacement discourses' which fuel positive social constructions with the intention not to 'replace one truth with another' but instead invoke 'a multiplicity of resistances' 'to the ubiquity of power' (Henry and Milovanovic, 1996: ix–xiii; Milovanovic, 1997b: 91).

Constitutive criminologists are thus opposed to imprisonment, which they consider to be merely incapacitation and an approach which simply presents a false separation between inside and outside, noting that the incarcerated actually commit more and worse crimes in their 'new architectural spaces'. Constitutive criminologists thus object to expenditure on prisons, which they propose is money which might be better spent on education and welfare provision. Prison expansion – it is noted – has been accompanied by an increased fear of crime, with the outcome that incapacitation simply offers the fiction of a safer society but actually offers more freedom for the powerful to commit more crimes (Henry and Milovanovic, 1996, 1994; Milovanovic, 1997b). The new contemporary criminological development of constitutive penology is considered later in this chapter. Meanwhile, we should note that constitutive criminologists are also opposed to the war on drugs and offer some support for mediation, conflict resolution and reconciliation programmes and the idea of relating crime more to wider society (Henry and Milovanovic, 2001: 174–75).

Mark Cowling (2006) nevertheless questions these core notions of constitutive criminology and asks, for example, whether the imprisonment of serial killers and rapists simply makes things worse, and queries whether it would be better for us all if the state did not interfere in domestic violence. He, moreover, asks whether it is an appropriate role for 'progressive' criminologists to be supporting 'resistances' by men who have been engaged in battering against the 'ubiquitous' power of the police and courts and proposes that such expansive claims need to be revealed and argued rather than merely asserted.

In the following section, we consider the application of the theoretical concepts of constitutive criminological to a critical reading of the 'war on terror' and its aftermath.

Constitutive criminology and the 'war on terror'

Shamila Ahmed (2014) observes that since the terrorist attacks of 11 September 2001, terrorism has become a global phenomenon with terrorist attacks occurring in numerous cities, including Mumbai, Bali, Madrid, London, Boston and Nairobi. The perpetrators are – she argues – motivated by a resistance to perceived 'Western occupation', they embrace, indeed perpetuate, the dualism of 'Western nations' versus Islam and Islamic nations. Indeed, this is an example of the 'clash of civilizations' we encountered in the previous chapter.

Ahmed argues that to understand how the harm created by terrorist actions can be appealing to its perpetrators requires an understanding of how the 'war on terror' discourse facilitates an alternative understanding. It is an alternative discourse which recognizes these harm creating actions as a reaction to the boundaries of difference created and instigated by the war on terror. Gunning (2007: 257) thus pertinently notes that 'terrorism and counterterrorism measures kill and harm real people in real places' and observes that this is clearly an important postmodern issue worthy of criminology study but not – it is proposed – by the traditional modernist methods of enquiry.

Early challenges to the traditional criminological approach came from critical criminologists such as Stanley Cohen (1988) and feminist criminologist Carol Smart (1995), who advocated abandoning the disciplinary frameworks of criminology, if not its subject matter. More recently, Zedner (2007: 268) has noted how criminology 'lacks any established, distinctive explanatory or methodological framework'. It is a failure that not only had consequences for the generation of new knowledge but has at the same time undermined any potential for progress and, more important, social justice. Hudson and Walters (2009: 604) later observed: 'If criminology is to be a dynamic and evolving discipline, it must engage with these significant international events, and extend its thematic scope beyond its well-worn topics'.

Ahmed (2014) proposes that constitutive criminology provides an affirmative postmodernist integrative holistic perspective which through the process of deconstruction exposes the underlying assumptions of socially constructed realities. It is a supposedly sophisticated interdisciplinary theory that incorporates an integrative framework which offers criminology the potential to investigate new phenomenon without imposing a self-limiting analytical framework as is the case with the traditional modernist criminological canon. Ahmed therefore uses holistic constitutive criminological analysis to explore how foreign policy, UK state policies and counter-terrorism legislation have intersected in the war on terror.

Beck (2006: 139) observes that it was 'only when the word "war" fell from the lips of the president – "a war has been declared on America" – did the terrorist attack become political terrorism and then global terrorism'. Beck notes that the response was socially constructed and highlights the significance of words such as *global* in his analysis. Howell (2006: 123) similarly argues that the phrase 'global war on terror' embraces 'the expression of a polarizing vision of the world, which pits modernity against backwardness, civilization against barbarism and freedom against oppression'. The war on terror incorporates dichotomies, with one side seen as the global enemy, thereby invalidating their narratives and 'alternative ways of knowing' (Arrigo, 1997b: 33).

President George W. Bush painted a frightening picture of 'tens of thousands of al-Qaida-trained terrorists in at least a dozen countries', and as Beck (2002: 44) notes, it is the powerful states that 'empower themselves by defining who is their terrorist enemy, their bin Laden'. The war on terror therefore constructed the global enemy along a religious binary, with Bush singling out the Islamic faith (Bush, 2001). Terrorism became seen as the 'dark side' of globalization', (Bosworth *et al.*, 2008: 263) with Islam singled out as the major threat to Western democracies and civil society, through accelerating and indeed encouraging terrorism (Turam, 2004; Howell, 2006).

Cosgrove (2000: 252) notes that words provide us with 'a system of categories' and in the constitutive criminological sense these categories represent 'symbols' which when taken together assist in providing a structured discourse.

Ahmed (2014) argues that in the case of the war on terror, it was the process by which language was used to legitimize state action that construction went from being an abstract discourse to one embodied in structure and thus capable of causing subjects harm. Words such as *war* and *global* conveyed – and continue to convey – not just the magnitude of threat and risk but also the constructed limits of the war on terror. It was thus the construction of threat and security actions conveyed as being necessary, which made controversial legislation appear imperative and in the quest for victory any limits, such as democracy and the rule of law were undermined.

Government officials argued that such measures were necessary to ensure national security and through doing so diminished and eroded universal values, 'civil liberties and human rights'. Furthermore, euphemisms such as 'collateral damage' rather than the killing of civilians and 'moderate physical pressure' rather than 'torture' become part of the normative discourse which serves the purpose of denying 'the psychological, political or moral consequences' that is part of the implied denial (Welch, 2004: 11). Bak (1999: 23) argues that social structures sustain discourses through ensuring they continue in 'everyday discourse'. Concepts of risk and threat were part of the war on terror discourse, permeating foreign policy and national security and thereby ensuring the institutionalization of the war on terror.

Deconstructing the UK's war on terror

Constitutive criminology claims that crime is 'a phenomenon that focuses upon the reduction and repression of the human subject that is inflicted by way of inequality through the discursive practices of social structures and of other human subjects' (Bak, 1999: 28). Indeed, 'it is necessary to explore the state, institutional processes and constitutively interrelated sets that bolster and legitimate some individuals or groups to accumulate the power to cause pain whether through cultural hegemony, organizational strategy or personal will' (Henry and Milovanovic (1996: 174). Ahmed (2014) thus examines the interrelated sets identified in the framework of constitutive criminology, which involves analysing law and examining how 'through the guise of law, the law legitimizes actions which create harm' (Bak, 1999 29).

The global war on terror is seen to have had an enormous impact on the UK and was used to create 'harm, injustice, pain and conflict' (Henry and Milovanovic, 1996: 116). The criminalization of terrorism and the global risk and fear of terrorism were thus used to expand domestic social control, thereby reinforcing global governance. Within this new security agenda, Islamic extremism was defined as the enemy or 'new terrorism' (Altheide, 2007; Findlay, 2007; Poynting and Mason, 2007; Mythen and Walklate, 2008).

Ahmed (2014) observes that one of the notable features of the war on terror in the UK was the exceptional measures taken through the inclusion of pre-crime in counter-terrorism legislation. It is noted that pre-crime has an enormous capacity to cause harm because it 'includes measures that expand the remit of the criminal law to include activities or associations that are deemed to precede the substantive offence targeted for prevention' (McCulloch and Pickering, 2009: 1). Zedner (2007) notes that the institutionalization of pre-crime in counter-terrorism legislation marked a deviation from the post-crime orientation of traditional modernist criminal justice. The legislation introduced simply expanded the remit of the criminal law at the expense of human rights and civil liberties.

The Prevention of Terrorism Act 2005 is one of the most controversial pieces of legislation to have emerged permitting 'control orders' to be made against any suspected terrorist, whether a UK national or a non-UK national or whether the terrorist activity is international or domestic. Control orders are preventive, designed to restrict the liberty of an individual to prevent a possible terrorist attack. Indeed, control orders provide very limited rights of appeal and due process. Liberty (2006) observe that control orders substitute long-term punishment based on secret intelligence for charges, evidence and proof.

The UK Institute of Race Relations (2007) argued that control orders are forms of collective punishment, which violate natural justice and international law. The Terrorism Act 2006 was subsequently introduced in response to the 7 July 2005 London bombings and legitimizes 28 days' detention without charge, which far exceeds that used by any other European state member (Liberty, 2007). It is perhaps not surprising that the legislation has received much criticism because suspects are stripped of capacity and responsibility.

It is possible therefore to argue that pre-crime legitimizes punishment on the basis of giving suspects no moral autonomy, thereby exacerbating the differences between counter-terrorism legislation and non-counter-terrorism legislation. The institutionalization of risk in counter-terrorism legislation mediates with other forms of risk management – cultural, symbolic and linguistic mechanisms (Arrigo, 2013) – to make the legal mechanism appear just and necessary. Suspects of terrorism are therefore excluded from the moral community through the construction and implementation of difference based on the threat and risk of terrorism (Deutsch, 2006). This itself is defined as crime by constitutive criminology.

Welch (2004: 11) observes that the construction of difference continues the dehumanization of those that might experience harm with 'the psychological, political, or moral consequences' denied. Kauzlarich et al. (2001: 185) note that 'victimizers often do not acknowledge the degree to which their policies have caused harm'. It is through constructing terrorism outside the political process and democracy that the suspect is dehumanized (Findlay, 2007; Tadros, 2007; Hudson, 2008; Stohl, 2008), that principles of liberalism and human rights are legitimized as not existing. In this way, suspects of terrorism 'suffer the pain of being denied their own humanity' (Henry and Milovanovic, 1994: 119). Through the use of constitutive criminology, it is thus possible, it is argued, to conceptualize counter-terrorism legislation itself as a crime (Ahmed, 2014).

Utilitarianism is usually used by governments to justify the introduction of controversial legislation, but criticisms of counter-terrorism legislation have gone further and been compared with laws introduced in Zimbabwe and apartheid South Africa, not least because the response has been absolute in the lack of rights afforded to terrorist suspects, with risk and suspicion determining punishment, in the form of control orders and detention (Mythen and Walklate, 2008). Punishment can only be considered reasonable when the court respects the concept of proportionality; the punishment reflects the severity of the crime committed, not a crime that an individual might commit; and the punishment is both reasoned and reasonable (Allan, 2001). Paye (2005) argues, that counter-terrorism legislation places suspicion over fact: house arrest can be imposed not on the basis of what a person has done, but according to what they could do.

The Human Rights Act 1998 was introduced and became the most comprehensive system of human rights, detailing legal rights in the UK. The legislation was introduced to ensure that the UK, as a European member state incorporated the rights and mechanisms to adhere to the European Convention on Human Rights (ECHR). Counter-terrorism legislation simply does not apply the Human Rights Act, and therefore, those suspected of terrorism suffer a 'form of deprivation, reduction or repression which another group does not' through not being afforded human rights (Henry and Milovanovic, 1999: 7). In 2013, the home secretary, Theresa May, said, in a drive to curb the appeal rights of 70,000 people who face deportation every year, that the Conservative Party was prepared to withdraw from the ECHR after the next election (May, 2013). Should the UK withdraw from the ECHR this would mark a further decrease in human rights and would mean that at the very least, foreign nationals suspected of terrorism could be deported and not afforded any rights which exist under ECHR.

Policing and the war on terror

Ahmed (2014) observes that constitutive criminology is particularly helpful in encouraging an analysis which allows one to explore the dialectic relationship between discourses and policing, with one impacting and maintaining the other. It is an approach which not only advocates a social constructionist analysis of crime but also incorporates ideas of difference and inequality, which have been the focus of critical criminologists for many years. Henry and Milovanovic (1991: 306) have thus stated, that institutions which practice discourses in which differences are amplified, harm and oppress citizens and the police are agents who 'both produce and sustain deviant categories'.

It is without doubt the purpose of the criminal justice system to maintain social control, but it is the police who are the most powerful social control institution. It is the police who are 'empowered to investigate crime, search for evidence, arrest suspected offenders and question them' (Allan, 2001: 2). The introduction of counter-terrorism legislation such as pre-crime and risk thus became part of counter-terrorism policing.

Constitutive criminology views crime as a socially constructed category, 'it is a categorization of the diversity of human conflicts and transgression into a single category "crime", as though these were somehow the same. It is the celebration of the homogeneous' (Henry and Milovanovic, 1994: 118). Interestingly, due to the preventive nature of this legislation, it encourages profiling and the celebration of the homogenous because, as McCulloch and Pickering (2009) argue, the 'preventive' counter-terrorism framework is concerned with targeting and managing through restricting and incapacitating those individuals and groups considered being a risk. The outcome is the construction of a 'suspect community' (Panthazis and Pemberton, 2009), one which is vulnerable to policing suspicion on the basis of possessing certain ethnic and religious traits. And it is the presence of such traits which determines, as Zedner (2007: 274) observes, 'those within and without protection', leading to their criminalization, which has had an enormous impact on policing, significantly increasing their power. It is thus inevitable that because there is a lack of human rights and a pre-occupation with attributing risk, innocent people will suffer (Mythen and Walklate, 2008).

Analysing the war on terror

Government policies were as equally important as actual counter-terrorism legislation in contributing to the war on terror discourse. Turam (2004: 276) states 'the key to understanding the relationship between Islam and civil society is the state'. Although the legislative response was an aggressive one, so was state political policy. Prime Minister Tony Blair referred to wars of 'values change', which really meant 'Muslim societies need to be forced to abandon "their values"' (Blair, 2006), which, in doing so, created the Islamic identities of Muslims as a problem. Kundnani (2007: 30) observed that the role of government policies had legitimized Islamophobia and those who were once abused as 'Pakis' were now also abused as 'Muslims'. Questions of the compatibility between Islamic identity and British identity emerged. Islam was homogenized and Muslims were constructed as being unable to make a commitment to the nation state (Johnson, 2002; Turam, 2004).

It could thus be argued that British Muslims experienced a loss in their standing through being constructed as a threat and not according to their national identity (Ahmed, 2014).

Sivanandan (2008) argues that the war on terror, the loss of civil rights and the erosion of democracy are intrinsically tied to Islamophobia. Interestingly, there are similarities between the construction of the terrorist and Islamophobia because both constructions incorporate the 'suspect and/or victim' being dehumanized and lacking moral autonomy. Islamophobia incorporates the belief that those of the Islamic faith (Muslims) are of such faith because they have no choice. The idea conveyed is that the Muslim lacks individuality and autonomous existence. Muslims are thus seen as a group that cannot escape the social forces that militate against individual expression and the individual freedoms exercised in liberal democratic states (Lea, 2005: 40).

The social construction of Islamophobia was founded on a failure to recognize intrinsic diversity because even as groups: 'Muslim communities can consist of Sunnis, Shiites or Ismailis, who differ greatly in doctrine and principle' (Lea, 2005: 40). The denial of diversity was to lead to the construction of one identity which is seen as a threat to the nation state and in legislation which denied suspects autonomy. It can be argued that it is through the maintenance of the imposed difference, that Islam is a threat which is located in language, that Muslims continue to be portrayed as the 'other'. Muslims are rendered powerless because they are labelled as potential criminals.

Ahmed (2014) observes that within the war on terror, each of the interrelated sets, (1) the international level (where the words *war on terror* were first used), (2) the UK state (which introduced counter-terrorism legislation and wider political policies to reflect the discourse) and (3) the police (maintain and sustain the discourse), not only influenced the war on terror discourse but also acted to reinforce and maintain the discourse. It is through using constitutive criminology – it is argued – that it is possible to see how the war on terror discourse became the 'normative discourse', one that influenced societal relations and indeed led to an increase in Islamophobia (see Sheridan, 2006).

Marginalized discourses

The war on terror discourse was to become 'pervasive', sustained 'conceptual and discursive practices' and sought to undermine 'any that seek to counter it' (Henry and Milovanovic, 1996: 174). But other non-state-centric discourses persist. In this way, constitutive criminology, whilst providing the framework to explore dominant discourses which cause harm, does not discount other, marginalized discourses. Where the war on terror is concerned, some critics claim that the war is truly a war on Islam itself. A poll conducted by the *Guardian* newspaper found that many Muslims saw the war against terrorism as a war against Islam (Travis, 2004). It was seen internationally to mean that when the administration said *war*, it meant war in the sense of people being commanded to go and kill other people, while critics argued that *war on terror* was used to justify human rights abuses (Amnesty, 2009). Hudson and Walters (2009: 604) observe that 'for numerous commentators, the war on terror has been a political, economical, environmental and humanitarian failure of colossal proportions'. Indeed, some politicians observed that the phrase actually empowered the very groups who wanted to cause harm and the director of public prosecutions, Sir Ken MacDonald, said, 'It is critical that we understand that this new form of terrorism . . . encourages a fear-driven and inappropriate response . . . it can tempt us to abandon our values' (Reynolds, 2007).

Ahmed (2014) observes that the war on terror was to become a dangerous phenomenon both in terms of the terrorist attacks and in the reaction to these attacks and argues that if the threat of terrorism is to be reduced or even eradicated in the future, then understanding, rather than privileging, should be the aim so that we can provide 'an alternative vision' (Henry and Milovanovic, 1996: 205) to military action abroad, the immense power exercised in labelling 'rogue' nations as terrorist nations and the violation of due process (presumption of innocence, right to silence, the right to a fair trial) and civil rights.

Ahmed observes that constitutive criminology has provided a non-state-centric perspective to the war on terror and that through encouraging critical theoretical engagement, it has been possible to see how, at the macro level, the UK state actively manufactured a victim discourse which was used to legitimize the expansion of social control and, at the micro level, how the state, as instigators of difference and therefore perpetuators of crime and harm, created victims that are vulnerable, reduced and disempowered. Therefore, the theory through offering a holistic and yet deconstructed apparatus of tools merges non-state defined harms, which had previously been outside the realms of criminology, with a progressive critical criminology that is cable of doing what 'politicians avoid and what academics must' examining 'the actions and consequences of those who govern' in the war on terror (Hudson and Walters, 2009: 607).

Having considered the validity of constitutive criminology in helping us to deconstruct the discourses surrounding the war on terror and provide possible alternatives, we consider constitutive penology.

Constitutive penology

Milovanovic and Henry (2005) advise us that constitutive penology is an extension of postmodernist constitutive criminological theory. Societal responses to crime are seen to interrelated with the wider society, particularly through 'crime and punishment' talk. Discursive distinctions are constructed and continuously reinterpreted – or iterated – through penal policy pronouncements, practical actions, discussions in popular culture and the proclamations, rules and practices of institutional structures such as the criminal justice system, penal institutions and punishment and rehabilitation. It is observed that these abstract distinctions obscure the numerous ways in which penological discourse and practices permeate the wider society. They also disguise the connections between the theory and practices of penology and the impacts, costs and consequences that these have for society.

Constitutive penologists thus call for (1) the integration of prison and related penological practices with society, (2) a demystification of the penological society and (3) the development of more holistic responses to criminal harm.

Milovanovic and Henry (2005) argue that conventional modernist penology provides the discursive reference for actions which create, develop and sustain prison. Discursive structures are thus embodied with ideological material, which provides the backdrop for socially constructed meaning. Debates about being in or out of prison, building more or less penal institutions, about overcrowding and overspending and about alternatives to and challenges, all continuously assume the taken-for-granted existence of the very structures that need to be questioned and explained. In short, they reinforce the prison as a necessary reality (Milovanovic and Henry, 2005.

Constitutive penologists see penal policy as part of a way of talking about dealing with offenders (discursive process) whereby aspects of existing practice are selected, emphasized, refined, given linguistic form and are formally discussed, while other aspects are ignored, subordinated, dispersed and relegated to the informal or conceptualized as abnormal. Conventional penologists are seen to distinguish between six general philosophical approaches which underpin their policies and inform sentencing practice: (1) incapacitation/social defence, (2) punishment/retribution/just deserts, (3) deterrence, (4) rehabilitation/treatment, (5) prevention and (6) restitution/reparation. Constitutive penologists, in contrast, argue that any one of these 'philosophies' constructs a false separation between the penal system and society. For example incapacitation does not separate offenders from society since being *in* prison is being *in* society; prison is physically, structurally and symbolically integrated into the broader community. Rather than 'walls of imprisonment', there is continuity between being 'in' or 'out'. The incarcerated are not incapacitated, since they do additional and, in many cases, more serious forms of offensive behaviour inside prison as a reaction to their confinement

Milovanovic and Henry (2005) observe that we pay the economical and social costs of massively expanded prison programmes. Socially, the 'new penology' of incapacitation has accentuated the issue of race in US society, in particular, where one in three African American males aged 20 to 29 is in prison, on probation or on parole. This permeates the minority perspective of those people of colour *outside* prison who withdraw support for formal institutions of society, especially from government and law enforcement. It, moreover, corrupts the views that the majority white population has of minorities, thereby contaminating day-to-day interactions.

Once moral sentiment has been withdrawn, people feel morally justified in violating all kinds of rules based on the rationalization that 'whites' and other dominant groups, in general, cannot be victims of specific crimes, since their racist violations of minorities make them the aggressors. Minorities are merely taking back what was seen as rightly taken from them, including dignity, self-determination, property and even life itself.

Constitutive penologists are concerned with how criminologists may – despite their best intentions – replicate the very system they try to understand and critique. Criminologists are seen to do this by constructing ideal-typical classifications that disguise how policy makers, practitioners, targeted agents and theorists de-emphasize some aspects of the reality of prison practice as aberrant, unofficial, informal or untypical to make claims about its operational identity. To avoid legitimating the prison while analysing penal policy, constitutive penologists argue that it is necessary to use a semiotic approach that deconstructs the role that language use plays in the construction of the penal system and its attendant philosophies and institutions. Transformation of crime and societal responses to it, they argue, requires a reintegration of crime and societal responses with the whole, of which each is a part, and they indicate that a change in the whole is necessary to bring about a change in any of its parts.

Milovanovic and Henry (2005) argue that an alternative direction would provide an opportunity for the development of a new 'replacement discourse'. It is a language of 'transpraxis' which connects the way we speak with our social relations and institutions so that we are continuously aware of the interrelatedness of our agency and the structures it reproduces. Transpraxis is a deliberate and affirmative attempt not to reverse hierarchies but, instead, to affirm those who victimize, marginalize and criminalize while renouncing their victimizing, marginalizing and criminalizing practices. Transpraxis is an effort to validate the act of resistance. The key is speech, words, grammar and how we talk about (and then act on) emancipation (Arrigo, 2001: 220). Constitutive penology asks us to rethink the discursive structures within which we situate our research on the penal question.

Milovanovic and Henry (2005) propose that genuinely alternative, replacement discourse would envelop not just the declarations of policy but also the ways practitioners and policy makers distinguish their reality from the totality and point toward ways these can be reintegrated. It would require a 'bringing back in' of the undervalued, informal, unofficial, marginalized practices (the unspoken) which are part of the totality of the prison business. Only with such a comprehension of the totality and the contribution of these excluded parts to the reality-making process is it possible to provide an alternative understanding of the phenomena of crime and crime control in our society. Only from such an understanding of the total constitutive process is it possible to generate a replacement discourse which begins the deconstruction of penology, the correction of corrections and the ultimate reconstruction of penal policy that is its own demise

Policy implications of constitutive criminology

The fundamental policy implication confronting constitutive criminology is how is it possible as a society to stop investing in structures of oppression whose appearance channels and sustains the very use of the power to harm, without at the same time actually exercising power. A related problem is how, given the nature of power and social structure, is it possible to change the reified products of discourse that we take to be structure, culture and nature. This is the major – some suggest insurmountable – problem facing the constitutive criminological project.

Perhaps most disappointing from this perspective is the discussion of how to overcome the problem that local action cannot transform wider structural, state and institutional systems. While Henry and Milovanovic argue that super-liberalism and chaos theory can create an 'empowered' democracy, they provide few practical strategies to indicate how this can be achieved and many of the strategies seem little more than 'old wine in new bottles' (Croall, 1996).

In considering policy, the connection between resistance and reconstruction is vital. Unlike some relevant critiques levied against the nihilistic forms of postmodern analysis, the affirmative version sees deconstruction and reconstruction as the necessary focus of attention. Simply separate one from the other and the roads to nihilism or romanticism are seductively inviting.

Given that the basis of crime – as harm – is the socially constructed and discursively constituted exercise of power through difference, it follows that human subjects whose investment in power relations harms others have the potential to reconstitute their use of human agency to be less harmful or have the potential to be reconstituted through interactive relations with the wider culture or structure. Such a perspective, as Colvin comments, 'opens the possibility for transformation of human subjects and the social structures we construct' (1997: 1450). The problem of policy, then, is not one of merely applying strategies but of closely linking deconstruction and reconstruction so that appreciation of difference, rather than domination based on difference, pervades the spirit of social life. Difference without domination is to be celebrated but will be inevitably difficult, indeed probably impossible to achieve, and here lies the practical problematic of constitutive criminology and the sub-field of constitutive penology.

Summary of main points

1 Constitutive criminology a significant attempt to consider the central principles of criminology in the context of postmodernism.
2 The two core theoretical foundations are (1) an interpretation of the post-Freudian Jacques Lacan and (2) chaos theory.
3 The ideas of Lacan centre on key Freudian concepts such as the unconscious, the castration complex and the ego, with the focus being on the importance of language to subjectivity.
4 Lacan essentially understands psychoanalysis to be a process involving four major discourses: (1) the discourse of the master, (2) the university, (3) the hysteric and (4) the analyst.
5 Constitutive criminologists argue that people who are repressed by the criminal justice system are very likely to be suffering oppression in other forms and would therefore benefit from assistance in articulating their needs.
6 As it is popularly understood, chaos theory deals with unpredictable complex systems and the theory originates, in part, from the work of Edward Lorenz, a meteorologist, who simulated weather patterns on a computer.
7 Constitutive criminologists adopt three main concepts from chaos theory: (1) the notion of undecidability or uncertainty, (2) the idea that one individual can make a significant difference and (3) the analysis of conditions being far from equilibrium.
8 Shamila Ahmed argues that in order to comprehend how the harm created by terrorist actions can be appealing to its perpetrators requires an understanding of how the war on terror discourse facilitates an alternative understanding.
9 It is argued that constitutive criminology provides an affirmative postmodernist integrative holistic perspective which through the process of deconstruction, the underlying assumptions of socially constructed realities are exposed.
10 Constitutive penology is an extension of postmodernist constitutive criminological theory where discursive distinctions are constructed and continuously reinterpreted through penal policy pronouncements, practical actions, discussions in popular culture and the proclamations, rules and practices of institutional structures such as the criminal justice system, penal institutions and punishment and rehabilitation.

Discussion questions

1 What are the core tenets of constitutive criminology?
2 How does the work of Jacques Lacan and chaos theory contribute to our understanding of constitutive criminology?
3 In what ways does traditional criminological policy and discourse explain the war on terror?
4 In what way does constitutive criminology offer alternative discourses to explain the war on terror?
5 What are the core tenets of constitutive penology?

Further reading

Henry and Milovanovic (1991, 1994, 1996, 1999, 2000, 2001) are the originators of constitutive criminology, and these texts give a thorough introduction to the theory and its applications. Ahmed (2014) produces a most comprehensive discussion of constitutive criminology and the war and terror.

References

Ahmed, S. (2014) 'Constitutive Criminology and the War on Terror', *Critical Criminology*, 22: 357–71.

Allan, M.J. (2001) *Criminal Law*, 6th ed. London: Blackstone Press Ltd.

Altheide, D. (2007) 'The Mass Media and Terrorism', *Discourse and Communication*, 1(3): 27–30.

Amnesty (2009) *Accountability for US Counter-terrorism Human Rights Violations*. Available from: www.amnesty.org/en/appeals-for-action/accountability-for-US-counter-terrorism-human-rights-violations [Accessed 26 June 2019].

Arrigo, B.A. (1997a) 'Dimensions of Social Justice in a Single Room Occupancy: Contributions from Chaos Theory, Policy and Practice', in D. Milovanovic (ed.) *Chaos, Criminology, and Social Justice: The New Orderly (Dis) Order*. Westport, CT: Praeger.

Arrigo, B.A. (1997b) 'Transcarceration: Notes on Psycholoanalyically-informed Theory of Social Practice in Criminal Justice and Mental Health Systems', *Crime, Law and Social Change*, 27: 31–48.

Arrigo, B.A. (2001) 'Praxis', in E. McLaughlin and J. Muncie (eds.) *The Sage Dictionary of Criminology* (pp. 219–21). London: Sage.

Arrigo, B.A. (2013) 'Managing Risk and Marginalizing Identities: On the Society-of-Captives Thesis and the Harm of Social Disease', *International Journal of Offender Therapy and Comparative Criminology*, 57(6): 672–93.

Bak, A. (1999) 'Constitutive Criminology: An Introduction to the Core Concepts', in S. Henry and D. Milovanovic (eds.), *Constitutive Criminology at Work: Applications to Crime and Justice*. Albany, NY: State University of New York Press.

Beck, U. (2002) 'The Terrorist Threat World Risk Society Revisited', *Theory, Culture and Society*, 19(4): 39–55.

Beck, U. (2006) *The Cosmopolitan Vision*. Cambridge: Polity Press.

Blair, T. (2006) *Tony Blair, Speech to the Los Angeles World Affairs Council, 1 August 2006*. Available from: http://news.bbc.co.uk/1/hi/uk/5236896.stm [Accessed 20 March 2019].

Bloland, H. (1995) 'Postmodernism and Higher Education', *Journal of Higher Education*, 66(5): 521–57.

Bosworth, M., Bowling, B. and Lee, M. (2008) 'Globalization, Ethnicity and Racism: An Introduction', *Theoretical Criminology*, 12(3): 263–73.

Brennan, C. (1995) 'Beyond Theory and Practice: A Postmodern Perspective', *Counselling and Values*, 39(2): 99–108.

Bush, G. (2001) *Presidential Address to the Nation: The Treaty Room*. Available from: http://georgewbush whitehouse.archives.gov/news/releases/2001/10/print/20011007–8.html. [Accessed 14 April 2020].

Cohen, S. (1988) *Against Criminology*. New Brunswick, NJ: Transaction.

Colvin, M. (1997) 'Review of Stuart Henry and Dragan Milovanovic's Constitutive Criminology', *American Journal of Sociology*, 102: 1448–50.

Cosgrove, L. (2000) 'Crying out Loud: Understanding Women's Emotional Distress as both Lived Experience and Social Construction', *Feminism and Psychology*, 10(2): 247–67.

Cowling, M. (2006) 'Postmodern Policies? The Erratic Interventions of Constitutive Criminology', *Internet Journal of Criminology*, November.

Croall, H. (1996) 'Crime: Understanding More and Condemning Less?', *Reviewing Sociology*, 10: 3.

Deutsch, M. (2006) 'A Framework for Thinking About Oppression and Its Change', *Social Justice Research*, 19(1): 7–41.

Findlay, M. (2007) 'Terrorism and Relative Justice', *Crime, Law and Social Change*, 47(1): 57–68.

Gunning, J. (2007) 'A Case for Critical Terrorism Studies?', *Government and Opposition*, 42(3): 363–93.

Hayles, K. (1990) *Chaos Bound*. Ithaca, NY: Cornell University Press.

Hayles, K. (1991) *Chaos and Order: Complex Dynamics in Literature and Science*. Chicago, IL: University of Chicago Press.

Henry, S. and Milovanovic, D. (1991) 'Constitutive Criminology, the Maturation of Theory', *Criminology*, 29(2): 293–316.

Henry, S. and Milovanovic, D. (1994) 'The Constitution of Constitutive Criminology', in D. Nelken (ed.) *The Futures of Criminology*. London: Sage.

Henry, S. and Milovanovic, D. (1996) *Constitutive Criminology: Beyond Postmodernism*. London: Sage.

Henry, S. and Milovanovic, D. (1999) *Constitutive Criminology at Work: Applications to Crime and Justice*. New York: State University of New York Press.

Henry, S. and Milovanovic, D. (2000) 'Constitutive Criminology: Origins, Core Concepts, and Evaluation', *Social Justice*, 27(2): 260–76.

Henry, S. and Milovanovic, D. (2001) 'Constitutive Definition of Crime: Power as Harm', in S. Henry and M.M. Lanier (eds.) *What Is Crime? Controversies over the Nature of Crime and What to Do about It*. Lanham, MA: Rowman and Littlefield.

Howell, J. (2006) 'The Global War on Terror, Development and Civil Society', *Journal of International Development*, 18(1): 121–35.

Hudson, B. (2008) 'Difference, Diversity and Criminology: The Cosmopolitan Vision', *Theoretical Criminology*, 12(3): 275–92.

Hudson, B. and Walters, R. (2009) 'Criminology and the War on Terror, Special Edition of the British Journal of Criminology', *The British Journal of Criminology*, 49(5): 603–8.

Institute of Race Relations (2007) 'Community Responses to the War on Terror', IRR briefing paper no 3. Available from: www.irr.org.uk/pdf/IRR_Briefing_No.3.pdf [Accessed 21 November 2019].

Johnson, R. (2002) 'Defending Ways of Life: The (Anti) Terrorist Rhetorics of Bush and Blair', *Theory, Culture and Society*, 19(4): 211–31.

Kauzlarich, D., *et al.* (2001) 'Towards a Victimology of State Crime', *Critical Criminology*, 10: 173–94.

Kundnani, A. (2007) 'Integrationism: The Politics of Anti-Muslim Racism', *Race and Class*, 4(4): 24–44.

Lea, D. (2005) 'Communitarianism vs, Individual Rights in the West and the Islamic World', *Middle East Policy*, 12(2): 36–48.

Liberty (2006) 'High Court Quashes Control Orders in Six Cases'. Available from: www.liberty-human-rights. org.uk/news-and-events/1-press-releases/2006/control-orders-quashed.shtml [Accessed 12 June 2019].

Liberty (2007) *Terrorism Pre-Charge Detention Comparative Study*. Available from: www.liberty-human-rights. org.uk/issues/pdfs/pre-charge-detention-comparative-law-study.pdf [Accessed 20 December 2019].

Markus, M. (2000) 'A Scientist's Adventures in Postmodernism', *Leonardo*, 33(3): 179–86.

May, T. (2013) 'Conservatives Promise to Scrap Human Rights Act after Next Election'. Available from: http://www.theguardian.com/law/2013/sep/30/conservitives-scrap-human-rights-act [Accessed 20 March 2019].

McCulloch, J. and Pickering, S. (2009) 'Pre-Crime and Counter Terrorism: Imagining Future Crime in the "War on Terror"', *The British Journal of Criminology*, 49(5): 628–45.

Milovanovic, D. (ed.) (1997a) *Chaos, Criminology, and Social Justice: The New Orderly (Dis) Order*. Westport, CT: Praeger.

Milovanovic, D. (1997b) *Postmodern Criminology*. New York: Garland Publishing.

Milovanovic, D. and Henry, S. (2005) 'Constitutive Penology', in M. Bosworth (eds.), *Encyclopedia of Prisons and Correctional Facilities*. Newbury Park, CA: Sage.

Mythen, G. and Walklate, S. (2008) 'Terrorism, Risk and International Security: The Perils of Asking "What If?"', *Security Dialogue*, 39(2–3): 221–42.

Panthazis, C. and Pemberton, S. (2009) 'From the "Old" to the "New" Suspect Community: Examining the Impacts of Recent UK Counter-terrorism Legislation', *The British Journal of Criminology*, 49(5): 646–66.

Paye, C. (2005) *The End of Habeas Corpus in Great Britain*. [Online] Available from: www.monthlyreview. org/1105paye.htm [Accessed 11 January 2019].

Poynting, S., and Mason, V. (2007) 'The Resistible Rise of Islamophobia: Anti-Muslim Racism in the UK and Australia before 11 September 2001', *Journal of Sociology*, 43(1): 61–86.

Reynolds, B. (2007) *Declining Use of 'War on Terror'*. Available from: http://news.bbc.co.uk/2/hi/uk_ news/politics/6562709.stm [Accessed 20 March 2019].

Sheridan, L. (2006) 'Islamophobia Pre- and Post-September 11th, 2001', *Journal of Interpersonal Violence*, 21(3): 317–36.

Simons, G.L. and Stroup II, W.F. (1997) 'Law and Social Change: The Implications of Chaos Theory in Understanding the Role of the American Legal System', in D. Milovanovic (ed.) *Chaos, Criminology and Social Justice: The New Orderly (Dis) Order*. Westport, CT: Praeger.

Sivanandan, A. (2008). *Nativism vs Integration*. Available from: http://www.irr.org.uk/200/may/ha000019.html [Accessed 11 March 2019].

Smart, C. (1995) *Law, Crime and Sexuality: Essays in Feminism*. London: Sage.

Sokal, A. and Bricmont, J. (1999) *Intellectual Impostures*. London: Profile Books.

Stohl, M. (2008) 'Networks, Terrorists and Criminals: The Implications for Community Policing', *Crime, Law and Social Change*, 50: 59–72.

Tadros, V. (2007) 'Rethinking the Presumption of Innocence', *Criminal Law and Philosophy*, 1: 193–213.

Travis, A. (2004) 'Desire to Integrate on the Wane as Muslims Resent "War on Islam"', *The Guardian*. www.theguardian.com/politics/2004/mar/16/race.polls [Accessed 14 June 2019].

Turam, B. (2004) 'The Politics of Engagement Between Islam and the Secular State: Ambivalences of Civil Society', *The British Journal of Sociology*, 55(2): 259–81.

Welch, M. (2004) 'Trampling Human Rights in the War on Terror: Implications to the Sociology of Denial', *Critical Criminology*, 12: 1–20.

Williams, C.R. and Arrigo, B.A. (2004) *Theory, Justice and Social Change: Theoretical Integrations and Critical Applications*. New York: Kluwer.

Young, T.R. (1999) 'A Constitutive Theory of Justice: The Architecture of Affirmative Postmodern Legal Systems', in S. Henry and D. Milovanovic (eds.) *Constitutive Criminology at Work: Applications to Crime and Justice*. New York: State University of New York Press.

Zedner, L. (2007) 'Pre-Crime and Post Criminology?', *Theoretical Criminology*, 11(2): 261–81.

Chapter 7

Anarchist criminology

Key issues

1   Anarchism and criminology
2   Peacemaking criminology
3   The peacemaking pyramid paradigm
4   Criticisms of peacemaking criminology
5   Restorative justice as an alternative to criminal justice

> Anarchism is an orientation toward social life and social relations that is ultimately no orien-
> tation at all. In fact, anarchism might best be thought of as disorientation; that is, an approach
> which openly values fractured, uncertain, and unrealised understandings and practices as the
> emerging essence of social life.
>
> – Ferrell (1998: 5)

Jeff Ferrell (1998) observes that unlike most modernist intellectual orientations, anarchism
and anarchist criminology do not seek to incorporate reasoned or reasonable critiques of
law and legal authority, but, in contrast, argue that progressive social change requires the
'unreasonable' and the 'unthinkable'. In other words, reason and 'common sense' notions
of the legal and illegal developed by the modernist state are seen to keep us trapped within
the present arrangements of authority and power, and it is thus in our interest to stop
making sense, to imagine the unimaginable and think the unthinkable (Ferrell, 1998).

Anarchist criminologists thus launch aggressive and 'unreasonable' critiques against law
and legal authority because they argue that these institutions fundamentally undermine
human community and diversity. Anarchist criminology is therefore different from the
modernist critical criminological tradition because it is not a careful criticism of criminal justice, a 'loyal opposition' to the state and state law, but stands instead as a disloyal
and disrespectful attack (Mazor, 1978), a 'counterpunch to the belly of authority' (Ferrell, 1996: 197). Moreover, it aims its disrespectable gaze both high and low: it not only
attacks the state structure and legal authority above us but also encourages those below
and beyond this authority to find ways of resisting it and finding more egalitarian alternatives. Anarchist criminology thus seeks to harass those comfortable with legal power and
privilege and to comfort those afflicted by its abuses.

Anarchist critiques of law and legality are nevertheless nothing new and have long-
established foundations in early anarchism itself, with prominent writers and activists like
William Godwin (1756–1836), Max Stirner (1806–56), Michael Bakunin (1814–76) and

Peter Kropotkin (1842–1921) focusing some of their most significant assaults on state authority and legal control. Godwin (1971: 275–76), for example, argued that 'whatever inconveniences may arise from the passions of men, the introduction of fixed laws cannot be the genuine remedy', in that such laws tend 'to fix the human mind in a stagnant condition', to inhibit lived solutions to human problems and to promote state-administered 'criminal justice' and punishment. Kropotkin (1975: 56), similarly, criticized the tendency of the law to crystallize that which should be modified and developed on a day-to-day basis and demanded the abolition of prisons and the law itself: 'In place of the cowardly phrase, "Obey the law", our cry is "Revolt against all laws!"' Stirner (1971: 157) called for 'war . . . against establishment itself, the State' – for the state to be 'abrogated, annihilated, done away with, not reformed' – and argued that crime in this context constituted a sort of individualistic rebellion against state law and authority. Bakunin also called for the destruction of the state and its replacement with the spontaneous and continuous action of the masses: 'the passion for destruction is a creative passion, too'.

Ferrell (1998) observes that such anarchist critiques have emerged not as the outcome of theoretical posturing but out of head-on confrontations between state legal authorities and anarchists attempting to construct alternative societal arrangements. Thus, for Bakunin and Kropotkin, anarchist criminology was part of revolutionary activity against the Russian oligarchy and the nation states that emerged with capitalism. In fact, Bakunin's notion of 'the spontaneous and continuous action of the masses' referred to an actual case of anarchist revolt: the Paris Commune of 1871. In the US, anarchists like Emma Goldman (1869–1940) and Alexander Berkman (1870–1936) also mixed labour and social activism with theoretical critique and spent large periods of their lives in prison. Most remarkable were the Wobblies, who blended deceptive strategies to avoid legal prosecution with out-and-out defiance of the law. With allied trade unions, they invented strategies to turn the law against itself and win labour and political victories; thus, for example, on occasion, in the workplace, they obeyed every rule and regulation so precisely as to finally grind all work to a halt, and in the streets, they systematically violated unjust laws in such large numbers as to overload courts and jails and force the dismissal of their cases (Ferrell and Ryan, 1995; Kornbluh, 1988; Ferrell, 1991).

Ferrell (1998) observes that anarchist criminology has actually flourished since the late 1960s in the US, and this may come as surprise to some of you at first sight. Harold Pepinsky (1997) had published an article advocating 'communist anarchism as an alternative to the rule of criminal law' and later transformed this approach into a 'peacemaking criminology' which is almost mainstream in the US and which is opposed to the violence seen to be inherent in the concept and practice of state law (Pepinsky, 1991; Pepinsky and Quinney, 1991) and which is discussed in the following section. Larry Tifft (1979) developed an anarchist criminology which argued for replacing state/legal 'justice' with a fluid, face-to-face form grounded in emerging human needs. Bruce DiCristina (1995) constructed a critique of criminology and criminal justice developed from the work of the anarchist philosopher of science Paul Feyerabend (1975). Ferrell (1994, 1995a, 1995b, 1996; Ryan and Ferrell, 1986) also developed an anarchist criminology aimed at examining the interplay between state/legal authority, day-to-day resistance to it and the practice of criminality.

Anarchist criminology thus incorporates the sort of 'visceral revolt' (Guerin, 1970) characteristic of anarchism itself, the passionate sense of 'fuck authority', to quote the old anarchist slogan, that is the outcome of being pushed around by police officers, judges, bosses, priests and other authorities. Ferrell (1997) notes that anarchists agree with many feminist and postmodernist theorists that intuitive passions are important as methods of understanding and resistance outside the usual confines of rationality and respect, while, at the same time, they seek to incorporate a relatively complex critique of state law and legality, which begins to explain *why* we might benefit from defying authority or standing 'against the law'.

Many contemporary critical criminologists agree that state law is so thoroughly lubricated by economic privilege, intertwined with patriarchal arrangements and protected by racist procedures as to constitute a mailed fist regularly brought down on the heads of women, the poor, ethnic minorities, young people and other outsiders to economic power or state authority (Ferrell, 1998). Anarchist criminologists certainly agree with this analysis but go further and argue that the practice of centralized state law, in fact, harms people, groups and the social fabric which joins them together even if it is not aimed directly at 'the powerless'. In other words, they are arguing that the administration of centralized state authority and legality destroys community, exacerbates criminality and expands the abusive power of the state machinery throughout the contemporary social order and then, through its discriminatory practices, doubles this harm for those pushed to the bottom of the system.

Ferrell (1998) observes four broad harms of state legality. First, there is the 'state-protection racket' (Pepinsky and Jesilow, 1984: 10), whereby cash and conformity are seen to be extorted from those unlucky enough to be caught up in it:

> From speed traps to parking fines, from the plethora of licensing fees to the bureaucratised bungling of the tax authorities, the state operates a vast revenue machine which serves itself and those who operate it, and which is enforced by a whole range of state-sanctioned strong-arm tactics such as impoundment, seizure and imprisonment. It is a system designed to perpetuate itself and to protect the powerful in and around it, obscuring its real intentions by an ideological veil of being in the best interests of the community.
>
> (Ferrell, 1998: 13)

Second, this labyrinth of state legality is seen to flourish in the absence of real human community and, once in place, suffocates any possibility of fluid and engaged human interaction:

> In a social world increasingly fractured by alienated labour and economic inequality, privatized leisure, and the paranoia of the lonely crowd, calls for police assistance and civil litigation multiply as does the sense that such disjointed, externalised tactics somehow constitute appropriate measures for solving disputes and achieving justice.
>
> (Ferrell, 1998: 14)

Third, there is recognition and acknowledgement of the crucial role of the labelling tradition with the confinement of people and groups within state-administered categories of criminality and systems of punishment and retribution, which, in reality, promotes not rehabilitative humanity but rather a downward spiral of crime, criminalization and inhumanity:

> This spiral interconnects state and media sponsored fears of crime, an ideology of state-sanctioned retaliation, and thus sudden outbreaks of objectification, dehumanisation,

and legal retribution. It is in this way that a system of state law and 'justice' is perpetuated within individual lives and larger social relations.

(Ferrell, 1998: 15)

Fourth, the 'rule of law' continues to proliferate, to penetrate further into all corners of
social and cultural life (Cohen, 1979) – as in Max Weber's (1964) notion of the 'iron cage
of bureaucracy' – while state legality constitutes a sort of bureaucratic cancer that grows
on itself, that produces an ever-expanding maze of legal control and that, in turn, generates an ever-expanding body of bureaucratic and legal sycophants employed to obfuscate
and interpret it:

> This proliferation of legal controls finally suspends what little protection the law once
> may have afforded. Every facet of social and cultural life is defined by legal control,
> and thus by state definitions of legality and illegality, we all remain continually vul-
> nerable to the flagrant exercise of state power.

(Ferrell, 1998: 16)

Anarchist criminology thus produces a profoundly radical critique of state law as a system
of inherent inhumanity, and its sense of standing 'against the law' leads logically to a
criminology of crime and resistance. Labour historians and sociologists of work have
long documented the pattern by which systems of authoritarian, alienating work generate among workers incidents of sabotage – of intentional rule-breaking and disruption –
as a means of resisting these systems and regaining some sense of humanity and control.
Anarchist criminologists suggest that this pattern may be found in the interplay of state
legal control and criminality. Rather than dismissing criminality as mindless misbehaviour or, worse, simply accepting the social construction of legality and illegality provided
by the state as definitive of good and bad human conduct, anarchist criminologists
seek to explore the situated politics of crime and criminality. In other words, anarchist
criminologists argue that the political (and politically inequitable) nature of state law
and criminalization means that acts of crime under such a system must also carry some
degree of political meaning.

Anarchist criminologists thus seek to blur and explore the boundaries between crime
and political resistance (Simon, 1991). This exploration does not, however, assume that
all crime constitutes conscious resistance to state authority, nor does it ignore the often,
but not always, negative consequences of criminality for people and communities. It
does, on the other hand, require that careful attention is paid to various criminal(ized)
activities – graffiti writing, 'obscene' art and music performances, pirate radio broadcasts,
illegal labour strikes, curfew violations, shoplifting, drug use, street cruising, gangbang-
ing, computer hacking (Ferrell, 1995a, 1996; Ferrell and Sanders, 1995) – as a means of
investigating the variety of ways in which criminal or criminalized behaviours may incorporate repressed dimensions of human dignity, self-determination and lived resistance to
the authority of state law.

Anarchist criminology calls for human communities which are decentralized, fluid, eclectic
and inclusive, and it is proposed that this sense of inclusive, non-authoritarian community
can benefit critical criminology itself. Ferrell (1998) observes that anarchist criminology shares much with the uncertainty and situated politics of feminist criminology, with
the decentred authority and textual deconstruction of the postmodern and constitutive

criminologies, the critical pacifism of peacemaking criminology and, of course, with the broader critique of legal injustice common to all critical criminologies. Ferrell observes that even left realists share with anarchist criminology a concern with identifying and exploring the situated consequences of crime and crime control. In the spirit of eclectic inclusivity, anarchist criminology argues against partitioning critical criminology into a series of small intellectual cubicles and then closing one critical cubicle to the occupants of another (Pepinsky, 1991). It instead calls for an ongoing critical conversation among perspectives, for a multifaceted critique of legal injustice made all the more powerful by its openness to alternatives. Stan Cohen (1988: 232) writes of his 'lack of commitment to any master plan (such as liberalism, left realism, or abolitionism), a failing, I would like to think, not of my own psyche but of the social world's refusal to correspond to any one theory'. Anarchist criminology shares this postmodern lack of commitment to master plans or grand narratives – including its own – and embraces instead fluid communities of uncertainty and critique.

Peacemaking criminology

Introduction

The general argument presented by peacemaking criminology is that the whole of the US criminal justice system is based on the continuance of violence and oppression (as seen in the prison system), war (as seen in the war on crime and the war on drugs) and the failure to account for how the larger social system contributes to the problem of crime (as seen in the failure to reduce poverty in society; Pepinsky and Quinney, 1991). Richard Quinney (1991: 3) a long-time critic of mainstream modernist criminology, observes:

> Let us begin with a fundamental realization: No amount of thinking and no amount of public policy have brought us any closer to understanding and solving the problem of crime. The more we have reacted to crime, the farther we have removed ourselves from any understanding and any reduction of the problem. In recent years, we have floundered desperately in reformulating the law, punishing the offender, and quantifying our knowledge. Yet this country remains one of the most crime-ridden nations. In spite of all its wealth, economic development, and scientific advances, this country has one of the worst crime records in the world.

Peacemaking criminology observes that crime is connected to suffering and proposes that, to end crime, we must end suffering. This means that poverty, racism, sexism, alienation, abuse within families, harassment and all other forms of suffering must be dealt with if crime is to be reduced. The state itself is seen to perpetuate crime (and violence) through repressive policies of social control, such as the death penalty, lengthy prison sentences and the criminalization of non-violent drug offences, while the criminological focus on individual offenders has been seen to be at the neglect of institutional arrangements in society that contribute to a very high crime rate. Criminology should therefore concern itself with promoting greater social equity, with a significant move away from traditional criminal justice to restorative justice.

Peacemaking criminology is thus not traditional mainstream criminology, and it is certainly not obsessed with the detailed statistical analysis of the causes of criminal behaviour, which is very much the dominant orthodoxy in the contemporary US (Young, 2011). This is not to say that peacemaking criminology is not interested in the causes of crime, but rather, it approaches the aetiology issue through non-traditional means. Thus, for example, in providing a summary of the intellectual foundations of peacemaking criminology, Quinney (1991: 3–4) attempts to encapsulate how the aetiology issue can be framed. First, the thought of the Western rational mode is conditional, limiting knowledge to what is already known. Second, the truth of reality is emptiness: all that is real is beyond human conception. Third, each life is a spiritual journey into the unknown and the unknowable, beyond the egocentric self. Fourth, human existence is characterized by suffering: crime is suffering, and the sources of suffering are within each of us. Fifth, through love and compassion, beyond the egocentric self, we can end suffering and live in peace, personally and collectively. Sixth, the ending of suffering can be attained in a quieting of the mind and an opening of the heart, in being aware. Seventh, crime can be ended only with the ending of suffering, only when there is peace – through the love and compassion found in awareness. Eighth, understanding, service, justice – all these flow naturally from love and compassion, from mindful attention to the reality of all that is, here and now. Ninth, a criminology of peacemaking, the nonviolent criminology of compassion and service, seeks to end suffering and thereby eliminate crime.

One of the greatest challenges for peacemaking criminology has been the development of a coherent, unifying theory. The kind of theorizing which has accompanied peacemaking criminology has been more general in tone and has a broader, less systematic nature.

The peacemaking pyramid paradigm

John Fuller (2003: 86–8) has developed a six-stage model of peacemaking criminology which deals with the criminal justice system:

1   *Non-violence.* Peacemaking criminology is first and foremost opposed to violence and the use of capital punishment as a criminal justice policy. The premeditated violence of the state is viewed as just as wrong as the violence of the offender.
2   *Social justice.* Social justice considers a broader concept of justice than traditional criminal justice, and issues of sexism, racism and inequality are key concerns. For example it is observed that a pattern of racial bias has long been apparent in capital punishment cases with the ethnicity of the offender and the victim having been shown to influence the death sentence. Ethnic minorities have been more likely to receive death penalties than whites, and while there are other reasons to argue against the death penalty, this obvious ethnic bias is quite clearly a violation of any notion of social justice. The minority offender may be guilty of a heinous crime, but the peacemaking perspective argues against the death penalty on social justice grounds when there are such extra-legal factors affecting the sentence.
3   *Inclusion.* It is argued that the criminal justice system needs to be more inclusive of the stakeholders in the community. In the current highly formalized concept of criminal justice, the offender is pitted against the state. There are nevertheless others who have an interest in the case and who can offer legitimate perspectives and alternatives. Families of the victim and the offender, as well as individuals from the neighbourhood, are all interested parties who have valuable insights. When the state takes such total control of a case, it deprives the affected parties of the opportunity to develop

their own creative solution. Christie (1977) likens this situation to the state taking away the property of the offender and victim. The concept of inclusion also entails giving the offender an opportunity to negotiate the outcome. Rather than having a sentence imposed on them, the offender agrees to the conditions and takes ownership of the offence and their treatment. The peacemaking perspective proposes that such conditions of inclusion will form more satisfactory and lasting solutions than conventional sentencing.

4   *Correct means.* There is an old saying that the ends do not justify the means, and this is seen to be especially true in the criminal justice system. A whole area of procedural law has been developed to ensure that criminal justice practitioners do not violate the legal and civil rights of the offender. Correct means entails ensuring that offenders and victims are not coerced into settlements of their cases with due process guarantees preserved and not sacrificed in order to ensure effectiveness. An example of this point offered is the extensive racial profiling used by many law enforcement agencies. While targeting ethnic minorities may seem justified to the police based on their expectations and experience, such incorrect means are inherently unfair and quickly become a self-fulfilling prophecy. When ethnic minorities are excessively targeted, they become disproportionately arrested and this is used as evidence in developing suspect profiles. It becomes a vicious circle where incorrect means contributes to the violations of social justice.

5   *Ascertainable criteria.* For victims, offenders and community members to fully participate in the criminal justice system, they must understand what is going on. There are two types of language barriers that inhibit equal access to the law. The first is the inability of many recent immigrants to understand English. While many jurisdictions provide adequate translators, many do not. It is clear that, when individuals cannot understand English, they cannot fully participate in the court proceedings. The second issue concerns the specialized jargon used in the criminal justice system. The language of the law is a highly specialized professional argot that is only completely understood by lawyers. The peacemaking concepts of ascertainable criteria and inclusion argue that efforts to ensure that all parties fully understand the procedures are desirable. This would include education efforts aimed at non-English-speaking individuals as well as clearly written legal guidelines aimed at educating victims and offenders.

6   *Categorical imperative.* When considering the problems of crime and the criminal justice system, the peacemaking perspective aims at developing a consistent and predictable viewpoint. Using Immanuel Kant's concept of the categorical imperative, the peacemaking perspective argues that responses to crime should reflect an underlying philosophy of non-violence and social justice that is extended throughout the criminal justice system. Victims and offenders, criminal justice practitioners and the public should all be treated with the respect and dignity we all deserve. To that end, criminal justice decisions should employ Kant's axiom: 'Act only according to that maxim whereby you can at the same time will that it should become a universal law'. Thus, the peacemaking perspective is not a haphazard and inconsistent policy guide. It aims at providing true equality under the law for all people.

A few observations can be made about this 'theoretical' perspective. First, it is not a traditional criminological theory, complete with hypotheses and propositions that can be tested. Second, it does not directly address the issue of crime causation or who commits crime and why. Third, it could be considered to be less peacemaking criminology and more peacemaking criminal justice. All three observations are not necessarily criticisms. Fuller provides an alternative and welcome social justice view to the dominant criminal justice perspective, which we should note is in harmony with the radical moral communitarianism promoted by this author in the penultimate chapter of this book. Moreover, his argument is a humanist and compassionate plea for human dignity while, at the same time, reminding us that perhaps criminologists should be as interested in victims as in offenders. Finally, Fuller has clearly implied that the contemporary criminologist should be actively engaged in the various struggles for social justice.

Criticism of peacemaking criminology

Peacemaking criminology has, perhaps not surprisingly, been the recipient of significant and often vitriolic criticism, having been viewed as 'utopian', 'soft on crime', 'unrealistic' and 'just not feasible'. One of its staunchest critics has been eminent US criminologist Ronald Akers, who noted in his 1997 book, *Criminological Theories: Introduction and Evaluation*, that

> [p]eacemaking criminology does not offer a theory of crime or of the criminal justice system that can be evaluated empirically. . . . It may be possible to construct a testable, parsimonious, and valid theory from peacemaking criminology, but at this point it remains a philosophy rather than a theory. It is a utopian vision of society that calls for reforming and restructuring to get away from war, crime, and violence. . . . This is a highly laudable philosophy of criminal justice, but it does not offer an explanation of why the system operates as it does or why offenders commit crime. It can be evaluated on other grounds but not on empirical validity.
>
> (183)

In a subsequent edition, Akers (2000) identifies four additional shortcomings. First, he argues that it is contradictory to claim Marxist/critical theory as one of the main foundations for peacemaking, because this perspective is based on class conflict and Marx himself endorsed violent revolution. Second, feminism is not consistent with peacemaking because the nurturing role of women is simply part of the patriarchal system of the oppression of women. Third, almost all the policies recommended by peacemaking criminology have long been mainstays of the policy recommendations of traditional criminology. Thus, peacemaking criminology is not really anything new or different. Fourth, peacemaking criminology does not provide a strategy for getting beyond the limitations of criminal justice policies to suggest how large-scale structural changes can be brought about to make society less violent.

Fuller (2003: 93–94) nevertheless responds to these objections. First, he observes that peacemaking criminology does not share all aspects of Marxism. Thus, it is committed to that part which demands equality and rejects that element which calls for violence, which we might observe is very much in accord with serious contemporary European thought. Second, he argues that feminism is consistent with peacemaking criminology; in particular, it demonstrates how rigid gender roles have had a negative impact on society, proposing that both women and men should have a nurturing role. Third, traditional criminologists may have advocated many changes in the criminal justice system, but the war-on-crime mentality still tends to dominate. Fourth, he argues that people practise 'peace-making' in their everyday lives and the extent to which this occurs will mean less crime.

Akers is not the only critic who asks how peacemaking criminology would propose a structural re-organization of society. Gibbons (1994: 172) observes that 'the Pepinsky and Quinney volume has little to say about how the grand-scale changes they propose might be achieved', but peacemaking criminologists have responded and point to structural innovations that could be undertaken in the US that could arguably reduce the suffering that causes crime. Among the changes proposed are the following:

1   Provision of universal health care based on the Canadian and European models
2   Replace the minimum wage law with one based on the idea of a liveable wage
3   Make poverty a priority and initiate a broad and sweeping national programme to reduce poverty through a system of guaranteed child support for all poor families
4   Provide free tuition for all students enrolled in community colleges
5   Provide free child care for all preschool children – with a minimal charge for affluent families
6   De-criminalize all drug laws and expand free treatment for addicts
7   De-institutionalize prisons and use these institutions predominantly for violent offenders
8   Shift the tax burden from the middle and working classes to the upper economic classes and corporations
9   Make a total commitment to the abolition of wage inequality based on sex
10 Redirect economic and social policies to inner cities, especially in housing
11 De-militarize the political economy of the US
12 Abolish the death penalty

Some of the proposed changes are clearly more radical than others, but some, such as the provision of free health care for all citizens and policies to help poor families become independent and productive members of society, have been in existence in Europe for many years, and these societies enjoy much lower crime rates than the US. To the average European, such policies are not radical but mainstream.

Restorative justice as an alternative to criminal justice

The single most important proposal by peacemaking criminologists centres on the notion of restorative justice, which is seen as an opportunity to restructure a significant part of the criminal justice system. It is recognized that the criminal justice system should be maintained for dealing with crimes of violence – murder, rape, robbery and assault – but it is proposed that many property and drug crimes could be dealt with through a non-criminal justice system.

Van Ness and Strong (2002: 38–43) note that restorative justice rests on three major propositions. First, justice requires that we work to restore those who have been injured: victims, communities and even offenders. Second, those most directly involved and affected by crime – victims, offenders and community – should have the opportunity to participate as fully in the intervention as they wish. Third, while the government is responsible for preserving a just social order, the role of the community in establishing and maintaining a just peace must be given special significance.

In other words, restorative justice is seen to be a system where the primary motive is healing, not punishment. It looks to bring victim and offender together, to promote restitution (both monetary and symbolic), to involve the community in decision-making and to seek non-violent (i.e. non-custodial) solutions to crime. It is not the traditional response to crime: it is not founded on principles of retribution, nor does it ignore victims, as the current dominant criminal justice orthodoxy in the US does. Restorative justice looks to options other than trial, plea-bargaining and imprisonment. In short, it is a peacemaking alternative to crime rather than the war model, which has come to dominate contemporary criminal justice in the US. Rick Sarre (2003: 102–7) offers some examples of what restorative justice looks like in actual practice:

- *Family conferencing.* This is where offenders, victims, family and community members and police are brought together to negotiate a settlement. Offenders confront their wrongs, and the aim is a mutually satisfactory reconciliation.
- *Family violence court.* This is an 'interventionist' court that deals with domestic violence issues and generally seeks treatment for offenders through anger management programmes and drug abuse treatment.
- *Mental health court.* This court takes referrals from police and lower-level magistrates for people who have non-severe mental disorders yet are in need of mental health intervention through various agencies.
- *Drug assessment and aid panels.* This is a pre-court diversionary programme now in use in South Australia which works with drug offenders to seek medical, not criminal, solutions for addiction. A 'panel' oversees the treatment regimen for these offenders.
- *Customary law.* This is the recognition of tribal and customary law among indigenous populations in solving many justice issues.
- *Victim Offender Reconciliation Program (VORP).* This is a programme that can operate at both the pre-court and post-conviction stages. It is designed around the principles of mediation and reconciliation, bringing offender and victim together to repair the damage done by the crime and to have the offender take responsibility for that damage.

Restorative justice is perceived to be a new way of thinking about crime and the way in which society responds and intervenes. It promotes bringing together offenders and victims and expects the former to accept responsibility for their actions. It promotes victim healing through reconciliation and offender rehabilitation through treatment, restitution and reparation. It emphasizes the need to effectively reintegrate offenders back into the community and the related responsibility of the community to play a positive role in that reintegration. Restorative justice is the principal proposal of peacemaking criminology for overhauling the criminal justice system. It may not be a workable proposal for some crimes – many crimes of violence, for instance – but, for many property crimes, drug offences and young offending, it is a very reasonable alternative to incarceration and punishment, which provide the foundations of the contemporary criminal justice system in the US and beyond.

Conclusion

[a]ll too often criminologists forget the social responsibility they bear as experts in the area of crime and justice. . . . By accepting their roles as experts on law-violating behaviour, criminologists place themselves in a position of power. The potential

consequences of their actions are enormous. Therefore, they must be both aware of the ethics of their profession and prepared to defend their work in the light of public scrutiny. Major ethical issues include what to study, whom to study, and how to conduct those studies.

Peacemaking criminology seeks to address these concerns in the following ways. First, crime is clearly identified as a significant part of peacemaking criminological study, but it is only a part. Peacemaking criminologists should also study the institutions that comprise the social structure with attention directed to the systems of court administration, law enforcement and the penal system. In other words, the focus should not only be on offenders but also on the societal response to crime with the peacemaking criminologist needing to examine those institutions that play a role in producing the suffering that is at the core of the crime problem. This means that criminologists should know more about economic inequality, poverty, racism, sexism and bias against gays and lesbians. It is necessary to know how schools reproduce academic and personal failure. The focus of peacemaking criminology must be on 'criminals' but *also* on the social dynamics which produce the suffering that causes criminals.

Second, it is proposed that peacemaking criminology must study those in positions of political and social power. It is necessary to know how law-makers function, what philosophies motivate judges, and what priorities drive police activities. Peacemaking criminologists should therefore study those who work in mainstream corrections (prison wardens, correctional officers) and those who would be part of the restorative justice process (mediators, teachers, counsellors, therapists). It needs to explore how community activists, religious leaders and social workers can be brought into ways of reducing suffering. In short, peacemaking criminologists should be as interested in the persons and agencies that respond to crime as in the criminals.

Third, peacemaking criminology has the responsibility to engage in only ethical research, committed to the principles of confidentiality and non-violence. Peacemaking criminologists must not conduct studies which contribute to suffering; they must be attentive to the human rights of their research subjects, whether they are criminals or the police. They must not allow their research to further a system of oppression, alienation and mistreatment of law offenders or law enforcers. Whether their work is based on case studies, large-scale survey research or participant observation, peacemaking criminologists must always be dedicated to finding constructive solutions to the social problems which generate crime. Peacemaking criminologists must themselves be agents of social change and be engaged in various struggles to promote social justice.

Peacemaking criminology has had a short history, but its adherents propose that it offers a realistic cause for crime (human suffering) and a practical response (restorative justice). It broadens the vision of the criminologist to the structure and processes of the social system, thus breaking away from the narrow vision of examining only offenders and, in doing so, revives and revitalizes the radical tradition in the US and brings it into line with contemporary radical developments in Australia and the UK.

Anarchist criminology revisited

It is widely accepted in the US that their criminal justice system is not working with US Senator Jim Webb (2009) observing that

America's criminal justice system has deteriorated to the point that it is a national disgrace. Its irregularities and inequities cut against the notion that we are a society founded on fundamental fairness. Our failure to address this problem has caused the nation's prisons to burst their seams with massive overcrowding, even as our neighbourhoods have become more dangerous. We are wasting billions of dollars and diminishing millions of lives.

During the major financial crisis that occurred between 2008 and 2010 – and which is discussed in more detail elsewhere in this book – the huge non-productive cost of incarceration in the US came to the fore of political debate with discussions centring on how to imprison fewer people and to lower the cost of keeping those who are detained. Not surprisingly, there were significant protests against efforts to change sentencing laws by people who still seemed to believe a nation can arrest its way to security. Equally unsurprising were the attacks from the correctional officer associations which seemed to be aimed at anything that might diminish the flow of inmates.

We should note that most people incarcerated in the US have been involved with illegal drugs, usually on the distribution and sales end of the business. The question thus started to be asked in respectable circles whether society is safer by making drugs illegal and, moreover, whether society can afford that particular safety. The response of society to these issues is inevitably determined by elites with the understandable concern about continuing to make good profits with the minimum of effort. The situation is moreover made worse by criminologists who continue to bolster these pro-incarceration elites with studies which can be interpreted to show the usefulness of a system which is obviously broken.

A criminal justice system which imprisons 1% of the total adult population and a much higher percentage of black people cannot be considered to be working. No other nation in the world comes close to approaching the incarceration rate of the US while, at the same time, paroled felons are forced into a netherworld of unemployability from which few escape. This rising tide of formerly incarcerated persons thus must be added to the currently incarcerated to get a true picture of the situation. Thus, more than 5.6 million Americans were in prison or had served time there, one in 33 of adults living in the US (Belk, 2006). Change in the US criminal justice system has nevertheless been all but impossible due to entrenched elites, supported by unionized middle-class employees, whose power is bound to the current system.

Anarchist criminology proposes that it can make a vast change in how citizens work with each other to keep social deviance within bounds acceptable to society. The following are some principles of an anarchist criminology which could also serve as principles of restorative justice:

1   Harm creates needs and responsibilities.
2   Collectives respond to harm by assessing the needs of those harmed and providing a process allowing those harmed and those responsible for the harm to meet the needs created with the assistance of the collective.
3   Collectives provide pro-social support for those engaged in responding to needs created by harm.
4   Collectives respect and celebrate efforts to respond to needs created by harm.
5   Collectives offer alternatives for those who are unable or unwilling to avoid causing harm, to assist the collective in avoiding harm.

Ron Claassen (1996) has listed 11 principles of restorative justice, and while divided into finer nuances, they are all consistent with the five principles outlined earlier. The focus of the five principles is on the work of the collective in addressing harm. No central authority is required for the operation of these principles, and they could be applied by a collective of any size.

These principles do not propose punishment as a goal because it does not repair harm. It may have some deterrent effect, but that is about all it does for a collective. If the only punishment used is imprisonment, it actually harms the collective by requiring the support of unproductive members in a relatively expensive way, followed by the need to rehabilitate a person who has been kept in an unproductive status for a time.

Policy implications of anarchism and peacemaking criminology

The earlier-discussed anarchist principles do not require a central authority for their operation. A collective at any level of societal organization can follow them. It is proposed that central authorities are actually a hindrance to the good use of these principles, since they remove those directly affected from the process, and tend to focus more on consistency than functionality of the remedies selected in a particular case. These principles do not, however, preclude the use of incarceration as a technique for protecting the collective from people who cannot or will not live without creating harm.

The policy implications of peacemaking criminology include a mixture of anarchism, humanism, socialism and Native American and Eastern philosophies: rejecting the idea that criminal violence can be reduced by state violence and the belief that reducing suffering will reduce crime. It is an approach which suggests that the solution to all social problems, including crime, is (1) the transformation of human beings, (2) mutual dependence, (3) reduction of class structures, (4) the creation of communities of caring people and (5) universal social justice.

Summary of main points

1 Anarchist criminologists launch aggressive and 'unreasonable' critiques against law and legal authority because they argue that the latter institutions undermine human community and diversity.
2 Anarchist criminology aims its disrespectable gaze both high and low: it not only attacks the state structure and legal authority above us but also encourages those below and beyond this authority to find ways of resisting it and finding more egalitarian alternatives.
3 It is argued that the administration of centralized state authority and legality destroys community, exacerbates criminality and expands the abusive power of the state machinery throughout the contemporary social order.
4 Peacemaking criminology argues that the whole of the US criminal justice system is based on the continuance of violence and oppression (as seen in the prison system), war (as seen in the war on crime and the war on drugs) and the failure to account for how the larger social system contributes to the problem of crime (as seen in the failure to reduce poverty in society).
5 Peacemaking criminology proposes that crime is connected to suffering and that, to end crime, we must end suffering. This means that poverty, racism, sexism, alienation,

abuse within families, harassment and all other forms of suffering must be dealt with if crime is to be reduced.

6 The state itself is seen to perpetuate crime (and violence) through repressive policies of social control, such as the death penalty, lengthy prison sentences for offenders and the criminalization of non-violent drug offences.

7 John Fuller has developed a six-stage model of peacemaking criminology which deals with the criminal justice system.

8 Peacemaking criminology has been the recipient of significant and often vitriolic criticism, having been viewed as 'utopian', 'soft on crime', 'unrealistic' and 'just not feasible'.

9 The single most important proposal by peacemaking criminologists centres on the notion of restorative justice, which is seen as an opportunity to restructure a significant part of the criminal justice system.

10 Restorative justice is perceived to be a new way of thinking about crime and the way in which society responds and intervenes.

Discussion questions

1 What are the main points of anarchist criminology?
2 What are the main points of peacemaking criminology?
3 Outline the six-stage model of peacemaking criminology?
4 What are the main criticisms of peacemaking criminology?
5 What are the theoretical links between peacemaking criminology and restorative justice?

Suggested further reading

Ferrell (1994, 1995a, 1995b) provides an excellent introduction to anarchist criminology. Pepinsky and Quinney's (1991) edited text provides an equally excellent introduction to peacemaking criminology and Fuller (2003) a more focused, comprehensive account and defence.

References

Akers, R.L. (1997) *Criminological Theories: Introduction and Evaluation*, 2nd ed. Los Angeles, CA: Roxbury.

Akers, R.L. (2000) *Criminological Theories: Introduction, Evaluation, and Application*, 3rd ed. Los Angeles, CA: Roxbury.

Belk, A.G. (2006) *A New Generation of Native Sons: Men of Color and the Prison-Industrial Complex*. Washington, DC: Joint Center for Political and Economic Studies.

Christie, N. (1977) 'Conflict as Property', *British Journal of Criminology*, 17(1): 1–14.

Claassen, R. (1996) *Restorative Justice Primary Focus on People, Not Procedures*. Available from: http://peace.fresno.edu/docs/rjprinc2.html. [Accessed April 2019].

Cohen, S. (1979) 'The Punitive City: Notes on the Dispersal of Social Control', *Contemporary Crises*, 3: 339–63.

Cohen, S. (1988) *Against Criminology*. New Brunswick, NJ: Transaction.

DiCristina, B. (1995) *Method in Criminology: A Philosophical Primer*. New York: Harrow and Heston.

Ferrell, J. (1991) 'The Brotherhood of Timber Workers and the Culture of Conflict', *Journal of Folklore Research*, 2: 163–77.

Ferrell, J. (1994) 'Confronting the Agenda of Authority: Critical Criminology, Anarchism, and Urban Graffiti', in G. Barak (ed.) *Varieties of Criminology: Readings from a Dynamic Discipline*. Westport, CT: Praeger.

Ferrell, J. (1995a) 'Urban Graffiti: Crime, Control, and Resistance', *Youth and Society*, 27: 73–92.

Ferrell, J. (1995b) 'Anarchy Against the Discipline', *Journal of Criminal Justice and Popular Culture*, 3: 6–91.

Ferrell, J. (1996) *Crimes of Style: Urban Graffiti and the Politics of Criminality*. Boston, MA: North-eastern University.

Ferrell, J. (1997) 'Criminological Verstehen: Inside the Immediacy of Crime', *Justice Quarterly*, 14: 3–23.

Ferrell, J. (1998) 'Against the Law: Anarchist Criminology', *Social Anarchism*, 25: 5–23.

Ferrell, J. and Ryan, K. (1995) 'The Brotherhood of Timber Workers and the Southern Lumber Trust: Legal Repression and Worker Response', *Radical America*, 19: 55–74.

Ferrell, J. and Sanders, C.R. (eds.) (1995) *Cultural Criminology*. Boston, MA: North-eastern University Press.

Feyerabend, P. (1975) *Against Method: Outline of an Anarchistic Theory of Knowledge*. London: New Left Books.

Fuller, J. (2003) 'Peacemaking Criminology', in M.D. Schwartz and S.E. Hatty (eds.) *Controversies in Critical Criminology*. Cincinnati: Anderson.

Gibbons, D.C. (1994) *Talking About Crime and Criminals: Problems and Issues in Theory Development in Criminology*. Englewood Cliffs, NJ: Prentice Hall.

Godwin, (1971) *Enquiry Concerning Political Justice*. London: Oxford.

Guerin, Daniel (1970). *Anarchism*. New York: Monthly Review.

Kornbluh, J. (ed.) (1988) *Rebel Voices: An IWW Anthology*. Chicago, IL: Charles H. Kerr.

Kropotkin, P. (1975) *The Essential Kropotkin*. New York: Liveright.

Mazor, L.J. (1978) 'Disrespect for Law', in R.J. Pennock and J.W. Chapman (eds.) *Anarchism*. New York: New York University.

Pepinsky, H.E. (1991) 'Peacemaking in Criminology', in B.D. MacLean and D. Milovanovic (eds.) *New Directions in Critical Criminology*. Vancouver, BC: The Collective Press.

Pepinsky, H.E. and Jesilow, P. (1984) *Myths That Cause Crime*, 2nd ed. Cabin John, MD: Seven Locks.

Pepinsky, H.E. and Quinney, R. (eds.) (1991) *Criminology as Peacemaking*. Bloomington, IN: Indiana.

Pepinsky, H.E. (1997) 'Communist Anarchism as an Alternative to the Rule of Criminal Law', *Contemporary Crises*, 2: 315–27.

Quinney, R. (1991) 'The Way of Peace: On Crime, Suffering, and Service', in H. Pepinsky and R. Quinney (eds.) *Criminology as Peacemaking*. Bloomington: Indiana University Press.

Ryan, K. and Ferrell, J. (1986) 'Knowledge, Power, and the Process of Justice', *Crime and Social Justice*, 25: 17–95.

Sarre, R. (2003) 'Restorative Justice: A Paradigm of Possibility', in M.D. Schwartz and S.E. Hatty (eds.) *Controversies in Critical Criminology*. Cincinnati: Anderson.

Simon, J.K. (1991) 'Michel Foucault on Attica: An Interview', *Social Justice*, 1: 26–34.

Stirner, M. (1971) *The Ego and His Own*. New York: Harper and Row.

Van Ness, D. and Strong, K.H. (1997) *Restoring Justice*. Cincinnati, OH: Anderson Publishing.

Van Ness, D. and Strong, K.H. (2002) *Restoring Justice*. Cincinnati, OH: Anderson Publishing.

Webb, J. (2009) 'Why We Must Fix Our Prisons', *Parade*, March 29.

Weber, M. (1964) *The Theory of Social and Economic Organization*. New York: Free Press.

Young, J. (2011) *The Criminological Imagination*. Oxford: Polity Press.

Chapter 8

Cultural criminology

Key issues

1 The focus of cultural criminology
2 Methods and applications
3 Psychosocial criminology
4 Deviant leisure
5 Cultural criminology and the mass media

The focus of cultural criminology

Cultural criminology seeks to explain crime and criminal behaviour, and its control, in terms of culture. In doing so has very close intellectual links with postmodern and anarchist criminology. Crime and the various agencies and institutions of crime control are seen to be cultural and creative constructs which should be understood in terms of the phenomenological meanings they carry. It follows in a tradition established by Marx and the later humanist Marxists who argue that the essence of 'humanity' is not that we are rational calculating beings but that we are productive and creative, carrying with us a 'world vision' and ideology which shapes our own version of what is right and wrong (Lukacs, 1970; Goldmann, 1970). We nevertheless live our lives in a social world, which is predominantly structured by an economic system that prioritizes the pursuit of scientific rationalism. In this context, 'crime' appears to the dominant political groups in society to be endemic and simply a reflection of their world turned 'upside down'. Mike Presdee observes that it is the overwhelming lure of transgression which produces for the cultural criminologist a 'fascination with the unacceptable' in scientific rational society:

> Culture delivers to us social sites where popular transgression – the breaking through of the constraints created around us – is considered a crime in itself and where order and its accompanying rationalisations actually herald the death and the destruction of spontaneous life.

> (2004: 276)

That spontaneity – by its very essence – defies and resists order, and this dynamic tension between order and disorder, in turn, creates a cultural energy that is immediately apparent in the culture of 'edge work', 'emotion work' and 'excitement', which provides a central thread in much of the work conducted by cultural criminologists.

David Garland (2001) notes that our lives are characterized by a 'culture of control' where we are policed at home, at work, at pleasure and in a surveillance society where it is impossible to escape the dominant gaze, as we are watched, tracked, trailed, filmed and photographed by the electronic panopticon of rational society. This experience has produced cultures which are characterized by the process of the dominance through which they are formed. Mainstream criminology has tended to view these cultures as non-cultural, deviant and pathological, but cultural criminology, in contrast, approaches human behaviour through an analysis of lived everyday life and, as a result, has come to understand that humans have the ability to twist, modify and oppose meanings produced by dominant rational groups (Willis, 1978).

Cultural criminology studies show how some cultures have come to be designated deviant, while others have not. It is argued that activities, whether strategies of resistance or otherwise, represent clear attempts to find meaning in a life lived through rules provided from above by our supposed betters. Presdee observes that

> [n]ow we can begin to see that much crime, but not all; much disorder, but not all, is no more or less than the everyday life of the oppressed and the 'excluded'. From this perspective, crime should be viewed as everyday responses to lives lived out within deprived, brutalised and often lonely social locations. Moreover, the responses from within the structures of domination are often truly masochistic in that the reaction to such disorder is often further acts of cruelty by the dominant over the dominated.
>
> (2004: 281)

Cultural criminologists consider the changing cultural significance of contemporary consumer cultures and their particular effect on feelings and emotions (see Hayward, 2004a). Thus, the desire to own, to have and to be, no longer respects the limits and cultural boundaries produced in the past. This new consumer culture creates a confused psyche where anxiety and its social antidotes are themselves producing much so-called social disorder and transgression, as groups and individuals attempt to make sense of a life increasingly mediated through consumerism in contemporary society (Presdee, 2000; Hayward, 2004b). It is argued that the search for the thwarted promise of happiness through consumption simply leads many to hedonism and seemingly irrational acts.

In a society based on consumption, to 'have' is to exist to 'have nothing' is to be nothing. Presdee asks rhetorically how we can emotionally live a life that is burdened with such shame and observes that it is through crime that we can 'have' and, as a result, 'be'. It is this nothingness and loss of social status which is often the source of social or personal harm, the trigger for violence as self-expression, whether it is directed inwardly (self-mutilation) or outwardly (the mutilation of others). Crime and disorder can provide a subjective solution to this conundrum and thus becomes a 'therapeutic action' to alleviate personally perceived loss and translates the nothingness of life into something, while the pain of life is translated into pleasure.

Katz (1988) observes the 'seductions of crime' in which disorder is itself a 'delight' to be sought after and savoured and whereby the causes of crime are constructed by the offenders themselves, in ways which are compellingly seductive. 'Hot-blooded' murder is, for example, described in terms of a triad of conditions: interpretive, emotional and practical. *Interpretive* conditions include the defence of morality, the role of teasing or daring the victim, the role of a supportive audience and the role of alcohol in casual settings of last resort, for example, in the home. *Emotional* conditions involve a process of transcending humiliation with rage via the intermediary of righteousness. *Practical* conditions are a marking, or desecration, of the body of the victim, for example, when offenders can recall precisely the number of stitches it took for a victim to survive.

The key term in all of this is *humiliation*, which is defined as a 'profound loss of control over one's identity, or soul' (Katz, 1988: 24). All forms of criminality are seen to be a moral response to the shame of humiliation with the notion of 'uncertainty' eliminating any inevitability in the event. Cursing by the attacker and silent prayers by the victim are treated as priestly omens and sacrificial service honouring the sacred, which must be approached by a 'leap into faith' and the final seduction into 'the unknown' (Katz, 1988: 43).

Katz (1988: 51) defines foreground as individual consciousness and associated mental processes, while the less important background involves factors such as social class and gender. Background differences can nevertheless vary the experience of humiliation and open up possibilities for rituals of forgiveness, but foreground, or what is going through the head of the offender at the time of the crime, is more important. Crimes such as shoplifting and pizza theft involve attributing sensual power to an object so that the seduction is like a 'romantic encounter'. Practical conditions involve flirting with the object and a tension of being privately deviant in public places. Emotional conditions involve transcending uncontrollable feelings of thrill. Interpretive conditions involve metaphors of self (bounding immorality), game (timeouts and goal lines), religion (secret defilement), sex (like an orgasm) and the interrelationship between deviance and charisma (reaching for mysterious forces). The resonating of these metaphors makes the seduction irresistibly compelling, and thus, 'it is not the taste for pizza that makes the crime happen but the crime that makes the pizza taste good' (Katz, 1988: 91).

Gang violence requires learning to be a 'badass' by projecting symbols of impenetrability, which Katz relates to the hardness of male phallic imagery and feels that such behaviour requires a commitment to firmness of purpose so that it is left to make the rational choice calculations of costs and benefits. Badasses engage in the 'accidental bump' and hog the pavement when they walk. Practical conditions involve the creation of an oppressive background image to emphasize the status of the person as a street survivor or a member of an elite. Emotional conditions involve 'getting over' from 'here' to 'there' and the personal insults involving others' violations of artificial turf space.

Katz (1988) considers robbery to be a prototypical 'breeding ground' for crime, and thus, those conducting hold-ups with weapons are those that seek 'continuous action' and embrace a death wish (thanatos). They will commit any degree of violence necessary, even to the point where it puts their own lives at risk. These 'stick-up men' also develop a sense of competence at superior perceptual ability – in exploiting contextual weaknesses in a target, be it victim or architecture – and claim a special morality about this. Uncertainty in this example is related to 'chaos', that is during a hold-up, the offender is required to maintain suspense and manage the impression of coming from an alien world.

It is the desire to seek continuous action – for example crime, drugs, sex and gambling – which distinguishes the persistent or career criminal. Such offenders – also known as 'heavies' or omnibus felons – will often pursue action to the point of physical and mental exhaustion and they do this by always being available for all spontaneous opportunities, maintaining permeable boundaries for associates and reckless, super-fast spending with the proceeds from crime.

Katz observes that the main problem for criminals is the transcendence of chaos and depicts the ongoing project to achieve this as a process of imposing discipline and control over one's life and doing so will often mean the humiliation and physical abuse of women and children. Imposing control is seeking to get caught by sarcastically thanking the authorities, doing some moral accountancy – thus 'got away withs' exceed 'got caughts' – and looking forward to the opportunities for action in prison.

Katz (1988: 247) observes that the attractions of crime are seen as extensions, or 'celebrations', of being male and being black, and cites research on childhood socialization to suggest that the main effect of being male is preparation for a life of pretensions. Being black means to live in a culture of continuous insult, even from fellow blacks, and this tradition prepares blacks for becoming 'bad' by overcoming insult with insult. Crime emerges in the process of establishing a gendered, ethnic identity.

The carnival of crime

O'Malley and Mugford (1994) argue the need a new phenomenology of pleasure if we are to recognize 'crime' as simply a *transgression* from the impermissible and as *transcendence* of the everyday mundane. Presdee (2000) captures this sense of the interrelationships between pleasure and pain through his notion of 'crime as carnival', whereby the latter is a site where the pleasure of playing at the boundaries is clearly catered for. Thus, festive excess, transgression, the mocking of the powerful, irrational behaviour and so on are all temporarily legitimized in the moment of carnival. Breaking rules is a source of joy, of humour, of celebration, and many acts that might otherwise be considered criminal or at the very least 'deviant' are momentarily tolerated. The 'Christmas period', the 'office party' and the pervasive, invariably inebriated, 'goings-on' afterwards provide the classic example. Moreover, such acts as sadomasochism, raving, joyriding, computer hacking, recreational drug use, reclaim the streets parties, gang rituals and extreme sports, Presdee finds enduring fragments from the culture of the carnival. Moreover, as Thornton's (1995) study of 1990s' youth club cultures found, there is a continual and shifting exchange between the boundaries of acceptability and illegality and between subcultural authenticity and media manufacture. Moral panics about deviancy no longer simply signify condemnation but are something to be celebrated by the subcultural participants themselves.

Cultural criminologists argue that we need to push deeper and deeper to capture the full meaning of social harm. They accept that the traditional concept of crime does have a place but one that is subjugated to, and set against, a multiple series of alternative discourses, incorporating transgression, disrespect, disorder and resistance, as well as loss, injury and troubles. Van Swaaningen (1999: 23) observes that such discourses themselves may also suggest a new sociology of deviance based on difference and 'otherness'. Once more, the discursive frame necessary to recognize these elements needs to shift not just from criminal justice to social justice, restoration and reconciliation but to delight, drama, tolerance, celebration, transcendence and the pursuit of pleasure. It is an ambitious and for some an exhilarating agenda.

The schizophrenia of crime

Hopkins Burke (2007) introduces the phrase 'the schizophrenia of crime' to refer to the apparently contradictory duality of attitude to criminal behaviour which has become endemic in contemporary societies characterized by the postmodern condition. Thus, on one hand, it is possible to observe widespread public demand for a rigorous intervention against criminality which has made the 'war against crime' a major political issue, and indeed, it is in this context that we can observe an extensive expansion in situational crime prevention strategies epitomized by the ubiquitous existence of closed-circuit television (CCTV) cameras (Hopkins Burke, 2004b), a whole raft of crime-control legislation which has placed increasing restrictions on our civil liberties and human rights (Hopkins Burke, 2004c), and the introduction of rigorous 'zero-tolerance-style' policing interventions (see Hopkins Burke, 1998, 2002, 2004a) that have occurred not as the outcome of the coercive strategies of a totalitarian regime but in response to overwhelming public demand in a liberal democratic society (Hopkins Burke, 2004b). *We* want it, *we* demand it and *we* get it (Hopkins Burke, 2007), even though we as individuals are invariably unaware of the ultimate implications for our freedom. Hopkins Burke (2012, 2013) has thus developed a left realist historical perspective, which incorporates both the embourgeoisement thesis of John Goldthorpe (1968) and the 'civilizing process' of Norbert Elias (1978, 1982), to explain how increasing demands for improved social conditions and material rewards among the respectable working classes – or more recently the new middle classes – have occurred alongside a fast-declining tolerance for the very visible criminality and incivilities in our midst.

Yet, on the other hand, we should observe that criminality or at least 'deviancy' has become widespread to the virtual point of universality. Many people have committed criminal offences, at some stage in their life, and a great many continue to do so. There is increasing empirical evidence to show that white-collar, corporate and business crime is extremely widespread and when considering, for example, recreational drug use (the smell of cannabis or 'skunk', a very strong variant of 'weed,' is with us virtually everywhere; see, e.g., Winlow and Hall, 2006), crimes of disorder and incivility associated with alcohol use (extremely extensive in any location, urban or rural, in the UK, particularly during weekend evenings; Hobbs *et al.*, 2000, 2005) and driving cars beyond the legal speed limit (virtually compulsory through peer group pressure on motorways; Hopkins Burke, 2007), the notion of the virtual universality of criminality is not as implausible as it may at first seem.

Hopkins Burke (2007) is clearly influenced by Mike Presdee's notion of 'second lives', where the usually law-abiding and pillars of 'straight society' enjoy an alternative part-time existence involving walking on the wild side (Presdee, 2000). There is thus – as Jock Young (1999, 2001) observed – a considerable 'blurring of boundaries' between the criminal and the legal and, significantly, in our perceptions and understandings of these supposedly polarized opposite behaviours, which enables us to make some sense of 'the schizophrenia of crime' in a world where crime has become both normal and indeed non-pathological (Garland, 1996). The increasing blurring of boundaries between honesty and dishonesty has been nowhere more apparent than in the realms of organized crime, corporate crime and legitimate business. The globalization of generic crime and criminal behaviour is considered in the following chapter.

Methods and applications

Theoretical orientations of cultural criminology are closely interconnected with its methods of research. Theoretical focus is on the meaning of crime, as it is constructed in particular situations, emotions and experiences, and the role of mediated representation and symbolism in shaping perceptions of crime and criminals. Methods are thus required which allow researchers to get inside particular criminal situations and experiences and which can enable them to comprehend emotion, meaning and symbolism. There is also a need for methods which can penetrate the dynamics of the mass media and grasp something of the loops and spirals which entangle crime and its image.

Cultural criminologists thus regularly adopt alternative methods of research to those of conventional criminology. Thus, survey research and the statistical analysis of results, for example, the most widely used methods in conventional criminology, preclude by their very design any deep engagement with meaning, emotion and the social processes by which these are generated. Such methods force the complexities of human experience and emotion into simplistic choices prearranged by the researcher and so reduce research participants to carefully controlled categories of counting and cross-tabulation. They remove the researcher from the people and situations which are to be studied, creating a sort of abstract, long-distance research that excludes those essential dynamics of crime and justice – ambiguity, surprise, anger – from the process of criminological research (Kane, 2004). Moreover, cultural criminologists argue, that such conventional methods are invariably used precisely because they produce safe findings and abstract statistics in the service of political agencies or criminal justice organizations, thereby forfeiting the critical, independent scholarship which cultural criminologists see as necessary for good criminological research and analysis. Cultural criminologists thus often use ethnography: long-term, in-depth field research with the people to be studied.

Cultural criminologists who are deeply immersed in the lives of criminals, crime victims or police officers can become part of the process by which such people create meaning and can witness the ways in which they make sense of their experiences through symbolic codes and shared language. Sharing with them their situations and experiences, while sensitive to their tragedies and triumphs, cultural criminologists can also learn something of the emotions which course through their research subjects of experiences of crime, victimization and criminal justice.

A similar difference can be seen in the cultural criminology study of the mass media that we consider later in this chapter. Conventional criminologists most often study media and crime by using content analysis, measuring static content categories within media texts. Cultural criminologists, in contrast, argue that the fluid interplay between media, crime and the criminal justice process cannot be captured in quantitative summaries of textual word frequency or source type. Numeric summaries of discrete textual categories miss the larger aesthetic within which a text takes shape and ignore the structural frames which shape the flow of meaning within a text. Furthermore, content analysis is invariably used with the intention of objectively proving the degree of divergence between the 'real' nature of a crime issue and a 'biased' media representation of it. Yet, it is observed, this approach misses the more complex dynamic of media loops and spirals and the multiplicity of audiences and interpretations that will confound the real and the representational as a crime issue runs its course.

In place of traditional content analysis, cultural criminologists use two alternative methods. The first is David Altheide's (1987) method of ethnographic content analysis, an approach which conceptualizes such analysis as a search for meaning and a process of intellectual give-and-take between researcher and research participant. It is a method designed to produce deep involvement with the text, such that the researcher develops a profound understanding of the text and its meanings. It is also designed to approach the media text not as a single entity but as an emergent cultural process incorporating various media, political and cultural dynamics. Like conventional content analysis, this method allows researchers to identify and analyze textual patterns, but it also draws out the fluid, looping media that increasingly define crime and justice. The second alternative approach goes a step further and in fact returns us to ethnography: fieldwork with criminals, criminal justice workers or others as they go about interacting with the mass media, developing images of their own lives or even inventing their own alternative media (Snyder, 2002).

Cultural criminologists have investigated the dynamics of symbolism, meaning and representation, amid a variety of criminal and criminal justice situations. Much renowned cultural criminological work has used ethnographic methods to explore illicit subcultures and their interactions with legal authorities and the media. This close attention to particular subcultural dynamics has allowed researchers to confront media and criminal justice stereotypes of these subcultures. Ferrell (1996), for example, conducted long-term participatory ethnographies of three urban subcultures: (1) hip-hop graffiti writers, (2) street-level political activists and (3) trash scroungers. In each case, his findings served to humanize the members of the subcultures, to reveal the ways in which they engage in meaningful collective action and to challenge the validity of aggressive criminal justice campaigns against them. Alternatively, Mark Hamm's (1997, 2002) long-term ethnographic research among various subcultures associated with extremist, right-wing terrorism has revealed hidden dimensions of their strategies and ideologies and so has helped strengthen legal efforts to contain them. Thus, from the perspective of the cultural criminologists, a deep understanding of the values and practices of a subculture can help shape more appropriate public and legal responses to them, whether those responses eventually become more tolerant or more condemnatory. In a similar fashion, other researchers have used cultural criminological perspectives in the in-depth ethnographic study of illegal street racers, youthful brawlers, police officers, immigrant communities, drug users and youth gangs.

As Ferrell's three ethnographies of urban subcultures suggest, cultural criminological models have been found to be especially applicable to the swirl of subcultures, images and interactions that animate urban life and criminality. Keith Hayward (2004a), in particular, has developed a comprehensive cultural criminological analysis of urban crime and urban social control in the context of consumer culture. Drawing on and revitalizing long-standing traditions in criminological theory and urban scholarship, Hayward has revealed the many ways in which consumer culture has come to penetrate urban life and urban spaces, intertwining with the practice of both legal control and crime and in many ways defining the city itself. With the cultural criminologist's eye for situated meaning and symbolic interaction, he has also documented the existence of two different sorts of city life, within large urban areas: on one hand, the regulated, rationalized city of urban planners and legal authorities and, on the other hand, the ambiguous, spontaneous city of underground economies and illicit urban subcultures.

A variety of cultural criminological studies have explored the interplay of crime, media and representation. Many of these studies have investigated the complex dynamics by which the mass media construct a particular crime concern or criminal justice issue and the ways in which these media dynamics, in turn, intertwine with public perceptions and criminal justice policy. In this way, cultural criminologists have studied, for example, mass media campaigns surrounding 'three strikes and you're out' sentencing policy and reform-minded 'get smart on crime' movements, and they have analyzed media representations of child sexual abuse, regional drug use, female criminals and popular music controversies. Cultural criminological perspectives have also been applied to a wide range of popular media forms, including heavy metal music, bluegrass music, cartoons and comic books, television shows (e.g. *CSI* [*Crime Scene Investigation*]) and films on prisons and policing. As suggested by the theory of media loops and spirals, however, cultural criminologists have also explored media and representation outside the conventional boundaries of the mass media, focusing especially on the ways in which mediated representation, crime and criminal subcultures are increasingly interwoven. Cultural criminologists have, for example, carefully studied the symbolism of the shrines constructed in memory of the 11 September 2001, attacks on the US and the symbolic reminders offered by roadside shrines to victims of motor accidents. They have also documented the ways in which graffiti, corporate advertising and political messages are confused within shared urban spaces and the ways in which criminal subcultures are increasingly defined by their ability to invent their own media and so to communicate beyond any one locality. We next consider the analogous methodological approach of psychosocial criminology.

Psychosocial criminology

Psychosocial criminology is a relatively niche field within criminology, but in the social sciences, in general, there has been an eruption of interest in such studies as a field of inquiry which cuts across the disciplines of sociology, social work, psychology, education, counselling and forensic psychotherapy. Central to this approach is the premise that psychological phenomenon (personalities, emotions, dispositions) and sociological phenomenon (class, gender, ethnicity, inequality, strain, poverty) are not as separate as usually thought. Psychosocial scholars thus seek to transcend the existing disciplinary formations of the psychological and social sciences and develop modes of thinking and acting capable of recognizing that both social issues and problems have psychological dimensions which always need to be addressed.

At the heart of psychosocial studies is a recognition that people are irreducible to group identities and this identification enables us to observe a capacity for human agency regardless of the circumstances of the individual. This is an important insight for criminology, the subject matter of which is more often than not the multiple forms of human suffering inflicted on and by some of the most disadvantaged. It is, nevertheless, an insight many criminologists are reluctant to exploit, probably because it involves speculating about elements of human subjectivity which cannot be verified through conventional social scientific methods. Alternative methods are thus required which enable to come to terms with the complexities of lived experience and the social damage inflicted on the least powerful in neoliberal society. It is thus necessary to address both the inner worlds of psychic suffering and the outer worlds of social structural oppression as epitomized by the perpetration of domestic and sexual violence, the fear of crime, reactions to sex offenders, racist crime, as well as homophobic hate crimes. Central to all of this work is a commitment to redressing the central criminological challenge of explaining crime and reactions to it in ways which neither shirk responsibility for coming to terms with the most monstrous manifestations of human behaviour or neglect the mundane, commonplace and essential normal nature of much crime and deviance (Gadd and Jefferson, 2007).

In seeking to overcome the 'expert' discourses of conventional criminology, psychosocial criminologists have concerned themselves with showing how apparently commonplace social and psychological reactions, reinforced by everyday social discourses and interactions, can in very specific circumstances lead to extreme or apparently sense-less behaviours becoming comprehensible. The collation and production of complex qualitative data about offenders, and offending has thus been critical to this work which is clearly compatible with generic cultural studies.

Whether trying to make sense of high-profile cases or attempting to understand the behaviour of little-known offenders, psychosocial analyses usually involve the assembling of a textual portrait of the people or community being studied. It is a portrait which enables a complex view of the subject to be grasped and one which seeks to hold onto apparently contradictory data, whether that be two conflicting accounts of the same event or attitudes that do not square logically with each other. The reason why psychosocial criminologists refuse to let go of contradictions in the data – or aggregate them away in favour of discovering some kind of norm, trait or propensity – has much to do with how they regard typicality.

Typicality is regarded as problematic from the psychosocial perspective, as it is proposed that one should not assume that people from any particular demographic group are likely to think and feel the same. Rather, it is only in understanding the particularity of any single case – whether typical or exceptional – that it is possible to extract conceptual lessons (Gadd and Jefferson, 2007; Hollway and Jefferson, 2013).

Sometimes, as in the case of high-profile offenders or widely publicized crimes, it is possible to assemble such complexity from secondary sources, including academic ones (Jefferson, 1997; Gadd, 2012). But when it is not possible, psychosocial criminologists have turned to qualitative methods, especially in-depth interview data, to produce them. Although not the only method used by psychosocial scholars, attempts by Hollway and Jefferson (2013) to do qualitative research differently through the development of an inter-view method geared to eliciting 'free associations' from participants has had a profound impact on the wider field. In terms of its core principles in the gathering of interview data, the method packaged together a set of techniques which were commonly used in oral history and biographical research, although these were not necessarily explained in pragmatic ways for English-speaking audiences. These included (a) the importance of ask-ing questions which invited storytelling, (b) the avoidance of 'why' questions that might encourage over-rationalization, (c) careful adherence to the utilization of the interviewee's words and meaning frame in the construction of questions and (d) minimalist facilitation.

The free association interview method is based on the premise that the meanings on which the prompted narratives of interviewees are founded are best accessed via links based on spontaneous association, rather than whatever consistency can be found in the account. This is a radically different conception of meaning because as Hollway and Jef-ferson (2013: 140) observe that

> free associations follow an emotional rather than a cognitively derived logic. . . . It gives priority to the meanings inherent in the links, rather than the meanings con-tained within statements. In the interstices, we believe, is revealed a subject beyond the unitary, rational subject of most social science.

It is in the theorization of emotionally charged links and interstices that the approach has invited the most controversy. One central question is whether researchers can ever access the worlds of others without recourse to well-rehearsed discourses, including the psy-choanalytic (Wetherell, 2005). The psychosocial approach assumes that one can and that a psychoanalytic interpretive perspective provides a means of sensitizing oneself, in mind and body, to the lived and not always speakable experiences of another (Hollway, 2011).

Hollway (2006) thus sought to capture the relational dynamics involved in the parenting of small children through a form of 'scenic understanding' which, like a piece of theatre or film, requires a form of academic engagement which is more holistic, closer to tacit, unconscious knowing, and capable of accessing societal-cultural unconscious' than might otherwise be expected. 'Scenic understanding' – like engaging with any good drama – involves being able, at least sometimes, to tolerate the 'absence of a consistent story' or a 'muddle', by 'using imagination' and 'arousing curiosity' (Balint, 1993: 11). Such an approach, of course, brings with it the danger of over-interpretation – or seeing connections that cannot be demonstrated empirically – and may have their origins as much in the mind of the researcher than in the mind of the research subject (Wengraf, 2001). But, we should observe that this danger is inherent in all social scientific methods and not exclusive to the psychosocial approach (Garfield et al., 2010).

First, the concept of *discourse* is central to the psychosocial approach but not in the conventional sense, which assumes that people are disciplined absolutely by its configuration of power and knowledge. Someone who has committed a racist crime, for example, might depict themselves as 'able to get along with everyone as long as they don't interfere', as well as being 'tolerant of other faiths', but nonetheless 'worried about unrestricted immigration' (Gadd and Dixon, 2011). Such depictions can involve the individual actively positioning themselves through a number of competing discourses – 'the laid-back individual', 'the multiculturally sensitive' and the 'economically rational and reasonable' man – that sometimes fit well together but can also fall into tension, for example when an immigrant is seen to be staking a claim that restricts the choices available to the individual. Identifying how offenders construct themselves discursively is thus a critical methodological task. In understanding violence, noticing what these discourses achieve in relation to the construction and attribution of vulnerability and invulnerability is often critical.

Second, in part, because of these different discursive positionings, psychosocial criminologists question the idea that people are only rational conscious beings whose thoughts all hang together in a unitary and uncomplicated way. Instead, they note that most people espouse attitudes which are at least a little contradictory. People tend also to hold quite contradictory feelings in their minds and bodies. This is obvious when people feel both love and hate for a particular individual on whom they are dependent, but it is common in all kinds of relationships, not just romantic ones. It happens in our work lives, schools, politics and local communities. All places where hateful attacks are mounted. Psychosocial criminologists take the psychoanalytic view that such contradictions are commonly managed using unconscious defence mechanisms which protect the individual from feelings of vulnerability. This can mean burying certain feelings – like shame, disgust and guilt as best we can – while running the risk that they will sometimes resurface in ways that are not always strictly controllable – that is slips of the tongue and sudden outbursts, as well as dreams. They can also be managed through psychic splitting and projection, processes whereby unwanted feelings are attributed to others where they can be attacked. This might be the case, for example, in a homophobic attack where someone who feels insecure about their heterosexuality will attack someone else for their perceived effeminacy, or when someone who is worried about their reputation for being unemployable attacks immigrants or disabled people for 'stealing our benefits' as if they are the 'real' problem. For this reason, psychosocial criminologists have to address the emotional work discursive investments achieve.

Third, there is the issue of identification: not only the identifications that the participant has of significant others which they reveal in their story but also the identification between the researcher and the researched, and particularly the extent to which the former feels moved, troubled, endeared, or repulsed by what is revealed by the latter. For the researcher-turned-analyst, this is liable to shift during and after the research as they become more acutely aware of the discursive and emotional linkages represented explicitly and latently in interview transcripts. This can require the researcher to confront some of their own defences, a process which is all the more difficult when the safeguard of anonymity is foregone, as it has to be in academic publishing, but one that can be facilitated through sharing parts of the analyses with colleagues and co-authors willing and able to provide critical comment.

Deviant leisure

Smith and Raymen (2016a) – heavily influenced by the neo-historical materialist inspired ultra-realist perspective we encounter in more depth in Chapter 19 – note that early work by cultural criminologists claims that deviant forms of leisure arise as a result of the timeless natural desire to seek thrills, pleasure and excitement. They recognize that it is a view that is pervasive across disciplines, forming part of a liberal orthodoxy, which tends to promote individual agency and a naturalist view of resistance to authority in narratives of harm. In this sense, the choice to seek thrills and excitement in a way which supposedly challenges authority is often celebrated and seen as politically inspired. Yet, elsewhere, the disapproval prompted by visible forms of violence and illegality detract from the more pertinent source of the violence and disorder and ignores the necessity to locate harm within the social structures of the fragmentation of modernity or postmodern condition. Continuation with the orthodox analysis of leisure and deviance simply serves to confuse the range of harms which, it is observed, occur as a direct or indirect result of commodified forms of leisure and their attendant cultural supply chains.

Smith and Raymen (2016b) not only acknowledge the highly significant role of morality in deciding what should be classified as harm but also take the view that ethical principles are the manipulated product of social structures and systems. It is thus the competitive individualism at the centre of the economic exchange mechanisms of consumer capitalism which is the driving impetus behind the willingness of individuals to inflict primary or secondary harms on others. Moral judgments are superseded by the *special liberty* which is synonymous with success in the hypercompetitive individualized environs of the current social order (Hall, 2012).

Thus, in contemporary neoliberal society, harms are embedded in culturally acceptable, value-normative behaviours, bound inextricably to the 'cultural injunction to enjoy' (Žižek, 2018). Not only are these harms often experienced as hidden, systemic forms of violence but in many cases are also largely preventable. In short, *prosocial* forms of leisure are possible but lie beyond a *hedonic realism*, the inability to see beyond the horizon of a social order where leisure identity is synonymous with the hyper-competitive and individualized arena of consumer capitalism. Smith and Raymen (2016a) produce a fourfold typology of deviant leisures and use the identified harm associated with various commodified leisure practices as their rationale.

First, *subjective harms* involve an easily identifiable perpetrator inflicting hurt on a clearly identifiable victim, in action related to a clearly defined leisure activity. A prime example is the commission of violence within the alcohol-based nighttime economy, an economy which has become synonymous with rising levels of interpersonal violence, which is often portrayed within the mainstream literature and media as the pathological behaviour of a minority of working-class men whose actions taint an otherwise unproblematic site of creativity and identity gain. The reality is that the nighttime economy is responsible for more than a million hospital visits a year (a somewhat conservative figure which is likely to underestimate the reality of the number of assaults). In addition, there are significant numbers of assaults on ambulance and emergency room staff who should also be considered victims of alcohol-based violence. Outside of these clearly subjective forms of violence are swathes of objective forms of violence, systemic and symbolic violence meted out against other consumers, bar workers, takeaway workers, taxi drivers and other peripheral victims of deviant leisure.

The marketized environment of the nighttime economy is key to creating an arena of sorts for violent encounters, as well as the creation and maintenance of leisure-based identity. It is characterized by a near-universal adherence to intoxication and the suspension of the moral regulation and behavioural norms of the daytime. Yet, it is this problematic and harmful form of determined drinking which is the most valuable from the perspective of the alcohol industry, accounting for 60% of its profits. These harms can be outward-facing as discussed earlier or can turn inwards on the participant, such as those involving poly-drug use, and other forms of risky or dangerous activities. In these instances of subjective harm, leisure behaviours incorporate an element of risk-taking that is barely managed and appears to be undertaken not without knowledge of danger but regardless of it.

Second, *environmental harms* are inflicted on the ecosystem as a result of non-criminal activities, alongside criminal and harmful behaviours which emanate from interaction with the global economy. A deviant leisure perspective not only interrogates the harms which result from engaging with leisure cultures but also explores the role of consumerism in the creation of individual desire and the cultivation of competitive individualism. Smith and Raymen (2016a) offer the example of the Maldives, an island chain of 26 atolls in the Indian Ocean. It is the lowest country in the world and probably the most vulnerable to the threat of sea-level change. Yet it also faces a multifaceted danger through the popularity of leisure and its desirability as a honeymoon or status destination. But this economic value comes at a cost, with waste disposal providing a specific challenge. It is observed that the most symbolic deviant leisure harm is the creation of the Thilafishu waste treatment and disposal site, which, in essence, amounts to the sacrifice of an island atoll and lagoon for the disposal and treatment of waste. The classic liberal defence of the tourist industry might rely on pointing to employment created by the tourist industry, in reality very few well-remunerated jobs go to indigenous islanders, with 42% of the population earning around US$1.50 per day (Scheyvens, 2011), while, at the same time, money leaks out of the country due to high levels of foreign ownership and a high proportion of expatriate employment consisting of 53% of the workforce (Shakeela *et al.*, 2011).

Smith and Raymen (2016a) observe that the challenges faced by the Maldives are not the product of tourism in an abstract sense but are synonymous with the commodification of a whole range of symbolism which is closely related to consumer culture. The ubiquitous image which adorns specialist honeymoon magazines – again an indication of the importance and reach of the honeymoon tourism industry – is of miles of white sands, empty but for the carefree linen-suited groom and his sarong-wearing new bride. However, the pristine beauty of the magazine is not as natural as we might suppose. Rather, the islands have been sanitized, depilated, shaved and plucked to the detriment of local ecosystems.

Third, *socially corrosive* leisure forms are those that contribute to the erosion of our shared social life. Baudrillard (1998) acknowledged the 'end of the social' with the dawn of neoliberalism, positioning consumer-citizens as increasingly atomized, cynical and disinterested in the possibility of collective interests. The social is constructed through a coherent and comprehensive socio-symbolic order, based on shared meanings and codes, which in their absence result in anxiety, unhappiness and despair, a constant state of emotional and existential precarity that can be temporarily assuaged by engagement in consumer markets.

Smith and Raymen (2016a) thus observe that a deviant leisure perspective examines the potential for leisure to cut individuals adrift from the social; contribute to the further erosion of social institutions such as family, class and community; and exacerbate the fragmented and individualized nature of the social in neoliberal societies. There are many forms of leisure which would fall into this category, but one example might be the creation of artificial scarcity, the privation of that which would otherwise be plentiful and free to the public. The creation of 'club goods' has the potential to create demarcated leisure zones of wealth and cultural capital. The example offered is that of Donald Trump's seizure of an enormous stretch of the Aberdeenshire coastline for the creation of a 'world-best' US$1.5-billion luxury golf course, club and hotel. Aided by a legal system which persistently protects the interest of private property, these leisure spaces create cultures of fragmentation. Notwithstanding the environmental damage done to local dune ecosystems, within such spaces of cultural exclusivity, the golf course and other similar country clubs become a no-go zone for those lacking the requisite social, cultural and financial capital.

Of course, Trump, in his role as a neoliberal 'undertaker' (Hall, 2012), has argued that he is simply doing what has to be done in order to revitalize the economy of the region, providing jobs and attracting tourism, despite vocal opposition. Despite promises of 6,000 jobs, only 200 jobs were actually created, while residents experienced interrupted water supply for several years. Exemplifying 'special liberty', Trump has transcended the ethical codes of the symbolic order to achieve his aims, irrespective of the effect it has on people.

Fourth, *embedded harm* leisure cultures are notable for becoming successfully entrenched within legitimate consumer markets and while imbued with potential for the creation of malleable identities based on the notion of cool, are deserving of closer criminological scrutiny. Perhaps the most illustrative example is the ubiquitous gambling industry, which has become legitimized and normalized through becoming embedded within other forms of leisure such as the consumption of professional sport, online social networks and the nighttime economy. With an increasing array of gambling opportunities, quite literally at our fingertips, it is likely that 'social' gambling, fiercely defended by the gambling industry as non-problematic, masks a range of damaging social and individual effects.

Once subject to wide-ranging state control, gambling has become increasingly embedded within the nighttime economy, sports fandom, and online forums of socialization. Perhaps nowhere is the legitimized democratization of betting and gambling more visible than in the explosion of sports-betting, specifically around football. It is impossible to watch any sports channel without being bombarded by targeted advertising of innumerable high-street and online bookmakers which visually situate the act of gambling within a wider weekend leisure experience of friends, football and beer at the pub or at home with friends. These individuals experience participation in organized gambling as integral to broader circuits of leisure, consumption and identity as gambling becomes imbued with more than the simple outcome of winning or losing.

An identity-based culture of sports betting combined with relentless promises of 'easy wins' encourages the chasing of losses and impulsive bets. In this way the cost of an afternoon watching football spirals, costs that can loop into other areas of life. In the face of financial losses, becoming trapped in the unforgiving and high-interest cycle of payday loans to cover gambling losses or even afford more simple domestic outgoings becomes a real possibility. The combination of the accumulation of social capital allied to the allure of the gambling win, underscored by readily available credit, has the potential to cast these young people into a new culture of indebtedness. The peaks and troughs of winning and losing, against the background of the 'objectless' anxiety of neoliberalism, perpetuates a leisure culture which, while culturally normalized, is characterized by the harms of stress, financial uncertainty, emotional volatility, depression and anxiety.

Cultural criminology and the mass media

Greg Barak (2012) notes that, when it comes to actual media coverage and/or representation of crime, there have been essentially two kinds: first, the more frequent inclusion of some type of felony or street crime, often involving an act of violence and, second, the less common insertion of white-collar offences, involving some type of public or private trust violation which usually concentrates its focus on individuals and their victims, not on societal institutions or social organizations and their victims. Not surprisingly, these mediated relations of delivering and receiving crime and justice 'information' are also reflected in the limited scholarly research, academic analysis and critical literature on media and crime. Thus, most of the documented work on the social construction of mediated crime and crime control has been restricted to the entertainment and news media spheres. There has also been relatively little research when it comes to the online sphere.

Barak (2012) cites the example of one barely explored, underdeveloped and potentially profitable area of research, which involves the emergence of what some have labelled pro-abuse cyberspace male peer support groups associated with certain types of shared pornography (DeKeseredy and Olsson, 2011; Kendall, 2003). While no causal relations have been established between viewing these types of pornography and engaging in abusive sexual behaviour with women, some researchers have speculated about an increasing number of men who are sharing and consuming derogatory, denigrating, racist and sexist pornographic materials online as 'part of a broader subculture of sexual deviance that legitimizes various forms of deviant sexuality' (Stack et al., 2004: 85).

Media, society and criminology

Throughout history the media has always shown a considerable interest in crime, criminals, punishment and justice. Print, sound, visual and the new online media alike have always depended on responsive audiences or 'ratings'. Through the processes of mass communication, these popular media have also made significant contributions – for better or worse – to the social construction of crime and justice. The media have also inconsistently mystified and demystified crime and justice while in reflecting the status quo – as well as in its capacity to lead, follow or resist social change – have not only facilitated the targeting of certain offenders, such as drug users, sex offenders, the poor or immigrants, but they have also omitted or treated lightly other offenders, such as the habitually law-violating corporations, or those city bankers, insurers and stockbrokers who have engaged in derivative Ponzi schemes[1] and subprime mortgaging,[2] or private security contractors who have thieved, raped and killed. The former category is typically portrayed as dangerous offenders who threaten the well-being of otherwise lawful societies, while the latter group are less frequently scrutinized. They are simply presented as anomalies, exceptions or glitches in the normative order, with these offenders and their offences not taken seriously or not considered real crime without any thought given to the systemic negative consequences for society (Barak, 1994; Potter and Kappeler, 1998; Bohm and Walker, 2006; Surette, 2007; Marsh and Melville, 2009; Stevens, 2010).

The radical criminological concept of 'moral panic' has greatly influenced the study of social problems, crime, media and collective behaviour. Barak (2012) nevertheless observes that, while intense, media-fuelled bursts of collective concern have typically distorted the danger or threat posed by targeted 'outsider' groups, with public outrage directed against those particular 'others' successfully labelled or identified by various 'moral entrepreneurs' (Becker, 1963) via the mass media as evil, the extent to which the new media has impacted or influenced the contemporary formation of postmodern folk devils and moral panics is unknown.

News representation and the social construction of crime

Barak (2012) argues that understanding news representation and the social construction of news-making requires an examination of the conscious and unconscious processes involved in the mass dissemination of symbolic consumer goods. These commodities of news production and the images of social reality that they invoke cannot be separated from their cultural histories. Moreover, mediated characterizations of crime and criminal justice, of criminals and social control, projected in news presentations are representations themselves of culturally shared visions, accessed through commonly unfolding historical narratives, in which average people and most journalists come to know crime and justice in developed societies. In other words, crime and justice stories produced by news media for mass consumption reflect and reveal much about the views those societies have of themselves.

These 'crime news' stories are not objective or value-neutral. All theoretical perspectives agree that, although crime and justice representations are highly selective and unrepresentative of their subject matter, they are, however, essential for disentangling the relationships between crime, control, justice and social order. These news stories thus respectively reproduce moral boundaries, legitimate law and order, and reinforce gender stereotypes, all of which helps to reify unequal power relations as well as inequality throughout society. Nevertheless, within and without the news business, there are also all kinds of sources and values which shape the processes of news-making, in general, and news-making criminology, in particular. Herbert Gans conducted a classic study of the national news in the US and observed that 'news is about the economic, political, social, and cultural hierarchies' with reporting focusing 'on those at or near the top of the hierarchies and on those, particularly at the bottom, who threaten them, to an audience, most of whom are located in the vast middle range between top and bottom' (1980: 284). News stories are divided into two categories: first, those stories about 'disorder' which report threats to all kinds of order as well as the measures taken to restore it and, second, those about 'routine activities' which are normative and usually pose no direct threats. Despite their differences, both categories help reproduce the dominant social order.

Gans (1980) noted that mediated crime and justice tends to focus its reporting primarily on external activities which threaten public peace and private security, typically those stories involving physical violence to persons and/or property (social disorder) and, secondarily, on reported transgressions of laws and mores which do not necessarily endanger the social order, such as many of the activities associated with 'victimless criminality' (moral disorder). The fundamental distinction between these types of disorder stories is the value of intentionality or culpability which can be attached to those who may be violating the social or moral orders.

Steve Chibnall (1977) and, more recently, Yvonne Jewkes (2004) have mapped out the news values which not only shape the reporting of crime but which also help locate these within the larger practices of journalism. For Chibnall, these values include immediacy, dramatization, personalization, simplification, titillation, conventionalism, structured access and novelty. Jewkes expands on this list and includes threshold, predictability, individualism, risk, sex, celebrity, proximity, violence, spectacle, graphic imagery and children. These journalistic values that increasingly rely over time on visual imagery – with respect to film/video and print – have also served as a primary device for defining normative and deviant behaviour, identity and reality. Moreover, they often make it difficult, if not impossible, to clearly distinguish between the perception, reaction and production of crime and justice. In the process of news crime construction, crime and crime control represents order, which 'provides people with preferred versions and visions of social order, on the basis of which they take action' (Ericson et al., 1991: 239).

At the end of the news-making day, the mediated construction of crime and justice becomes the socially constructed reality, when, in fact, this is the socially constructed subjective reality. Surette (2007) identifies four stages in the social construction of crime and five contemporary crime and justice frames which provide fully developed socially constructed templates, which allow claims and claim makers to succeed in making their representations of crime and justice stick to the media overload of information. Stage one consists of 'the physical world' enclosed by conditions, events and properties that establish the boundaries or background in which the other stages must frame their interactions. Stage two consists of the 'competing social constructions' or differing descriptions of the physical world of crime and justice offered up by various claim makers.

It is at stage three that the media play their most powerful role, filtering out competing constructions, typically favouring those positions which 'are dramatic, sponsored by powerful groups, and are related to pre-established cultural themes' or to the five prevailing crime and justice frames described by Sasson (1995: 13–17):

1   The 'faulty system' thematic which proposes that crime stems from criminal justice leniency and inefficiency. The proposed solution is to 'get tough' and 'tighten up'. Popular symbols used have included 'handcuffed police' and 'revolving door justice'.

2   The 'blocked opportunities' thematic argues that crime arises from poverty and inequality. The proposed solution is to address the 'root causes' of crime by creating jobs, community development and reducing poverty. Popular symbols used have included 'dead-end, low-paying jobs' and high unemployment rates.

3   The 'social breakdown' thematic argues that crime stems from family and community breakdown. The proposed solution is citizen involvement and community efficacy/policing. Popular symbols used have included 'family values' and 'take back the streets'.

4   The 'racist system' thematic proposes that the problem of crime arises from a criminal justice system which operates in a discriminatory fashion. The proposed solution is greater sensitivity to racial justice and to the empowerment of those groups discriminated against. Popular symbols used include 'profiling' and the 'differential application' of the criminal law.

5   The 'violent media' thematic proposes that crime, particularly violent crime, stems from the amount of extreme violence in the mass media. The proposed solution is more government regulation of the production and distribution of violent imagery. Popular symbols used include 'life imitating art' and 'copycat crimes'.

Stage four represents the emergence of dominant news themes or the 'winning social construction', which often drives – if not determines – criminal justice and crime control policies.

Crime, entertainment and the postmodern imagination

Barak (2012) observes that, regardless of the changing discourses in mediated crime and justice, in the fictional and nonfictional entertainment spheres of television soap operas and documentaries, respectively, the representations of 'good' and 'evil', 'non-violent' and 'violent', 'in control' and 'out of control' typically distort the images of perpetrators, victims, criminal justice and criminal punishment. In the case of criminal harm, depictions are primarily of individuals rather than of organizations or institutions. Although criminal victimization may be located at home, it is usually represented in the street and rarely viewed from the executive suite. In the process, myths and stereotypes about various types of violent 'offenders' and 'non-offenders' are projected onto large and small screens alike (Barak, 2003).

Frus observes that, when it comes to fictional accounts of gender and violence, Hollywood films 'are expert at providing [an] illusion of reality, no matter how fantastic the story, they are an important source of our mythology about family violence' (2001: 227). The portrayal of women in US cinema operates according to age-old myths, for example, wife 'batterers' are not like ordinary men, women who are abused are asking for it, beatings leave no permanent scars, women can leave their abusers and so on and so forth. In the mediums of film and literature more generally, criminal violence is often put to use through shifting mythic and ideological imperatives, in the service of constructing audience awareness and a world view sympathetic to extreme individualism and free enterprise. These themes are not so much the product of a manufactured consensus as they are the product of reflexivity, reification and reproduction, grounded in an integrating political economy and a dynamically developing collective unconscious (Barak, 2003).

Barak (2012) observes that no book or film (in this case both) has captured the dilemma of mediated criminal violence and the postmodern imagination better than *American*

Psycho, Bret Easton Ellis's twisted satire on serial murder. This best-selling novel was first published in 1991, and in 1999, it was released as a semi-successful film. Despite the movie's controversial portrayal of a high-class Wall Street wheeling-and-dealing serial killer – or perhaps because of it – the film became a cult classic as a video rental and is still shown regularly on cable television. In a strange way, the representations of graphic violence were of a serial killer gone mainstream, suggesting that, in accordance with the 'risk society' thesis, harm and dangers can come from anywhere.

Media, crime and social control

Barak (2012) observes that, despite differences, all theories of communication associate the workings of the mass media with contributing to the maintenance of social conformity, order and control. Historically, the roots of mass media involvement in social control can be traced back to the 1960s with 'the success of prosocial entertainment programs and public information campaigns' and to the 'development of a number of media-based anti-crime programs and the widespread adoption of media technology in the criminal justice field' a decade later (Surette, 2007: 171). Today, in addition to the anti-crime advertising, case processing using media technology and police surveillance systems based on the older technologies of audio- and videotaping, there is an abundance of newer media technologies 'capable of both facilitating and constraining communication, interaction, mobility, and the creation and realisation of fluid identities' (Greer, 2010: 491).

Chris Greer (2010) further observes that the digitized, computerized and networked information and communication technologies exemplified by the Internet have created virtual worlds with their own changing norms, values and codes of practice, altering the ways in which 'people engage and interact in time and space', giving 'new meaning to what it is to be "social"' (2010: 491). These technological transformations have created new opportunities and risks for crime and victimization, and for surveillance and crime control. For example CCTV, information gathering, and data processing have transformed how people perceive and negotiate their social worlds with caution and reserve, aware that 'cybercrime' is all about. At the same time, while the news media, law enforcement and external observers have raised concerns over the rise of 'Big Brother' and '1984', the public has tended to resign itself to a lack of privacy and to the installation of surveillance cameras in public places to prevent crime (Surette, 2007).

In this, the third decade of the twenty-first century, the mass media can be used to influence the attitudes people have about crime and criminal justice, for better or worse. The popular media can be used to provide the police with more crime-related information. Media technology has also become a staple used to speed the processing of criminal cases and to videotape police patrols, vehicle stops and subsequent interrogations. It can be useful in the investigation, surveillance and deterrence of crime and in the prevention of victimization by intercepting, for example, potential terrorist bombers foiled by Transportation Security Administration full-body video scanners when trying to pass through airport security. In these applications of media technology to crime and social control, the question typically asked by enquiring minds is: what are the costs or benefits to the public?

Barak (2012) observes that, while programmes designed to increase public cooperation by advertising crime have proved effective in gathering information and in solving some crimes, the overall effect on crime is not significant. Media programmes that teach the public about crime prevention techniques are quite popular. They also increase public knowledge and change attitudes about crime prevention but not actual crime prevention behaviour. Similarly, while surveillance programmes do show deterrence effects, their ability to do so without displacement remains unproved. Surette (2007) is ambivalent, at best acknowledging that media technologies can enhance the administration of justice, but his concern is that the message conveyed by the news media, in conjunction with the entertainment message that crime is caused by individuals, is that the resolution of crime becomes overly dependent on technological rather than social interventions.

Mediatized crime and crime control – direct and indirect effects

Barak (2012) considers whether mass communication (text and visual) can be used to stop war, abolish the death penalty, cultivate genocide, reduce ethno-political conflict or mediatize peace and non-violence. He acknowledges that is not the typical set of questions pondered by most people trying to understand the impact of mass media on non-conforming – or conforming – behaviour. Yet, he observes that in 1997, the Nobel Peace Prize was awarded to the International Campaign to Ban Landmines, recognizing the power of the internet to mobilize and enlist worldwide support. It had all begun a few years earlier when Jody Williams, from Putney, Vermont, used her email account to coordinate the activities of more than 700 organizations from over 60 countries. Direct effect? Indirect effect? What about the ultimate cases of ethnic cleansing and the extraordinary crime of genocide or the denial of it by millions of people? Direct effect? Indirect effect? No effect? Contradictory effect? (Barak, 2012).

In terms of genocidal murder or rape, for example, or more generally in the context of collective and/or organizational violence (or non-violence), the causes of ethnic conflicts (or peace) involve 'structural factors', including economic, social and political dimensions relating to both the distribution of wealth and inter-ethnic relations, 'facilitating factors', such as the degree of politicization and ethnic consciousness, and 'triggering factors' including sharp economic shocks, intergroup tensions and collapsed central authority. In the genocidal cases of Nazi Germany, the former Yugoslavia and Rwanda, while the ethnic and national media could not be blamed directly for the creation of ethno-political conflicts, the media and mediation played an important role in negotiation across all three causal spheres, especially in shaping evil 'Others', messages of hatred and the need for extermination (Costy and Gilbert, 1998).

Barak (2012) observes that, since the inception of mass mediatized words and images, concerns have been selectively raised over the real and imagined impact of deviant or taboo behaviours, especially as these have been associated with graphic or explicit depictions of sex, interpersonal violence and other 'morally' transgressive behaviours involved in both crime and crime control. The issue has always been whether the various mass media and mediatized representations of these behaviours elicit fear or imitation from their audiences. Thus, whether there is a direct effect, an indirect effect, no effect or perhaps all three. Barak observes that, despite an abundance of research studies both in the laboratory and in the field examining the effects of televised violence, sexual and non-sexual, on aggressive and non-aggressive behaviour, which tend to support the third possibility of both mixed and contradictory effects at the same time, most, if not all, of these studies are subject to a number of criticisms regarding the validity and appropriateness of the theories and methods and, in many instances, the moral politics that have traditionally underpinned the direct-effects model of mediated research.

Importantly, media studies of violence and aggression of a sexual or non-sexual nature have been able to differentiate among media consumers. Moreover, these studies have also been able to examine the indirect effects of media in relation to the reciprocal roles of other contributing factors. In arguing for an 'indirect-effects' model of hypothesized environmental influences on the development of antisocial behaviour against women, Neil Malamuth summarized the work that he and his colleagues had conducted on sexually violent media, thought patterns and antisocial behaviour as 'no influence works in a vacuum, and media influences are viewed as combining and interacting with a variety of other individual and cultural factors – sometimes counteracting them, sometimes reinforcing them, and at other times, not having much of any effect' (1989: 162).

Barak (2012) observes that, as the indirect-effects model of mediatized sexual violence simply emphasizes the direct-effects model of crime and crime control, it is too simplistic for serious consideration. On the other hand, the indirect-effects model of mass media effects leaves the door wide open for exploring the reciprocal relations between media and crime and proposes this as a useful future research agenda.

The future of cultural criminology

Among the recent trends in cultural criminology are those seeking to expand the substantive range of cultural criminological analysis, especially in the direction of greater diversity and inclusivity. Originally, for example, the cultural criminological concept of 'edgework' developed from the experiences and ethnographic research of male scholars involved predominantly masculine forms of illicit risk-taking. Now the concept is increasingly being explored in the context of the lives of women, with a focus on the distinctive ways in which women experience and make sense of high-risk activities. Recent research by female and male researchers has investigated women who lead BASE jumping underground, women who are members of search-and-rescue teams or whitewater-rafting expeditions and even women who hone their skills so as to push the dangerous, outer boundaries of anorexia and bulimia. Similarly, cultural criminology has expanded worldwide from its origins in the US and the UK. Cultural criminologists are now studying, for example, illegal street racing in Finland, immigration cultures and criminal law in the Netherlands, violence against Filipino women in Australia, crime discourse in Japan, the culture of Russian prisons and the international affiliations of urban street gangs.

Cultural criminologists are also developing new methodologies designed to mirror particular theoretical orientations and to resonate with the specific nature of contemporary social and cultural life. For example ethnographic research and the quest for criminological verstehen have traditionally been defined by the long-term participation of the researcher with the individuals being studied, on the assumption that the more time the former spends inside a group or situation, the more deeply he or she can understand its cultural dynamics. Although this can certainly still be the case, the rapid-fire pace of contemporary crime and culture – as embodied in virtual crime and communications, instant news and entertainment, and short-term employment – have suggested to cultural criminologists new possibilities for ethnographic research.

Consequently, cultural criminologists have developed the notion of instant ethnography (Ferrell et al., 2008) – the immediate and deep immersion in fleeting moments of criminality or transgression – and have begun to use this method in studying BASE jumpers and other groups. The new notion of liquid ethnography has developed from a similar rethinking of the nature of research (Ferrell *et al.*, 2008). Ethnography had previously focused on a single, definable group or subculture which occupies a distinct geographical location but in the contemporary world groups and subcultures are often on the move, migrating into new locations or mixing with other entities as global economies and migration blur distinct boundaries and identities. Moreover, as we have already seen with the concept of media loops and spirals, social groups are today more and more likely to be mystified with their own image, as representations of their own entity come to shape the group itself and to flow among alternative media, the mass media, and other institutions. Liquid ethnography is thus a type of ethnography attuned to these circumstances, that is a form sensitive to the dynamics of transitory communities, immersed in the ongoing interplay of images and aware of the ambiguous, shifting nature of contemporary social life.

Utilizing this form of research strategy, cultural criminologists are now beginning to explore, for example, the ways in which urban street gangs move beyond crime to combine political resistance, community empowerment and religious practice in their shifting collective identities. These cultural criminologists are also finding that global forces regularly intersect with local dynamics, with gangs embodying multi-ethnic identities, responding to the effects of immigration and mediated communication and forming global alliances with other groups. British cultural criminologists are now conducting liquid ethnographies with prostitutes, immigrants, asylum seekers and others who are pushed to the legal margins of the global economy, and in this research, they are using alternative media, such as art, photography, and street performance (O'Neill *et al.*, 2007). Such research allows cultural criminologists to collaborate with even the most transitory and contingent communities in defining their meaning and identity, developing the verstehen of shared emotional knowledge and working toward a holistic sense of social justice.

Appropriately enough for cultural criminology, a final trajectory focuses not so much on subject matter, theory or methodology but on representation and style. Cultural criminologists argue that issues of crime, violence and criminal justice lie at the very heart of contemporary society and its challenges. Because of this, researchers must find ways to disseminate their scholarship, contribute to public debate and so help work toward a safer and more just society. Conventional, mainstream criminology, they argue, is poorly equipped to meet this challenge: far too often, criminologists talk and write only for each other, and they do so through dry and confusing academic language, needlessly abstract concepts and impenetrable graphs and tables. The outcome is a forbidding and exclusionary style with the potential contribution of criminology to wider society lost, while at the same time, criminologists and their scholarship are often left on the sidelines of public debate and efforts at social progress.

In response to this predicament while being sensitive to issues of style and representation, cultural criminologists are increasingly experimenting with new styles of scholarship and alternative modes of communication, with the intention of making criminology more engaging for students, policymakers and the public. In place of lengthy reports, they at times issue manifestos, short, sharply written texts that can communicate succinctly key ideas and issues. Instead of relying on traditional forms of academic writing, they on occasion write short stories that embody cultural criminological themes, or craft true fiction, that is stories that blend a number of actual, existing crime issues into a narrative form that is more appealing to the reader. Responding to a world awash in media images, they also increasingly turn to the analysis of these images as visual documents, and they produce their own photographs, photographic collections, documentary films and web-sites as a way of making criminology conversant with this world (Redmon, 2005).

Cultural criminology emphasizes the essential role of symbolism, meaning, and emo-tion in shaping the complex reality of crime and its control for all involved: criminals, victims, crime control agents, politicians, the media and the public. In this way, it is designed to operate as a double challenge: to simplistic public assumptions about crime and criminal justice and to the theories and methods of mainstream criminology which exclude analysis of cultural forces. There can be no useful study of crime that is not also the study of culture.

Policy implications of cultural criminology

Keith Hayward and Jock Young (2012) respond to the frequent criticisms of cultural criminology that it has little potential for crime policy. They observe that this theo-retical perspective is in an appreciative approach which totally eschews 'correctionalism', although that does not inevitably mean to romanticize the offender, nor does it necessitate a non-intervention approach to crime. The emphasis is on the cultural meanings of the activities to those doing the crime.

Young (2011) recognizes the complete neglect of the cultural nature of crime in the current predestined actor model–dominated criminological orthodoxy in the US, in par-ticular, which invariably involves entirely inadequate attempts to measure – and some-times the collection of – toxic data. With this in mind, Hayward and Young (2012) observe that the issue becomes not whether cultural criminology is capable of providing legitimate policy interventions but rather whether much of the current funding directed at positivistic intervention is simply a waste of money.

Summary of main points

1   Cultural criminology seeks to explain crime and criminal behaviour and its control in terms of culture and has very close intellectual links with postmodern and anarchist criminology.
2   Our lives are characterized by a 'culture of control' in which we are policed at home, at work, at pleasure and in a surveillance society, where it is impossible to escape the dominant gaze (Garland, 2001).
3   Katz (1988) notes the 'seductions of crime' in which disorder is itself a 'delight' to be sought after and savoured.
4   Presdee (2000) captures this sense of the interrelationships between pleasure and pain through his notion of 'crime as carnival', where the latter is a site where the pleasure of playing at the boundaries is clearly catered for.
5   Psychosocial criminologists have concerned themselves with showing how appar-ently commonplace social and psychological reactions, reinforced by everyday social discourses and interactions, can lead to extreme or apparently senseless behaviours.
6   Methods used by psychosocial criminologists usually involve being critically attuned to what is said and produced in interaction and conversation.
7   A deviant leisure perspective examines the potential for leisure to cut individuals adrift from the social, contribute to the further erosion of social institutions such as

family, class, community and exacerbate the fragmented and individualized nature of the social in neoliberal societies.

8 Throughout history the media has always shown a massive interest in crime, criminals, punishment and justice. Print, sound, visual and the new media alike depend heavily on responsive audiences or 'ratings'.

9 Through the processes of mass communication, popular media have made significant contributions – for better and worse – to the social construction of crime and justice.

10 Cultural criminology emphasizes the essential role of symbolism, meaning and emotion in shaping the complex reality of crime and its control for all involved: criminals, victims, crime control agents, politicians, the media and the public.

Discussion questions

1 Explain the focus of cultural criminology.
2 What are the 'carnival of crime' and the 'schizophrenia of crime'?
3 What is psychosocial criminology, and what are its methods?
4 Explain the deviant leisure perspective.
5 How does the mass media present 'the crime problem'?

Suggested further reading

Ferrell and Sanders (1995), Ferrell (1998) and O'Malley and Mugford (1994) provide a good introduction to cultural criminology. Katz (1988) provides an excellent study of the seductions and pleasures of crime, Presdee (2000) the 'carnival of crime' and Hopkins Burke (2007) 'schizophrenia of crime'. Gadd and Carr (2015) provide an excellent introduction to psychosocial criminology, and likewise, Smith and Raymen (2016a) provide the essential introduction to the deviant leisure perspective. Jewkes (2004) provides an excellent introduction to the relationship between the media and crime and Barak (2012) a more recent account.

Notes

1 The Ponzi Scheme is named after Charles Ponzi, a clerk in Boston who first orchestrated such a scheme in 1919. It is a fraudulent investing scam promising high rates of return with little risk to investors and generates returns for older investors by acquiring new investors. This scam actually yields the promised returns to earlier investors, as long as there are more new investors. These schemes usually collapse on themselves when the new investments stop.

A Ponzi scheme is similar to a pyramid scheme in that both are based on using new investors' funds to pay the earlier backers. One difference between the two schemes is that the Ponzi mastermind gathers all relevant funds from new investors and then distributes them. Pyramid schemes, on the other hand, allow each investor to directly benefit depending on how many new investors are recruited. In this case, the person on the top of the pyramid does not at any point have access to all the money in the system.

2 A subprime mortgage is a type of mortgage that is normally made out to borrowers with lower credit ratings. As a result of the borrower's lowered credit rating, a conventional mortgage is not offered because the lender views the borrower as having a larger-than-average risk of defaulting on the loan. Lending institutions often charge interest on subprime mortgages at a rate that is higher than a conventional mortgage in order to compensate themselves for carrying more risk.

Borrowers with credit ratings below 600 often will be stuck with subprime mortgages and the higher interest rates that go with those mortgages. Making late bill payments or declaring personal bankruptcy could very well land borrowers in a situation in which they can only qualify for a subprime mortgage. Therefore, it is often useful for people with low credit scores to wait for a period and build up their scores before applying for mortgages to ensure they are eligible for a conventional mortgage.

References

Altheide, D. (1987) 'Ethnographic Content Analysis', *Qualitative Sociology*, 10(1): 65–77.

Balint, E. (1993) *Before I was I*. London: Free Association Books.

Barak, G. (ed.) (1994) *Media, Process, and the Social Construction of Crime: Studies in Newsmaking Criminology*. New York: Garland.

Barak, G. (2003) *Violence and Nonviolence: Pathways to Understanding*. Thousand Oaks, CA: Sage.

Barak, G. (2012) 'Media and Crime', in W. DeKeseredy and M. Dragiewicz (eds.) *Routledge Handbook of Critical Criminology*. London: Routledge.

Baudrillard, J. (1998) *Selected Writings*. Stanford, CA: Stanford University Press.

Becker, H. (1963) *Outsiders: Studies in the Sociology of Deviance*. New York: Free Press.

Bohm, R. and Walker, J. (eds.) (2006) *Demystifying Crime and Criminal Justice*. Los Angeles: Roxbury.

Chibnall, S. (1977) *Law and Order News: An Analysis of Crime Reporting in the British Press*. London: Tavistock.

Costy, A. and Gilbert, S. (1998) *Conflict Prevention and European Union: Mapping the Actors, Instruments, and Institutions*. London: International Alert.

DeKeseredy, W. and Olsson, P. (2011) 'Adult Pornography, Male Peer Support, and Violence Against Women: The Contribution from the "Dark Side" of the Internet', in M.V. Martin, M.A. Garcia-Ruiz and A. Edwards (eds.) *Technology for Facilitating Humanity and Combatting Social Deviation: Interdisciplinary Perspectives*. Hershey, PA: IGA Global.

Elias, N. (1978) *The Civilising Process, Vol. 1: The History of Manners*. Oxford: Blackwell.

Elias, N. (1982) *The Civilising Process, Vol. 2: State-Formation and Civilisation*. Oxford: Blackwell.

Ericson, R.V., Baranek, P. and Chan, J. (1991) *Representing Order: Crime, Law, and Justice in the News Media*. Toronto, ON: University of Toronto Press.

Ferrell, J. (1996) *Crimes of Style: Urban Graffiti and the Politics of Criminality*. Boston, MA: North-Eastern University.

Ferrell, J. (1998) 'Against the Law: Anarchist Criminology', *Social Anarchism*, 25: 5–23.

Ferrell, J., Hayward, K. and Young, J. (2008) *Cultural Criminology: An Invitation*. Beverly Hills, CA: Sage.

Ferrell, J. and Sanders, C.R. (eds.) (1995) *Cultural Criminology*. Boston, MA: North-Eastern University Press.

Frus, P. (2001) 'Documenting Domestic Violence in American Films', in J.D. Slocum (ed.) *Violence and American Cinema*. New York: Routledge.

Gadd, D. (2012) 'In-Depth Interviewing and Psychosocial Case Study Analysis', in D. Gadd, S. Karstedt and S.F. Messner (eds.) *The SAGE Handbook of Criminological Research Methods*. London: Sage.

Gadd, D. and Carr, M.L. (2015) 'Psychosocial Criminology: Making Sense of Senseless Violence', in J. Miller and W.R. Palacio (eds.) *Advances in Criminological Theory*. Piscataway, NJ: Taylor and Francis.

Gadd, D. and Dixon. B. (2011) *Losing the Race*. London: Karnac.

Gadd, D. and Jefferson, T. (2007) *Psychosocial Criminology*. London: Sage.

Gans, H. (1980) *Deciding What's News: A Study of CBS Evening News, NBC Nightly News, Newsweek and Time*. New York: Vintage.

Garfield, S., Reavey, P. and Kotecha, M. (2010) 'Footprints in a Toxic Landscape: Reflexivity and Validation in the Freeonx Association Narrative Analysis Method', *Qualitative Research in Psychology*, 7: 156–69.

Garland, D. (1996) 'The Limits of the Sovereign State: Strategies of Crime Control in Contemporary Society', *British Journal of Criminology*, 34(4): 445–71.

Garland, D. (2001) *The Culture of Control*. Oxford: Oxford University Press.

Goldmann, L. (1970) 'The Sociology of Literature: Status and the Problem of Methods', in M.C. Albrecht, J.H. Barnett and M. Griff (eds.) *The Sociology of Art and Literature: A Reader*. London: Duckworth.

Goldthorpe, J.H. (1968) *The Affluent Worker in the Class Structure*, 3 Vols. Cambridge: Cambridge University Press.

Greer, C. (ed.) (2010) *Crime and Media: A Reader.* London: Routledge.

Hall, S. (2012) *Theorising Crime and Deviance: A New Perspective.* London: Sage.

Hamm, M. (1997) *Apocalypse In Oklahoma: Waco and Ruby Ridge.* New York: Northeasten.

Hamm, M. (2002) 'In Bad Company: America's Terrorist Underground', *Critical Criminology*, 11(3): 265–7.

Hayward, K.J. (2004a) *City Limits: Crime, Consumer Culture and the Urban Experience.* London: Glass House Press.

Hayward, K.J. (2004b) 'Crime and Consumer Culture in Late Modernity', in C. Sumner (ed.) *The Blackwell Companion to Criminology.* Oxford: Blackwell.

Hayward, K.J. and Young, J. (2012) 'Cultural Criminology', in M. Maguire, R. Morgan and R. Reiner (eds.) *The Oxford Handbook of Criminology*, 5th ed. Oxford: Oxford University Press.

Hobbs, D., Lister, S., Hadfield, P., Winlow, S. and Hall, S. (2000) 'Receiving Shadows: Governance and Liminality in the Night-time Economy', *British Journal of Sociology*, 51(4): 701–17.

Hobbs, D., Winslow, S., Lister, S. and Hadfield, P. (2005) 'Violent Hypocrisy: Governance and the Night-Time Economy', *European Journal of Criminology*, 42(2): 352–70.

Hollway, W. (2006) *The Capacity to Care: Gender and Ethical Subjectivity: Women and Psychology.* London: Routledge.

Hollway, W. (2011) 'Psycho-Social Writing from Data', *Journal of Psycho-Social Studies*, 5(2): 92–101.

Hollway, W. and Jefferson, T. (2013) *Doing Qualitative Research Differently*, 2nd ed. London: Sage.

Hopkins Burke, R.D. (ed.) (1998) *Zero Tolerance Policing.* Leicester: Perpetuity Press.

Hopkins Burke, R.D. (2002) 'Zero Tolerance Policing: New Authoritarianism or New Liberalism?', *The Nottingham Law Journal*, 2(1): 20–35.

Hopkins Burke, R.D. (ed.) (2004a) *'Hard Cop/Soft Cop': Dilemmas and Debates in Contemporary Policing.* Cullompton: Willan Publishing.

Hopkins Burke, R.D. (2004b) 'Policing Contemporary Society', in R.D. Hopkins Burke (ed.) *'Hard Cop/Soft Cop': Dilemmas and Debates in Contemporary Policing.* Cullompton: Willan Publishing.

Hopkins Burke, R.D. (2004c) 'Policing Contemporary Society Revisited', in R.D. Hopkins Burke (ed.) *'Hard Cop/Soft Cop': Dilemmas and Debates in Contemporary Policing.* Cullompton: Willan Publishing.

Hopkins Burke, R.D. (2007) 'Moral Ambiguity, the Schizophrenia of Crime and Community Justice', *British Journal of Community Justice*, 5(1): 43–64.

Hopkins Burke, R.D. (2012) *Criminal Justice Theory: An Introduction.* Abingdon, Oxon: Routledge.

Hopkins Burke, R.D. (2013) 'Theorizing the Criminal Justice System: Four Models of Criminal Justice Development', *Criminal Justice Review*, September(3): 335–53.

Jefferson, T. (1997) 'Masculinities and Crime', in M. Maguire, R. Morgan and R. Reiner (eds.) *The Oxford Handbook of Criminology*, 2nd ed. Oxford: Clarendon.

Jewkes, Y. (2004) *Media and Crime.* London: Sage.

Kane, S.C. (2004) 'The Unconventional Methods of Cultural Criminology', *Theoretical Criminology*, 8(3): 304–21.

Katz, J. (1988) *Seductions of Crime: Moral and Sensual Attractions in Doing Evil.* New York: Basic Books.

Kendall, L. (2003) 'Cyberporn', in M.S. Kimmel and A. Aronson (eds.) *Men and Masculinities: A Social, Cultural, and Historical Encyclopedia.* Santa Barbara, CA: ABC-CLIO.

Lukacs, G. (1970) *Writer and Critic.* London: Merlin Press.

Malamuth, N. (1989) 'Sexually Violent Media, Thought Patterns, and Antisocial Behavior', *Public Communication and Behavior*, 2: 159–204.

Marsh, I. and Melville, G. (2009) *Crime, Justice and the Media.* London: Routledge.

O'Malley, P. and Mugford, S. (1994) 'Crime, Excitement and Modernity', in G. Barak (ed.) *Varieties of Criminology.* Westport, CT: Praeger.

O'Neil, M., Campbell, R., Hubbard, P., Pitcher, J. and Scoular, J, (2007) 'Living with the Other: Street Sex Work, Contingent Communities and Degrees of Tolerance', *Crime, Media, Culture*, 4: 73–93.

Potter, G. and Kappeler, G. (eds.) (1998) *Constructing Crime: Perspectives on Making News and Social Problems.* Prospect Heights, IL: Waveland.

Presdee, M. (2000) *Cultural Criminology and the Carnival of Crime*. London: Routledge.

Presdee, M. (2004) 'Cultural Criminology: The Long and Winding Road', *Theoretical Criminology*, (3): 275–5.

Redmon, D. (Producer/Director) (2005) *Madi Gras: Made in China {Motion Picture}*. New York: Carnivalesque Films.

Sasson, T. (1995) *Crime Talk: How Citizens Construct a Social Problem*. New York: Aldine de Gruyter.

Scheyvens, R. (2011) 'The Challenge of Sustainable Tourism Development in the Maldives: Understanding the Social and Political Dimensions of Sustainability', *Asia Pacific Viewpoint*, 52(2): 148–164.

Shakeela, A., Ruhanen, L., and Breakey, N. (2011) 'The Role of Employment in the Sustainable Development Paradigm: The Local Tourism Labor Market in Small Island Developing States', *Journal of Human Resources in Hospitality & Tourism*, 10(4): 331–53.

Smith, O. and Raymen, T. (2016a) 'Deviant Leisure: A Criminological Perspective', *Theoretical Criminology*, 22(2): 63–2.

Smith, O. and Raymen, T. (2016b) 'What's Deviance Got to Do With It? Black Friday Sales, Violence, and Hyper-Conformity', *British Journal of Criminology*, 56(2): 39–405.

Snyder, F. (2002) *Globalisation and Power Disparities*. London: Butterworths LexisNexis.

sStack, W., Wasserman, I. and Kern, R. (2004) 'Adult Social Bonds and Use of Internet Pornography', *Social Science Quarterly*, 5: 75.

Stevens, D. (2010) *Media and Criminal Justice: The CSI Effect*. Boston: Jones and Bartlett.

Surette, R. (2007) *Media, Crime, and Criminal Justice: Images, Realities, and Policies*, 3rd ed. Belmont, CA: Thomson Wadsworth.

Thornton, S. (1995) *Club Cultures*. Cambridge: Polity Press.

Van Swaaningen, R. (1999) 'Reclaiming Critical Criminology', *Theoretical Criminology*, 3(1): 5–2.

Wengraf, T. (2001) *Qualitative Research Interviewing*. London: Sage.

Wetherell, M. (2005) 'Unconscious Conflict or Everyday Accountability?', *British Journal of Social Psychology*, 44: 169–73.

Willis, P. (1978) *Profane Culture*. London: Routledge & Kegan Paul.

Winlow, S. and Hall, S. (2006) *Violent Night: Urban Leisure and Contemporary Culture*. Oxford: Berg.

Young, J. (1999) *The Exclusive Society: Social Exclusion, Crime and Difference in Late Modernity*. London: Sage.

Young, J. (2001) 'Identity, Community and Social Exclusion', in R. Matthews and J. Pitts (eds.) *Crime, Disorder and Community Safety*. London: Routledge.

Young, J. (2011) *The Criminological Imagination*. Oxford: Polity Press.

Žižek, S. (2018) *Like a Thief in Broad Daylight: Power in the Era of Post-Humanity*. London: Allen Lane.

Chapter 9

Globalization and organized crime

Key issues

1   Globalization and neoliberalism
2   Crime as normal and nonpathological
3   Globalization and organized crime
4   The UK and European organized crime
5   Dance culture – the globalization of deviance

Globalization and neoliberalism

While globalization and neoliberalism are not the same things, they are closely linked and highly interdependent. For the past four decades, neoliberalism has dominated economic policymaking in the US and the UK. It has strong advocates in Western Europe and Japan, but substantial popular resistance there has limited its influence despite continuing US efforts to impose neoliberal policies. In much of the third world and in the transition countries – with China being a notable exception – the US has been successful in dictating neoliberal policies, acting partly through the International Monetary Fund and World Bank and partly through direct pressure.

As we have seen elsewhere in this book, neoliberalism is a contemporary version of the classical liberal economics that was dominant in the US and UK prior to the Great Depression of the 1930s. From roughly the mid-1930s to the mid-1970s, a new interventionist approach replaced classical liberalism, and it became the accepted belief during that period that capitalism requires significant state regulation in order to be viable. Then, in the 1970s, classical liberalism returned, first in the academy and then in the realm of public policy.

Neoliberalism is thus both a body of economic theory and a policy stance. The theory claims that a largely unregulated capitalist system – a free-market economy – not only embodies the ideal of free individual choice but also achieves optimum economic performance with respect to efficiency, economic growth, technical progress and distributional justice. The state is assigned a very limited economic role: defining property rights, enforcing contracts and regulating the money supply. State intervention to correct market failures is considered likely to create more problems than it solves.

The policy recommendations of neoliberalism are concerned mainly with dismantling what remains of the welfare state. These recommendations include deregulation of business; privatization of public activities and assets; elimination of, or cutbacks in, social welfare programs; and reduction of taxes on businesses and the investing class. In the international sphere, neoliberalism calls for the free movement of goods, services, capital and money across national boundaries. Thus, corporations, banks and individual investors should be free to acquire and move their property across national boundaries, although free cross-border movement by individuals is not part of the neoliberal programme.

The increasing process of globalization has been closely linked to neoliberalism and involves the distribution of products, technology, information and jobs across national borders and cultures. In economic terms, it describes an interdependence of nations around the globe which is fostered through free trade. From a positive perspective, it can raise the standard of living in poor and less developed countries by providing job opportunities, modernization and improved access to goods and services. From a negative perspective, it can destroy job opportunities in the more developed and high-wage countries as the production of goods moves across borders. Motives for globalization are idealistic, as well as opportunistic, but the development of a global free market has benefitted large corporations based in the Western world. Its impact nevertheless remains mixed for workers, cultures and small businesses around the globe, in both developed and emerging nations.

Globalization is not of course a new concept. Traders travelled vast distances in ancient times to buy commodities that were rare and expensive for sale in their homelands. More recently the great Industrial Revolution of the late eighteenth and early nineteenth centuries brought considerable advances in transportation and communication which helped facilitate trade across borders. The process of globalization stalled after the First World War as nations moved towards protectionist policies and introduced import taxes to more closely guard their industries in the aftermath of the conflict. This trend continued throughout the Great Depression of the 1930s and the Second World War until the US took the lead in reviving international trade.

Globalization has subsequently accelerated at an unprecedented pace with public policy changes and communications technology innovations cited as the two main driving factors. One of the critical steps in the path to globalization came with the North American Free Trade Agreement (NAFTA) signed in 1993. A significant impact of NAFTA was to give US auto manufacturers the incentive to relocate a portion of their manufacturing to Mexico where they could save on labour costs. The new US–Mexico–Canada Agreement is a supposedly mutually beneficial win for North American workers, farmers, ranchers and businesses. When finalized and implemented on the 1 July 2020, the agreement is intended to create more balanced, reciprocal trade that supports high-paying jobs for both Americans and the North American economy.

Governments worldwide have integrated a free-market economic system through fiscal policies and trade agreements over the past 20 years with the core of most being the removal or reduction of tariffs. This evolution of economic systems has increased industrialization and financial opportunities in many nations with governments now focusing on removing barriers to trade and promoting international commerce.

Contemporary corporations gain a competitive advantage on multiple fronts through globalization. They can reduce operating costs by manufacturing abroad. They can buy raw materials more cheaply because of the reduction or removal of tariffs. Most of all, they gain access to millions of new consumers. Globalization is a social, cultural, political and legal phenomenon. Socially, it leads to greater interaction among various populations. Culturally, it represents the exchange of ideas, values and artistic expression among cultures as will see with our discussion of the contemporary dance culture later in this chapter. Globalization thus represents a trend toward the development of single world culture. Politically, globalization has shifted attention to intergovernmental organizations like the United Nations and the World Trade Organization (WTO). Legally, globalization has moreover altered how international law is created and enforced.

Proponents of globalization believe it allows developing countries to catch up with industrialized nations through increased manufacturing, diversification, economic expansion and improvements in their standards of living. Outsourcing by companies brings jobs and technology to developing countries. Trade initiatives increase cross-border trading by removing supply-side and trade-related constraints.

One clear disadvantage of globalization is that an economic downturn in one country can create a domino effect through its trade partners. For example the great financial crash that occurred in 2008 had a severe impact on Portugal, Ireland, Greece and Spain. All these countries were members of the EU which had to step in to bail out debt-laden nations, and they became known thereafter by the acronym PIGS. Globalization detractors argue that it has created a concentration of wealth and power in the hands of a small corporate elite which can consume smaller competitors around the globe with federations of nations such as the EU helping to encourage and protect this transfer of wealth from the poor (through reduced wages in the name of competition) to the conglomerates and super-rich in the name of profits and hence capital.

Globalization has become a polarizing issue in the US and the UK, with the disappearance of entire industries to new locations abroad, and is seen as a major factor in the economic squeeze on the middle classes. For better and worse, globalization has also increased homogenization. Starbucks, Nike and Gap dominate commercial space in many nations. The sheer size and reach of the US had made the cultural exchange among nations largely a one-sided affair.

The global criminal economy

Globalization is thus the increasing interconnectedness of societies with what happens in one locality being invariably shaped by – or itself shaping – distant events. For many the world has become a global village. Held *et al.* (1999) observe a similar globalization of crime, with an increasing interconnectedness of criminality across national borders. Thus, the same process which has brought about the globalization of legitimate activities has also brought about the spread of transnational organized crime with some of the same advantages not least economies of scale and increased profits.

David Garland (1996) observed that, as crime became more frequent, it simply ceased to be an exceptional or pathological event, which caused surprise when it has occurred. It has become a standard, normal, background feature of our lives with the parallel and increasing blurring of boundaries between honesty and dishonesty nowhere more apparent than in the realms of organized crime, corporate crime and legitimate business. As Ruggiero (2000) pertinently observed, organized crime has become a branch of big business which is simply the illegal sector of capital. Manuel Castells (1998) noted that, by the middle of the 1990s, the 'gross criminal product' of global organized crime had made it the 20th-richest organization in the world and richer than 150 sovereign states, while De Brie (2000) noted that the total world gross criminal product was estimated at 20% of world trade. There is no evidence to suggest that this situation has in any way changed for the better in the intervening years.

Ruggiero (2000) further observed that legitimate business both actively seeks relations with criminal organizations while adopting methods akin to those of organized crime. Thus, immigrant smuggling eases labour supply problems in a variety of manufacturing sectors such as clothing and food, construction and agriculture and in 'dirty economies' where semi-legal employment is interspersed with employment in more directly criminal activity. Moreover, as De Brie (2000) observed, the global sphere of multinational corporations has enabled the export of the most brutal aspects of cheap labour to convenient locations in the Southern Hemisphere. Meanwhile, the legal financial sector may well go out of its way to attract criminal investments. Kochan and Whittington (1991) note that the closure of the Bank of Credit and Commerce International in 1991 showed how private banks and investment traders openly tout for legal and illegal funds without being too concerned about the distinction between the two.

Castells (1998) proposed that as a result of globalization there was a global criminal economy worth over £1 trillion per annum and which takes a number of forms. First, there is the highly profitable business of smuggling of illegal immigrants with, for example, the Chinese Triads alone making an estimated US$2.5 billion annually. Second, the trafficking of women and children which is often linked to prostitution or slavery with nearly half a million people trafficked to Western Europe annually. Third, there is the trafficking in body parts for organ transplants in rich countries with an estimated 2,000 organs taken annually from condemned or executed criminals in China. Fourth, there are cybercrimes such as identity theft and child pornography. Fifth, there are green crimes which damage the environment such as the illegal dumping of toxic waste in third-world countries. Sixth, there is international terrorism with much activity based on ideological links made via the internet and other forms of information communication technology, rather than on the local territorial links of the past. Sixth, there is the mammoth global drugs trade that was worth an estimated US$300 to $400 billion annually at street prices and which has been a provider of much employment worldwide.

David Wall (2007/10) identifies four categories of cybercrime. First, cyber-trespass – crossing boundaries into the cyber property of others – includes hacking and sabotage such as spreading viruses. Second, cyber-deception and theft include identity theft, 'phishing' (obtaining identity or bank account details by deception) and the violation of intellectual property rights (e.g. software piracy, illegal downloading and file sharing). Ninety-five per cent of music available online is downloaded illegally, according to a report by the International Federation of the Phonographic Industry which found that despite record growth in digital music sales during the previous year, the majority of music was downloaded for free with no payments made to artists (Swash, 2009). Third, cyber-pornography includes porn involving minors and opportunities for children to access porn on the net. Fourth, cyber-violence involves doing psychological harm or inciting physical injury and includes cyber-stalking (e.g. sending unwanted threatening or offensive emails) and hate crimes against minority groups, as well as bullying by text.

Policing cyber-crime is particularly difficult partly because of the sheer scale of the internet and the limited resources of the police, not least because of its globalized nature which poses problems of jurisdiction. Police culture also gives cyber-crime a low priority because it is seen as lacking the excitement of more conventional policing. The new advances in information communications technology nevertheless provide the police and state with greater opportunities for surveillance and control of the population. Yvonne Jewkes (2003) argues that this new information technology permits routine surveillance through the use of closed-circuit television cameras, electronic databases, digital finger-printing and 'smart' identity cards.

The global criminal economy has both a demand and a supply side. Thus, a highly significant explanation for scale of transnational organized crime is demand from the rich West. Nonetheless, the global criminal economy simply could not survive without a supply side which provides the source for demands of the West, such as drugs and prostitutes. This supply is linked to the globalization process. For example third-world drug-producing countries, such as Colombia, have large populations of impoverished peasants. For them, drug investment is attractive for it is simple to produce and commands high prices. In Colombia, 20% of peasants rely on cocaine production for their livelihood, and the drug outsells all other exports. Thus, to understand drug crime, we cannot focus only on countries where drugs are consumed.

Globalization creates new insecurities and produces a new mentality of risk consciousness which is global rather than localized in what might be conceived as an international postmodern condition. For example, people in Western societies are anxious about immigration and the media helps to create this panic with reference to the UK being 'flooded' with immigrants. The media thus creates moral panics of supposed threats from immigrants and these are often encouraged and given respectability by politicians. Negative coverage of immigration has moreover led to hate crimes being committed against minorities throughout the EU. An outcome has been the intensification of social control at the national level. UK border control, for example, is thus toughened, airlines who bring in undocumented passengers are fined and there is now no limit to how long a person may be held in immigration detention. Immigrants are seen as 'folk devils', and so the police become more aware of crimes by such people, and so more crime is found which may lead to a moral panic and the deviancy amplification of ethnic minority crimes.

Ian Taylor (1997) argued that globalization had led to changes in the pattern and extent of crime. By giving a free hand to market forces, globalization has created greater inequality and rising crime with the resulting increase occurring at both ends of the social spectrum. It has thus allowed transnational corporations to switch manufacturing to low-wage countries, producing job insecurity, unemployment and poverty; for example many high street fashion clothes are produced in the third world. Deregulation nevertheless means that governments have little control over their own economies, for example, to create jobs or raise taxes while state spending on welfare has declined. Marketization has moreover encouraged people to see themselves as individual consumers thereby undermining social cohesion and communities. Increasingly the materialistic culture promoted by the global media portrays success in terms of lifestyle consumption.

Taylor acknowledged that multinational corporations had shifted activities from country to country simply in search for greater profitability. These changes have reduced the job security of full-time staff and increased the amount of part-time, temporary and insecure employment. The state has moreover reduced its role in social and economic planning, its involvement in the 'provision of public goods in areas like health and welfare, transport, housing and urban planning' with many of these areas increasingly opened up to market forces and competition which has led to cutbacks in the provision of welfare. The EUhas increasingly become an exclusively economic community with its primary emphasis on growth and on trying to gain an increasing share of world markets and commercial edge. Ruggerio *et al.* (1998) observed that in Europe, the emphasis on the market has left little space for the development of public and state institutions and for their consequent production of social cohesion and social justice. The EU has become dominated by corporations, monopolies and oligarchies and is a ready tool and supporter of neoliberal values, exporting cheap labour from the East, in particular, and forcing down labour costs in the Western countries of Europe.

These changes have increasingly resulted in a change in the culture of towards marketization. Thus, ordinary members of society are more and more encouraged to see their social life in market terms: calculate the economic costs and see the benefits of making particular decisions. Taylor (1997) included criminals in these developments where people are encouraged to see themselves as consumers who are entitled to be able to buy what they want. It is a discourse promoted by the media as

> [a] discourse which identifies the viewer or the listener as a consumer of 'goods', and which glorifies the idea of choice across a range of different marketplaces (unlimited tourist experiences, multiple channel television, a range of private health and personal insurance schemes.)
>
> (Taylor, 1998: 20)

Some sociologists thus argue that growing globalization and marketization have resulted in more opportunities for criminality, while both have encouraged crime because of the potential to make vast sums of money. Capitalism has therefore encouraged corporate greed with the outcome being more criminal activity within legitimate businesses which extend their influence throughout the world. The deregulation of financial markets has provided increased opportunities for crimes such as insider trading. Taylor (1997) lists the example of Wall Street stockbrokers Drexel, Burnham and Lambert, who were accused of manipulating the US stock market in 1990 and paid US$650 million to the Securities and Exchange Commission in compensation. Globalization and marketization have also increased the opportunities for various types of crime based directly on the growth of market and consumer societies, for example insurance fraud by claimants and salespeople.

The growth and expansion of the EU have provided an enormous opportunity for defrauding the body of money by making false claims for various subsidies. Taylor (1997) observed that by the end of the twentieth century, the EU was losing some US$7 billion per year due to fraud and the situation is unlikely to have improved. The failure to clamp down on this fraud has simply encouraged others to try their luck. While such crimes may not be 'sexy' and fail to attract too much media attention, they are still crimes. Ultimately, the money lost to fraud could have funded good causes within the EU. So, while the crime might appear to be painless, it still can have a marked impact on society.

Other crimes are related to the changing nature of employment and unemployment. Taylor (1998) identified a fundamental shift in employment patterns in capitalist societies. Both mass manufacturing and public-sector employment areas have experienced substantial job losses. At present there is little prospect of anything like a return to suitable, reasonably well-paid full employment in countries like the UK. Those with modern and technical skills are in a position to do better during the changed economic circumstances of neoliberal society, but those with dated or no skills – and there are many of these – are likely to find it impossible to find well paid full-time employment. Zero-hours contracts and precarious employment in the gig economy are fast expanding, and there are only two wage rates in most employment in the contemporary UK, the minimum wage for most and the 'living wage' for those with better employers. At the same time, multinational corporations continue to move out of the UK to countries where there is an even cheaper and larger source of labour. Countries in Asia have without doubt benefited greatly from this process, but this clearly has not been the case for the workforce of the UK.

It is areas most affected by unemployment and more latterly underemployment as draconian assaults of welfare benefits have forced most into low-paid precarious (often multiple) jobs that have suffered the massively destructive effects that this joblessness clearly has had on the self-respect of individuals and communities. Areas blighted by high levels of unemployment have little hope of major improvement, and the longer this situation continues, the greater the cumulative effects. In such circumstances, criminality in some form becomes an increasingly more rational choice for many.

Changing patterns of work have also created more opportunities and incentives for criminal activity based on work. Ruggerio *et al.* (1998) believe subcontracting encourages the employment of people who are working illegally, fraudulent benefit claims and those employed in conditions or with wage levels which fail to conform to national laws. This often happens in the clothing, food and building industries. Subcontractors may break rules to cut costs to get and retain contracts in competitive industries and to maximize their profits.

All of these factors create insecurity and widening inequality which encourages people, especially the poor to commit crime. The lack of legitimate opportunity destroys self-respect and drives the unemployed or under-employed to look for illegitimate prospects such as the huge employer of the highly profitable drugs trade. At the same time, globalization creates criminal opportunities for elite groups on a grand scale. For example the deregulation of financial markets creates opportunity for movement of funds across the globe to avoid taxation. Taylor thus usefully linked global trends in the capitalist economy to changes in the patterns of crime. It, of course, does not explain why these changes lead some people in these changed global criminogenic circumstances to choose crime as a viable option and not others.

Global criminal networks involve complex interconnections between a range of criminal networks which transcend national boundaries including the American Mafia, Colombian drug cartels, the Russian Mafia, Chinese Triads and the Sicilian Costa Nostra. Global criminal networks have developed because of the growth of an information age in which knowledge as well as because goods and people can move quickly and easily across national boundaries.

Misha Glenny (2008) argued that these networks form a global criminal economy which accounts for 15% of global trade. In order of importance (in economic terms), the main crimes organized criminal gangs engage in are (1) drug trafficking estimated at 8% of world trade, (2) money laundering estimated at 2% to 5 % of global gross domestic product (GDP) and (3) 4 to 5 million people are trafficked each year with profits of up to US$9.5 billion.

In addition, these criminal networks also trade in weapons, pharmaceuticals, nuclear materials, body parts, metals, precious stones/natural resources, stolen cars, art, antiques, rare animals and counterfeit goods. They provide and control illicit services, most notably, gambling and prostitution, they engage in cybercrime, robbery, kidnapping, extortion, corruption and piracy, and finally, there is also terrorism.

Glenny (2008) suggests that organized criminal gangs are especially important in facilitating the trade in illegal goods and services. Organized criminal gangs (basically the

Mafia) have become especially influential in those areas of the world where there is weak rule of law (failed and transitional states), distrust of the state (Italy and Mexico), inaccessible terrain (Peru and Colombia), high levels of corruption and easy access to weapons and transnational networks. One of the most significant criminal networks which impacts significantly on Europe operates from Bulgaria – a country which is a 'hub' between the rich and poor parts of the world and where the Mafia have held considerable power since the collapse of communism in the late 1980s. Most of the drugs people take in the UK and many of the prostitutes British men sleep with have been shipped by the Bulgarian Mafia.

Dick Hobbs and Colin Dunningham (1998) in their ethnographic study conducted in the 1990s examined how organized crime has expanded on the back of globalization. They nevertheless suggest that criminal organizations like the Mafia are not dominant, but most global crime operates through a glocal system – that is there is a global distribution network built from local connections. Local growers of cannabis thus deliver their product to a supply chain feeding a global network of users. In this way, Colombian drug barons use glocal systems to deliver their product to the world.

Organized crime in Europe and the UK

An EU-funded Organized Crime Portfolio project has estimated that organized crime costs the EU economy about €110 billion per annum or approximately 1% of EU GDP. The main illicit markets in the EU generate around 110 billion euro each year. Illicit drugs (heroin, cocaine, cannabis, amphetamines and ecstasy) remain the most profitable 'traditional' market (€28 billion yearly at EU level). Among emerging criminal activities, fraud appears to the most lucrative (€29 billion each year from missing trader intra community value-added tax fraud alone). Illicit revenues are shared by a plurality of organized crime groups and criminal actors. The use of business facilitators and of legitimate companies to cover illicit trade is also widespread. The poly-crime nature of criminal groups in Europe expands the economies of scale among illicit markets, reduces operational costs and increases profit margins (Savona and Riccardi, 2015).

Illicit proceeds are widely laundered in the European legal economy with evidence of organized crime investments in almost all EU countries. Investments nevertheless tend to concentrate in areas with a strong presence of organized crime (e.g. Southern Italy), ones strategic for illicit trafficking (e.g. Andalusia), with key ports and airports (e.g. Amsterdam/Rotterdam), border regions (e.g. north-western Italy and south-western France), tourist areas (e.g. Costa del Sol) and large cities (e.g. Rome, Madrid, London, Paris, Berlin, Bucharest).

Bars and restaurants, construction, wholesale and retail trade (especially of food products and clothing), transportation, hotels and real estate are traditional sectors of infiltration. There is, moreover, growing evidence of infiltration into renewable energy, waste and scrap management, logistics, money transfer businesses, slot machines, betting and gaming. Chinese organized crime groups, Russian/Georgian organized crime groups, Italian mafias, Motorcycle gangs and organized crime groups of British, Dutch and Turkish origin constitute the majority of cases. Differences in terms of investment strategy nevertheless exist among criminal groups and countries. Drivers of criminal investments were found to be profit, money laundering, control of the territory, influence on the political sphere, social consensus, personal benefit or concealment of criminal activities (Savona and Riccardi, 2015).

Both the National Security Strategy and the Serious and Organised Crime Strategy have identified organized crime as a significant risk to the security of the UK (HM Government, 2013). Drug supply, organized fraud and organized immigration crime have all had a major impact on both the UK economy and society more broadly. Child sexual exploitation and abuse, criminal use of firearms, cyber-crime, economic crime and organized theft are identified as key threats. In terms of geographical impact, organized criminal activity seems to be mainly concentrated in London and the South-East, the North-West and West Midlands, but other areas of the country are affected to a lesser extent.

One of the key concerns in the UK has been the structure of organized crime groups and the extent to which they reflect or differ from the socio-geographically based mafia groups found in Italy and elsewhere. The picture of organized crime in the UK nevertheless leans away from the traditional Mafia model towards conglomerations of career criminals who temporarily join with others to commit crimes until they are completed and then reform with others to commit new crimes.

As of December 2013, the number of organized crime groups operating in the UK was estimated by the National Crime Agency (NCA) to be about 5,300, comprising about 36,600 organized criminals. A Home Office (2013) study of criminal profiles of organized criminals in the UK has shown that the vast majority (87%) were UK nationals. While the majority had been convicted for drug-related offences (73%), only 12% of them specialized in a particular crime type – most are generalists.

Perhaps the most interesting finding of the recent EU-funded Organised Crime Portfolio project is that if you take the large Italian mafia groups out of the equation such as La Cosa Nostra, 'Ndrangheta, Camorra and others, then the pattern of organized crime groups in the UK is roughly similar to the rest to Europe. Most studies characterize them as polymorphous, adaptable and fluid multi-commodity criminal networks. While kinship and ethnicity remain important factors for group cohesion, multiple cross-ethnic linkages also play an important role in group formation, and such mixed networks may be more viable, successful, continuous and respected. The evidence points to domestic groups and networks, but there is some indication of activity by foreign-based organized groups operating legal businesses in the UK (Savona and Riccardi, 2015).

These constantly adapting organized crime groups are shifting towards less risky and less violent – but still lucrative – market niches where detection is more difficult. Savona and Riccardi (2015) found that fraud, drug trafficking, counterfeiting and tobacco smuggling are currently the largest organized illicit markets in the UK. Other profitable markets are trafficking for sexual exploitation and organized vehicle crime. Alongside traditional markets of organized crime such as drugs and human trafficking, there is growing evidence of its presence in the financial sector, renewable energy, waste and recycling.

The Organised Crime Portfolio project found that the estimated profits of particular criminal enterprises can vary considerably from tens of thousands to hundreds of millions of pounds. Contrary to popular belief, not all organized crime is associated with vast profits. Many offenders make just enough to cover living expenses they 'offend and spend', which is partly an outcome of the Proceeds of Crime Act 2002, which empowers various agencies to seize the profits of crime.

When criminals do invest, their main motivation is to satisfy personal and family consumption needs and lifestyle preferences. They may also create illegitimate businesses or use their profits to facilitate further crime, such as money laundering, rather than accumulate wealth. Criminals do tend nevertheless to buy themselves 'toys'. It is thus common to see high-value assets and consumer goods such as properties, cars, bikes, number plates, boats – even private jets and helicopters. They are important as symbols of success and patterns of a luxury lifestyle. High-value antiques, art and jewellery are particularly favoured investments and a way to launder money. Criminals may also make functional investments in businesses used as fronts for unlawful activities, to launder illicit proceeds or to perform criminal activities.

These businesses tend to be wholesale and retail trade, bars and restaurants or transport companies. Convenience stores and off licences can be used to sell illicit goods (e.g. smuggled alcohol) or act as fronts for other criminal activities. Other profitable sectors for organized groups are construction; sports and gaming; money service businesses; payday loan companies; sex, tattoo and other personal activities; hotels; sports; and casinos.

The image of organized crime to emerge from the Organised Crime Portfolio project is that of an evolving, adaptable transnational business model which clearly points to the need for a fundamental change in the general approach towards policing organized crime in the UK. The current hierarchical and rigid model we have is perhaps more suited to targeting traditional socio-geographical mafia-type organizations, but twenty-first-century organized crime requires more thought (Savona and Riccardi, 2015). But it is not just traditional organized crime that has undergone a process of globalization. The same is true of other aspects of deviant activities such as youth subcultures and associated illegal behaviour, such as the consumption of illicit party drugs.

Dance culture – the globalization of deviance

Ben Carrington and Brian Wilson (2002) observed that, like all youth cultures, and especially those formed through associations with music cultures, the evolution of 'club cultures' around the world could be attributed, at least in part, to ongoing global processes of cultural borrowing. The term *club cultures* refers to the youth cultural phenomenon associated with all-night dance parties at nightclubs or other venues, the production and consumption of various dance music genres – music 'mixed' or electronically created by DJs – and with the use of amphetamine drugs – particularly MDMA or 'Ecstasy' – to enhance the dance/music experience. The roots of this culture have their foundations in the 1970s and early 1980s American dance music scenes of New York, Chicago and Detroit, and latterly in Britain, where 'rave culture' emerged in 1988 during what came to be known as the 'second summer of love'. In Britain, in particular, the subsequent criminalization of the rave scene – a partial outcome of moral panics about rave-related drug use – and the incorporation of the rave scene by the mainstream music industry led the culture to become grounded in 'nightclub venues and that is how ravers, in effect, became clubbers' (Carrington and Wilson, 2002). Chambers argues that

> [t]he international medium of musical reproduction underlines *a new epoch of global culture contact*. Modern movement and mobility, whether through migration, the media or tourism, have dramatically transformed both musical production and publics and intensified cultural contact.
>
> (1994: 80)

DJs and promoters thus travelled to foreign countries, were exposed to fresh varieties of music and nightclubs and ultimately integrated ideas gleaned from these experiences into their domestic dance music cultures. Touring DJs and imported albums – in turn – were to influence local music-makers who combined the new material with their current work, thus creating something 'new again'. Images and ideas extracted from mass and alternative media were incorporated into local music production, fashion styles and club venues. In retrospect, what was to emerge from years of cultural 'cutting and mixing' (Hebdige, 1987) was a fascinating but hazy relationship between a 'global' club culture and various 'local club cultures'.

Carrington and Wilson (2002) noted an increasing tendency for youth to travel to foreign scenes as 'post-rave tourists' which has meant that local cultures were to became further defined by their diverse and transient membership. These mobile formations could well be described as *reflexive* communities in the extent to which they dissolve the boundary between producers and consumers, are actively entered into by their members rather than being proscribed by social location, are not delimited by simple time–space boundaries and are based on cultural and symbolic practices.

Researchers and scholars at the Centre for Contemporary Cultural Studies (CCCS) had previously shown how youth 'reactively and proactively' expressed their dissatisfaction with the status quo of post-war British society. By articulating themselves through spectacular forms of 'style', youth were believed to be symbolically and creatively resisting and, in so doing, finding 'solutions' to their problems. CCCS theorists referred to these 'magical solutions' as a way of recognizing that subcultural involvement is only a temporary form of empowerment and escape that does not (necessarily) substantially challenge the dominance/hegemony of the ruling classes. Hopkins Burke and Sunley (1996, 1998) later noted the coexistence of a number of different subcultures and argued that this was a product of the postmodern condition where specific groups of young people had come together to create solutions to their specific socio-economic problems with the possibility of choice being central to their account.

Carrington and Wilson (2002) recognize that these earlier studies were to provide significant foundations for later studies of youth culture, but among a number of identified limitations was the recognition that insufficient attention had been paid to the ways in which youth cultures were influenced by subcultural traditions in other countries. Others were simply dismissive of such developments and even announced the death of youth subcultures, while Redhead (1990) proposed that subcultural authenticity was now 'impossible' because of the tendency of contemporary culture to be self-referential, shallow, flat and hyper-real or, in other words, a culture of effervescent, spectacular, fast-moving, ever-present, 'better than real' images. Muggleton (1997, 2000) was thus able to suggest that the postmodern condition was inhabited by 'post-sub-culturalists' whose 'neo-tribal' identities are multiple and fluid, whose consumption was no longer 'articulated through the modernist structuring relations of class, gender or ethnicity' and who were defined by their fragmented/multiple stylistic identities. They now had a low degree of commitment to any subcultural group with high rates of subcultural mobility; while any fascination with style and image was generally apolitical, with a 'positive attitude toward media and a celebration of the inauthentic' (Muggleton, 2000: 52). From this perspective, dance cultures became invariably seen as the archetypal postmodern youth formation.

Appadurai (1990) nevertheless provides us with an alternative evaluation and to this end identifies 'five dimensions of cultural flow' which are seen to describe the dynamics of global cultural transmission. He proposes that these five dimensions – *ethnoscapes*, *mediascapes, technoscapes, finanscapes* and *ideoscapes* – work in ways which actually prevent the construction of a homogenous culture. *Ethnoscapes* refers to the flow of people around the world, for example tourists, immigrants, refugees, exiles, guest workers and other moving groups. *Technoscapes* refers to the flow of technology, for example the export of technology to countries as part of transnational business relocations. *Finanscapes* refers to the patterns of global capital transfer.

Augmenting these first three scapes are *mediascapes* and *ideoscapes*. The former refers to mass media images, to the modes of image distribution, for example electronic or print media, and to the ways that these images allow viewers to gain access to other parts of the world and thus become part of 'imagined communities'. The latter refers to images which are invested with political-ideological meaning, for example images presented by governmental groups justifying a military action or images created by social movements attempting to overthrow power groups. The crux of Appadurai's framework is the assumption that the various 'disjunctures' or interactions that occur between global cultural flows – as they relate to the various scapes – provide the analyst with crucial information about the complex ways that local cultures relate to global forces.

Carrington and Wilson (2002) have adapted this framework to their discussion of the globalization of dance music cultures and observed that this more elaborate approach to theorizing 'the local' encourages researchers to consider the intricacies of youth tastes, for example preferences for various genres of dance music, such as house or jungle or trance; interpretations of the music, for example as an escape, as a form of resistance; and uses of it, for example making a living in dance-music-related occupations. This more flexible and integrated interpretive framework has also allowed the analyst to consider how youth might simultaneously be interpreters and producers of culture, the creators of 'alternative' media which reflects personal understandings of global culture while, at the same time, making a significant contribution to this same culture.

Carrington and Wilson (2002) observed that the history of rave and club culture shows how travellers – within the ethnoscape – contributed to the transmission of dance music culture from the US and Ibiza to Britain and then, subsequently, back from Britain to the US and parts of Europe. The 'post-rave tourist' has also emerged, as a clubber who travels to locations around the world with the explicit purpose of experiencing the club/rave culture of the area. The authors argue that it would be a mistake to simply read the consumption (and production) of young people within this scene as an index of cultural manipulation. There is a sense of agency in the ways in which young people, through their engagement with the dance scene, have developed a degree of scepticism around the truth claims made by the scientific knowledge industries. For example the attempt to define dance cultures through a public health discourse, as inherently dangerous sites of unknown and indeterminate risk, spectacularly failed to prevent young people from embracing, adapting and exploring the possibilities of dance culture. It is argued that this is why, despite the attempt of most Western governments to prohibit the consumption of drugs, especially among the 'vulnerable' young, rates of consumption of Ecstasy – among other drugs – were to remain high. Carrington and Wilson (2002) thus suggested that the dance scene, by the extent and degree of its normalization of drug use, was to challenge the hegemony of the anti-drug discourse to the extent that a number of governmental agencies and states came to radically rethink the effectiveness of the war on drugs.

Responding to organized crime in the UK

Serious and organized crime nevertheless affects more UK citizens, more often, than any other national security threat and leads to more deaths in the UK each year than all other national security threats combined (National Crime Agency, 2018). It costs the UK at least £37 billion annually (Home Office, 2018). It undermines public services, communities, national reputation and our culture. The NCA assesses that the threat from organized crime is increasing, and serious and organized criminals are continually looking for ways to sexually or otherwise exploit new victims and novel methods to make money, particularly online.

The National Crime Agency (NCA; 2018) reports that a large amount of serious and organized crime remains hidden or underreported which means that the true scale is likely to be greater than we currently know. Although the impact may often be difficult to see, the threat is real and occurs every day all around us. Serious and organized criminals prey on the most vulnerable in society, including young children, and their abuse can have a devastating, lifelong effect on their victims. They target members of the public to defraud, manipulate and exploit them, sell them deadly substances and steal their personal data in a ruthless pursuit of profit. They use intimidation to create fear within communities and undermine the legitimacy of the state.

Enabled by their lawyers and accountants, corrupt elites and criminals set up fake companies to help them to hide their profits, fund lavish lifestyles and invest in further criminality. Serious and organized crime knows no borders, and many offenders operate as part of large networks spanning multiple countries. Technological change allows criminals to share indecent images of children, sell drugs and hack into national infrastructure more easily from all around the world while communicating more quickly and securely through encrypted phones. Continuously evolving technology has meant that the exploitation of children online is becoming easier and more extreme, from livestreaming of abuse to grooming through social media and other sites. Serious and organized criminals also exploit vulnerabilities in the increasing number of global trade and transport routes to smuggle drugs, firearms and people. Criminals have learned to become more adaptable, resilient and networked. Some think of themselves as untouchable.

In some countries overseas, criminals have created safe havens where serious and organized crime, corruption and the state are interlinked and self-serving. This creates instability and undermines the reach of the law, hindering the ability of the UK to protect itself from other national security threats such as terrorism and hostile state activity. The scale of the challenge faced by law enforcement agencies is considerable and it is the aim of the NCA to equip the whole of government, the private sector, communities and individual citizens to play their part in a single collective endeavour to rid society of the harms of serious and organized crime. The intention is to confront the threat globally before it comes to the UK. The intervention strategy is intended to improve powers and capabilities to identify, freeze, seize or otherwise deny criminals access to their finances, assets and infrastructure, both at home and overseas. At the heart of this approach is a new data, intelligence and assessment capability which will allow government and their agencies to penetrate and better understand serious and organized criminals and their vulnerabilities more effectively and target proposed disruptions to greater effect.

Policy implications of globalization and organized crime

The globalization of crime is evolving just as major social change encroaches increasingly on society. The fight against transnational crime and its threats to democracy will require global approaches like mutual assistance between states, extradition and international crime conferences as well as tribunals. It is only through the globalization of democratic values and human rights that the challenge of global violent crime can be met effectively. This does not mean an abdication of the state from its power to accomplish its intrinsic functions to act and mobilize resources. In addition, the increasingly passive role of the states regarding global economic activity should shift to regulatory initiatives.

The beneficial effects of globalization, consisting of a greater international division of labour, a more efficient allocation of capital through pooling of resources should nevertheless not erode the capacity of governments to manage crime. To achieve this goal, the global social, political, economic and cultural interdependence of countries worldwide demands concerted integrative developmental policies. In this way, the attainment of higher incomes should be coupled with re-distributive policies and social security nets, which will largely eliminate the incentive for local crimes.

The role of an ethically inspired education in the prevention of organized crime is essential. The distribution of the knowledge of the physical and psychological harm caused by transnational and local crimes should generate the moral outrage which might facilitate cooperation in its management. To address the root causes of global crime, it is essential to acquire an actual sense of global social responsibility and moral consciousness, beyond international conventions and national legal efforts. Only a renewed ethical force can educate and inspire society; fight against corruption, economic and moral poverty; and the all-pervasive culture of indifference and irresponsibility.

Summary of main points

1   The increasing process of globalization has been closely linked to neoliberalism and involves the distribution of products, technology, information and jobs across national borders and cultures.
2   In economic terms, it describes an interdependence of nations around the globe which is fostered through free trade.
3   Contemporary corporations gain a competitive advantage on multiple fronts through globalization.
4   Globalization is thus the increasing interconnectedness of societies with what happens in one locality being invariably shaped by – or itself shaping – distant events. The world is a global village.
5   The same process which has brought about the globalization of legitimate activities has also brought about the spread of transnational organized crime.
6   Legitimate business both actively seeks relations with criminal organizations while adopting methods akin to those of organized crime.
7   Castells (1998) proposes that as a result of globalization there is now a global criminal economy worth over £1 trillion per annum, and this takes a number of different forms.
8   Global criminal networks involve complex interconnections between a range of criminal networks which transcend national boundaries including the American Mafia, Colombian drug cartels, the Russian Mafia, Chinese Triads and the Sicilian Costa Nostra.

9 A recent EU-funded Organised Crime Portfolio project has estimated that organized crime costs the EU economy about €110 billion per annum or approximately 1% of EU GDP.
10 Serious and organized crime affects more UK citizens, more often, than any other national security threat and leads to more deaths each year than all other national security threats combined (National Crime Agency, 2018).

Discussion questions

1 What are the links between globalization and neoliberalism?
2 Explain what we mean by the term *global village*.
3 In what ways are legitimate businesses using the same methods as organized crime?
4 How would you explain the growth in global organized crime?
5 What do we mean by the term *glocal*?

Suggested further reading

Giddens (2002) provides a good introduction as to how the processes of globalization are changing our lives. Castells (1998) and Findlay (2000) provides an excellent introduction to the globalization of crime and criminality, while Glenny (2008) an interesting discussion of the global underworld. Carrington and Wilson (2002) and (2004) provide a good introduction to the globalization of youth subcultures and the moral ambiguities of internationalization of deviance. The Home Office (2018) discusses the scale and social and economic costs of organized crime in the UK, while the NCA (2018) produce a strategy for dealing with the problem.

References

Appadurai, A. (1990) 'Disjuncture and Difference in the Global Cultural Economy', *Theory, Culture and Society*, 7(2/3): 295–310.
Carrington, B. and Wilson, B. (2002) 'Global Clubcultures: Cultural Flows and Late Modern Dance Music Cultures', in M. Cieslik and G. Pollock (eds.) *Young People in Risk Society: The Restructuring of Youth Identities in Late Modernity*. Aldershot: Ashgate.
Carrington, B. and Wilson, B. (2004) 'Dance Nations: Rethinking British Youth Subcultural Theory', in A. Bennett and K. Kahn-Harris (eds.) *After Subculture: Critical Studies in Contemporary Youth Culture*. London: Palgrave.
Castells, M. (1998) *End of Millennium (The Information Age: Economy Society and Culture III)*. Oxford: Blackwell.
Chambers, I. (1994) *Migrancy, Culture, Identity*. London: Routledge.
De Brie, C. (2000) 'Thick as Thieves', *Le Monde Diplomatique*, April.
Findlay, M. (2000) *The Globalisation of Crime*. London: Cambridge University Press.
Garland, D. (1996) 'The Limits of the Sovereign State: Strategies of Crime Control in Contemporary Society', *British Journal of Criminology*, 34(4): 445–71.
Giddens, A. (2002) *Runaway World: How Globalisation Is Reshaping Our Lives*, 2nd ed. London: Profile Books.
Glenny, M. (2008) *McMafia: A Journey Through the Global Underworld*. New York: Vintage Books.
Hebdige, D. (1987) *Cut 'n' Mix: Culture, Identity and Caribbean Music*. London: Comedia.
Held, D., McGrew, A., Goldblatt, D. and Perraton, J. (1999) *Global Transformations: Politics, Economics and Culture*. Stanford: Stanford University Press.
HM Government (2013) *Serious and Organised Crime Strategy*. London: HMSO.
Hobbs, D. and Dunningham, C. (1998) *Global Organised Crime: Context and Pretext*. London: Routledge.

Home Office (2018) *Understanding Organised Crime: Estimating the Scale and the Social and Economic Costs.* London: HMSO.

Hopkins Burke, R.D. and Sunley, R. (1996) 'Hanging Out' in the 1990s: Young People and the Post-modern Condition', Occasional Paper 11, COP Series. Scarman Centre for the Study of Public Order, University of Leicester, Leicester.

Hopkins Burke, R.D. and Sunley, R. (1998) 'Youth Subcultures in Contemporary Britain', in K. Hazlehurst and C. Hazlehurst (eds.) *Gangs and Youth Subcultures: International Explorations.* New Brunswick, NJ: Transaction Press.

Kochan, N. and Whittington, B. (1991) *Bankrupt: The BCCI Fraud.* London: Victor Gollancz.

Muggleton, D. (1997) 'The Post-Subculturalist', in S. Redhead (ed.) *The Clubcultures Reader: An Introduction to Popular Cultural Studies.* Malden, MA: Blackwell.

Muggleton, D. (2000) *Inside Subculture: The Postmodern Meaning of Style.* New York: Berg.

National Crime Agency (2018) *National Strategic Assessment of Serious and Organised Crime 2018.* [Online] Available from: www.nationalcrimeagency.gov.uk/ publications/905-national-strategic-assessment-for-soc-2018; and www.gov.uk/government/publications/ national-security-strategy-and-strategic-defence-and-security-review-2015 [Accessed 1 May 2019].

Redhead, S. (1990) *The End-of-the-Century Party: Youth and Pop towards 2000.* New York: St Martin's Press.

Ruggiero, V. (2000) *Crimes and Markets: Essays in Anti-Criminology.* Oxford: Oxford University Press.

Ruggerio, V., South, N. and Taylor, I. (eds.) (1998) *The New European Criminology: Crime and Social Order in Europe.* London: Routledge.

Savona, E.U. and Riccardi, M. (eds.) (2015) 'From Illegal Markets to Legitimate Businesses: The Portfolio of Organised Crime in Europe', *Final Report of Project OCP: Organised Crime Portfolio (www.ocportfolio.eu).* Trento: Transcrime – Università degli Studi di Trento.

Swash, R. (2009) 'Online Piracy: 95% of Music Downloads Are Illegal', *The Guardian,* 17 January.

Taylor, I. (1997) 'Crime and Social Insecurity in Europe', *Criminal Justice Matters,* 27(Spring): 3–5.

Taylor, I. (1998) 'Crime, Market-Liberalism and the European Idea', in V. Ruggerio, N. South, and I. Taylor (eds.) *The New European Criminology: Crime and Social order in Europe.* London: Routledge.

Wall, D.S. (2007/10) 'Policing Cybercrimes: Situating the Public Police in Networks of Security within Cyberspace', *Police Practice & Research: An International Journal,* 8(2): 13–205.

Chapter 10

Southern theory and criminology

Key issues

1 North/South and global convergence in the digital era
2 Rethinking criminology from the global South
3 Crimes outside the metropole: the many worlds of violence
4 Gendered crime and victimization in the global South
5 Penality, punishment and Southern criminology

Introduction

Raewyn Connell (2007) argues that a structural imbalance in the economy of knowledge has produced a hegemony of social scientific thought based on the experience of a small number of societies in the global North, namely, the countries of Western Europe (including the UK) and the US. The conventional (Northern) account with which we are familiar depicts the rise of social science as a response to the profound problems – of social dislocation, urban change, migration, industrial conflict and moral anomie – experienced by these societies as they underwent the processes of rapid industrialization, urbanization and modernization in the nineteenth century. In this narrative, the global North, comprising countries depicted as *leading* the way to capitalist modernity, is treated as the normative benchmark for the economic, political and social development of other countries seeking to modernize. The social sciences produced from the experience of these Northern societies afford, it is assumed, a sure guide for understanding and confronting processes and problems common to all societies undergoing modernization.

Connell argues that social science thus succeeded in representing itself, and being widely accepted, as universal, timeless and placeless. According to this logic, social phenomena in the 'periphery' would be investigated from the standpoint of universal theories and laws of development generated in 'modern' or 'Western' societies of the global North. The South could be mined for data, as for other raw materials, and empirical studies might be conducted in Southern settings applying imported (Northern) theory, but little in the way of novel ideas or theoretical insights of anything more than local interest would be yielded by the social scientific enterprise in the South. Connell calls this 'metropolitan' thinking (Connell, 2007: 215). Carrington *et al.* (2018) suggest that this argument applies with equal force to the field of criminology.

Metropolitan thinking rests on a linear, panoramic, unifying and modernist standpoint in which space and geopolitical and social differences are erased in the imperial narrative of time. In this worldview, North Atlantic global dominance and leadership was a matter of historical precedence (Connell, 2007: 38). It submerges the fundamental historical reality that the processes of Western industrialization, modernization and dominance were not endogenous to a few, particularly innovative or fortunate countries which led in some notional race but depended critically on their imperial reach and power, the conquest and colonization of much of the rest of the world by North Atlantic powers in the period from the sixteenth to the nineteenth centuries which provided them with the resources, labour, markets and often know-how essential to their economic development. As dependency and world-systems theorists have argued over many years, capitalist modernity was global from the outset. Being 'underdeveloped' or economically 'backward' was not the 'normal' or 'natural' condition of particular countries so labelled but commonly a consequence of their subordinate place in the global economic order (Frank, 1970; Gregory, 2004; Beckert, 2014). Likewise, social scientific knowledge and many of its key categories and concepts were not simply a product of efforts to confront the problems associated with modernization in countries of the global North but were crucially shaped by the imperial context; they 'embodied an intellectual response to the colonised world' (Connell, 2007: 9). Theories and concepts that grounded criminology's early claims to be a scientific endeavour, like 'atavism' and the 'born criminal', were even more obviously beholding to the traffic in ideas and artefacts between imperial metropole and periphery (Carrington and Hogg, 2017).

(Re)conceptualizing the South in criminology

There are various ways of conceiving the South and North/South global relationships. The more conventional view depicts it in essentially geographical and binary terms as the division between the rich and poor countries of the world. The rich comprise the old imperial states of Europe and certain of their wealthy settler offshoots like the US, Canada, Australia and New Zealand (although the latter two are geographically located in the Asia-Pacific). The poor are the rest. A successor to the older 'developed/developing' discourse, the currency of North/South rose with the establishment and reports of the Independent Commission on International Development Issues in the 1970s and 1980s, perhaps more well-known as the Brandt Commission, after its chairperson, Willy Brandt, former chancellor of West Germany (Independent Commission on International Development Issues, 1980, 1983). Understood in these terms, the global South comprises three continents (Asia, Africa and Central and South America) and parts of Oceania and is home to roughly 85% of the world's population with most of those living in extreme poverty. These include the parts of the world most severely torn by violent conflict, the destructive depletion of natural resources, environmental degradation, population dislocation and by political corruption and poor, often autocratic, governance. Carrington et al. (2018) observe that this collection of mutually reinforcing threats to human security dwarfs the crime problems which preoccupy most criminologists in the global North. Issues of vital criminological research and policy significance therefore abound in the global South. Although manifestly destructive to the lives and life chances of 'the bottom billion' in the global population, they are, in a shrinking world with increasingly porous national borders, also highly consequential for South/North relations and global security and justice.

The conventional, geographical, rich/poor dichotomous image of North/South is helpful for putting some of these issues into context, but it is complicated by a range of factors with which Southern theory and Southern criminology seek to grapple. There is the fundamental point already made that the global South, and its forms of economic and political life, does not exist apart from the historical, highly unequal pattern of relationships with imperial countries of the global North. Also, it should not be forgotten that lines on maps, national borders and geographical boundaries are contingent constructions in worlds, both past and present, where the powerful are often enabled to draw them to suit their own economic and geopolitical interests, to create their own social and geographical realities on the ground and to erase those of weaker, more vulnerable peoples.

This power is a defining feature of the colonial project, but its effects have perhaps been most profound in settler-colonial societies whether classified as North or South: the US, Canada, Australia, New Zealand, Israel, South Africa, Zimbabwe (Rhodesia), Kenya, Algeria and the countries of South America. Settler colonialism was only one of the forms taken by European expansion, but it did, as James Belich (2011: 23) observes, 'reach further and last longer than empire'. These then are not *post*colonial societies: independence did not deliver sovereignty into the hands of the first nations of these lands but into those of their white settler populations. And the struggles of these settler populations for national independence invariably rested on vigorous assertions of white identity and supremacy as well as racist immigration policies aimed at further 'whitening' the population (Gott, 2007; Belich, 2011). This legitimized the expropriation, exploitation and marginalization of indigenous populations. At the same time, settlement in what were often harsh environments and climates inhospitable to the 'white man' frequently necessitated that labour be forcibly extracted from the native population or that slaves or bonded labour be imported to meet labour needs.

These patterns of expropriation, exploitation and forced migration was to leave enduring imprints on colonial settler societies, whether they happen to be in the North or the South and whether they are gross domestic production-rich or not. In the US, slavery, convict leasing, Jim Crow segregation laws and the mass incarceration of African Americans (Alexander, 2010) are all evidence of the South within the North. In other colonial-settler states, extreme poverty, serious levels of violence and massively disproportionate incarceration rates are commonly found in indigenous populations (United Nations Department of Economic and Social Affairs, 2009). Carrington *et al.* (2018) observe that Australia is invariably near the top of the UN Human Development Index (HDI), but the HDI of its indigenous peoples is roughly the same as that of Cape Verde and El Salvador, about 103rd in the world (United Nations Department of Economic and Social Affairs, 2009). This has led some to compare conditions in remote parts of the country where indigenous people live in disproportionate numbers to 'failed states' (Dillon and Westbury, 2007).

Conventional North/South discourse also tends to be 'top-down, national, and "terra-centric"' (Christopher *et al.*, 2007). It is non-reflexive in relation to 'cartographic structures of power' and 'scales of value which privilege large landmasses as uniquely important for human history' (Samson, 2011: 244). Oceans appear as no more than 'big empty spaces' on maps, neglected as 'connector, facilitator and challenger' for those living on, with and around them (Samson, 2011: 249). This may be particularly so of the vast Pacific region stretching from Asia to the east coast of the Americas and comprising numerous island states. Samson suggests that perhaps climate change along with space travel 'will challenge the old prejudices, showing us images of the planet, which do not respect our Eurocentric "up" and "down" orientations, and reminding us that all living things are dependent on Pacific weather systems' (Samson, 2011: 249). More urgently, rising sea waters caused by climate change threaten many of the island states of the Pacific with extinction. The Carteret Islanders of Papua New Guinea have already suffered this fate, being forced to relocate to Bougainville, itself an island that has recently experienced the traumas of decolonization and civil war (Beldi, 2016). Climate-induced conflict, human dislocation and an emerging 'climate apartheid' are among the many pressing issues attracting the attention of green criminologists influenced by a Southern perspective.

Carrington *et al.* (2018) observe that criminology has been highly urban–centric as well as 'terra-centric'. It has tended to maintain a highly selective focus on crime and justice in large population centres to the exclusion of the many more spaces and places that lie beyond them. The rural has often been treated as a naturally cohesive space, an exemplar of a stable community prior to the disruptive impacts of industrialization and urbanization. From the standpoint of the colonial periphery, however, it was not the domestic urban context that was the primary site of world-shattering, frequently violent, social change but the global countryside (Beckert, 2014). Moreover, contemporary economic, social and technological change is intensifying the divides between city and country across both North and South, giving rise to novel crime problems and posing challenging questions in relation to the delivery of justice in rural and remote communities (Donnermeyer and DeKeseredy, 2013; Barclay *et al.*, 2007; Hogg and Carrington, 2006). At the same time, marginalized and neglected spaces often afford opportunities for innovation in justice strategy and, equally, for rethinking received concepts and the role of traditional legal institutions such as the coronial inquest.

Finally, the criminological gaze has to an overwhelming extent been narrowly focused on crimes and crime control within the boundaries of pacified nation states (Barberet, 2014), whose typical form is traceable to the democratic capitalist states in the global North. Criminology has, in large part, been a peacetime endeavour, albeit with a rising number of exceptions (Aas, 2011; Bowling, 2011; Barberet, 2014; Hogg, 2002; Walklate and McGarry, 2015; Braithwaite and Wardak, 2013; Green and Ward, 2004; Hagan, 2003; Hagan and Rymond-Richmond, 2008). It has had little to say about the violence of state and nation building, of empire and settler colonialism, of the expropriation of indigenous peoples (Cunneen, 2001) and of enslavement and other forms of forced labour migration. The impacts of colonization live on in contemporary patterns of armed conflict, organized crime, gang wars and violence against women and children in settings where state agencies are often too weak, indifferent or corrupt to provide security for their citizens or, worse, are themselves directly complicit in genocidal violence, extrajudicial killings and other systematic human rights abuses.

Carrington *et al.* (2018) argue that Southern criminology must develop a more complex, dynamic conceptualization of the South and North/South relationships if the intellectual biases noted earlier are to be corrected. Rather than a conceptualization based on a fixed geographical or economic binary, a more productive approach may use 'the South' as a metaphor for the 'rupture with a static view of the international order'. In this usage, South references not only (or primarily) geographical regions, landmasses, nations and sharply drawn lines on a map of the globe but seeks to capture the flows and interrelationships – of force, influence, unequal exchange, domination – that connect peoples and practices across the globe. The approach would broaden knowledge and understanding and serve as a salve for the insularity of metropolitan thinking in which hegemonizing theoretical generalization is rooted in partial and limited experiences and views of the world.

North/South and global convergence in the digital era

Carrington *et al.* (2018) observe that while modernity, and indeed the world which preceded it, was always in some sense global, the changes occurring today are affecting North/South relations in novel ways. There is talk of the 'rise of the South' and 'epochal global rebalancing' (United Nations Development Programme, 2013), a dramatic shift in economic power away from the West and the North, as growth has taken off in the so-called BRIC, the expanding bloc of traditionally low- to middle-income countries represented by the big four (Brazil, Russia, India and China; O'Neill, 2013). As a result, quite massive strides have also been taken in the reduction of global poverty which has also brought about a decline in global inequality. On the other hand, while inequality between countries has fallen, inequality *within* them has increased just about everywhere (Bourguignon, 2016).

As we have seen elsewhere in this book, the incomes of wealthy elites in the South have been surging ahead of advances by the poor and others. The same is true in the heartlands of the North, where both the working and middle classes are facing the impacts of deindustrialization and offshoring. Corporations have increasingly outsourced operations to low wage/low tax/lax regulatory jurisdictions leading to weakened trade unions, increased job insecurity, high long-term youth unemployment and stagnant incomes. The divides between rich and poor – economic, social, spatial – thus remain in the South and have greatly sharpened across the North (most dramatically so in the US, UK and the eurozone). This appearance of 'a South' within the North is seeing countries and regions with huge and growing problems of unemployment and poverty (Southern Europe, the industrial wastelands of the North of England and the Rust Belt in the US) increasingly pitted against political, corporate and financial elites intent on advancing their own interests while imposing austerity on others (on the crisis in the eurozone and the impact on Greece, see Varoufakis, 2016). There is too a deeply disturbing revival of racist extremism, a backlash against immigrants and other visible minorities, calls to restore 'law and order' and growing government recourse to authoritarianism.

Carrington *et al.* (2018) observe that the technological, economic and other forces driving these shifts also reflect a profound transformation in the ways power is projected in the contemporary world. No longer a matter simply of territorial control or expansion by states, practices of rule are increasingly embodied in information and knowledge-based economic and financial circuits, often presided over by placeless elites who owe fidelity to no nation. Digital technologies permit the organization and coordination of economic, political and cultural life without reference to national borders or the territorial boundaries of legal systems. One effect has been to unleash new policing and surveillance strategies as we observed in the previous chapter. At the same time, the costs of organizing crime and violence on an extra-territorial scale are also much reduced, producing criminal activities in new forms with amplified harmful effects: cybercrimes, online frauds, terrorism, people trafficking and so on as we also observed in the previous chapter.

These developments are also facilitating a convergence of illicit with legitimate practices: reputable international banks aided by corps of professional lawyers and accountants provide the 'financial getaway vehicles' needed to successfully execute all manner of crimes, from money laundering for drug cartels to the corporate bribery of foreign governments to global tax evasion by corporations. The worlds of North and South and rich and poor are thus connected in novel ways by these and other criminal activities, including environmental crime and corruption. There is a shading of crime into politics, and in extreme cases – as with the war on terror and the war on drugs – into armed conflict and warfare. Crime takes on a novel geopolitical and strategic significance, especially as impacts readily flow across borders. Responses in turn blur the boundaries between domestic criminal justice administration and the deployment of force for defence and national security purposes. They also blur, where they do not blatantly flout, the boundaries between legality and illegality: the use of drones to undertake assassinations in foreign countries in violation of their sovereignty, the outsourcing of war to private warlords and corporate mercenaries and the return of state-sponsored torture (Carrington et al., 2018).

Carrington et al. (2018) observe that the massively increased salience of knowledge and information in the organization of contemporary social and economic life further emphasizes the critical importance of issues of cognitive justice which lie at the heart of the Southern criminology project. For, notwithstanding the evidence of declining global inequality, countries outside the North Atlantic metropole continue to occupy a subordinate position in the global organization of social scientific (and criminological) knowledge. That criminologies in the South have, until recently, tended to accept their subordinate place (Carrington et al., 2016) has stunted the intellectual development and vitality of criminology, in the South, across Asia and globally. It has also perpetuated the relative neglect of pressing criminological issues which affect both North and South.

Carrington et al. (2018) observe that Southern criminology is a theoretical, empirical and political project of redemption. It seeks to modify the criminological field to make it more inclusive of histories and patterns of crime, justice and security outside the global North. It seeks to introduce a perspective based on the analysis of crime and justice in the global South and of the historical and contemporary relationships linking South and North which have been constitutive of forms of life and thought in both but which have been obscured by the metropolitan hegemony over criminological knowledge. It approaches these relationships as layered and dynamic rather than fixed, binary and forever oppositional. It acknowledges the obstacles to knowledge production and dissemination presented by the growing dominance of the English language as a global medium for sharing ideas, publishing, conference organization and research evaluation. The impact is nonetheless not confined to the South. There is a need therefore to foster stronger links and dialogues not only across the South but between South and North.

Southern criminology is thus a theoretical project. It seeks to encourage and support theoretical innovation and not just the application of theory imported from the global North. It is moreover a democratizing epistemology which challenges the power imbalances which have privileged knowledges produced in the metropolitan centres of the global North. Its purpose is not to dismiss the conceptual and empirical advances which the social sciences have produced over the last century but to correct biases by decolonizing and democratizing the toolbox of available criminological concepts, theories and methods (Carrington et al., 2016).

Rethinking criminology from the global South

Southern theory thus draws attention to the way concepts based on empirical specificities of the English-speaking global North have been inappropriately generalized to the global South or neglected their specific differences (Carrington et al., 2016). The tendency to overlook or marginalize major historical and contemporary forms and trends in criminal justice practice that lie outside the Northern metropole have also skewed criminological theorizing. Southern experiences have been dismissed or neglected as sources for theoretical elaboration and reconstruction. Even where the more recent impacts of globalization have been a focus of criminological theorizing, it has also been too readily assumed that Northern trends – like neoliberal penality – simply spread across the globe. There has been a failure to do justice to difference and diversity in the sources and trajectories of economic, social and penal policy (Connell and Dados, 2014). While aspects of neoliberal crime control are evident in some of the trends in punishment in these countries, their penal practices are diverse, being shaped by distinctive local political economies and cultures of crime control.

Feminist concepts, produced largely in the Anglophone world in the Northern Hemisphere, have likewise tended to travel from North to South and West to East (Dongchao, 2017), neglecting the distinctive forms of gendered crime and violence which occur outside the Anglophone world. This is not to suggest that these analyses are faulty, simply that they are selective in privileging empirical referents and theoretical concepts derived from the geopolitical specificities of the metropolitan centres of the global North. Like criminology more generally, feminist criminology needs to broaden its conceptual and spatial horizons by globalizing its research agendas to add voices from the global South.

Recently, Asian criminology has grown rapidly with the establishment and growing strength of the Asian Society of Criminology, the creation of *The Asian Journal of Criminology* and a proliferation of research and publications dedicated to criminological issues in Asia (Liu *et al.*, 2012). These initiatives are all important steps in creating an institutional basis for an Asian criminology which resists the importation of metropolitan assumptions and theory, like contemporary strain theory (Agnew, 2015; Lin, 2012) to study crime in Asian societies and which might therefore align with the concerns of Southern criminology. As John Braithwaite (2015: 1) has observed, 'Asia's most important contribution to global criminology is . . . in opening its eyes to completely new ways of seeing, as opposed to adjusting, testing, or revising western theories in light of eastern experience'. He thus identifies a number of distinctive ways which the restorative shaming, peacebuilding, and reconciliation practices of Indonesia, East Timor, Pakistan, Afghanistan, Nepal and Polynesia create the basis for the development of an Asian criminology from which the rest of the world can learn. After all, muses Braithwaite, these societies have been more successful at preventing crime than the societies from which general theories of crime originate, a view shared not so surprisingly by other prominent scholars committed to the advancement of Asian criminology (Liu, 2009).

In the following two sections, we consider the different perceptions of, first, violence and, second, gendered crime offered by a Southern criminology perspective.

Crimes outside the metropole: the many worlds of violence

Carrington *et al.* (2016) observe a glaring contrast between the different worlds of violence to be found in the North and South which emphasizes the myopia of so much metropolitan criminology. In addition to poverty and multiple deprivations, organized violence in all its forms and manifestations is also heavily concentrated in the global South. The World Bank (2011: 2) estimated that 'one in four people on the planet, more than 1.5 billion, live in fragile and conflict-affected states or in countries with very high levels of criminal violence.' While, the incidence of both interstate and civil wars have declined since the 1990s, other forms of large-scale criminal violence and 'cycles of repeat violence' (drug wars, political violence and high levels of violent crime) have increased. The condition no longer fits comfortably within twentieth-century paradigms of conflict. It cannot usefully be described as either one of 'war' or of 'peace' (World Bank, 2011: 2). Many countries (including South Africa and the Central American republics) have made progress in relation to political conflict only to continue to be afflicted by high levels of criminal violence. Homicide rates in Latin America, for example, are 'the highest in the world (rate 27.5 per 100,000 pop.), over three times greater than those for the European Region' (Briceno-Leon et al., 2008: 752).

Violence and organized crime are intimately related to other problems, of governance, poverty and environmental destruction. Lucrative criminal activities – such as drug trafficking – finance political movements and corrupt public officials (as in Mexico; see Morris, 2012). Countries experiencing such violence are also much more likely to fall behind others in addressing their high levels of poverty and inequality (World Bank, 2010, 2011). Today, as in the past, many of these problems are conditioned not merely by forces from within (the idea that crime is local) but by the pattern of wider relationships within which countries are embedded. In a globally interconnected world, the collateral effects of violence also increasingly flow over national borders, spreading conflict and instability outward to neighbouring and, increasingly, also faraway countries.

Carrington et al. (2016) note that the dominant traditions within criminology have largely avoided interest in such forms of violence and conflict. Developed on the foundations of nineteenth-century practical social inquiry, medical science and moral statistics (Levin and Lindesmith, 1937), both the rational actor and the sociological variant of the predestined actor models have considered the urban context of metropolitan societies as the natural laboratory of criminological inquiry and theory (Hogg and Carrington, 2006). A central concern was with the disruptive effects of migration and urbanization on traditional patterns of social control in predominantly agrarian societies. The mass movement of people (both within and across national borders) from rural to urban was seen as a major source of social disorganization, fractured communities, cultural conflict and myriad associated pathologies of urban life – gangs, ghettos, organized crime, drunkenness, sexual promiscuity, suicide and so on – necessitating enlarged criminal justice powers and institutions and measures like organized philanthropy, social work and slum clearance (Baldwin and Bottoms, 1976). In these theories and research programmes, the countryside and 'traditional' rural worlds were largely seen as an undeveloped, naturally cohesive space, the alter ego of the fearful, crime-infested inner cities, although in reality, in countries of the North, this was mostly assumed rather than actually researched (Bottoms, 1994). The role of patriarchy and coerced social control in the maintenance of cohesive, hierarchical social relations in the countryside was also generally overlooked (Alston, 1995; Carrington and Scott, 2008).

From a Southern standpoint, this perspective simply ignored the historical role of states and the actual direction of movement of people, institutions and ideas which were central to shaping societies of the South as they were drawn into the orbit of the European imperial order. In other words, empire was missing from the analysis. It overlooked the fact that European capitalism was engaged from the outset in the transformation of the global countryside in what was often a violent process (Beckert, 2014). From the standpoint of the colonial periphery, it was not the domestic urban context that was the primary site of world-shattering social change. The periphery, far from being an undeveloped rural arcadia, bears the heavy imprints of a 'globe-spanning system' which in different times and places involved (amongst other things): the transportation of African slaves (some 8 million between 1500 and 1800) to plantations in the Caribbean, parts of Latin America and the southern states of the US; the heavy reliance on other forced labour regimes (including convict labour and indentured labour systems such as that involving Pacific Islanders on the plantations of north Queensland); the expropriation of the lands of indigenous peoples; the violent suppression and criminalization of resistance; and the deindustrialization of domestic manufacturing and local moral economies in the South to serve the demands of metropolitan capitalists for raw materials and a mass supply of cheap wage labour (Beckert, 2014). The advance of industrial capitalism in the metropole in the nineteenth century worked hand in glove with the extension and intensification of state-sponsored 'war capitalism' (Beckert, 2014) in the periphery. Similarly, today the worlds of violence are interconnected by markets in drugs and guns and political intervention in new forms. Latin America's lethal drug wars, for example, persist due to Northern demand for illicit drugs and trade with Southern American countries in weapons (Grillo, 2014).

Carrington *et al.* (2016) observe that while metropolitan criminology focused on the urban context of industrializing countries of the North, the issue in many colonial-settler states (Australia being a classic example) was not primarily one of managing the migration of people from the countryside into fledgling cities but of how to populate the countryside with white settlers and contend with the resistance of its existing inhabitants to their physical and cultural dispossession (Reynolds, 1989; Goodall, 1996). The resulting conflicts and tensions are far from being of mere historical interest. The impact of past expropriation, frontier violence, segregation and autocratic administrative controls under supposed 'protection' and 'welfare' laws, concerted efforts at cultural decimation (breaking up families and removing children), reach into the present, adversely impacting indigenous health and well-being in myriad ways (Australian Institute of Health and Welfare [AIHW], 2014).

Problems persist due to the impacts of contemporary global economic and social change on the rural and remote periphery, affecting non-Indigenous, as well as Indigenous, people. As the most marginal section of local populations with the strongest ties to place, Indigenous communities tend to suffer the most grievous effects, but many of the forces in question are driving demographic change and shrinking economic opportunities and access to health, education and other services which affects everyone in the periphery. The always-fragile white presence has become increasingly so. In many places, there are also the exacerbating effects of multiple, interrelated conflicts over title to land (native title claims), over land use and over environmental degradation and the impacts of climate change (Cleary, 2014). All these factors have sharpened existing divisions (e.g. around race), brought others to the surface (around gender) and introduced new ones (amongst farmers, miners and environmentalists; White, 2013a).

Carrington *et al.* (2016) observe that a growing body of criminological research is being undertaken into the historical and contemporary forces transforming the global countryside. It reveals both high levels of crime (particularly violence) and very different responses to it (Hogg and Carrington, 2006; Barclay *et al.*, 2007; Donnermeyer and DeKeseredy, 2013). In Australia, rates of violence are on average considerably higher in regional and rural communities than in the cities (Hogg and Carrington, 2006). Most of it is blamed on Indigenous people, prompting angry demands for law and order crackdowns. High levels of violence in Indigenous communities is undeniable, but depicting the problem as solely an Indigenous one masks the fact that disproportionately high levels of violence exist in white rural populations (Hogg and Carrington, 2006). The temptation to externalize, or *other*, social problems to sustain idealized images of rural cohesion is a recurrent feature of public discourse around crime in many rural communities. Cloaking violence, especially sexual and domestic violence, in a culture of denial safeguards such images at the expense of the well-being of victims and their right to live without fear and threat (Hogg and Carrington, 2006).

The selective popular, official and criminological gaze which settles on the crimes of the socially excluded, overlooks, or normalizes, violence and harm elsewhere. At the present time, the global countryside across both North and South (including in some of the poorest countries in the world like Laos, Mozambique, Papua New Guinea, Peru and Sudan) is being transformed at the hands of a globalized resources sector eager to access natural resources – coal, iron ore, oil and so on – to meet exploding demand caused by the rapid industrialization of China, India and other Asian nations (World Bank, 2011). Poor, conflict-ridden countries and regions in the global South with weak political institutions are particularly vulnerable to powerful corporations looking to maximize short-term profits without regard for long-term consequences. Corruption, violence, expropriation of landowners, environmental degradation and diversion of scarce public resources are commonplace and mutually reinforcing in their harmful effects. Instead of their rich resource base delivering benefits to ordinary citizens, poverty, poor health, degraded living conditions and conflict are perpetuated and often exacerbated (Green and Ward, 2004; Ruggiero and South, 2013). Even Australia has not managed to escape some of the destructive environmental, social and criminological impacts of the global resource industry's appetite to tap its rich resource base (Carrington *et al.*, 2010, 2011; Cleary, 2014).

Carrington *et al.* (2016) observe that if stable, prosperous, democratic states cannot avoid corruption, cronyism, economic distortions and other symptoms of the 'resource curse', we can only ponder the vulnerability of poor and fragile states confronting the power of global corporations.

Gendered crime and victimization in the global South

The development of feminist criminology put gender at the centre and not the periphery of criminological theorizing and research. The default assumptions of feminist criminology nevertheless tended to mirror those of the discipline, by elevating and reproducing certain forms of metropolitan thinking (see Carrington, 2015). The particular forms of feminist theory which elevated sexual difference as a central homogenizing category of analysis led to a narrowing of the feminist gaze to localized gendered power relations and structures, such as patriarchy. Feminist scholars of colour argued that when women are positioned as a universal category, abstracted from the specificity diverse experiences of women across time, class, space, history, religion, economics, culture and geopolitics, women outside feminist normative constructions become colonized.

Like much of criminology, feminist criminologists have tended to confine their critical gaze mostly to domestic issues of criminal justice, at least until recently (Renzetti, 2013; Barberet, 2014; Carrington, 2015). There were good reasons for this given that feminist scholars focused their critical attention on the invisibility of women as victims and their unjust treatment by state-based masculinist justice systems (Gelsthorpe, 1989; Naffine, 1997). Carrington *et al.* (2016) observe that while these developments should be applauded, a theory nevertheless based singularly on gender is and always was insufficient to explain how women of colour, rural women, Indigenous women and women from impoverished backgrounds are uniquely susceptible to policing, criminalization and imprisonment (Carlen, 1983; Potter, 2015). Many of these women are, moreover, situated outside the metropole.

Pat Carlen (1992) had observed that is only by incorporating a tapestry of interconnections encompassing social position, race, ethnicity, location and gender that the chronic over-representation of particular groups of women in the criminal justice systems begin to be understood. Intersectionality has been posited as the theoretical antidote to the metropolitanism of feminism (see Chapter 13 for a full discussion). Hence, a transnational feminist criminology which adopts an intersectional approach can be seen as a significant advance on essentialist feminist frameworks which privileged a unified monocultural, transhistorical conception of gender (Henne and Troshynski, 2013; Renzetti, 2013; Barberet, 2014; Potter, 2015). Intersectionality is, as Henne and Troshynski (2013: 468) observe 'a corrective concept', but we are warned against emptying it of its postcolonial and geopolitical importance. Thus, whilst feminist criminology has come a long way, some argue that it still needs to internationalize and cast its gaze outside the boundaries of the nation state (Barberet, 2014), to examine global inequities and 'gendered experiences of colonization' (Renzetti, 2013) and 'to widen its research agendas to include the distinctively different gendered patterns of crime and violence which occur across the globe' (Carrington, 2015: 2).

Carrington *et al.* (2016) observe that since the 1960s, the growing internationalization of the economy has seen massive migration of former colonial populations to Europe and America in pursuit of economic opportunity and to meet the demand for cheap labour. Manufacturing operations have also relocated from North to South in search of cheap labour, often in countries with unstable political regimes, low levels of unionization, weak labour laws and high unemployment. Global demographic change has resulted in the mass incorporation of women from the global South into domestic work, export-processing and labour-intensive industries. Carrington *et al.* (2016) observe that this is the geo-economic context to one of the largest unsolved crimes (or series of crimes) of femicide of recent times. Between 1993 and 2010, an estimated 878 women were killed in the Mexican city of Juarez, a city of around 2.5 million people, perched on the border with the US. In the 1990s, thousands of jobs became available in the factories that located there following the establishment of the North American Free Trade Agreement (see the previous chapter).

For two decades, the Mexican criminal justice system failed to adequately investigate the murders of factory workers, many of native Indian descent who had migrated from poor rural areas of Mexico in search of jobs in 2004. Their journeys to and from work (often at night) in a city where drug cartels operated with impunity and corruption was rife made them highly vulnerable targets for sexual predators. While globalization opened up opportunities for these impoverished rural women to seek a measure of economic independence (Thayer, 2010), it also exposed them to exploitation and violence. They were stigmatized as outsiders, as public women, who drank, worked and socialized like men and aligned with the stigma of prostitution (Wright, 2005). The victims were blamed for their own fate, diverting public attention from the corrupt government officials, police dereliction of duty, drug cartels and complicit factory owners (Wright, 2005).

Over a longer period elsewhere in the global South, a very different pattern of gendered violence was experienced by women.

Zina is defined in centuries' old Islamic law as sex outside marriage (Mir-Hosseini, 2011). Where this particular Islamic law operates, it can result in a sentence of a hundred lashes or even death by stoning if adultery is involved (Khan, 2004). These traditional Islamic offences emerged in the eighth-century Islamic world to regulate sexuality, promiscuity and prostitution at a time when the patriarchal rule over women and slaves was a pregiven social reality. Over the intervening centuries, slavery was abolished, and Zina laws became legally obsolete in almost all Muslim countries and communities (Mir-Hosseini, 2011). That changed in the 1970s. Islamic fundamentalism revived Zina laws across the Muslim majority countries of Libya, Sudan, Aceh in Indonesia, Palestine, Algeria, Somalia, Iran, Pakistan, Iraq, Somalia, parts of Syria, Yemen, Afghanistan, Nigeria and Malaysia (Mir-Hosseini, 2011). Khan (2003), who undertook a study of women punished for Zina offences in Pakistan, argues that the revival of Zina laws in the twentieth century is a transnational feminist issue of significant and global concern.

Carrington *et al.* (2016) observe that an emergent feminist scholarship within the Muslim faith has taken issue with interpretations of Islamic law used to justify the revival of Zina offences (Khan, 2004; Rahat, 2005; Mir-Hosseini, 2011). They observe that the revival of Zina offences is based on patriarchal interpretations of Sharia law which have 'led to regressive gender policies, with devastating consequences for women: compulsory dress codes, gender segregation, and the revival of out-dated patriarchal and tribal models of social relations' (Mir-Hosseini, 2011: 12). They also argue that women punished for Zina are rendered invisible by a cultural relativist acceptance that Zina is a justifiable religious or customary practice (Khan, 2004). Islamic fundamentalism (like other contemporary fundamentalisms) is a modern phenomenon, a reaction to contemporary conditions, which consciously mixes carefully selected elements of the past with present political projects which have nothing traditional about them (Ruthven, 2004). Hence, the specific forms and effects of systemic violence and discrimination experienced by women where oppressive Islamic laws criminalize consensual adult sex outside marriage are considered to be an important project for a Southern criminology.

Carrington *et al.* (2016) observe that there is also much which feminists from the global North can learn from the struggles for justice by women in the global South. One example is the development of women–only police stations as an effective, although imperfect, method of combatting violence against women (Hauztinger, 2010). Established for the first time in Brazil in 1985 (which now has 475) women–only police stations have spread across Latin America, including Argentina, Bolivia, Brazil, Ecuador, Nicaragua, Peru and Uruguay. They deal exclusively with female victims of sexual and domestic violence. Evaluations have found they enhance the willingness of women to report, increase the likelihood of conviction and enlarge access to a range of other services such as counselling, health, legal, financial and social support (UN Women, 2011). Although their effectiveness depends on a range of local factors (Hauztinger, 2010), the overall success has led to their introduction in other parts of the world, including India, the Philippines, Sierra Leone, South Africa and Uganda.

Penality, punishment and Southern criminology

The trajectories and dynamics of modern penal development have been the focus of a prolific body of criminological scholarship since the 1970s, much of it influenced by the work of Foucault and the revival and revision of classical sociological theorizing around punishment (Garland, 1990). In generalizing from certain experiences in the metropole – the rise of the penitentiary in the nineteenth century, the contemporary global spread of neoliberal penal ideas – this scholarship conforms to a familiar (Northern) pattern. Carrington *et al.* (2016) observe one notable omission, more striking because of the particular historical focus of this work, relates to the connections between punishment and colonization and how they impact the contemporary understanding of penal practice. Empire is therefore, once again, an important connecting thread in the relationship between penal practices in the North and South. Mark Brown (2014) has argued that existing conceptions of the penal field need to be broadened if an account is to be taken of colonial penal practices. The broadening, he suggests, is not just geographical in nature but must also encompass the complex, shifting and contingent ways in which penal practice was articulated with forms of colonial rule according to local circumstances, in countries like India, for example, which is the focus of his research.

Carrington (2016) observe that quite apart from how colonial rule and penal practice were articulated *within* colonial settings, punishment was itself an instrument for projecting imperial power and culture across the globe. Penal transportation and the founding of convict colonies in the global South was a critical component of the statecraft of modern imperial powers. It was central to British domestic and colonial penality for more than three centuries until its cessation in the early twentieth century. Transportation to the Australian colonies was the most significant of these penal projects but was not the only one. Other European imperial states also used transportation as a penal measure, albeit not on the same scale as Britain (Thayer, 2010).

Transportation has nevertheless received little attention in the criminological literature on penal modernism (although see Rusche and Kirchheimer, 1939). Ignoring or substantially writing it out of the history of penal modernism overlooks not only its role in shaping the societies founded and/or developed as penal colonies but also the significant impacts it had on metropolitan penal developments. It also severs the genealogy of modern punishment from other experiences and histories which are constitutive of global modernity: colonialism, enclosure and dispossession, migration and forced labour in its many different forms.

Carrington *et al.* (2016) note that in more recent times, restorative justice ideas and practices have been developed in the South, drawing in particular on New Zealand Maori and other Indigenous forms of dispute resolution (Richards, 2009). In other parts of the global South, including South Africa, Latin America and Timor Leste, similar (often Indigenous) traditions have informed the building of new justice institutions and processes – truth and reconciliation commissions and other transitional justice mechanisms – to support the transition from colonial domination or military dictatorship to democracy, to address gross human rights abuses of the past and to protect against future outbreaks of violent conflict (Tutu, 2000; Liu, 2009; Richards, 2009; Braithwaite, 2013, 2015). These initiatives, often with their roots in the periphery of the periphery, suggest wholly new ways of looking at the world and at how the struggle for justice and democracy might be pursued. Grappling with such questions in war-torn Afghanistan, John Braithwaite has identified some hopeful signs for building peace and democracy in certain surviving traditional localized justice practices. He makes the general point that 'criminologists need to be part of a debate about the path to democracy that starts at the periphery of a society rather than at the centre' (Braithwaite, 2013: 209). Elsewhere, he points out that other Asian societies, those in the East, have generally been successful at preventing crime – even as they grappled with the legacies of colonization, the challenges of modernization and combatting widespread poverty – and might therefore offer some relevant lessons for Northern societies which manage to produce a lot of criminology but enjoy less success when it comes to crime prevention (Braithwaite, 2015).

In recent years, the neoliberal thesis on penality has become a widely accepted way of thinking about the punitive turn in criminal justice. This thesis is nevertheless based on specific experiences of the global North, in the main that of the US since the 1970s. It is a narrative which describes the contemporary penal field as being heavily colonized by a trend of increasing punitiveness, driven by the emergence of neoliberalism which we have seen is a political project designed and developed by an increasingly transnational elite which has radically transformed the character of the state in the spheres of economic, social and penal interventions. This narrative is embedded most strongly in the work of Wacquant (2009a, 2009b), who argues that what happened to criminal justice initially in the US spread as the neoliberal political project with which it is connected reached across the world. He provides examples from the global North, especially from Europe (Britain and France) to support his argument, although acknowledging more complexity in the process in his most recent version (Wacquant, 2009b). It is a thesis which has also been extended to penality in countries of the global South, particularly in Latin America (in relation to Brazil, see Wacquant, 2003, 2008; and more generally, see Iturralde, 2010a, 2010b: 3012). Wacquant and his legacy are discussed in more detail in Chapter 18.

Carrington et al. (2016) note that neoliberalism was promoted in South America during the 1970s, 1980s and 1990s, in different times and contexts and by different government, economic and social reforms. Neoliberal reforms in that continent occurred under the auspices of both dictatorial and democratic governments, which followed the lead of international agencies like the World Bank and the International Monetary Fund. Simultaneously, there has also been a punitive turn in those societies, as measured by incarceration rates (an imperfect but the only available indicator), as in Colombia and Brazil. This does not necessarily mean that in such cases, the relationship between the influence of neoliberalism and this punitive turn can be considered simple or automatic, as the example of Argentina illustrates. At the beginning of the 1990s, neoliberal reforms under the auspices of 'Menemism' – the political alliance built around the figure of President Menem who governed Argentina between 1989 and 1999 – was combined with a moderate growth of some indicators of punitiveness but also with a certain stability in others. This changed in the second half of the 1990s, when penal populism emerged from a crisis of legitimacy in the context of the strong politicization of crime (Sozzo, 2011). After a strong trend towards increased punitiveness from the mid-1990s, the incarceration rate continued to increase during the 'Kirchnerist' process of political change which began in 2003 but to a much lower degree (Sozzo, 2011). Something similar has occurred in Uruguay since 2005. Furthermore, there are also other national cases in the region in which the simultaneous presence of reforms inspired by neoliberal principles and a punitive turn are not evident, at least in terms of incarceration rates, as in Venezuela during the 1990s or Bolivia between mid-1990 and mid-2000 (Sozzo, 2011).

Carrington et al. (2016) observe that the use of the neoliberal penality thesis to describe and explain the penal system present in this region of the global South is also hampered by another crucial element. In several national contexts, from the late 1990s, political change has seen the rise of political alliances and programmes which have built their identities around being 'post-neoliberal', reflecting different levels of radicalism and connections with local traditions of the Left (in Venezuela since 1999, Brazil and Argentina since 2003, Uruguay since 2005, Bolivia since 2006 and Ecuador since 2007). Of course, there is variation between these nation states. But in all of them, there are some important manifestations such as the expansion of social policies, strengthening of state intervention in the market, non-alignment with the US in international relations and the nationalization of previously privatized public services.

In some of these countries, only more recently has there been a strong punitive turn, at least as measured by the indicator of the rate of imprisonment, as in Bolivia or, even more dramatically, in Venezuela. But in other cases, the growing punitive trend observed in the recent past has continued, such as in Brazil (Carrington *et al.*, 2016). It is, therefore, impossible to assume recent trends toward increased punitiveness in these scenarios are simply the consequence of neoliberalism and treat them as an integral part of some uniform, transnational political project. The link between these governmental experiences and penality is more complex (O'Malley, 2014).

This brief exploration of penal trends in the global South – as with the earlier examples – provokes a radical rethink of criminological arguments based on experiences in the global North. Metropolitan criminology has too readily generalized from the impact of neoliberalism in its own societies to the rest of the world. Globalization is often depicted as westernization or the simple extension of the neoliberal commitment to free markets, small government and harsh punishment across the globe. Such simplification simply fails to do justice to global diversity in the sources and trajectories of neoliberalism (Connell and Dados, 2014) and its impacts on penal policies, practices and developments, including diversity within the US itself.

Policy implications of Southern theory

Carrington *et al.* (2016) see Southern criminology as a theoretical, empirical and political project aimed at bridging global divides and democratizing epistemology by levelling the power imbalances which privilege knowledges produced in the metropolitan centres of the global North, particularly those located in the Anglo world. As an empirical project, it seeks to modify the criminological field to make it more inclusive of patterns of crime, justice and security outside the boundaries of the global North (see also Walklate, 2015). The authors propose a dual purpose: first, to highlight certain distinctive forms and patterns of crime and trends in criminal justice practice in the global South which substantially elude criminological theory that generalizes from Northern experience and, second, to show that North and South are globally interconnected in ways and with effects, both historical and contemporary, which warrant inclusion in criminological research, theoretical and policy agendas. Southern criminology is also a theoretical project which seeks to adjust the theoretical lens of interpretation and to recover histories rooted in colonialism to enable it to more usefully account for the divergent patterns of crime, violence and justice which occur outside the metropole and their power effects on everyday life in the global South.

Summary of main points

1   Raewyn Connell (2007) argues that a structural imbalance in the economy of knowledge has produced a hegemony of social scientific thought based on the experience of a small number of societies in the global North.

2   Criminology has been highly urban-centric as well as 'terra-centric', pursuing a highly selective focus on crime and justice in large population centres to the exclusion of the many more spaces and places that lie beyond them.

3   Southern criminology must develop a more complex, dynamic conceptualization of the South and North/South relationships if the intellectual biases are to be corrected.

4   Massive strides have been made in the reduction of global poverty which has also brought about a decline in global inequality between countries but at the same time inequality *within* them has increased just about everywhere (Bourguignon, 2016).

5   Southern criminology seeks to modify the criminological field to make it more inclusive of histories and patterns of crime, justice and security outside the global North.

6   Violence and organized crime are intimately related to other problems, of governance, poverty and environmental destruction.

7   The default assumptions of feminist criminology have mirrored those of the discipline by elevating and reproducing certain forms of metropolitan thinking.

8   An emergent feminist scholarship within the Muslim faith has taken issue with interpretations of Islamic law used to justify the revival of Zina offences.

9   Punishment was itself an instrument for projecting imperial power and culture across the globe. Penal transportation and the founding of convict colonies in the global South were critical components of the statecraft of modern imperial powers.

10 In more recent times, restorative justice ideas and practices have been developed in the South, drawing in particular on New Zealand Maori and other Indigenous forms of dispute resolution.

Discussion questions

1   What is the focus of Southern theory?
2   How do Southern theory criminologists explain different levels of violent crime in the south?
3   In what way has Southern theory contributed to global feminist debates?
4   How would you explain the re-emergence of fundamentalist religious responses to crime since the 1970s?
5   What contributions has Southern criminology made to the global criminological project?

Suggested further reading

Raewyn Connell (2007) provides the definitive introduction to Southern theory, but Connell and Dados (2014) discuss the market and neoliberalism in a southern context. Carrington *et al.* (2016, 2018) provide excellent introductions to the impact of Southern theory on criminology and develop the themes covered in this chapter in more detail.

References

Aas, K. (2011) 'Visions of Global Control: Cosmopolitan Aspirations in a World of Friction', in M. Bosworth and C. Hoyle (eds.) *What Is Criminology?* Oxford: Oxford University Press.

Agnew, R. (2015) 'Using General Strain Theory to Explain Crime in Asian Societies', *Journal of Asian Criminology*, 10(2): 131–147. https://doi.org/10.1007/ s11417-014-919-2 [Accessed 6 May 2015].

Alexander, M. (2010) *The New Jim Crow: Mass Incarceration in the Age of Colorblindness*. New York: The New Press.

Alston, M. (1995) *Women on the Land*. Sydney: University of NSW Press.

Australian Institute of Health and Welfare (AIHW) (2014) National Key Performance Indicators for Aboriginal and Torres Strait Islander Primary Health Care: Results from December 2013, Cat. no. IHW 146, AIHW.

Baldwin, J. and Bottoms, A.E. (1976) *The Urban Criminal*. London: Tavistock.

Barberet, R. (2014) *Women, Crime and Criminal Justice*. London and New York: Routledge.

Barclay, E., Donnermeyer, J., Scott, J., and Hogg, R. (eds.) (2007) *Crime in Rural Australia*. Leichhardt, NSW: Federation Press.

Beckert, S. (2014) *Empire of Cotton: A New History of Global Capitalism*. London: Allen Lane.

Beldi, L. (2016) 'Carteret Climate Refugees Seek Home', *ABC Pacific Beat*. Available from: www.abc. net.au/news/2016-0-07/carteret-climate-refugees-new-home/7693950. [Accessed 6 May 2019].

Belich, J. (2011) *Replenishing the Earth: The Settler Revolution and the Rise of the Anglo-World, 173–1939*. Oxford: Oxford University Press.

Bottoms, A. (1994) 'Environmental Criminology', in M. Maguire, R. Morgan and R. Reiner (eds.) *The Oxford Handbook of Criminology*. Oxford: Oxford University Press.

Bourguignon, F. (2016) Inequality and Globalization: How the Rich Get Richer as the Poor Catch Up. *Foreign Affairs*, 95(1), 11–15.

Bowling, B. (2011) 'Transnational Criminology and the Globalisation of Harm Pro-duction', in M. Bosworth and C. Hoyle (eds.) *What Is Criminology?* Oxford: Oxford University Press.

Braithwaite, J. (2013) 'Truth, Reconciliation and Peacebuilding', in R. King, V. MacGill and R. Wescombe (eds.) *Peace in Action: Practices, Perspectives and Policies That Make a Difference*. Sydney: King.

Braithwaite, J. (2015) 'Rethinking Criminology Through Radical Diversity in Asian Reconciliation', *Asian Journal of Criminology*, 10(3): 11–3. https://doi.org/10.1007/s11417-014-9200-z [Accessed 6 May 2019].

Braithwaite, J. and Wardak, A. (2013) 'Crime and War in Afghanistan, Part 1: The Hobbesian Solution', *British Journal of Criminology*, 53(2): 179–96. https://doi.org/10.1093/bjc/azs066 [Accessed 6 May 2019].

Briceno-Leon, R., Villaveces, A. and Concha-Eastman, A. (2008) 'Understanding the Uneven Distribution of the Incidence of Homicide in Latin America', *International Journal of Epidemiology*, 37: 751–7.

Brown, M.D. (2014) *Penal Power and Colonial Rule*. Abingdon, Oxon: Routledge.

Carlen, P. (1983) *Women's Imprisonment*. London: Routledge & Kegan Paul.

Carlen, P. (1992) 'Criminal Women and Criminal Justice: The Limits to, and Potential of, Feminist and Left Realist Perspectives', in R. Matthews and J. Young (eds.) *Issues in Realist Criminology*. London: Sage.

Carrington, K.B. (2015) *Feminism and Global Justice*. Abingdon: Routledge.

Carrington, K.B. and Hogg, R. (2017) 'Deconstructing Criminology's Origin Stories: A View from the Global South', *Asian Journal of Criminology*. https://doi.org/10.1007/s11417-017-924-7 [Accessed 6 May 2019].

Carrington, K.B., Hogg, R. and McIntosh, A. (2011) 'The Resource Boom's Underbelly: The Criminological Impact of Mining Development', *Australian and New Zealand Journal of Criminology*, 44: 335–54.

Carrington, K.B., Hogg, R., Scott, J. and Sozzo, M. (2018) 'Criminology, Southen Theory and Cognitive Justice', in K.B. Carrington, R. Hogg, J. Scott and M. Sozzo (eds.) *The Palgrave Handbook of Criminology and the Global South*. London: Palgrave Macmillan.

Carrington, K.B., Hogg, R., and Sozzo, M. (2016) 'Southern Criminology', *British Journal of Criminology*, 56(1): 1–20. https://doi.org/10.1093/bjc/azv03 [Accessed 7 May 2019].

Carrington, K.B., McIntosh, A. and Scott, J. (2010) 'Globalization, Frontier Masculinities and Violence: Booze, Blokes and Brawls', *British Journal of Criminology*, 50: 393.

Carrington, K.B. and Scott, J. (2008) 'Masculinity, Rurality and Violence', *British Journal of Criminology*, 48: 641–66.

Christopher, E., Pybus, C., and Rediker, M. (2007) 'Introduction', in E. Christopher, C. Pybus, and M. Rediker (eds.) *Many Middle Passages: Forced Migration and the Making of the Modern World*. Berkeley: University of California Press.

Cleary, P. (2014) 'Native Title Contestation in the Pilbara', *International Journal of Crime, Justice and Social Democracy*, 3: 132–4.

Connell, R.W. (2007) *Southern Theory: The Global Dynamics of Knowledge in Social Science*. Sydney: Allen and Unwin.

Connell, R.W. and Dados, N. (2014) 'Where in the World Does Neoliberalism Come From? The Market Agenda in Southern Perspective', *Theory and Society*, 43(2): 117–3. https://doi.org/10.1007/s1116-014-9212-9.

Cunneen, C. (2001) *Conflict, Politics & Crime: Aboriginal Communities & Police*. Crows Nest, NSW: Allen and Unwin.

Dillon, M. and Westbury, N. (2007) *Beyond Humbug: Transforming Government Engagement with Indigenous Australia*. West Lakes: Seaview Press.

Dongchao, M. (2017) *Translation and Travelling Theory: Feminist Theory and Praxis in China*. London: Routledge.

Donnermeyer, J. and DeKeseredy, W. (2013) *Rural Criminology*. Oxon and New York: Routledge.

Frank, A. (1970) 'The Development of Underdevelopment', in R. Rhodes (ed.) *Imperialism and Underdevelopment: A Reader*. New York: Monthly Review Press.

Garland, D. (1990) *Punishment and Modern Society: A Study in Social Theory*. Chicago: University of Chicago Press.

Gelsthorpe, L. (1989) 'Sexism and the Female Offender: London: Gower Look in the Mirror', *The Daily World*, June 3.

Goodall, H. (1996) *Invasion to Embassy: Land in Aboriginal Politics in New South Wales 1770–1972*. Sydney: Allen & Unwin.

Gott, R. (2007) 'Latin America as a White Settler Society', *Bulletin of Latin American Research*, 26(2): 269–89. https://doi.org/10.1111/j.1470-9856.2007.00224.x [Accessed 6 May 2019].

Green, P. and Ward, T. (2004) *State Crime: Governments, Violence and Corruption*. London: Pluto Press.

Gregory, D. (2004) *The Colonial Present*. Oxford: Blackwell Publishing.

Grillo, I. (2014) 'Mexico's Deadly Narco-Politics', *New York Times*, October 9.

Hagan, J. (2003) *Justice in the Balkans: Prosecuting War Crimes in the Hague Tribunal*. Cambridge: Cambridge University Press.

Hagan, J. and Rymond-Richmond, W. (2008) *Darfur and the Crime of Genocide*. Chicago: Chicago University Press.

Hauztinger, S. (2010) 'Criminalising Male Violence in Brazil's Women's Police Stations: From Flawed Essentialism to Imagined Communities', *Journal of Gender Studies*, 11: 243–51.

Henne, K. and Troshynski, E. (2013) 'Mapping the Margins of Intersectionality: Criminological Possibilities in a Transnational World', *Theoretical Criminology*, 17: 455–73.

Hogg, R. (2002) 'Criminology beyond the Nation State: Global Conflicts, Human Rights and the "New World Disorder"', in K. Carrington and R. Hogg (eds.) *Critical Criminology: Issues, Debates, Challenges*. Cullompton: Willan.

Hogg, R. and Carrington, K. (2006) *Policing the Rural Crisis*. Leichardt, NSW: Federation Press.

Independent Commission on International Development Issues (1980) *North-South: A Programme for Survival*. London: Pan Books.

Independent Commission on International Development Issues (1983) *Common Crisis: North-South Cooperation for World Recovery*. Cambridge, MA: MIT.

Iturralde, M. (2010a) 'Democracies without Citizenship: Crime and Punishment in LatinAmerica', *New Criminal Law Review*, 13: 309–22.

Iturralde, M. (2010b) 'Emergency Penality and Authoritarian Liberalism: Recent Trends in Colombian Criminal Policy', *Theoretical Criminology*, 12: 377–97.

Khan, S. (2003) 'Zina and the Moral Regulation of Pakistani Women', *Feminist Review*, 75: 75–94.

Khan, S. (2004) 'Locating the Feminist Voice: The Debate on the Zina Ordinance', *Feminist Studies*, 30: 660–2.

Levin, Y. and Lindesmith, A. (1937) 'English Ecology and Criminology of the Past Century', *Journal of Criminal Law and Criminology*, 27: 1–16.

Lin, W.-H. (2012) 'General Strain Theory in Taiwan: A Latent Growth Curve Modeling Approach', *Asian Journal of Criminology*, 7(1): 37–54. https://doi.org/10.1007/s11417-010-9101.

Liu, J. (2009) 'Asian Criminology: Challenges, Opportunities and Directions', *Asian Journal of Criminology*, 4(1): 1–9. https://doi.org/10.10007/s11417-009-9066-7.

Liu, J., Hebenton, B. and Jou, S. (2012) *Handbook of Asian Criminology*. New York: Springer.

Mir-Hosseini, Z. (2011) 'Criminalising Sexuality: Zina Laws as Violence against Women in Muslim Contexts', *Sur International Journal on Human Rights*: 7–32.

Morris, S. (2012) 'Corruption, Drug Trafficking and Violence in Mexico', *Brown Journal of World Affairs*, 18: 29–44.

Naffine, N. (1997) *Feminism and Criminology*. Sydney: Allen & Unwin.

O'Malley, P. (2014) 'Prisons, Neoliberalism and Neo-liberal States. Reading Loïc Wacquant and Prisons of Poverty', *Thesis Eleven*, 3: 9–96.

O'Neill, J. (2013) *The Growth Map: Economic Opportunity in the BRICs and Beyond*. London: Portfolio Penguin.

Potter, H. (2015) *Intersectionality and Criminology: Disrupting and Revolutionizing Studies of Crime*. Abingdon: Routledge.

Rahat, I. (2005) 'Legal Injustices: The Zina Hudood Ordinance of Pakistan and Its Implications for Women', *Journal of International Women's Studies*, 7: 7–100.

Renzetti, C. (2013) *Feminist Criminology*. Abingdon: Routledge.

Reynolds, H. (1989) *Dispossession: Black Australians and White Invaders*. Sydney: Allen & Unwin.

Richards, K. (2009) 'Rewriting and Reclaiming History: An Analysis of the Emergence of Restorative Justice in Western Criminal Justice Systems', *International Journal of Restorative Justice*, 5: 104–2.

Ruggiero, V. and South, N. (2013) 'Green Criminology and Crimes of the Economy: Theory, Research and Praxis', *Critical Criminology*, 21: 359–73.

Rusche, G. and Kirchheimer, O. (1939) *Punishment and Social Structure*. New York: Russell & Russell.

Ruthven, M. (2004) *Fundamentalism: The Search for Meaning*. Oxford: Oxford University Press.

Samson, J. (2011) 'Pacific History in Context', *Journal of Pacific History*, 46(2): 244–250. https://doi.org/10.1080/00223344.2011.607273 [Accessed 6 May 2019].

Sozzo, M. (2011) *Transition to Democracy and Penal Policy: The Case of Argentina*. Straus Working Paper 03/11, School of Law, New York University.

Thayer, M. (2010) *Making Transnational Feminism*. Oxon: Routledge.

Tutu, D. (2000) *No Future without Forgiveness*. London: Random House.

United Nations Department of Economic and Social Affairs (2009) *State of the World's Indigenous Peoples*. New York: United Nations.

United Nations Development Programme (UNDP) (2013) *The Rise of the South: Human Progress in a Diverse World*. Human Development Report 2013. New York: United Nations.

UN Women (2011) *Women's Police Stations in Latin America Case Study: An Entry Point for Stopping Violence and Gaining Access*. Available from: www.endvawnow.org/uploads/browser/files/security_wps_case_study.pdf [Accessed 12 May 2019].

Varoufakis, Y. (2016) *And the Weak Suffer What They Must? Europe, Austerity and the Threat to Global Stability*. London: Vintage.

Wacquant, L. (2003) 'Towards a Dictatorship Over the Poor: Notes on the Penalization of Poverty in Brazil?', *Punishment and Society*, 5: 197–205.

Wacquant, L. (2008) 'The Militarization of Urban Marginality Lessons from Brazilian Metropolis', *International Political Sociology*, 1: 56–74.

Wacquant, L. (2009a) *Prisons of Poverty*. Minneapolis: University of Minnesota Press.

Wacquant, L. (2009b) *Urban Outcasts: A Comparative Sociology of Advanced Marginality*. Cabridge: Polity Press.

Walklate, S. and McGarry, R. (eds.) (2015) *Criminology and War: Transgressing the Borders*. Cullompton: Routledge.

White, R. (2013a) 'Resource Extraction Leaves Something Behind: Environmental Justice and Mining', *International Journal for Crime, Justice and Social Democracy*, 2: 50–64.

World Bank (2010) *Indigenous Peoples: Still among the Poorest of the Poor, Policy Brief*. Available from: https://academic.oup.com/bjc/article-abstract/56/1/1/246242 [Accessed 9 May].

World Bank (2011) 'World Development Report 2011: Conflict, Security, and Development: Overview', *World Development Report*, World Bank Group. Available from: http://documents.worldbank.org/curated/en/2011/01/1421992/world-development-report-2011-conflict-security-development-overview.

Wright, M. (2005) 'Paradoxes, Protests, and the Mujeres de Negro of Northern Mexico', *Gender, Place, and Culture*, 12: 177–92.

Chapter 11

Critical race theory

Key issues

1   Core themes and
2   Theoretical framework
3   Critical race criminology
4   Hip-hop: from South Bronx to global footprint
5   Sharing a parallel universe

Defining critical race theory

Critical race theory is another key component of the critical criminological armoury and refers to a historical and contemporary body of scholarship which aims to interrogate the discourses, ideologies and social structures which have produced and maintained conditions of racial injustice. Critical race theory thus analyses how race and racism are foundational elements in historical and contemporary social structures and social experiences.

In defining critical race theory, it is important to make a distinction between the long-established historical tradition of critical theorizing about race and racism and a specific body of legal scholarship which emerged in the US during the 1970s and 1980s in response to the successes and failures of the civil rights movement struggles for the freedom and liberation of black people during the 1950s and 1960s. While this new school of legal thought created the term *critical race theory* to indicate a new critical analysis of the role of the law in propagating and maintaining racism, this movement is nevertheless part of a broader intellectual tradition of critical theories of race and anti-racist struggle which has political roots in the work of pioneering scholar-activists like Frederick Douglass, Ida Wells-Barnett and W.E.B. Du Bois. Using this broader framework, critical race theory can be viewed as a diagnostic body of 'intellectual activism' scholarship which has sought to identify the pressure points for anti-racist struggle. Given the historical scope of critical race theories, the following section highlights several core themes which have brought together this eclectic body of explicitly political theorizing.

Core themes

The first core theme deals with how critical race theories frame their two focal objects of study: race and racism. First, critical race theory understands the concept of race as a social construction which is produced as a result of the cultural and political meanings ascribed to it through social interactions and relationships across multiple levels of social organization. Thus, since the seventeenth century, race has been a constitutive feature of global social, political, economic and cultural organization. Critical race theories demonstrate how race concepts and their accompanying racisms were foundational to the administration of colonial social systems, the rise and expansion of global capitalism and the emergence of the human biological sciences and medicine of the eighteenth, nineteenth and twentieth centuries.

Critical race theorists have rejected the notion that racism is limited to malign individual prejudice and have embraced a more structural understanding of racism. An organizing theme of critical race theory is that there is not, and has never been, one monolithic and universal form of racism. In 1967, black radicals Stokely Carmichael and Charles V. Hamilton devised the term 'institutional racism' to identify how racism is embedded in social structures and multiple institutions. In highlighting the structural dynamics of racism, critical race theorists challenge the idea that black people are solely responsible for their own oppression. Drawing on these formulations, contemporary critical race theories understand racism as a vast and complicated system of institutionalized practices that structure the allocation of social, economic and political power in unjust and racially coded ways.

The second core theme is that critical race theories are grounded in the lived experiences, unique experiential knowledge and narrative voice of racialized and subordinated communities. Strongly influenced by previous freedom movements against colonialism, segregation and racial violence, these theorists have engaged pragmatically in 'intellectual activism' which has aimed not only to theorize but also resist these conditions of racial oppression. These lived experiences are not, however, always reflected in the activities of scholars located in professional academia. Critical race theorists have thus helped to produce and have drawn upon social and intellectual movements for liberation and empowerment in the US and elsewhere, such as the Harlem Renaissance, Black Nationalism and Afrocentrism. Not only have critical race theorists tended to emerge from subordinated social groups, but their theories also attempt to use the voices and experiences of black people in the pursuit of social and economic justice. We reflect further on this argument when we consider the parallel emergence and rise of the 'hip-hop nation' later in this chapter.

The third core theme is that critical race theory has traditionally used and continues to represent an interdisciplinary approach to the study of race and racism. The interdisciplinary and, indeed, extra-disciplinary nature of critical race theory enables the analysis of a wide range of social, economic and political phenomena which shape race and racism as social structures. Critical race theory draws on an interdisciplinary body of scholarship that has intellectual roots and practitioners in sociology (Brown et al., 2003), critical legal studies (Bell, 1989, 1993, 2004; Matsuda et al., 1993), political theory and philosophy (Goldberg, 1993, 2002), neo-Marxist British cultural studies (CCCS, 1982; Hall, 1992), African American literary criticism (Murray, 1970; Carby, 1998), history (Fredrickson, 2002; Marable, 2000) and philosophy (Outlaw, 1996; West, 1999).

In sociology, critical race theories draw heavily on the theoretical and philosophical orientations of Marxism, pragmatism and poststructuralism. Drawing on psychoanalytic and literary theories, critical race theorists have analysed the relationships between forms of cultural racism and colonial domination and have also documented and critiqued the role of nation states in the formation of racial categories in the enactment of different forms of political oppressions. From these various disciplinary locations, critical race

theories entail the illumination and critique of these discursive and institutional relationships between social constructions of race and the social practices of racism in terms
which makes opposition to these racial discourses and racist practices possible.

A fourth core theme is that critical race theories embrace and deploy quantitative,
qualitative and discursive methodologies to illuminate different aspects of race and racism
as social structural phenomena. Critical race theorists have used quantitative methodologies to map the contours of economic and spatial segregation, racist attitudes and
ideologies and racially coded health disparities. They have also deployed qualitative methodologies to understand the lived experiences and narratives of racially designated peoples
and discursive approaches to investigate the relationships between racial discourses and
the construction of racial subjects. As is discussed later, critical race theories also draw
heavily on historical and comparative frameworks which allow for the analysis of race and
racism as historically embedded social phenomena. This methodological pluralism, partly
a consequence of the interdisciplinary scope of critical race theory, has enabled the formulation of a response to the dominant social, political and scientific practices and ideas
which constitute race and racism in different historical periods.

Fifth, critical racial theories have long recognized and opposed the centrality of science
to the construction of racial meanings and practices. In fact, in what might be considered
the first treatise of critical race theory, the detailed analysis produced by W.E.B. Du Bois
in *The Philadelphia Negro* (1899) was intended to refute the claims that rates of poverty
and destitution among the black population of that city were the result of inherent biological and cultural inferiorities. Scientific racism consists of ideas of race based on pre-
sumed physiological, biological and/or genetic differences and the practices of deploying
such ideas as essentialist explanations for racial stratification and oppression. Critical race
theory has long contested these scientific claims which upheld racial hierarchies and have
justified ideologies of white supremacy. Whereas science had long been a tool of racial
oppression, it has nevertheless emerged as the spearhead and epistemic foundation of the
critical race theories of the post–Second World War era.

Core theoretical framework

While critical race theories have relied on a wide range of theoretical approaches, a
core framework embraced by many contemporary critical race theorists is that of *racial
formation*, which emerged in the 1990s as an explicitly historical and political approach
to analysing race as an organizing system of knowledge and power which combines
both discursive and institutional elements (Omi and Winant, 1994; Winant, 2001). The
racial formation framework stands in stark contrast to demographic approaches to race
which conceptualize race as a quantitative variable trait in population studies, biological
approaches which view race as something rooted in biology and/or genetics and colour-
blind approaches which wish to abandon the study of race concepts altogether. The racial
formation understands the construct of race as 'a concept that signifies and symbolizes
socio-political conflicts and interests in reference to different types of human bodies' (Omi
and Winant, 1994: 72). Analytically, this means always interpreting the meaning of race
in relation to the discursive practices which produce the idea of race; the social processes
through which racial categories are created, embodied, transformed and destroyed; and
the institutionalized power relations which are brought to bear in shaping racial conflicts
and interests (Omi and Winant, 1994).

These discursive and institutional elements form what are called 'racial projects' in which social and political conflicts and interests are waged over race bodies and racialized groups. This idea of racial projects is central to the racial formation approach because it draws the discursive and institutional elements of race and racism together into a single analytic framework. Omi and Winant (1994: 56) define racial projects as the discursive and institutional deployments of race which are both an interpretation, representation or explanation of racial dynamics and/or an effort to organize and distribute resources using racial categories. Racial projects combine what race means in a particular discursive practice and the ways in which both social structures and everyday experiences are racially organized based on that meaning (Winant, 2001, 2004).

Some critical race theorists, particularly black feminist theorists, have also articulated an intersectional theoretical approach to analysing the ways in which systems of gender, sexuality and nationalism are implicated in the production and maintenance of racial subordinations (Collins, 1990, 1998; Matsuda et al., 1993). Drawing on this earlier work, critical race theorists have continued to direct their attention to the ways in which the formulation, production and dissemination of cultural images and representations are placed in the service of white supremacy (Collins, 2005; hooks, 1981, 1990).

The myths of US democracy

In the post–civil rights era, critical race theorists have exposed and criticized the ways in which the myths of US democracy, meritocracy and progress and the ideology of individualism function to justify changing forms of racial domination (Delgado and Stefancic, 2001). In particular, critical race theorists have analysed new forms of colour-blind racism which enable and conceal the reproduction of racial inequality without direct reference to the social constructions of race (Bonilla-Silva, 2003; Williams, 1997). Colour-blind racism assumes that racial inequalities are the outcome of natural, economic and/or cultural differences between racialized groups and advocate that not using constructions of 'race' is necessary for the principled end of racism.

A major trajectory in this analysis of colour-blind racism is the analysis of the law and legal institutions as crucial sites for the production of colour-blind policies and practices. Legal scholar Derrick Bell (1989, 1993, 2004), considered to be the intellectual inspiration for the consolidation of critical race theories of the law, has demonstrated that conditions of racial segregation have ideological and pragmatic foundations in discourse about socially denigrated groups. His primary target is the absolutist position on the First Amendment protection of free speech and how this virtually inviolable constitutional right allows racist speech ideology to ripple throughout society, especially in universities.

Bell and his followers have also challenged the assumption that racial progress has been achieved in the post–civil rights era. Bell thus illuminates the partial truths of racial progress in US society by a close rereading of American political and legal history armed with the notion of silent covenant, a backdoor agreement among white elites to advance black interests and civil rights if and only they will also benefit whites. The implication of his analysis is that political freedom for oppressed racial groups is only achieved when it can be accomplished in the context of furthering white political domination. Bell recounts key moments in US social history which illustrate this relationship: the signing of the Constitution, the Emancipation Proclamation and, most important, the *Brown* decision, the landmark US Supreme Court case in which state laws establishing separate public schools for black and white students were declared unconstitutional. Bell argues that conditions of racial injustice are so entrenched in the US that, when modest gains for racial equality are achieved, they are too often interpreted as evidence that the struggle for racial equality is complete.

A final theme is illustrated in a recent exemplar of contemporary critical race theory. Many critical race theories go beyond diagnosis and critique to offer arguments and proposals for specific social policies which, if implemented, can work to undo the systemic disadvantages that impair the life chances and conditions of black people in the US. These theories continue to challenge entrenched racial inequalities in health, education, criminal injustice, political representation and economic opportunity (Brown *et al.*, 2003; Guiner and Torres, 2002; Shapiro, 2004). In an exemplar of contemporary critical race theory, a group of prominent sociologists attacked racial realism, a variant of colour–blind ideology, in which it is claimed that racism is largely over and the racial inequalities which remain are the result of the natural inclinations and cultural pathologies of black people (Brown *et al.*, 2003).

Critical race criminology

Michael Coyle (2010) argues that we can build on the use of language critique, which is fundamental to the critical justice theory research tradition, to develop a significant critical race criminology. Specifically, language studies can unmask the racism of modern 'criminal justice' discourse and modern 'criminal justice system' practices. It is thus proposed that researchers can identify the construction and maintenance of race work in the discourse and practices of 'criminal justice' in at least two important ways.

The first is to conduct individual investigations into any word or phrase commonly used in 'criminal justice discourse'. It is exactly because everyday justice discourse takes place within a body of interpretations, metaphors, rhetorical frames and, ultimately, ideology that can be and sometimes is racist that the study of the very words and phrases used in 'criminal justice discourse' will disclose the presence of racism.

Second, it is proposed that researchers can engage in a critical examination of the language they encounter in their research, regardless of its topic. Thus, for example, an ethnography of incarcerated black youth in a juvenile facility in the US can not only unveil the voice and meanings which these young people give to their experience but can also trace what the very words they use show about racism in incarcerated and everyday life.

From its very inception, the legal system in the US has been developed and refined by the privileged and the powerful, or by those individuals who have little to no experience or realistic understanding of poverty, despair, noiselessness, or for a legal system which can and should be developed from the bottom up. The US prison system is a good example of this 'top-down' approach. Thus, in general, many who favour harsh legislation and imprisonment as a means of deterrent punishment and retribution are from the privileged groups in society, while many of those that favour humane legislative enactments and rehabilitation as a means of punishment and imprisonment are typically those who feel and understand how life is messy, seedy and rarely as perfect as it is for the privileged (Johnson, 2008).

Critical race theory was to fully disrupt the analytical gaze which had captured the law and the legal academy since the beginning. Scholars were to literally stun the traditional academy which had likely expected gratitude and platitudes for racial advances accomplished, not insurrection or ingratitude. Critical race theory was to profoundly influence the academy as a whole, not just the legal academy. As a result, critical race theory programmes and scholars now thrive in universities throughout the US, its power and influence continuing and growing.

A.D.P. Cummings (2010) observes that in surprising ways, the origin and evolution of critical race theory parallel many of the paths traversed by the cultural movement of hip hop in its origin, development and calculated bottom–up assault on white privilege and black oppression.

Hip-hop: from South Bronx to global footprint

Forged in the fires of the South Bronx, New York, and Kingston, Jamaica, hip-hop became the clarion call of youth rebellion and a generation-defining movement. In the post–civil rights era defined by the de-industrialization and globalization we have encountered elsewhere in this book, hip-hop music and culture formed a multi-racial, poly-cultural worldview of a whole generation with the outcome of significantly changing US politics and values (Cummings, 2010).

In the early 1970s, a Jamaican disc jockey (DJ) known as DJ Kool Herc moved from Kingston, Jamaica, to the West Bronx in New York City. In his new home, Kool Herc adapted his style of chanting improvised rhymes over the instrumental or percussion sections of the day's popular records. This simple act of rhyming in verbal cadence over the hooks and loops of popular records was to become a runaway cultural phenomenon which captured the imagination of not just disaffected black and Latino youth but, ultimately, young people around the world as well (Light, 1999).

In October 1979, Sugar Hill Records released a single, titled 'Rapper's Delight' by The Sugarhill Gang, who sampled the funky rhythm of Chic's 'Good Times' (1979) and expressed a memorable stream of rhymes over the familiar hooks. The single sold more than two million copies worldwide and peaked at No. 4 on the Billboard R&B charts and No. 36 on the pop charts. For the burgeoning culture that would come to be known as hip-hop, this moment was a fulcrum. 'Rapper's Delight' was not the first hip-hop recording, but it marked the first time that the genre would be recognized by a national and even international audience. This revolutionary new sound and style, developed by poor black and Latino youth in the 1970s, had been captured on wax with an undeniable commercial outcome.

Following success in the street and parks of the South Bronx, young African American and Latino youngsters began mimicking Kool Herc by reciting their own original phrases and rhyming over familiar records' loops and instrumental sections. 'Call and response' became a trendy style of DJing in which a popular or catchy phrase 'rapped' by the DJ 'would evoke a response from a crowd who began to call out their own names and slogans. As this phenomenon evolved, the party shouts became more elaborate', giving young African American and Latino youth a chance to freely express themselves (Light, 1999: 13–20).

Hip-hop flourished immediately as it was accessible to all-comers. It was not necessary to have a lot of money or expensive resources to rhyme. Rapping was a verbal skill which could be practised and honed to perfection at almost any time. It appealed to young disaffected minority youth because it offered unlimited challenges and opportunities: as a cultural movement it allowed the individual to accurately and efficiently inject personality. If an MC was laid back, the MC could rap at a slow pace. If the MC was fast-paced, the MC could rap quickly and rhythmically. No two MCs rapped the same, even when reciting the same words, Thus, hip-hop nestled comfortably into the historic tradition of reflecting African American culture in its musical expression (Tanner et al., 2010).

Throughout history, music originating from African American communities has always included an accompanying subculture reflective of the political, social, and economic conditions of the time (Burton, 2009). Hip-hop culture – like all black art forms before it – embraced its own specific subculture, including graffiti art, break dancing, DJing (cutting and scratching), and rapping. Hip-hop culture was to become a lifestyle with its own language, style of dress, music and mindset. Initially, all major facets of hip hop were forms of countercultural self-expression accompanied by an express disregard for the law. But when it originated in the 1970s, hip-hop reflected the political, social and economic conditions at the time directly following the civil rights movement.

Hip-hop originated, in part, as a direct response to the civil rights generation's perceived rejection of the values and needs of urban young people. Additionally, hip-hop came about because of some major format changes that took place within black radio during the early 1970s. Prior to hip-hop, black radio stations played an important role in the community by being a musical and cultural storyteller. It reflected the customs and values of the day in particular communities. It set the tone and created the climate for which people governed their lives as this was a primary source of information and enjoyment (Light, 1999).

Martin Luther King, Jr., himself acknowledged the critical role that black radio played in the civil rights movement. In his August 1967 address to the National Association of Radio Announcers, Dr. King lauded black radio DJs for the intricate role they played in keeping the civil rights movement alive (Cummings, 2010).

Nevertheless, due in part to the narrowing of radio ownership, and the nationalization of radio station ownership rules, the influence of black radio decreased following the civil rights movement. National radio became dominated by disco and rock, with little space for black expression. Hip-hop culture and rap then began filling the void for urban African Americans. It was thus a direct response to the diminishment of black public radio and the watered-down, Europeanized disco music which permeated the airwaves in the 1970s and early 1980s.

To many, hip-hop spelled liberation and a return to authentic black music and expression. The dance and disco music of the 1970s buried the emotionally charged, folk-based soul music of the 1960s, which had been fuelled by the victorious poetic rhetoric of civil rights and black power. Rap and hip-hop meant that performers were free again to talk openly (Folami, 2007).

In addition to the disappearance of black public radio and the disaffection of minority youth with the civil rights generation, other crucial factors contributing to the platform from which the hip-hop revolution emerged included a US societal malaise represented by Vietnam, national political unrest, rampant stimulant/narcotic abuse, law-and-order mentality, unemployment and inner-city disenfranchisement. Another event precipitating the eventual intensity of hip-hop was the election of Richard Nixon as president of the US and a massive military conscription of urban black and Latino 18- to 20-year-olds creating, virtually overnight, a community-disrupting void. A result of this historical convergence was a spontaneous movement of ferocious intensity: the hip-hop nation was born (Cummings, 2010).

Hip-hop music and culture conquered the world. From its humble beginnings, it became in just three decades, a US phenomenon and a global cultural and entertainment movement. Hip-hop artists regularly top the US and international record sales charts. Motion pictures with hip-hop themes chart regularly on box office reports, both in the U.S. and internationally. Hip-hop artists have become record company moguls, international movie stars, clothing line designers, stars of reality television programming and world-renowned collaborators. Hip-hop studies programs have sprung up throughout the academy in the US, and a burgeoning body of literature has documented this global ascent. In a relatively short time, hip-hop has become a dominant cultural force in the world and, in many ways, has become the voice of a generation (Holloway, 2002).

This global movement had nevertheless emerged from very modest roots. Rap music and hip-hop culture were dismissed at their inception as a fad and were widely panned by critics and the majority public as an unimportant 'flash in the pan' musical movement. The public seemed content to ignore hip-hop and its trappings (break dancing, graffiti, DJing, etc.) when the movement was confined to the inner cities of major US metropolitan areas (Collins, 1988). Thus, when the 1970s and 1980s saw the releases of The Sugarhill Gang's 'Rapper's Delight', Africa Bambaataa's 'Planet Rock', Kurtis Blow's 'Basketball' and 'If I Ruled the World' and Whodini's 'Five Minutes of Funk', legislators and law enforcement paid little heed to this nascent movement, although the genre was becoming an increasingly powerful force (Light, 1999).

However, in the 1980s, when hip hop began creeping into the cassette players and minds of white American suburban youth, particularly with aggressive, violent, and counterculture lyrics, the US general public, legislators, and law enforcement began to take urgent notice (Collins, 1988). With the releases of Public Enemy's *It Takes a Nation of Millions to Hold us Back* (1988) and *Fear of a Black Planet* (featuring 'Don't Believe the Hype', 'Black Steel in the Hour of Chaos' and 'Fight the Power'; 1990), N.W.A.'s *Straight Outta Compton* (featuring 'Fuck tha Police' and 'Gangsta Gangsta'; (1988), Boogie Down Productions' *Criminal Minded* (1987), *By All Means Necessary* (1988) and Ice-T's single '6 in the Mornin'' (1988) and the heavy metal and punk-influenced 'Cop Killer' (1992), hip-hop suddenly attained considerable attention and criticism. This newfound status as controversial lightning rod emerged not just because of the explicit political and violent countercultural messages but also because these were being heard and received widely by inner-city youth as well as white suburban youth across the US (Cummings, 2010).

Despite a period of intense criticism and attempts to discredit and eradicate hip-hop, including aggressive attacks by the Federal Bureau of Investigation, Central Intelligence Agency and local law enforcement across the US, hip-hop has not just survived but has also influenced and dominated a generation: the hip-hop generation (Kitwana, 2005). From the 1980s to the present day, hip-hop culture has grown in its power and influence. A big debate has raged during these four decades as to whether this influence has been a positive force or a destructive mechanism, but few still believe or argue that hip-hop will fade as a mere cultural footnote.

The genuine power and robust influence of hip-hop and its generation were on clear display during the 2008 US presidential election cycle. Many diverse constituencies fuelled President Barack Obama's victory, but the hip-hop generation was certainly one of the most important. Socially conscious rapper Talib Kweli backed and campaigned for President Obama and referred to him as not just the first black president but the first hip-hop president. Barack Obama, mused:

I would go as far as to suggest that there's a good chance there wouldn't even be an "Age of Obama" without hip hop, given the fundamental role . . . young people played in galvanizing Obama's campaign. I was there in Iowa where there was just a few of us; . . . disproportionately young, disproportionately white, and when we stole away, they were all listening to hip hop. And I am not talking about just Eminem. . . . Hip hop doing what? Opening young people to the humanity of other young black people whose conditions have been overlooked.

(Cited in Cummings, 2010: 517)

In recognizing the sizeable global footprint that hip-hop has created; two things would seem clear. First, as the hip-hop generation grows up, some of its members will become leaders: legislators, educators, lawyers, labourers, scholars and philosophers. Second, these leaders, educators and professionals will bring to their specific roles the images, lessons and stark critiques which accompany all authentic members of their generation. As hip-hop is truly impacting an emerging generation of leaders and scholars, it would seem that society needs to pay very close attention to the messages and lessons which hip-hop has taught and continues to impart.

Cummings (2010) pertinently observes that as hip-hop has established its place as a global phenomenon, the origin and evolution of this movement shares a startling parallel development with critical race theory. He argues that this relationship is one grounded in the foundations of race and the manner in which the law intersects with racism and racial discrimination. Hip-hop music and culture have deeply influenced the second generation of critical race theorists, and this is seen to have the potential to radically influence race scholarship and lawyers.

Sharing a parallel universe

From the outset, critical race theorists championed storytelling and narrative as valuable empirical proof of reality and the human experience while rejecting traditional forms of legal studies, pedagogy and various forms of civil rights leadership. Hip-hop, at its root, is narrative in form, while the best, most recognizable hip-hop artists use storytelling as their most fundamental communicative method. Moreover, early hip-hop culture and rap music rejected the traditional legal, judicial and educational systems, denouncing the status quo system established by the white majority (Delgado and Stefancic, 2001). At the same time, there was a rejection of the straight white male perspective and privilege pervasive throughout the legal academy, proposing instead a much different approach to teaching, writing, legal learning and perspective-sharing within the law school classroom.

The striking similarities between critical race theory and hip-hop begin with the intellectual underpinnings of both movements. Thus, both serve the dual purpose of providing a race-based interdisciplinary theoretical framework for analysing laws, policies and administrative procedures which have a negative impact on racial minorities. But hip-hop reinforces the basic insights of critical race theory, including the notion that racism is a normal and relentless fact of daily life. In addition, personal experience and narrative storytelling are used extensively and creatively to challenge the existing social construction of race. Both classical race theory and hip-hop recognize that white elites will tolerate or encourage racial advances for blacks only when such advances promote white self-interest. In response to the inevitable result of cultural marginalization, African

Americans have utilized hip-hop lyrics to disempower the white cultural elite. Hip-hop serves as white America's introduction to the rest of minority society, exposing traditional America to life in the inner city. Both KRS-One and Chuck D began using their voices in hip hop as a revolutionary mechanism to politicize youth: a tool for consciousness, education and awareness of the common stereotypes of the day. Due to hip-hop's bold and unapologetic representation of the culture of inner-city youth to mainstream America, the public eventually had no choice but to listen and accept a different reality (Collins, 1988)

Many critical race theorists believe that a principal obstacle to genuine racial reform in the US is the majoritarian mindset: an experientially limited bundle of presuppositions, received wisdoms and shared cultural understandings which persons in the majority bring to discussions of race. To analyse and challenge these power-laden beliefs, many critical race pioneers employed counter-stories, parables, chronicles, and anecdotes aimed at revealing the contingency, cruelty and self-serving nature of majoritarian rule (Collins, 1988). Similarly, hip-hop revolves around storytelling. In educating the hip-hop generation, Grandmaster Flash and the Furious Five recorded 'The Message'; Public Enemy famously recorded 'Fight the Power', 'Don't Believe the Hype', 'Black Steel in the Hour of Chaos' and '911 Is a Joke'; N.W.A. notoriously released 'Fuck Tha Police' and '100 Miles and Runnin''; Tupac Shakur released 'Brenda's Got a Baby', 'Keep Ya Head Up' and 'Changes'; Ice Cube released the explosive *AmeriKKKas Most Wanted* featuring 'Endangered Species (Tales from the Darkside)' and later *Dead Homiez*; KRS-One released an entire album he styled edutainment featuring 'Love's Gonna Getcha'. Each release represented an urban tale, a story known intimately by the authors/artists; likewise, each was an effort on the part of the artist to educate and enlighten the hip-hop generation. Particularly, these stories illuminated fans and listeners to the inequities and discrimination inherent in a criminal justice system that to this day systematically targets and disproportionately imprisons minority and urban youth (Cummings, 2010).

Like the aforementioned seminal hip-hop records, critical race theorist founders dropped narrative and intellectual bombs in their early countercultural legal writing. In educating the legal academy, and the world in general, to the deeply entrenched racism underlying US institutions, Derrick Bell wrote the profound *The Space Traders, Serving Two Masters, Minority Admissions*, the *Usual Price of Racial Remedies* and *The Interest Convergence Theory*; Richard Delgado published the explosive *The Imperial Scholar* and *A Plea for Narrative*; Kimberlé Crenshaw authored the inspired *Race, Reform, and Retrenchment*; Charles Lawrence published the groundbreaking *The Id, The Ego, and Equal Protection: Reckoning with Unconscious Racism*; Mari Matsuda wrote *Looking to the Bottom*; and Neil Gotanda published *A Critique of 'Our Constitution Is Color-Blind'* (Cummings, 2010). Each publication represented an effort on the part of pioneer critical race theorists to educate and enlighten the civil rights generation, emerging scholars of colour and the rest of the legal world to the inequities and discrimination inherent in a legal system which systematically disadvantages minority citizens in the US.

Both critical race theory and hip-hop were to find a post–civil rights era voice and used this to express fiery and furious critiques of a system which was, and remains, fundamentally unfair. Without doubt, both movements also found an audience that was yearning for a vehicle to speak truth to power. Indeed, they had been waiting in vain for a representative voice to expose a reality known by so many of the oppressed and voiceless. Hip-hop was a source of validation and acknowledgement for a generation which had been shut out and shut down. Critical race theory served a similar function for a professional movement which had become frustrated with the failure of the US to live up to its promise of equality and social justice. Together, these two movements converged in extraordinary ways.

But in the 1980s, as hip-hop began to expand its reach into suburban US and its youth, and as artists and groups began to wield political power and deliver countercultural messages which resonated with those youth, an aggressive and hostile backlash was to emerge from law enforcement, activist groups and government agencies. Yet, despite intense criticism and myriad attempts at its eradication, hip-hop not just survived but was to flourish and exact a dominant influence over a generation (Kitwana, 2005). While the initial backlash against hip-hop proved ineffective, criticism was to continue, some for good reason. The devastating misogyny, homophobia and violence prevalent in some hip-hop work to deter many from hearing and feeling the transformative messages contained in thousands of hip-hop anthems and lyrics. This criticism must be acknowledged and needs to reconcile with hip-hop's message of empowerment and self-realization (Cummings, 2010).

Similarly, when critical race theory emerged and began to find genuine traction in the legal academy, the backlash from the establishment was acerbic and intense. Of course, those invested and entrenched in protecting traditional legal scholarship criticized the emerging critical race scholarship as ungrounded, overly passionate and polemic and neither academic nor intellectual. The traditional academy sought to expose the narrative tradition of critical race theory as non-scholarly, unempirical, unrepresentative and untrustworthy. In addition, opponents of the movement criticized critical race theory as promoting a 'myth' that people of colour share a specific or unified voice and therefore should not be recognized as fundamentally important on issues of race.

Nonetheless, notwithstanding the early acerbic critiques and backlash, both hip-hop and critical race theory shook off the criticism and controversy and continued to offer powerful alternatives to mainstream legal scholarship and contemporary music. Critical race theory rejected the critique and scorned the invitation to ground its relevance in traditional 'accepted' methodologies. True to its purpose and the power of its narrative, critical race theory scholars endeavoured to produce scholarship and advocate for the oppressed and voiceless. They continue to do so today. Critical race theory's slow burn continues today as evidenced by its powerful movement across disciplines and a deep legitimacy gained through its urgency and adherents. Hip-hop similarly rebuffed the backlash, and its artists created – for a time – the most powerfully relevant and critical music of its generation. Both continued to grow in influence and reach out across the world

Conclusion

For four decades, critical race theory and hip-hop have radically engaged the traditional majority in the US. Curiously, both of these radical engagements have shared many of the same characteristics and goals. In furiously challenging norms prevalent in the US, critical race theory has advocated and hip-hop artists have brashly suggested a reality completely different from the rest of the country and the world. Through narrative storytelling and funky bass lines, critical race theory and hip-hop have sought to educate, inspire and motivate a generation. Despite weaknesses in both movements, critical race theory and hip-hop have informed and changed society in compelling ways. The hip-hop nation is growing up and joining the ranks of lawyers, doctors, engineers, teachers, labourers, professors and service industry employees. The critical race theory founders are not only actively writing and engaging but also looking to a new generation of scholars and teachers to assume the weight and responsibility of continuing their message. The perfect storm bringing together the coming of age of the hip-hop generation with the passing of the torch of critical race scholarship is beginning to emerge.

Epilogue: from slavery to Black Lives Matter

Ed Pilkington (2020) tells the story of when George King, a black man in South Carolina, was freed from slavery by the 13th Amendment to the US constitution in 1865. His former slave owner came to him to clarify how things were going to work from now on. 'The Master, he says we are all free', King later recalled. 'But it don't mean we is white. And it don't mean we is equal.'

Pilkington observes the true horror of those words, and the blast of racial terrorism such sentiments ignited across the deep south in the immediate aftermath of the civil war, are laid bare in a harrowing new report by the Equal Justice Initiative (EJI). *Reconstruction in America* (EJI, 2020) documents more than 2,000 black victims of racial terror lynchings killed between the end of the Civil War in 1865 and the collapse of federal efforts to protect the lives and voting rights of black Americans in 1876.

In that brief 12-year period – known as Reconstruction – a reign of terror was unleashed by Confederate veterans and former slave owners in a brazen effort to keep black people enslaved in all but name. Technically freed slaves were lynched at an average rate of almost one every two days, thus ending any hope that emancipation offered millions of black people and effectively terrorizing them into submission. It is a prequel to a previous report (EJI, 2015) which identified and recorded more than 4,400 black victims of racial terror lynchings from the post-Reconstruction period, 1877 to 1950. The new report allows that grim tally to be further expanded with the addition of the 2,000 documented victims from the Reconstruction era itself – bringing the total number of documented cases of black people who were supposedly free yet were lynched in the most sadistic fashion to a staggering 6,500 men, women and children.

EJI (2020) depicts the paradox of how quickly the promise of freedom was stolen from freed black Americans. In the first flush of emancipation, more than 3 million black people living overwhelmingly in the South rushed to claim the benefits of citizenship. A swath of equal rights groups popped up encouraging freed slaves to register to vote. By the summer of 1867, about 80% of eligible black male voters had registered in all but one of the 11 former Confederate states. Black representation followed, with some 2,000 black men holding elected office during Reconstruction. In 1870, Hiram Revels from Mississippi took a seat in the US Senate, the first African American to serve in Congress. Such an extraordinary surge of black political participation was nevertheless matched by an equal and opposite surge of white violence designed to put black people back in the box.

On Christmas Eve, 1865, less than three weeks after the 13th Amendment was ratified abolishing slavery, six former Confederate leaders came together to form the first chapter of the Ku Klux Klan and began what W.E.B. Du Bois (1903) described as 'armed guerilla warfare'. Appalling acts of sadistic homicidal terrorism, targeted frequently against nascent black leaders who were at the forefront of the movement to claim the benefits of citizenship, were swift to follow. EJI has documented 34 mass lynchings during Reconstruction.

The deadliest of them took place in 1868 in Opelousas, Louisiana, where an orgy of white violence over two weeks claimed the lives of 200 black people who were mercilessly hunted down through fields and swamps.

It was no coincidence that what motivated the murderers was a desire to suppress black voter turnout in Opelousas in the run-up to the 1868 presidential election. Withholding the vote from the country's new citizens was seen as a crucial means of reimposing white supremacy in the absence of the physical chains of slavery. Other acts of mass violence were committed against black people who had the audacity, after slavery was ended, to ask to be paid for their work in the fields. Still others were killed because they tried to leave the cotton plantations where they had been enslaved or because they set up schools to teach black children how to read. Most of the violence occurred in the South, but the North was not exempt or guiltless.

EJI (2020) honours the memory of Octavius Catto, an African American veteran of the Union army who worked hard to organize black citizens in Philadelphia. He was killed by a white supremacist in October 1871 as he was on his way back home, having voted in a mayoral election. In 12 short years, the white supremacists managed through a whirlwind of violence to change the entire course of US history, putting the country on the path towards inequality and discrimination under which it still labours today.

Black Lives Matter: an activist movement

Black Lives Matter is an activist movement which began as a hashtag (#BlackLivesMatter) after George Zimmerman was acquitted in the shooting death of Trayvon Martin, an unarmed African American teenager killed in Florida in July 2013. The movement became more widely known and popularized after two high-profile deaths in 2014 of unarmed African-American men (Eric Garner in Staten Island, New York, and Michael Brown in Ferguson, Missouri). Neither of the police officers involved in their deaths was indicted formally charged with a crime.

There is a larger context and history of African American men and boys who have been killed at the hands of the police, many of whom, like George Floyd (2020), were unarmed. Since 2014, other high-profile deaths include Tamir Rice (2014), Laquan McDonald (2014), John Crawford (2014), Freddie Gray (2015), Walter Scott (2015), Alton Sterling (2016), Philando Castile (2016), Terence Crutcher (2016), Antwon Rose (2018) and others. Black women and girls are also targets of police violence, a reality that sparked the "Say Her Name" movement to highlight how this violence often goes unnoticed. Women who have died as a result of police interactions include Sandra Bland (2015), Deborah Danner (2016), Atatiana Jefferson (2019) and Breonna Taylor (2020).

Ongoing local and national protests and other actions – often sparked by the deaths of other unarmed African Americans – have brought the Black Lives Matter movement to the public consciousness and conversation. Black Lives activists released 'Campaign Zero,' which includes ten policy solutions developed in conjunction with activists, protestors and researchers across the US, integrating community demands, input from research organizations and the President's Task Force on 21st Century Policing.

On 4 March 2016, the US Department of Justice announced the findings in two separate investigations related to Ferguson. One report found a pattern of civil rights violations on the part of the Ferguson Police Department. A second report determined that 'the evidence examined in its independent, federal investigation into the fatal shooting of Michael Brown does not support federal civil rights charges against Ferguson Police Officer Darren Wilson.' Two weeks later, on 17 March, the Department and the city of Ferguson formally announced an agreement 'aiming to remedy the unconstitutional law enforcement conduct that the Justice Department found during its civil pattern-or-practice investigation.' The announcement resolved a pending federal lawsuit against Ferguson and addressed a range of issues including bias-free police and court practices, protecting all individuals' First Amendment rights, and reorienting Ferguson's use of force policies.

A week that shook a nation

Chris McGreal (2020) observed that not for half a century had the US seen such large protests – and never with a president whose response was to be so callous. The country had been here before, divided by racial division which left its cities in flames and its citizens demanding a different state – but not for half a century and never with a president whose responses to demands for basic justice were so belligerent and divisive that even his former top military officials were to turn on him. The fires lit in Minneapolis by a police officer squeezing the life out of George Floyd, by kneeling on his neck for nearly nine minutes, ignited the biggest protests since the anti–Vietnam War and the civil rights movement of the 1960s.

Most of the demonstrations were peaceful, and where they were not, that was frequently down to the police. But rioters left a five-mile-long scar through southern Minneapolis as they burned and looted their way along one of the main shopping thoroughfares after ransacking the police station at the centre of the storm over Floyd's death. From there, a surge of anger radiated across the country, driven in good part by the nature of the nine-minute video of Floyd's killing, but also the frustration that for all the promises made with each police killing of an unarmed black man, they do not stop.

When the traumatic video of Floyd begging for his life met the tinder of weeks of coronavirus pandemic lockdown, surging unemployment and a collapsing economy the fire raced through the US. It ignited protests and riots from New York to Los Angeles and the South and then London, Berlin and beyond. As 50 years previously, the National Guard were called out to face down the demonstrators, although this time it was also to stand guard over the violent dispersal of a legal and peaceful protest to provide a photo opportunity for Trump. Now, as then, the president accused 'outside agitators' – Trump called them terrorists – of stirring up trouble. But this time, voices from the USA establishment spoke up in support of those demands and warned that the country was at an inflection point. The power of the nearly nine minutes of Floyd's suffering as the police office charged with his murder, Derek Chauvin, looked into the camera was taken as a statement of police contempt for African American lives and the Black Lives Matter movement.

McGreal (2020) observes that it was the moment when many of the doubters in the US – the people always prepared to give the police the benefit of the doubt – were confronted with the indisputable evidence that police treat black people differently. If further evidence was required it came in the swirl of recordings of officers beating peaceful unarmed demonstrators that in some cities, including New York, drew accusations of a police riot. By the end of the week, the entire culture and practice of policing in America were on trial and not just over Floyd. But it was more than just policing.

Tim Walz, the governor of Minnesota, where the protests began, described the uprising as a singular opportunity in the history of his state to break the chain of

> systemic racism and the lack of accountability up and down our society that led to a daytime murder of a black man on a street in Minneapolis. . . . I think this is probably our last shot as a state and a nation to fix this systemic issue.
>
> (cited in McGreal, 2020)

The Rev Al Sharpton, a central figure in the US civil rights movement, put it more succinctly in a rallying cry at the Minneapolis memorial service for Floyd. White America needed 'to get off our neck'. He went on to say:

> The reason we could never be who we wanted and dreamed of being is you kept your knee on our neck [*he cried to shouts of agreement*]. We could do whatever anyone else could do. But we couldn't get your knee off our neck. What happened to Floyd happens every day in this country in education and health services and in every area of American life. It's time for us to stand up in George's name and say: get your knee off our necks.
>
> (Cited in McGreal, 2020)

As McGreal (2020) observes, there are signs that the rest of the US is more willing to hear that message than ever. Almost no one was willing to try to defend the abuse of Floyd by Chauvin. Moreover, whereas construction workers had turned on the anti-war protesters who marched through New York after the National Guard shot demonstrators at Kent State University in 1970, this time 'hard hats' working in the city were seen clapping the demonstrators demanding justice.

As the police teargassed and shot at people protesting legally from Portland to Kansas City, those on the receiving end included Americans not usually found marching to demand police accountability. Even some Republicans normally quick to defend the police were alarmed enough by the video of Floyd's death to turn out to march. In many places, the violent police response to legitimate protest only strengthened the sense that the problem lies deep in the culture of militarized police departments that act like occupation forces in minority communities.

Yet there were also glimpses of progress. Police officers in other parts of the country – in Texas, Kentucky, Florida and other Trump states – went down on bended knee in a show of solidarity with the demands of demonstrators. Among them was the police chief of Ferguson, Missouri – the birthplace of the Black Lives Matters movement six years previously following riots and protests over the police killing of Michael Brown.

The president instinctively lashed out over a crisis he could not control, with his tested attempts to create division and mayhem. But it proved to be the week when lines began to be drawn on the limits of Trump's power to subvert. He had already neutralized the US justice department, freeing his allies from prison and compromising investigations. The Supreme Court is weighted in favour of his agenda, thanks to the highly politicized nomination process placing ideology over competence under a Republican-run Senate afraid of Trump.

That left the military as the remaining branch of government over which his malign influence was not yet decisive. Then came what was quickly tagged the Battle of

Lafayette Square, a small patch of park in front of the White House. A large and noisy group of protesters had gathered there to make known their support for demands that all of the police officers involved in Floyd's death be arrested. Ever sensitive to criticism, Trump was feeling humiliated by a report that suggested he had bolted for a bunker under the White House a few days previously when demonstrators tried to climb its fence.

Trump decided to prove his courage by wading manfully into Lafayette Square to have his photo taken holding a Bible in front of a church. That would have the added benefit of playing to the evangelical vote. But first the peaceful protesters had to be cleared. Trump's attorney general, William Barr, ordered the police to empty the square, which they did with teargas and baton charges backed by soldiers of the national guard.

Not long after, the sight of the chairman of the Joint Chiefs of Staff, General Mark Milley, in combat fatigues marching behind the president as he strode across Lafayette Square seemed to give a stamp of approval to Trump's threat to turn out the military against those, he was labelling domestic terrorists. The defence secretary, Mark Esper, had told state governors to 'dominate the battle space' by which he meant up the use of force in their cities. The president's allies in Congress upped the ante, with Senator Tom Cotton proposing to send in the 82nd Airborne or 'whatever it takes' against those he called 'insurrectionists'. Trump, as ever on Twitter, gave that idea the thumbs-up.

Faced with this situation, the military establishment chose a side. The first to break cover was James Mattis, the marine general who resigned as Trump's defence secretary in December 2018 and had kept silent until now. He described himself as 'angry and appalled' by Trump's response to the protests and called him a threat to the constitution: 'Donald Trump is the first president in my lifetime who does not try to unite the American people – does not even pretend to try. Instead, he tries to divide us'. His specific point of contention was the use of the military to clear protesters 'to provide a bizarre photo op for the elected commander-in-chief, with military leadership standing alongside' (cited in McGreal, 2020).

Admiral Mike Mullen, the former chairman of the Joint Chiefs of Staff, said he was 'sickened' to see the national guard and other security forces used to 'forcibly and violently' clear a path for the president's 'stunt'. He accused Trump of disdain for the right of peaceful protest and said he was 'deeply worried' that the military will be co-opted for political purposes. The head of the National Guard, General Joseph Lengyel, felt it necessary to stake out a position just in case anyone thought he was siding with the president on the value of black lives. He said he was 'sickened' by the killing of Floyd and 'enraged' at the deaths of unarmed black men at the hands of 'police brutality and extra-judicial violence'.

Defence secretary Esper retreated. He now rejected the idea of sending the military in to control the streets of the cities. Not long after, the Pentagon began pulling out 1,600 troops moved to the Washington, D.C., area during the protests. Few now expected Esper to survive in his job for very much longer. But the real damage was inflicted on Trump. His chaotic handling of the COVID-19 pandemic, with deaths close to 110,000 and rising, had already damaged his diminishing prospects for re-election.

The pandemic has also badly hit the one issue on which many Trump voters were prepared to forgive him all else: the economy. More than 20 million jobs had been lost in April. May saw 2.5 million of those return, although unemployment for African Americans kept rising. It then gets even more bizarre.

Trump's response to the employment figures was to describe it as a 'great day' for Floyd. 'Hopefully, George is looking down right now and saying, 'This is a great thing happening for our country. A great day for him, a great day for everybody', he said. For his critics, the comment was another piece of the president's casual callousness mixed with self-obsession. But for all his boasts, Trump could no longer make claims for a booming economy, even if stock market growth had not translated into better standards of living for most Americans.

As Minneapolis picked up the pieces, Al Sharpton led the memorial service for George Floyd. Alongside his demand for white America to 'get off our necks', and the heart-rending glimpses into Floyd's life from his family, perhaps the most torturous part for the mourners was when Sharpton asked them to stand in silence for 8 minutes 46 seconds to understand just how long Chauvin kept his knee pressing down on the African American man's neck. But Sharpton is a preacher, and he was not going to leave his audience without a brighter future to cling to.

'I'm more hopeful today than ever', he told the mourners. 'When I looked this time and saw marchers were in some cases young whites outnumbering the black marchers, I know that it is a different time and a different season'. Sharpton described an incident at a civil rights march many years previously and being confronted by a white woman who looked him in the face and said: 'Nigger go home.'

This week he had come face-to-face with a young white girl. 'I braced myself and she looked at me and said: no justice, no peace', Sharpton recalled to a roar of approval from the mourners. 'This is the time. We won't stop. We'll keep going until we change the whole system of justice' (McGreal, 2020).

An alternative discourse

> This is a transformational moment. Let's use it to challenge structural injustice, not to elicit or wallow in guilt.
>
> – Malik (2020)

Kenan Malik (2020) wryly observes that the transformation has been bewilderingly swift. Six years previously, most people in the US had thought that police killings of black suspects were 'isolated events'. Now, three out of four accept that there is a systemic problem. Support for Black Lives Matter had risen more in the previous two weeks than over the past two years. And far from feeding Donald Trump's base, the flames consuming US cities had diminished the stature of the president while, to date, not exacerbating the polarization of the nation.

The attitudes not just of the public but of major institutions, too, had metamorphosed. The National Football League, which for the past four years had condemned players 'taking the knee' to the national anthem in protest at racist killings, now acknowledged that it was wrong. The National Association for Stock Car Auto Racing, that most Trumpian of US sports, now banned Confederate flags. Corporation after corporation publicly affirmed support for Black Lives Matter.

In Britain, too, the ground had now shifted. From nationwide mass protests to a new national conversation about statues and history, from footballers and politicians taking the knee, to Yorkshire Tea telling a critic of Black Lives Matter 'Please don't buy our tea again', public life seemed irrevocably changed. When demonstrators toppled the statue of slaver Edward Colston in Bristol, only a minority of Britons supported their actions. A majority nevertheless thought the statue should be taken down legally, something unimaginable even a few months previously.

Malik (2020) observes that the stress on 'white privilege' nevertheless turns a social issue into a matter of personal and group psychology. Thus, one perspective, the shift in public attitudes expresses something positive: the rejection of racism, the understanding that Black Lives Matter means not 'only black lives matter' but 'black lives matter, too'. Yet – he observes – attitudes rarely change as if at the flick of a switch. The speed of the recent transformation had reflected also the febrile character of contemporary politics. Volatility and polarization are expressions of the same phenomenon: the detachment of politics from its traditional social moorings. It is an issue much discussed – as we have observed elsewhere in this book in recent years – in the context of the rise of populism and of the shifting allegiances of working-class voters. Over the past few weeks, we had witnessed one of the unpredictable expressions of the current unpredictability of politics.

Malik (2020) observes that as the old moorings have become detached, so politics has become driven as much by cultural or psychological anxieties as it is by material concerns – witness the influence of identity politics or the reframing of working-class grievances in terms of cultural loss.

Malik (2020) observes that politics has always relied on symbols, rituals and performance. But now it could feel as if politics has been consumed by performance. Thus, consider the way that we now talk more about 'white privilege' rather than about 'racism'. The problem of racism is primarily social and structural – the laws, practices and institutions that maintain discrimination. The stress on 'white privilege' turns a social issue into a matter of personal and group psychology.

'White people, you are the problem,' writes the *Chicago Tribune* columnist Dahleen Glanton (2020). 'For white people,' the US-based British writer Laurie Penny insists, 'acknowledging the reality of racism means acknowledging our own guilt and complicity' (cited in Malik, 2020). White people wash the feet of black faith leaders as atonement for their sins and religiously acknowledge their guilt. Such demonstrations of public obsequiousness are performances that not only make individuals feel better about themselves but also keep the structures of power and discrimination untouched.

Malik (2020) observes that viewing white people – all white people – as 'guilty and complicit' distorts political issues and deflects from real causes. In the US, black people are, as the Sentencing Project observes, 'more likely than white Americans to be arrested; once arrested, they are more likely to be convicted; and once convicted, and they are more likely to experience lengthy prison sentences. And more likely to be killed by the police, too'. Yet studies also show that the problems faced by African Americans are not due simply to white people, or even to white police officers (Menifield *et al.*, 2018), but to a system of justice that is structurally deeply unjust. Thus, some analysts suggest that the best predictor of police killings is not race but income levels.

Nor is it just African Americans whose lives are devastated by the injustices of the justice system. More than half of those killed by US police are white (Fryer, 2019) and while, proportionately, police killings of African Americans have fallen in recent years, that of white people has sharply risen. Some analysts suggest that the best predictor of police killings is not race but income levels – the poorer you are, the more likely you are to be killed. Other studies have shown that the startlingly high prison numbers in the US are better explained by class than race and that 'mass incarceration is primarily about the systematic management of the lower classes, regardless of race' (Lewis, 2019: 32). African Americans, disproportionately working class and poor, are also likely to be disproportionately imprisoned and killed (Menifield *et al.*, 2018).

In Britain, there are far fewer police killings (292 deaths in custody and 40 fatal shootings over the past 15 years), but here, too, black people are disproportionately the victims – forming 3% of the population but 8% of deaths in custody. The majority of killings are, nevertheless, of white people – 249 of the 292 deaths in custody and 26 of the 40 shootings – and probably mainly poor and working class (although these figures are harder to obtain).

Or take COVID-19 deaths. The disproportionate impact of the virus on BAME communities is well documented. But class inequalities are also important. People living in the most deprived areas in England and Wales have died from coronavirus at twice the rate as those in the least deprived areas (Devlin and Barr, 2020). Thus, race and class are not competitive causal categories to be set against each other. Minorities are an integral part of the working class, and they often have similar experiences of state authority. Race and class shape the lives of people in complex ways.

Malik (2020) observes that given the volatility of politics, what might feel at the time of writing to be a fundamental transformation of public consciousness may seem less so in a month or in a year. What is certain, however, is that inequalities, whether of race or of class, cannot be reduced to the question of white privilege or challenged by eliciting guilt. Symbolism and rituals are important. But the heart of the problem lies in warped social relations and deformed institutional structures. As we search for new political moorings, we need to think not just of identity and psychology but also of the material and the social.

Policy implications of critical race theory

Critical race theorists observe that systematic oppression has pervaded policy making both historically and currently in the US. Public policies related to voting, school funding, the criminal justice system and health care reflect both overt and subtle forms of prejudice. Rather than addressing the US legacy of racism, these policies propagate inequity. The outcomes of this oppression are evident in racial and ethnic disparities in criminal justice outcomes.

While much has been written about the outcomes of racist policies, very little has been written about the policy-making processes which result in these inequitable policies. Democratic principles ensure that public policy-making processes include input from diverse constituent groups. However, the actual development, framing and deliberation in relation to public policies are fraught with the same racist undertones prevalent in US culture. Critical race theory developed by legal scholars, provides a strong theoretical framework by which to analyse the influence of racism on policy making.

The Black Lives Matter movement's platform, titled *A Vision for Black Lives: Policy Demands for Black Power, Freedom and Justice*, goes much further and is an altogether more radical vision. The platform has six demands:

1   End the war on black people
2   Reparations
3   Invest–divest

4   Economic justice
5   Community control
6   Political power

Each demand outlines the demands, the problem, the solution and the actions that need to be taken at the local, state and federal levels. The intention of the platform was to establish a unifying agenda that would provide advocacy groups with the necessary steps to transform the political, economic and social circumstances of black communities in the US.

Although the Movement for Black Lives' platform was 'launched in the context of the Democratic National Convention,' the coalition seeks to implement and create their own change within US society as it recognizes that neither major 'political party has our interests at heart'. While the movement's platform largely focuses on the implementation of domestic policies that will advance black communities in the US, it also recognizes 'that patriarchy, exploitative capitalism, militarism, and white supremacy know no borders', and thus, it is necessary that people acknowledge both the goals and demands beyond those represented by the platform's policies.

Summary of main points

1   Critical race theory refers to a historical and contemporary body of scholarship which aims to interrogate the discourses, ideologies and social structures which have produced and maintained conditions of racial injustice.
2   Critical race theories are grounded in the lived experiences, unique experiential knowledge and narrative voice of racialized and subordinated communities.
3   Critical race theory has traditionally used and continues to represent an interdisciplinary approach to the study of race and racism. It embraces and deploy quantitative, qualitative and discursive methodologies to illuminate different aspects of race and racism as social structural phenomena.
4   A core theoretical framework embraced by many contemporary critical race theorists is that of *racial formation* – an explicitly historical and political approach to analysing race as an organizing system of knowledge and power.
5   Some black feminist theorists have also articulated an intersectional theoretical approach to analysing the ways in which systems of gender, sexuality and nationalism are implicated in the production and maintenance of racial subordinations.
6   Michael Coyle (2010) argues that we can build on the use of language critique, which is fundamental to the critical justice theory research tradition, to develop a significant critical race criminology.
7   Cummings (2010) observes that in surprising ways, the origin and evolution of critical race theory parallel many of the paths traversed by the cultural movement of hip-hop in its origin, development and calculated bottom–up assault on white privilege and black oppression.
8   As the hip-hop generation grows up, some of its members will become leaders: legislators, educators, lawyers, labourers, scholars and philosophers.
9   The striking similarities between critical race theory and hip-hop begin with the intellectual underpinnings of both movements. Thus, both serve the dual purpose of providing a race-based interdisciplinary theoretical framework for analysing

laws, policies and administrative procedures which have a negative impact on racial minorities.

10   Many critical race theorists believe that a principal obstacle to genuine racial reform in the US is the majoritarian mindset.

Discussion questions

1   How would you define criminal justice theory?
2   What are the key themes of criminal justice theory?
3   How would you explain racial formation as a theoretical framework?
4   What are the striking similarities between critical race theory and hip-hop?
5   What is the majoritarian mindset?

Suggested further reading

This chapter suggests much further reading in both the areas of critical race theory and hip-hop. Not forgetting the many musical tracks that can be accessed to provide the reader with enlightenment of the classical hip-hop canon. Derrick Bell (1989, 1993, 2004) is considered to be the intellectual inspiration for the consolidation of critical race theories of the law and provides an excellent introduction to the subject. Likewise, A.D.P. Cummings (2010) provides a detailed and scholarly account for those interested in the close parallels between the development and influence of critical race theory and hip-hop, an excellent introduction to the subject.

References

Bell, D.A. (1989) *And We Are Not Saved: The Elusive Quest for Racial Justice.* New York: Basic Books.

Bell, D.A. (1993) *Faces at the Bottom of the Well: The Permanence of Racism.* New York: Basic Books.

Bell, D.A. (2004) *Silent Covenants: Brown v. Board of Education and the Unfulfilled Hopes for Racial Reform.* New York: Oxford University Press.

Bonilla-Silva, E. (2003) *Racism Without Racists: Color-Blind Racism and the Persistence of Racial Inequality in the United States.* Lanham: Rowman & Littlefield.

Boogie Down Productions (1988) By All Means Necessary (Jive Records).

Boogie Down Productions (1987) Criminal Minded (B-Boy Records).

Brown, M.D., Carnoy, M.K., Currie, M., Duster, T., Oppenheimer, T., Shultz, D.B.M. and Wellman, D. (2003) *Whitewashing Race: The Myth of a Colorblind Society.* Berkeley, CA: University of California Press.

Burton, W.P. (2009) *Lift Every Voice: The History of African American Music.* New York: Rowman & Littlefield.

Carby, H. (1998) *Race Men.* Boston: Harvard University Press.

Centre for Contemporary Cultural Studies (CCCS) (1982) *The Empire Strikes Back: Race and Racism in 70s Britain.* London: Hutchinson.

Chic (1979) Good Times (Atlantic Records).

Collins, G. (1988) 'Rap Music, Brash and Swaggering, Enters Mainstream', *New York Times*, August 29. Available from: www.nytimes.com/19/0/29/arts/rap-music-brash-and-swaggering-enters- mainstream.html [Accessed 1 May 2019].

Collins, P.H. (1990) *Black Feminist Thought: Knowledge, Consciousness, and the Politics of Empowerment.* New York: Routledge.

Collins, P.H. (1998) *Fighting Words: Black Women and the Search for Justice.* Minnesota: University of Minneapolis Press.

Collins, P.H. (2005) *Black Sexual Politics: African Americans, Gender, and the New Racism.* New York: Routledge.

Coyle, M.J. (2010) 'Notes on the Study of Language: Towards a Critical Race Criminology', *Western Criminology Review*, 11(1): 11–19.

Cummings, A.D.P. (2010) 'Thug Life: Hip-Hop's Curious Relationship with Criminal Justice', *Santa Clara Law Review*, 50: 515. Available from: https://digitalcommons.law.scu.edu/lawreview/vol50/iss2/5 [Accesed 17 May 2019].

Delgado, R. and Stefancic, J. (2001) *Critical Race Theory: An Introduction*. New York: New York University Press.

Devlin, H. and Barr, C. (2020) 'Poorest Areas of England and Wales Hit Hardest by Covid-19-ONS', *The Guardian*, June 12.

Du Bois, W.E.B. (1899) *The Philadelphia Negro: A Social Study*. Philadelphia: University Press.

Du Bois, W.E.B. (1903) *The Souls of Black Folk*. Chicago: A.G. McClurg.

EJI (2015) *Lynching in America: Confronting the Legacy of Racial Terror*. Montgomery, AL: Equal Justice Initiative.

EJI (2020) *Reconstruction in America: Racial Violence after the Civil War, 165–176*. Montgomery, AL: Equal Justice Initiative.

Folami, A.N. (2007) 'From Habermas to "Get Rich or Die Tryin": Hip Hop, the Telecommunications Act of 1996, and the Black Public Sphere', *Michigan Journal of Race and Law*, 12(2): 235–304.

Fredrickson, G.M. (2002) *Racism: A Short History*. Princeton, NJ: Princeton University Press.

Fryer, R.G. (2019) 'An Empirical Analysis of Racial Differences in Police Use of Force', *Journal of Political Economy*, 127(3): 1210–61.

Glanton, D. (2020) 'White America, If You Want to Know Who's Responsible for Racism, Look in the Mirror', *The Daily World*, June 3.

Goldberg, D.T. (1993) *Racist Culture: Philosophy and the Politics of Meaning*. Oxford: Blackwell.

Goldberg, D.T. (2002) *The Racial State*. Malden: Blackwell.

Guiner, L. and Torres, G. (2002) *The Miner's Canary: Enlisting Race, Resisting Power, Transforming Democracy*. Cambridge, MA: Harvard University Press.

Hall, S. (1992) 'New Ethnicities', in H.A. Baker, Jr., M. Diawara and R.H. Lindeborg (eds.) *Black British Cultural Studies: A Reader*. Chicago: University of Chicago Press.

Holloway, L. (2002) 'The Angry Appeal of Eminem Is Cutting Across Racial Lines', *New York Times*, October 2. Available from: www.nytimes.com/2002/10/2/business/the-angry-appeal-of-eminem-is-cutting-across-racial-lines [Accessed 1 May 2019].

hooks, b. (1981) *Ain't I a Woman: Black Women and Feminism*. Boston, MA: South End Press.

hooks, b. (1990) *Yearning, Race, Gender, and Cultural Politics*. Boston, MA: South End Press.

Ice-T (1992) Cop Killer, (Sire/Warner Bros. Records).

Ice-T, 6 (1988) In the Mornin, (Sire/Warner Bros. Records).

Johnson, D. (2008) 'Racial Prejudice, Perceived Injustice, and the Black-White Gap in Punitive Attitudes', *Journal of Criminal Justice*, 36(2): 19–206.

Kitwana, B. (2005) 'The Cotton Club', *The Village Voice*, June 21. Available from: www.villagevoice.com/2005-06-21/music/the-cotton-club/ [Accessed 21 May 2019].

Lewis, N. (2019) *Mass Incarceration New Jim Crow, Class War, or Both?* Washingto, DC: People's Policy Project.

Light, A. (1999) *The Vibe History of Hip Hop*. New York: Three Rivers.

Malik, K. (2020) 'White Privilege' Is a Distraction, Leaving Racism and Power Untouched', *The Observer*, June 14.

Marable, M. (2000) *How Capitalism Underdeveloped Black America: Problems in Race, Political Economy, and Society*. Boston, MA: South End Press.

Matsuda, M.J., Lawrence, III, C.R., Delgado, R. and Crenshaw, K.W. (1993) *Words that Wound: Critical Race Theory, Assaultive Speech, and the First Amendment*. Boulder, CO: Westview Press.

McGreal, C. (2020) 'A Week That Shook a Nation: Anger Burns as Power of Protests Leaves Trump Exposed', *The Observer*, June 7.

Menifield, C.E., Shin, G. and Strother, L. (2018) 'Do White Law Enforcement Officers Target Minority Suspects?', *Public Administration Review*, 79(1): 56–6.

Murray, A. (1970) *The Omni Americans: Black Experience and American Culture*. New York: Outerbridge & Dienstfrey.

N.W.A. (1988) Straight Outta Compton (Ruthless/Priority Records).

Omi, M. and Winant, H. (1994) *Racial Formation in the United States*. New York: Routledge.

Outlaw, Jr., L.T. (1996) *On Race and Philosophy*. New York: Routledge.

Pilkington, E. (2020) 'Racial Terror: 2,000 Black Americans Were Lynched in Reconstruction Era, Report Says', *The Guardian*, 16 June.

Public Enemy (1988) It Takes a Nation of Millions to Hold Us Back (Def Jam Records 19).

Public Enemy (1990) Fear of a Black Planet (Def Jam Records 1990).

Shapiro, T.M. (2004) *The Hidden Costs of Being African American: How Wealth Perpetuates Inequality*. New York: Oxford University Press.

Tanner, J., Asbridge, M. and Wortley, S. (2010) *Listening to Rap: Cultures of Crime, Cultures of Resistance*. Chapel Hill, NC: The University of North Carolina Press.

West, C. (1999) *The Cornell West Reader*. New York: Basic Civitas Books.

Williams, P.J. (1997) *Seeing a Color-Blind Future: The Paradox of Race*. New York: Noonday.

Winant, H. (2001) *The World Is a Ghetto: Race and Democracy Since World War II*. New York: Basic Books.

Winant, H. (2004) *The New Politics of Race*. Minneapolis: University of Minnesota Press.

Chapter 12

Terrorism and state violence

Key issues

1   Social science explanations of terrorism
2   Contemporary criminological explanations of terrorism
3   The war on terrorism
4   State violence as state terrorism
5   Terrorism and postmodernism revisited

Introduction

The topic of terrorism is both complex and emotive. It is complex because it combines so many different aspects of human experience, including subjects such as politics, psychology, philosophy, military strategy and history, to name a few. Terrorism is also emotive both because experiences of terrorist acts arouse tremendous feelings and because those who see terrorists as justified often have strong feelings concerning the rightness of the use of violence. Without a doubt, terrorism evokes strong feelings whenever it is discussed. Thus, a key challenge of understanding terrorism is both acknowledging the moral outrage at terrorist acts while at the same time trying to understand the rationale behind terrorism which is not a new phenomenon.

Violence has been used throughout human history by those who have chosen to oppose the politically dominant of the time. Yet this sort of violence should be differentiated from what is termed terrorism. Violence in opposition to a government is often targeted against the military and those who govern. Terrorism is invariably characterized by the use of violence against civilians, with the expressed desire of causing terror or panic in the population, although there can be some ambiguity as we will discover.

Terrorism is not unique to the twentieth and twenty-first centuries. It existed in eighteenth-century revolutionary France during the Reign of Terror, as well as among the Zealots of Palestine in opposition to Roman rule some 2,000 years ago. Today, terrorist activity can be found in Israel, Indonesia, the UK, Sri Lanka, Colombia, France and the US, to name but a few. Of particular concern in this chapter are the 11 September suicide attacks against the World Trade Center and the Pentagon and the attempted attack which resulted in the plane crash in Pennsylvania. The outcome of which was the 'war against terror'.

The suicide attacks began when a passenger jetliner, hijacked en route from Boston to Los Angeles, slammed into New York's World Trade Center at 8:45 a.m. About 18 minutes after the first crash, a second plane – United Airlines flight 175, also originating in Boston and bound for Los Angeles, with 92 crew and passengers – struck the South Tower. The action was so well executed that the authorities concluded that the hijackers had their own pilot aboard.

Plumes of smoke filled the skyline of lower Manhattan as other terror attacks were underway. American Airlines flight 77, bound for Los Angeles from Washington, D.C., with 64 people aboard, was hijacked by men wielding knives and box cutters shortly after its take-off at 8:21 a.m. Veering off course, the passenger plane took aim at the Pentagon just 25 miles away, crashing into the western facade at 9:45 a.m.

Meanwhile, in New York, bedlam had gripped the financial district around the World Trade Center (also the target of a 1993 terrorist bomb, which exploded in the basement, killing six). Thousands of people fled the buildings and surrounding area. Others who had not yet escaped the building were helping the injured or were simply riveted by what they saw fell victim to another tragedy. At about 10 a.m., the 410-foot-tall South Tower suddenly began to collapse, one floor collapsing onto the one below. Forty minutes later, the second tower collapsed. In the meantime, there were reports of another hijacked airline, United Airlines flight 93, crashing in Somerset County, Pennsylvania, southeast of Pittsburgh.

For a time, panic set in, marked by incorrect reports of bombings at the US Capitol, as well as the State Department. The White House was evacuated. The US–Mexico border was closed, and the Federal Aviation Administration grounded all US commercial airline flights. International flights bound for the US were hastily diverted to Canada.

Using the military, law enforcement, diplomacy (including coalition formation), the treasury department and other instruments of state, the US government undertook a campaign against bin Laden and his al-Qaeda group taking great pains to state that its efforts were not directed against Islam but against the terrorism and its sponsors.

Social science explanations of terrorism

There is a well-known adage that 'one man's terrorist is another man's freedom fighter', and it is clear that those involved in the aforementioned al-Qaeda terrorist attacks undoubtedly considered their actions to be justified acts of war, just as the retaliatory strikes against Afghanistan and Iraq were subsequently considered just acts in the war against terrorism by the governments of the US, the UK and their allies. Contemporary politicians invariably go to great lengths to describe terrorists as being no different from common criminals, but this has not always been the case. During the nineteenth century, Britain obtained a reputation for being a safe haven for political 'agitators' and refugees from Europe, but this situation was to change significantly during the following century when 'political criminals' were to become synonymous with 'terrorists' and abhorred by governments throughout the world.

Terrorism is thus an emotive word which emphasizes the extreme fear caused by apparently indiscriminate violent actions of individuals claiming to be operating on behalf of some particular cause. Sometimes terrorist activities are funded by states (state-sponsored terrorism) and the West has been keen to accuse countries such as Libya, Iran, (previously) Iraq and Syria of this. Western states have nevertheless supported terrorism when it has been in their political interests to do so, and thus during the Cold War backed many right-wing movements invariably as a bulwark against communism.

Israel readily condemns terrorism but ironically the state itself came into being as the outcome of a terrorist campaign. One of the actions of the Jewish organization Irgun Zvai Leumi was to blow up the King David Hotel in Jerusalem in July 1946 without giving any warning, killing over seventy people, many of them British. The leader of Irgun, Menachem Begin, was sought by the British as a terrorist and a murderer and was sentenced to death in his absence. He was later to become prime minister of Israel and was awarded the Nobel Peace Prize in 1978. Similarly, Nelson Mandela spent over 25 years in prison for acts of terrorism and subsequently became president of South Africa within five years of his release, as well as a global icon.

Most of the major theories which seek to explain terrorism – and individual and group involvement – are derived from theories of collective violence developed in the field of political science. Terrorism is not a form of governance as such, but anarchism is. Most anarchists reject terrorism, but in a theoretical sense, anarchism justifies such actions as a form of criminal action which attacks the values of an organized, complacent society. Anarchism is (as we have previously seen in this book) a theory of governance which rejects any form of central or external authority, preferring instead to replace it with alternative forms of organization, such as shaming rituals for deviants, mutual assistance pacts between citizens, syndicalism (any non-authoritarian organizational structure which gives the greatest freedom to workers), iconoclasm (the destruction of cherished beliefs), libertarianism (a belief in absolute liberty) and straightforward individualism. Anarchism is often referred to as providing the nineteenth-century foundations of terrorism with the actual term first introduced in 1840 by Pierre-Joseph Proudhon. Other major nineteenth-century anarchist figures – such as Karl Heinzen and Johann Most – argued that murder, especially murder–suicide, constituted the highest form of revolutionary struggle and both advocated the use of weapons of mass destruction.

It was minor figures in the history of anarchism, such as Charles Gallo, Auguste Vaillante, Emile Henry and Claudius Konigstein, who advocated the influential idea that, to be most effective, the targets must be innocents – in places such as crowded dance halls or shopping centres – or symbols of economic success – like banks and stock exchanges. It is nevertheless important to note that present-day anarchists – and certainly not the anarchist criminologists such as Jeff Ferrell who we encountered earlier in this book – do not support terrorism. Moreover, it is important to recognize that only a small minority of terrorists have ever been anarchists, and only a small minority of anarchists have ever been terrorists.

Passmore (2002) proposes that fascism – a form of government with strong links to state-sponsored terrorism – can be defined as the consolidation of an ultranationalist ideology which is unashamedly racist. The word itself comes from the Latin *fasces*, which means to use power to scare or impress people, and it generally refers to the consolidation of all economic and political power into some form of super-patriotism which is devoted to genocide or endless war. So-called Islamo-Fascism has links with the birth of Nazi 'national socialist' fascism in 1928 when the Muslim Brotherhood (Al Ikhwan Al Muslimun, parent organization of numerous terrorist groups) was formed in reaction to the abolition of the caliphate in 1924 by the secularist Turkish government. Passmore (2002) proposes that the term 'Islamic Fascism' is a better term with which to describe the agenda of contemporary radical Islam, for this captures the twin thrusts of reactionary fascism. In one sense, fascism is born out of insecurity and a sense of failure, but in another sense, it thrives in a once-proud, humbled but ascendant people. Envy and false grievances are the characteristics of such reactionary fascism, while believers are subject to all kinds of conspiratorial delusions that setbacks were caused by others and can be erased through ever more zealous action.

Fascism supports terrorism at home and abroad, and its inevitably charismatic leaders are usually given supreme powers to crackdown on dissidents. With the frequent wars and militaristic ventures that come with fascism, an effort is made to demonize the enemy as sub-humans who deserve extinction, while, at the same time, they are transformed into scapegoats and blamed for all the past problems a country has experienced. Fascism simply appeals to the frustrations and resentments of an ethnic group of people who think they ought to have a bigger place at the global table. When combined with an anti-Western slant (the US as the Great Satan, the UK the lesser Satan), fascism becomes a means of social identity (pan-Africanism, pan-Arabism, Islamo-Fascism) as well as a facilitator of terrorism.

Hoffman (1993) notes that about a quarter of all terrorist groups and about half of the most dangerous ones on earth are primarily motivated by religious concerns, believing that God not only approves of their action but also demands it. Their cause is thus sacred and consists of a combined sense of hope for the future and vengeance for the past. Of these two components, the backward-looking desire for vengeance may be the more important trigger for terrorism because the forward-looking component – called apocalyptic thinking or eschatology – tends to produce wild-eyed fanatics who are more a danger to themselves and their own people.

The successful use of terrorism in the name of religion rests on convincing believers or the converted that a 'neglected duty' exists in the fundamental, mainstream part of the religion. Religious terrorism is thus not about extremism, fanaticism, sects or cults but is instead about a fundamentalist or militant interpretation of the basic tenets. Most religious traditions are filled with plenty of violent images at their core and destruction or self-destruction is a central part of the logic behind religion-based terrorism (Juergens-meyer, 2001). Evil is often defined as malignant narcissism from a theological point of view and religion easily serves as moral cover for self-centred terrorists and psychopaths. We should note that religion has always absorbed or absolved evil and guilt in what is called theodicy or the study of how the existence of evil can be reconciled with a good and benevolent God (Kraemer, 2004).

Economics has produced many concepts which are relevant to an understanding of terrorism, such as supply and demand, costs and benefits, and we saw in the discussion of rational choice theory in the second chapter of this book – a significant component of the contemporary variant of the rational actor model of crime and criminal behaviour – proposes that people will engage in crime after weighing the costs and benefits of their actions. Criminals thus come to believe that their actions will be beneficial (to themselves, their community or society), and they must come to see that crime pays or is at least a risk-free way to better their situation (Cohen and Felson, 1979). It is in this theoretical context that 'the Olson (1982) hypothesis' suggests that participants in revolutionary violence base their behaviour on a rational cost–benefit calculus to pursue the best course of action given the social circumstances (Olson, 1982). Rational choice theory, in political science, follows a similar line and holds that people can be collectively rational, even when making what appear to be irrational decisions for themselves as individuals, after perceiving that their participation is important and their personal contribution to the public good outweighs any concerns they may have for the 'free rider' problem (Muller and Opp, 1986).

Martha Crenshaw (1998) is a rational choice theorist who proposes that terrorism is far from a pathological phenomenon or aberration and argues that the central focus of study should be on why it is that some groups find terrorism useful to further their aims and equally why it is that other groups do not find it useful. Thus, some groups may continue to work with established patterns of dissident action, while others may resort to terrorism because they have tried other alternatives. Still other groups may choose terrorism as an early choice because they have learned from the experiences of others that alternative strategies do not work. Crenshaw calls the latter the contagion effect and claims it has distinctive patterns similar to the copycat effect in other theories of collective violence (Gurr, 1970). There may also be circumstances in which the terrorist group wants to publicize its cause to the world, a process she had previously called the globalization of civil war.

Nassar (2004) argues that the processes and promises of globalization contribute to dreams, fantasies and rising expectations but, at the same time, lead rather inevitably to dashed hopes, broken dreams and unfulfilled achievements. Terrorism breeds in the gap between expectations and achievements, and this is an argument resonant with that contained in Merton's version of anomie theory. Indeed, we might observe that the only thing unique with this version of globalization theory is that it adds a rich–poor dichotomy. Thus, rich people – or nations – are seen as wanting power and wealth, and poor people – or nations – are seen as wanting justice. From this perspective, rich people are part of the causes of terrorism, since they contribute to the conditions which give rise to it, while the perpetrators are never seen as being born or socialized with any specific predispositions towards it. In short, globalization theory proposes that, if the oppressed and disgruntled poor people of the world were simply given the chance to find peaceful means for achieving justice, terrorism would not thrive.

Modern sociological perspectives are primarily concerned with the social construction of fear or panic and how institutions and processes, especially the media, primary and secondary groups, maintain that expression of fear. O'Connor (1994) thus makes use of a neo–functionalist framework to chart the way terrorism impacts on the whole of society by affecting core values of achievement, competition and individualism. Some societies become 'softer' targets after terrorism – especially after short-term target hardening – while other societies become stronger in the long term. It depends upon interaction patterns, stabilities and interpenetrations among the structural subsystems (economy, polity, religion, law).

O'Connor (1994) identifies five sociological theories of terrorism. First, the *frustration-aggression hypothesis* proposes that every frustration leads to some form of aggression and that every aggressive act relieves that frustration to some extent. Second, the *relative deprivation hypothesis* proposes that, as a person goes about choosing their values and interests, they compare what they have and do not have, as well as what they want or do not want, with real or imaginary others. The person then usually perceives a discrepancy between what is possible for them and what is possible for others and reacts to it with anger or an inflamed sense of injustice. Third, the *negative identity hypothesis* proposes that, for whatever reason, a person develops a vindictive and covert rejection of the roles and statuses laid out for them by their family, community or society. Thus, a child raised in an affluent family might secretly sabotage every effort to give them a good start in life, until the day comes, with some apparent life-altering experience – like engaging in terrorism – when the long-nurtured negative identity comes to the fore, and the subject can then make it feel more like a total identity transformation. Fourth, the *narcissistic rage hypothesis* is a generic explanation for all the numerous things which can go wrong in child-rearing, such as too much mothering, too little mothering, ineffective discipline, overly stringent discipline, psychological trauma and coming from a broken home, which leads to a damaged self-concept and a tendency to blame others for our own inadequacies. Fifth, the *moral disengagement hypothesis* follows the work of David Matza on 'techniques of neutralization' which proposes the ways that a person neutralizes or removes any inhibitions they have about committing acts of horrific violence. Thus, some common patterns include imagining oneself to be a hero, portraying oneself to be a mere functionary with limited – or diminished – responsibility, minimizing the harm done, dehumanizing the victim or insulating oneself in routine activities. O'Connor (1994) observes that organized crime figures, for example, usually hide behind family activities with their wives and children, although we should also be aware that there are numerous other ways that violence can be rationalized and neutralized (see Hacker, 1996). Terrorist rationalizations usually involve a complete shift in the way government and civil society is perceived by the individuals and groups concerned.

Psychological explanations of terrorism have tended – with a few exceptions (Ross, 1996, 1999) – to be clinical and invariably futile attempts to find something pathological in the terrorist personality. Merari (1990) provides a good overview of psychological approaches and factors which have been implicated in the formation of supposedly terrorist personalities, and these include the familiar explanations of ineffective parenting, rebellion against parents, a pathological need for absolutism and a variety of other 'syndromes' and hypotheses, which it is observed have yielded little valid and reliable information about the psychology of terrorists other than a few generalizations. There have been several promising attempts to merge or combine psychology with sociology into what might be called terrorist profiling (Russell and Bowman, 1977; Bell, 1982; Galvin, 1983; Strentz, 1988; Hudson, 1999). When suicide bombing came to the fore, Merari (1990) conducted interviews with terrorists and found that most who commit suicide attacks are between the ages of 16 and 28. Most are male, but 15% are female, with that proportion increasing. Many come from poor backgrounds and have limited education, but some have university degrees and come from wealthy families.

What sociological and psychological approaches basically tell us is that individuals join terrorist organizations to commit acts of terrorism and that this process is the same as when individuals join criminal subcultures to commit acts of crime. Moreover, there appears to be no unique terrorist personality but there do appear to be unique subcultural phenomena that develop, support and enhance an enthusiasm for cold-blooded, calculated violence, which, if not satisfied within a terrorist organization, *might* well be fulfilled elsewhere. Terrorism is a social activity, and individuals join a terrorist group usually after they have tried other forms of political involvement. The emotional links between individuals and the strength of commitment to their ideology appear to become stronger by the group living in the underground and facing adversity in the form of counter-terrorism.

Socialization in the terrorist underground is quite intense and the identity of an individual may become tied to the identity of the group, but it is just as likely that emotional relationships become as important as – if not more important than – the purpose of the group. This means that the distribution of beliefs among members in a terrorist group may be uneven and there may be major differences between individual and group ideology (Ferracuti, 1982). Thus, ideology may not necessarily be the main component of motivation.

We have observed in our discussion above how some of the traditional criminological theories – in particular, the US anomie tradition as developed via deviant subculture theories but also social control theories – have helped to explain why people join terrorist groups. In other words, this is part of a long-established criminological tradition which proposes that people choose to act in certain criminal ways because of where they are born and who they associate with, and this is as much applicable to involvement in terrorism as it is to white-collar, professional and hate crimes. Ruggiero (2005) follows in this sociological criminological tradition and commences his discussion with Durkheim, and we should observe that the latter's notion of the 'normality of crime', which is functional to the requirements of society, is commensurate with an understanding of terrorist activity. Terrorist activities seem to make the most sense at times of rapid social change (when there is a prevailing sense of normlessness or Durkheimian anomie) and when an unfair or forced division of labour is readily apparent to many. In the following section, we consider some more recent criminological explanations of various aspects of terrorism.

Contemporary criminological explanations of terrorism

Understanding the reasons behind the rise and persistence of terrorism and the ways that it can be stopped has become one of the more prominent political priorities of the early twenty-first century, and there has been a growing focus within criminology since the twentieth century. Rigorous scholarship relies on theoretical explanations and their extensions as guides to scientifically assess terrorist behaviour and to evaluate the many popularly held myths promoted by politicians and media. Such evaluations are now possible because systematically collected terrorism data and advanced analytic techniques are increasingly available to test these theories. Furthermore, because criminologists and others have been studying law-breaking and efforts to stop it for at least three centuries, the field offers a unique perspective which is often overlooked by others who study terrorism.

A growing body of literature bridges the gap between the many different criminological theories that explain why people commit crimes and the number of terrorist attacks vary across times and space.

Rational choice theories

Rational choice theories – as we know – assume that humans are self-interested beings with free will who seek to maximize pleasure and minimize pain. When applied to terrorism, this perspective draws on an extensive literature from criminology and other social sciences and which has been used to examine a wide variety of central issues relating to terrorism. Some of these studies nevertheless draw on the principles of rational choice without necessarily explicitly discussing the theory. In fact, one of the most well-cited studies on terrorism, Pape (2003) analyses all suicide terrorist attacks from 1980 to 2001 and discovers a pattern of strategic logic for the attacks, producing evidence that terrorists use the tactic to pressure democratic occupiers to withdraw from a territory. Perry *et al.* (2016) also assess the logic of suicide terrorists by questioning whether they are indeed rational and explore their motivations. After reviewing the personal, social and religious incentives, this study suggests that suicide terrorists display a commitment toward maximizing self-gratifying behaviour rather than altruism.

The idea that terrorists might rely on strategic logic has nevertheless been questioned by other scholars. McCartan et al. (2008) assess the strategic choices of Chechen rebels during the Chechen/Russian conflict between 1997 and 2003 and test whether civilian targets are more likely in Russia than in Chechnya, whether weather influences their attack frequency and whether the Chechens are likely to increase the costs to Russians with time. Wilson et al. (2010) examine whether strategic and tactical patterns can be found in assassinations and bombing attacks perpetrated by Euzkadi Ta Askatasuna (ETA) terrorists in between 1980 and 2007. LaFree and Miller (2008) examine whether the spatial and temporal patterns of terrorist attacks by ETA between 1970 and 2007 reflect rational strategic planning, finding that the diffusion patterns of attacks after ETA declared a prolonged war of attrition with Spain shifted from contagion diffusion to hierarchical diffusion extending beyond the Basque region. All of these scholars find evidence that rebel groups operate strategically during ongoing conflicts.

Other research directly relies on rational choice theory to assess responses to interventions. Dugan et al. (2005) examine the impact of government counter-terrorism interventions (target hardening) – or cost-based interventions which increase the severity of punishment – and how these are related to a decreased risk of aerial hijacking. Dugan and Chenoweth (2012) later use a rational choice framework to broaden the strategies of counter-terrorism beyond those of deterrence – which simply punish terrorists – to include government actions which reward abstention from terrorism. The model is tested by using data on government actions by Israel directed toward Palestinian civilians and terrorists. Argomaniz and Vidal Diez (2015) explore competing hypotheses which are aligned with rational choice theory to examine the consequences of counter-terrorism policies aimed at reducing the rational justification for terrorism by the Basque separatist group ETA, finding evidence that backlash motivated ETA attacks.

While rational choice is an especially appealing theory to inform potential interventions, Pete Fussey (2011) challenges its application to terrorism and discusses the increasing attention given to crime prevention approaches aimed at reducing terrorism. He argues that rational choice theories erroneously assume that terrorist organizations engage in value-free strategic and operational decision-making, concluding that these are limited in their ability to explain terrorism.

Deterrence theories

Deterrence has been one of the most dominant perspectives within the literature on terrorism not least because most governments rely heavily on the threat of punishment to end terrorist violence. Much in this category uses deterrence theory to test whether interventions which threaten to punish are effective in reducing the risk of terrorism. Le Vine and Salert (1996) thus examined the impact of official responses to terrorism sponsored or directed by the Palestine Liberation Organization (PLO) between 1968 and 1986 and found that some deterrent impacts were short-lived, which suggests that coercive responses to terrorism by government were more valuable for providing political defences than for deterring terrorism. LaFree et al. (2009) similarly use deterrence theory to evaluate the impact of a range of different counter-terrorist strategies used by the British government in Northern Ireland to see how they affect the risk of terrorist violence. Carson (2014) later used deterrence theory to assess whether four federal sentencing acts were able to deter radical ecoterrorism in the US, specifically examining the impact of each change in legal sanctions on the additional incidents, serious incidents and ideologically specific incidents. Some evidence for legislation and outcome specific deterrence was found.

Other research draws on other theoretical perspectives to better understand how deterrence efforts might actually play out when directed toward reducing terrorism. Tyler *et al.* (2010) use ideas of legitimacy to explore conditions which foster voluntary cooperation by members of the US Muslim community with police efforts to combat terrorism. Their analysis of data covering the period between March and June 2009 suggests that focusing on procedural justice in designing counter-terrorism policing strategies may help nurture community cooperation. Frey and Luechinger (2003) nevertheless question the perceived effectiveness of deterrence strategies by theoretically examining the likely consequences of such interventions and suggest alternative strategies which could also reduce terrorism and propose that increasing the opportunity cost and making terrorist attacks less attractive may be superior strategies for reducing terrorism. Hua and Bapna (2012) simply dismiss the value of deterrence theory by pointing out structural difficulties when applying and measuring such strategies for cyberterrorism. They highlight the legal and technical challenges to tracking terrorists and provide a series of suggestions to address these practical constraints and present some key structural considerations which are needed to improve the deterrent capacity of existing methods on cybersecurity. Trivizas and Smith (1997) apply deterrence theory differently by making terrorism the independent variable and asking whether terrorism can be a deterrent for other forms of crime. They thus examine whether salient terrorist attacks affect rates of luggage theft in railway and underground stations and found a sharp and brief decline in thefts after a major terrorist incident. The researchers discuss whether this was due to increased police vigilance (deterrence) or concern that the luggage might contain explosives.

Strain theories

Strain theories have had a large impact on the study of crime and have developed to encompass a number of theoretical predictions within the criminological literature. Since 1992, scholars have directed general strain theory (GST) toward terrorism in an effort to better predict its patterns. Agnew (2010) provides an overview of how GST can be applied to terrorism and argues that such acts of are most likely to occur when people experience 'collective strains' which substantially affect civilians, are widely perceived to be unjust and are inflicted by substantially more powerful others. Rice and Agnew (2013) offer an updated framework of GST and argue that negative affect and emotions more generally hold theoretical value for examining radicalization and terrorism. They provide a detailed framework for understanding how emotions, affect and GST may contribute to the understanding of terrorism, and suggests ways to pursue this research agenda. Fodeman (2015) empirically assesses the impact of strain on anti-abortion terrorism in the US and suggests that anti-abortion responses varied in accordance with political frustrations. González *et al.* (2014) explore the involvement of women in terrorism and extremist violence in the US and provide a theoretical framework which uses GST and other theories. Rice (2009) discusses GST and other criminological theories and provides a research agenda for examining the role that emotions may play in terrorism and argues that numerous criminological theories, including GST, can be used to better understand terrorism.

Others have applied the concept of strain without explicitly using GST. Cottee (2011) thus suggests that the formation of a terrorist organization can be understood as a collective response to the strains encountered by members of these groups and found that they imposed by the circumstances that individuals experience. Dugan and Young (2010) offer a provocative policy proposal based on the premise that strains derived from policy implemented in the US may provide the impetus for terrorism. They argue that increasing political participation by extremists and giving them a voice in the policymaking process may reduce subsequent terrorist violence. Piazza (2012) examines the role that discrimination against minorities – an obvious strain – might have on terrorist attacks across 166 nations between 1991 and 2006 and found that only socio-economic discrimination against minorities consistently predicted terrorism.

Social disorganization theories

Social disorganization theories have again been influential within criminology for more than a century, but their application to the study of terrorism has only occurred within the past decade. Some studies explicitly apply social disorganization to terrorism while others use its components without referencing the theory. Freilich and Pridemore (2007) provide one of the earliest empirical examinations which explicitly links social disorganization to terrorism by using cross-sectional data of US states to examine violence committed against abortion clinics in the US. LaFree and Bersani (2014) also apply social disorganization to terrorism by examining whether county-level geographic patterns of terrorism in the US are consistent with its predictions. Fahey and LaFree (2015) examine the impact of country-level social disorganization on terrorist attacks and resulting fatalities in 101 countries between 1981 and 2010. They operationalize social disorganization as the presence of revolutionary and ethnically motivated wars, government regime changes and the presence of genocides.

Other studies have empirically examined the components of social disorganization. Akyuz and Armstrong (2011) investigate the links among ethnic heterogeneity, residential mobility, poverty and terrorism in Turkey between 2005 and 2007, and their findings suggest that all three factors may be related to subsequent terrorism in that country. Mullins and Young (2012) with their theory of *legitimation-habituation* offer predictions that are similar to social disorganization, in that they both test their hypotheses across nations, explore how the overall volume of violence within societies influences the likelihood of political dissidents engaging in terrorism. Using data from between 1970 and 1997, the authors find evidence to suggest that the volume of legitimate and illegitimate violence within a society holds predictive value for terrorism. Hamm (2004) and Pisoiu (2015) both explore the social histories of neo-Nazis to investigate the impact that subcultures (a component of some social disorganization theories) may have on terrorism. Wormeli (2014) emphasizes the importance of examining the origin of previous terrorist attacks at the neighbourhood level so that an effort can be made to prevent terrorism during the planning stages instead of responding to it only afterwards. She argues that information sharing among government agencies is necessary to prevent terrorism

Situational theories

Criminologists have used situational theories to explain the geographical and strategic distribution of crime and terrorism in order to reduce its occurrence. Clarke and Newman (2006), in a seminal text, present a framework for minimizing opportunities to commit terrorist acts to reduce their occurrence. They argue that regardless of the reasons underlying the decisions to attack a government, opportunities that allow for terrorism should be identified and removed. Gruenewald *et al.* (2015) draw on this framework and examine the vulnerability and attractiveness of eco-terrorism targets in the US. Their findings indicate general support for the claim that the vulnerability and attractiveness of targets inform targeting decisions by eco-terrorists.

Others have used situational theories to better explain the behaviour of terrorists. Parkin and Freilich (2015) assess whether differences between ideological and non-ideological homicides can be explained by predictors of routine activities and lifestyle theories and find empirical support for both. Hsu and Apel (2015) explore different forms of displacement and diffusion of benefits in response to airport metal detectors on acts of terrorism occurring between 1970 and 1977. Their study suggests that the response of terrorist organizations to the implementation of situational counter-terrorism strategies is more complex than is often assumed. Perry *et al.* (2016) evaluate the effectiveness of the 'West Bank Barrier', constructed by the Israeli government, as a defence against suicide bombings and other terrorist attacks. Their findings suggest a reduction in suicide terrorist attacks and a movement toward more opportunistic attacks. Smith and Damphousse (1998) had previously looked at the situational context of federal court processing and assess whether terrorist defendants are processed in a more consistent manner than other defendants for the same crime by using structural contextual theory and the liberation hypothesis.

Applying situational theory to terrorism can nevertheless provide significant challenges. Lynch (2011) thus highlights a number of statistical and theoretical difficulties in producing conclusions from the literature on evaluating the success of terrorism prevention measures, arguing that the absence of terrorism does not necessarily suggest counter-terrorism efforts are successful, since terrorism is a rare event. Morris (2015) discusses the environmental elements of terrorism and summarizes the previous literature on target selection by terrorists, concluding that the implementation of situational crime prevention may yield counter-terrorism benefits, particularly for specific vulnerable places.

Developing areas of research

Many scholars have argued that the terrorism literature has overlooked criminological theory with a number of potentially useful perspectives underexplored. We here briefly consider a number of different perspectives which have received less attention than those mentioned earlier or which have investigated concepts relevant to a broader range of theories. As such, the only commonality in the research presented here is that each pushes the boundaries of existing theoretical frameworks to include terrorism.

Criminologists have of course extensively studied why people desist from crime. LaFree and Miller (2008) argue that desistance research can be applied to terrorism, discuss the implications of this approach from the existing criminological literature and identify a number of objectives for future research. Rice (2009) thus draws on the intersection of psychology and criminology to suggest that research should incorporate the emotional processes of terrorists and their communities. Akers and Silverman (2004) outline the potential value of applying differential association and social learning theories to terrorism, arguing that terrorists adopt an ideology and identity, which includes values, beliefs and attitudes which justify terrorism, specifically, and killing, more generally.

Oliverio and Lauderdale (2005) explore the roles that different forms of social control may play in terrorism and argue that families and other groups can emulate mechanisms established by a government to control terrorism and other violence. They also suggest that particular forms of societal control structures could be used to justify terrorism. Freilich *et al.* (2009) apply developmental theories to four white supremacist groups to examine the factors that could influence their growth and longevity, with their research suggesting that the capability of leadership to advance ideological messages and goals and to take advantage of political opportunities is connected with the growth and longevity of these groups. Appleby (2010) uses labelling theory to examine whether government created labels related to Islam makes counter-terrorism efforts better or worse, arguing that government rhetoric fails to allow for multiple identities and homogenizes individual identity, resulting in outcomes which are detrimental to counter-terrorism goals.

Hayward (2011) explores the similarities and differences between early twenty-first-century research in critical terrorism studies and cultural criminology. He makes a number of suggestions for future research and highlights the importance of having focused goals for communicating between disciplines. Gaskew (2009) examines the fundamental concepts of peacemaking criminology through sixteen months of ethnographic fieldwork in a Muslim American community in Florida after the passage of the US Patriot Act. The study describes in detail their difficulties and recommends ways to improve relations between law enforcement and Muslim American communities. We now turn our attention to a critical discussion of the 'war on terrorism'.

The war on terrorism

The term *war on terrorism* is used to describe the US-led global counter-terrorism campaign launched in response to the terrorist attacks of 11 September 2001. In its scope, expenditure and impact on international relations, it was comparable to the Cold War and was intended to represent a new phase in global political relations, and it has subsequently had important consequences for security, human rights, international law, cooperation and governance.

The war on terrorism was a multidimensional campaign of almost limitless scope. Its military dimension involved major wars in Afghanistan and Iraq, covert operations in Yemen and elsewhere, large-scale military-assistance programs for cooperative regimes and major increases in military spending. Its intelligence dimension comprised institutional reorganization and considerable increases in the funding of US intelligence-gathering capabilities, a global programme of capturing terrorist suspects and interning them at Guantanamo Bay, expanded cooperation with foreign intelligence agencies and the tracking and interception of terrorist financing. Its diplomatic dimension included continuing efforts to construct and maintain a global coalition of partner states and organizations and an extensive public diplomacy campaign to counter anti-Americanism in the Middle East. The domestic dimension entailed new anti-terrorism legislation, such as the USA Patriot Act; new security institutions, such as the Department of Homeland Security; the preventive detainment of thousands of suspects; surveillance and intelligence-gathering programmes by the National Security Agency, the Federal Bureau of Investigation and local authorities; the strengthening of emergency-response procedures; and increased security measures for airports, borders and public events.

The successes of the first years of the war on terrorism included the arrest of hundreds of terrorist suspects around the world, the prevention of further large-scale terrorist attacks on the US mainland, the toppling of the Taliban regime and the subsequent closure of terrorist-training camps in Afghanistan, the capture or elimination of many of the senior members of al-Qaeda, and increased levels of international cooperation in global counter-terrorism efforts.

Critics nevertheless argued that the failures of the US counter-terrorism campaign outweighed its successes. They contended that the war in Afghanistan had effectively scattered the al-Qaeda network, thereby making it even harder to counteract, and that the attacks in Afghanistan and Iraq had increased anti-American feeling among Muslims throughout the world, thereby amplifying the message of militant Islam and uniting disparate groups in a common cause. Others alleged that the war on terrorism was a contrived smokescreen for the pursuit of a larger US geopolitical agenda which included controlling global oil reserves, increasing defence spending, expanding the country's international military presence and countering the strategic challenge posed by various regional powers.

By the time of the re-election of President George W. Bush in 2004, the drawbacks of the war were becoming readily apparent. In Iraq, US forces had overthrown the government of Saddam Hussein in 2003 with relative ease and limited casualties. But war planners had underestimated the difficulties of building a functioning government from scratch and neglected to consider how this effort could be complicated by sectarian tensions in Iraq, which had previously been held in check by Saddam's repressive regime but were unleashed by his removal. By late 2004, it was clear that Iraq was sinking into chaos and civil war. Estimates of the number of Iraqi civilians killed during the period of maximum violence – roughly 2004 to 2007 – vary widely but generally exceed 200,000. US casualties during this period far outnumbered those suffered during the initial 2003 invasion. Afghanistan, which for several years had seemed to be under control, soon followed a similar trajectory, and by 2006, the US was facing a full-blown insurgency there led by a reconstituted Taliban.

The Bush administration faced increasing domestic and international criticism for actions which it deemed necessary to fight terrorism, but which critics considered to be immoral, illegal or both. These included the detention of accused enemy combatants without trial at Guantánamo Bay and at several secret prisons outside the US, the use of torture against these detainees in an effort to extract intelligence, and the use of unmanned combat drones to kill suspected enemies in countries far beyond the battlefields of Iraq and Afghanistan.

By the last years of the Bush presidency, public opinion was strongly negative concerning his handling of the Iraq War and other national security matters. This discontent helped Barack Obama – an outspoken critic of Bush's foreign policy – to win the presidency in 2008. Under the new administration, the expression *war on terrorism* – still closely associated with Bush policies – quickly disappeared from official communications. Obama made the rejection explicit in a speech made in 2013 in which he stated that the US would eschew a boundless, vaguely defined 'global war on terrorism' in favour of more focused actions against specific hostile groups.

During the Obama administration, the wars in Iraq and Afghanistan were gradually wound down, although at the end of his presidency in 2016, there were still US troops in both countries. It is worth noting that beneath Obama's rejection of the war on terrorism as a rhetorical device and as a conceptual framework for national security there were important continuities with the policies of his predecessor. The Obama administration, for example, greatly expanded the campaign of targeted killings carried out with drones, even eliminating several US citizens abroad whom it deemed threatening. Special operations forces were greatly expanded and increasingly deployed to conduct low-profile military interventions in countries outside of acknowledged war zones. And US security agencies continued to exercise the wide-ranging surveillance powers that they had accumulated during the Bush administration despite protests from civil liberties groups.

State violence as state terrorism

Introduction

Blakely (2012) observes that much state violence is used to coerce populations into complying with the wishes of elites and is usually intended to achieve certain political objectives, particularly curtailing political opposition. When used in this way, state violence constitutes state terrorism. A defining feature of state terrorism, and that which distinguishes it from other forms of state violence, is that it involves the illegal targeting of individuals that the state has a duty to protect with the aim of instilling fear in a target audience beyond the direct victim.

Defining state terrorism and violence

Totalitarian regimes throughout history – including those of Stalin, Hitler and Pol Pot – have used violence to terrorize populations into complying with their demands. European colonial powers used violence in this way to establish and maintain their empires, and later, to try to thwart independence movements in their colonies. During World War II, the Allies bombed civilians in German cities to try to incite them to turn against Hitler. During the Cold War, Latin American states – invariably with the support of the US – deployed violence, including disappearances and torture, to try to curtail support for opposition movements. When non-state actors use violence to intimidate an audience beyond the direct victim of that violence, we refer to it as terrorism. Yet there has been considerable resistance to the notion that states can be perpetrators of terrorism, even though the vast majority of state violence, in particular that against domestic populations, is intended to terrorize and results in far higher casualties than non-state terrorism. It is frequently assumed that because state violence is based on its monopoly of coercive power, there is a fundamental difference between the two.

Blakely (2012) thus observes that as states are permitted to use violence, we should not refer to their use of violence as terrorism. Non-state actors, on the other hand, are afforded no such right in pursuit of their political objectives. Hence, we refer to their actions as terrorism. There are nevertheless two significant problems with these assumptions. First, terrorism and state violence are considered differently on the basis of who the perpetrator of the act is rather than on the nature of the act itself. Second, there is the incorrect assumption that because the state has a monopoly on violence, any such use by the state is permissible. The key difference between state terrorism and other forms of state violence is that state terrorism involves the illegal targeting of individuals that the state has a duty to protect with the intention of creating extreme fear among an audience beyond the direct victim of the violence. That audience may be a domestic one, and it may be limited, consisting of only the immediate acquaintances of the actual victim. This is nevertheless significant because it helps us to make an important distinction between isolated incidents of criminal activity or state violence, on one hand, and state terrorism, on the other. The case of torture is helpful for exploring the significance of the target audience.

Many victims of state violence are subjected to torture. In some cases, torture is carried out covertly and is aimed primarily at tormenting the victim. It, of course, violates international law, but for torture to constitute state terrorism, it must be aimed at, or have the effect of, terrorizing an audience beyond the direct victim. Torture was used in history, very publicly, as not only a form of punishment but also as a means of deterring criminal behaviour (Beccaria, [1764] 1995; Foucault, 1977; Peters, 1985; Vidal-Naquet, 1963). Torture continues to be used as a means of terrorizing other incarcerated detainees to compel certain behaviour by ensuring that they hear the torture occurring or see the physical harm inflicted on their fellow captives. Torture is often intended to alter behaviour among a much wider audience well beyond the walls of the torture chamber. It was used in this way by the Guatemalan state during the counter-insurgency war of the 1970s and 1980s, during which – as Amnesty International reported – newspapers were permitted to publish photographs of dead torture victims with the intention of terrorizing the populations of entire cities. In some cases, a much more specific organization or set of individuals will be the intended audience.

Blakely (2012) observes that if torture occurs in complete secret – and there is no audience to witness it – it is difficult to argue that this is state terrorism. For example if an isolated individual or group of prison guards or members of the armed forces secretly uses torture, goes to great lengths to ensure that no one else knew of it, with there being no evidence that higher authorities had sanctioned the torture, we might conclude that this was the criminal act of an individual or group, rather than an act of state terrorism. On the other hand, if such an act was carried out with the sanction of higher authorities, but the perpetrators and the higher authorities went to great lengths to ensure that no one else knew of it, we might conclude that this was an act of state violence, since it was perpetrated very clearly on behalf of the state. We could not, however, conclude that it was state terrorism if there was no audience to witness it. In practice, most torture committed by state agents is part of a wider pattern of state repression and in many cases, state terrorism. Nevertheless, it is important to make this distinction between criminal activities by individuals, state violence, and state terrorism, thereby reserving the label of state terrorism for those acts which are both condoned at some level by the state and are intended to or have the effect of terrorizing a wider audience.

The difficulties of identifying state terrorism

Both state terrorism and the illicit use of other forms of violence by the state are prosecutable under international law. But it is important to try to determine when states are using illicit violence as a means of intimidating an audience beyond the direct victim of the violence, thereby committing state terrorism. This is because in so doing they are

committing not just one but two serious crimes – illegal use of force and an act of terrorism. Determining the intentions of state actors is not easy. Often, their purposes will,
at best, be ambiguous. This is largely because in most cases governments seek to conceal
the extent to which they use terrorism, and when such activities are exposed, they tend
to be justified as 'necessary measures' or more benignly as 'police action' (Mitchell, 1986;
Nicholson, 1986). Obtaining data on acts of terrorism committed by states is extremely
difficult, since they tend not to advertise their terrorist activities or intent (Chambliss,
1989; Gibbs, 1989; Mitchell, 1986; Nicholson, 1986). When such activities are exposed,
considerable analytical effort is required to determine whether such an act does constitute
state terrorism, since they are unlikely to be included in the major data sets of terrorist
incidents. This also means that drawing concrete conclusions about whether certain acts
constitute state terrorism may not always be possible, and instead, we might need to make
inferences from other context-specific evidence.

In some cases, groups within a society may be terrorized as a consequence of other acts
of state violence. This raises the question of whether we can argue that state terrorism
has occurred if it is not the primary or only outcome of state violence. Mitchell (1986)
observes that if the terror was unintentional, we could not argue that this was 'true' terrorism. But this assumes that we can determine that the terror was not intentional but
rather than one of a number of intentions of the act. If we apply this condition, an act of
violence cannot be defined as state terrorism if it is primarily aimed at harming the victim, a secondary effect of which is to terrorize other groups within a population. Mitchell
illustrates this argument with the example of the policies of the Khmer Rouge that were
aimed at the destruction of a particular sector of society and which therefore constituted
genocide. While this will have instilled terror throughout society, this was not the primary intention. By contrast, they argue, policies such as US Operation Phoenix in South
Vietnam, which involved terrorizing people associated with members of the National
Liberation Front by publicly rounding them up, torturing and assassinating them, do
constitute state terrorism, because terrorizing the target audience was the primary objective (Mitchell, 1986).

Blakely (2012) observes that such a sharp distinction should not be made between terrorism as a secondary effect, especially in cases where the act itself is illegitimate. A parallel can be drawn here with the work of Michael Walzer (2000) on the legitimacy of acts
in war which are likely to have evil consequences. He argues that, in line with the *jus in
bello* principles, such an act is only permissible providing four conditions hold:

> that the act is good in itself or at least indifferent, which means . . . that it is a legitimate
> act of war; that the direct effect is morally acceptable . . . that the intention of the actor
> is good, that is, he aims only at the acceptable effect; the evil effect is not one of his
> ends, nor is it a means to an ends; that the good effect is sufficiently good to compen-
> sate for allowing the evil effect; it must be justifiable under the proportionality rule.
>
> (Walzer, 2000: 153)

Blakely (2012) observes that these conditions can be usefully applied to state terrorism,
where it appears to be a secondary effect of some other act of state violence. State terrorism in such cases is not the unintended secondary effect of some good or indifferent
act. It is a consequence of a policy which itself is illegitimate, repressive and evil. Furthermore, if the state seeks to commit genocide, for example, against a specific group, are

they not assisted because others outside of that group are sufficiently fearful of the consequences for themselves if they were to intervene in an attempt to prevent the genocide? And could the terror that arises among other groups not be an intended effect, whether primary or secondary? In the case of the genocide by Nazi Germany against Jews, gypsies and homosexuals, individuals outside of those groups may not have intervened because they had been sufficiently terrorized by the increasing intensity of efforts by the Nazis to single these groups out, round them up and transport them to unknown places and subsequently by the rumours they had heard of concentration camps and of others outside those groups who had attempted to protect the vulnerable themselves disappearing. Indeed, as Gurr notes, Adolf Hitler, while in power, was explicit about the fact that his genocidal policies also served as a tool of terror to deter opposition:

> I shall spread terror through the surprising application of all means. The sudden shock of a terrible fear of death is what matters. Why should I deal otherwise with all my political opponents? These so-called atrocities save me hundreds of thousands of individual actions against the protestors and discontents. Each one of them will think twice to oppose me when he learns what is [awaiting] him in the [concentration] camp.
>
> (Adolf Hitler, cited in Gurr, 1986: 46–47)

Even where the terrorism is not a secondary objective, it might prove expedient to the state and should be labelled state terrorism. Walzer argues that to conclude that a secondary effect was unintentional there would have to be evidence that the actors involved sought to minimize the secondary effect. It is difficult to envisage that a state involved in a genocidal policy would be too concerned about minimizing the ensuing terror among others outside of the targeted group, particularly where the terror may be instrumental to its overall objectives.

The same principle applies if terrorism arises as a secondary effect of an act which may be considered legitimate. The case of the targeting of electrical power during the first Gulf War is useful here. In Operation Desert Storm, the US-led campaign against Iraq in 1990–91, civilians were never intended as direct targets. Indeed, according to the Gulf War Air Power Surveys (an analysis carried out by the US Air Force following the Gulf War) 'there was widespread agreement from the outset of the planning process that directly attacking the people of Iraq or their food supply was neither compatible with US objectives nor morally acceptable to the American people' (Keaney and Cohen, 1993: 268).

The target categories drawn up by the planners also indicate that civilians were not intended as direct targets. The authors of the surveys claim that the air campaign had not only been 'precise, efficient and legal, but had resulted in very few civilian casualties'(Keaney and Cohen, 1993: 305). A Greenpeace International study in 1991 estimated that countrywide civilian casualties were 2,278 dead and 5,976 injured (Arkin et al., 1991: 46–47). The Greenpeace figure is cited by the Gulf War Air Power Surveys and is not disputed by its authors (Keaney and Cohen, 1993: 482). There was nevertheless considerable controversy surrounding the reporting of civilian casualties in the Gulf War, since the Pentagon made no attempt to keep records of civilian deaths. In 1993, Greenpeace revised its estimate to 3,500 civilian deaths as a result of coalition bombing. The US Army War College estimated that 3,000 had been killed, and the government of Iraq put the figure at 2,248. Greenpeace did conclude that they found no evidence of deliberate targeting of civilians. They did nevertheless highlight the catastrophic human impact of the air campaign, caused by the devastation of the Iraqi infrastructure and the intense environmental degradation caused by the bombing. This was a result of the intensity of the air campaign. According to the Greenpeace report, '[i]n one day of the Gulf War, there were as many combat missions flown against Iraq as Saddam Hussein experienced in the entire Iran-Iraq war' (Arkin et al., 1991).

Blakely (2012) observes that is no indication in the Gulf War Air Power Surveys that measures were taken to minimize the secondary effect of terrorizing the population, which would undoubtedly arise from aerial bombardment of targets deemed to be legitimate, especially given the extensive nature of the bombing campaign. The opposite was true. There was a view among a number of those involved in the planning of the air campaign that harming the morale of the civilian population would be a welcome secondary effect of the targeting of Iraq's electricity generating capacity:

> As for civilian morale, some of the air planners, including General Glosson, felt that 'putting the lights out on Baghdad' would have psychological effects on the average Iraqi. . . . By demonstrating that Saddam Hussein could not even keep the electricity flowing in Baghdad, it was hoped the Ba'th Party's grip on the Iraqi population could be loosened, thereby helping to bring about a change in the regime.
>
> (Keaney and Cohen, 1993: 292)

Aerial bombardment that was sufficient to cripple the entire electricity generation capacity of modern cities, such as Baghdad and Basra, is likely to have resulted in considerable levels of fear among the civilian population. This was not seen by the planners as an illegitimate secondary effect but instead as a welcome means by which to undermine the regime. In warfare, attacking the morale of enemy soldiers is considered an appropriate means by which to attempt to avoid having to fight each and every battalion one by one. Walzer's argument nevertheless requires that measures are taken to minimize the secondary effect, in this case, terrorizing large sectors of the population. No such measures were taken by the air campaign planner. Indeed, they hoped that the population would be sufficiently 'psychologically affected' – a euphemism for 'terrorized' – that opposition to the regime would increase. Rather than try and prevent the terrorizing of the population, those involved in planning the air campaign actively encouraged it, even though this is illegitimate.

The problem of agency

Before concluding that an act of violence by a representative of the state was an act of state terrorism, we are confronted with a number of challenges relating to agency. We must first rule out the possibility that the act was simply an isolated, criminal act by an individual as opposed to an act of state violence. We then need to be able to demonstrate that the act was intended to or had the effect of terrorizing a wider audience than the direct victim of the violence. Even then, the state still holds a degree of responsibility for the actions of its representatives. Whether we conclude that a state sanctioned the act and was therefore complicit in state terrorism through its agents might depend on how the state responds afterwards. If the state fails to prosecute the individual to the full extent of the law and fails to compensate the victims, and if the state attempts to excuse the actions in some way, the state is condoning the actions of that individual. We can argue therefore that the state was complicit. Blakely (2012) argues that with reference to the use of torture at Abu Ghraib prison in Iraq, it is essential to demonstrate the importance of context-specific evidence in determining, first, whether acts of violence by state agents were acts of state terrorism and, second, whether those acts were part of an institutionalized policy of state terrorism.

To differentiate between the odd isolated criminal act of a prison officer or member of the armed forces and an act sanctioned by the state, it is important to examine the reaction of the relevant officials and the state. If measures are taken, swiftly, to try and punish the perpetrator(s) through proper legal and disciplinary channels, and there is no evidence of the state sanctioning such activities, we might conclude that this was a criminal act by an individual or group and not an act of state violence. This was indeed what the Pentagon and Bush administration claimed once the photographs emerged in 2004 revealing that detainees at the Abu Ghraib prison in Iraq had been tortured by US personnel. Nevertheless, this claim cannot be sustained, since there have been very few prosecutions, sentences have been light and punitive measures have been limited to lower-ranking soldiers, rather than the senior officers involved, or indeed the officials in the Bush administration who fought to ensure that methods tantamount to torture be permitted against terror suspects. In a speech on Iraq on 24 May 2004, shortly after the public had learned of the torture, President Bush declared:

> Under the dictator [Saddam Hussein], prisons like Abu Ghraib were symbols of death and torture. That same prison became a symbol of disgraceful conduct by a few American troops who dishonoured our country and disregarded our values.
>
> (cited in Milbank, 2004)

The same conclusions were drawn by Major General Antonio Tabuga in his initial inquiry. He concluded that the torture was the work of a few bad apples in need of improved training (Taguba, 2004). Yet the record of events uncovered through various leaked documents, traced by Seymour Hersh (2004) and subsequently compiled by Karen Greenberg and Joshua Dratel (2005), shows that despite the public statement condemning torture, the administration had been behind numerous attempts to allow torture of detainees in the war on terror. Policies outlined in the various memos which passed between the upper echelons of the administration, including the White House, the Department of Justice and the senior counsel to the president, were enacted. These included not affording protection under the Geneva Conventions to detainees and allowing torture, including the use of stress positions, extremes of temperature and light, hooding, interrogations for 20 hours, forced grooming and removal of clothing, waterboarding and the use of scenarios designed to convince the detainee that death or severe pain were imminent, as advocated in a memo from Major General Dunlavey, dated 11 October 2002, requesting approval for such techniques (Dunlavey, 2002). These techniques were subsequently sanctioned by Secretary of State Donald Rumsfeld on 2 December 2002 (Haynes, 2002).

The response of the administration to the abuses at Abu Ghraib involved proceedings in military courts against nine reservists involved in the abuses, three of whom were convicted; the other six made plea deals (Gutierrez, 2005). None of the senior officers implicated was brought to trial, and there was no attempt to hold to account those in the Bush administration who had themselves been involved in efforts to legitimize torture.

Without examining the wider context of the Abu Ghraib case, it would be possible to conclude that this was an isolated incident committed by a small number of miscreants, and this was certainly the message that the administration attempted to portray. The reality is that there were many cases of abuse in the war on terror at numerous camps in Iraq and Afghanistan, as well as at Guantanamo Bay, at the hands of US and allied forces. Furthermore, the policy of extraordinary rendition has resulted in torture and abuse, sanctioned by the US and various liberal democratic allies, and carried out by security agents from many countries with appalling human rights records (Blakeley, 2009). Abu Ghraib was not therefore an isolated incident but part of a much bigger pattern of state violence sanctioned by the US state. We can also conclude that it is indicative of a pattern of state terrorism, since these practices have had the effect of terrorizing a wider audience than the direct victims of the disappearances and torture.

Blakely (2012) observes that states have frequently used violence against their own or external populations as a means of achieving their political objectives. State violence frequently also constitutes state terrorism because it is used to instil fear in a wider audience than the direct victim of the violence. This is what distinguishes state terrorism from other forms of state violence. It also helps explain why much of the violence deployed by states against its own or another population also constitutes state terrorism. States have found terrorism to be functional to the achievement of their political objectives, as the examples explored here have demonstrated.

Terrorism and postmodernism revisited

Whether the terrorist activities outlined earlier can be considered to be 'just' wars in terms of international law in any objective sense has been widely debated, but it does seem that these can be considered perfectly normal, albeit violent and extremely unpleasant, activities, which make perfect subjective sense to the participants and the groups supporting them. The significance for our discussion of terrorism is that the events of 11 September 2001 – and those which followed – seemingly signposted the end for any positive notion of a postmodern society. From that date, the very idea of societies being founded on widely accepted and legitimate moral ambiguities where there are a range of different discourses that can be legitimate and hence right for different people, at different times, in different contexts has become seriously problematic.

Postmodern societies can only function successfully if there is a reciprocal acceptance of diverse values from all participant groups. It was always a deeply problematic notion in societies with a very pronounced 'forced-division-of-labour' (Durkheim, 1933), and it appears seemingly impossible when groups become so totally opposed to the values and activities of others that they are prepared to use any means to destroy them. At that point, such groups become enemies and anyone – however tangentially associated with them – will become a legitimate target for surveillance and risk assessment. Government cannot afford not to take the issue of state security seriously, and the notion of the risk society becomes entrenched and virtually unassailable in public policy discourse.

Policy implications of terrorism and state violence

The war on terror needs to focus on more than just transnational terrorism, because domestic terrorism – and home-grown terrorists – pose a greater threat in terms of lives and property loss than the former. This is also true because domestic terrorism tends to spill over into transnational terrorism as local terrorists seek greater world recognition.

For transnational terrorism, enhanced defensive counter-terrorism precautions and the increasing dominance of religious fundamentalist terrorists have made the hardest-to-defend private targets the most popular. The changing targeting of transnational and domestic terrorists has made public places – shopping malls, department stores, public squares, public transport, sporting events – likely attack venues. For domestic terrorism, private parties have been the prime target for 30 years. Targeting differences between domestic and transnational terrorism can inform the allocation of security resources.

For all target types, there is an increased targeting of people over property, which makes defensive security measures more challenging. As defensive action becomes more difficult and costly, more resources must be put into proactive measures that dismantle terrorist groups and their infrastructure and discourage membership of extremist groups. More radical measures will be those that target global inequalities and lead to a more equal global division of labour and thus remove the substantive motivation for terrorist involvement.

Summary of main points

1   The topic of terrorism is both complex and emotive, not least to those who see terrorists as justified and often have strong feelings concerning the rightness of the use of violence.

2   Terrorism is invariably characterized by the use of violence against civilians, with the expressed desire of causing terror or panic in the population.

3   Sometimes terrorist activities are funded by states (state-sponsored terrorism) and the West has been keen to accuse countries such as Libya, Iran, (previously) Iraq and Syria of this.

4   Western states have nevertheless supported terrorism when it has been in their political interests to do so, and during the Cold War backed many right-wing movements invariably as a bulwark against communism.

5   Most of the major theories which seek to explain terrorism – and individual and group involvement – are derived from theories of collective violence developed in the field of political science.

6   Theoretically understanding the reasons behind the rise and persistence of terrorism and the ways that it can be stopped has become one of the more prominent political priorities of the early twenty-first century.

7   A growing body of literature bridges the gap between the many different criminological theories which explain why people commit crimes and the number of terrorist attacks vary across times and space.

8   The term *war on terrorism* is used to describe the US-led global counter-terrorism campaign launched in response to the terrorist attacks of 11 September 2001 It was a multidimensional campaign of almost limitless scope.

9   A defining feature of state terrorism is that it involves the illegal targeting of individuals that the state has a duty to protect with the aim of instilling fear in a target audience beyond the direct victim.

10 The events of 11 September 2001 – and those which followed – signposted the end for any positive notion of a postmodern society.

Discussion questions

1   How would you define terrorism?
2   What are the links between fascism and terrorism?
3   How do political scientists explain terrorism?
4   How would explain state terrorism?
5   What does terrorism tell us about the possibilities for a postmodern society?

Suggested further reading

Martha Crenshaw (1998) provides the definitive discussion of terrorism as rational choice. O'Connor (1994) identifies and discusses five sociological theories of terrorism. There are a multitude of criminological theories explaining different aspects of terrorism, and these are signposted in the text. There are too many to cite here, and you can take your choice depending on your area of interest. Likewise, the war on terrorism. Blakely (2012) provides an excellent critical discussion of state violence as state terrorism.

References

Agnew, R. (2010) 'A General Strain Theory of Terrorism', *Theoretical Criminology*, 14(2): 131–53.
Akers, R.L. and Silverman, A.L. (2004) 'Toward a Social Learning Model of Violence and Terrorism', in M.A. Zahn, H.H. Brownstein and S.L. Jackson (eds.) *Violence: From Theory to Research*. Newark, NJ: LexisNexis.
Akyuz, K. and Armstrong, T. (2011) 'Understanding the Sociostructural Correlates of Terrorism in Turkey', *International Criminal Justice Review*, 21(2): 134–55.
Appleby, N. (2010) 'Labelling the Innocent: How Government Counter-Terrorism Advice Creates Labels that Contribute to the Problem', *Critical Studies on Terrorism*, 3(3): 421–36.
Argomaniz, J. and Vidal-Diez, A. (2015) 'Examining Deterrence and Backlash Effects in Counterter-rorism: The Case of ETA', *Terrorism and Political Violence*, 27(1): 160–81.
Arkin, W., Durrant, D. and Cherni, M. (1991) *On Impact: Modern Warfare and the Environment: A Case Study of the Gulf War*. Available from: www.greenpeace.org/raw/content/international/press/reports/on-impact-
Beccaria, C. ([1764] 1995) *On Crimes and Punishments and Other Writings*. Cambridge: Cambridge University Press.
Bell, B. (1982) 'Psychology of Leaders of Terrorist Groups', *International Journal of Group Tensions*, 12: 84–104.
Blakeley, R. (2009) *State Terrorism and Neoliberalism: The North in the South, Routledge Critical Terrorism Studies*. London: Routledge.
Blakely, R. (2012) 'State Violence as State Terrorism', in M. Breen-Smyth (ed.) *The Ashgate Research Companion to Political Violence*. London: Ashgate.
Carson, J.V. (2014) 'Counterterrorism and Radical Eco-Groups: A Context for Exploring the Series Hazard Model', *Journal of Quantitative Criminology*, 30(3): 485–504.
Chambliss, W. (1989) 'State-Organized Crime: The American Society of Criminology, Presidential Address', *Criminology*, 27(2): 183–208.
Clarke, R.V.G. and Newman, G.R. (2006) *Outsmarting the Terrorists. Global Crime and Justice*. Westport, CT: Praeger Security International.
Cohen, L.E. and Felson, M. (1979) 'Social Inequality and Predatory Criminal Victimization: An Exposition and Test of a Formal Theory', *American Sociological Review*, 44: 5–60.
Cottee, S. (2011) 'Jihadism As a Subcultural Response to Social Strain: Extending Marc Sageman's "Bunch of Guys" Thesis', *Terrorism and Political Violence*, 23(5): 730–51.
Crenshaw, M. (1998) 'The Logic of Terrorism: Terrorist Behavior as a Product of Strategic Choice', in W. Reich (ed.) *Origins of Terrorism*. New York: Woodrow Wilson Center Press.

Dugan, L. and Chenoweth, E. (2012) 'Moving beyond Deterrence: The Effectiveness of Raising the Expected Utility of Abstaining from Terrorism in Israel', *American Sociological Review*, 77(4): 597–624.

Dugan, L., LaFree, G. and Piquero, A.R. (2005) 'Testing a Rational Choice Model of Airline Hijackings', *Criminology*, 43(4): 1031–65.

Dugan, L. and Young, J. (2010) 'Allow Extremist Participation in the Policymaking Process', *Paper presented at the meeting of the American Society of Criminology held* November 4–7, 2009 in Philadelphia. In Contemporary Issues in Criminal Justice Policy: Policy Proposals from the American Society of Criminology Conference, edited by N.A. Frost, J.D. Freilich and T.R. Clear. Belmont, CA: Wadsworth Cengage Learning.

Dunlavey, M. (2002) *Counter-Resistance Strategies (Memorandum for Commander, US Southern Command)*, October 11. Available from: www.torturingdemocracy.org/documents/20021011.pdf [Accessed 18 October 2018].

Durkheim, E. (1933 originally 1893) *The Division of Labour in Society*. Glencoe, IL: Free Press.

Fahey, S. and LaFree, G. (2015) 'Does Countrylevel Social Disorganization Increase Terrorist Attacks?', *Terrorism and Political Violence*, 27(1): 81–111.

Ferracuti, F. (1982) 'A Sociopsychiatric Interpretation of Terrorism', *Annals of American Academy of Political & Social Science*, 463: 129–41.

Fodeman, A.D. (2015) 'Safety and Danger Valves: Functional Displacement in American Anti-abortion Terrorism', *Behavioral Sciences of Terrorism and Political Aggression*, 7(3): 169–83.

Foucault, M. (1977) *Discipline and Punish: The Birth of the Prison*. London: Allen Lane.

Freilich, J.D., Chermak, S.M. and Caspi, D. (2009) 'Critical Events in the Life Trajectories of Domestic Extremist White Supremacist Groups', *Criminology & Public Policy*, 8(3): 497–530.

Freilich, J.D. and Pridemore, W.A. (2007) 'Politics, Culture, and Political Crime: Covariates of Abortion Clinic Attacks in the United State', *Journal of Criminal Justice*, 35(3): 323–36.

Frey, B.S. and Luechinger, S. (2003) 'How to Fight Terrorism: Alternatives to Deterrence', *Defence and Peace Economics*, 14(4): 237–49.

Fussey, P. (2011) 'An Economy of Choice? Terrorist Decisionmaking and Criminological Rational Choice Theories Reconsidered', *Security Journal*, 24(1): 85–99.

Galvin, D. (1983) 'The Female Terrorist: A Socio-Psychological Perspective', *Behavioral Science & Law*, 1: 19–32.

Gaskew, T. (2009) 'Peacemaking Criminology and Counter-Terrorism: Muslim Americans and the War on Terror', *Contemporary Justice Review*, 12(3): 345–66.

Gibbs, J. (1989) 'Conceptualization of Terrorism', *American Sociological Review*, 54(3): 329–40.

González, A.L., Freilich, J.D. and Chermak, S.M. (2014) 'How Women Engage Homegrown Terrorism', *Feminist Criminology*, 9(4): 344–66.

Greenberg, K. and Dratel, J. (eds.) (2005) *The Torture Papers: The Road to Abu Ghraib*. Cambridge: Cambridge University Press.

Gruenewald, J., Allison-Gruenewald, K. and Klein, B.R. (2015) 'Assessing the Attractiveness and Vulnerability of Ecoterrorism Targets: A Situational Crime Prevention Approach', *Studies in Conflict & Terrorism*, 38(6): 433–55.

Gurr, T.R. (1970) *Why Men Rebel*. Princeton, NJ: Princeton University Press.

Gurr, T.R. (1986) 'The Political Origins of State Violence and Terror: A Theoretical Analysis', in M. Stohl and G. Lopez (eds.) *Government Violence and Repression: An Agenda for Research*. New York: Greenwood Press.

Gutierrez, T. (2005) 'Lynndie England Convicted in Abu Ghraib Trial', *USA Today*, September 26.

Hacker, F. (1996) *Crusaders, Criminals, Crazies: Terror and Terrorists in Our Time*. New York: Norton.

Hamm, M.S. (2004) 'Apocalyptic Violence: The Seduction of Terrorist Subcultures', *Theoretical Criminology*, 8(3): 323–39.

Haynes, W.J. (2002) *Counter-Resistance Techniques (Action Memo from William J Haynes, General Counsel, to Secretary of State for Defense Donald Rumsfeld)*, November 27. Available from: www.torturingdemocracy.org/documents/20021127-1.pdf [Accessed 18 October 2018].

Hayward, K.J (2011) 'The Critical Terrorism Studies: Cultural Criminology Nexus: Some Thoughts on How to "Toughen Up" the Critical Studies Approach', *Critical Studies on Terrorism*, 4(1): 57–73.

Hersh, S. (2004) *Chain of Command: The Road from 9/11 to Abu Ghraib*. London: Penguin Books.

Hoffman, B. (1993) *Holy Terror*. Santa Monica, CA: RAND.

Hsu, H.Y. and Apel, R. (2015) 'A Situational Model of Displacement and Diffusion Following the Introduction of Airport Metal Detectors', *Terrorism and Political Violence*, 27(1): 29–52.

Hua, J., and Bapna, S. (2012) 'How Can We Deter Cyber Terrorism?', *Information Security Journal: A Global Perspective*, 21(2): 102–14.

Hudson, R. (1999) *Who Becomes a Terrorist and Why*. Guilford, CT: Lyons Press.

Juergensmeyer, M. (2001) *Terror in the Mind of God: The Global Rise of Religious Violence*. Berkeley, CA: University of California Press.

Keaney, T. and Cohen, E. (1993) *Gulf War Air Power Surveys (Volume II, Part II)*. Available from: www.airforcehistory.hq.af.mil/Publications/Annotations/gwaps.htm [Accessed 30 July 2019].

Kraemer, E. (2004) 'A Philosopher Looks at Terrorism', in A. Nyatepe-Coo and D. Zeisler-Vralsted (eds.) *Understanding Terrorism*. Upper Saddle River, NJ: Prentice Hall.

LaFree, G. and Bersani, B.E. (2014) 'County-Level Correlates of Terrorist Attacks in the United States', *Criminology & Public Policy*, 13(3): 455–81.

LaFree, G., Dugan, L. and Korte, R. (2009) 'The Impact of British Counterterrorist Strategies on Political Violence in Northern Ireland: Comparing Deterrence and Backlash Models', *Criminology*, 47(1): 17–45.

LaFree, G. and Miller, E. (2008) 'Desistance from Terrorism: What Can We Learn from Criminology?', *Dynamics of Asymmetric Conflict*, 1(3): 203–30.

Le Vine, V.T. and Salert, B.A. (1996) 'Does a Coercive Official Response Deter Terrorism? The Case of the PLO', *Terrorism and Political Violence*, 8(1): 22–49.

Lynch, J.P. (2011) 'Implications of Opportunity Theory for Combating Terrorism', in B. Forst, J.R. Greenemand, J.P. Lynch (eds.) *Criminologists on Terrorism and Homeland Security* (pp. 151–82). Cambridge Studies in Criminology. Cambridge: Cambridge University Press.

McCartan, L.M., Masselli, A., Rey, R. and Rusnak, D. (2008) 'The Logic of Terrorist Target Choice: An Examination of Chechen Rebel Bombings from 1997–2003', *Studies in Conflict & Terrorism*, 31(1): 60–79.

Merari, A. (1990) 'The Readiness to Kill and Die: Suicidal Terrorism in the Middle East', in W. Reich (ed.) *Origins of Terrorism*. Cambridge: Cambridge University Press.

Milbank, D. (2004) 'Bush Seeks to Reassure Nation on Iraq', *Washington Post*, May 25.

Mitchell, C. (1986) 'State Terrorism: Issues of Concept and Measurement', in M. Stohl and G. Lopez (eds.) *Government Violence and Repression: An Agenda for Research*. New York: Greenwood Press.

Morris, N.A. (2015) 'Target Suitability and Terrorism Events at Places', *Criminology & Public Policy*, 14(2): 417–26.

Muller, E. and Opp, K.-D. (1986) 'Rational Choice and Rebellious Collective Action', *American Political Science Review*, 80: 471–87.

Mullins, C.W. and Young, J.K. (2012) 'Cultures of Violence and Acts of Terror: Applying a Legitimation–Habituation Model to Terrorism', *Crime & Delinquency*, 58(1): 28–56.

Nassar, J. (2004) *Globalization and Terrorism*. Lanham, MD: Rowman and Littlefield.

Nicholson, M. (1986) 'Conceptual Problems of Studying State Terrorism', in M. Stohl and G. Lopez (eds.) *Government Violence and Repression: An Agenda for Research*. New York: Greenwood Press.

O'Connor, T. (1994) 'A Neofunctional Model of Crime and Crime Control', in G. Barak (ed.) *Varieties of Criminology*. Westport, CT: Greenwood Press.

Oliverio, A. and Lauderdale, P. (2005) 'Terrorism as Deviance or Social Control: Suggestions for Future Research', *International Journal of Comparative Sociology*, 46(1–2): 153–69.

Olson, M. (1982) *The Rise and Decline of Nations*. New Haven, CT: Yale University Press.

Pape, R.A. (2003) 'The Strategic Logic of Suicide Terrorism', *American Political Science Review*, 97(3): 343–61.

Parkin, W.S. and Freilich, J.D (2015) 'Routine Activities and Rightwing Extremists: An Empirical Comparison of the Victims of Ideologically and Non-Ideologically Motivated Homicides Committed by American Far-Rightists', *Terrorism and Political Violence*, 27(1): 182–203.

Passmore, K. (2002) *Fascism: A Very Short Introduction*. New York: Oxford University Press.

Perry, S., Apel, R., Newman, G.R. and Clarke, R.V.G. (2016) 'The Situational Prevention of Terrorism: An Evaluation of the Israeli West Bank Barrier', *Journal of Quantitative Criminology*, 32: 1–25.

Peters, E. (1985) *Torture*. New York: Basil Blackwell.

Piazza, J.A. (2012) 'Types of Minority Discrimination and Terrorism', *Conflict Management and Peace Science*, 29(5): 521–46.

Pisoiu, D. (2015) 'Subcultural Theory Applied to Jihadi and Rightwing Radicalization in Germany', *Terrorism and Political Violence*, 27(1): 9–28.

Rice, S.K. (2009) 'Emotions and Terrorism Research: A Case for a Socialpsychological Agenda', *Journal of Criminal Justice*, 37(3): 248–55.

Rice, S.K. and Agnew, R. (2013) 'Emotional Correlates of Radicalization and Terrorism', in J.B. Helfgott (ed.) *Criminal Psychology. Vol. 2: Typologies, Mental Disorders, and Profiles*. Westport, CT: Praeger.

Ross, J.I. (1996) 'A Model of the Psychological Causes of Oppositional Political Terrorism', *Peace and Conflict: Journal of Peace Psychology*: 2–11.

Ross, J.I. (1999) 'Beyond the Conceptualization of Terrorism: A Psychological-Structural Model', in C. Summers and E. Mardusen (eds.) *Collective Violence*. New York: Rowen and Littlefield.

Ruggiero, V. (2005) 'Political Violence: A Criminological Analysis', in M. Natarajan (ed.) *Introduction to International Criminal Justice*. New York: McGraw Hill.

Russell, C. and Bowman, M. (1977) 'Profile of a Terrorist', *Terrorism: An International Journal*, 1(1): 17–34.

Smith, B.L. and Damphousse, K.R. (1998) 'Terrorism, Politics, and Punishment: A Test of Structural-Contextual Theory and the "Liberation Hypothesis"', *Criminology*, 36(1): 67–92.

Strentz, T. (1988) 'A Terrorist Psychological Profile', *Law Enforcement Bulletin*, 57: 11–12.

Taguba, M.G.A. (2004) *Article 15–6 Investigation of the 800th Military Police Brigade*. Washington, DC: US Department of Defence.

Trivizas, E. and Smith, P.T. (1997) 'The Deterrent Effect of Terrorist Incidents on the Rates of Luggage Theft in Railway and Underground Stations', *British Journal of Criminology*, 37(1): 63–74.

Tyler, T.R., Schulhofer, S. and Huq, A.Z. (2010) 'Legitimacy and Deterrence Effects in Counterterrorism Policing: A Study of Muslim Americans', *Law & Society Review*, 44(2): 365–402.

Vidal-Naquet, P. (1963) *Torture: Cancer of Democracy*. Middlesex: Penguin Books.

Walzer, M. (2000) *Just and Unjust Wars*, 3rd ed. New York: Basic Books.

Wilson, M.A., Scholes, A. and Brocklehurst, E. (2010) '"A Behavioural Analysis of Terrorist Action: The Assassination and Bombing Campaigns of ETA between 1980 and 2007", in Special Issue: Terrorism: Criminological Perspectives', *British Journal of Criminology*, 50(4): 690–707.

Wormeli, P. (2014) 'Developing Policies for Countering Terrorism', *Criminology & Public Policy*, 13(3): 493–7.

Chapter 13

Gender, feminism and masculinity

Key issues

1   The historical development of feminism
2   Perspectives in feminist theory
3   Criminology and women
4   Crime and masculinities
5   Queer criminology

Introduction

The victimized actor model we encountered in the second chapter of this book proposes that the criminal is in some way the victim of an unjust and unequal society. Feminists take that argument further and observe that it is men who are the dominant group in society, and it is they who make and enforce the rules which are invariably to the detriment of women.

We should note from the outset that a distinction is usually made between the biological characteristics which define and distinguish males and females and the cultural expectations inherent in the social roles defined by societies as being applicable to men and women. *Sex* is thus a biological term used to describe the anatomical differences between males and females, while the term *gender* refers to learned behaviour associated with men and women which has developed through the socialization process. Gender is thus considered to be the social construction of non-biological differences between men and women and can be further explained by the identification of at least two sub-groups such as masculinity and femininity, which are partially based on physical difference. Well, that has become the orthodox way of considering these matters in recent social studies teaching and beyond. Yet it is a reality which has nevertheless been challenged in recent years. We consider the contentious issue of whether there is a simple binary biological divide between men and women (absolutism) or whether individuals are simply located on a continuum between male at one end and female at the other, as suggested by transgenderism, later in this chapter.

This is therefore more than the customary women and crime chapter found in criminology textbooks about women and crime, which invariably discusses why the issue has been ignored by traditional criminology, not least because so few women, in comparison to men, apparently engage in such behaviour. This chapter essentially examines such core issues but nevertheless goes further, considering other matters related to gender and sexuality. The outcome is that this chapter is long in comparison to others in this book, but this is rather inevitable in view of the breadth of territory it covers. We nevertheless start with the remarkably influential feminist criminology which has informed and heavily influenced the wider agenda.

The emergence of feminist criminology came to challenge the androcentrism – or male-centredness – of criminology (Daly and Chesney-Lind, 1988) and crucially noted that the failure of traditional 'malestream' criminological theory had been its inability to understand the significance of gender and sex roles (Gelsthorpe and Morris, 1990). For some, this significance is reflected in the ongoing differential in sex roles and gender inequality; for others, the inequalities are structural within patriarchy – a situation where the rights and privileges of males are considered superior to those of females – and which are a fundamental principle of societal organization. Labelling and conflict theories had previously recognized male–female differences in power, but feminist theory proposes that the power differential between men and women is at least as important as – if not more important than – the power differentials of race, class and age.

Feminist criminologists maintain that the criminal justice system reflects this inherent male dominance and functions to support patriarchy by discriminating against women and reinforcing traditional sex and family roles (Mann, 1984; Messerschmidt, 1986; Morris, 1987; Chesney-Lind, 1988, 1989; Daly and Chesney-Lind, 1988; Daly, 1989, 1992, 1994a, 1994b; Simpson, 1989, 1991; Gelsthorpe and Morris, 1990; Chesney-Lind and Shelden, 1992).

It is nevertheless important to recognize at the outset that feminism is not a unitary system of thought but a collection of different theoretical perspectives with each explaining the oppression of women in a different way. Consequently, there is no one feminist explanation of female criminality and it will thus be useful to briefly consider the different variations of feminist thought or feminisms and their development in a historical context.

The historical development of feminism

The French term *feminisme* was first used in the late nineteenth century as a synonym for the emancipation of women (Jaggar, 1983; Pilcher, 1983) and referred in the broadest sense to a 'women's movement' made up of a number of diverse groups seeking to advance the position of women in society. In the early twentieth century, when the term was introduced in the US, its meaning was limited to referring only to a group which asserted the uniqueness of women's experience and their social and sexual purity (Jaggar, 1983). The term is no longer so restricted, although there is still confusion about its exact meaning and use.

Feminism is one of the most important social movements of the past two centuries and certainly one which has brought about an enduring transformation of human society on a global scale. It is customary to divide the history of feminism into a first, second and third wave, with each period indicating a different era in the struggle to attain equality between the sexes. At the time of writing, we are currently experiencing the relatively early stages of a fourth wave. Feminism currently means many different things to different people, but at its core, if we go back to its origins in the late eighteenth century, it was primarily a social movement for the emancipation of women, and in its early stages, proponents were mainly isolated voices advocating 'women's rights' in a clearly unequal world.

One of the earliest self-consciously feminist tracts was Mary Wollstonecraft's *A Vindication of the Rights of Woman* (1792) written at the height of the French Revolution. In this extremely influential text, she introduced themes that were to become familiar in later feminist writing and conducted a closely linked two-part critique of the completely male-dominated society of the time. First, she criticized the unjust limitations placed on the rights of women, as well as their lack of opportunity for education, self-expression and economic independence, while, second, she was critical of women themselves for their blind adherence to femininity which, in her view, turns women into mere 'spaniels' and 'toys'. Her proposed solution was better education for young women but not the granting of equal rights. It could thus be said that feminism begins not with Wollstonecraft but rather with the various women's suffrage movements that emerged during the early nineteenth century.

The achievement of full voting rights for all women regardless of age, ethnicity or marital status took more than a century of struggle. Nevertheless, the focus on voting rights, as important as this was, has tended to obscure the reality that it was to be several decades before full equality was obtained, and many would argue that still has not been achieved today.

Throughout the long first wave of feminism women fought against several other injustices, three of which were crucial. First, women were restricted in terms of the ownership of property, requiring them to marry so as to inherit and thus preventing them from attaining true independence (it is this issue which exercised significant proto-feminist writers of the nineteenth century like Jane Austen and Charlotte Bronte). Second, women did not have full rights over their own body, which meant they had no legal protection against sexual violence (e.g. the notion that a husband could rape his wife did not become part of the legal code until late in the twentieth century). Third, women were discriminated against in the workplace, which not only meant that they were paid less than men for doing the same work but there were also restrictions on them applying for certain jobs, with promotion denied, and no allowance made for maternity leave. Many of these issues persist today.

Once the vote had been achieved, the women's rights movement fell into decline and remained inactive until the late 1950s and early 1960s when it was revitalized by a new generation of activists who called themselves second-wave feminists. Betty Friedan's *The Feminine Mystique* (1963) is widely considered to be the crucial text that ignited this new era of political struggle. Following directly in the footsteps of Mary Wollstonecraft, she argued that women were victims of a false belief in the promise of femininity and urged them to look beyond their domestic situation for fulfilment. The National Organization for Women was formed in 1966 and became the central focus for feminist activism in the US. The goal was the ratification of an Equal Rights Amendment to the Constitution, and although major steps towards this objective were made it was not achieved in full. Second-wave feminists also took the view that equality between the sexes would only come about if there were very significant changes in cultural attitudes on the part of both women and men. Writers such as Germaine Greer and Kate Millett demanded sexual liberation, arguing that women could alter their status as the second sex (to borrow the title of Simone de Beauvoir's important book [1971, originally 1949]) by overturning the double standards applied to their sexuality and behaviour.

Second-wave feminism came to an end in the early 1980s partly as a result of its successes – thus, many women felt that all the relevant battles had been fought and won – but primarily because of the change in the general political climate. The Reagan–Thatcher era – which introduced the dominant contemporary neoliberal hegemony – was extremely unfriendly to equal rights, and it rolled back many of the gains that had been achieved. This is the period of the so-called culture wars when feminism was caricatured as mere 'political correctness' and its political agenda was scorned in the press. Third-wave feminist scholar Susan Faludi documents this in her *Backlash: The Undeclared War Against Women* (1991). But there were also problems within feminism. Feminist scholars of colour, particularly those from the third world, argued very forcefully that feminism had significantly neglected race and class. Subsequently, these issues were to be central to third-wave feminism, which many argue began with the outraged response of feminist critics to the treatment of Anita Hill during the Senate confirmation hearings for US Supreme Court nominee Clarence Thomas in 1991. Hill testified that Thomas had sexually harassed her when she was working in the Department of Education and later at the Equal Employment Opportunity Commission. Thomas categorically denied these allegations but was subsequently confirmed by the Senate.

The third wave of feminism emerged during the mid-1990s in the US and was led by Generation Xers – those born during the 1960s and 1970s – and who had been brought up in a media-dominated, culturally and economically diverse world. Although they benefitted significantly from the legal rights and protections obtained by the earlier feminists, they were nevertheless critical of the current status quo, arguing that their predecessors had not gone far enough. The third wave was nevertheless enabled by the greater economic and professional power plus status achieved by their second-wave predecessors, the massive expansion in opportunities for the dissemination of ideas created by the information revolution of the late twentieth century and the coming of age of Generation X scholars and activists.

Some early third wavers were literally daughters of the second wave, and these women and others like them grew up with the expectation of achievement and examples of female success as well as an awareness of the barriers presented by sexism, racism and classism. They chose to battle such obstacles by inverting sexist, racist and classist symbols, fighting patriarchy with irony, answering violence with stories of survival and combatting continued exclusion with grassroots activism and radical democracy. Moreover, rather than becoming part of the 'machine', third wavers began both sabotaging and rebuilding the machine itself.

Influenced by the postmodernism which provides one of the central themes of this book, third-wave feminists sought to question, reclaim and redefine the ideas, words and media that have transmitted ideas about womanhood, gender, beauty, sexuality, femininity and masculinity, among other things. There was a decided shift in perceptions of gender, with the notion that there are some characteristics which are strictly male and others which are strictly female, giving way to the concept of a gender continuum. From this perspective, each person is seen as possessing, expressing and suppressing the full range of traits that had previously been associated with one gender or the other. For third-wave feminists, the concept of 'sexual liberation', a major goal of their predecessors, was expanded to mean a process of first becoming conscious of the ways one's gender identity and sexuality have been shaped by society and then intentionally constructing (and becoming free to express) one's *authentic* gender identity.

Third-wave feminists inherited an institutional power base created by their predecessors, including women's studies programs at universities, long-standing feminist organizations and well-established publishing outlets such as *Ms.* magazine and several academic journals. These outlets were nevertheless a less important part of the culture of the third wave than for their predecessors.

In expressing their concerns, third-wave feminists actively subverted, co-opted and played on seemingly sexist images and symbols. This was evident in the double entendre and irony of the language commonly adopted by people in their self-presentations. Slang used derogatorily in most earlier contexts became proud and defiant labels. The spirit and intent of the third wave were demonstrated through the raw honesty, humour and horror of Eve Ensler's play (and later book) *The Vagina Monologues*, which explored the feelings of women about sexuality and included vagina-centred topics as diverse as orgasm, birth and rape; the righteous anger of punk rock's riot grrrls movement; and the playfulness, seriousness and subversion of the Guerrilla Girls, a group of women artists who donned gorilla masks in an effort to expose female stereotypes and fight discrimination against female artists.

The third wave was, moreover, much more inclusive of women and girls of colour than their predecessors. In reaction and opposition to stereotypical images of women as passive, weak, virginal and faithful, or alternatively as domineering, demanding, slutty and emasculating, the third wave redefined women and girls as assertive, powerful and in control of their own sexuality. In popular culture, this redefinition gave rise to icons of powerful women that included the singers Madonna, Queen Latifah and Mary J. Blige, among others, and the women depicted in television series such as *Buffy the Vampire Slayer* (1997–2003), *Sex and the City* (1998–2004), and *Girlfriends* (2000–08). Media programming for children increasingly depicted smart, independent girls and women in lead roles, including Disney heroines such as Mulan (1998) and Helen Parr and her daughter Violet (The Incredibles, 2006) and television characters such as Dora (*Dora the Explorer*, 1999–2006), Carly and Sam (*iCarly*, 2007–12), and *Sesame Street*'s first female lead, Abby Cadabby, who debuted in 2006. The sassy self-expression of 'Girl Power' merchandise also proved popular.

The increasing ease of publishing on the Internet meant that e-zines (electronic magazines) and blogs were everywhere. Many serious independent writers, not to mention organizations, found that the internet offered a forum for the exchange of information and the publication of essays and videos that made their point to a potentially huge audience. The internet quite simply radically democratized the content of the feminist movement with respect to participants, aesthetics and issues.

But third-wave feminism did not avoid criticism, with some writers declaring themselves to be postfeminist and arguing that the movement had lived beyond its usefulness. Moreover, established feminists of the previous generation argued that the issues had not really changed and that the younger women were not adding anything of substance. Around the turn of the century, some writers from inside and outside feminism announced that the third wave was over. Moreover, questions surrounding sexualized behaviour raised debate on whether such things as revealing clothing, designer-label stiletto heels and amateur pole dancing represented true sexual liberation and gender equality or were simply the old oppressions in disguise.

As with any other social or political movement, fissures and disagreements were present in each wave of feminism. The third wave, to an extent almost unimaginable to the previous waves before it, was plural and multifaceted, comprising people of many gender, ethnic and class identities; experiences; and interests. With the outcome that its greatest strength, multivocality, was attacked by some as its greatest weakness. Its proponents nevertheless responded to this criticism by proposing that the creation of a unified agenda or philosophy was not only unrealistic but actually undesirable.

Many commentators were to argue at this juncture that the internet has enabled a shift from 'third-wave' to 'fourth-wave' feminism. What is certain is that the internet has created a 'call-out' culture, in which sexism or misogyny can be 'called out' and challenged. This culture is indicative of the continuing influence of the third wave, with its focus on micropolitics and challenging sexism and misogyny insofar as they appear in everyday rhetoric, advertising, film, television and literature, the media and so on. The existence of a feminist fourth wave has been challenged by those who maintain that increased usage of the internet is not enough to delineate a new era. It is nevertheless clear that the internet has facilitated the creation of a global community of feminists who use the medium both for discussion and activism. According to #FemFuture: Online Feminism, a report published by the Barnard Center for Research on Women at Columbia University, females aged between 18 and 29 are the 'power users of social networking'. According to this research, the number of women using digital spaces is increasing. There is evidence, too, that the uptake of new technologies such as Twitter is growing in geographical localities where women still face social injustices: in Turkey, for example, women make up 72% of social media users. Several large corporations have fallen afoul of the speed with which feminist campaigns can garner support on the internet. Facebook, for example, was forced to confront the issue of gender-based hate speech on its web pages after initially suggesting that images of women being abused did not violate its terms of service. In the UK, websites such as *The F Word* and *The Women's Room* and online campaigns such as *The Everyday Sexism Project* and *No More Page 3* have attracted thousands of supporters who find that the internet works both as a forum for discussion and as a route for activism.

Whether internet campaigning actually enables change is arguable, and there is considerable concern that online discussion and activism is increasingly divorced from real-world conflicts. *Slacktivism* is a term used to describe 'feel-good' campaigns that garner plenty of public support – such as a petition circulated via Facebook – but that do not necessarily address pressing issues. So, while research points to the fact that feminism is being reinvigorated by the internet, whether this is leading to transformative political action is hotly debated. Julia Schuster (2013) discusses feminist engagement in New Zealand and notes that online activism is often the preserve of the young and that due to the closed nature of some social networks, feminist discussion is often 'hidden' from those who are not sufficiently networked. Schuster observes that this may create a divide between young feminists and older activists, as the new wave of feminists unwittingly hide their politics from their older peers. Many of those academics in a position to research and publish on feminism belong to this older age group; hence, academic feminism is arguably guilty of failing to properly examine the shape that the fourth wave is currently taking.

One of the key issues for contemporary feminism is *intersectionality* – the idea that different axes of oppression intersect, producing complex and often contradictory results. As bell hooks (the writer spells her name in the lower case) (2007) showed, the experiences of working-class black and white women in the US are insurmountably different – yet each belongs to the category 'woman'. Academic feminists have been comfortable with the idea of intersectionality since at least the 1980s, when prominent third-wave feminists such as hooks, Gloria Anzaldua and Audre Lord spoke out about women of colour being sidelined within feminism. These feminists undermined the idea that gender alone was a sound basis for identification.

In an effort to draw attention to these axes of difference, contemporary feminists advocate several tactics, including the much-maligned practice of 'privilege-checking' which is about reminding someone that they cannot and should not speak for others. The phrase 'check your privilege' itself was born on the internet, and young activists who grew up communicating via chat rooms appear to have considerably less trouble with the phrase than older feminists. As Sadie Smith has nevertheless noted in the *New Statesman*, 'check your privilege' is often abused as a phrase – used as a means of deflection rather than with any hope of understanding or rapprochement.

The emergence of privilege-checking nevertheless reflects the reality that mainstream feminism remains dominated by the straight white middle-classes. Parvan Amara interviewed self-identified working-class feminists for a piece published on Internet magazine *The F Word* and noted that many of those she spoke to found themselves excluded from mainstream feminism both on the internet and 'in real life'. Amara notes that many women tend to encounter feminism at university. Thus, women who do not go on to higher education face a barrier when attempting to engage with those academic debates that drive feminism.

The realization that women are not a homogenous group has brought with it a set of new terminologies which attempt to ensure that those who hold a given identity are not spoken for by inappropriate others, or carelessly pigeonholed. For newcomers, the vocabulary can be dizzying, from 'cis' (a neologism referring to those individuals whose gender and sexual identities map cleanly on to one another) to 'WoC' (women of colour) and 'TERFs' (trans-exclusionary radical feminists). On the internet, you may have your privilege checked, or in extreme cases, you might be 'doxed' (have your personal files hacked and distributed – the term *dox* is derived from the .docx file format where much virtual data are stored). 'Doxing' has been used predominantly by anti-trans activists to release information about the identities of trans people. The proliferation of these new technologies – most notably the internet – points to how central they are to contemporary feminist debate and activism. Terms such as *WoC*, *cis* and *TERF* are invaluable given the word limit imposed by Twitter and lend themselves to the practice of hashtagging, an online practice that allows information to be quickly retrieved and linked.

Feminism is regularly declared to be dead but it can be argued that such widespread negativity is unwarranted. Whether or not we are living through a fourth wave of feminism, it is clear that women's understanding of their position in the world and their political struggles are changing. With more and more young feminists turning to the internet, it would seem imperative that academics consider the effects that new technologies are having on feminist debate and activism. While controversy abounds concerning the delineation between second-, third- and fourth-wave feminism, it is clear that several key issues animate contemporary feminism. Intersectionality and the exclusionary nature of mainstream feminism remain a real concern. The political potential of the fourth wave centres on giving voice to those women still marginalized by the mainstream.

Perspectives in feminist theory

Feminist thought has had a considerable impact on the social sciences and other academic fields with new areas of research opened up and designed to make previously invisible women visible. While the feminist enterprise has not come without criticism, there are six main – often competing – sub-groups which invariably permeate the different waves of feminism and are often closely linked to wider political perspectives.

Liberal feminism has its roots in the notions of individual rights and freedoms which were central to the rise and consolidation of modern societies in the eighteenth and nineteenth centuries. From this perspective, the subordination of women is examined as part of an analysis of the wider social structures and inequalities with the central concern being to locate discrimination in social practice, specifically within the public sphere, and extend rights to women to equal those enjoyed by men through the process of legal reform. It is a perspective which has been criticized for its inability to confront the deep-rooted levels of gender inequality. In short, there is an identified failure to challenge fundamental male values, while the solutions offered are limited and to some extent superficial. But the legacy of sex discrimination and equal pay legislation introduced predominantly during the second-wave era can be attributed to the influence of liberal feminism, and there is recognition of its value to the broader feminist paradigm (Jaggar, 1983; Tong, 1988).

Radical feminism emerged very much with the second wave during the 1970s and focuses on the importance of *patriarchy*, or the 'set of hierarchical relations between men, and solidarity between them, which enables them to control women' (Hartmann, 1981: 447). Patriarchy describes a power relationship inherent in the structures and social relations within which the subordination and exploitation of women occurs and it is used to explain the institutionalization of male power and domination over women (see Walby, 1980: 173–201). The slogan 'the personal is political' has been used to identify the basis of the oppression of women within the private realm of personal relationships and private lives. Thus, the need to expose the hidden secrets of personal relationships and social practice within the private sphere was recognized by radical feminists and was to lead to the examination of issues such as reproductive freedom, pornography, domestic violence and child abuse. Radical feminists have advocated separatism from men to different degrees and this can be seen either partially, in the provision of women-only institutions or events, or wholly, including the withdrawal of women from personal and sexual relationships with men, indeed in more recent third-wave years, the encouragement and promotion of same-sex lesbian relationships.

Radical feminism has been criticized for its biological determinism, that is the belief that by nature all men are the same and so are all women. Further criticism has been directed at the notion that patriarchy is an all-pervasive universal principle operating in the same way in all geographical locations at all times and thus failed to recognize differences in the experiences of women across time and space, including class and ethnic differences (Jaggar, 1983). These issues were to be addressed by the third and more recent fourth waves of feminism and, in particular, the key concept of intersectionality.

Marxist feminists argue that the subordination of women is located in the wider capitalist exploitation of their domestic role and identify the existence of a dominant ideology which presents women as primarily carers within the domestic sphere and which is used to justify low-wage, low-status and part-time jobs, and which is, in turn, used to deny women the right to economic independence (Beechey, 1977). Women are also considered to be part of a reserve army of labour, available to be drawn into the workforce when the needs of capitalism demand it and easily rejected when there is surplus labour (Bruegel, 1978), for example, during and after the two World Wars.

Marxist feminists have been criticized for their overuse of economic explanations of women's oppression while failing to examine the complexity of family relationships. Tong (1988) nevertheless notes the increasing relevance of the Marxist feminist critique, as more and more women have become employed in the market economy, a process that has greatly accelerated during the intervening years.

Socialist feminism thus provides a synthesis of the radical and Marxist feminist perspectives crucially identifying that both capitalist and patriarchal systems play a part in the subordination of women. This 'dual systems theory' recognizes the systems of capitalism and patriarchy are separate but, at the same time, mutually accommodating systems of oppression, while 'unified system theorists' have developed unifying concepts as central categories of analysis. Jaggar (1983), for example, identified the concept of 'alienation' which provides a theoretical synthesis of Marxist, radical and liberal feminist thought. The potential of socialist feminism to bring together the diverse accounts of different feminist approaches is significant but has nevertheless been criticized by black feminists for the tendency to deny the diversity of experiences which different women encounter. But surely this is not an insurmountable issue.

Black feminism was thus to examine the structures of domination prevalent in the personal, cultural and institutional levels and experiences of the lives of black women, with the axes of race, gender and class all identified as forming the basis of their oppression within which, it is argued, there exists a 'more generalized matrix of domination'. This matrix was described by bell hooks (1988: 174–76) as a 'politic of domination', which is grounded in a hierarchical, ideological belief system. In their critique of feminist accounts of the family, education, reproduction and patriarchy, black feminist writers identified the relationship of black women to the structures, ideologies and institutions of oppression. Accusations of racism made by black feminists towards the broader, often white middle-class feminist movement were productive for they opened up a discourse of difference, recognizing the diversity of female experience which was to become extremely influential in third-wave feminism.

The notion of difference is also central to any understanding of the relationship of feminism to *postmodernism*. Some such as the prominent feminist Carol Smart (1990) welcomed postmodernism, but others found the theoretical development problematic. Radical feminists criticized the emphasis on – and celebration of – individual difference by arguing that it is the collective voice which makes women strong, but others argue that the challenge is to find a way to think both women *and* 'women' recognizing diversity and collective experience.

Criminology and women

Criminology was traditionally one of the most androcentric (male-centred) fields of study in the social sciences. The majority of the research and theories were based on the study of male criminality and the ways in which the criminal justice system has responded to male offenders (Rafter and Heidensohn, 1985). Women were invariably invisible, but when they were considered, biological and (bio)psychological theories were used to explain their criminality with the emphasis being on female sexual deviance (Downes and Rock, 1998). Moreover, as criminology sought wider recognition and acceptance in the criminal justice sphere outside the academy, there was to be a focus on objective empirical research, using official records and large national surveys. The outcome was a failure to consider important differences in male and female pathways into crime, types of crime, victimization and punishments. Feminist criminology has sought to address these limitations by enhancing our understanding of both male and female offending as well as criminal justice system responses to their crimes.

The scope of feminist criminology

Males have historically committed far more offences than women, especially those crimes which have been deemed important by the criminal justice system. It is thus perhaps not surprising that the criminal involvement of women was largely ignored by criminology until the 1970s. At the same time, the orthodox Weberian value-free approach to the study of crime had produced a non-reflective assumption that data and theories about boys and men are generalizable to girls and women (Einstadter and Henry, 1995) It was thus assumed that the study of male crime was simply the generic study of crime with female involvement more of an anomaly than a research subject in its own right. The feminist approach emerged from the critique of this practice (see Smart, 1977; Heidensohn, 1994).

It is only in the past 30 years that feminist criminology has developed a recognizable perspective within the wider discipline. Yet, the term itself is misleading, and it might be more appropriate to use that of feminist criminologies in reference to a wide range of theoretical perspectives and methodologies. which have focused on a broad range of issues related to women and crime. These include theoretical explanations of crime, responses to female offending, women working in the criminal justice system and the particular needs of women in prison. We noted earlier that feminism does not provide a homogeneous approach to women and crime, but there is a common focus on the ways in which the gendered structure of society is related to crime.

The emergence of feminist criminology

Until the later decades of the twentieth century, most criminology had thus focused on male offenders and the criminal justice system response to male crime. The lack of attention to female offending can best be explained by the reality that most crime was committed by males. Yet, by the last two decades of that century, female incarceration rates were increasing rapidly, in particular, in the US, with the outcome being a surge in research on girls, women, crime and the criminal justice system. The war on drugs and the federal sentencing reforms of the 1980s help explain much of the large increase in female prisoners in the US, but the roots of feminist criminology predate these changes and can be located in the second-wave feminism of the 1960s and the 1970s. Three major themes can be identified.

I The gender equality argument

Early feminist interest in female crime first emerged in Canada and the UK (Bertrand, 1969; Heidensohn, 1968). Two important books were published in the early 1970s with their origins clearly located in the second-wave liberal feminist focus on gender equality: Freda Adler's (1975) *Sisters in Crime* and Rita Simon's (1975) *Women and Crime*. They focused on different aspects of the issue and reached somewhat different conclusions, but both argued that the mid-twentieth-century women's movement had changed both female participation in crime and perceptions of their involvement in criminality. Indeed, the central thesis of these two works was not only that women would engage in more crime as a result of women's liberation but also that, with the growing emphasis on equal treatment, the criminal justice response to female offending would become harsher and less 'chivalrous'.

These two books were important because they brought more attention to the issue of female criminality and the response of the criminal justice system but the focus on increased criminal opportunities for women as a result of increased gender equality received widespread criticisms from feminist criminologists with two broad themes emerging. First, it was asked whether lower-class female offenders were acting out of a desire to achieve equality with male offenders or whether increases in female crime might be due to the 'feminization of poverty', at a time when the composition of families in poverty was increasingly dominated by female-headed single-parent households. Moreover, it was observed that lower-income female offenders tended to have more traditional and stereotypical views of the role of women, thus questioning the idea that these offenders were trying to compete with male criminals (Daly and Chesney-Lind, 1988). Second, careful analysis of data failed to support the contention that the gap between male and female offending was narrowing (Steffensmeier and Allan, 1996).

Box and Hale (1983) neatly and influentially summarize the many and varied criticisms of Adler and Simon's general thesis by noting merely a historical overlap between women's liberation and an increase in female crime. It was also noted that the rate of male violent crime continued to rise faster than the female rate (Mukherjee and Fitzgerald, 1981), and thus, the 'new violent' female was considered a myth (Box, 1983). Walklate (1995) later concluded that men and women commit similar types of crime, although the latter offend at a much lower rate and commit far less serious crimes less frequently than men.

Heidensohn (2000/1) noted that offences committed by women tend to be concentrated in the areas of theft, handling stolen goods and drug offences, with little involvement in acts of violence, while Graham and Bowling (1995) established that female offending tends to peak at the age of 13 to 14, a much earlier age than for males. But we might note that none of the preceding observations totally refutes the propositions of Adler and Simon that, in short, a reduction in the extent of informal social controls for girls and young women – indeed in our changing perceptions of what is acceptable behaviour for 'young ladies' – has provided them with opportunities to engage in previously less thinkable criminal activities, although a simple causal relationship between female emancipation and criminality was never likely to exist.

2 The influence of radical criminology

The second major factor in the rise of feminist criminology was the emergence of the 'new criminologies' which viewed crime as the outcome of gender, race and class oppression. Both radical and feminist criminologies emerged during the highly political, socially conscious 1960s and 1970s. In the US and much of the Western world, this was an era of rapid social change and political unrest. Existing ideologies and power structures were challenged, with the emergence of new social action groups, including the anti-war, civil rights and women's liberation movements.

But feminist criminologists quickly became disenchanted with the overly idealistic and still male-centred focus of radical criminology. The 'new criminology' view of the offender as a noble warrior engaged in a struggle with a powerful state (Young, 1979) also angered radical feminists working to end intimate violence and rape, and they consequently began to focus their attention on the ways in which a patriarchal society enabled the abuse of women. It was thus radical feminism – with its focus on the consequences of patriarchy – which was to contribute significantly to the burgeoning body of feminist criminological scholarship.

Radical feminists sought to change the public response to crimes such as rape and intimate violence in which victims had often been blamed for their own victimization. Susan Brownmiller's (1975) *Against Our Will* was a devastating analysis of the role of male dominance in the crime of rape, while Carol Smart (1977) criticized mainstream criminological theories not only for their failure to look at crime through a gendered lens but also for their assumption that victimization was a similar experience for all victims.

The contribution of radical feminism to the development of feminist criminology is important for two reasons. First, in collaboration with community activists, radical feminist scholars were able to effect social change. Violence against women became a matter of public concern. Shelters for battered women began emerging throughout the USA and the UK, and rape laws were reformulated to protect the victims from undue scrutiny. Until the mid-1970s, victims of rape were essentially placed on trial themselves. Proof of rape required evidence that the victim had resisted as well as corroborating evidence. Moreover, the victim's past sexual conduct could be introduced as evidence of their apparent promiscuity by the defence. The feminist approach to rape, in contrast, incorporated the perspective of the victim, and ultimately, legislation was introduced which barred the introduction of the victim's past sexual behaviour as evidence.

Second, feminist scholarship on rape and intimate violence had an impact on mainstream criminology, and this was to lead to a revised understanding of the complexities of victimization. For example, women are far more likely to be victimized by someone close to them, which is not the case for men who are more likely to become victims outside the home. From the radical feminist perspective, this anomaly is explained because social institutions and norms facilitate the victimization of women in the home.

In the case of domestic violence, the whole issue is now considered far more serious than previously by the criminal justice system. As recently as 1984, Sir Kenneth Newman, then Metropolitan Police commissioner, had tried to exclude the police, invariably the first port of call for victims of domestic violence, from responding to such cases, as he called this 'rubbish work' akin to dealing with 'lost dogs'. It was not proper police work (Radford and Stanko, 1994: 149–58). There are now special legal provisions established to protect women and children from domestic violence, although some critics argued that this actually made matters worse, for it allows these offences to be dealt with less seriously than would be the case in incidents of street violence. Second, although there is now a greater emphasis than before in dealing with these cases, domestic violence has continued to remain under-reported (see Hanmer and Saunders, 1984; Dobash and Dobash, 1992; Heidensohn, 2003).

Feminist scholarship on sexual violence has impacted greatly on our understanding of violence within the home and between partners. Much of the early research on intimate violence stemmed from work using the Conflict Tactics Scale, but feminists were to note that while this scale measures the incidence of a wide range of aggressive tactics, it simply fails to locate them in context. Stanko's (1990) examination of everyday violence provided evidence that victimization of women was frequently unreported. Thus, research conducted by feminist criminologists, in conjunction with activism, examined not only legislation but also police practices. Eventually, the National Crime Victimization Survey in the US was reformulated to address the experiences of female victims. Questions about rape and sexual assault were added, as were questions about violent victimization in the home (Britton, 2000), and subsequently the Federal Violence Against Women Act 1994 was passed. Prevention and intervention programmes were developed, aggressive prosecution was pursued and funding for research became available. More recently, the International Violence Against Women Act has carried this focus on the rights of women to safety into the international arena.

3 Criminological theories from a feminist perspective

Some writers have modified the 'control theory' originally proposed by Hirschi (1969) and applied this to the situation of women. Heidensohn (1985) argued that the reason why there were so few women criminals is because of the formal and informal controls which constrain them within male-dominated society and proposed that, to understand more about the transmission of gender inequality and the control of women by familial roles, it was necessary to consider the practical and ideological constraints imposed by family life. It was these very practices and policies that limited the involvement of women in activities outside of the home and which drove them back into the family where they are subject to greater control. Heidensohn observed that, while women can be seen as responsible for the behaviour of others within the home and within the community, they are acting as the agents of male authority when carrying out that control function. There, thus, exists the stereotype of the mother reprimanding a child by saying, 'Wait until your father gets home'.

Heidensohn noted that, while women may act as agents of control on behalf of men, they are themselves controlled both at home and outside. The sexual division of labour is related to the notion of separate spheres – public and private – for men and women, and the latter were expected to function chiefly within the 'private' sphere of the home. Moreover, the privacy afforded this sphere was a contributing factor in the oppression that women experience, for it is within the home that they are vulnerable to isolation and its consequences. Lacking alternative definitions of themselves and their roles, they are affected by those around them, particularly their husbands. Male dominance may result in the subtle undermining of the woman's confidence and self-esteem and this may lead to overt violence and bodily harm (Ditton, 1979; Dobash and Dobash, 1980). Wives who were housebound, isolated and dependent, were also the major victims of neurosis and depression (Brown and Harris, 1978). Furthermore, paid employment for women often entailed subjection to male power and supervision. Heidensohn claimed that, in short, their socialization and the conditions of their existence effectively control women. It was thus little wonder that so few women engaged in criminal activity. An area of criminality in which women were involved, while at the same time clearly being controlled by men – although this latter point is challenged by some – is that of prostitution, and feminism has been at the forefront of challenging the notion of this being a victimless crime.

But feminist criminological theorizing has not been limited to one approach with different perspectives having been adopted as we will see.

A MAINSTREAM THEORIES AND FEMINIST CRIMINOLOGY

A major thrust of feminist criminology has been the critique of the development of mainstream theories based on research with boys and men. The 'add women and stir' approach has meant that gender, if considered at all, has frequently been used only as a control variable. Although this has provided confirmation that males are indeed more criminal than females, virtually no information about female criminality has been collected through this type of research. There are two unspoken assumptions with which feminist criminologists take issue. First, there is the tacit assumption that, because males are far more likely than females to engage in criminal behaviour, females are somehow unimportant to the field. Second, there is the inference that males and females are alike and that what works to explain male criminality will work equally well to explain female criminality.

Thus, the extremely influential strain theory (Merton, 1938) was to be criticized by feminist criminologists for the focus on economic goals and the failure to consider how personal relationships may contribute to criminality. Merton had argued that crime was largely the result of having the American Dream of significant material success as a goal but lacking the opportunities to achieve this in a legitimate manner. Feminist criminologists argue in response that strain theory is not equally applicable to women because, although they certainly have had their access to financial reward more restricted than men, they have committed far less crime (Belknap and Holsinger, 2006). Social learning and differential association theories, with their focus on peer attitudes and behaviours, have also been criticized for the failure to take into account the gendered nature of peer relationships. Whereas male delinquency is strongly linked to having peers with delinquent behaviours and attitudes, this is far less so for females. Indeed, females who are intimately involved with older delinquent males may be introduced to crime and delinquency by these intimate partners rather than by their peers. Although this is certainly not an exhaustive list of mainstream theories which has been criticized by feminist criminologists, it does give an idea of the male-dominated approach taken by supposedly gender-neutral theories.

Other feminist criminologists have nevertheless argued that mainstream theories may be legitimate if they are restructured and operationalized in a manner more sensitive to the predictors of crime in both men and women. This is the case with Agnew's (1992) general strain theory which attempts to be gender-sensitive. Thus, by incorporating a broader range of sources of strain in the theory, Agnew has attempted to address the concerns voiced by feminists, explicitly focusing on relationship strains as well as on negative life experiences, both of which are important predictors of female delinquency. Men and women are seen to have different emotional reactions to strain, possess different coping skills and resources and commit different types of offences (Broidy and Agnew, 1997). A feminist operationalization of general strain theory could therefore explicitly examine the role of abuse histories in predicting female crime.

Agnew has argued that it is not strain *per se* but rather negative emotional responses to strain which leads to crime. Again, a thoughtful and gendered analysis would focus on how emotional responses and coping resources are gendered and how this would help clarify the different relationships between life experiences of males and females and their subsequent participation in crime. Indeed, general strain theory lends itself more to a gendered analysis than most mainstream criminological theories.

Life course theories may offer an opportunity for a gendered exploration of the criminality of women. These theories not only look at factors important in the initiation of criminal behaviour but also examine occurrences which may change the pathways from criminal to noncriminal or vice versa. In a broad sense, life course theories suggest that it is the significance of an event or reason which determines the likelihood that someone engaging in criminal behaviour will cease. In the case of men, this may be marriage or career, but for women, it may be important to examine other reasons. In particular, the birth of a child may provide sufficient motivation for a woman engaging in criminality to change her trajectory to a non–criminal one.

In general, the gendered use of mainstream theories has not been well received by feminist criminologists. Many argue that these theories fail to explore in detail the ways in which the experiences of girls and women shape their lives. In contrast, feminist path-ways theory focuses explicitly on the relationship between life experiences and future criminality, arguing that one must consider the role of patriarchal society if one truly wishes to understand female crime and criminality.

B FEMINIST PATHWAYS THEORY

Feminist pathways theory is perhaps the furthermost development in feminist crimino-logical theory and research in recent years. Seeking to demonstrate how female crime is inseparably linked to the life experiences of women and girls, it focuses on the ways in which their location in society leads them into criminal lifestyles. In numerous articles and books, Meda Chesney-Lind (see, e.g., Chesney-Lind and Pasko, 2004) has established how childhood abuse and a patriarchal juvenile justice system shape the opportunities of girls, ultimately forcing them into criminal lifestyles. She argues that, unlike boys, the initial encounters that girls have with the juvenile justice system are invariably the outcome of status offences, such as running away or engaging in sexual activity. The patriarchal double standard means that girls engaging in these behaviours are seen as immoral and in need of 'correction'. Girls and women have historically faced institution-alization for engaging in behaviours which have been, at the most, mildly frowned on in males. Indeed, girls suspected of sexual 'misconduct' have often been treated more harshly than either boys or girls engaging in criminal activity. It is this patriarchal, paternalistic approach to the social control of females which pushes them into contact with the juve-nile justice system.

Moreover, there has invariably been a failure to recognize that early sexual behaviours, as well as running away from home, are frequently the outcome of abuse within the home. But, instead of intervening in the lives of abused girls, society has reacted with a double standard which labels these girls as incorrigible and/or immoral. By punishing them for behaviours which may actually be self-preserving – for example running away from abu-sive or neglectful homes – society may be further limiting their life chances by identifying them as delinquents. This perspective also examines the relationship between abuse and substance abuse, the number one offence leading to the imprisonment of women. Sub-stance abuse is invariably a coping mechanism with girls and women often using alcohol and drugs to self-medicate their trauma, which has resulted from abuse they have experi-enced. This is an important point, because the majority of incarcerated girls and women have substance abuse problems. Moreover, the majority of these 'offenders' have histories of physical, sexual, or emotional abuse. Feminist pathways theory seeks to illuminate the connections between the abuse and exploitation of young females and their subsequent offending. It is arguably the dominant approach in contemporary feminist criminology.

C SOCIALIST FEMINIST CRIMINOLOGY

It would be negligent in any discussion of feminist criminology to exclude a discussion of how feminist criminology has led to an examination of masculinity and crime. Messerschmidt (1986) thus produced an analysis highly influenced by socialist feminism and focused on the ways in which patriarchal capitalism structures the experiences of both males and females, arguing that one cannot ignore either economic structures or gender relationships in any true explanation of crime. He proposes that marginalized lower class and minority males engage in street crimes because of their blocked opportunities and their limited legitimate roles as males in a patriarchal capitalist society. In contrast, the structure of gender relations in society tends to relegate crimes committed by women to low-level larceny and fraud.

Messerschmidt (1986) also explored the sexual exploitation of women in the sex trade in third-world countries, showing how patriarchy and capitalism combined to place these women in desperate situations where they submit to exploitation to survive. In addition, he drew links between economic inequality and male–dominated family patterns in his discussion of male violence against women. Finally, he synthesized theories about male privilege as well as those about capitalism in his examination of higher-level white-collar and corporate crimes, which are committed primarily by males. His work is extremely important to the development of feminist criminology because he directly addresses the feminist criticism that most criminology ignores how gender relations structure crime. His theory illustrates that the feminist approach is relevant to both the experiences of men and women seeking to illustrate how gender is intrinsically related to crime. We shall return to the work of Messerschmidt in a wider discussion of masculinities later in this chapter

D FEMINIST CRIMINOLOGY AND MULTIPLE MARGINALITIES

Early feminist criminology was criticized for its assumption that the experiences of all women are similar. This was to subsequently lead to a feminist scholarship which acknowledges the interlinked effects of gender, race, class and sexual identity. In many ways, the critical race critique of feminist criminology has been similar to the feminist critique of mainstream criminology. Feminist criminologists had in many ways essentialized the experiences of women, assuming them all to be alike. Proponents of intersectionality and multiple marginality argue, in contrast, that race, class and gender are each impacted by the social structure and, in turn, have an impact on individuals. Furthermore, these impacts interact. It is not simply being female, ethnic minority, lesbian or poor that matters. Neither are the effects cumulative. Instead, there is an interaction that evolves from the intersection of statuses. The actions and opportunities that one has are structured by our position along each of these dimensions. Thus, the experiences of, for example, Hispanic women are different from those of Hispanic men as well as white or black women (Burgess-Proctor, 2006).

E THE SCOPE OF FEMINIST CRIMINOLOGICAL SCHOLARSHIP

Feminist criminology covers a broad range of topics with theory having an important focus and the study of violence against women being central to the agenda. Feminist criminology recognizes that there is not a clear-cut dichotomy between victims and offenders: female offenders are quite likely to also be victims, whether of childhood abuse or abuse as adults (Belknap, 1996). Moreover, the motherhood role must also be considered, and numerous feminist criminologists have explored the effects of large-scale female incarceration on both the women and their children (Sharp, 2003).

Extensive research has examined the offending of women and girls but the majority of feminist criminological scholarship since the mid-1980s has focused on the response of the criminal justice system. This has especially been the case in the US, where the war on drugs and the federal sentencing guidelines of the 1980s resulted in massive increases in the number of women sent to state and federal prisons. Changes, moreover, designed to reduce the inequities of indeterminate sentencing resulted in mandatory sentences for lower-level female offenders. In particular, aggressive prosecution of drug offences was to impact notably on women, especially those of colour. By the end of 2007, more than 100,000 women were incarcerated for felony convictions on any given day.

This recognition has led to extensive research on the arrest, prosecution, conviction and incarceration of female offenders (cf. Sharp, 2003). Feminist scholars have consistently argued that as women and men have essentially different life experiences as well as motivations for crime and engage in different types of crime, the criminal justice system should not be designed to treat women in the same way as men. Some have gone as far as to challenge the gender equity of the system, arguing that applying the punitive approach designed for men is a form of 'vengeful equity', a sort of backlash against women demanding equality (see Chesney-Lind, 1989).

Substance abuse treatment, vocational rehabilitation and therapy in prisons are also viewed through a gendered lens. During the 1990s, the therapeutic communities and boot camp programme became common forms of rehabilitation in US prisons, but these were not equally suited to males and females. Women, for example, respond less positively to confrontation, a central component of both types of programmes (Marcus-Mendoza et al., 1998), and tend to have gender-specific health problems which may preclude their participation in physically demanding activities (Sharp, 2003). Finally, motherhood has to be seriously considered in a system where two-thirds of female prisoners are mothers of children who are minors.

As feminists came to focus on the criminal justice system and its response to women, their attention became directed towards women working within that system. The increasing number of female prisoners contributed to an increase of women police officers, lawyers and in the prison service. Criminal justice has long been dominated by men but with a significant increase in both feminist criminology and female prisoners, there became a fast-expanding body of feminist work taking a gendered approach to studying all aspects of the criminal justice system. It is a perspective which has primarily focused on two aspects of the gendered nature of criminal justice employment. First, there is a consideration of how women and men differ in the practices of their jobs and, second, an examination of the ways in which the structure of law enforcement, courts and imprisonment continues to lead to gender inequality (Britton, 2000).

CONCLUSION

Feminist criminology has expanded greatly in the past 20 years, but it remains marginalized in the context of the wider discipline. Mainstream journals publish only a minor feminist contributions, and textbooks pay limited attention to feminist criminological theory. Thus, new generations of criminologists are educated and given relatively little information about feminist criminology, although this is perhaps less the case in the UK and continental Europe than is the case in the US.

Crime and masculinities

Maureen Cain (1989, 1990) and Carol Smart (1990) both argued that feminism itself had 'transgressed criminology' and had identified a significant need to answer the fundamental question of what it is about 'maleness' which leads a disproportionate number of men to become criminals. It was in response to this feminist discourse that a growing literature began to emerge which sought to 'take masculinity seriously'. Central to this development was the work of the transgender Australian academic Bob Connell (1987, 1995; later Rae Connell), who – in response to the one-dimensional absolutist notion of male dominance presented by radical feminism – recognized the existence of 'multiple masculinities'. Thus, masculinities can be black as well as white, homosexual or heterosexual, working class or middle class, with all subject to challenge and change over time. Connell accepted that there is a dominant hegemonic masculinity in society, which is based on the notions of heterosexual power and authority but proposed that other forms can challenge this orthodoxy and consequently, male power should not be considered absolute but historically variable and indeed a social construction.

James Messerschmidt (1993) was to apply this analysis of diverse and contested masculinities to youth crime, arguing that the types of offences committed by young males are patterned through various interpretations of masculinity generated by 'structures of labour and power in class and race relations'. In an apparent development of Robert Merton's anomie theory, he argues that crime provides a means of 'doing masculinity' when there is no access to other resources. The nature of the actual offence committed takes on different forms according to how different class and ethnic groups define their masculinities.

For white working-class youth, masculinity is seen to be constructed around physical aggression and, for some, hostility to all groups considered to be inferior in a racist and heterosexual society. Lower-working-class ethnic minorities, on the other hand, find their masculinity in the street gang. Whereas the white middle class may envisage a future in mental labour and the white working class in manual labour, both of these routes are invariably inaccessible to many youths from ethnic minority backgrounds, and offences, such as robbery, provide the opportunity to accomplish a particular form of masculinity based on toughness and physical power. Messerschmidt argues that each form of masculinity represents an attempt to meet the cultural ideal of the dominant form of masculinity that is denied to young people elsewhere, whether it is in the home, school or even work.

Tony Jefferson (1997) is nevertheless sceptical of such structurally determinist arguments, which he observes tell us little of why it is that only a particular minority of young men from a given ethnic group or social class choose to accomplish their masculinity by 'doing crime', while the majority do not. He thus follows Katz (1988) and Presdee (1994) in noting that criminological knowledge has repeatedly failed to recognize the pleasure that is involved in 'doing masculinity' and 'doing crime'. Both these latter two writers argue that, unless we come to understand these pleasures, we will never have a complete picture of why it is that young people, in particular, become involved in criminal behaviour. If masculinity – or at least different variants of masculinity – is a social construction and hence not a characteristic biologically inherent in the male sex, it follows logically that there is a false duality between the male and female genders, with the outcome being that women may well do masculinity. Connell observes that 'unless we subside into defining masculinity as equivalent to men, we must acknowledge that sometimes masculine conduct or identity goes together with a female body' (2000: 16). If this is the case, it becomes necessary to analyse how crime and violence committed by women and girls are related to masculinities.

Messerschmidt (2005) argues that both traditional malestream pre-feminist and liberal feminist criminological theories create an artificial dualism in gender constructions and reduce all masculinities and femininities to one normative standard case for each – the 'male sex role' and the 'female sex role' – with the outcome being a reification of gender. He observes that these criminological theories require that we examine masculinity exclusively done by men and boys and femininity by women and girls while ignoring the creation of masculinities and femininities by people. If masculinities and femininities are not determined biologically, it is important to identify and examine possible masculinities by women and girls (and femininities by men and boys) and their relation to crime. Indeed, there remains a necessity in criminological research to uncover not only gender diversity among girls/women but also their relations to crime and violence and whether such social action constructs masculinity or femininity.

Jody Miller (2001, 2002) shows that certain girls involved in gangs identify with the boys and she describes such groupings as 'masculinist enterprises'. While gender inequality is rampant in the mixed-gender gangs of which the girls were members – for example male leadership, a double standard with regard to sexual activities, the sexual exploitation of some girls and the exclusion of most from serious gang crime – some of the girls differentiated themselves from others through a construction of being 'one of the guys'. In other words, the notion 'one of the guys' is not fashioned by being similar to boys – because of the inequalities – but, rather, certain girls are perceived and perceive themselves as being different from other girls.

Messerschmidt (2004) conducted a life-history study of adolescent involvement in violent assault and found numerous gender constructions by violent girls and that some of them 'do' masculinity by, in part, displaying themselves in a masculine way, by engaging primarily in what they and others in their milieu consider to be authentically masculine behaviour and by an outright rejection of most aspects of femininity. Messerschmidt (2005) later observes that the task of contemporary criminologists is not to reify gender by concentrating research and theory solely on gender differences in crime but proposes that the goal should be to examine and explain both gender differences and gender similarities – that is gender diversity – in the commission of crime. Contemporary debates on male rape make a major contribution to that debate.

Stanko (1985) argued that men rape other men for exactly the same reasons they rape women: to exercise power and control over the victim. Rape is consequently a violent act which, along with a consideration of hegemonic masculinity, helps us understand why male rape has been largely overlooked. For over 30 years, feminist researchers and activists pronounced sexual assault and rape to be essentially a 'women's issue', but some theories of male dominance – or patriarchy – have been criticized for being too descriptive instead of analytical, incapable of explaining the foundations of male supremacy or offering strategies for weakening male power structures (Bryson, 1992). Walby (1980) had observed that the concept of patriarchy does *not* suggest that every single male person oppresses every single female person in society: the 'enemy' is male supremacy, which is perceived to be a social construction rather than an innate determination.

Much feminist theory has nonetheless tended to concentrate on men as rape offenders and women as victims. There is an unquestioned assumption that men control and dominate women, and that sexual assault and other types of sexual violence carried out against females strengthens male primacy (Abdullah-Khan, 2008). Yet, men do get raped, while, at the same time, rape crisis centres in the UK have provided no systematic provision for male victims, even though the Ministry of Justice provides public funding so that all victims of sexual violence can be provided with support. Male rape victims seeking help have simply been turned away from these centres (Cohen, 2014; Pitfield, 2013), leaving them isolated and unable to obtain help. Donnelly and Kenyon (1996) argue that feminist-based rape crisis centres have been less ready to recognize and manage male rape victims because they do not believe that men can be raped or that they were raped only because they 'wanted to be'. Because of the fewer social, physical and cultural provisions available for men, this helps explain why they are reporting sexual assault at much lower rates than women. Gillespie (1996) appears to conclude from this that there is no urgent need for rape crisis centres to include help for male rape victims since their numbers are small.

Cohen (2014) argues that feminist discourse has colonized particular areas of victimization as inherently female with rape and sexual violence being crucial examples. She argues that it is vital to highlight male victimization not only to develop a greater understanding of the issue but also to alert researchers and funders to the relegation of male rape. Feminist neglect of male rape can only help maintain and reinforce patriarchal power relations and 'hegemonic masculinities'.

Susan Brownmiller's (1975) influential text had nevertheless previously argued that male victims are not neglected, nor are they actively 'forgotten', but female victims are simply considered more 'acceptable'. Neither, however, can we – or indeed should we – equate male victims with female victims and parallel the motivation for, and experience of, male rape with same as/more than/less than statements. Cohen (2014) warns us that comparing and contrasting male rape with female rape is destructive because it fuels the continued polarization of debate and places limits on our understandings of harm, rendering male rape invisible, or at least consigns them to the margins. Reductionist and essentialist understandings of rape simply affect negatively the recording, prosecution and reporting practices in sexual violence against men.

Accounts of sexual violence are at least partly attributed to deep-rooted gender expectations of masculinity. While social constructions of women as sexually vulnerable and physically weak fits a stereotypical view of the victims of sexual violence, expectations of what is required of men (tough, powerful, strong, invulnerable, impenetrable and self-sufficient) challenge perceptions of victimization in general (Lees, 1997). While 'real' men are forced to take on a masculine role and avoid behaviours linked to femininity, male rape victims may be judged to have failed as men for not fighting off their aggressor (Lees, 1997). Feminizing or gendering victimization is mostly seen through the use of derogatory labels ascribed to men who have not achieved expectations of hegemonic masculinity (Connell, 2002), and men who have been the victim of a sexual attack undermine the dominant, social ideal of masculinity (Weiss, 2010).

Hegemonic masculinity – together with heterosexuality – has been presented by feminists as the dominant norm in which society fundamentally expects 'real' men to want, initiate and pursue sex only with women (Connell, 2002). In a culture which emphasizes male superiority, power and control, subordination and powerlessness are unacceptable (Lees, 1997). Thus, men are seen to commit most conventional and serious crime, including sexual violence, and are not the victims. Men who report sexual violence appear to confirm that they have been powerless and contest codes of male (hetero)sexuality (Weiss, 2010). Men as the victims of sexual assault simply undermine the dominant, social ideals of masculinity, which, in turn, contributes to the neglect of male rape victims as a subject for empirical study. So clearly do gay men.

Queer criminology

LGBTQ is the usual acronym for lesbian, gay, bisexual, transgender and queer or questioning. These terms have been in use since the 1990s and are used to describe the sexual orientation or gender identity of a person, while the alternative term *gay* has also been used to collectively describe a community usually considered to be united by a common culture and social movement. L is for lesbian: a woman who is attracted to other women. G is for gay: a man who is attracted to other men or more broadly people who identify as homosexual. B is for bisexual: a person who is attracted to both men and women. T is for transgender: a person whose gender identity is different from the sex the doctor put down on their birth certificate. Q is for queer: originally used as a hate term, some people want to reclaim the word, while others find it offensive. It can be a political statement, suggesting that someone does not want to identify with 'binaries' (e.g. male v female, homosexual v straight) or that they do not want to label themselves only by their sexual activity. Q can thus be for questioning: a person who is still exploring their sexuality or gender identity.

There has been very little data on LGBTQ experiences of crime, whether as victims or offenders, while the bulk of criminological research over the past four decades has focused almost exclusively on bias or hate crime/bullying and intimate partner violence (Peterson and Panfil, 2014). Although these growing bodies of research help to increase our knowledge about certain aspects of LGBTQ experiences, their applicability has been limited because of the narrow focus on victimology.

Second, the overwhelming majority of criminological engagement with sexual orientation and gender identity occurred prior to the 1980s and focused on whether 'homosexuality' should be considered a type of criminal (or non-criminal) sexual deviance and was very much a reflection of the stigma attached to LGBTQ people in legal, social and political spheres. Anti-sodomy and sexual psychopath laws were central to these discussions with LGBTQ people invariably deemed criminals and psychopaths.

Third, there has been little or no theoretical engagement with sexual orientation from mainstream criminological theory. This poses the question as to whether existing criminological methods and theories apply to the experiences of LGBTQ people and whether queer criminologists can and should modify them to address sexual orientation and gender identity. It also raises key questions about the role of queer theories – which have been virtually excluded from criminology – to create new criminological frameworks. These themes parallel prior and ongoing discussions among feminist scholars about the propriety of working within existing criminological frameworks to provide a complete understanding of the relationship between gender and crime (Cain, 1990).

The treatment of sexual orientation and gender identity in early biological theories of crime needs to be seen in the context of societal changes during the second half of the twentieth century (Woods, 2014). Homosexuality had been previously viewed as a series of abominable acts as opposed to a distinct identity (Weeks, 1981), but as city spaces and populations became increasingly mobile following industrialization and urbanization, a diversity of sexual and gender non-conforming behaviours became more visible in the public sphere (Bullough, 1979; Weeks, 1979). Because Victorian ideology had restricted government intervention in regulating private sexual conduct, bourgeois society turned to medical experts to resolve moral dilemmas and generate new definitions of sexual normalcy (Hamowy, 1977; Greenberg, 1988).

A science of sexology consequently emerged with homosexuality now being studied in greater detail, with societal conceptions shifting from abominable committed acts to individual biological characteristics (Foucault, 1976; Greenberg, 1988). German and French doctors Johann Ludwig Casper (1852) and Ambroise Tardieu (1857) were to advance the first suggestions that homosexuality is a congenital disease and less than a decade later, German Karl Heinrich Ulrichs articulated the first comprehensive medical conception of homosexuality (Herrn, 1995; Kennedy, 1997). Soon after, a number of prominent physicians proposed that homosexuality was biologically innate and a 'natural' feature of human sexuality. But other late nineteenth-century physicians combined medical advancements with emerging theories of degeneracy to situate homosexuality outside the realm of sexual normalcy. Austrian psychiatrist Richard von Krafft-Ebing (1999, originally 1886) produced the most popular example of this perspective, and although he later changed his position to argue that homosexuality was a harmless and natural variant of human sexuality, his early positions defined heterosexuality as the biological norm and ostracized homosexuals as a class of biological degenerates (Makari, 2008).

Evolving conceptions which proposed that homosexuality was something people were, as opposed to something that people did, were present in early biological theories of crime (Woods, 2013). Cesare Lombroso thus argued that crime was a natural phenomenon rooted in the physical constitutions of individuals and assumed that external physical features mirrored internal moral states (Gibson and Rafter, 2006). Two important themes emerged from his writings which demonstrate the multidimensional stigma attached to LGBTQ people in early biological perspectives. First, homosexual men were considered to be a distinct category of 'insane criminal' or 'pederasts' who could be identified by their physical attributes, mannerisms and clothing. Pederasts were simply odd and strange (Lombroso, 1875). Second, the patriarchal sexual ideology of late Victorian society shaped his comprehension of sexual intimacy between women, describing lesbianism as a form of 'sexual perversion', but not a distinct type of criminal identity (Lombroso and Ferrero, 1885). Although Lombroso acknowledged a connection between prostitution and lesbianism, his conception of female sex criminality was largely shaped by societal demands on women to uphold gendered expectations.

The history of the relationship between LGBTQ populations and the psychological and psychiatric professions is marked with tension. From the 1950s until the 1970s, homosexuality was widely understood to be a mental illness (Bayer, 1981; Kitzinger and Coyle, 2002). A pathological view that was reinforced by the inclusion of homosexuality as a mental disorder in the American Psychiatric Association's *Diagnostic and Statistical Manual of Mental Disorders* (*DSM*) from 1952 until 1973.

Psychoanalytic and psychopathological perspectives developed before the 1980s focused on whether homosexuality should be considered a crime, mental illness, both or neither. Psychoanalytic perspectives, with their origins in the work of Sigmund Freud, displayed more favourable attitudes towards homosexuality. Thus, a cohort of psychoanalytic criminologists argued strongly against the criminalization of homosexuality based on Freud's (1905, 1911) characterization of homosexuality as a non-harmful and natural variation of psychosexual development (Alexander and Staub, 1931, originally 1929); Friedlander, 1947). Psychoanalytic criminologists nevertheless resisted embracing sexual and gender non-conforming behaviours in youth, arguing that the inclination of children to engage in such activities should be altered during the early stages of psychosexual development through proper education and programming (Aichhorn, 1951, originally 1925; Alexander and Staub, 1931 originally 1929; Friedlander, 1947).

More hostile attitudes towards homosexuality appeared in psychopathological perspectives which focus on mental illness. Freud's position on homosexuality had prevailed in the psychiatric profession until the 1940s when a group of researchers prompted a major shift in the profession, which now decided homosexuality and gender non-conformity were mental illnesses which could, and should, be cured (Bergler, 1956; Rado, 1940; Socarides, 1968). As these pathological conceptions of homosexuality and gender non-conformity gained force, they shaped the treatment of LGBTQ people within the legal and political spheres. The clearest example of this treatment was the wave of 'sexual psychopath laws' which swept across the US from the late 1930s to the early 1970s.

During the mid-1970s, pathological conceptions of homosexuality were to significantly lose their influence in the psychiatric profession. Homosexuality was removed from the *DSM* manual in 1973, and 21 US states repealed their sexual psychopath laws during the 1960s and early 1970s. Two key factors contributed to this shift. First, an increasing body of empirical research, especially from the behaviourist perspective, rejected the notion that homosexuality was a disease (Ford and Beach, 1951; Hooker, 1956, 1957, 1958; Kinsey, 1948; Kinsey *et al.* 1953; Szasz, 1970). Second, gay and lesbian organizations started to gain political influence and advance their social status in the US. Official publications sponsored by such organizations provided a public forum for emerging research which discounted orthodox pathological conceptions of homosexuality. The advocacy approach of gay and lesbian political organizations also took a more radical turn during the 1960s as demonstrated by the popular Stonewall riots of 1969. These more radical followers prioritized combatting the 'gay is sick' stigma and protested frequently at psychiatric professional meetings to eliminate that stigma (Barnhouse, 1977).

Even after pathological conceptions of homosexuality became less influential, some forensic psychiatrists continued to stress the connection between homosexuality and sexual criminality. In 1984, British forensic psychiatrists collaborated to release a co-edited volume on forensic psychiatry in which, although homosexuality was not considered to be a criminal status *per se*, they nevertheless stressed that 'the lifestyle of males with homosexual preferences may inevitably put them at risk of contravening the law' (Craft *et al.*, 1984: 65). The investigators also emphasized that 'boys, young men and indeed the public at large, should be protected against "unnatural acts"' (Craft and Craft, 1984: 403). The stigma of the sexual deviancy framework consequently survived in forensic psychiatric perspectives even during the late twentieth century.

Other major psychological perspectives to gain popularity after the 1970s – when anti-sodomy and sexual psychopath laws were very much in decline – were to largely omit discussions of sexual orientation and gender identity. Personality trait theories, for instance, focus on the structural components of the human personality and three models were widely used to study crime: (1) the Psychoticism–Extraversion–Neuroticism

(PEN) model (Eysenck, 1977), (2) the three-factor model and (3) the Five Factor Model (McCrae and Costa, 1990). With the exception of Eysenck, each of these personality theorists neglected sexual orientation and gender identity. When briefly discussing homosexuality in his criminological application of the PEN model, Eysenck recognized that societies differed in terms of whether it was criminalized, observing that it was 'a crime in some American states but not in Germany' and acknowledged that '[i]f homosexuality is a crime in England but not in France, then criminologists would be engaged in quite different pursuits on the two sides of the Channel. This, they argue, is absurd' (1977: 23). These statements of course reflected changing legal attitudes, but their focus still centred on homosexuality as a disputed type of deviance.

Sexual orientation and gender identity were largely omitted from the developmental and life course theories which were to gain popularity in the 1990s. Many discussions of sexual behaviour and gender within these theories simply assume that their subjects are heterosexual and/or have gender identities which conform to binary conceptions of biological sex.

The similar neglect of sexual orientation and gender identity from early sociological theories can probably be explained by theorists considering these to be individual conditions with no bearing on social structure or organization (McIntosh, 1968; Seidman, 1996). It is perhaps not surprising that sexual orientation and gender identity are neglected in most theories of crime which view structural conditions such as poverty, unemployment, racism and poor education as the key determinants of crime.

Sexual orientation and gender identity were to bear the stigma of sexual deviancy the few times they were discussed. Albert Cohen (1955: 22) characterized homosexuality as a form of 'sexual immorality' and later described homosexuals as a 'community of deviants' who had 'in common a propensity to some activity that is stigmatized and penalized by the larger society' (1966: 86–87).

Most sociological–criminological engagement with sexual orientation and gender identity has operated at the micro-level in social process theories, which view criminality as a function of the socialization process and the interactions that people have with different social institutions, including peer groups, families and schools. These theories have focused largely on the ways in which socialization processes sustain homosexuality as a pattern of sexual deviance.

Social learning theories have mostly characterized homosexuality as a form of sexual deviance which is learned and sustained through environmental interactions. Jeffery (1965: 295) in his 'differential reinforcement theory' stressed that '[t]he homosexual selects a male rather than a female as the sex object because of his past conditioning in the sexual area'. Akers (1973) later viewed subcultures as a mechanism of reinforcement for homosexuals to continue engaging in their deviant sexual patterns. Later social learning studies simply omit any discussion of sexual orientation and gender identity concepts (e.g. Akers, 1997).

Social control theories discuss homosexuality as a form of sexual deviance. Reiss (1961) examined a specific form of male prostitution in which adult homosexual males ('queers') hired delinquent youth hustlers ('peers') for sexual services and concluded that norms within these groups defined sexual transactions in ways which stopped them from viewing themselves as sexual deviants. Matza (1964) similarly described homosexuality as a type of deviance and characterized homosexual subcultures as deviant ones which reinforced the behaviour of its members. Later social control theories omit any discussion of LGBTQ populations entirely (Gottfredson and Hirschi, 1990; Hagan, 1988; Hirschi, 1969).

The dominance of the sexual deviancy framework in early victimized actor perspectives is established in labelling theories. Lemert (1951) thus used the 'homosexual' as an example of a deviant status and identified homosexuality as a type of deviance sustained through associations of people with similarly deviant sexual preferences. Becker (1963: 30) stressed that the homosexual 'makes deviance as a way of life' and 'organizes his identity around a pattern of deviant behaviour'. John Braithwaite's (1989) later sole mention of homosexuality was governed by the sexual deviancy framework, and in his view, most crimes in contemporary societies are considered as such by a strong social consensus, but this was not the case with a small number of victimless crimes such as homosexuality.

In the more radical variants of the victimized actor model, there is little or no engagement with LGBTQ populations with again the sexual deviance framework framing the few discussions of homosexuality, and these are in the context of the debate over the criminalization of homosexuality (Chambliss, 1984, 1988; Quinney, 1970). There has simply been no comprehensive radical analysis of crime which considers how sexual orientation and gender identity relate to capitalist production or the occurrence of crime in capitalist societies. This gap in the literature further supports the need for macro-level analyses of crime which engage with sexual orientation and gender identity differences.

Few feminist criminological perspectives have focused on the experiences of queer and transgender women, but there has been greater engagement with sexual orientation and gender identity in this area of criminology. Generally, this engagement has taken two forms. First, some feminist perspectives have drawn attention to specific areas of LGBTQ victimization, including sexual harassment (MacKinnon, 1979) and hate crime (Messerschmidt, 1993; Stanko, 1990). Second, some feminist perspectives have articulated a need to deconstruct a heterosexist social order which subordinates LGBTQ people (Collier, 1998; Messerschmidt, 1993), although these calls have remained highly abstract.

A new trend emerging in feminist criminology from the 1990s has focused on the role of men and their performance of masculinity in offending as we saw earlier (Collier, 1998; Messerschmidt, 1993), and although this area of criminology has provided meaningful insight into how gender norms are socially constructed, it has nevertheless largely focused on deconstructing the 'heterosexual male'. Consequently, this enterprise has yet to further the understanding of how gender norms may lead LGBTQ people – and those who identify as male in particular – to commit crime. Neither does it provide much insight into how race, class and religious differences may intersect with sexual orientation and gender identity to shape motivations for offending.

Left-realism has largely ignored LGBTQ people but some authors have briefly discussed anti-gay hate crimes and essentialism in recognizing homosexual identity and subcultures in late or fragmented modernity (Young, 1999; Young and Matthews, 1992).

This brief overview of mainstream criminological theory has demonstrated a need for theoretical and empirical advancements which bring the experiences of LGBTQ people out of the shadows. An enterprise which seeks to 'queer' criminology is nevertheless not straightforward. One potential challenge arises from conflicting definitions of the term *queer* itself. Although academics and community activists disagree over its precise meaning, the term has been generally used in two ways. First, it has been used as an umbrella term to describe people who assume an array of defined sexual orientation and gender identity categories, including 'gay', 'lesbian', 'bisexual' and 'transgender' (Jargose, 1996).

Second, the term has been used to challenge and subvert phenomena which is viewed as stable and determined. Thus, from this perspective, the term *queer* can debunk the notion that sex, gender and sexuality are essential and fixed identity concepts. It may also challenge the stability of concepts, methods and assumptions of conventional social science research (Plummer, 2005).

Woods (2014) observes that although queer criminology attempts to bring sexual orientation and gender identity issues to the fore of criminological inquiry, it cannot neglect how intersecting differences of race, gender, class and religion shape LGBTQ experiences of crime, both in terms of victimization and offending. These intersections can thus cause a queer woman of colour to experience marginalization on the basis of her sexuality and a transgender woman of colour to experience marginalization on the basis of her gender identity in different ways than a white gay man experiences marginalization on the basis of his sexuality (Pharr, 1977; Smith, 1993). This observation is especially valuable given the dearth of criminological research on queer women, transgender individuals and LGBTQ people of colour. Critical race scholarship – especially theories of intersectionality (Crenshaw, 1991) – offers valuable frameworks to investigate intersections of race/ethnicity, class, age, religion, sexual orientation and gender identity in criminological contexts. Encouraging intersectionality approaches in the queer criminological enterprise thus assists in capturing the range of LGBTQ experiences of crime and inhibits it from becoming an exclusive criminal justice movement for economically well-off white gay men.

Gender, feminism and masculinity revisited

In this final section, we reflect on three very controversial but growing issues, which can be conceptualized in the broad category of gender studies, and their links with criminality.

TERF wars

In November 2018, the *New York Times* reported on a leaked memo from the Department of Health and Human Services which, if adopted, would reverse the Obama-era federal decision to interpret Title IX[1] as prohibiting discrimination on the basis of gender identity in addition to biological sex (Kearns, 2018). According to the *New York Times*, this would mean that transgender people 'could be defined out of existence'.

In the US, trans rights are the latest battle in the left–right culture war, but in Britain they have created a bitter left-on-left conflict in which the most fearless opponents of trans militants have not been conservatives but a cohort of liberal women, or, as their detractors call them, 'TERFs': trans–exclusionary radical feminists.

Between July and October 2018, the British Conservative Party considered whether to reform the Gender Recognition Act (GRA) 2004 so that any person could change his or her legal gender simply by filling out a form. The existing provisions of the legislation require that a person provides medical proof of gender dysphoria and live for at least two years as a member of their preferred gender. (The law does not require surgical transitions, as laws in some US states do.) Trans activists nevertheless maintain that the requirements are too demanding.

Kearns (2018) observes that if any man can become a woman without so much as shaving his beard, where does that leave natal females? Earlier that year, a sex offender named

Karen White was incarcerated in a British women's prison, where 'she' sexually assaulted fellow inmates. And how did this 'woman' sexually abuse other women? The prosecution explained: her penis was erect and sticking out of the top of her trousers.

TERFs do not accept that boys identifying as girls should be allowed to shower with girls or that trans women (natal males) should be allowed to compete in women's sports or be peer counsellors for women who have been raped. In this they are following their feminist foremothers, who argued for a clear distinction between two now much-abused concepts: sex and gender. Feminists of the latter half of the twentieth century had argued – as we have seen – that gender was a social construct used to oppress the female sex (sex being, as the Trump administration has suggested, an immutable biological trait). But trans activists are now pushing the opposite idea: that a person's self-identified gender is a liberating absolute that may, legally and medically, veto his or her sex.

TERFs, having realized that the proposed change to the GRA would undermine sex-based rights for women, started a number of grassroots women's groups – such as Fair Play for Women, Standing for Women and Women's Place – aimed at educating the public. But they were to face obstacles. For instance, Standing for Women funded a billboard campaign to spread a dictionary definition of *woman* ('an adult human female'). Then trans activists complained and the billboard company, Primesight Direct, removed the billboards. Its owner said his company had been 'misled' about them. A museum in London, Wellcome Collection, decided to use the term *womxn* instead of *women* in a marketing campaign, explaining that it's 'important to create a space/venue that includes diverse perspectives'. (The museum later disavowed the unorthodox spelling.)

Kearns (2018) observes that such pandering to trans activists is indicative of a prevail-ing sense of fear, with this group resorting to bullying tactics against those who do not comply. For example, after Rosa Freedman, a law professor at Reading University, argued against the GRA reform, a male student called her a 'transphobic Nazi who should get raped'. For merely retweeting an announcement of a TERF event, the rector of the University of Edinburgh was accused by official student groups of enabling transphobia. Dame Jenni Murray, the presenter of BBC's *Woman's Hour*, who had questioned whether trans women are 'real women', was deterred from speaking at Oxford University by cam-pus activists. Maria MacLachlan, a 61-year-old TERF, was assaulted at a feminist rally by a trans woman named Tara Wolf, who had posted on Facebook, "I wanna f*** up some TERFs. They're no better than fash [fascists]." Wolf, who is a biological male, has since been prosecuted and fined.

Perhaps intimidation from loud grassroots thugs also helps explain why a ComRes poll – taken during discussion of the GRA change – found that 69% of Conservative members of Parliament (MPs) supported keeping the requirement for medical verifica-tion of gender dysphoria, yet 63% were afraid to voice their opinion lest they receive social media abuse or be labelled 'transphobic'. Or why the speaker of the House of Com-mons rejected a parliamentary request known as an 'urgent question' (which requires a government minister to respond in person on the same day) from a Tory MP to discuss the issues raised by the case of Karen White, the transgender rapist. Or why the Conser-vative Party allowed consideration of the GRA reform in the first place.

Kearns (2018) observes that there is another reason why the Conservative Party is terri-fied of the trans mob, of course: trans activists have piggybacked on the gay rights move-ment and claimed a stripe of the rainbow flag. This is problematic for the Conservative Party because of the legacy of the now widely despised Section 28 of its Local Government

Act of 1988, which banned the public promotion of homosexuality and was repealed in the early 2000s. Although in practice there are many gay people who dissent from trans orthodoxy, the prevailing political wisdom is to see the LGBT crowd as one uniform electoral congregation, and people have decided that it better to say nothing at all.

It is nevertheless a mistake to suppose that trans dogma is professed by all trans people who are first and foremost *people*, who, like anyone, may have a range of viewpoints or change their mind. They are not inevitably analogous with trans *activists*, who aggressively pursue a specific ideological agenda. For example Jamie Shupe, born male, is the first legally non-binary person (i.e. neither legally male nor legally female) in the US. Previously, as a trans woman, Shupe had penned a letter to the *New York Times* consistent with the trans party line, insisting that he was, in fact, a woman. But after years of hormone treatment that he found both physically and emotionally unsuccessful, Shupe came to the conclusion that trans orthodoxy is a 'cult'. Shupe now does not like being classified as female and identifies as non-binary, preferring to be referred to as 'they' and 'their'.

Shupe's experience illustrates a common TERF objection to trans ideology – the reinforcement of gender stereotypes feeling that it is necessary to 'appear like a female,' which means 'big breasts, long hair, and lots of makeup'. But the emphasis on hyper-femininity only increased his gender dysphoria. He felt a 'crushing expectation' to 'look like a woman', and despite a high dosage, hormones did not help.

It is nevertheless not just men opting *in* to womanhood that worries TERFs; it is also young girls opting *out* of it. In Britain, the number of teenage girls referred for transition treatment to become boys has risen from 40 to 1,806 between 2010 and 2018 – an increase of over 4,000%. Historically, gender dysphoria has affected more boys than girls, but now the situation has changed.

Lisa Littman, an assistant professor at the Brown University School of Public Health, conducted a study of parental reports to find out and concluded that 'social and peer contagion' may be a factor. After pressure from activists, Brown University, nevertheless, distanced itself from her study, removing the press release from its website. Littman told the *National Review*, 'When activists shut down gender-dysphoria research about potential risks and contraindications of transition, they are depriving the transgender community of their right to receive accurate information' (Kearns, 2018).

Other stories commonly ignored by trans militants involve post-surgical regret. Julie Bindel, a TERF and a UK *Guardian* contributor who has fought for decades to protect women from violence, began writing about transgenderism in 2003 after she met Claudia, a gay man who had felt pressured into sex-change surgery by a partner. In an illuminating recent episode, the *Guardian* ran an editorial outlining 'where rights collide' between trans activists (who want gender recognition) and feminists (who want sex-based protections). The editorial rejected 'the idea that one of these positions is the right one – and the other wrong.' But the staff of the US *Guardian* were so alarmed by the editorial that they wrote a rebuttal accusing their British counterparts of promoting 'transphobic viewpoints' that included 'some of the same assertions about gender that US politicians are citing in their push to eliminate trans rights'.

'Trans rights are human rights' is the standard slogan of pro-trans activists. But in practice, trans rights have been a chaotic means of state-sponsored censorship and coercion. Obviously, *all* people should be free from discrimination, harassment, and abuse. One could say, then, that human rights are trans rights. And that – as the TERFs suggest – women need them, too (Kearns, 2018).

Misandry: the invisible hatred of men

Joe Kort (2016) notes that microaggressions are those subtle (and sometimes not so subtle) things we do to distance ourselves from minorities, be they someone from another ethnic group or culture. The term itself was first used by psychiatrist and Harvard University professor Chester M. Pierce in 1970 to describe insults and dismissals he regularly witnessed non-black Americans inflict on African Americans. Most people are well intentioned and do not mean to be offensive, but they are. Some of these include the following:

- 'What are you?' (to a person of mixed heritage)
- 'You don't act like a black person'.
- 'I am colour-blind'.
- 'Why do you sound white?'
- 'Is that really your hair?'
- 'Are you the first in your family to go to university?'

Today the term *microaggression* is also being used to describe insults and dismissals of women and LGBT people. Kevin Nadal (2013) provides examples of microaggressions against the latter group which include

- 'I'm not being homophobic; you're being too sensitive'.
- 'Have you ever had real sex?'
- 'So, who's the man in the relationship?'
- 'That's totally cool with me as long as I can watch'.
- 'You are so Jack on *Will and Grace* or Cam on *Modern Family*'.
- 'I would never date a bisexual man he can't commit or make up his mind'.
- 'What's going on down there' (to a transgender person)?

Kort (2016) observes the following microaggressions he has witnessed against women:

- 'I wouldn't work for a woman'.
- 'If you dress like a slut, you're asking for it'.
- 'She thinks like a man' (intended complement).
- 'You're being too emotional. You need to look at this logically'.
- 'I'm impressed that a woman could do that'.
- 'Why don't you just get back in the kitchen' (supposed joke).

Kort (2016) has increasingly noticed more and more microaggressions against men but has nevertheless observed surprisingly little discussion of this trend but does note, a word most people have never heard of *misandry*. Misandry means hatred of men, and it parallels misogyny, hatred of women. Kort argues that noting microaggressions directed against men, we can uncover a lot of 'hidden' misandry and he observes the following examples:

- 'Men only think with their dicks'.
- 'A man wouldn't understand'.
- 'Men just want a hole to put it in'.
- 'Men can't hear the word *no*' (when rejected sexually).

- 'Men are obsessed with lesbian porn'.
- 'Really? You don't like sports?'
- 'He's, you know, "artistic"'.
- 'Be a man'.
- 'Men are womanizers, man-whores, man-sluts'.

Kort (2016) notes that he has even heard women say things like 'Balls are gross. I hate them', observing that if a woman overheard men talking about vaginas being dirty and disgusting, this would be considered misogyny and microaggression, yet this is not the case the other way around. Thus, many otherwise enlightened people seem to think that putting a man down by shaming him for the transgressions of a few criminal men or for his inadequate physicality is a sort of privilege or entitlement. They are not even aware of their misandry.

Mostly we know that men, especially heterosexual white men, have privileged status in our society; that they are mostly blind to their privilege; and that we live in a patriarchal world. But let us critically consider our assumptions. What does it mean, for instance, when we tell someone to 'man up' or 'toughen up'?

We often think of patriarchy as hurting women, but we do not talk about how it also hurts men. Patriarchy includes a rigid standard of looks and behaviour, and men who fail to follow the standard are tormented ruthlessly. Conforming men may be 'blind to their privilege', but nerds and sissies are fair targets for contempt. A man who dares not be 'manly' is scorned by women as well as men. Those 'cry-babies' are seen to deserve what they get. Terrence Real (1998) observes that 'boys and men are granted privilege and special status, but only on the condition that they turn their backs on vulnerability and connection to join in the fray. Those who resist, like unconventional men or gay or bisexual men, are punished for it'.

Kort (2016) notes that the adage 'sticks and stones may hurt my bones, but words can never hurt me' is simply wrong. Words can and do wound. They perpetuate 'norms' which give rise to 'bigotry, misogyny, misandry, racism, homophobia, and more'. Given how 'manliness' is enforced by both men and women, it is not surprising that men have become 'fair targets' for a running commentary of contempt. Even the absence of online discussions of microaggressions against men is itself a microaggression because the absence renders the problem invisible. Some discussions of microaggressions toward women and minorities even say that since men are privileged, they cannot experience microaggressions. But many men are not privileged. These men have been rendered invisible and at the same time marked as fair game.

It pathologizes men when we assume something is wrong with one who does not like sports, is not 'tall, dark, and handsome', or otherwise does not fit a 'manly' stereotype. It also pathologizes men when we assume the worst transgressions of a few are characteristics of all. It does not help women (or blacks or LGBT individuals) engage in the sport of putting down men. We might begin by extending to men our sensitivity about the harm done by microaggressions. It could open the door to compassion and help us build a more humane world. Yet this is a position rejected by many feminists.

In September 2018, Labour MP Stella Creasy successfully campaigned for the government to review whether offences motivated by misogyny should fall under hate crime legislation. The following month, it was announced that the Law Commission in Britain would also look at whether other groups of people should be considered and covered by hate crime legislation – including the elderly, goths and men.

Among those calling for misandry to be considered a hate crime was the organization Fathers 4 Justice which said that it risked stereotyping men as perpetrators and women as victims and stated that abuse has no gender.

Feminist writer Sian Norris (2018) argues that the problem with this analysis is it simply does not match the facts. She acknowledges that some men are victims and survivors of gender-based violence and that they deserve support and justice. Yet it is impossible to ignore the reality that violence and abuse are gendered. The majority of perpetrators of violent crime against both men and women are male. According to the Office for National Statistics Crime Survey for England and Wales (2017), 78% of perpetrators of violent crime are men, for domestic abuse, 89% of those experiencing more than four incidents are women. When it comes to sexual offences, the majority of victims are women, and perpetrators men. Norris thus argues that to say that 'abuse has no gender' is not true.

Hate crimes – which can include verbal, physical and sexual abuse – are 'aggravating offences' that attract longer prison sentences than those not motivated by hate and is a reflection of how these crimes spread fear among the group to which the victim belongs. According to the Home Office (2016), hate crime can have an impact beyond individual victims and lead to increased feelings of isolation and fear across whole communities. Norris (2018) notes that this is arguably true of misogyny. Thus, acts of violence against women influence the way they feel able to live their lives, in the same way hate crimes motivated by ethnicity or sexuality have a repressive impact on an entire community. The threat of male violence restricts the freedoms of women in a way we simply do not see when it comes to violent crimes committed against men – the vast majority of which is perpetrated by other men. At the same time, the abuse of women online has been condemned by Amnesty International (2018) as an attempt to prevent women from fully exercising their right to participate in public life. Misogyny succeeds in repressing the freedom of women in all sorts of blatant and insidious ways. Does misandry have the same impact on the lives of men?

Involuntary celibates (incels)

Shortly after the May 2014 Isla Vista shooting, in which a gunman opened fire outside a University of California, Santa Barbara, sorority house, a chilling video circulated on social media. The attacker, 22-year-old former student Elliot Rodger, bluntly declared his motivation: 'If I can't have you girls', he said, 'I will destroy you'.

As has now become a fixture of mass shootings both in the US and elsewhere, the gunman emailed his 107,000-word manifesto, titled *My Twisted World*, to 34 addresses in order to both presage and publicize the attack. The manifesto, which was widely quoted in news reports, revealed the existence of an aggressive, hateful and rapidly proliferating online community of young men frustrated at their inability to find sexual partners. They call themselves 'incels', short for 'involuntary celibate' (Hoffman and Ware, 2020).

The term is derived from a website created by a female undergraduate student at Canada's Carleton University in 1993, named Alana's Involuntary Celibacy Project. Although originally conceived as a site where lonely individuals of both sexes could meet, exchange experiences and provide support, both the concept and its online manifestation were taken over by men complaining about their own involuntary celibacy and debating the causes behind their frustrations. Rodger was among those who adopted the 'incel' label.

Indeed, he is now considered by fellow incels to be the 'patron saint' of their movement – a cultural touchstone and inspirational figure – to be imitated and emulated.

The incel ideology, as such as it is, rails against 'Stacys', the idealized women they desire but believe deny them sex, as well as 'Chads', the similarly idealized males who are assailed for corralling all the apparently best women for themselves. Five years ago, these incels congregated on websites including PUAHate.com ('PUA' stands for pick-up artist); now, they trawl Reddit, 8chan and its replacement 8kun, and have also created their own forums and moved to the dark web.

The incel ideology is nevertheless real and it is lethal. In the deadliest incel-linked attack to date, in April 2018, ten pedestrians were killed in a vehicle-ramming attack on Toronto's busy Yonge Street. Other deadly attacks that have cited incel ideology or inspiration have occurred at Umpqua Community College in Roseburg, Oregon, in October 2015; Aztec High School in Aztec, New Mexico, in December 2017; Marjory Stoneman Douglas High School in Parkland, Florida, in February 2018; and the Tallahassee Hot Yoga studio in Tallahassee, Florida, in November 2019. The death toll in the US and Canada now stands at nearly 50 people. And incel ideology has spread to Europe, although it has yet to inspire, at least directly, any deadly attacks.

There are thus reasons to believe that the incel movement, and the terrorism threat it poses, are both here to stay and a matter to be taken seriously. First, this violence is indisputably terroristic in that it seeks to repress and subjugate women as part of the movement's vision of a paternalistic, gendered society. As J.M. Berger (2018) argues, statements issued by incels showcase

> all the standard components of extremist belief, including an in-group (the group to which an extremist belongs, in this case, the sexually deprived incels) and an out-group (the group targeted by the extremist group, in this case, Chads and Stacys, which translates from incelspeak as people with normal sex lives).

Berger also disputes the dismissal of incel violence as perpetrated by 'obviously troubled' or mentally ill young men, even in cases where mental health issues are confirmed, ideology plays a role and the terrorism label is still applicable. By advocating bloodshed as a means of broader societal intimidation, incel ideology conforms to the core definition of terrorism as violence designed to have far-reaching psychological effects.

Second, the incel movement has benefitted from the same social mobilization and online communication tools that have propelled the Islamic State of Iraq and Syria (ISIS) and violent far-right extremists to increasing prominence and attention. With just a Google search, curious outsiders can discover an entire online world populated by incels, complete with their own sites, language and culture. Once there, initiates are exposed to a variegated menu of extremist topics, propagated by forum dwellers eager to radicalize newcomers.

Relatedly, the threat posed by incels is growing harder to ascertain, because increased law enforcement and media attention has forced the movement into darker and more private online locales. Public forums today, while still unambiguously misogynistic in their rhetoric, now rarely advocate violence as brazenly as they once did because they are relatively effectively self-policed by site administrators. Fringes of the movement have migrated to smaller, less-policed sites, including Telegram, the encrypted app favoured by the Islamic State and other terrorist groups, and Discord, the popular gaming site (Hoffman and Ware, 2020).

Third, the fact that incel violence has come from breakaway lone actors rather than organized groups represents a formidable challenge to law enforcement efforts to prohibit and prevent the violence espoused by the proponents of the ideology. Moreover, like most violent far-right and modern jihadist terrorism, incel violence has not been dictated by leaders of an identifiable network who design a plot and finance and train the attackers. Without any kind of traditional command–and–control apparatus, these incel attacks have instead been conceived by individuals who design and execute their plots alone. In this lone-actor model, it becomes nearly impossible for law enforcement agencies to intercept would-be attackers and stop the violence before it occurs, as we have seen with terrorists inspired by ISIS. In most cases, the perpetrators leave no traceable footprint online until they post their manifestos or digital attack advertisements. When they do, they are easily drowned out or overwhelmed by an army of 'shitposters,' who enjoy spreading increasingly extreme and often violent rhetoric through their anonymous online profiles but rarely have any intention of committing attacks in the real world.

Fourth, the incel movement should be of grave concern because of its increasing interaction with violent far-right extremists and their own bedrock talking points of hatred and intolerance. Rodger's manifesto was not only virulently misogynistic, it was also racially charged. Since its publication in 2014, the incel movement has been infiltrated by far-right extremists, who see so-called men's rights activism as a common ground. Male supremacy thus has gone hand in glove with white supremacy. As such, the increasing spread of extremist far-right views online and the success of far-right terrorists in launching major attacks from El Paso to Pittsburgh will likely continue to embolden incels.

In addition – like their far-right counterparts – some incels may have benefitted from prior military service. Indeed, four of the six incel attackers cited earlier had some degree of military experience, and at least one other incel attack (in which only the gunman was killed) involved a US Army veteran who opened fire outside a Dallas courthouse. In this respect, even those who left military service prematurely may have used the weapons training they received in their attacks.

Finally, the rise of the incel movement is concerning because of its accessibility. This is not an ideology that requires training in arcane religious doctrine or indoctrination through complex political texts. Instead, it plays off emotions and frustrations experienced daily by young men around the world, and it appeals more effectively to individuals who are simply angry or lonely than to those with pre-existing extremist tendencies. The incel ideology co-opts these feelings of isolation and sexual frustration and then weaponizes them into a hateful ideology that attacks women, men, and, in some instances, minorities and individuals with mental illness. And, with its online presence, a catalogue of incel chatrooms is only a few clicks away for anyone with an internet connection. Compared to Islamic extremism or white supremacism, inceldom is an ideology that any young man, in any community, could fall into and become deeply enmeshed.

Perhaps the most challenging aspect of the incel movement's mobilization to violence is that there are no obvious legal measures or counter-terrorism intelligence initiatives available. The movement is completely decentralized, without any hierarchy or leaders, and therefore no targetable offline organizing or funding streams. It is also difficult to identify and enlist persons with similarly extremist views but who eschew violence to serve as interlocutors, as is done with other programmes to counter violent extremism. Domestic law enforcement agencies cannot of course legally track online speech or police language and, even so, incels pride themselves on their aforementioned penchant for 'shitposting'. Policing social media forums and their content might potentially risk creating new monitoring problems by forcing incels into the darker web, where oversight is more difficult and violent rhetoric can more safely be propagated.

Moreover, the fact that, as Berger (2018) notes, many incels themselves claim to be suffering from psychological issues such as depression or evidence some degree of autism suggests the need for more proactive intervention from therapists and other mental health professionals. But, this is more easily said than done, as journalist Aja Romano (2018), who has studied incels, notes:

> outreach for incels shouldn't start with enabling the community's violent misogyny or its collective sense of entitlement to the bodies and emotional support of women. . . . Romano it should start with improving men's access to mental health treatment – and, crucially, their faith that it can do them any good.

Hoffman and Ware (2020) observe that alongside the far-right and Islamic extremist homegrown violent extremists, incels conform to an increasingly pervasive trend of terrorist attacks perpetrated by individuals without any connection to an existing organization with known leaders and an identifiable command-and-control structure. It is part of a broader rise of domestic terrorism threat – in fragmented modernity and the postmodern condition – and needs to be taken equally seriously by law enforcement and the counter-terrorism community before the movement continues to grow in size and threat.

Policy implications of the gendered criminal

Gender plays a critical role throughout the criminal justice process. A review of the life circumstances and of the backgrounds of female offenders in the system would suggest that there are more effective ways to prevent and address the criminal behaviour of women than are currently in use. Feminists thus propose that criminal justice practice could be improved by addressing the pathways that women take into the criminal justice system, the differences in their patterns of offending from those of male offenders, their experiences in the criminal justice system and their responses to programmes.

Feminists argue, for example, that it is important to re-examine the gendered effects of public policies that criminalize substance abuse, which often results in the overrepresentation of women in prison. Mandatory minimum-sentencing statutes for drug offences in the US – in particular – have had a devastating effect on women and have unfairly punished them as well as their children. Standard gender-neutral correctional procedures have also disadvantaged women in that such procedures do not take into account the histories of abuse of many female offenders. The criminal justice system, it is argued, must become trauma-informed to provide effective interventions and services for women.

At present, both the availability of programming for women offenders and the types of services offered fall short of what is needed. For example, because women in treatment find recovery complicated by trauma, child care issues, inadequate social support systems and lack of financial resources, proposed strategies must take these issues into account. Additionally, it is critical that programmes provide appropriate screening and assessment of the needs – not risks – of individual clients, along with a range of services designed to meet those needs.

In creating appropriate services that truly take into account and respond to gender and cultural factors it is necessary to first re-examine our current criminal justice policies. We can then work to adjust those policies so that the response to offending by women is one that emphasizes human needs, specifically those that reflect the realities of the lives of women.

Rather than focusing solely on punitive sanctions, a feminist-inspired policy perspective would propose that we begin to systematically consider the least restrictive appropriate alternatives to incarceration. The savings to society from a reduction in the imprisonment of women and from the improved reintegration of female offenders into the community would be of benefit, it is argued, not only to the women themselves but also to future generations.

Summary of main points

1   Feminists argue that it is men who are the dominant group in society. It is they who make and enforce the rules, which are invariably to the detriment of women.
2   Feminist criminologies challenge the male-centredness of criminology and propose that the main weakness of traditional 'malestream' criminological theory is the failure to understand the significance of gender and sex roles.
3   An area where feminism has been particularly influential has been in focusing our attention on the nature of crimes committed against women by men, with the two areas most frequently studied being rape and domestic violence.
4   Separate studies of women and their experiences of crime have had a threefold influence in criminology: (1) the development of different explanations of female criminality and conformity, (2) a 'gendering' of crime which includes gendered explanations of certain male criminality and (3) a recognition of different female 'experiences' of crime, victimization and the criminal justice system.
5   It was in response to feminist discourse that a growing literature began to emerge that sought to 'take masculinity seriously'.
6   Messerschmidt observes that, as masculinities and femininities are not determined biologically, it is important to identify and examine possible masculinities by women and girls (and femininities by men and boys) and their relation to crime.
7   There has been very little data on LGBTQ experiences of crime, whether as victims or offenders, while the bulk of criminological research over the past four decades has focused almost exclusively on bias or hate crime/bullying and intimate partner violence.
8   A brief overview of mainstream criminological theory has demonstrated a need for theoretical and empirical advancements which bring the experiences of LGBTQ people out of the shadows.
9   In the US, trans rights are the latest battle in the left–right culture war, but in Britain, they have created a bitter left-on-left conflict where the most fearless opponents of trans militants have been not conservatives but a cohort of liberal women – or, as their detractors call them, 'TERFs': trans-exclusionary radical feminists.
10   Among those calling for misandry to be considered a hate crime was the organization Fathers 4 Justice which called to make misogyny a hate crime as it risked stereotyping men as perpetrators and women as victims and stated that abuse has no gender.

Discussion questions

1   Discuss the notion that feminist criminology has had no impact on the law and criminal justice system.
2   In what ways do feminists explain increasing female involvement in crime?
3   What impact has feminism had on the study of male criminality?
4   What are the implications of trans-exclusionary radical feminist thinking for LGBT rights?
5   Should misandry be considered a hate crime?

Suggested further reading

Key feminist texts in the field of explaining crime and criminal behaviour are Carlen (1988, 1992), Gelsthorpe and Morris (1990), Heidensohn (1985, 1994), Leonard (1983) and Smart (1977, 1981, 1990). Dobash and Dobash (1992) and Hanmer and Saunders (1984) are essential reading on violent crime against women. For key texts on masculinity and crime, consult Connell (1987, 1995, 2002), Messerschmidt (1993, 2004, 2005), Miller (2001, 2002) and Jefferson (1997).

Note

1   Title IX is a federal civil rights law that prohibits discrimination on the basis of sex in any educational program or activity that receives federal funding. This includes most schools, including private institutions and grades K through 12.

References

Abdullah-Khan, N. (2008) *Male Rape: The Emergence of a Social and Legal Issue.* Hampshire: Palgrave Macmillan.
Adler, F. (1975) *Sisters in Crime: The Rise of the New Female Criminal.* New York: McGraw-Hill.
Agnew, R. (1992) 'Foundation for a General Theory of Crime and Delinquency', *Criminology*, 30: 47–87.
Aichhorn, A. (1951, originally 1925) *Wayward Youth.* New York: Meridian Books.
Akers, R.L. (1973) *Deviant Behavior: A Social learning approach (1st ed.),* Belmont, CA: Wadsworth Publishing.
Akers, R.L. (1997) *Criminological Theories: Introduction and Evaluation,* 2nd ed. Los Angeles, CA: Roxbury.
Alexander, F. and Staub, H. (1931, originally 1929) *The Criminal, the Judge and the Public.* New York, NY: Macmillan.
Amnesty (2018) *Women Have the Right to Use Twitter Equally, Freely and Without Fear.* Available from: www.amnesty.org/en/latest/research/2018/03/online-violence-against-women-chapter-5/#topanchor
Barnhouse, R.T. (1977) *Homosexuality: A Symbolic Confusion.* New York, NY: The Seabury Press.
Bayer, R. (1981) *Homosexuality and American Psychiatry: The Politics of Diagnosis.* New York, NY: Basic Books.
Becker, H. (1963) *Outsiders: Studies in the Sociology of Deviance.* New York: Free Press.
Beechey, V. (1977) 'Some Notes on Female Wage Labour in Capitalist Production', *Capital and Class*, Autumn: 45–66.
Belknap, J. (1996) *The Invisible Woman: Gender, Crime and Justice.* Belmont, CA: Wadsworth.
Belknap, J. and Holsinger, K. (2006) 'The Gendered Nature of Risk Factors for Delinquency', *Feminist Criminology*, 1: 48–71.
Berger, J.M. (2018) 'The Difference between a Killer and a Terrorist', *The Atlantic*, April 26.

Bergler, E. (1956) *Homosexuality: Disease or Way of Life*. New York, NY: Hill and Wang.

Bertrand, M. (1969) 'The Myth of Sexual Equality before the Law', in *Proceedings of the Fifth Research Conference on Delinquency and Criminality*. Montreal: Quebec Society of Criminology.

Bieber, I., Dain, H.J., Dince, P., Drellich, M.G., Grand, H.G. and Gundlach, R.H., (1962) *Homosexuality: A Psychoanalytic Study of Male Homosexuals*. New York, NY: Basic Books.

Box, S. and Hale, C. (1983) 'Liberation and Female Criminality in England and Wales', *British Journal of Criminology*, 23(1).

Braithwaite, J. (1989) *Crime, Shame and Reintegration*. Cambridge: Cambridge University Press.

Britton, D.M. (2000) 'Feminism in Criminology: Engendering the Outlaw', *Annals of the American Academy of Political and Social Science*, 571: 57–76.

Broidy, L.M. and Agnew, R. (1997) 'Gender and Crime: A General Strain Theory Perspective', *Journal of Research in Crime and Delinquency*, 34: 275–306.

Brown, G.W. and Harris, T. (1978) *Social Origins of Depression*. London: Tavistock.

Brownmiller, S. (1975) *Against Our Will: Men, Women and Rape*. New York: Simon & Schuster.

Bruegel, I. (1978) 'Women as a Reserve Army of Labour: A Note on Recent British Experience', *Feminist Review*, 3: 12–23.

Bryson, V. (1992) *Feminist Political Theory*. Women in Society Series. London: Palgrave.

Bullough, V.L. (1979) *Homosexuality: A History*. New York, NY: New American Library.

Burgess-Proctor, A. (2006) 'Intersections of Race, Class, Gender, and Crime: Future Directions for Feminist Criminology', *Feminist Criminology*, 1: 27–47.

Cain, M. (ed.) (1989) *Growing Up Good*. London: Sage.

Cain, M. (1990) 'Towards Transgression: New Directions in Feminist Criminology', *International Journal of the Sociology of the Law*, 18(1): 1–18.

Carlen, P. (1988) *Women, Crime and Poverty*. Milton Keynes: Open University Press.

Carlen, P. (1992) 'Criminal Women and Criminal Justice: The Limits to, and Potential of, Feminist and Left Realist Perspectives', in R. Matthews and J. Young (eds.) *Issues in Realist Criminology*. London: Sage.

Casper, J.L. (1852) 'Über Nothsucht und Päderastie und deren Ermittelung seitens des Gerichtsarztes', *Vierteljahrschrift für gerichtliche und öffentliche Medicin*, 1: 21–78.

Chambliss, W.J. (1988). *Exploring Criminology*. New York, NY: Macmillan.

Chambliss, W.J. (ed.). (1984) *Criminal Law in Action*. New York, NY: Wiley.

Chesney-Lind, M. (1988) 'Girls in Ggaril', *Crime and Delinquency*, 34: 150–68.

Chesney-Lind, M. (1989) 'Girls' Crime and Woman's Place: Toward a Feminist Model of Female Delinquency', *Crime and Delinquency*, 35: 5–29.

Chesney-Lind, M. and Pasko, L. (2004) *The Female Offender: Girls, Women and Crime*, 2nd ed. Thousand Oaks, CA: Sage.

Chesney-Lind, M. and Shelden, R.G. (1992) *Girls, Delinquency, and Juvenile Justice*. Pacific Grove, CA: Brooks/Cole.

Cohen, A.K. (1955) *Delinquent Boys: The Culture of the Gang*. New York: Free Press.

Cohen, A.K. (1966) *Deviance and Control*. Englewood Cliffs, NJ: Prentice Hall.

Cohen, C. (2014) *Male Rape Is a Feminist Issue: Feminism, Governmentality, and Male Rape*. Hampshire: Palgrave Macmillan.

Collier, R. (1998) *Masculinities, Crime and Criminology: Men, Heterosexuality and the Criminal(ised) Other*. London: Sage.

Connell, R.W. (1987) *Gender and Power*. Cambridge: Polity Press.

Connell, R.W. (1995) *Masculinities*. Cambridge: Polity Press.

Connell, R.W. (2000) *The Men and the Boys*. Sydney: Allen and Unwin.

Connell, R.W. (2002) 'On Hegemonic Masculinity and Violence: Response to Jefferson and Hall', *Theoretical Criminology*, 6(1): 89–99.

Craft, A. and Craft, M. (1984) 'Treatment of Sexual Offenders', in M. Craft and A. Craft (eds.) *Mentally Abnormal Offenders*. London: Butler and Tanner Ltd.

Craft, A., Craft, M. and Spencer, M. (1984) 'Sexual Offences: Intent and Characteristics', in M. Craft and A. Craft (eds.) *Mentally Abnormal Offenders*. London: Butler and Tanner Ltd.

Crenshaw, K. (1991) 'Mapping the Margins: Intersectionality, Identity Politics, and Violence against Women of Color', *Stanford Law Review*, 43: 1241–99.

Daly, K. (1989) 'Neither Conflict Nor Labeling Nor Paternalism Will Suffice: Intersections of Race, Ethnicity, Gender, and Family in Criminal Court Decisions', *Crime and Delinquency*, 35: 136–68.

Daly, K. (1992) 'Women's Pathways to Felony Court: Feminist Theories of Lawbreaking and Problems of Representation', *Review of Law and Women's Studies*, 2: 11–52.

Daly, K. (1994a) *Gender, Crime, and Punishment*. New Haven, CT: Yale University Press.

Daly, K. (1994b) 'Gender and Punishment Disparity', in G.S. Bridges and M. Myers (eds.) *Inequality, Crime and Social Control*. Boulder, CO: Westview Press.

Daly, K. and Chesney-Lind, M. (1988) 'Feminism and Criminology', *Justice Quarterly*, 5(4): 487–535.

De Beauvoir, S. (1977, originally 1949) *The Second Sex*. New York: Alfred A. Knopf.

Ditton, J. (1979) *Controlology: Beyond the New Criminology*. London: Macmillan.

Dobash, R.E. and Dobash, R.P. (1980) *Violence against Wives*. London: Open Books.

Dobash, R.E. and Dobash, R.P. (1992) *Women, Violence and Social Change*. London: Routledge & Kegan Paul.

Donnelly, D.A. and Kenyon, S. (1996) 'Honey We Don't Do Men: Gender Stereotypes and the Provision of Services to Sexually Assaulted Males', *Journal of Interpersonal Violence*, 11: 441–8.

Downes, D. and Rock, P. (1998) *Understanding Deviance*, 3rd ed. Oxford: Oxford University Press.

Einstadter, W. and Henry, S. (1995) *Criminological Theory*. Fort Worth, TX: Harcourt Brace.

Eysenck, H.J. (1977) *Crime and Personality*. London: Routledge and Kegan Paul.

Faludi, S. (1991) *The Undeclared War against Women*. New York: Crown.

Ford, C.S. and Beach, F.A. (1951) *Patterns of Sexual Behavior*. New York, NY: Harper and Brothers.

Foucault, M. (1976) *The History of Sexuality*. London: Allen Lane.

Freud, S. (1905) 'Three Essays on the Theory of Sexuality', *Standard Edition*, 7: 125–245.

Freud, S. (1911) 'Psychoanalytical Notes on the Autobiographical Account of a Case of Paranoia (Dementia Paranoides)', *Standard Edition*, 12: 1–82.

Friedan, B. (1963) *The Femine Mystique*. New York: W.W. Norton.

Friedlander, K. (1947) *The Psychoanalytic Approach to Juvenile Delinquency*. London: Kegan Paul.

Gelsthorpe, L. and Morris, A. (eds.) (1990) *Feminist Perspectives in Criminology*. Milton Keynes: Open University Press.

Gelsthorpe, L. and Morris, A. (eds.) (1990) *Feminist Perspectives in Criminology*. Milton Keynes: Open University Press.

Gibson, M. and Rafter, N.H. (2006) 'Editor's Introductio', in M. Gibson and N.H. Rafter (eds.) *Criminal Man*. Durham, NC: Duke.

Gillespie, T. (1996) 'Rape Crisis Centres and Male Rape: A Face of the Backlash', in M. Hester, L. Kelly and J. Radford (eds.) *Women Violence and Male Power*. Buckingham: Open University Press.

Gottfredson, M.R. and Hirschi, T. (1990) *A General Theory of Crime*. Stanford, CA: Stanford University Press.

Graham, J. and Bowling, B. (1995) *Young People and Crime, Home Office Research Study No. 145*. London: HMSO.

Greenberg, D.F. (1988) *The Construction of Homosexuality*. Chicago, IL: University of Chicago Press.

Hagan, J. (1988) *Structural Criminology*. Cambridge: Polity Press.

Hamowy, R. (1977) 'Medicine and the Crimination of Sin: "Self-Abuse" in 19th Century America', *Journal of Libertarian Studies*, 1(3): 229–70.

Hanmer, J. and Saunders, S. (1984) *Well-Founded Fear*. London: Hutchinson.

Hartmann, H. (1981) 'The Family as a Locus of Class, Gender and Political Struggle: The Example of Housework', *Signs*, 6: 360–94.

Heidensohn, F.M. (1968) 'The Deviance of Women: A Critique and an Enquiry', *British Journal of Criminology*, 19(2): 160–76.

Heidensohn, F.M. (1985) *Women and Crime*. London: Macmillan.

Heidensohn, F.M. (1994) 'Gender and Crime', in M. Maguire, R. Morgan and R. Reiner (eds.) *The Oxford Handbook of Criminology*. Oxford: Oxford University Press.

Heidensohn, F.M. (2000/2001) 'Women and Violence: Myths and Reality in the 21st Century', *Criminal Justice Matters*, 42: 20.

Heidensohn, F.H. (2003) 'Gender and Policing', in T. Newburn (ed.) *Handbook of Policing*. Cullompton: Willan Publishing.

Herrn, R. (1995) 'On the History of Biological Theories of Sexuality', *Journal of Homosexuality*, 28(1–2): 31–56.

Hirschi, T. (1969) *Causes of Delinquency*. Berkeley, CA: University of California Press.

Hoffman, B. and Ware, J. (2020) 'Incels: America's Newest Domestic Terrorism Threat', *Lawfare: Hard National Security Choices*, January 12.

Hooker, E. (1956) 'A Preliminary Analysis of Group Behavior of Homosexuals', *Journal of Psychology*, 42: 217–25.

Hooker, E. (1957) 'The Adjustment of the Male Overt Homosexual', *Journal of Projective Techniques*, 21: 18–31.

Hooker, E. (1958) 'Male Homosexuality in the Rorschach', *Journal of Projective Techniques*, 22: 33–54.

hooks, b. (1988) *Talking Back, Thinking Feminist, Thinking Black*. Boston, MA: South End Press.

Jaggar, A.M. (1983) *Feminist Politics and Human Nature*. Lanham, MD: Rowman and Littlefield.

Jargose, A. (1996) *Queer Theory: An Introduction*. New York, NY: New York University Press.

Jefferson, T. (1997) 'Masculinities and Crime', in M. Maguire, R. Morgan and R. Reiner (eds.) *The Oxford Handbook of Criminology*, 2nd ed. Oxford: Clarendon.

Jeffery, C.R. (1965) 'Criminal Behavior and Learning Theory', *Journal of Criminal Law, Criminology, and Police Science*, 56(3): 294–300.

Katz, J. (1988) *Seductions of Crime: Moral and Sensual Attractions in Doing Evil*. New York: Basic Books.

Kearns, M. (2018) 'TERF Wars'. *National Review*, November 15.

Kennedy, H. (1997) 'Karl Heinrich Ulrichs: First Theorist of Homosexuality', in V. Rosario (ed.) *Science and Homosexualities*. New York, NY: Routledge.

Kinsey, A.C., Pomeroy, W.B. and Martin, C.E. (1948) *Sexual Behavior in the Human Male*. Philadelphia, PA: Saunders.

Kinsey, A.C., Pomeroy, W.B., Martin, C.E. and Gebhart, P.H. (1953) *Sexual Behavior in the Human Female*. Philadelphia, PA: Saunders.

Kitzinger, C. and Coyle, A. (2002) 'Introducing Lesbian and Gay Psychology', in A. Coyle and C. Kitzinger (eds.) *Lesbian and Gay Psychology: New Perspectives*. Oxford: Blackwell.

Kort, J. (2016) 'Misandry: The Invisible Hatred of Men', *Psychology Today*, August 7.

Lees, S. (1997) *Ruling Passions: Sexual Violence, Reputation and the Law*. Buckingham: Open University Press.

Lemert, E. (1951) *Social Pathology*. New York, NY: McGraw-Hill.

Leonard, E. (1983) *Women, Crime and Society*. London: Longmans.

Lombroso, C. (1875) *L'uomo delinquente (The Criminal Man)*. Milan: Hoepli.

Lombroso, C. and Ferrero, G. (1885) *Criminal Woman, the Prostitute, and the Normal Woman*. Durham, NC: Duke University Press.

MacKinnon, C. (1979) *Sexual Harassment of Working Women: A Case of Sex Discrimination*. New Haven, CT: Yale University Press.

Makari, G. (2008) *Revolution in Mind: The Creation of Psychoanalysis*. New York, NY: Harper Collins.

Mann, C.R. (1984) *Female Crime and Delinquency*. Birmingham, AL: University of Alabama Press.

Marcus-Mendoza, S., Klein-Saffran, J. and Lutze, F. (1998) 'A Feminist Examination of Boot Camp Prison Programs for Women', *Women & Therapy*, 2: 173–85.

Matza, D.M. (1964) *Delinquency and Drift*. New York: Wiley.

McCrae, R.R. and Costa, P.T. (1990) *Personality in Adulthood*. New York, NY: Guilford Press.

McIntosh, M. (1968) 'The Homosexual Role', *Social Problems*, 16(2): 182–92.

Merton, R.K. (1938) 'Social Structure and Anomie', *American Sociological Review*, 3: 672–2.

Messerschmidt, J.W. (1986) *Capitalism, Patriarchy and Crime: Toward a Socialist Feminist Criminology*. Totowa, NJ: Rowman and Littlefield.

Messerschmidt, J.W. (1993) *Masculinities and Crime*. Lanham, MD: Rowman and Littlefield.

Messerschmidt, J.W. (2004) *Flesh and Blood: Adolescent Gender Diversity and Violence*. Lanham, MD: Rowman and Littlefield.

Messerschmidt, J.W. (2005) 'Masculinities and Crime: Beyond a Dualist Criminology', in C. Renzetti, L. Goodstein and S. Miller (eds.) *Gender, Crime, and Criminal Justice: Original Feminist Readings*. Los Angeles, CA: Roxbury.

Miller, J. (2001) *One of the Guys: Girls, Gangs, and Gender*. New York: Oxford University Press.

Miller, J. (2002) 'The Strengths and Limits of "Doing Gender" for Understanding Street Crime', *Theoretical Criminology*, 6(4): 433–60.

Morris, A. (1987) *Women, Crime and Criminal Justice*. Oxford: Blackwell.

Mukherjee, S.K. and Fitzgerald, M.K. (1981) 'The Myth of Rising Crime', in S.K. Mukherjee and J.A. Scutt (eds.) *Women and Crime*. London: Allen & Unwin.

Nadal, K. (2013) *That's So Gay: Microaggressions and the Lesbian, Gay, Bisexual, and Transgender Community*. Washington, DC: American Psychological Society.

Norris, S. (2018) 'Why Misandry and Misogyny Should Be Treated Differently When It Comes to Hate Crimes', *The New Statesmen*, October 16.

Peterson, D. and Panfil, V. (eds.) (2014) *The Handbook of LGBT Communities, Crime, and Justice*. New York: Springer.

Pharr, S. (1977) *Homophobia: A Weapon of Sexism*. Berkeley, CA: Chardon Press.

Pilcher, J. (1983) 'I'm not a Feminist, But . . . Understanding Feminism', *Sociology Review*, 3: 2.

Pitfield, C. (2013) *Male Survivors of Sexual Assault: To Tell or Not to Tell?* Available from: http://webcache. googleusercontent.com/search?q=cache:BBMfwrMnd34J:roar.uel.ac.uk/3442/1/2013_DClinPsych_ Pitfield.pdf+&cd=1&hl=en&ct=clnk&gl=uk&client=safari [Accessed 5 December 2019].

Plummer, K. (2005) 'Critical Humanism and Queer Theory: Living With the Tensions', in N.K. Denzin and Y.S. Lincoln (eds.) *The SAGE Handbook of Qualitative Research*, 3rd ed. Thousand Oaks, CA: Sage.

Presdee, M. (1994) 'Young People, Culture and the Construction of Crime: Doing Wrong versus Doing Crime', in G. Barak (ed.) *Varieties of Criminology*. Westport, CT: Praeger.

Quinney, R. (1970) *The Social Reality of Crime*. Boston, MA: Little, Brown, and Co.

Radford, J. and Stanko, E.A. (1994) *The Contradictions of Patriarchal Crime Control*. London: Routledge.

Rado, S. (1940) 'A Critical Examination of the Concept of Bisexuality', *Psychosomatic Medicine*, 2: 459–67.

Rafter, N.H. and Heidensohn, F. (eds.) (1985) *International Feminist Perspectives: Engendering a Discipline*. Buckingham: Open University Press.

Real, T. (1998) *I Don't Want to Talk About It: Overcoming the Secret Legacy of Male Depression*. New York: Prentice Hall.

Reiss, A.J. (1961) 'The Social Integration of Queers and Peers', *Social Problems*, 9(2): 102–20.

Romano, A. (2018) 'What a Woman-led Incel Support Group Can Teach Us About Men and Mental Health'. *Vox*. Available from: https://www.vox.com/2018/6/20/17314846/incel-support-group-therapy-black-pill-mental-health

Schuster, J. (2013) 'Invisible Feminists? Social Media and Young Women's Political Participation', *Political Science*, 65(1): 8–24.

Seidman, S. (1996) 'Introduction', in S. Seidman (ed.) *Queer Theory/Sociology*. Oxford: Blackwell.

Sharp, S.F. (2003) *The Incarcerated Woman: Rehabilitative Programming in Women's Prisons*. Upper Saddle River, NJ: Prentice Hall.

Simon, R.J. (1975) *Women and Crime*. London: Lexington Books.

Simpson, S.S. (1989) 'Feminist Theory, Crime and Justice', *Criminology*, 27: 605–27.

Simpson, S.S. (1991) 'Caste, Class and Violent Crime: Explaining Differences in Female Offending', *Criminology*, 29: 115–35.

Smart, C. (1977) *Women, Crime and Criminology*. London: Routledge & Kegan Paul.

Smart, C. (1981) 'Response to Greenwood', in A. Morris and L. Gelsthorpe (eds.) *Women and Crime*. Cambridge: Cropwood Conference Series.

Smart, C. (1990) 'Feminist Approaches to Criminology; or Postmodern Woman Meets Atavistic Man', in L. Gelsthorpe and A. Morris (eds.) *Feminist Perspectives in Criminology*. Buckingham: Open University Press.

Smith, B. (1993) 'Homophobia: Why Bring It Up?', in H. Abelove, M. Barale and D. Halperin (eds.) *The Lesbian and Gay Studies Reader*. New York, NY: Routledge.

Socarides, C.W. (1968) *The Overt Homosexual*. New York, NY: Aronson.

Stanko, E.A. (1985) *Intimate Intrusions: Women's Experience of Male Violence*. London: Routledge & Kegan Paul.

Stanko, E.A. (1990) *Everyday Violence*. London: Pandora Press.

Steffensmeier, D., and Allan, E. (1996) 'Gender and Crime: Toward a Gendered Theory of Female Offending', *Annual Review of Sociology*, 22: 459–88.

Szasz, T.S. (1970) *Ideology and Insanity*. New York, NY: Doubleday.

Tardieu, A. (1857) *Étude Médico-légale Fur Les Attentats Aux Moeurs [Medico-legal Studies of Offences Against Morals]*. Paris, FR: Librairie JB Baillière et Fils.

The Incredibles (2006) *Walt Disney Pictures*. Los Angeles, CA: Hollywood.

Tong, R. (1988) *Feminist Thought: A Comprehensive Introduction*. London: Routledge.

von Krafft-Ebing (1999, originally 1886) *Psychopathia Sexualis*. Berlin: Bloat Books.

Walby, S. (1980) *Theorizing Patriarchy*. Oxford: Basil Blackwell.

Walklate, S. (1995) *Gender and Crime: An Introduction*. Hemel Hempstead: Prentice Hall/Harvester.

Weeks, J. (1979) *Coming Out: Homosexual Politics in Britain, from the Nineteenth Century to the Present*. London: Quartet Books.

Weeks, J. (1981) *Sex, Politics, and Society: The Regulation of Sexuality Since 1880*. New York, NY: Longman.

Weiss, K.G. (2010) 'Male Sexual Victimization: Examining Men's Experiences of Rape and Sexual Assault', *Men and Masculinities*, 12: 275–98.

Wollstonecraft, M. (1792) *A Vindication of the Rights of Women with Strictures on Moral and Political Subjects*. London: Joseph Johson.

Woods, J.B. (2013) 'The Birth of Modern Criminology and Gendered Constructions of Homosexual Criminal Identity', *Journal of Homosexuality*, 62(2): 131–66.

Woods, J.B. (2014) 'Queering Criminology: An Overview of the State of the Field', in D. Peterson and V. Panfil (eds.) *The Handbook of LGBT Communities, Crime, and Justice*. New York: Springer.

Young, J. (1979) *Capitalism and the Rule of Law*. London: Hutchinson.

Young, J. (1999) *The Exclusive Society: Social Exclusion, Crime and Difference in Late Modernity*. London: Sage.

Young, J. and Matthews, R. (eds.) (1992) *Rethinking Criminology: The Realist Debate*. London: Sage.

Chapter 14

Green and species criminology

Key issues

1. Green criminology
2. Animal rights
3. From the beginning – a selective history
4. Philosophical and legal approaches
5. (Il)legitimate cruelty to animals

Introduction

Green criminology is a branch of criminology which involves the study of harms and crimes against the environment. The term *green criminology* was introduced by Michael J. Lynch in 1990 and expanded on in Nancy Frank and Michael J. Lynch's 1992 book, *Corporate Crime, Corporate Violence*, which examined the political–economic origins of green crime and injustice, and the scope of environmental law. The term became more widely used following publication of a special issue on green criminology in the journal *Theoretical Criminology* edited by Nigel South and Piers Bierne in 1998.

The study of green criminology has expanded significantly in recent years and is supported by groups such as the *International Green Criminology Working Group*. There are increasing empirical and theoretical intersections between the study of green criminology, which focuses on environmental harms and crimes, and mainstream criminology and criminal justice, with criminologists studying the 'greening' of criminal justice institutions and practices in efforts to become more environmentally sustainable and the involvement of people in prison or on probation in ecological justice initiatives.

The second major variation of green criminology is the non-speciesist argument proposed by Piers Beirne (1999), who argues that the study of harms against nonhuman animals is an important criminological topic which requires attention and at the same time illustrates the limits of current criminological theorizing about, crime/harm, law and justice with its focus almost exclusively on humans (Beirne, 2009). This approach includes discussions of animal rights and this debate provides a major focus of this chapter.

Criminology is, of course, and eclectic subject which incorporates inputs from various different disciplines in the study of crime and its meanings. This is demonstrated in this chapter which includes elements from history, philosophy and evolutionary biology in a lively discussion of what could be the most important issue in contemporary society. This clearly seems to be the case with the arrival of the COVID-19 pandemic.

The case for a green criminology

During the 1990s, a number of scholars began to write about a range of issues and concerns which reflected engagement with the environment and what could be identified as an emerging 'green' criminology (Lynch, 1990; Beirne, 1995; Halsey and White, 1998; South, 1998; South *et al.*, 2013). Yet green criminology does not represent an entirely new perspective within criminology, for several criminologists had previously examined different environmental hazards and crimes (Lynch, 1990), but its impact has been in building on that past work (South and Beirne, 1998; White, 2009).

Green criminology can be defined as a framework of intellectual, empirical and political orientations toward primary and secondary harms, offences and crimes which impact in a damaging way on the natural environment, diverse species (human and non-human) and the planet. Introducing such a framework into criminology does not promote any one theory but rather introduces a perspective (South, 1998) which can inform theoretical and empirical work. It is a common principle of green criminology that it should be an inter- and multidisciplinary meeting place for critical discussion of global warming and environmental degradation involving various social and environmental sciences.

There are various ways of differentiating and highlighting topics and themes for legitimate green criminological inquiry (Carrabine *et al.*, 2009; Wolfe, 2011). White (2008: 98–9) has developed a threefold typology of 'brown', 'green' and 'white' issues: 'brown' defined in terms of urban life and pollution, 'green' meaning conservation and 'wilderness' concerns and 'white' referring to the impact of new technologies and various laboratory practices. Lynch and Stretesky (2007: 251) alternatively propose that green criminology should be concerned with the critical examination of environmental policies, offering meaningful alternatives where appropriate and environmental justice.

Major themes and topics of green criminology include pollution and regulation, corporate criminality and environmental impacts, health and safety breaches with environmentally damaging consequences; syndicated crime and official corruption in legal and illegal waste disposal, impacts of law enforcement and military operations on landscapes, water supply, air quality and living organisms and forms of law enforcement and rule regulation relevant to all these (South *et al.*, 2013; Eman *et al.*, 2009).

There are close links between green criminology and the concept of the risk society (Beck, 1992) which – which we have seen elsewhere – considers environmental problems and challenges to be threats created by modernity, globalization and transnational production and reproduction. It is highly relevant to criminology to maintain awareness of new technologies – for example, in biosciences and nanotechnology – while also critically reflecting on past mistakes, such as the dangerous disposal of radioactive waste and more recently of e-waste.

A key development in green criminology has been the call for a greater awareness of the harms and criminal acts committed against non-human species. The concept of speciesism has been employed to describe the devaluing and prejudicial treatment of other species as less worthy of concern, compassion or justice than humans. Best and Nocella (2004: 13) define speciesism as being critical of assumptions 'that non-human species exist to serve the needs of the human species, that animals are in various senses inferior to human beings, and therefore that one can favour human over non-human interests according to species status alone'.

Mainstream criminology tends to be anthropocentric, positioning and privileging human beings as the central and most significant species. A critique of speciesism questions this and the denial of the extension of rights to other non-human species (Beirne, 2009, 1995; Sollund, 2013). The huge international trade in wildlife as live bodies or as harvested 'parts and products' has largely been overlooked until recently but is now widely recognized, with trafficking and related animal abuse now better understood and the subject of a growing number of studies (Schneider, 2012; Beirne, 2009; Wyatt, 2012).

Some are uneasy about the label 'green' which, in some situations and some countries, particularly where green political parties are well established, can be seen as politically loaded. This view does not dispute that academic studies should engage with environmental matters but argues for the need to avoid political and politicized associations and banners. In some cases, where emotion and controversy may coincide, some may feel that their scientific neutrality and credibility will be questioned if they are associated with an explicitly 'green' position, group or body of work. Of course, there are other writers and researchers who positively embrace a political statement about their research because they believe this can add critical weight and transparency. Modest debate may continue regarding the most appropriate label or name for a criminology concerned with the environment, and some criminologists will argue that most relevant work can be carried out under the headings of 'corporate crime' and 'organized crime'. Quite simply, the term *green criminology* need not be employed by those who do not find it useful.

Spencer and Fitzgerald (2013) criticize green criminology for neglecting the field of victimology and victims and for being insufficiently reflexive about its attributed modernist assumptions. There is nevertheless considerable variety in the analytical and theoretical positions taken by those who might be called green criminologists, so the criticism may not apply to all or be accepted as valid or useful even if 'accurate' in some cases. Spencer and Fitzgerald also observe that green criminology pays less attention to victims than to offenders or offences. Yet a considerable amount of work in green criminology and environmental justice is concerned with victimization.

Walters (2010) notes that many acts of eco crime create devastating conditions for the lives of local people. The contamination of drinking water, the degradation of soil and the pollution of air and land all expose people – usually those in poor and developing countries – to substantial health risks. Acts of eco crime are linked to poverty and social dislocation, as well as the mental and physical debilitation, of people who are victims of corporations and states which deliberately violate environmental agreements.

White (2013: 243) argues that green criminology has been surprisingly neglectful of political economy, after all, 'environmental harm takes place within the overarching context of a distinct global political economy'. Thus, while much work has exposed

> specific types of criminal or harmful environmental actions or omissions . . . what is less common are examples of study which locate these harms, crimes, injustices and corrupt practices within the context of an explicit theoretical understanding of the state or economic relations.

Long *et al.* (2012) nevertheless have applied the 'treadmill of production' theoretical model to examine how environmental harms are the direct result of processes of production, growth and capital accumulation, supported by an alignment of corporate and state interests. Such interests favour forms of 'business as usual' which embed resistance to calls for action on urgent matters such as the causes of climate change (Lynch *et al.*, 2010; Fussey and South, 2012; Kramer and Michalowski, 2012).

Ruggiero and South (2013) argue that a political economy approach to environmental harms should pose questions about the long-term outcomes of development processes and how these impact on the limited resources of the planet, while gross domestic product (GDP), which they argue is the most powerful number in the world, should be carefully deconstructed. Thus, for decades the GDP mantra has dominated public debate and the media, with countries being ranked and hierarchies arranged accordingly. Policies are designed with an eye to their potential effect on this number, and even the necessity to curb greenhouse gas emissions is subordinated to the power of this artificial measurement (Fioramonti, 2013). During World War II, monitoring the GDP was meant to provide the US with regular statistical data about its economic performance in relation to its rival countries or enemies. After the war, the GDP was not just a number but also a propaganda tool, supposedly signalling the superiority of the US over the Soviet Union, which also resorted to that powerful number to boast about its economic performance.

Currently, with the EU seeking stability and growth, the value of GDP determines austerity cuts to public provision in areas such as health and education. The principles of equity, social justice and collective well-being are overshadowed by calculations of output and development. In the US, the defeat of the current economic crisis, as well as that of terrorism, is linked with economic growth as citizens are encouraged to shop and buy anything, whether needed or not, to assist the economy via consumerist patriotism.

Ruggiero and South (2013) nevertheless observe that GDP does not adequately capture costs to the environment, nor does it assess the sustainability of the growth that is occurring. In fact, GDP counts costs to the environment in a positive manner as officially these reflect enterprise, productivity and wealth. The alternative view is that depletion of resources should equate to diminishing wealth and a declining economic future. The authors observe that this type of rampant and damaging economic development should enter the domain of criminological interest as, in the past, have other acts that deplete resources and actors who evade public policies which aim to protect the public good.

Traditional neoliberal thinkers such as Hayek (1973) have informed us that economic initiative forges a 'spontaneous order', a utopian state of affairs to which market actors will attempt to adhere but only rarely will they approximate. Deviant elites harming the environment translate this utopia into concrete practice, albeit such translation requires violation of rules and illegality. In their case, total freedom 'spontaneously' leads to crime, a form of 'creative destruction' which is more real than metaphorical. Such destruction targets not only institutional frameworks and traditional forms of state sovereignty but also 'social relations, welfare provisions, ways of life and thought, reproductive activities, attachment to the land and habits of the heart' (Harvey, 2005: 3). In advocating the maximization of the reach and frequency of market transactions, neoliberalism has sought to bring all human action into the domain of the market. The consequences of this economic belief system are that markets are required to replace governments and economics should be entrusted with the task of abolishing politics, seen as a cumbersome obstacle to freedom of choice. Economics as a 'science' conceived by neoliberalism cannot accept being hindered by human and political choice (Terni, 2011).

Challenging growth implies a critique of consumption, rendered by into a critique of wants. This involves a comparison between what one wants and what others have and a realization that an achieved level of material wealth is likely to be less satisfying while others possess more (Skidelsky and Skidelsky, 2012). 'Wants' come in the form of 'status spending', namely consumption which makes us feel superior to others, or as indicators of our own success in accumulating money. Ruggiero and South (2013) pertinently observe that this dual critique of economic neoliberalism and of consumption-driven social life could be a powerful future direction for green criminology. Some of this is captured in proposals for an international law of ecocide and the accompanying promotion of a green sensibility and green economy (Higgins *et al.*, 2013).

Like all variants of critical criminology, the green one addresses social and political dynamics which cause collective harm and aims to investigate how this shapes lawmaking and determines the very definition of what is officially identified as crime. It is within this analytical tradition that green criminology seems set to continue its empirical and theoretical work. This is very much the case in the following discussion of animal rights and their treatment by human beings.

Animal rights

Animal rights proponents argue that all, non-human animals are entitled to the possession of their own existence and that their most basic interests – for example the need to avoid suffering – should receive the same consideration as similar interests of human beings. Animals have the *right* to be treated as the individuals they are, with their own desires and needs, rather than as unfeeling property. They should no longer be viewed as food, clothing, research subjects, entertainment or beasts of burden.

Critics of animal rights argue that nonhuman animals are unable to enter into a social contract and thus cannot possess rights, a view made by the philosopher Roger Scruton (1998), who argues that, as only humans have duties and responsibilities, only they can have rights, which is a rather interesting take on the communitarianism we encounter elsewhere in this book. Utilitarianism argues that animals may be used as resources so long as there is no unnecessary suffering. Certain forms of animal rights activism, such as the destruction of fur farms and animal laboratories by the Animal Liberation Front, have also attracted criticism, including from within the animal rights movement itself, as well as prompted reaction from the authorities and legislators. But these debates are not new and have been with us in some form since antiquity, which demonstrates that history does not necessarily and in all cases follow a simple social progress model (Hopkins Burke, 2012).

From the beginning . . . a selective history

In the *Book of Genesis* Adam is given 'dominion over the fish of the sea, and over the fowl of the air, and over the cattle, and over all the earth, and over every creeping thing that creepeth upon the earth'. Dominion nevertheless need not entail property rights, but it has been interpreted, by some, over the centuries to imply ownership.

Philosopher Bernard Rollin (2010: 112) thus argues that '*dominion* does not entail or allow abuse any more than does dominion a parent enjoys over a child' and notes that the Ten Commandments 'required that animals be granted a day of rest along with humans'. Moreover 'plowing with an ox and an ass together' is forbidden (Deut. 22: 10–11), and this is said to originate from the hardship that an ass would suffer by being compelled to keep up with an ox, which is, of course, far more powerful. Similarly, we find the prohibition against 'muzzling an ox when it treads out the grain' (Deut. 25: 4–5) and even an environmental prohibition against destroying trees when besieging a city (Deut. 20:

19–20). These ancient regulations – now, virtually forgotten – speak of an ancient aware-ness of the status of animals as ends in themselves.

Pythagoras (ca. 580–ca. 500 BCE) urged respect for animals, believing that human and nonhuman souls were reincarnated from human to animal and vice versa. Aristotle (384–22 BCE) later took a different view and argued that nonhuman animals have no interests of their own, ranking them far below humans in the Great Chain of Being. In creating a taxonomy of animals, he observed some similarities between humans and other species, but stated that for the most part animals lacked reason (*logos*), reasoning (*logismos*), thought (*dianoia, nous*), and belief (*doxa*). Theophrastus – a student of Aristotle – nonetheless later argued that animals do possess reasoning (*logismos*) and was opposed to the eating of meat on the grounds that it robbed them of life and was therefore unjust. Sorabji (1993) observes that later and current attitudes to animals can be traced to the heirs of the Western Christian tradition which appropriated the hierarchy that Aristotle sought to preserve.

Animal protection

The first known animal protection legislation in Europe was passed in Ireland in 1635. It prohibited pulling wool off sheep and the attaching of ploughs to the tails of horses, refer-ring to 'the cruelty used to beasts'. In 1641, the first legal code to protect domestic ani-mals in North America was passed by the Massachusetts Bay Colony, whose constitution was based on The *Body of Liberties* by the Reverend Nathaniel Ward (1578–1652), who proposed that 'no man shall exercise any Tirrany or Crueltie toward any brute Creature which are usually kept for man's use'.

Animal welfare laws were passed in 1654 as part of the ordinances of the government of Oliver Cromwell – who personally hated blood sports – and which lasted from 1653 to 1659, following the English Civil War. The Puritans interpreted the biblical domin-ion of man over animals to mean responsible stewardship, rather than ownership. But, the opposition to blood sports became part of what was seen as Puritan interference in people's lives – a kind of seventeenth-century 'nanny state thesis' – and the animal protec-tion laws were overturned during the Restoration when Charles II was returned to the throne in 1660.

The greatest influence of the seventeenth century – and a lasting one – was the French philosopher Rene Descartes (1596–1650), whose *Meditations* (Decartes, 1641) informed attitudes about animals well into the twentieth century. Descartes – writing during the scientific revolution – proposed a mechanistic theory of the universe with the aim of showing that the world could be mapped without allusion to subjective experience (Kete, 2002) and it was an approach he extended to the issue of animal consciousness. Mind, for Descartes, was a thing apart from the physical universe, a separate substance, linking human beings to the mind of God. Non-humans, on the other hand, were simply com-plex automata, with no souls, minds or reason.

The English philosopher John Locke (1632–1704) nonetheless commented, in *Some Thoughts Concerning Education* (1693), that animals do have feelings and that unnecessary cruelty toward them is morally wrong, but the right not to be harmed adheres either to the owner of the animal or to the human being who is damaged by being cruel. Discussing the importance of preventing children from tormenting animals, he wrote: 'For the custom of tormenting and killing of beasts will, by degrees, harden their minds even towards men'.

This is a position which resonates with that of Thomas Aquinas (1225–74) whose argument can be found at 1 Corinthians 9: 9–10, when Paul asks: 'Is it for oxen that God is concerned? Does he not speak entirely for our sake? It was written for our sake'. Christian philosophers have interpreted this to mean that humans have no direct duty to non-human animals but do have a duty to protect them from the effects of engaging in cruelty (Waldau, 2001).

The German philosopher Immanuel Kant (1724–1804) – following in the tradition established by Aquinas – was opposed to the idea that humans have direct duties toward nonhumans. For Kant, cruelty to animals was wrong only because it was bad for human-kind. 'Cruelty to animals is contrary to man's duty to *himself*, because it deadens in him the feeling of sympathy for their sufferings, and thus a natural tendency that is very useful to morality in relation to other *human beings* is weakened' (1785: part II, paras 16 and 17).

Jean-Jacques Rousseau (1712–78) argued for the inclusion of animals in natural law on the grounds of sentience (the capacity to feel, perceive, or experience subjectively) and encouraged parents to raise their children on a vegetarian diet, believing that the food of the culture a child was raised eating, played an important role in the character and dispo-sition they would develop as adults. Four years later, one of the founders of modern utili-tarianism, the English philosopher Jeremey Bentham (1748–1832) – although opposed to the concept of natural rights – argued that it was the ability to suffer that should be the benchmark of how we treat other beings. It is the capacity for suffering which gives the right to equal consideration. If rationality were the criterion, he argued, many humans, including infants and the disabled, would also have to be treated as though they were things. He did not conclude that humans and non-humans had equal moral significance but argued that the interests of the latter should be taken into account.

The nineteenth century saw an explosion of interest in animal protection, particularly in England. Legge and Brooman (1997) note that the educated classes became concerned about attitudes toward the old, the needy, children and the insane, while this concern was extended to non-humans. Before the nineteenth century, there had been prosecutions for poor treatment of animals but only because of the damage to the animal as property. But from 1800 onwards, there were attempts to introduce animal protection legislation. In 1809, for example, Lord Erskine (1750–1823) introduced a bill to protect cattle and horses from malicious wounding, wanton cruelty and beating. The bill was passed by the Lords but opposed in the Commons because it was said that it would be used against the 'lower orders' when the real culprits would be their employers (Phelps, 2007).

In 1821, the Treatment of Horses bill was introduced by Colonel Richard Martin (1754–1834), a member of Parliament for Galway in Ireland, but was lost amongst laugh-ter in the House of Commons that the next thing would be rights for asses, dogs and cats. Nicknamed 'Humanity Dick' by George IV, Martin finally succeeded in 1822 with his 'Ill Treatment of Horses and Cattle Bill' – or 'Martin's Act' as it became known – which was the first major piece of animal protection legislation in the world.

Other countries followed in passing legislation or making decisions that favoured ani-mals. In 1822, the courts in New York ruled that wanton cruelty to animals was a mis-demeanour at common law. In France in 1850, Jacques Phillippe Delmas de Grammont succeeded in having the *Loi Grammont* passed, outlawing cruelty against domestic ani-mals, and leading to years of arguments about whether bulls could be classed as domes-tic to ban bullfighting. The state of Washington followed in 1859, New York in 1866, California in 1868 and Florida in 1889. In England, a series of amendments extended the reach of the 1822 Act, which became the Cruelty to Animals Act 1835, outlawing cockfighting, baiting, and dog fighting, followed by another amendment in 1849 and again in 1876 (Phelps, 2007).

Richard Martin soon realized that magistrates did not take his act seriously, and it was not reliably enforced. But the legislation was supported by various social reformers who were not parliamentarians and an informal network had gathered around the efforts of Reverend Arthur Broome (1779–1837) to create a voluntary organization which would promote kindness toward animals. Broome made several – at first unsuccessful – attempts to form a Society for the Prevention of Cruelty to Animals (SPCA) that would bring together the patronage of persons who were of social rank and committed to social reforms. The society became the Royal Society in 1840, when it was granted a royal charter by Queen Victoria, herself strongly opposed to vivisection (Phelps, 2007).

The development in England of the concept of animal rights was strongly supported by the German philosopher Arthur Schopenhauer (1788–1860), who wrote that Europeans were 'awakening more and more to a sense that beasts have rights, in proportion as the strange notion is being gradually overcome and outgrown, that the animal kingdom came into existence solely for the benefit and pleasure of man'. He nevertheless stopped short of advocating vegetarianism, arguing that, so long as an animal's death was quick, men would suffer more by not eating meat than animals would suffer by being eaten. Schopenhauer also argued that the reason people succumbed to the *'unnatural diet'* of meat-eating was because of the unnatural cold climate and the necessity of meat for survival in such a climate, for fruits and vegetables could not be dependably cultivated at that time. He nonetheless applauded the animal protection movement in England and argued against the dominant Kantian orthodoxy that animal cruelty is wrong only insofar as it brutalizes humans (Phelps, 2007).

The first animal protection group in the US – the American Society for the Prevention of Cruelty to Animals (ASPCA) – was founded by Henry Bergh in 1866. Bergh had been appointed by President Abraham Lincoln to a diplomatic post in Russia and had been disturbed by the mistreatment of animals he witnessed there. He consulted with the president of the RSPCA in London and returned to the US to speak out against bullfights, cockfights and the beating of horses. He created a 'Declaration of the Rights of Animals' and in 1866 persuaded the New York state legislature to pass anti-cruelty legislation and to grant the ASPCA the authority to enforce it.

In 1875, the Irish social reformer Frances Power Cobbe (1822–1904) founded the Society for the Protection of Animals Liable to Vivisection, the world's first organization opposed to animal research, which became the National Anti-Vivisection Society. In 1880, the English feminist Anna Kingsford (1846–88) became one of the first English women to graduate in medicine, after studying for her degree in Paris, and the only student at the time to do so without having experimented on animals. She published *The Perfect Way in Diet* (1881), advocating vegetarianism, and in the same year founded the Food Reform Society. She was also vocal in her opposition to experimentation on animals. In 1898, Cobbe set up the British Union for the Abolition of Vivisection, with which she campaigned against the use of dogs in research, coming close to success with the 1919 Dogs (Protection) Bill, which almost became law.

As the interest in animal protection grew in the late 1890s, attitudes towards animals among scientists began to harden. They embraced the idea that what they saw as anthropomorphism – the attribution of human qualities to nonhumans – was unscientific.

Animals had to be approached as physiological entities only, as Ivan Pavlov wrote in 1927, 'without any need to resort to fantastic speculations as to the existence of any possible subjective states'. It was a position that takes us back to Descartes in the seventeenth century, non-humans are purely mechanical, with no rationality and perhaps even no consciousness (Ryder, 2000).

Friedrich Nietzsche (1844–1900) found other reasons to defend animals, observing that 'the sight of blind suffering is the spring of the deepest emotion'. Writing 'for man is the cruelest animal. At tragedies, bull fights, and crucifixions hath he hitherto been happiest on earth; and when he invented his hell, behold, that was his heaven on earth'. Throughout his writings, he speaks of the human being as an animal (Nietzsche, 2008).

Even the leading advocates of animal rights seem to have recoiled from basing their claim on the only argument which can ultimately be held to be a really sufficient one: the assertion that animals, as well as humans, however, of course, to a far less extent, are possessed of a distinctive individuality and, therefore, are in justice entitled to live their lives with a due measure of that 'restricted freedom' to which Herbert Spencer alludes when he argued that there was no point in claiming rights for animals if those rights were subordinated to human desire and took issue with the idea that the life of a human might have more moral worth (Salt, 1894).

In 1902, Lizzy Lind af Hageby (1878–1963), a Swedish feminist, and a friend, Lisa Shartau, travelled to England to study medicine at the London School of Medicine for Women, intending to learn enough to become authoritative anti-vivisection campaigners. In the course of their studies, they witnessed several animal experiments and published the details as *The Shambles of Science: Extracts from the Diary of Two Students of Physiology* in 1903. Their allegations included that they had seen a brown terrier dog dissected while conscious, which prompted angry denials from the researcher, William Bayliss, and his colleagues. After Stephen Coleridge of the National Anti-Vivisection Society accused Bayliss of having violated the Cruelty to Animals Act 1876, Bayliss sued and won, convincing a court that the animal had been anaesthetized as required by the act (Mason, 1997).

In response, anti-vivisection campaigners commissioned a statue of the dog to be erected in Battersea Park in 1906, with the plaque: 'Men and Women of England, how long shall these Things be?' There was uproar among medical students, leading to frequent vandalism of the statue and the need for a 24-hour police guard. The affair culminated in riots in 1907 when 1,000 medical students clashed with police, suffragettes and trade unionists in Trafalgar Square. Battersea Council removed the statue from the park under cover of darkness two years later (Mason, 1997).

The significance of the affair lay in the relationships that formed in support of the 'Brown Dog Done to Death', which became a symbol of the oppression the women's suffrage movement felt at the hands of the male political and medical establishment. Both sides saw themselves as heirs to the future. The students saw the women and trade unionists as representatives of anti-science sentimentality, and the women saw themselves as progressive, with the students and their teachers belonging to a previous age (Mason, 1997).

The development of veganism

Members of the English Vegetarian Society who avoided the use of eggs and animal milk in the nineteenth and early twentieth century were known as strict vegetarians. The

International Vegetarian Union cites an article informing readers of alternatives to shoe leather in the Vegetarian Society's magazine in 1851 as evidence of the existence of a group that sought to avoid animal products entirely. There was increasing unease within the Society from the start of the twentieth century onwards with regards to egg and milk consumption, and in 1923 its magazine wrote that the 'ideal position for vegetarians is [complete] abstinence from animal products' (Leneman, 1999).

Mahatma Gandhi (1869–1948) argued in 1931 before a meeting of the Society in London that vegetarianism should be pursued in the interests of animals and not only as a human health issue. In 1944, several members, led by Donald Watson (1910–2016), decided to break from the Vegetarian Society over the issue of egg and milk use. Watson coined the term 'vegan' for those whose diet included no animal products, and they formed the British Vegan Society in that year (Davis, 2009).

On coming to power in January 1933, the German Nazi Party had passed a comprehensive set of animal protection laws. Arluke and Sax (1992) observe that the Nazis tried to abolish the distinction between humans and animals, to the point where many people were regarded as less valuable than animals. In April 1933, they passed laws regulating the slaughter of animals. One of their targets was kosher slaughter. In November the *Tierschutzgesetz*, or animal protection law, was introduced, with Adolf Hitler announcing an end to animal cruelty: '*Im neuen Reich darf es keine Tierquälerei mehr geben*' (In the new Reich, no more animal cruelty will be allowed). It was followed in July 1934 by the *Reichsjagdgesetz*, prohibiting hunting; in July 1935, by the *Naturschutzgesetz*, environmental legislation; in November 1937, by a law regulating animal transport in cars; and, in September 1938, by a similar law dealing with animals on trains. Hitler was a vegetarian in the later years of his life; several members of his inner circle, including Rudolf Hess, Joseph Goebels and Heinrich Himmlers, adopted some form of vegetarianism (Arluke and Sax, 1992).

Despite the proliferation of animal protection legislation, animals still had no legal rights. Legge and Brooman (1997) observe that existing legislation was very much tied to the idea of human interests, whether protecting human sensibilities by outlawing cruelty or protecting property rights by making sure animals were not harmed. The over-exploitation of fishing stocks, for example, is viewed as harming the environment for people; the hunting of animals to extinction means that humans in the future will derive no enjoyment from them; poaching results in financial loss to the owner; and so on.

Notwithstanding the interest in animal welfare of the previous century, the situation for animals deteriorated in the twentieth century, in particular, after the Second World War, as billions of animals were raised and killed for food on a scale considered impossible before the war. This was in part because of the increase in the numbers used in animal research – 300 in the UK in 1875, 19,084 in 1903 and 2.8 million in 2005 (50–100 million worldwide), and a modern annual estimated range of 10 million to upwards of 100 million in the US – but mostly because of the industrialization of farming on a scale that would have been unthinkable before the war (Williams and DeMello, 2007).

Development of direct action

In the early 1960s in England, support for animal rights began to coalesce around the issue of blood sports, particularly hunting deer, foxes and otters, using dogs, an aristocratic and middle-class English practice, stoutly defended in the name of protecting rural traditions. The psychologist Richard D. Ryder – who became involved with the animal rights movement in the late 1960s – observes that the new chair of the League Against Cruel Sports tried in 1963 to steer it away from confronting members of the hunt, which triggered the formation that year of a direct-action breakaway group, the Hunt Saboteurs Association. This was set up by a journalist, John Prestige, who had witnessed a pregnant deer being chased into a village and killed by the Devon and Somerset Staghounds. The practice of sabotaging hunts (e.g. by misleading the dogs with scents or horns) spread throughout south-east England, particularly around university towns, leading to violent confrontations when the huntsmen attacked the 'sabs' (Ryder, 2000).

The controversy spread to the RSPCA, which had grown away from its radical roots to become a conservative group with charity status and royal patronage. It had failed to speak out against hunting, and indeed counted huntsmen among its members. As with the League Against Cruel Sports, this position gave rise to a splinter group, the RSPCA Reform Group, which sought to radicalize the organization, leading to chaotic meetings of the group's ruling council and successful (although short-lived) efforts to change it from within by electing to the council members who would argue from an animal rights perspective and force the RSPCA to address issues such as hunting, factory farming and animal experimentation. Ryder himself was elected to the council in 1971 and served as its chair from 1977 to 1979 (Ryder, 2000).

Formation of the Oxford Group

The same period saw writers and academics begin to speak out again in favour of animal rights. Ruth Harrison published *Animal Machines* (1964), an influential critique of factory farming, and on October 10, 1965, the novelist Brigid Brophy had an article, 'The Rights of Animals', published in *The Sunday Times* (Ryder, 2000). She wrote:

> The relationship of homo sapiens to the other animals is one of unremitting exploitation. We employ their work; we eat and wear them. We exploit them to serve our superstitions: whereas we used to sacrifice them to our gods and tear out their entrails in order to foresee the future, we now sacrifice them to science, and experiment on their entrails in the hope – or on the mere off chance – that we might thereby see a little more clearly into the present. . . . To us it seems incredible that the Greek philosophers should have scanned so deeply into right and wrong and yet never noticed the immorality of slavery. Perhaps 3000 years from now it will seem equally incredible that we do not notice the immorality of our own oppression of animals.
>
> (Ryder, 2000: 5–6)

These publications led to an explosion of interest in the relationship between humans and nonhumans. Brophy's article was discovered by a group of postgraduate philosophy students at the University of Oxford, Rosalind and Stanley Godlovitch (husband and wife from Canada), John Harris and David Wood, who now became known as the Oxford Group. They decided to put together a symposium to discuss the theory of animal rights (Ryder, 2000). Around this time, Ryder wrote several letters to *The Daily Telegraph* criticizing animal experimentation, based on incidents he had witnessed in laboratories. The letters, published in April and May 1969, were seen by Brigid Brophy, who put Ryder in touch with the Godlovitches and Harris. Ryder also started distributing pamphlets in

Oxford protesting against experiments on animals; it was in one of these pamphlets in 1970 that he coined the term 'speciesism' to describe the exclusion of nonhuman animals from the protections offered to humans (Waldau, 2001).

From 1982 onwards, a series of articles by Tom Regan led to his *The Case for Animal Rights* (1984), in which he argues that non-human animals are 'subjects-of-a-life' and therefore possessors of moral rights, a work regarded as a key text in animal rights theory. Regan (2001) observed that philosophers had written more about animal rights in the previous 20 years than in the 2,000 years before that.

Animal Liberation Front

In 1971, a law student, Ronnie Lee formed a branch of the Hunt Saboteurs Association in Luton, later calling it the Band of Mercy after a nineteenth-century RSPCA youth group. The Band attacked hunters' vehicles by slashing tyres and breaking windows, calling it 'active compassion'. In November 1973, they engaged in their first act of arson when they set fire to a Hoechst Pharmaceuticals research laboratory, claiming responsibility as a 'nonviolent guerilla organization' dedicated to the liberation of animals from all forms of cruelty and persecution at the hands of mankind (Molland, 2004: 74).

Lee and another activist were sentenced to three years in prison in 1974, paroled after 12 months. In 1976, Lee brought together the remaining Band of Mercy activists along with some fresh faces to start a leaderless resistance movement calling it the Animal Liberation Front (ALF). ALF activists see themselves as a modern Underground Railroad passing animals removed from farms and laboratories to sympathetic veterinarians, safe houses and sanctuaries. Some activists also engaged in threats, intimidation, and arson, acts which lost the movement sympathy in mainstream public opinion. From the 1980s through to the early 2000s, there was an increased level of violence by animal rights extremist groups directed at individuals and institutions associated with animal research.

In the 1980s, animal rights became associated with punk subculture and ideologies, particularly straight-edge hardcore punk in the US and anarcho-punk in the UK. This association continues on into the twenty-first century, as evidenced by the prominence of vegan punk events such as Fluff Festival in Europe.

Philosophical and legal approaches to animal rights

The two main philosophical approaches to animal rights are utilitarian and rights-based. The former is exemplified by Peter Singer and the latter by Tom Regan and Gary Francione. Their differences reflect a distinction between ethical theories that judge the rightness of an act by its consequences (consequentialism/teleological ethics or utilitarianism), and those that focus on the principle behind the act, almost regardless of consequences (deontological ethics). Deontologists argue that there are acts we should never perform, even if failing to do so entails a worse outcome.

Utilitarian approaches

Nussbaum (2004) observes that utilitarianism – starting with Jeremy Bentham and John Stuart Mill – has contributed more to the recognition of the moral status of animals than any other ethical theory. The utilitarian philosopher most associated with animal rights is

Peter Singer, professor of bioethics at Princeton University. Singer is not a rights theorist but nonetheless uses the language of rights to discuss how we ought to treat individuals. He is a preference utilitarian meaning that he judges the rightness of an act by the extent to which it satisfies the preferences (interests) of those affected.

His position is that there is no reason not to give equal consideration to the interests of human and non-humans, although his principle of equality does not require identical treatment. A mouse and a man both have an interest in not being kicked, and there are no moral or logical grounds for failing to accord those interests equal weight. Interests are predicated on the ability to suffer, nothing more, and once it is established that a being has interests, those interests must be given equal consideration. Singer quotes the English philosopher Henry Sidgwick (1838–1900): 'The good of any one individual is of no more importance, from the point of view . . . of the Universe, than the good of any other' (Singer, 1990: 111).

Singer argues that equality of consideration is a prescription, not an assertion of fact: if the equality of the sexes were based only on the idea that men and women were equally intelligent, we would have to abandon the practice of equal consideration if this were later found to be false. But the moral idea of equality does not depend on matters of fact such as intelligence, physical strength or moral capacity. Equality therefore cannot be grounded on the outcome of scientific investigations into the intelligence of non-humans. All that matters is whether they can suffer.

Commentators on all sides of the debate now accept that animals suffer and feel pain, although it was not always so. Bernard Rollin professor of philosophy, animal sciences, and biomedical sciences at Colorado State University, observes that the influence of Descartes continued to be felt until the 1980s. Veterinarians trained in the US before 1989 were taught to ignore pain and at least one major veterinary hospital in the 1960s did not stock narcotic analgesics for animal pain control. In his interactions with scientists, he was often asked to 'prove; that animals are conscious, and to provide 'scientifically acceptable' evidence that they could feel pain (Rollin, 2012).

Scientific publications have nevertheless made it clear since the 1980s that the majority of researchers do believe animals suffer and feel pain, although it continues to be argued that their suffering may be reduced by an inability to experience the same dread of anticipation as humans or to remember the suffering as vividly. The problem of animal suffering, and animal consciousness in general, arose primarily because it was argued that animals have no language. Singer (1990) observes that, if language were needed to communicate pain, it would often be impossible to know when humans are in pain, though we can observe pain behaviour and make a calculated guess based on it. He argues that there is no reason to suppose that the pain behaviour of nonhumans would have a different meaning from the pain behaviour of humans.

Rights-based approach

Tom Regan, professor emeritus of philosophy at North Carolina State University, argues in *The Case for Animal Rights* (1984) that nonhuman animals are what he calls 'subjects-of-a-life' and as such are bearers of rights. He argues that, because the moral rights of humans are based on their possession of certain cognitive abilities, and because these abilities are also possessed by at least some non-human animals, such animals must have the same moral rights as humans. Although only humans act as moral agents, both marginal-case humans, such as infants, and at least some non-humans must have the status of 'moral patients'.

Moral patients are unable to formulate moral principles and as such are unable to do right or wrong, even though what they do may be beneficial or harmful. Only moral agents are able to engage in moral action. Animals for Regan have 'intrinsic value' as subjects-of-a-life and cannot be regarded as a means to an end, a view that places him firmly in the abolitionist camp. His theory does not extend to all animals but only to those that can be regarded as subjects-of-a-life. He argues that all normal mammals of at least one year of age would qualify.

Whereas Singer is primarily concerned with improving the treatment of animals and accepts that, in some hypothetical scenarios, individual animals might be used legitimately to further human or non-human ends, Regan believes we ought to treat non-human animals as we would humans. He applies the strict Kantian ideal – which Kant himself applied only to humans – that they ought never to be sacrificed as a means to an end and must be treated as ends in themselves.

Abolitionism

Gary Francione, professor of law and philosophy at Rutgers Law School in Newark, is a leading abolitionist and argues that animals need only one right, the right not to be owned. Everything else would follow from that paradigm shift. He observes that, although most people would condemn the mistreatment of animals, and in many countries, there are laws that seem to reflect those concerns, 'in practice the legal system allows any use of animals, however abhorrent'. The law only requires that any suffering not be 'unnecessary'. In deciding what counts as 'unnecessary', the interests of an animal are weighed against the interests of human beings, and the latter almost always prevail (Francione, 1995).

Francione's *Animals, Property, and the Law* (1995) was the first extensive jurisprudential treatment of animal rights where the situation of animals is compared to the treatment of slaves in the US, where legislation existed that appeared to protect them, but the courts ignored that, and the institution of slavery itself rendered the protection unenforceable. He offers as an example the US Animal Welfare Act, which he describes as an example of symbolic legislation, intended to assuage public concern about the treatment of animals but was, in practice, difficult to implement.

He argues that a focus on animal welfare, rather than animal rights, may worsen the position of animals by making the public feel comfortable about using them and entrenching the view of them as property. He calls animal rights groups who pursue animal welfare issues, the 'new welfarists', arguing that they have more in common with nineteenth-century animal protectionists than with the animal rights movement; indeed, the terms *animal protection* and *protectionism* are increasingly favoured.

Critics and criticisms

R.D. Frey professor of philosophy at Bowling Green State University, is like Singer – a preference utilitarian – but reaches a very different conclusion, arguing in *Interests and Rights* (1980) that animals have no interests for the utilitarian to take into account. He argues that interests are dependent on desire and that no desire can exist without a corresponding belief. Animals have no beliefs, because a belief state requires the ability to hold a second-order belief – a belief about the belief – which he argues requires language.

Carl Cohen professor of philosophy at the University of Michigan, argues that rights holders must be able to distinguish between their own interests and what is right. He rejects Singer's argument that, since a brain-damaged human could not make a moral judgement, these cannot be used as the distinguishing characteristic for determining who is awarded rights. Cohen argues that the test for moral judgement is not a test to be administered to humans one by one but should be applied to the capacity of members of the species in general (Cohen, 1986).

Judge Richard Posner debated the issue of animal rights in 2001 with Peter Singer and posits that his moral intuition tells him that human beings prefer their own. If a dog threatens a human infant, even if it requires causing more pain to the dog to stop it than the dog would have caused to the infant, then we favour the child. It would be monstrous to spare the dog (Posner and Singer, 2001).

Singer challenges this by arguing that formerly unequal rights for gays, women and certain races were justified using the same set of intuitions. Posner replies that equality in civil rights did not occur because of ethical arguments, but because facts mounted that there were no morally significant differences between humans based on race, sex, or sexual orientation that would support inequality. If and when similar facts emerge about humans and animals, the differences in rights will erode too. But facts will drive equality, not ethical arguments that run contrary to instinct. Posner calls his approach 'soft utilitarianism', in contrast to Singer's 'hard utilitarianism'. He argues:

> The "soft" utilitarian position on animal rights is a moral intuition of many, probably most, Americans. We realize that animals feel pain, and we think that to inflict pain without a reason is bad. Nothing of practical value is added by dressing up this intuition in the language of philosophy; much is lost when the intuition is made a stage in a logical argument. When kindness toward animals is levered into a duty of weighting the pains of animals and of people equally, bizarre vistas of social engineering are opened up.
>
> (Posner, 2004: 116)

Roger Scruton, the British philosopher, argues that rights imply obligations. Every legal privilege imposes a burden on the one who does not possess that privilege; that is 'your right may be my duty'. Scruton therefore regards the emergence of the animal rights movement as 'the strangest cultural shift within the liberal worldview', because the idea of rights and responsibilities is, he argues, distinctive to the human condition, and it makes no sense to spread them beyond our own species (Scruton, 1998).

He accuses animal rights advocates of 'pre-scientific' anthropomorphism, attributing traits to animals that are, he says, Beatrix Potter–like, where 'only man is vile'. It is within this fiction that the appeal of animal rights lies. The world of animals is non-judgemental, filled with dogs who return our affection almost no matter what we do to them, and cats who pretend to be affectionate when, in fact, they care only about themselves. It is a fantasy, a world of escape. Scruton (1998: 76) singled out Peter Singer, observing that his works

> [c]ontain little or no philosophical argument. They derive their radical moral conclusions from a vacuous utilitarianism that counts the pain and pleasure of all living

things as equally significant and that ignores just about everything that has been said in our philosophical tradition about the real distinction between persons and animals.

All arguments which allow those involved in the routine brutalizing torture and murder of animals, techniques of neutralization to explain and even subjectively excuse their behaviour. We next consider the widespread brutality and cruelty towards animals that is the 'legitimate' central component of factory farming.

(Il)legitimate cruelty to animals

Yuval Noah Harari (2019), professor of world history at the Hebrew University of Jerusalem, takes an evolutionary psychology perspective and argues most convincingly that the fate of industrially farmed animals is one of the most pressing ethical questions of our time. Tens of billions of sentient beings, each with complex sensations and emotions, live and die on a production line. Animals are the main victims of history, and the treatment of domesticated animals is perhaps the worst crime in history. The march of human progress is strewn with dead animals. Even tens of thousands of years ago, our stone-age ancestors were already responsible for a series of ecological disasters. When the first humans reached Australia about 45,000 years ago, they quickly drove to extinction 90% of its large animals. This was the first significant impact that *Homo sapiens* had on the ecosystem of the planet. It was not to be the last.

About 15,000 years ago, humans colonized America, wiping out in the process about 75% of its large mammals. Numerous other species disappeared from Africa, from Eurasia and from the myriad islands around their coasts. The archaeological record of country after country tells the same sad story. The tragedy opens with a scene showing a rich and varied population of large animals, without any trace of *Homo sapiens*. In scene two, humans appear, evidenced by a fossilized bone, a spear point, or perhaps a campfire. Scene three quickly follows, in which men and women occupy centre stage and most large animals, along with many smaller ones, have gone. Altogether, *Homo sapiens* drove to extinction about 50% of all the large terrestrial mammals of the planet before they planted the first wheat field, shaped the first metal tool, wrote the first text or struck the first coin.

The next landmark in human–animal relations was the agricultural revolution: the process by which we turned from nomadic hunter-gathers into farmers living in permanent settlements. It involved the appearance of a completely new life-form on Earth: domesticated animals. Initially, this development might seem to have been of minor importance, as humans only managed to domesticate fewer than 20 species of mammals and birds, compared with the countless thousands of species which remained 'wild'. Yet, with the passing of the centuries, this novel life-form became the norm. Today, more than 90% of all large animals are domesticated ('large' denotes animals that weigh at least a few kilograms). Consider the chicken, for example. Ten thousand years ago, it was a rare bird that was confined to small niches of South Asia. Today, billions of chickens live on almost every continent and island, bar Antarctica. The domesticated chicken is probably the most widespread bird in the annals of planet Earth. If you measure success in terms of numbers, chickens, cows and pigs are the most successful animals ever.

Alas, domesticated species paid for their unparalleled collective success with unprecedented individual suffering. The animal kingdom has known many types of pain and misery for millions of years. Yet the agricultural revolution created completely new kinds of suffering, ones that only worsened with the passing of the generations.

At first sight, domesticated animals may seem much better off than their wild cousins and ancestors. Wild buffaloes spend their days searching for food, water and shelter and are constantly threatened by lions, parasites, floods and droughts. Domesticated cattle, by contrast, enjoy care and protection from humans. People provide cows and calves with food, water and shelter, they treat their diseases, and protect them from predators and natural disasters. True, most cows and calves sooner or later find themselves in the slaughterhouse. Yet does that make their fate any worse than that of wild buffaloes? Is it better to be devoured by a lion than slaughtered by a man? Are crocodile teeth kinder than steel blades?

Harari (2019) argues that what makes the existence of domesticated farm animals particularly cruel is not just the way in which they die but above all how they live. Two competing factors have shaped the living conditions of farm animals: on one hand, humans want meat, milk, eggs, leather, animal muscle-power and amusement; on the other, humans have to ensure the long-term survival and reproduction of farm animals. Theoretically, this should protect animals from extreme cruelty. If a farmer milks his cow without providing her with food and water, milk production will dwindle, and the cow herself will quickly die. Unfortunately, humans can cause tremendous suffering to farm animals in other ways, even while ensuring their survival and reproduction. The root of the problem is that domesticated animals have inherited from their wild ancestors many physical, emotional and social needs that are redundant in farms. Farmers routinely ignore these needs without paying any economic price. They lock animals in tiny cages, mutilate their horns and tails, separate mothers from offspring and selectively breed monstrosities. The animals suffer greatly, yet they live on and multiply.

Harari (2019) asks whether these observations contradict the most basic principles of Darwinian evolution? The theory of evolution maintains that all instincts and drives have evolved in the interest of survival and reproduction. If this is the case, does not this mean that the continuous reproduction of farm animals prove that all their real needs are met? How can a cow have a 'need' that is not really essential for survival and reproduction?

Harari observes that in order to survive and reproduce, ancient wild cattle had to communicate, cooperate and compete effectively. All instincts and drives evolved in order to meet the evolutionary pressures of survival and reproduction. When these pressures disappear, however, the instincts and drives they had shaped do not evaporate instantly. Even if they are no longer instrumental for survival and reproduction, they continue to shape the subjective experiences of the animal. The physical, emotional and social needs of present-day cows, dogs and humans do not reflect their current conditions but rather the evolutionary pressures their ancestors encountered tens of thousands of years ago.

Harari asks a series of rhetorical questions. First, why it is that people today love sweets so much? Well, it is not because in the early twenty-first century, we must gorge on ice cream and chocolate in order to survive. Rather, is it because if our stone-age ancestors came across sweet, ripened fruits, the most sensible thing to do was to eat as many of them as they could as quickly as possible? Second, why is it that young men drive recklessly, get involved in violent rows and hack confidential internet sites? Because they are obeying ancient genetic decrees. Seventy thousand years ago, a young hunter who risked his life chasing a mammoth outshone all his competitors and won the hand of the local beauty – and we are now stuck with his macho genes.

Harari observes that exactly the same evolutionary logic shapes the life of cows and calves in our industrial farms. Ancient wild cattle were social animals. To survive and reproduce, they needed to communicate, cooperate and compete effectively. Like all social mammals, wild cattle learned the necessary social skills through play. Puppies, kittens, calves and children all love to play because evolution implanted this urge in them. In the wild, they needed to play. If they did not, they would not learn the social skills vital for survival and reproduction. If a kitten or calf was born with some rare mutation that made them indifferent to play, they were unlikely to survive or reproduce, just as they would not exist in the first place if their ancestors had not acquired those skills. Similarly, evolution implanted in puppies, kittens, calves and children an overwhelming desire to bond with their mothers. A chance mutation weakening the mother–infant bond was a death sentence.

What happens when farmers now take a young calf, separate her from her mother, put her in a tiny cage, vaccinate her against various diseases, provide her with food and water and then, when she is old enough, artificially inseminate her with bull sperm? From an objective perspective, this calf no longer needs either maternal bonding or playmates to survive and reproduce. All her needs are being taken care of by her human masters. But from a subjective perspective, the calf still feels a strong urge to bond with her mother and to play with other calves. If these urges are not fulfilled, the calf suffers greatly.

Harari (2019) observes that this is the basic lesson of evolutionary psychology: a need shaped thousands of generations ago continues to be felt subjectively even if it is no longer necessary for survival and reproduction in the present. Tragically, the agricultural revolution gave humans the power to ensure the survival and reproduction of domesticated animals while ignoring their subjective needs. In consequence, domesticated animals are collectively the most successful animals in the world, and at the same time, they are individually the most miserable animals that have ever existed.

The situation has only worsened over the last few centuries, during which time traditional agriculture gave way to industrial farming. In traditional societies such as ancient Egypt, the Roman empire or medieval China, humans had a very limited understanding of biochemistry, genetics, zoology and epidemiology. Consequently, their manipulative powers were limited. In medieval villages, chickens ran free between the houses, pecked seeds and worms from the garbage heap and built nests in the barn. If an ambitious peasant tried to lock 1,000 chickens inside a crowded coop, a deadly bird-flu epidemic would probably have resulted, wiping out all the chickens, as well as many villagers. No priest, shaman or witch doctor could have prevented it. But once modern science had deciphered the secrets of birds, viruses and antibiotics, humans could begin to subject animals to extreme living conditions. With the help of vaccinations, medications, hormones, pesticides, central air-conditioning systems and automatic feeders, it is now possible to cram tens of thousands of chickens into tiny coops and produce meat and eggs with unprecedented efficiency.

Harari (2019) observes that the fate of animals in such industrial installations has become one of the most pressing ethical issues of our time, certainly in terms of the numbers involved. These days, most big animals live on industrial farms. We imagine that our planet is populated by lions, elephants, whales and penguins. That may be true of the National Geographic channel, Disney movies and children's fairy tales, but it is no longer true of the real world. The world contains 40,000 lions but, by way of contrast, there are approximately 1 billion domesticated pigs, 500,000 elephants and 1.5 billion domesticated cows, 50 million penguins and 20 billion chickens.

In 2009, there were 1.6 billion wild birds in Europe, counting all species together. That same year, the European meat and egg industry raised 1.9 billion chickens. Altogether, the domesticated animals of the world weigh about 700 million tonnes, compared with 300 million tonnes for humans and fewer than 100 million tonnes for large wild animals.

Harari (2019) argues that this is why the fate of farm animals is not an ethical side issue. It concerns the majority of Earth's large creatures: tens of billions of sentient beings, each with a complex world of sensations and emotions but which live and die on an industrial production line. We observed in the previous section, that 40 years ago, the moral philosopher Peter Singer (1990) published *Animal Liberation*, which has done much to change people's minds on this issue. Singer claimed that industrial farming is responsible for more pain and misery than all the wars of history put together.

The scientific study of animals has played a dismal role in this tragedy. The scientific community has used its growing knowledge of animals mainly to manipulate their lives more efficiently in the service of human industry. Yet this same knowledge has demonstrated beyond a reasonable doubt that farm animals are sentient beings, with intricate social relations and sophisticated psychological patterns. They may not be as intelligent as us, but they certainly know pain, fear and loneliness. They too can suffer, and they too can be happy.

Harari (2019) argues most convincingly that it is high time that we take these scientific findings to heart, because as human power keeps growing, our ability to harm or benefit other animals grows with it. For 4 billion years, life on Earth was governed by natural selection. Now it is governed increasingly by human intelligent design. Biotechnology, nanotechnology and artificial intelligence will soon enable humans to reshape living beings in radical new ways, which will redefine the very meaning of life. He observes that when we come to design this brave new world, we should take into account the welfare of all sentient beings, and not just of Homo sapiens.

Policy implications of green and species criminology

Green criminology examines mechanisms for disrupting and preventing environmental crime and reducing harms to non-human animals and the environment (Wellsmith, 2010, 2011; Nurse, 2015). Traditional reactive policing models of detection, apprehension and punishment (Bright, 1993) tend to be inadequate in the case of environmental harm where irreparable environmental damage or loss of animal life may have already been caused. Likewise, traditional justice systems are also often inadequate to redress the impact of environmental harm. Hall (2017) makes a case for the wider utilization of restorative justice and mediation-based approaches as a means of providing alternative or parallel justice mechanisms for both human and non-human victims of environmental crimes and broader environmental harms. Such consideration of alternatives is integral to the critical approach of green criminology, which also seeks to promote preventive or disruptive enforcement activity aimed at preventing environmental harm before it occurs.

As a form of critical criminological discourse, green criminology arguably shines a light on the failure of mainstream and traditional justice approaches to deal with such complex crimes. Progress is not steady. There will always be periods in which we seem to be treading water or even going backwards. Periodically articles appear about the resurgence of fur, for example, but I doubt that fur will ever be as acceptable as it was

40 years ago. The fact that newspapers give extensive coverage to stories about the abuse of animals being slaughtered for food (not only about abused dogs, cats or horses) is itself a sign of progress.

Peter Singer (2015) observes quite simply that the abuse of animals will not stop until people stop buying meat and hence making huge profits for those in industrialized food production. For central to neoliberalism is – as readers of this book should now be well aware – the essential need to make such profit. So can capitalism continue to make these huge profits and abandon meat production? Well, it is possible not least considering the recent worldwide massive expansion in veganism which is no longer a fringe activity but is now a successful business enterprise which is going mainstream. And then came the COVID-19 pandemic.

Stephen Bush (2020) observes that the battle against novel diseases rests on two contingencies: that governments tell the World Health Organization (WHO) everything they know as soon as they know it, and that the WHO tells everyone else, as soon as they know it. Neither happened in the case of the COVID-19 novel coronavirus.

He observes that a novel organization would almost certainly help in keeping an eye on the danger zones that could produce a new pandemic. The great ones of the modern era – HIV-AIDS and the novel coronavirus – both emerged from animals. The various near misses – variant Creutzfeldt-Jakob disease, the Zika virus, the H1N1 flu – also came from animal-to-human transmission. And as with the novel coronavirus, the zone of maximum risk comes from unsafe agricultural practices: in the case of the novel coronavirus, from Chinese agri-business and that country's wet markets, but H1N1 emerged from factory farms in Mexico and spread via agri-businesses, while mad cow disease, and with it variant CJD, spread from unsafe animal feed here in the UK.

The evidence for the increasing regularity of the emergence of major life-threatening epidemics/pandemics in contemporary neoliberal society seems to lie unassailably in the mass exploitation, abuse and murder of non-humans for human gratification. The radical policy implication offered by species criminology is clearly the complete abolition of human exploitation of non-humans, and that includes eating them. You know it makes sense.

Summary of main points

1   Green criminology is a framework of intellectual, empirical and political orientations toward primary and secondary harms, offences and crimes which impact in a damaging way on the natural environment, diverse species (human and non-human) and the planet.
2   Mainstream criminology tends to be anthropocentric, positioning and privileging human beings as the central and most significant species. The concept of speciesism has thus been used to describe the devaluing and prejudicial treatment of other species as less worthy of concern, compassion or justice than humans.
3   The huge international trade in wildlife as live bodies or as harvested 'parts and products' was largely overlooked until recently but is now widely recognized, with trafficking and related animal abuse now better understood.
4   Ruggiero and South (2013) argue that a political economy approach to environmental harms should pose questions about the long-term outcomes of development processes and how these impact on the limited resources of the planet.

5   Like all variants of critical criminology, the green one addresses social and political dynamics which cause collective harm and aims to investigate how this shapes law-making and determines the very definition of what is officially identified as crime.

6   Animal rights proponents argue that all, non-human animals are entitled to the possession of their own existence and that their most basic interests – for example the need to avoid suffering – should receive the same consideration as similar interests of human beings.

7   Critics of animal rights argue that nonhuman animals are unable to enter into a social contract and thus cannot possess rights, a view made by the philosopher Roger Scruton (1998), who argues that, as only humans have duties and responsibilities, only they can have rights.

8   In the early 1960s in England, support for animal rights began to coalesce around the issue of blood sports, particularly hunting deer, foxes and otters, using dogs.

9   The two main philosophical approaches to animal rights are utilitarian and rights-based. Their differences reflect a distinction between ethical theories that judge the rightness of an act by its consequences and those that focus on the principle behind the act, almost regardless of consequences.

10 Yuval Noah Harari (2019) argues that the fate of industrially farmed animals is one of the most pressing ethical questions of our time. Tens of billions of sentient beings, each with complex sensations and emotions, live and die on a production line. The march of history is littered with the dead bodies of animals.

Discussion questions

1   What are the areas of interest considered by green criminology, and why a political approach inevitably appropriate?
2   How would you define speciesism?
3   Should animals be afforded the same rights as humans?
4   Explain the two main philosophical arguments in favour of animal rights?
5   Do you agree with Yuval Noah Harari that the destruction of billions of animals by human beings is one of the greatest crimes of all time? If so, how would end such practices.

Suggested further reading

Ruggiero and South (2013) provide the quintessential account of a green criminology located in the context of a political economy critique of neoliberalism. Regan (1984, 2001), Rollin (2010) and Singer (1990) provide essential introductions to animal rights. Yuval Noah Harari (2015) outlines his views on factory farming and much more in a provocative book that should be read by everyone who is interested in the history of our species and the crimes against the planet for which we are responsible.

References

Arluke, A. and Sax, B. (1992) 'Understanding Nazi Animal Protection', *Anthrozoos: A Mdisciplinary Journal of The Interactions of People & Animals*, 5(1): 16–31.
Beck, U. (1992) *Risk Society*. London: Sage.

Beirne, P. (1995) 'The Use and Abuse of Animals in Criminology: A Brief History and Curent Review', *Social Justice*, 22(1): 5–31.

Beirne, P. (1999) 'For a Nonspeciesist Criminology: Animal Abuse as an Object of Study', *Criminology*, 37(1): 117–14.

Beirne, P. (2009) *Confronting Animal Abuse: Law, Criminology, and Human-Animal Relationships*. London: Rowman & Littlefield Publishers.

Best, S. and Nocella, A. (eds.) (2004) *Terrorists or Freedom Fighters? Reflections on the Liberation of Animals*. Herndon, VA: Lantern Books.

Bright, J. (1993) 'Crime Prevention: The British Experience', in K. Stenson and D. Cowell (eds.) *The Politics of Crime Control*. London: Sage.

Bush, S. (2020) 'Morning Call', *The New Statesman*, June 24.

Carrabine, E., Cox, P., Lee, M., Plummer, K. and South, N. (2009) *Criminology: A Sociological Introduction*. New York, NY: Routledge.

Cohen, C. (1986) 'The Case for the Use of Animals in Bioimedical Research', *New England Journal of Medicine*, 315(14): 65–70.

Davis, J. (2009) 'History of Vegetarianism: The Source of Some Words', *International Vegetarian Union*, 6 April.

Decartes, R. (1641) 'Meditationes De Prima Philosophia', in *Qua Dei Existentia et Animae Immortalitas Demonstrantur*. Paris: Michel Soly. Available from: https://gallica.bnf.fr/ark:/12148/btv1b86002964.r=.langEN

Eman, K., Meško, G. and Fields, C. (2009) 'Crimes against the Environment: Green Criminology and Research Challenges in Slovenia', *Journal of Criminal Justice and Security*, 11(4): 574–92.

Fioramonti, L. (2013) *Gross Domestic Problem: The Politics Behind the World's Most Powerful Number*. London: Zed Books.

Francione, G. (1995) *Animals, Property, and the Law*. New York: Temple University Press.

Frey, R.G. (1980) *Interests and Rights: The Case against Animals*. London: Clarendon Pre.

Fussey, P. and South, N. (2012) 'Heading toward a New Criminogenic Climate: Climate Change, Political Economy and Environmental Security', in R. White (ed.), *Climate Change from a Criminological Perspective*. New York: Springer.

Hall, M. (2017) *Exploring the Cultural Dimensions of Environmental Victimization*. Available from: https://doi.org/10.1057/palcomms.2017.76

Halsey, M. and White, R. (1998) 'Crime, Ecophilosophy and Environmental Harm', *Theoretical Criminology*, 2(3): 345–71.

Harari, Y.N. (2015) *Sapiens: A Brief History of Humankind*. London: Harvill Secke.

Harari, Y.N. (2019) 'Industrial Farming Is One of the Worst Crimes in History', *The Guardian*, January 7 2020.

Harrison, R. (1964) *Animal Machines: The New Factory Farming Industry*. London: Stuart.

Hayek, F.A. (1973) *Law, Legislation and Liberty*. London: Routledge.

Higgins, P., Short, D. and South, N. (2013) 'Protecting the Planet: A Proposal for a Law of Ecocide', *Crime, Law and Social Change*. doi:10.1007/s10611-013-9413-6

Hopkins Burke, R.D. (2012) *Criminal Justice Theory: An Introduction*. Abingdon, Oxon: Routledge.

Kant, I. (1785) *Groundwork of the Metaphysic of Morals*. London: Jonathan Bennett.

Kete, K. (2002) 'Animals and Ideology: The Politics of Animal Protection in Europe', in N. Rothfels (ed.) *Representing Animals*. Indianapolis: Indiana University Press.

Kramer, R. and Michalowski, R. (2012) 'Is Global Warming a State-Corporate Crime?', in R. White (ed.) *Climate Change From a Criminological Perspective*. London: Springer.

Kramer, R.C. (1984) 'Corporate Criminality: The Development of an Idea', in E. Hochstetler (ed.) *Corporations as Criminals*. Beverly Hills, CA: Sage.

Legge, D. and Brooman, S. (1997) *Law Relating to Animals*. London: Cavendish Publishing.

Leneman, L. (1999) 'No Animal Food: The Road to Veganism in Britain, 1909–1944', *Society and Animals*, 7: 1–5.

Locke, J. (1693) *Some Thoughts Concerning Education*. Cambridge: Cambridge University Press.

Long, M., Stretesky, P., Lynch, M. and Fenwick, E. (2012) 'Crime in the Coal Industry: Implications for Green Criminology and Treadmill of Production', *Organization and Environment*, 25: 328–46.

Lynch, M.J. (1990) 'The Greening of Criminology: A Perspective on the 1990s', *Critical Criminologist*, 2(3–4): 11–12.

Lynch, M.J., Burns, R. and Stretesky, P. (2010) 'Global Warming and State-Corporate Crime: The Politicalization of Global Warming under the Bush Administration', *Crime Law and Social Change*, 54: 213–39.

Lynch, M.J. and Stretesky, P. (2007) 'Green Criminology in the United States', in P. Berine and N. South (eds.) *Issues in Green Criminology: Confronting Harms against Environments, Humanity and Other Animals*. Cullompton: Willan.

Mason, P. (1997) *The Brown Dog Affair*. London: Two Sevens Publishing.

Molland, N. (2004) 'Thirty Years of Direct Action', in S. Best and A.J. Nocella (eds.) *The Animal Liberation Front*. London: Lantern Books.

Nietzsche, F. (2008) *The Selected Writings of Friedrich Nietzsche*. London: Wilder Publications.

Nurse, A. (2015) *Policing Wildlife: Perspectives on the Enforcement of Wildlife Legislation*. London: Palgrave Macmillan.

Nussbaum, M. (2004) 'Beyond Compassion and Humanity: Justice for Nonhuman Animals', in C. Sunstein and M. Nussbaum (eds.) *Animal Rights: Current Debates and New Directions*. Oxford: Oxford University Press.

Nussbaum, M. (2006) *Frontiers of Justice: Disability, Nationality, Species Membership*. Cambridge, MA: Belknap Press.

Phelps, R. (2007) *The Longest Struggle: Animal Advocacy from Pythagoras to PETA*. London: Lantern Books.

Posner, R.A. (2004) 'Animal Rights: Legal, Philosophical, and Pragmatic Perspectives', in M. Nussbaum and C.R. Sunstein (eds.) *Animal Rights: Current Debates and New Directions*. Chicago, IL: Chicago University Press.

Posner, R.A. and Singer, P. (2001) 'Posner-Singer Debate', *Slate*, July 10.

Regan, T. (1984) *The Case for Animal Rights*. Berkley, CA: University of California Press.

Regan, T. (2001) *Defending Animal Rights*. Chicago: University of Illinois Press.

Rollin, B.E. (2010) *Animal Rights and Human Morality*. New York: Promethus Books.

Ruggiero, V. and South, N. (2013) 'Green Criminology and Crimes of the Economy: Theory, Research and Praxis', *Critical Criminology*, 21: 359–73.

Ryder, R. (2000) *Animal Revolution: Changing Attitudes towards Speciesism*. New York: Berg.

Salt, H.S. (1894) *Animal's Rights: Considered in Relation to Social Progress*. London: Mamillan & Co.

Schneider, J. (2012) *Sold into Extinction: The Global Trade in Endangered Species*. Westport: Praeger.

Scruton, R. (1998) 'Animal Rights', *City Journal*, Summer.

Singer, P. (1990) *Animal Liberation*. New York: Review Books.

Singer, P. (2015) 'The Abuse of Animals Won't Stop Until We Stop Eating Meat', *The Guardian*, February 11.

Skidelsky, R. and Skidelsky, E. (2012) *How Much is Enough? The Love for Money and the Case for the Good Life*. London: Allen Lane.

Sollund, R. (2013) 'The Victimisation of Women, Children and Non-Human Species through Trafficking and Trade: Crimes Understood through an Ecofeminist Perspective', in N. South and A. Brisman (eds.) *The Routledge International Handbook of Green Criminology*. London: Routledge.

Sorabji, R. (1993) *Animal Minds and Human Morals*. Ithaca, NY: Cornell University Press.

Spencer, D., and Fitzgerald, A. (2013) 'Three Ecologies, Transversality and Victimization: The Case of the British Petroleum Oil Spill', *Crime, Law and Social Change*, 59: 209–23.

South, N. (1998) 'A Green Field for Criminology? A Proposal for a Perspective', *Theoretical Criminology*, 2(2): 211–33.

South, N. and Beirne, P. (1998) 'Editors' Introduction', *Theoretical Criminology*, 2(2): 147–58.

South, N., Brisman, A. and Beirne, P. (2013) 'A Guide to a Green Criminology', in N. South and A. Brisman (eds.) *The Routledge International Handbook of Green Criminology*. London: Routledge.

Terni, M. (2011) *La mano invisibile della politica. Pace e guerra tra stato e mercato*. Milan: Garzanti.

Waldau, P. (2001) *The Specter of Speciesism: Buddhist and Christian Views of Animals*. Oxford: Oxford University Press.

Walters, R. (2010) 'Eco Crime', in J. Muncie, D. Talbot and R. Walters (eds.) *Crime: Local and Global*. Cullompton: Willan.

Wellsmith, M. (2010) 'The Applicability of Crime Prevention to Problems of Environmental Harm: A Consideration of Illicit Trade in Endangered Species', in R. White (ed.) *Global Environmental Harm: Criminological Perspectives*. Cullompton: Willan Publishing.

Wellsmith, M. (2011) 'Wildlife Crime: The Problems of Enforcement', *European Journal of Criminal Policy Research*, 17: 125–40.

White, R. (2008) *Crimes against Nature: Environmental Criminology and Ecological Justice*. Cullompton: Willan.

White, R. (2009) 'Introduction: Environmental Crime and Eco-Global Criminology', in R. White (ed.), *Environmental Crime: A Reader*. Willan: Cullompton.

White, R. (2013) 'The Conceptual Contours of Green Criminology', in R. Walters, D. Westerhuis and T. Wyatt (eds.) *Emerging Issues in Green Criminology: Exploring Power, Justice and Harm*. Basingstoke, Hampshire: Palgrave Macmillan.

Williams, E.E. and DeMello, M. (2007) *Why Animals Matter*. New York: Prometheus Books.

Wolfe, B. (2011) 'Green-Collar Crime: Environmental Crime and Justice in the Sociological Perspective', *Sociology Compass*, 5(7): 499–511.

Wyatt, T. (2012) *Green Criminology and Wildlife Trafficking: The Illegal Fur and Falcon Trades in Russia Far East*. Saarbrücken: LAP Lambert Academic Publishing.

Chapter 15

Bio-critical criminology

Key issues

1   Biosocial theory
2   The postmodern critique of science
3   Bio-critical criminology
4   Recent sociobiological explanations of childhood delinquency
5   ACE (adverse childhood experiences)

Introduction

A number of the biological studies which are part of the predestined actor model tradition suggest that some individuals are born with a physiological condition which predisposes them to commit crime. But as we observed, closer investigation suggests that social and environmental background are at least equally important.

There have nevertheless been attempts in recent years to rehabilitate biological explanations by incorporating social and environmental factors into a 'multifactor' approach. These socio-biologists argue that the presence of certain biological predispositions – and the introduction of foreign chemical agents – may increase the likelihood, but not determine absolutely, that an individual will offend (Mednick *et al.*, 1987).

Biosocial theory

An interest in biological explanations of crime and criminal behaviour was revived during the 1970s, following the publication of Edmund O. Wilson's book *Sociobiology*, where Wilson argued that people are biosocial organisms whose behaviours are influenced by both their physical characteristics and the environmental conditions in which they live. Thus, rather than viewing criminals as people whose behaviours are totally controlled or predetermined by their biological traits, modern biosocial theorists believe that physical, environmental and social conditions interact in complex ways to produce human behaviour (see Englander, 2007; Ellis, 2005; Fishbein, 2001; Yaralian and Raine, 2001).

Biosocial scholars ask why it is that, when faced with the same environmental stressors, some people engage in violence, yet most people do not, and they propose that it is the presence of certain biological abnormalities or physical disabilities which makes some individuals more prone to violence or aggression than others. The perspective of many socio-biologists has been neatly captured by Van den Bergle:

What seems no longer tenable at this juncture is any theory of human behaviour which ignores biology and relies exclusively on sociocultural learning. Most scientists have been wrong in their dogmatic rejection and blissful ignorance of the biological parameters of our behaviour.

(1974: 779)

Biosociology is thus an emerging paradigm, one which seeks to understand human behaviour by integrating relevant insights from the natural sciences into traditional sociological thinking. It is not a 'biological' perspective, as such, it is argued, but a biosocial perspective which recognizes 'the continuous, mutual, and inseparable interaction between biology and the social environment' (Lancaster *et al.*, 1987: 2). Biosociology thus proposes no ultimate causes of human behaviour but rather seeks to understand how biological factors interact with other dynamics to produce observed behaviour. It does not seek to 'reduce' complex behaviour to the level of biological processes in isolation from environmental influences but merely insists that such processes must be recognized and included in any analysis of behaviour.

The work of Sarnoff Mednick and associates (1977, 1987) provides a good example of the orientation of criminological biologists working in the context of the biosocial paradigm. Mednick *et al.* (1987: 68) argue that the biological characteristics of an individual are only part of the explanation of criminal behaviour, with other factors involved being the physical and social environment:

Where the social experiences of the antisocial individual are not especially antisocial, biological factors should be examined. The value of the biological factors is more limited in predicting antisocial behaviour in individuals who have experienced criminogenic social conditions in their rearing.

Mednick proposes in his *biosocial theory* that all individuals must learn to control natural urges which drive us towards antisocial and criminal behaviour. From this perspective, it is acknowledged that the learning process we all experience takes place in the context of the family and during the course of interaction with peer groups, and it is based on the punishment of undesirable behaviours. The punishment response is mediated by the autonomic nervous system. If the reaction is short-lived, the individual is said to have rewarded him- or herself, and criminal behaviour is inhibited. A slow physiological recovery from punishment though does little to teach the individual to refrain from undesirable behaviour. Mednick ultimately proposes that criminals are those who have slow autonomic nervous system responses to stimuli.

Jeffery (1977) was to strongly argue that this new biological criminology is not simply 'neo-Lombrosian' and has been highly critical of those criminological theories which have ignored or rejected biological components. In contrast, he has argued that biological, psychological and sociological characteristics should be seen as interacting together in a systems model to produce criminal behaviour. Central to his argument is the notion that individuals are born with particular biological and psychological characteristics or propensities which may not only predispose them to but also may actually cause certain forms of behaviour. This criminal 'nature' is independent of the socialization process present in the social environment. But there is, nonetheless, a good deal of interaction between nature and nurture through the physical environment and the feedback mechanisms which exist in human biochemical systems.

Jeffery (1977) further observes that it is poor people who tend to experience a poor-quality, vitamin-deficient diet and are more likely to be geographically exposed to pollutants. The resulting nutrients and chemicals are transformed by the biochemical system into neurochemical compounds within the brain, which can have a significant impact on their behaviour. Bio-criminologists maintain that minimum levels of vitamins and minerals are required for normal brain functioning and cite medical research which suggests that proper nutrition is essential during early childhood. Thus, nutritional deficiencies at this crucial stage in child development can result in serious physical, mental and behavioural problems (Liu and Wuerker, 2005; Neisser, 1996). Research has also suggested that improving diet quality can reduce delinquency while dramatically improving the mental functioning and the academic performance of adolescents (see Schoenthaler and Bier, 2000). Other studies have indicated that diets which are deficient in potassium, calcium, amino acids, sodium, peptides and other nutrients can lead to depression, mania and cognitive problems. Such mental health issues can, in turn, significantly increase the probability of violent behaviour. Similarly, studies have found a strong link between antisocial behaviour and insufficient quantities of vitamins B3, B6 and C (Siegel and McCormick, 2006; Liu and Wuerker, 2005).

Diets that are high in sugar and carbohydrates have also been linked to violence, aggression and other behavioural issues (Gans, 1991). One experiment with incarcerated youths, for example, found that reducing sweet foods and drinks in the prison diet produced a 45% decline in institutional violence (Schoenthaler and Doraz, 1983). But other, more recent studies suggest that most people with high sugar/carbohydrate diets never engage in serious violence and that, for some individuals, sugar actually has a calming effect which reduces aggression (Gray, 1986).

Other studies have explained that apparent discrepancy by suggesting that it is how the brain metabolizes glucose that may determine whether sugar causes antisocial behaviour. Hypoglycaemia, for example, is a condition that causes glucose to fall below the level needed to maintain normal brain functioning (the brain is the only organ that obtains all of its energy from glucose). Symptoms of hypoglycaemia include anxiety, depression, insomnia, nervousness, mood swings, phobias and temper tantrums. A number of studies have found a significant relationship between hypoglycaemia and violence – including assault, homicide and rape. Furthermore, studies of prison populations have found higher than normal rates of hypoglycaemia among habitually violent inmates (Virkkunen, 1986).

Sociobiological researchers have also established a connection between exposure to dangerous contaminants – including copper, mercury, chlorine, artificial colouring, food dyes, and so on – and both aggressive and antisocial behaviour (see Rappaport and Thomas, 2004; Ellis, 2005), while a great deal of more recent research has focused on the possible relationship between lead poisoning and violence. One study, for example, found that communities with the highest concentrations of lead in the air also reported the highest levels of homicide and other forms of violence (Stretesky and Lynch, 2001). A number of studies have also found that lead poisoning is one of the most significant predictors of male delinquency and persistent adult criminality (see Denno, 1993; McCall and Land, 2004). Needleman et al. (1996), for example, tracked several hundred boys from the age of 7 to 11 and found that those with high concentrations of lead in their bones were much more likely to demonstrate attention deficit problems, poor language skills, delinquency and aggression. High lead ingestion has also been linked to lower IQ scores – a factor which can contribute to youth violence (Neisser, 1996).

In short, the sociobiological perspective proposes that poverty leads to behavioural differences through the interaction of individual and environment and it is an argument which has been taken up and developed by key 'right realist' criminological theorists in sometimes highly contentious formulations. Sociobiology is thus not politically neutral, and this is an important point well worth remembering.

Right realists, Wilson and Herrnstein (1985) thus argue that an amalgam of gender, age, intelligence, body type and personality factors constitute the individual, who is projected into a social world where they learn what kind of behaviour is rewarded in what circumstances. Heavily by psychological behaviourism, the authors argued that individuals learn to respond to situations according to how their behaviour has been previously rewarded and punished, and their environment should therefore be changed to produce the desired conduct and hence discourage involvement in criminality. Thus, to understand the propensity to commit crime, it is important to identify the ways in which the environment might operate on particular individuals to produce this response. Within this general learning framework, the influence of the family, school and wider community is identified as being crucial.

The early biological positivists had sought to demonstrate through the use of the natural sciences research methods that physiological processes control human behaviour. In response to a predominantly social constructionist challenge to this predestined actor model tradition, biological positivism, certainly in its purist form, went out of fashion as the dominant form of criminological explanation for the latter part of the twentieth century. Yet this tradition was to nevertheless return to the forefront with a revamped version of biological explanation incorporating sociological explanation.

These *socio*-biological theories proposed that biological processes are inextricably intertwined with socially constructed dynamics which also inform behaviour. Yet, as will be seen later in this chapter, bio-critical criminology has not just challenged the assumptions of this new biologism but goes further and seriously questions whether science itself provides clear and value-free information – as it proposes – or whether it is itself a socially constructed process which presupposes certain ideologies.

The postmodern critique of science

Let us briefly consider the traditional scientific principles that provide the fundamentals of the natural sciences in modern society before questioning those tenets from a postmodern perspective.

Traditional scientific principles

First, the principle of *scientific progress* states that there should be a quest for truth about the universe, ignoring all forces who want to deny truth and defend their superstitions.

Second, with *scientific objectivity*, scientists are supposed to be objective observers. They study nature by direct observation, indirect observation or through controlled experiments intended to rule out bias.

Third, the notion of *scientific rationality* proposes that science should be rational, and scientists use inductive or deductive logic to (1) outline a problem or question, (2) interpret an observation, (3) formulate a hypothesis, (4) articulate the logical implications of a hypothesis and (5) test the hypothesis.

Fourth, a formulated *hypothesis* is but one possible explanation for a phenomenon. Once a hypothesis is formed, it must be tested under conditions where falsifiability is possible, and it must predict the outcome of experiments.

Fifth when *handling data*, scientists should not select data to match their hypotheses but try to discover whether their hypotheses really match all available data.

Sixth, although the *beginning assumptions* of science cannot be demonstrated by scientific methods, they should be accepted anyway as reasonable beginning points. Scientists are not consistent with their own method unless they admit their own presuppositions are not certain.

Some of the presuppositions of the sciences include the following: (1) an external world exists, (2) nature is understandable, (3) the rules of logic are valid, (4) language is adequate to describe the natural realm, (5) human senses are reliable, (6) mathematical rules are descriptive for the physical world, (7) unexplained things can be used to explain other phenomena (e.g. gravity is thus far unexplained, but it is used to explain the movement of planets and the bending of light) and (8) observable phenomena provide knowledge about unobservable phenomena (e.g. cosmic background radiation provides insight into the Big Bang).

The postmodern critique of science

First, science actually arrives at its 'truths' in response to social forces both within and without the scientific community. Periodic shifts in outlook come as a result of irrational conversions on the part of influential scientific leaders, not from systematic searches.

Second, observations do not interpret themselves. They are interpreted by 'a mind' and the biases of any particular person or group conducting the experiment. These minds are affected by their culture and language to such an extent that the 'actual' nature of things may be unknowable.

Third, some postmodernists question not whether science is rational but whether rationality provides any real insights into the world. It is thus argued that there is no such thing as objective reason and feminist Andrea Nye (1990), for example, claims that logic has meant different things in different eras, depending on the world view in vogue at the time. All agree that the rules of logic only apply within a given cultural paradigm, or model based on a given language/thought system.

Fourth, some historians of science and psychologists argue that when scientists form hypotheses, they lose objectivity. In a number of cases, scientists have refused to see data that has contradicted their current understandings. For instance, nobody saw a red-shift of light from the sun until the theory predicted it, then everybody that looked 'saw' it (Collins and Pinch, 1993). Joseph Lister had found it very difficult to convince his fellow physicians to wash their hands between the dissection room and the operating table in spite of overwhelming evidence that the physicians were causing the spread of a deadly disease. His notions of infection were not the prevalent view for how disease was caused, so the data were ignored.

Fifth, hypotheses do not simply rise up from raw data but originate in the mind of the observer, who then imposes the hypothesis on the data as a way of organizing it. How does a scientist decide which information is useful and which is not? The world is full of physical data, much of which we never notice. For instance, suppose you wanted to study the cause(s) of light emission by certain fungi. What data would you collect? Is the time of day relevant; the ambient temperature; the cycle of the moon; the presence of dog urine? To collect data, you must first decide what is important. But once you do that, you have already decided what causes can safely be excluded from consideration. In so doing, scientists may impose an artificial order on the observations.

Sixth, the beginning points of modern science cannot be obviously true because many cultures deny them. These beginning points along with the questionable bases for building on them constitute the basis for calling science a purely subjective exercise, telling Western man or woman only what they want to hear.

Seventh, mystical scientists have allied themselves with other postmodernists to charge that quantum physics prove the Eastern mystical view of the universe – a universe that is interconnected, irrational and spiritual.

Thus, from a postmodernist perspective, science is not neutral, objective and '*the* truth' as natural scientists would claim.

Bio-critical criminology

We here consider the debate between biosocial scientists (defending science and biology) and critical criminologists (utilizing critical realism as a tool to challenge biology and science). Again, much of the tension in the following debate is due to a fundamental difference in assumptions between these two perspectives.

In terms of epistemology, those on opposite sides of the debate have different views about what constitutes knowledge (Slife and Williams, 1995). Bio-criminologists assume a positivist epistemology which requires no subjective interpretation. Data are gathered which can be quantified and counted, genetic codes and criminal convictions, for example. If the former correlates strongly with the latter, no interpretation is required. The data speak for themselves, and the relationship between variables is provable. This objective certainty saves the scientist from the seemingly unreasonable relativism of social constructionism. But as Draper *et al.* (2015) pertinently observe this position overlooks crucial similarities between objectivism and relativism.

Some biosocial criminologists argue that there is no such thing as naïve data and actually take a critical realist perspective (Heylen *et al.*, 2015). An epistemology which entails an iterative refinement of observations and improvement of theoretical models rather than proof through experimentation on dependent and independent variables (Coller, 1994; Bhaskar, 1998). Critical realists argue that processes may potentially exist which remain inactivate at a particular time and context which cannot be observed. Thus, even if a given mechanism or process is not observed, it may still exist (Coller, 1994).

Critical realists explicitly take up a social constructionist or hermeneutic approach to understanding both what knowledge is and how it can be obtained. Knowledge from this perspective is developed by human relationships and language so that it is only possible to know something within the specific and broader context of language and culture (Gergen, 2014). Thus, any knowledge or truth claim made by a criminologist is situated in, and informed by, the cultural, social, and linguistic context of the research. It can nevertheless be deconstructed to show that the 'objective' or 'scientific' truth claim made by the researcher arose (in part) out of the socio–cultural context of the research. For example, if a researcher finds a strong relationship between a particular ethnic group and criminal behaviour, the constructionist would ask whether this is this really due to genetic differences or rather endemic and intractable racism. Their concerns have arisen through observing the relationship between racism and crime and that oppressed minorities (who assumedly share some genetic similarities) are more heavily involved in crime because (in part) of the desperation caused by their oppression (Unnever, 2015). Should a biosocial criminologist find a relationship between genetics and criminal behaviour, in this example, what they are actually finding is an artefact of racism and oppression.

Critical realism and constructionism share common characteristics but arrive at these from different sides of the debate (Draper *et al.*, 2015). Fundamentally, there is the uncertainty of the iterative nature of knowledge. For the critical realist, engaging in research is an ongoing matter of refinement, looking and looking again, reflecting on criticism of the research and building new models. Knowledge is thus always approximate and ultimately uncertain because of its fluidity and constructed nature.

Bio-critical criminologists are concerned that all actions of human beings from the baseness of their crimes to the heights of their altruism can be reduced ultimately to genetics, but they are not alone in their concerns. Reductionism – the assumption that any given object or process is caused by and reducible to its components (Slife and Williams, 1995) – is not without its critics within the behavioural sciences. For a reductionist, an object is not merely less than the sum of its parts, but the object is only the component part. This is an atomistic approach which involves the belief that the cause of an object is the atoms which compose it, the fundamental and irreducible parts of the object (Slife *et al.*, 2005). Thus, if the object in question is crime (a very complex socio-cultural, socio-legal, moral and ethical issue), it is reducible to its most fundamental irreducible unit. These 'atoms' from the perspective of these biosocial researchers are the irreducible 'cause of causes' that genetics represent for them. This does not discount the complex relationship of these atoms (genetics) or even their effect on the environment. But, even in the face of all of this complexity, the assumption or assertion remains the same: the ultimate cause of all these other events (like crime rates in a community) is ultimately reducible, at least in part, to the genetics of those committing the crime. Bio-critical criminologists challenge that assumption because they tend to view crime as not reducible to any atoms and view crime as situated in a time, place, and culture and comprehensible only within a macro-context which criminalizes certain actions.

Associated with the assumption of reductionism is the tacit assumption of determinism which is the belief that these atoms (genetics) determine behaviour and that human agency does not actually play a role. In the writings of some socio-biologists, human agency seems epiphenomenal to the criminal behaviours they seek to measure, because it is actually caused by other forces. Hence. the experience of agency is disregarded or ignored in their theory and research.

The assumptions of reductionism and determinism are important because they complicate questions of 'guilt' and 'innocence' in the world of crime and jurisprudence. In Western philosophy and culture, there is a strong conceptual link between agency (some semblance of genuine choice on the part of a subject) and moral and ethical culpability for the commission of crime (Osborne, 2014). In essence, someone accused of a crime can only be found guilty if they actually have the capacity to choose to commit the crime and have done so. If they did not have the capacity to choose rationally whether to commit a crime, then they would be found not guilty (e.g. 'not guilty by reason of insanity'). Rational choice is so important because both the state-of-mind at the time of the crime as well as competency to stand trial are both assessed in cases where these are an issue and inform the process of jurisprudence greatly (Perlin and Dlugacz, 2007).

Some biosocial criminologists leave room for agency, but others are compatibilist and deterministic in their language. Compatibilism is a philosophical position which in this situation involves both the causes of behaviour as well as some degree of free will or human agency (Kane, 2005). Biosociologists who are epistemologically critical realists may nevertheless leave room for human agency, thus considering the role genetics have in terms of the 'influences' of biology on crime or 'tendencies' of certain people with certain genotypes to behave in a criminal way. Their research attempts to uncover the degree to which a criminal act may have a genetic or biological basis, which may potentially inform the courts of the degree of moral and legal culpability of the accused. But, in the research of other biosociologists, the self is seen as constrained by forces outside the control of the individual who is seen as merely a biological mechanism which reacts to environmental cues, rather than a person who chooses to grapple with the elements of their complex and sometimes difficult environment. Carrier and Walby (2014: 11) characterize the work of the biosocial criminologist as 'the biopathologization of a brain's structure', 'nomothetic, socio-historically non-contingent', and based on a 'neo-positivist Poperian conception of science', which only gives credence to testable predictions of behaviour which are 'falsifiable'.

Because the subject matter of biosocial criminology is humanity itself, the social constructionist has good reason to be concerned about the scientific hubris earlier. Davis (1996) pertinently observes that views which assume too readily that humanity can be encapsulated and 'totalized' have done severe damage to the lives of people. The methodological assumptions of the constructionist radically reject any attempt to capture the human as a social person within any kind of 'scientific' framework which insists it understands humanity in terms which reject the infinite flexibility of the human. At the same time, they take a rather sceptical approach to the natural sciences in general, which are themselves seen as social constructions. The psychiatrist, the neuroscientist and the psychologist are simply another set of storytellers whose methods are different, but no better, than the methods of the shaman or the priests.

A look at the history of social science over the past 100 years gives us plenty of examples. Stephen J. Gould (1996), for example, famously described how 'science' found a difference in intelligence between members of certain racial groups on IQ scores, when these differences are actually due to socio-economic and socio-cultural processes, not race. Likewise, after examination and thorough inquiry of slaves who ran away, certain scholars coined the diagnosis 'drapetomania' a disease which caused slaves to attempt to flee their bondage (Naragon, 1994). Moreover, such 'scientific' diagnoses existed well into the twentieth century. For years, as we saw earlier, homosexuality was considered a mental illness requiring treatment. Fully scientifically verifiable, what was at stake was not the scientific data but the value-based assumptions of the scientists. In the Soviet Union, political dissidents were diagnosed with 'sluggish schizophrenia' by psychiatrists, and this diagnosis was used to silence dissidents (Draper et al., 2015). In the previously mentioned cases, value assumptions of the researchers guided their interpretation of the data.

Carrier and Walby (2014) observe that biosocial criminology has the potential for the worst kind of social control and are keen to rule out that kind of psychological manipulation, but Draper et al. (2015) argue that their critique may be going too far. The foolishness of past overly simplistic biological determinism is acknowledged, but it is considered inappropriate to condemn all attempts to look for biological causal antecedents. There is thus room for the view of the self as a biologically embodied agent, constrained by their own biologies, even if they are not determined by that biology in all instances. This may in fact be the kind of agent that we indeed are. But if this is the kind of agency – we as individuals enjoy – then there is real room for exploring the causal antecedents of (some of) our behaviour, even while admitting that these causal factors do not entirely undermine our self-determination.

Next, we consider some recent sociobiological explanations of childhood delinquency and bear in mind the earlier bio-critical observations, before considering a very contemporary example of the dubious impact of such research.

Sociobiology revisited – recent sociobiological explanations of childhood delinquency

In recent years, there has been substantial interest among sociobiological researchers in the US in antisocial behaviour, with this being seen to emerge early in childhood in some individuals and persist into adulthood. Contributing to that research interest has been the growing evidence that 5% to 6% of the most persistent offenders are responsible for 50% of known crimes (Aguilar et al., 2000) and that these individuals are difficult – if not impossible – to rehabilitate and most likely to become recidivists (Kazdin, 1987; Moffitt, 1993a). It is thus argued that identifying risk factors of early antisocial behaviour has important implications for improving both intervention and prevention.

Raine (2002) has proposed the development of a biosocial model to account for the contribution of both biologically and environmentally related risk factors in the development of antisocial behaviour. One group of studies which has sought to test this model has focused on perinatal complications and environmental adversity. A consistent interaction between the presence of both of these factors and the development of serious antisocial behaviour in adulthood (Raine et al., 1997; Piquero and Tibbetts, 1999; Arseneault et al., 2002).

Research has suggested that there are multiple risk factors and pathways associated with the development of antisocial behaviour during early and middle childhood (Cicchetti and Rogosch, 1996). One such risk factor is the health status of the mother, which, when compromised during pregnancy, has been associated with impaired functioning of the central nervous system of the child and subsequent problems in its well-being (Moffitt, 1993a, 1993b). Complications during the prenatal – conception to seventh month of pregnancy – and perinatal – seventh month of pregnancy through to 28 days after birth – periods have been found to be early factors affecting the development of the central nervous system and have been tested individually as predictors of deviant outcomes (see Brennan and Mednick, 1997). The most consistent correlation has been found between complications during the perinatal stage and later antisocial behaviour (Kandel and Mednick, 1991). Direct relations between perinatal complications and antisocial behaviour have not typically been demonstrated (Rantakallio et al., 1992). However, in the context of family adversity, high levels of perinatal complications have been associated with increased risk of child antisocial behaviour (Drillien, 1964; Werner et al., 1971; Broman et al., 1975).

More recent empirical research testing the biosocial interaction hypothesis has clearly suggested that the correlation between perinatal complications and later antisocial behaviour is moderated by environmental adversity (Brennan and Mednick, 1997; Piquero and Tibbetts, 1999; Laucht et al., 2000; Arseneault et al., 2002). In their study of a Danish male birth cohort, Raine *et al.* (1997) found that boys who suffered both perinatal complications and early maternal rejection were most likely to become violent offenders in adulthood. Arseneault *et al.* (2002) also found support for the biosocial model in a low-income sample of 849 boys, with their results suggesting that a combination of perinatal complications posing imminent harm to the infant predicted increased rates of physical aggression at ages 6 to 17 years when the children were reared in impoverished environments.

A whole body of research has linked aspects of the environment inhabited by the child – such as the quality of parenting and marital conflict – to the development of antisocial behaviour. Several studies suggest that the quality of early parental care – such as unresponsiveness and rejection – plays a significant role in the development of early-onset antisocial behaviour (Campbell *et al.*, 2000; Shaw *et al.*, 2003). Parental responsiveness, sensitivity to social cues and emotional availability are all associated with positive outcomes in young children, such as behavioural regulation and social competence (Martin, 1981; Bost *et al.*, 1998; Wakschlag and Hans, 1999). A lack of parental responsiveness during infancy has nevertheless been associated with negative outcomes, such as antisocial behaviour later in childhood (Shaw *et al.*, 1994a; Shaw *et al.*, 1998b; Wakschlag and Hans, 1999). Parental rejection, the combination of harsh and controlling parenting practices coupled with unacceptance of the child, have also been linked with the development of later antisocial behaviour (Dishion, 1990; Dodge *et al.*, 1994; Campbell *et al.*, 1996; Younge *et al.*, 1996). A number of studies support a 'cumulative risk hypothesis' wherein the number of environmental stressors rather than the particular combination of stressors has been associated with child behaviour problems both in the short and long term (Rutter *et al.*, 1975a; Rutter *et al.*, 1975b; Sameroff *et al.*, 1987; Sanson *et al.*, 1991; Shaw *et al.*, 1994b; Shaw *et al.*, 1998a; Deater-Deckard *et al.*, 1998).

In what is now widely considered to be a classic study, Rutter and his colleagues (1975a, 1975b) found a dramatic rise in the probability of child adjustment difficulties as the number of family stressors increased. Sameroff *et al.* (1987) thus tested the impact of three sets of variables on the behaviour of the children in their sample and found that those with high multiple environmental risk scores had much worse outcomes than children with low multiple risk scores.

Thus, there does seem to be research evidence to demonstrate a close correlation between biological factors, multiple environmental factors, in particular poor parenting skills, poverty and inadequate living conditions, and the onset and persistence of antisocial behaviour. Whether possession of these factors can be legitimately considered to be the fault or responsibility of the family involved – as would be suggested by right realists such as Wilson and Herrnstein (1985) – or at least partially the responsibility of wider society and government is a matter of some conjecture.

Sociobiological research has nevertheless been extremely influential, widely accepted and dangerously unquestioned by welfare organizations as the following case study shows.

Case study: ACE (adverse childhood experiences)

The Adverse Childhood Experiences (ACEs) Study was conducted by the health maintenance organization Kaiser Permanente and the Centers for Disease Control and Prevention in the US (Felitti *et al.*, 1998). Participants were recruited between 1995 and 1997 and have been in long-term follow-up for health outcomes.

Overview of ACEs

ACEs are stressful events occurring in childhood including:

- domestic violence,
- parental abandonment through separation or divorce,
- a parent with a mental health condition,
- being the victim of abuse (physical, sexual and/or emotional),
- being the victim of neglect (physical and emotional),
- a member of the household being in prison and
- growing up in a household in which there are adults experiencing alcohol and drug use problems.

ACEs are common. The original study found that almost two-thirds of participants experienced one or more, while more than one in five experienced three or more. Subsequent surveys conducted in Britain found that in Wales almost 50% experienced one ACE and 14% experienced four or more; in England, almost 50% experienced one and over 8% four or more.

Research found that a relationship with one trusted adult during childhood can mitigate the impacts of ACEs on mental and physical well-being.

The term was originally developed in the US for the Adverse Childhood Experiences Survey which found that as the number of ACEs increased in the population studied, so did the risk of experiencing a range of health conditions in adulthood. There have been numerous other studies which have found similar findings including in Wales and England.

ACEs and health inequalities

Preventing ACEs should be seen within the wider context of tackling societal inequalities. While ACEs are found across the population, there is more risk of experiencing ACEs in areas of higher deprivation.

ACEs have been found to have life-long impacts on health and behaviour, and they are relevant to all sectors in society. All of us are seen to have a part to play in preventing adversity and raising awareness of ACEs. Resilient communities thus have an important role in action on ACEs. An ACE survey with adults in Wales found that compared to people with no ACEs, those with four or more are more likely to

- have been in prison,
- develop heart disease,
- frequently visit the general practitioner,
- develop type 2 diabetes,
- have committed violence in the last 12 months and
- have health-harming behaviours (high-risk drinking, smoking, drug use).

The influential orthodoxy proposes that when children are exposed to adverse and stressful experiences, it can have a long-lasting impact on their ability to think, interact with others and on their learning. But ACE has been widely criticized.

Criticisms of ACE

Jessica Eaton (2019) has identified a number of reasons why we should be critical of ACEs, which is being used uncritically as a predictive model to forecast outcomes of abused and harmed children. This means that your score is being used to predict your potential, your outcomes, your lifestyle, your health, your well-being, your mental health and your criminality. Thus, those of us with ACE scores over 4 are reportedly much more likely to commit suicide, have hepatitis, commit domestic violence, have heart disease, have liver failure and even be raped by someone. ACEs are literally being used to predict our outcomes and those of children all over the world. These approaches pathologize and label children, arguing that those kids with the high scores are destined for doom, drugs, prison, illness and early death.

The crucial issue is whether abused and traumatized children go on to have such poor outcomes and whether it is possible to generalize so much. Let us consider some basic logic and stats. One in five British adults said they were abused in childhood according to the Office for National Statistics (2017) which would suggest that our population literally collapsed under the weight of suicides, chronic illness, criminality and serious mental health issues. Yet it seems that so many 'successful' people were abused in childhood. In reality, many kids make it out of the ghetto and council estates and go on to university, get careers, bring up their own kids and live a safe and happy life. But, if ACEs was correct, all these success stories would just be 'anomalies'. The exception to the rule. OK. Let us consider that possibility.

A study conducted by Eaton and Holmes (2017) showed that 51% of the children's social work workforce in the UK had been abused in childhood. Were these all exceptions to the rule. Eaton (2019) ponders why it is that so many abused and traumatized children can go to university, get a social work degree and work in child safeguarding and protection when they are supposedly so damaged by their ACEs.

The reality is that you cannot predict outcomes for humans who are complex, weird and wonderful. Sometimes a child who escapes trafficking and slavery goes on to become a lawyer and a national advocate. Yet ACEs would argue that this person should be ill, dead on drugs or committing violent crime. Moreover, you can also meet people with extremely low to zero ACEs scores (about 20%–30% of the population) who have mental health issues, have attempted suicide, are addicted to drugs, are violent criminals or have become very unwell.

Eaton (2019) proposes that scoring systems will always fail us. Quantifying human experience and predicting human behaviour will never work. We are too unpredictable and too diverse.

Lots of people have hailed ACEs as a 'trauma-informed approach', but such philosophies are strength-based. This means that if you truly adopt a trauma-informed approach to your work or your understanding of human development and suffering, then you do not label that human with diagnoses or numbers based on what other people have done to them. ACEs are largely things other people have done to us, or which we have witnessed being done to others. Eaton (2019) pertinently observes that trying to predict the outcomes of children based on harm committed towards them by a third party is *not* strengths-based or trauma-informed.

The trauma-informed approach to trauma and suffering would be to support the human with the reactions, responses and consequences of being traumatized and harmed by others or by an event. In which case, it would not then use those events to predict their future. Argued from a strengths-based, trauma-informed approach, no matter what horrors that young person has lived through, they are capable of anything. They could be a famous dancer, a genius engineer, a CEO of a company, a doctor, a politician or an author. From this perspective, their 'ACEs' do not define them and cannot be used to predict their well-being, worth or behaviours. ACEs is thus a true deficit framework which calculates the horrible things that have happened – or done – to children or young people to try to predict their futures, as if they are not changeable or recoverable.

Eaton (2019) provides two examples of how ACEs is currently – or has recently been – used to harm victims and survivors of abuse. The first example comes from Australia. In recent news, insurance underwriters for life and buildings insurance have started to use ACEs as a way to make decisions on policies and insurance decisions. Yes. If your ACE score is too high, maybe you are uninsurable. ACEs positions you as a risk to that company. What if they insure your life for £500,000 and then you commit suicide with your 1222% chance of suicide as predicted by the ACEs study?

The second example comes from a local authority in the UK where ACEs scores were being used on pregnant women when they went to antenatal classes or scans, to decide whether to begin pre-birth assessments to check their capability of being a safe mother. Women were being asked to fill in an ACEs quiz and if their score reached a threshold, they were referred to social care for an assessment on their capability to be a mother. This project was pulled after 12 months and never spoken about again.

Eaton (2019) asks those who support ACEs whether they had considered what might happen if we start to label people with numbers based on their traumas. How might those numbers be used against them? Does it truly have the predictive power it claims to have? She asks how professionals can keep using it, making comments about the outcomes of children, when they know they have lived those same lives. She observes that thankfully, ACEs is not accepted by many psychologists, academics, victims and survivors.

Parliamentary submission

On 12 December 2017, six eminent academics made a submission to the House of Commons Science and Technology Select Committee Inquiry into the evidence base for early-years intervention (Edwards *et al.*, 2017). The aim was to encourage the committee to consider that, as in any area of science and policy, evidence concerning the existence of – and cure for –ACEs is unresolved and still contested. Their concern was that the remit of the committee might be limited by a presumption that evidence for both ACEs and successful preventive intervention was already established, pre-empting the aim of the inquiry to 'examine the strength of the evidence linking adverse childhood experiences with long-term negative outcomes'.

The submission observed good reasons to be circumspect. The notion of ACEs is the latest in a long line of diagnoses of – and simple solutions to – complex social issues in the search for interventions that 'work'. The ACEs approach is nevertheless not a neutral, evidence-based diagnosis. Rather, it reflects certain presumptions and is driven by particular agendas and interest groups (e.g. what has been labelled the 'First Three Years Movement'). The ACEs approach, as with other attempts to diagnose and label sections of the population as deficient, has the potential for damaging consequences for the children and adults who are said to possess such deficiencies. Furthermore, viewing social issues through the prism of ACEs may well inhibit our ability to identify and respond to human needs.

Embracing the promise of prevention sounds positive and common sense, but the scientific basis for early intervention programmes is open to question, with evidence of success quite ambiguous and the negative consequences of prevention thinking rarely acknowledged. It is also important to note that researchers who critique the current policy thinking do not do so from the same terrain as those who develop new policy initiatives and intervention programmes. They are often scholars with a depth of knowledge of previous social intervention projects (successful and unsuccessful), alert to questionable scientific-sounding claims and with a knowledge of the global origins of new policy agendas. The level of resources directed to providing the quick evidence for early intervention programmes is disproportionate to the funding available to those wishing to investigate and question the foundations of the early intervention paradigm. It is seen to be important that committee members pay attention to informed critical voices where they do exist.

The submission was written as a group of social scientists with considerable knowledge of social policy interventions stretching back beyond the beginnings of the welfare state. The group had all engaged in the study of early intervention and the use and abuse of scientific claims-making and the misuse of scientific language and metaphors to build the case for public funding.

The conclusions reached in the submission argued that the campaign encouraging teachers, health and social care professionals to be 'ACEs-aware' should be subject to serious questioning. While, of course, they should be looking out sympathetically and proactively for the children in their care, this is seen to be very different from performing amateur diagnoses of children as having high or low ACE scores. The further rolling out of the ACEs approach was seen to be a very dangerous way to proceed. The misidentification of individuals as being at-risk and then subject to intervention could have serious consequences for them and their families. On a broader scale, it could create the stigmatization of sections of the population whose social position or conditions of existence are identified as destined to create dysfunctional individuals.

They conclude their submission by posing a crucial question which they thought deserving of consideration: Would a life lived in the miserable conditions created by adverse situations be wrong even if there were no long-lasting biological effects? It is a very good question.

At the time of writing – June 2020, and in the midst of the COVID-19 pandemic – we the public have been instructed to adhere to the advice of the experts – the scientists – and 'follow the science'. But what happens when that advice is wrong? Or even fraudulently wrong? Sometimes with disastrous consequences.

The natural sciences revisited – do vaccines cause autism?

Friday 29 January 2010

The doctor who sparked the measles–mumps–rubella (MMR) vaccine controversy was 'dishonest, irresponsible and showed callous disregard for the distress and pain' of children, the General Medical Council (GMC) has ruled. The ruling has been reported by many newspapers.

The GMC said Dr Andrew Wakefield 'abused his position of trust' when conducting research into a proposed link between the MMR vaccine, autism and bowel disorders. He carried out clinically unnecessary and invasive tests on children without ethical approval or appropriate qualifications.

Wakefield also failed to disclose conflicts of interest to the *Lancet* medical journal, which in 1998 published the research paper that sparked the MMR scare. The paper has since been withdrawn by the *Lancet* and discredited. The scare nonetheless led to a dramatic drop in MMR vaccination rates and a rise in cases of measles.

The ruling comes after a two-and-a-half-year investigation by the GMC.

Autism rates in developing countries have risen remarkably in the past 30 years. For children born in 1992, according to the US Centers for Disease Control and Prevention, about 1 in 150 would be diagnosed with an autism spectrum disorder (ASD). For children born in 2004, about 1 in 68 children would receive an ASD diagnosis. (CDC, 2018). It is nevertheless difficult to compare autism rates from the 1990s and later with rates from the 1940s through the 1980s: in earlier years, autism was associated primarily with very severely affected individuals, and the rate of autism was estimated to be only about 1 in 10,000 people (Rice *et al.*, 2012). Beginning in the 1990s, understanding of the spectrum of autism has expanded greatly, and now individuals who would most likely previously not have been thought of as having autism may be classified with one of a variety of ASDs (Hertz-Picciotto and Delwiche, 2009).

Whether the high rates of autism today are due to increased diagnosis and reporting, changing definitions of autism or an actual increase in the development of ASD is unknown (CDC, 2018). Regardless, researchers and worried parents alike have speculated about the causes of autism, and the issue has been widely studied. The role of vaccines has been questioned, along with other possible risk factors for ASD, such as genetic predisposition, advanced parental age and other environmental factors. Vaccines have perhaps received more scrutiny that any other speculated cause of ASD, and the great majority of scientists, physicians and public health researchers have come to the conclusion that there is no association between vaccines and autism (CDC, 2018). But some still question whether vaccines play a role in ASD development, and so the public health and medical establishments continue to address these concerns.

The MMR hypothesis

The story of how vaccines came to be questioned as a cause of autism dates back to the 1990s. In 1995, a group of British researchers published a cohort study in the *Lancet* showing that individuals who had been vaccinated with the measles–mumps–rubella vaccine (MMR) were more likely to have bowel disease than individuals who had not received MMR (Thompson *et al.*, 1995). One of those researchers was gastroenterologist Andrew Wakefield, MD, who went on to further study a possible link between the vaccine and bowel disease by speculating that persistent infection with vaccine virus caused disruption of the intestinal tissue that, in turn, led to bowel disease and neuropsychiatric disease (specifically, autism). Part of this hypothesis – that vaccination was associated with autism – had been suggested previously by a few researchers. For example Fudenberg (1996) posited this relationship in a small pilot study published in a non-mainstream journal, as did Gupta (1996) in a review of possible treatments for autism. This hypothesis had not been systematically investigated when Wakefield began to interrogate it

In 1998, Wakefield, along with 12 co-authors, published a case series study in the *Lancet* claiming that they had found evidence, in many of the 12 cases they had studied, of the measles virus in the digestive systems of children who had exhibited autism symptoms after receiving the MMR vaccination (Wakefield *et al.*, 1998). Although in the paper they stated that they could not demonstrate a causal relationship between MMR vaccination and autism, Wakefield suggested in a video released to coincide with the publication of the paper that a causal relationship existed between the MMR and autism: 'the risk of this particular syndrome [what Wakefield termed autistic enterocolitis] developing is related to the combined vaccine, the MMR, rather than the single vaccines' (cited in Deer, 2011). He then recommended that the combination MMR vaccine be suspended in favour of single-antigen vaccinations given separately over time. (Wakefield himself had filed for a patent for a single-antigen measles vaccine in 1997 and so would seem to have had a potential financial interest in promoting this view; Deer, 2011.)

Reaction to the Wakefield publication was immediate. Press outlets covered the news widely and frightened parents began to delay or completely refuse vaccination for their children, both in Britain and the US. MMR vaccination rates in Britain plummeted (Offit, 2008).

Over the next 12 years, the possibility of a link between MMR and autism was studied exhaustively. But no reputable, relevant study confirmed the findings of Wakefield. Quite the opposite. Many well-designed studies found no link between MMR and bowel disease or MMR and autism (CDC, 2018).

In 2004, Dr. Richard Horton, editor of the *Lancet*, wrote that Wakefield should have revealed to the journal that he had been paid by attorneys seeking to file lawsuits against vaccine manufacturers (Horton, 2004). In television interviews, Horton now claimed that Wakefield's research was 'fatally flawed' (Laurance, 2004). Most of the co-authors of the study now retracted the interpretation in the paper, and in 2010, the *Lancet* formally retracted the paper itself.

Three months after the retraction, in May 2010, Britain's GMC banned Wakefield from practicing medicine in Britain, stating that he had shown 'callous disregard' for children in the course of his research. The council also cited previously uncovered information about the extent to which Wakefield's research was funded by lawyers hoping to sue vaccine manufacturers on behalf of parents of children with autism (Meikle and Boseley, 2010).

On 6 January 2011, the *BMJ* published a report by Brian Deer, a British journalist who had previously reported on flaws in Wakefield's work. For this new report, Deer spoke with parents of children from the retracted study and found evidence that Wakefield committed research fraud by falsifying data about the conditions of the children (Deer, 2011). He specifically reported that while the paper claimed that 8 of the 12 children in the study showed either gastrointestinal or autism-like symptoms days after vaccination, records instead show that at most two children experienced these symptoms in this time frame. Additionally, while the paper claimed that all 12 of the children were 'previously normal' before the MMR vaccination, at least two had developmental delays that were noted in their records before the vaccination took place. After examining the records of all 12 children, Deer noted that the statements made in the paper did not match numbers from the records in any category: the children having regressive autism, those with non-specific colitis or those showing first symptoms within days after receiving the MMR vaccine. The *Lancet* paper claimed that six of the children had all three of these conditions; according to the records, not a single child actually did.

In an accompanying editorial, *BMJ* editor in chief Fiona Godlee and co-authors Jane Smith and Harvey Marcovitch examine the damage to public health caused by a tiny study based on parental recall with no control group – a study that turned out to be almost entirely fraudulent but whose impact continues to this day (Godlee *et al.*, 2011). Although the findings of Wakefield's paper have long been discredited by scientists, the evidence that the data themselves were falsified makes this report by the *BMJ* a landmark moment in the history of vaccines. Evidence is strong that the original study should not have been published, not merely because it was poorly conducted but also because it was a product of research fraud.

The thimerosal hypothesis

MMR is not the only vaccine or vaccine component that has been targeted for scrutiny by those who suspect vaccination might be related to autism. After the MMR controversy died down, critics turned their questions to thimerosal, a mercury-containing preservative used in some vaccines. (Thimerosal had never been used in MMR, as antimicrobial agents are not used in live vaccines; WHO, 2006.)

In the late 1990s, legislators, environmentalists and medical and public health workers became concerned about environmental exposures to mercury, particularly from the consumption of fish. With heightened attention to known and potential harmful effects of such exposures, the US Food and Drug Administration (FDA) in 1999 requested that drug companies report on amounts of mercury in their products. The results for mercury in vaccines, in the form of thimerosal, exceeded FDA guidelines for exposures to the kind of mercury found in fish. Mercury in fish appears in the form of methylmercury, which is not readily metabolized and excreted in the human body. It is known to cause, at certain levels of high exposure, harmful neurological effects. The mercury in thimerosal metabolizes in the body to ethylmercury, a compound which, while not widely studied at the time, was thought to be much less harmful than methylmercury.

The FDA had a dilemma: there were no recommendations for exposure to levels of ethylmercury. So, should they apply the methylmercury guidelines to ethylmercury? Was there cause for concern about exposure to mercury in childhood vaccines? Unable to answer these questions immediately, together with the American Academy of Pediatrics and other groups, they called for vaccine companies to reduce or eliminate the use of thimerosal in vaccines. Additionally, studies were planned to investigate whether there were harmful effects in children exposed to the amount of mercury in vaccines.

At this point, activists and others became concerned about the safety of thimerosal, and they speculated that autism could be an outcome of exposure to mercury in vaccines. The Institute of Medicine consequently undertook a comprehensive safety review of the issue. Their preliminary report, published in 2001, stated that the committee did not find enough evidence to support or reject a causal relationship between mercury in vaccines and neurodevelopmental disorders (Immunization Safety Review Committee, 2001). But, their final report, published in 2004, reached the conclusion that the large body of evidence gathered on the question since 2001 favoured rejecting the hypothesis that mercury in vaccines was associated with neurodevelopmental disorders. Since then, evidence from many studies has continued to support rejecting an association between thimerosal and autism. Thimerosal is thus no longer used in most childhood vaccines, although some forms of influenza vaccine available in multi-dose vials may contain the preservative (CDC, 2018).

Other hypotheses

But, after thimerosal was removed from most vaccines, autism rates did not drop. Rather, they continued to rise (CDC, 2018). Some vaccine critics then shifted their attention from a hypothesized mercury exposure/autism connection to other targets. One such target is the number of vaccines given to children. Many vaccines have been added to the childhood immunization schedule since the 1980s, and some critics have voiced concern that this increase in vaccine exposure results in autism. Yet no evidence of an association between increased exposure to vaccines and autism has appeared (DeStephano *et al.*, 2013). Others have focused on the aluminium adjuvant in some vaccines as a potential cause of autism. Yet the amounts of aluminium used in vaccines are small in comparison to other exposures to aluminium, such as in breast milk and infant formula. Aluminium in vaccines has not been implicated in any infant or childhood health problems (CDC, 2018)

Conclusion

Most scientific and medical experts are satisfied that no connection exists between vaccines and autism and other neurodevelopmental disorders. But still critics continue to question the issue. Not only do they question the relationship between MMR and thimerosal and autism, but they also bring up further culprits they believe might play a role in the development of autism. Researchers continue to examine these questions, but there is no evidence that these factors play a role in autism development. Most autism researchers hold that the causes of autism are many and include genetic and environmental factors but do not involve vaccines (CDC, 2018).

Vaccines are one of the great pillars of modern medicine. Life used to be especially brutal for children before vaccines, with huge numbers being felled by diseases like measles, smallpox, whooping cough or rubella, to name just a few. Today these ailments can be completely prevented with a simple injection. So, as science continues to advance and tackle new challenges, people should not forget how many deaths and illnesses vaccines have prevented and how they continue to protect us from potentially devastating forms of infectious disease.

Summary of main points

1   There have been attempts to rehabilitate biological explanations of criminal behaviour by incorporating social and environmental factors into a 'multifactor' approach. This proposes that the presence of certain biological predispositions may increase the likelihood that an individual will offend.

2   Individuals born with particular biological and psychological characteristics or propensities may not only predispose them to but also may actually cause certain forms of behaviour.

3   This sociobiological perspective proposes that poverty leads to behavioural differences through the interaction of individual and environmental elements and is an argument taken up and developed by key 'right realist' theorists.

4   Bio-criminologists assume a positivist epistemology which requires no subjective interpretation.

5   Biocritical criminologists are concerned that all actions of human beings from the baseness of their crimes to the heights of their altruism can be reduced ultimately to genetics.
6   Social constructionists are concerned about scientific views which assume that humanity can be encapsulated and 'totalized' and which it is argued has done severe damage to the lives of people.
7   In recent years, there has been substantial interest among sociobiological researchers in the US in antisocial behaviour which is seen to emerge early in childhood in some individuals and persist into adulthood.
8   A whole body of research has linked aspects of the environment inhabited by the child – such as the quality of parenting and marital conflict – to the development of antisocial behaviour.
9   Adverse childhood experiences (ACEs) are being used as a predictive model to forecast outcomes of abused and harmed children.
10 A submission by six eminent academics to a House of Commons Science and Technology Select Committee Inquiry concluded that the campaign encouraging teachers, health and social care professionals to be 'ACEs aware' should be seriously questioned.

Discussion questions

1   In what ways do sociobiological explanations of criminal behaviour differ from their traditional biological predecessors?
2   In what ways have right realists incorporated sociobiological research into their explanations of criminal behaviour?
3   Briefly explain the biocritical of socio-biology.
4   What are ACEs and why are they said to be usual?
5   What are the criticisms of ACES?

Suggested further reading

Wilson and Herrnstein (1985), Mednick (1977) and Mednick *et al.* (1987) provide essential introductory readings for those interested in sociobiology. Wilson and Herrnstein (1985) provide the links between this approach and right realism. Draper *et al.* (2015) provide the introduction to biocritical criminology. The case for ACEs is put by Felitti *et al.* (1998) and is questioned by Eaton and Holmes (2017). The submission to the House of Commons Science and Technology Select Committee Inquiry is provided by Edwards *et al.* (2017).

References

Aguilar, B., Sroufe, A., Egeland, B. and Carlson, E. (2000) 'Distinguishing the Early-Onset/Persistent and Adolescent-Onset Antisocial Behavior Types: From Birth to 16 Years', *Development and Psychopathology*, 12(2): 109–32.
Arseneault, L., Tremblay, R.E., Boulerice, B. and Saucier, J. (2002) 'Obstetrical Complications and Violent Delinquency: Testing Two Developmental Pathways', *Child Development*, 73(2): 496–50.
Bhaskar, R. (1998) *The Possibility of Naturalism: A Philosophical Critique of the Contemporary Human Sciences*, 3ird ed. London: Routledge.

Bost, K.K., Vaughn, B.E., Washington, W.N., Cielinski, K.L. and Bradbard, M.R. (1998) 'Social Competence, Social Support, and Attachment: Construct Domains, Measurement, and Paths of Influence for Preschool Children', *Child Development*, 69: 192–218.

Brennan, P. and Mednick, S.A. (1997) 'Medical Histories of Antisocial Individuals', in D.M. Stoff, J. Breiling and J. Maser (eds.) *Handbook of Antisocial Behavior* (pp. 269–79). New York: John Wiley & Sons.

Broman, S.H., Nichols, P.L. and Kennedy, W.A. (1975) *Preschool IQ: Prenatal and Early Developmental Correlates*. Hillsdale, NJ: Erlbaum.

Campbell, S.B., Pierce, E.W., Moore, G. and Marakovitz, S. (1996) 'Boys' Externalizing Problems at Elementary School Age: Pathways From Early Behavior Problems, Maternal Control, and Family Stress', *Development and Psychopathology*, 4: 701–19.

Campbell, S.B., Shaw, D.S. and Gilliom, M. (2000) 'Early Externalizing Behavior Problems: Toddlers and Pre-Schoolers at Risk for Later Maladjustment', *Development and Psychopathology*, 12(3): 467.

Carrier, N. and Walby, K. (2014) 'Ptolemizing Lombroso: The Pseudo-Revolution of Biosocial Criminology', *Journal of Theoretical and Philosophical Criminology*, 6(1): 1–45.

Centers for Disease Control and Prevention (CDC) (2018) *Data and Statistics on Autism Spectrum Disorder*. Available from: www.cdc.gov/ncbddd/autism/data.html [Accessed 25 January 2019].

Cicchetti, D. and Rogosch, F.A. (1996) 'Equifinality and Multifinality in Developmental Psychopathology', *Development & Psychopathology*: 597–600.

Coller, A. (1994) *Critical Realism: An Introduction to Roy Bhaskar's Philosophy*. London: Verso.

Collins, H. and Pinch, T. (1993) *The Golem: What Everyone Should Know About Science*. Cambridge: Cambridge University Press.

Davis, A. (1996) 'Risk Work and Mental Health', in H. Kemshall and J. Pritchard (eds.) *Good Practice in Risk Assessment and Risk Management*. London: Jessica Kingsley.

Deater-Deckard, K., Dodge, K.A., Bates, J.E. and Pettit, G.S. (1998) 'Multiple Risk Factors in the Development of Externalizing Behavior Problems: Group and Individual Differences', *Development and Psychopathology*, 10: 469–93.

Deer, B. (2011) 'How the Case Against the MMR Vaccine', *BMJ*, 342: c5347.

Denno, D. (1993) 'Considering Lead Poisoning as a Criminal Defence', *Fordham Urban Law Journal*, 20: 377–400.

DeStefano, F., Price, C.S., Weintraub, E.S. (2013) 'Increasing Exposure to Antibody-Stimulating Proteins and Polysaccharides in Vaccines is Not Associated with Risk of Autism', *The Journal of Pediatrics*, 163(2): 561–7.

Dishion, T.J. (1990) 'The Family Ecology of Boys' Peer Relations in Middle Childhood', *Child Development*, 61: 74–92.

Dodge, K.A., Pettit, G.S. and Bates, J.E. (1994) 'Socialization Mediators of the Relation between Socioeconomic Status and Child Conduct Problems', *Child Development*, 65: 649–65.

Draper, M.R., Olsen, J.M., McGraw, J. and Sturtevant, D. (2015) 'An Interpretivist Introduction', *Journal of Theoretical and Philosophical Criminology*, 7(1): 42–60.

Drillien, C.M. (1964) *The Growth and Development of the Prematurely Born Infant*. Edinburgh: Livingstone.

Eaton, J. (2019) 'Why You Need to Remain Critical of ACEs (Adverse Childhood Experiences)', *Victimfocus*, March 15.

Eaton, J. and Holmes, D. (2017) *Working Effectively to Address Child Sexual Exploitation: Evidence Scope*. Birmingham: Research In Practice.

Edwards, R., Gillies, V., Lee, E., Macvarish, J., White, S. and Wastell, P. (2017) 'The Problem with ACEs', *Submission to the House of Commons Science and Technology Select Committee Inquiry into the Evidence-Base for Early Years Intervention (EY10039)*, December 12.

Ellis, L. (2005) 'Theory Explaining the Biological Correlates of Criminality', *European Journal of Criminology*, 2(3): 27–314.

Englander, M. (2007) 'Persistent Psychological Meaning of Early Emotional Memories', *Journal of Phenomenological Psychology*, 3: 11–216.

Felitti, V.J., Anda, R.F., Dale, M.S., Nordenberg, M.D., Williamson, D.F., Spitz, A.J., Edwards, V., Koss, M.P. and Marks, J.S. (1998) 'Relationship of Childhood Abuse and Household Dysfunction to Many of the Leading Causes of Death in Adults: The Adverse Childhood Experiences (ACE) Study', *American Journal of Preventive Medicine*, 14(4): 245–5.

Fishbein, D. (2001) *Biobehavioural Perspectives in Criminology*. Belmont, CA: Wadsworth.

Fudenberg, H.H. (1996) 'Dialysable Lymphocyte Extract (DLyE) in Infantile Onset Autism: A Pilot Study', *Biotherapy*, 9(1–3): 143–7.

Gans, D. (1991) 'Sucrose and Unusual Childhood Behaviour', *Nutrition Today*, 26: 14.

Gergen, K. (2014) 'Social Constructionism', in T. Thomas (ed.) *Encyclopedia of Critical Psychology* (pp. 1772–6). New York, NY: Springer.

Godlee, F., Smith, J. and Marcovitch, H. (2011) 'Wakefield's Article Linking Wakefield's Article Linking MMR Vaccine and Autism Was Fraudlent', *BMJ*, 342: c7452.

Gould, S.J. (1996) *The Mismeasure of Man*. New York, NY: W.W. Norton.

Gray, G. (1986) 'Diet, Crime and Delinquency: A Critique', *Nutrition Reviews Supplement*, 44: 9–94.

Gupta, S. (1996) 'Immunology and Immunologic Treatment of Autism', *Proc Natl Autism Assn Chicago*: 455–60.

Hertz-Picciotto, I. and Delwiche, L. (2009) 'The Rise in Autism and the Role of Age at Diagnosis', *Epidemiology*, 20(1): 84.

Heylen, B., Pauwels, L., Beaver, K. and Ruffinengo, M. (2015) 'Defending Biosocial Criminology: On the Discursive Style of our Critics, the Separation of Ideology and Science, and a Biologically Informed Defense of Fundamental Values', *Journal of Theoretical and Philosophical Criminology*, 7(1): 3–96.

Horton, R.A. (2004) 'Statement by the Editors of the Lancet', *The Lancet*, 363(9411): 820–1.

Immunization Safety Review Committee, Institute of Medicine (2001) 'Immunization Safety Review: Measles-Mumps-Rubella Vaccine and Autism', *National Academies Press*, January 25.

Jeffery, C.R. (1977) *Crime Prevention Through Environmental Design*. Beverly Hills, CA: Sage.

Kandel, E. and Mednick, S. (1991) 'Perinatal Complications Predict Violent Offending', *Criminology*, 29(3): 519–29.

Kane, R. (2005) *A Contemporary Introduction to Free Will*. New York, NY: Oxford University Press.

Kazdin, A.E. (1987) *Conduct Disorder in Childhood and Adolescence*. Newbury Park, CA: Sage.

Lancaster, J.B., Sherrod, L., Rossi, A.S. and Altmann, J. (1987) *Parenting Across the Life Span*. Piscataway, NJ: Aldine Transaction.

Laucht, M., Esser, G., Baving, L., Gerhold, M., Hoesch, I., Ihle, W., Steigleider, P., Stock, B., Stoehr, R., Weindrich, D. and Schmidt, M. (2000) 'Behavioral Sequelae of Perinatal Insults and Early Family Adversity at Years of Age', *Journal of the American Academy of Child and Adolescent Psychiatry*, 39: 122.

Laurance, J. (2004) 'How Was the MMR Scare Sustained for So Long When the Evidence Showed That It Was Unfounded?', *The Independent*, September 19.

Liu, J. and Wuerker, A. (2005) 'Biosocial Bases of Aggressive and Violent Behaviour: Implications for Nursing Studies', *International Journal of Nursing Studies*, 42(2): 229–41.

Martin, J. (1981) 'A Longitudinal Study of the Consequences of Early Mother: Infant Interaction: A Microanalytic Approach', *Monographs of the Society for Research in Child Development*, 190: 46.

McCall, P. and Land, K. (2004) 'Trends in Environmental Lead Exposure and Troubled Youth', *Social Science Research*, 33(2): 339–59.

Mednick, S.A. (1977) 'A Biosocial Theory of the Learning of Law-Abiding Behavior', in S.A. Mednick and K.O. Christiansen (eds.) *Biosocial Bases of Criminal Behavior*. New York: Gardner.

Mednick, S.A., Moffitt, T.E. and Stack, S. (eds.) (1987) *The Causes of Crime: New Biological Approaches*. Cambridge: Cambridge University Press.

Meikle, J., Boseley, S. (2010) *MMR Row Doctor Andrew Wakefield Struck Off Register*, May 24.

Moffitt, T.E. (1993a) 'Adolescent-Limited and Life-Course-Persistent Antisocial Behavior: A Developmental Taxonomy', *Psychological Review*, 100: 674–701.

Moffitt, T.E. (1993b) 'The Neuropsychology of Conduct Disorder', *Development and Psychopathology*, 5: 135–51.

Naragon, M.D. (1994) 'Communities in Motion: Drapetomania, Work and the Development of African-American Slave Cultures', *Slavery and Abolition: A Journal of Slave and Post-Slave Studies*, 153: 63–7.

Needleman, H., Reiss, J., Tobin, M., Biesecker, G. and Greenhouse, J. (1996) 'Bone Lead Levels and Delinquent Behaviour', *Journal of the American Medical Association*, 275: 363–9.

Neisser, U. (1996) 'Intelligence: Knowns and Unknowns', *American Psychologist*, 51: 77–101.

Nye, A. (1990) *Words of Power: A Feminist Reading of the History of Logic*. London: Routledge.

Office for National Statistics (2017) *Crime in England and Wales: Year Ending June 2017*. London: ONS.

Offit, P.A. (2008) *Autism's False Profits*. New York: Columbia University Press.

Osborne, T. (2014) 'Desperate Equilibrium: On the Guilt, Law, and Rationality', *Economy and Society*, 43(1): 40–54.

Perlin, M. and Dlugacz, H. (2007) *Mental Health Issues in Jails and Prisons: Cases and Materials*. Durham, NC: Carolina Academic Press.

Piquero, A. and Tibbetts, S. (1999) 'The Impact of Pre/Perinatal Disturbances and Disadvantaged Familial Environment in Predicting Criminal Offending', *Studies on Crime and Crime Prevention*: 52–70.

Raine, A. (2002) 'Biosocial Studies of Antisocial and Violent Behavior in Children and Adults: A Review', *Journal of Abnormal Child Psychology*, 30(4): 311–26.

Raine, A., Brennan, P. and Mednick, S. (1997) 'Interaction between Birth Complications and Early Maternal Rejection in Predisposing Individuals to Adult Violence: Specificity to Serious, Early-Onset Violence', *American Journal of Psychiatry*, 154(9): 1265–71.

Rantakallio, P., Koiranen, M. and Moettoenen, J. (1992) 'Association of Perinatal Events, Epilepsy, and Central Nervous System Trauma with Juvenile Delinquency', *Archives of Disease in Childhood*, 67: 1459–61.

Rappaport, N. and Thomas, C. (2004) 'Recent Research Findings on Aggressive and Violent Behaviour in Youth: Implications for Clinical Assessment and Intervention', *Journal of Adolescent Health*, 35(4): 260–77.

Rice, C.E., Rosanoff, M., Dawson, G., Durkin, M., Croen, L.A., Singer, A., Yeargin-Allsopp, M. (2012) 'Evaluating Changes in the Prevalence of the Autism Spectrum Disorders (ASDs)', *Public Health Reviews*, 34(2): 1.

Rutter, M., Cox, A., Tupling, C., Berger, M. and Yule, W. (1975a) 'Attainment and Adjustment in Two Geographical Areas: 1. The Prevalence of Psychiatric Disorder', *British Journal of Psychiatry*, 126: 493–509.

Rutter, M., Yule, B., Quinton, D., Rowlands, O., Yule, W. and Berger, W. (1975b) 'Attainment and Adjustment in Two Geographical Areas: 3. Some Factors Accounting for Area Differences', *British Journal of Psychiatry*, 126: 520–33.

Sameroff, A., Seifer, R., Zax, M. and Barocas, R. (1987) 'Early Indicators of Developmental Risk: The Rochester Longitudinal Study', *Schizophrenia Bulletin*, 13: 33–94.

Sanson, A., Oberklaid, F., Pedlow, R. and Prior, M. (1991) 'Risk Indicators: Assessment of Infancy Predictors of Pre-School Behavioural Maladjustment', *Journal of Child Psychology and Psychiatry*, 32(4): 609–26.

Schoenthaler, S.J. and Bier, I. (2000) 'The Effect of Vitamin-Mineral Supplementation on Juvenile Delinquency among American Schoolchildren: A Randomized Double-Blind Placebo-Controlled Trial', *Journal of Alternative and Complementary Medicine*, 6: 7–1.

Schoenthaler, S.J. and Doraz, W. (1983) 'Diet and Crime', *International Journal of Biosocial Crime*, 4: 74–94.

Shaw, D.S., Ingoldsby, E., Gilliom, M. and Nagin, D. (2003) 'Trajectories Leading to School-Age Conduct Problems', *Developmental Psychology*, 3: 40–91.

Shaw, D.S., Keenan, K. and Vondra, J.I. (1994a) 'Developmental Precursors of Externalizing Behavior: Ages 1 to 3', *Developmental Psychology*, 30(3): 355–64.

Shaw, D.S., Vondra, J.I., Hommerding, K., Keenan, K. and Dunn, M. (1994b) 'Chronic Family Adversity and Early Child Behavior Problems: A Longitudinal Study of Low Income Families', *Journal of Child Psychology and Psychiatry*, 35(6): 1109–22.

Shaw, D., Winslow, E., Owens, E. and Hood, N. (1998a) 'Young Children's Adjustment to Chronic Family Adversity: A Longitudinal Study of Low-Income Families', *Journal of the American Academy of Child and Adolescent Psychiatry*, 37(5): 545–53.

Shaw, D.S., Winslow, E., Owens, E., Vondra, J., Cohn, J. and Bell, R. (1998b) 'The Development of Early Externalizing Problems among Children from Low-Income Families: A Transformational Perspective', *Journal of Abnormal Child Psychology*, 26(2): 95–107.

Siegel, L.J. and McCormick, C. (2006) *Criminology in Canada: Theories, Patterns, and Typologies*, 3rd ed. Toronto, ON: Thompson, Nelson.

Slife, B., Reber, J, and Richardson, F. (2005) *Critical Thinking about Psychology: Hidden Assumptions and Plausible Alternatives*. Washington, DC: American Psychological Association.

Slife, B. and Williams, R. (1995) *What's Behind the Research? Discovering Hidden Assumptions in the Behavioral Sciences*. Thousand Oaks, CA: Sage.

Stretesky, P. and Lynch, M. (2001) 'The Relationship between Lead Exposure and Homicide', *Archives of Paediatric Adolescent Medicine*, 155: 579–2.

Thompson, N.P., Pounder, R.E., Wakefield, A.J. and Montgomery, S.M. (1995) 'Is Measles Vaccination a Risk Factor for Inflammatory Bowel Disease?', *The Lancet*, 345(8957): 1071–4.

Unnever, J.D. (2015) 'Causes of African American Juvenile Delinquency', in M.D. Krohn, J. Lane and J. Malden (eds.) *The Handbook of Juvenile Delinquency and Juvenile*. Cambridge, MA: Wiley Blackwell.

Van den Bergle, P. (1974) 'Bringing the Beast Back In: Towards a Biosocial Theory of Aggression', *American Sociological Review*, 39: 779.

Virkkunen, M. (1986) 'Reactive Hypoglycaemic Tendency among Habitually Violent Offenders', *Nutritional Reviews Supplement*, 44: 94–103.

Wakefield, A.J., Murch, S.H., Anthony, A., Linnell, J., Casson, D.M., Malik, M. and Walker-Smith, J.A. (1998) 'Ileal-Lymphoid-Nodular Hyperplasia, Non-Specific Colitis, and Pervasive Developmental Disorder in Children', *The Lancet*, 351(9103): 637–41.

Wakschlag, L.S. and Hans, S.L. (1999) 'Relation of Maternal Responsiveness during Infancy to the Development of Behavior Problems in High-Risk Youths', *Developmental Psychology*, 35(2): 569–79.

Werner, E.E., Bierman, J.M. and French, F.E. (1971) *The Children of Kauai: A Longitudinal Study from the Prenatal Period to Age Ten*. Honolulu, HI: University of Hawaii Press.

WHO (2006) 'Thimersol in Vaccines', *World Health Organization*, January 25.

Wilson, J.Q. and Herrnstein, R.J. (1985) *Crime and Human Nature*. New York: Simon and Schuster.

Yaralian, P. and Raine, A. (2001) 'Biosocial Approaches to Crime: Psychophysiology and Brain Dysfunction', in R. Paternoster and R. Bachman (eds.) *Explaining Criminals and Crime*. Los Angeles: Roxbury Publishing.

Younge, S.L., Oetting, E.R. and Deffenbacher, J.L. (1996) 'Correlations among Maternal Rejection, Dropping Out of School, and Drug Use in Adolescents', *Journal of Clinical Psychology*, 52(1): 96–102.

Chapter 16

Abolitionism and convict criminology

Key issues

1   Abolitionism
2   Critical carceral studies
3   New abolitionism meets criminology
4   Studying the lessons and experiences of the new abolitionists
5   Convict criminology

Introduction

Abolitionism is a sociological and political perspective which analyses criminal justice and penal systems as being social problems in themselves which actually intensify rather than diminish crime and its impact. Thus, prisons – the initial focus of study – reinforce dominant ideological constructions of crime, reproduce social divisions and, by concentrating on crimes committed by the poor and powerless, divert attention from crimes committed by the powerful. Abolitionists thus advocate the radical transformation of the prison and punishment systems and propose their replacement with a reflexive and integrative strategy for dealing with these complex social phenomena.

Convict criminology is a relatively new and controversial perspective in the practical field of criminal justice and the academic field of criminology which has emerged in the US in recent years. It provides an alternative view to the way crime and criminal justice problems are usually seen by researchers, policy makers, and politicians, many of whom have had minimal contact with prisons and convicts. It is a view informed by a rather different but candid form of participant observation.

Abolitionism

Liberal approaches to the study of the prison and notions of punishment have been built on a number of often competing and contradictory goals: rehabilitation, general prevention, incapacitation, punishment and specific and general deterrence. Abolitionism, which emerged out of the social and civil rights movements of the late 1960s, challenges these liberal perspectives by arguing that in practice the criminal justice system and prisons contribute little to the protection of the individual and the control of crime. The Dutch abolitionist Willem De Haan thus observes that the prison 'is counter-productive, difficult to control and [is] itself a major social problem'. Crime is understood to be a complex, socially constructed phenomenon which 'serves to maintain political power relations and lends legitimacy to the crime control apparatus and the intensification of surveillance and control' (De Haan, 1991: 206–7). Abolitionists are furthermore critical of the unquestioning acceptance of prison reform by liberals.

For abolitionists like Thomas Mathiesen, liberal reform can never have a positive effect because it reinforces and strengthens the system, perpetuating processes of brutalization for the confined. In contrast, 'negative reforms' are supported for their potential to challenge and undermine the system leading eventually to the demise of prisons. Abolitionists thus advocate a system which deals with crime as a socially constructed phenomenon. The response should not be based on punitive exclusion but by a reflexive and participatory system of inclusion built on redress, social policy, mutuality and solidarity: 'the aim is compensation rather than retaliation; reconciliation rather than blame allocation. To this end, the criminal justice system needs to be decentralized and neighbourhood courts established as a complement or substitute' (De Haan, 1991: 211–12). Abolitionism thus 'implies a negative critique of the fundamental shortcomings of the criminal law to realize social justice', while simultaneously offering both an alternative way of thinking about crime and a 'radical approach to penal reform' (Wilson and Herrnstein, 1985).

It is important to note that abolitionism is not a homogeneous theoretical and political movement but one which varies across cultures. It is a predominantly European phenomenon (Davies, 1998), but there have also been different strands to the movement with some pointing to the distinct differences between European and UK movements. In Europe, early abolitionists such as Mathiesen, Christie, Bianchi and Hulsman advocated an alternative vision for criminal justice politics. Second-generation abolitionists – neo-abolitionists – accept many of the earlier principles, including the rejection of both the concept of crime and 'penality as the ultimate metaphor of justice' (Wilson and Herrnstein, 1985).

British neo-abolitionists such as Box-Grainger, Ryan, Ward, Hudson and Sim have also advocated engaging in more interventionist work to develop a 'criminology from below', which, in utilizing a complex set of competing, contradictory and oppositional discourses, providing support on the ground for the confined and their families, has challenged the hegemony around prison that has US servants, traditional reform groups and many academics on the same pragmatic and ideological terrain. In a number of areas, such as deaths in custody, prison conditions, medical power, visiting, censorship and sentencing, these groups have conceded key points to the abolitionist argument and have moved onto a more radical terrain where they, too, have contested the construction of state-defined truth around penal policy (Sim, 1994: 275–76).

In view of the huge increase in prison populations around the globe and the continuing rise in both reported crimes and crimes audited in victimization and self-report studies, abolitionism offers an important series of insights into the role of the prison and its failures at the beginning of the twenty-first century. There have nevertheless been a number of issues raised and criticisms made of the abolitionist position. Most have come from those who – like abolitionists – would see themselves as part of a theoretical and political tradition on the critical wing of politics and social science. Left realists thus criticize abolitionists for their idealism and for their 'anarcho–communist position' which is 'preoccupied with abolishing or minimizing state intervention rather than attempting to make it more effective, responsive and accountable'.

Abolitionists nevertheless reject the charge of idealism and point to the influence they have had on a number of political debates and social policies in terms of making the state more accountable. For example, the issue of deaths in custody which became a major political debate in the UK in the 1980s and 1990s, not only involved individuals who were part of the abolitionist movement; it also had a significant hegemonic impact on liberal reform groups, by pulling them onto a more radical and critical terrain in terms of demanding political action to deal with the devastating impact of these deaths on the families and friends of the deceased (Sim, 1994). Abolitionists would also say that the problem with criminology is that it suffers from too little utopian and idealistic thought rather than too much.

Feminist writers have drawn attention to the problem of violent men and what should be done to protect women from, for example, men who rape. This raises the broader issue of dangerousness and the nature of the response needed to deal with dangerous individuals such as serial killers who are invariably men. Abolitionists would agree that violence against women is a major issue across societies, which should be taken seriously, but would also argue that simply incarcerating violent men can only mean detaining them in institutions where the pervasive culture of masculinity is likely to reinforce misogynist views around male power and women (Sim, 1994). They thus say that the nature of the institutions and the broader culture which objectifies women and equates heterosexuality with domination and power should be addressed.

Moreover, abolitionists would argue that dangerousness is a social construction encompassing a range of behaviours which can have immense implications for individual and group safety, but which are rarely, if ever, labelled dangerous, for example, the non-implementation of health and safety laws. Finally, abolitionists would suggest that the distinction between normal and abnormal, which lies at the heart of positivist thought and which dominates debates about violence and dangerousness, is itself problematic. The killings carried out by, and the non-prosecution of, the 'normal' men who murdered hundreds of innocent men, women and children in Vietnam in 1968 is given as an example of the social construction of dangerousness. This crime took place fifteen months before the infamous Manson Family murders in the US, with the latter case becoming deeply embedded in popular and political consciousness while the former was to be largely forgotten.

Angela Davies (1998: 102–3) has also noted that while the European abolitionist tradition has offered many important insights into the nature of the prison, 'there is no sustained analysis of the part anti-racism might play in the theory and practice of abolitionism'. This is particularly important when it is recognized that prison populations around the world contain a disproportionate number of people who are drawn from ethnic minority backgrounds and this is very much the case in her home, the US.

Abolitionists have nevertheless become increasingly attached to the emerging discourses and debates surrounding human rights and social justice which they see as mechanisms for developing negative reforms, thereby promoting a response to social harm that is very different from the destructive prison and punishment systems which currently exist. We now consider these issues further in the context of the case for a critical carceral studies which seek more than the simple abolition of the prison.

Critical carceral studies

Brown and Schept (2017) argue that criminology has been slow to open up a conversation about decarceration and abolition in comparison with other disciplines, such as history, geography, gender, race and critical ethnic studies. Scholars from those areas and actors on the ground – those close up to confinement – have done most of the organizing against mass incarceration and the theorizing of alternative possibilities. Why those experiences – and the theoretical traditions which inform their work – have been less recognized and developed in criminology and this should be an essential concern for criminologists. The extent to which criminology can sustain an alternative or abolitionist politics nevertheless remains an open question. Amid growing conversations about decarceration and shifting rhetoric on punishment, the authors identify some of the obstacles that limit criminology as a site from which to engage the abolitionist project, asking where criminologists might turn for interventionist models which move away from imprisonment and the violence of the carceral state itself.

Brown and Schept (2017) observe that the rise of the carceral state remains a peculiar failure or a success of unprecedented proportions depending on your criminological perspective. Thus, if one considers the managerialist benevolence of criminology to be both an intention toward and an exercise of reform, then the unforeseen historical possibility and structural dimensions of the scope and scale of the carceral state truly indicate a failure on the part of the discipline to anticipate the punitive turn. If, on the other hand, one sees from a criminological perspective an historical approach to reform that has always expanded and stabilized the very systems it claims to change, then the rise of mass incarceration marks, in fact, the continued success of the discipline, which offers important credibility to the expansion of police power and imprisonment.

Importantly, this latter position should not be seen as an endorsement of some conspiracy between the discipline and the state. Rather, it is steeped in an historical examination of the patterns of imprisonment across centuries, performed by scholars and activists concerned with the ways that criminology has rescued the carceral state from crises of legitimacy (Foucault, 1980; Rothman, 1980; Murakawa, 2014). Thus, in the US, a growing research literature in the socio-legal and sociological study of punishment takes racial injustice and the criminalization of poverty and everyday life, as its primary frame for understanding criminal justice (Beckett, 2000; Beckett and Herbert, 2009; Muhammad, 2010; Alexander, 2010; Murakawa, 2014). Moreover, this work has taken place alongside a wave of anti-racism movements which have challenged mass incarceration, police violence and the historical frames of criminology.

Brown and Schept (2017) observe that while criminology has often played an active role in providing both material and ideological support and legitimacy for expansions and exercises of police power and mass imprisonment (Cohen, 1988; Foucault, 1980; Schept et al., 2015), there is, at the same time, a part of the history of the discipline which includes lines of radical and activist scholarship even though this development is uneven and interrupted. Thus, as we have seen elsewhere in this book, criminologists active in the 1960s and 1970s were shaped by the social movements surrounding them and of which they were a part. Entire departments coalesced around radical political commitments. Foundational work on abolition (Mathiesen, 1974; Hulsman and De Celis, 1982) and decarceration (Scull, 1977) emerged during this period, alongside broader engagements with police power and capital (Taylor et al., 1973; Quinney, 1977; Hall et al., 1978). Moreover, criminologists became involved in the International Conference on Penal Abolition, which brought together academics, former prisoners, activists, and journalists into a 'conference-movement' occurring biennially in a variety of places throughout the world. Since the late 1990s, a number of edited criminological volumes have emerged engaging with abolition specifically, as well as visions of transformative justice, alongside entire monographs engaging abolition and decarceration (Miller, 1996; Ruggiero, 2010; Schept, 2015).

European and Australian criminologists have played a significant role in bringing discussions of abolition to the forefront of critical criminology with much of this work emerging from radical forms of Christian liberation theology, Marxist critiques, and post-Enlightenment forms of reasoning, which trace utopian thinking within the context of Western liberal ideologies (Mathiesen, 1974; Christie, 1981; Hulsman, 1991; Ruggiero, 2010). The themes include transformation over reform through long-term structural change, the problems of institutional assimilation and neutralization, the persistence and violence of the prison and the refocusing of harm over crime, all which, at first glance, have much in common with US abolition movement (Carlen, 2013; Hillyard, 2015; Ryan and Ward, 2015). Similarly, in the Australian context, important attention to settler colonialism and intersectionality in relation to abolition has found a foothold but largely in terms of a critique of criminal justice system reform efforts (Baldry *et al.*, 2012; Russell and Carlton, 2013; Cuneen and Tauri, 2015).

Criminological engagement with abolition has allowed for a reflexive critique of the discipline itself. Thus, Foucault (1980: 47–48) refers to the 'garrulous discourses' of criminology, full of 'endless repetitions' and 'indispensability' in grafting intellectual credibility onto juridical or political power. But, several critics within the discipline have taken up alternative positions. Thus, Jock Young has noted the 'elective affinity' between positivist criminology and the state, both in the supply of necessary technocratic data and in the form of 'shared notions of ontology and of social order', a position shared by many others operating from within the discipline (Agozino, 2003; Morrison, 2004; Loader and Sparks, 2010; Schept *et al.*, 2015; Piche, 2016).

New abolitionists and critical carceral studies scholars nevertheless show little interest in a public sociology or criminology dedicated to questions of the political tenability in policy discussions. Rather, their work emanates from experiences, practices and movement-generated theories grounded in surviving the threat of captivity, torture, and social death over the generations. A critical carceral studies approach – in solidarity with the project of abolition and meaningful decarceration – requires us to rethink the keywords of criminology to understand if abolition is a project to which the discipline can contribute.

New abolition meets criminology

Brown and Schept (2017) observe that criminology has been a key site – in its varied forms – for the reproduction of the very carceral logics which critical scholars aim to dismantle. Thus, the ways in which we assume, write and lecture about carceral and police power, play an important role in carrying the regime forward, reproducing and reforming its logics, training the next generation of its players and, in the prison industrial complex will require the abolition – the dismantling, changing and building anew – of the normative discourses and vocabularies, the ways of thinking and being, which constitute the conditions of the prison–industrial complex that derives their legitimacy in part from criminology (Foucault, 1980).

One key contribution of new abolitionist work is the disruption of dominant understandings of crime, law, punishment, safety and accountability, justice and the generation of alternative vocabularies and analyses from which to begin the escape from the carceral state. This work asks us to reconceptualize violence, victims, perpetrators, rehabilitation, safety and accountability, through the affective and emotional lives of the actors closest to – and locked within – the prison – industrial complex. Such work goes far to ensure that survival and precarity become visible as political events within the structural context of US criminal justice. This pursuit is one avenue by which to create the conditions for the legibility of everyday racialized state violence and its associated oppressions, out of which may come a transformative set of questions and possibilities about the nature of injury, harm and accountability (Martinot and Sexton, 2003).

Crime

Brown and Schept (2017) pertinently observe that mass incarceration – and the US criminal justice system – depends on criminalization. It is dependent on the production of vulnerability through forms of neoliberal dispossession and its consequent criminalization on an unprecedented scale. This is apparent in the criminalization of poverty, addiction, homelessness and mental illness (Beckett and Herbert, 2009; Wacquant, 2009b); children and youth (Rios, 2011); women (Richie, 2012); migrants (Moran et al., 2013; Mountz and Loyd, 2014; Weber and Pickering, 2011); race (Alexander, 2010); sexuality (Spade, 2011; Stanley and Smith, 2011); and disability (Ben-Moshe et al., 2014). Thus, creating a vast swathe of new carceral subjects. Quite simply, the carceral subject is a form of life which inhabits states of precarity continuously and is thus dedicated to projects of survival.

Criminologists must therefore deal with the reality that the interdependency of the discipline with the state agencies which comprise 'criminal justice' is what produces (and reproduces through reformation) criminalization and the carceral (Morrison, 2004). Normative treatments of violence as fundamentally interpersonal, individualized, and natural deny the multiple forms of structural violence inflicted by the neoliberal state through its institutions (policing, prisons, detention, etc.), legislative and administrative policies (dismantling of welfare, criminalizing of poverty, perpetual wars) and collusions with corporate power to secure accumulation and divest from the social wage. Without an understanding of these structural relations, most efforts to respond to crime reproduce configurations of violence. A move away from criminalization means an effort to reconceptualize crime and address violence without sole reliance (or, in some cases, any reliance) on criminal justice, specifically law enforcement or imprisonment.

Brown and Schept (2017) observe that in the US, these efforts are increasingly prevalent across cities where organizers share training, curricula and workshops which emphasize emergent strategies pushing back against community violence, school-to-prison pipelines, imprisonment and police violence. But following Davies (2003) and Gilmore (2007) it is observed that we must resist the urge to visualize abolition as an alternative metaphorical and material structure which can replace the prison (Davies, 2003: 107). Seen rather as a set of relationships, abolition and abolitionist reforms should focus on building up health, education, housing, jobs and alternative approaches to harm as they also dismantle the prison. In this manner, abolition is founded on the nature and possibility of freedom and emancipated forms of life. A key lesson for criminologists in this pursuit is the acknowledgement of criminal justice as foundational to the exercise of violence and one of our largest obstacles in the pursuit of social change. Criminology must ask what it offers in terms of an understanding of the needs of survivability and its contribution to life-extending, liberating work.

Law

Brown and Schept (2017) observe that in the US, jurisprudence, the subject of the law, is only intelligible as a rights-bearing individual. Notions of individual culpability and responsibility justify the exertion of police and carceral power; notions of a free-will rational actor compromised through addictions, mental illness or prior victimizations might mitigate the severity of the state response but still creates an individualized subject prone to coerced incapacitation and treatment by the state. Groups who have suffered violence at the hands of the state – for example racial minorities, LGBTQ (lesbian, gay, bisexual, transgender, queer/questioning) communities, immigrants and refugees – do not gain the kind of recognition through law and rights claims which supports structural transformation. Reliance on the law as a space for claims to dignity (Christie, 1981; Simon, 2014) too often risk reproduction of these liberal formations. The vast majority of policy reform efforts in the US criminal justice system begin at the compromised locus of law and the individualized neoliberal subject. A critical carceral study is attuned to the convergence of liberal legal constructs with neoliberal penality reliance on responsibilization and governance through risk (Harcourt, 2010).

Critical carceral studies increasingly take up a nuanced approach to law, critically examining reification and even reliance on law in pursuits of social justice while considering the effectiveness of legal strategies to secure certain 'non-reformist reforms' (Gorz, 1967), such as increased environmental justice victories, decriminalization and decarceration strategies that shrink the carceral net and minimum wage or guaranteed employment campaigns (Stein, 2014). Non-reformist reforms aim to prevent additional harms such as economic displacement and racialized social control. While the logic of visibility and inclusion is one of the main attractions of rights claims, abolitionists are, in general, wary of legal reforms which have created more insidious ways to entrench carceral practices (Murakawa, 2014).

Punishment

Brown and Schept (2017) observe that the keyway in which criminology and abolition challenge the legitimacy of punishment is in the historical prison–crime disconnect (Garland, 2001; Mauer, 2006). This, they argue, remains a disconnection which requires uncoupling in popular thinking and public discourse. They observe that while there is nothing novel about pointing out that state punishment is predominantly reserved for poor people (Reiman and Leighton, 2015) and people of colour (Alexander, 2010; Mauer, 2006), in the carceral era, punishment is still undertheorized by criminologists as criminogenic in its own right, having produced social, psychic, political and economic harms of unprecedented proportions which are the conditions for current abolitionist projects. But the violence of the state and capital is barely recognized as such, let alone subject to the kinds of sanctions which the criminal law metes out to those in violation of its most minute provisions. The rise of the debtor's prison, the criminalization of everyday life through regulatory infractions that fill municipal budgets, and the uprisings in various cities are distinctive ways in which to understand this carceral project in the current US (Kilgore, 2014; Shapiro, 2014).

Brown and Schept (2017) further argue that we should also pay attention to the terms we deploy to label such political projects. While the term *mass incarceration* undoubtedly draws attention to the sheer volume of people under forms of penal control, terminology like the *carceral state*, *prison nation* and *prison-industrial complex* are able to locate mass imprisonment in the political-economic and socio-cultural changes of divestment and austerity – deindustrialization, the loss of jobs, the retreat of the welfare state, privatization and the fortification of police power and security, the ongoing project of racialized criminalization – that have produced and characterize the carceral era. This broader treatment extracts the prison from its narrow place in the popular imagination as being just about crime and punishment and instead relocates it in conversations about employment, economies, imperialism, racial justice, uneven development, public health, climate change and environmental justice, land use and neoliberal ideology. This more acute, historicized discussion can begin to apprehend the complicated – and even contradictory – nature of punishment: its centrality to mass imprisonment (Clear and Frost, 2014), the cultural work it performs outside of the edifices of the prison (Brown, 2009) and, crucially, the ideological ways it operates, particularly within criminology, to obscure the broader social forces which sustain the carceral state.

Safety and accountability

Brown and Schept (2017) observe that the ultimate shared question for criminology and abolition may be the one of safety. Whereas criminologists refer to this as the mandate of crime control, abolitionists see the desire for safety as emergent at the level of everyday experience, without the borders or boundaries of criminological frames. They consider how we can create safe, healthy communities and flourishing lives. The kind of community (world) we want to live in. Mass incarceration, they observe, is a failed project in establishing safety for a host of reasons, but the primary one is of deadly significance: the life disruptions of criminal justice shorten existence for its subjects, their families and communities. And its markers are so normalized as to be largely overlooked: the carceral separation of families, especially parents and children; the individual and collective loss of family members to violence and prisons; school- and cradle-to-prison pipelines which exclude the lives of children in custody and suspension (Meiners, 2007); the chronic stress diseases and premature deaths of loved ones who engage in the exhausting daily work of job, home, and justice, attempting to bring public attention to carceral conditions and maintain contact with their loved ones in confinement (Gilmore, 2007); and the mortal entropy of labelling social problems as criminal offences.

In these contexts, the resourcing of criminal justice is considered more important and actively sequesters from education, health care, employment and, ultimately, safety. Rendering life less liveable and more precarious through criminalization and incarceration does not reduce harm or future harm and is at cross-purposes with stopping abuse and violence. For abolitionists and critical carceral studies scholars, safety is a product of structural transformation and is collective at its core. For criminology, both the neoliberal construct of the individual at the crux of crime and criminal justice limit both the conceptualization and actualization of safety. Safety, then, is not simply about those who have harmed or been harmed, but a movement beyond disciplinary neoliberal frames of responsibilization and internalization to community and state accountability, a kind of insurrectionary safety operating within an abolitionist habitus (Schept, 2015).

Abolitionists do not assume that we will ever exist in harm-free spaces. Rather, they emphasize that vulnerability is bound up with the human condition, that the pursuit of total security is a life-damaging pursuit, and that there are ways to better address, collectively, the harms we face and produce. To that effect, queer and feminist activist scholars from the anti-violence movement have produced important interventions in dominant approaches to problems of violence that all too often extend violence – state violence – into the very lives of victims and survivors on whose behalf advocates had reached out to police. Intervening in the traditional notion that the state provides safety, these authors argue against what they call 'carceral feminism' and argue for approaches to gender and sexual violence which can bring safety through addressing harms while transforming the structural conditions that produced them (Musto, 2013; Richie, 2012; Law, 2014; Thuma, 2015).

Justice

Brown and Schept (2017) observe that US opinion broadly understands justice as fundamentally equating to individual rights, responsibilities, culpability and retribution. This construct is affirmed as it circulates heavily through cultural production, reproducing itself as much in courtroom and police dramas as it does in actual courtrooms and police stations (Brown, 2009). But the hegemony of this narrow understanding has been subject to scathing critique, theorization and mobilization from community organizers and scholars developing and practising transformative justice, a vision which places interpersonal harm and accountability in the context of and inseparable from structural harm and state accountability. If notions of justice are separated from state punishment and instead understood as fundamentally social – joined inextricably to individual and collective safety from all violence, including that of precarity and of the state – then we may begin to imagine new ways of addressing our needs. In this way, we transform our situations as we also un-imagine the contemporary criminal justice system, an abolitionist project that is both political and epistemological (Armstrong, 2013; Carlen, 2013).

Reframing the key concerns of criminology, like abolition, is less about foreclosure and more about opening up possibilities for life. It is an empirical project, which asks what people are doing otherwise to deal with harm and violence and to produce flourishing lives and communities, to build health, education and employment in terms that both respond to the conditions of violence and harm and limit the former on as many levels as possible. That local and everyday project is how we might more fully theorize justice and a world beyond prisons (Gilmore (2011).

The lessons and experiences of the new abolitionists

Critical carceral studies remain distinctive from current arenas of criminological thought in important ways. The empirical record and lived experience of capture and confinement, quite formidably, exceed the frames of what we have historically conceived of as punishment. Prison–like conditions, the criminalization and segregation of everyday life and the reliance on exclusion and containment at borders, in urban centres and across poor and racialized communities and societies extend beyond traditional treatments of punishment (Beckett and Herbert, 2009; Beckett and Murakawa, 2012; Loyd *et al.*, 2012; Hannah-Moffat and Lynch, 2012; Story, 2015).

The carceral subject of a critical carceral study complicates and exceeds categories of criminality, penality and victimhood. Instead, this subject is an actor subjected to intersecting contemporary social forces and penal histories, whose identity is produced in the course of navigating dispossession, oppression and the production of social suffering (Brown, 2014). The carceral subject is distinctive from others in that they are precisely a mode of surplus life, created by forces of governance under global neoliberal capitalism, the inhabitant criminalized precisely because they live in conditions of precarity, included within different forms of carceral confinement. Consequently, studies of the carceral state place centre-stage analyses of late capitalist political economies, racialized regimes of state power and multilevel explications of state violence in examinations of criminalization, political resistance and crime (Murakawa, 2014; Gottschalk, 2015; Camp, 2016).

Work which engages the important structural relations between intimate violence, police violence, and incarceration (Kelly, 2011; Kim, 2009, 2011; Richie, 2012; Smith et al., 2006; Smith, 2015) refuses a singular focus on any one kind of violence and accuses the normative reliance on police and imprisonment to provide safety and accountability for the individuals, families and communities most hard hit by interpersonal harm, addiction and economic despair, It is an account of interpersonal, state and structural violence.

Conclusion

Among the many disastrous lessons of the rise of the carceral state is an important one for criminology. Criminologists have simply underestimated the crisis of credibility that the US criminal justice system now faces.

Jonathan Simon (2014: 3) observes argues that 'beyond the numbers, the quantitative story of mass incarceration, we as a society know shockingly little about what this far-from-natural disaster has wrought, the qualitative story of mass incarceration'. The 'depth of depravity' exceeds the violence done to the daily lives of prisoners and extends into the lived experiences of their families, loved ones and communities. Brown (2012) argues that attention must be given to the affective life of pain and suffering that the communities hardest hit by incarceration experience (Brown, 2012). In that pursuit, we must study the knowledges that experience has produced, a rich subaltern history of fugitivity, abolition, and transformation.

We consider the carceral (or penal) society thesis further in Chapter 18, but the one group with a significant lived experience of traditional penal incarceration on which they can legitimately critically reflect are ex-convicts. We thus now turn our attention to convict criminology.

Convict criminology

Convict criminology is a relatively new and controversial perspective in the practical field of criminal justice and the academic field of criminology which has emerged in the US in recent years. It provides an alternative view to the way crime and criminal justice problems are usually seen by researchers, policymakers and politicians, many of whom have had minimal contact with prisons and convicts. It is a view informed by a rather different but candid form of participant observation.

Convict criminology emerged in the 1990s among a group of ex-convict academics frustrated by reading the existing literature on crime and criminal justice which they found to be a reflection of the views of prison administrators or university academics and which largely ignored the lived experiences of convicts themselves. These former prisoners, who had subsequently obtained higher university degrees – along with sympathetic critical criminologists and abolitionists – sought research which reflected the observations and critical assessments of the men and women who had been incarcerated. The emerging field of convict criminology has thus consisted primarily of essays, articles, and books written by convicts or ex-convicts studying for or already in possession of doctorates some of whom are now employed as full-time academics.

An academically qualified ex-convict who merges his or her real-life experience and the perspectives derived from it with scholarly research into crime or prisons is generally referred to as a convict criminologist but having a criminal record is not a necessary precondition with so-called cleanskin researchers – with publications and work in the field – may also choose to join the group. Together, the collective intention is to conduct research which incorporates the experiences of defendants and prisoners and attempts to balance the representations of media and government. The value of this knowledge is that it may open the door to crime control strategies which are enlightened, humane and, it is hoped, more effective than what are currently in place.

There have been numerous ex-convicts who have worked at universities in a variety of disciplines. Most of them have chosen to 'stay in the closet', perhaps because their criminal histories were not relevant to their studies or maybe because they were afraid of negative reactions from their colleagues or employers. One early exception was Frank Tannenbaum, sometimes referred to as the 'grandfather of labelling theory', political activist, former federal prisoner, professor at Columbia University in the 1930s and one of the first to openly self-identify as an ex-convict. Tannenbaum served one year in prison but subsequently had a successful career first as a journalist and then as a celebrated scholar.

The contemporary intellectual origins of convict criminology have their beginnings in the published work of John Irwin – especially his books *The Felon* (1970), *Prisons in Turmoil* (1980) and *The Jail* (1985) – who served five years in prison for armed robbery in the 1950s. In the late 1960s, he was a student of David Matza and Erving Goffman when he completed his PhD at the University of California at Berkeley. He later became a prominent prison ethnographer, and although many of his colleagues knew his background, his ex-convict history was apparent only to the close reader of his texts. Irwin was now out of the closet, conducting inside-prison research, but still nearly alone in his representation of the convict perspective. Others were to nevertheless slowly follow.

Richard McCleary, wrote *Dangerous Men* (1978), a book informed by his experience and doctoral research when he was on parole from prison in Minnesota. He later developed a well-respected career as a quantitative criminologist at the University of California. Ten years later, in Canada, an influential academic journal began which specialized in publishing the work of convict and ex-convict authors. Robert Gaucher, Howard Davidson, and Liz Elliot started *The Journal of Prisoners on Prisons* following their disappointment with presentations at the International Conference on Penal Abolition III held in Montreal in 1987 and the lack of prisoner representation. The concept of convict criminology finally emerged with a series of seminars held during the late 1990s sponsored by the American Society of Criminology which recognized the dehumanizing conditions of the criminal justice system and the lives of those defined as criminal. Currently, the convict criminology group includes men and women ex-convict academics from Australia, Canada, Finland, New Zealand, Sweden, the UK and the US. The latter has the largest prison population in the Western world and thus – not surprisingly – continues to contribute the most members.

Convict criminologists are, of course, not the first to research prisons and penological practices but build on the foundations provided by chosen intellectual mentors. Erving Goffman, for example, made a very considerable contribution with his insightful analysis of asylums (1961) and the development of the notion of stigma (1963). The scholarly work of Frank Tannenbaum (1938) on the dramatization of evil is also significant, as is the prolific work of radical criminologists such as Richard Quinney and William Chambliss. Many others have deconstructed myths, challenged the taken-for-granted and searched for alternative meanings and these have had a substantial impact.

In the US – perhaps more than in other Western country – offenders suffer discrimination nearly everywhere they go in respectable society, in particular when applying for employment. Many end up giving in, opting instead for marginal lives and/or a return to crime which seems a rational choice to them in the circumstances in which they find themselves.

Like other released prisoners, educated ex-convicts have also suffered discrimination when they enter universities. Academia, for all its liberal pretences, quest for diversity and support for affirmative action, is often a hostile environment for ex-convict students and staff. Many universities ask criminal history questions on student admission forms, and applicants may be denied financial aid, accommodation and employment because of their past convictions. Ex-convicts can legally be denied admission to graduate programmes or financial assistance in some states in the US.

Similarly, academic appointments, promotions, and tenure may be subject to criminal background checks. Ex-convicts with doctorates may find it difficult getting employment or, if they do, may be passed over for tenure, promotion or consideration for administrative positions. Some university administrators may feel uneasy about having their photos taken with ex-convict academics. Other universities may be concerned that employing ex-convict academics will tarnish the image or reputation of their institutions. In some institutions, ex-convict students and junior academics have been advised not to disclose their past, conceal their identity or simply keep a low profile, for example by refusing media interviews or publishing without discussing their criminal histories.

Convict criminology has nevertheless continued to grow as numerous articles and books are added to the literature and the perspective is discussed in textbooks including this one. The convict criminology group emphasizes the use of direct observation and real-life experience in understanding the different processes, procedures, and institutional settings which comprise the criminal justice system. The methodology used includes correspondence with prisoners, face-to-face interviews, retrospective interpretation of past experiences, and direct observation inside correctional facilities. The group is especially skilled in gaining entry to prisons, writing research questions, composing interview questionnaires in language that convicts can understand and in analyzing prison records and statistics.

Convict criminology proposes two policy strategies. First, they wish to see a cessation of what Austin and Irwin (2001) called the 'imprisonment binge' in the US, which began in the 1980s and has caused the prison population to more than double since 1990. The outcome has been millions of people incarcerated at an immense cost to the taxpayer in terms of prison construction, operation and maintenance, overcrowded courts, overworked parole and probation authorities and overburdened welfare agencies to which falls the task of supporting families whose primary breadwinner has been removed. Second, there is a demand for improved prison conditions. Conditions have deteriorated, partially as the result of a rapidly increasing prison population, rising incarceration costs,

crowded prison conditions and a thinning of resources (Ross, 2008). Budgets have tightened, and many prison programmes have similarly disappeared. The article written by
Robert Martinson in 1974 in which he argued strongly that 'nothing works' in prison
reform, added weight to arguments that spending money on rehabilitation programmes
is a waste of time. This encouraged many jurisdictions in the US, already struggling with
rising numbers, to abandon such programmes and invest instead in expensive high-tech
surveillance and security to manage prisoners. Thus, many prisons became warehouses
for offenders, where criminals are essentially kept in cold storage until they are paroled
or their sentences expire (Irwin, 2005). Unprepared for life in the real world after years
of stagnation in the artificial environment of the prison, it is not surprising that so many
are unable to survive upon their release and end up back inside, a situation where further
offending is again a rational choice.

Convict criminologists are committed to understanding and attempting to remedy the
processes which have given the 'land of the free' the largest and fastest-growing prison
population in the history of the Western world. Within the context of the prison itself,
they have shared a determination to expose and address a carceral environment which,
although ostensibly created to prevent a prisoner from future offending, in fact, produces
the socially disabled, whose return to an offending lifestyle and where further incarceration is virtually ensured (Irwin, 1970, 1980, 1985, 2005).

Prisoners should be provided with opportunities for better-paid institutional employment, advanced vocational training, higher education and family skills development.
Although it is true that most institutions have token programmes that serve a small number
of prisoners – for example a prison may have paid jobs for 20% of its prisoners, low-tech
training and occasional classes in life skills or group therapy – the great problem is that
these services are dramatically limited in scope and availability.

Another matter which concerns convict criminologists is the issue of voting rights.
The US (and the UK) are two of the few advanced industrial countries that continue to
deny prisoners and felons voting rights. If convicts could vote, it is argued, many of the
improvements suggested here might become policy, because politicians would be forced
to campaign for convict votes. State and federal governments will begin to address the
conditions in prisons only when prisoners and felons become voters. One would not
expect prisoners to be any less interested than free persons in exercising their right to
vote. To the contrary, if polling booths were installed in prisons, voter turnout would
likely be higher than in most outside communities.

To prevent relapses into offending caused by desperation, convict criminologists advocate that prisoners released from prison should have enough 'gate money' to allow them
to pay for up to three months of rent and food. They could earn some of this money
working in prison industries, with the balance provided by the state. All persons exiting
correctional institutions should have clothing suitable for applying for employment, eye-
glasses (if needed) and identification (social security card, state ID or driver's license and
a copy of their institutional medical records).

The final and perhaps most controversial policy recommendation is eliminating the
"snitch" system in prison (i.e. using inmates as informants). The snitch system is used
by guards in old-style institutions to supplement their surveillance of convicts. It is used
to control prisoners by turning them against each other and is thus seen to be responsible for ongoing institutional violence. If convict criminologist recommendations for
a smaller prison population, single-cell housing, better food and clothing, voting rights

and well-funded institutional programming were implemented, it is then argued that the snitch system would become redundant. Small units are easier to manage and the demoralizing and dangerous recruitment of snitching inmates to assist in operational functions would be unnecessary.

Conclusion

Since the start of the convict criminology group more than a decade ago, there has been a steady increase in the number of ex-convict academics willing to step forward and become a part of it. In doing so, they show a willingness to challenge the taken-for-granted and offer fresh insights into some of the oldest questions in sociology and criminology/criminal justice. As the group grows and these observations accumulate, a more complete and relatively current picture of modern prisons begins to emerge (see Jones and Schmid, 2000; Ross and Richards, 2002, 2003; Terry, 2003; Irwin, 2005; Newbold, 2007). Members of the group are able to write with authority about what they have observed or experienced in prisons located in different states and different countries.

Summary of main points

1   Abolitionism is a sociological and political perspective which analyses criminal justice and penal systems as being social problems in themselves which actually intensify rather than diminish crime and its impact.
2   Liberal approaches to the study of the prison and notions of punishment have been built on a number of often competing and contradictory goals: rehabilitation, general prevention, incapacitation, punishment and specific and general deterrence.
3   Abolitionism emerged out of the social and civil rights movements of the late 1960s, challenges these liberal perspectives by arguing that in practice the criminal justice system and prisons contribute little to the protection of the individual and the control of crime.
4   In view of the huge increase in prison populations around the globe and the continuing rise in both reported crimes and crimes audited in victimization and self-report studies, abolitionism offers an important series of insights into the role of the prison and its failures at the beginning of the twenty-first century.
5   Abolitionists have nevertheless become increasingly attached to the emerging discourses and debates surrounding human rights and social justice which they see as mechanisms for developing negative reforms, thereby promoting a response to social harm that is very different from the destructive prison and punishment systems that currently exist.
6   Brown and Schept (2017) argue that criminology has been slow to open up a conversation about decarceration and abolition in comparison with other disciplines, such as history, geography, gender, race and critical ethnic studies.
7   The rise of the carceral state remains a peculiar failure or a success of unprecedented proportions depending on your criminological perspective and what you are seeking to achieve.
8   Criminological engagement with abolition has allowed for a reflexive critique of the discipline itself.

9 A key contribution of new abolitionist work is the disruption of dominant understandings of crime, law, punishment, safety and accountability, justice and the generation of alternative vocabularies and analyses from which to begin the escape from the
carceral state.

10 Convict criminology is a relatively new and controversial perspective which emerged
in the 1990s among a group of ex-convict academics frustrated at reading the existing
literature on crime and criminal justice.

Discussion questions

1 Outline the liberal perspective on the reform of the prison.
2 In ways do abolitionist criminologists disagree with the liberal perspective on
incarceration?
3 How would you explain the carceral state?
4 Are critical carceral scholars simply idealistic and ignoring the reality of pervasive
criminality?
5 Explain the contribution of convict criminology to the discipline.

Suggested further reading

Willem De Haan (1991) provides an excellent introduction to the notion of abolitionism and try Austin and Irwin (2001) as an introduction to convict criminology and their
discussion of the 'imprisonment binge'. Brown and Schept (2017) provide an excellent
introduction to the links between the new abolitionists, criminology and critical carceral
studies.

References

Agozino, B. (2003) *Counter-Colonial Criminology: A Critique of Imperialist Reason*. London: Pluto Press.
Alexander, M. (2010) *The New Jim Crow: Mass Incarceration in the Age of Colorblindness*. New York: The
New Press.
Armstrong, S.C. (2013) 'Using the Future to Predict the Past: Prison Population Projections and the
Colonisation of Penal Imagination', in M. Malloch and B. Munro (eds.) *Crime, Critique and Utopia*.
Series: Critical Criminological Perspectives. Basingstoke: Palgrave Macmillan.
Austin, J. and Irwin, J. (2001) *It's About Time: America's Imprisonment Binge*. Belmont, CA: Thomson
Learning.
Baldry, E., Carlton, B. and Cunneen, C. (2012) 'Abolitionism and the Paradox of Penal Reform in
Australia: Indigenous Women, Colonial Patriarchy and Co-option', *Social Justice*, 41(3): 16–19.
Beckett, K. (2000) *Making Crime Pay: Law and Order in Contemporary American Politics*. New York:
Oxford University Press.
Beckett, K. and Herbert, S. (2009) *Banished: The New Social Control in Urban America*. New York:
Oxford University Press.
Beckett, K. and Murakawa, N. (2012) 'Mapping the Shadow Carceral State: Toward an Institutionally
Capacious Approach to Punishment', *Theoretical Criminology*, 16(2): 221–44.
Ben-Moshe, L., Chapman, C. and Carey, A.C. (2014) *Disability Incarcerated: Imprisonment and Disability
in the United States and Canada*. London: Palgrave Macmillan.
Brown, M.D. (2009) *The Culture of Punishment: Prison, Society, and Spectacle*. New York: New York
University Press.

Brown, M.D. (2012) 'Empathy and Punishment', *Punishment & Society*, 14(4): 33–401.

Brown, M.D. (2014) *Penal Power and Colonial Rule*. Abingdon, Oxon: Routledge.

Brown, M.D. and Schept, J. (2017) 'New Abolition, Criminology and a Critical Carceral Studies', *Punishment and Society*, 19(4): 440–62.

Camp, J. (2016) *Incarcerating the Crisis: Freedom Struggles and the Rise of the Neoliberal State*. Berkeley: University of California Press.

Carlen, P. (2013) *Imaginary Penalities*. Portland, OR: Willan Publishing.

Christie, N. (1981) *Limits to Pain: The Role of Punishment in Penal Policy*. Eugene, OR: Wipf and Stock.

Clear, T.R. and Frost, N.A. (2014) *The Punishment Imperative: The Rise and Failure of Mass Incarceration in America*. New York: New York University Press.

De Haan, W. (1991) 'Abolitionism and Crime Control: A Contradiction in Terms', in K. Stenson and D. Cowell (eds.) *The Politics of Crime Control*. London: Sage.

Foucault, M. (1980) *Power/Knowledge: Selected Interviews and Other Writings 1972–77*, edited by C. Gordon. Brighton: Harvester Press.

Gilmore, R.W. (2007) *Golden Gulag: Prisons, Surplus, Crisis, and Opposition in Globalizing California*. Berkeley: University of California Press.

Gilmore, R.W. (2011) 'What is to Be Done?', *American Quarterly*, 63(2): 245–65.

Goffman, E. (1961) *Asylums: Essays on the Social Situation of Mental Patients and Other Inmates*. Garden City, NY: Anchor Books.

Goffman, E. (1963) *Stigma: Notes on the Management of a Spoiled Identity*. Englewood Cliffs, NJ: Prentice Hall.

Gorz, A. (1967) *Strategy for Labor*. Boston: Beacon Press.

Gottschalk, M. (2015) *Caught: The Prison State and the Lockdown of American Politics*. Princeton, NJ: Princeton University Press.

Hall, S., Critcher, C., Jefferson, T., Clarke, J. and Roberts, B. (1978) *Policing the Crisis*. London: Macmillan.

Hannah-Moffat, K. and Lynch, M. (2012) 'Theorizing Punishment's Boundaries: An Introduction', *Theoretical Criminology*, 16(2): 119–21.

Harcourt, B.E. (2010) 'Neoliberal Penality: A Brief Genealogy', *Theoretical Criminology*, 14(1): 74–92.

Hillyard, P. (2015) 'Criminal Obsessions: Crime Isn't the Only Harm', *Criminal Justice Matters*, 102(1): 39–41.

Hulsman, L. (1991) 'Abolitionist Case: Alternative Crime Policies', *The Israel Law Review*, 25: 61.

Hulsman, L. and De Celis, J.B. (1982) *Peines Perdues: Le Syste'me Pe'nal en Question*. Paris: Le Centurion.

Irwin, J. (1970) *The Felon*. Englewood Cliffs, NJ: Prentice Hall.

Irwin, J. (1980) *Prisons in Turmoil*. Boston: Little, Brown.

Irwin, J. (1985) *The Jail*. Berkeley: University of California Press.

Irwin, J. (2005) *The Warehouse Prison: Disposal of the New Dangerous Class*. Los Angeles: Roxbury.

Jones, R.S. and Schmid, T. (2000) *Doing Time: Prison Experience and Identity among First Time Inmates*. Stamford, CT: JAI Press.

Kelly, E.L. (2011) 'Philly Stands Up: Inside the Politics and Poetics of Transformative Justice and Community Accountability in Sexual Assault Situations', *Social Justice*, 37(4): 44–57.

Kilgore, J. (2014) *Tackling Debtors' Prisons: Reflecting on the Death of Eileen DiNino*. Available from: http://truth-out.org/news/item/2447-tackling-debtors-prisons-reflecting-on-the-death-of-eileen-dinino [Accessed 12 February 2020].

Kim, M. (2009) 'Alternative Interventions to Intimate Violence: Defining Political and Pragmatic Challenges', in J. Ptacek (ed.) *Restorative Justice and Violence against Women*. New York: Oxford University Press.

Kim, M. (2011) 'Moving Beyond Critique: Creative Interventions and Reconstructions of Community Accountability', *Social Justice*, 37(4): 14–35.

Law, V. (2014) 'Against Carceral Feminism', *Jacobin Magazine*. Available from: www.jacobinmag.com/2014/10/against-carceral-feminism/ [Accessed 12 February 2020].

Loader, I. and Sparks, R. (2010) *Public Criminology?* London: Routledge.

Loyd, J.M., Mitchelson, M. and Burridge, A. (2012) *Beyond Walls and Cages: Prisons, Borders, and Global Crisis.* Athens, GA: University of Georgia Press.

Martinot, S. and Sexton, J. (2003) 'The Avant-Garde of White Supremacy', *Social Identities*, 9(2): 169–11.

Martinson, R. (1974) 'What Works?: Questions and Answers about Prison Reform', *The Public Interest*, 35: 22–54.

Mathiesen, T. (1974) *The Politics of Abolition.* London: Martin Robertson.

Mauer, M. (2006) *Race to Incarcerate.* New York: The New Press.

McCleary, R. (1978) *Dangerous Men: The Sociology of Parole.* New York: Harrow & Heston.

Meiners, E.R. (2007) *Right to Be Hostile: Schools, Prisons, and the Making of Public Enemies.* New York: Routledge.

Miller, J. (1996) *Last One Over the Wall: The Massachusetts Experiment in Closing Reform Schools.* Columbus, OH: Ohio State University Press.

Moran, D., Gill, N. and Conlon, D. (eds.) (2013) *Carceral Spaces: Mobility and Agency in Imprisonment and Migrant Detention.* Burlington, VT: Ashgate.

Morrison, W. (2004) 'Reflections With Memories: Everyday Photography Capturing Genocide', *Theoretical Criminology*, 3: 341–35.

Muhammad, K.G. (2010) *The Condemnation of Blackness: Race, Crime, and the Making of Modern Urban America.* Cambridge, MA: Harvard University Press.

Murakawa, N. (2014) *The First Civil Right: How Liberals Built Prison America.* New York: Oxford University Press.

Musto, J.L. (2013) 'Domestic Minor Sex Trafficking and the Detention-to-Protection Pipeline', *Dialectical Anthropology*, 37: 257–76.

Newbold, G. (2007) *The Problem of Prisons.* Wellington, New Zealand: Dunmore.

Piche, J. (2016) 'Assessing the Boundaries of Public Criminology: On What Does (Not) Count', *Social Justice*, 42(2): 70.

Quinney, R. (1977) *Class, State and Crime.* New York: David McKay.

Reiman, J. and Leighton, P. (2015) *The Rich Get Richer and the Poor Get Prison: Ideology, Class, and Criminal Justice*, New York: Routledge.

Richie, B, (2012) *Arrested Justice: Black Women, Violence, and America's Prison Nation.* New York: New York University Press.

Rios, V. (2011) *Punished: Policing the Lives of Black and Latino Boys.* New York: New York University Press.

Ross, J.I. (2008) *Special Problems in Corrections.* Upper Saddle River, NJ: Prentice Hall.

Ross, J.I. and Richards, S.C. (2002) *Behind Bars: Surviving Prison.* New York: Alpha/Penguin.

Ross, J.I. and Richards, S.C. (2003) *Convict Criminology.* Belmont, CA: Wadsworth.

Rothman, D. (1980) *Conscience and Convenience: The Asylum and Its Alternatives in Progressive America.* Boston: Little, Brown.

Ruggiero, V. (2010) *Penal Abolitionism.* New York: Oxford University Press.

Russell, E. and Carlton, B. (2013) 'Pathways, Race and Gender Responsive Reform: Through an Abolitionist Lens', *Theoretical Criminology*, 17(4): 474–92.

Ryan, M. and Ward, T. (2015) 'Prison Abolition in the UK: They Dare Not Speak Its Name?', *Social Justice*, 41(3): 107–19.

Schept, J. (2015) *Progressive Punishment: Job Loss, Jail Growth, and the Neoliberal Logic of Carceral Expansion.* New York: New York University Press.

Schept, J., Wall, T. and Brisman, A. (2015) 'Building, Staffing, and Insulating: An Architecture of Criminological Complicity in the School-to-Prison Pipeline', *Social Justice*, 41(4): 96–115.

Scull, A. (1977) *Decarceration.* Englewood Cliffs, NJ: Prentice Hall.

Shapiro, J. (2014) *Unpaid Court Fees Land the Poor in 21st Century Debtor's Prisons.* Available from: www.npr.org/2014/05/20/314137/unpaid-court-fees-landthe-poor-in-21st-century-debtors-prisons [Accessed 12 February 2020].

Sim, J. (1994) 'The Abolitionist Approach: A British Perspective', in A. Duff, S. Marshall, R.E. Dobash and R.P. Dobash (eds.) *Penal Theory and Practice: Tradition and Innovation in Criminal Justice.* Manchester: Manchester University Press.

Simon, J.K. (2014) *Mass Incarceration on Trial: A Remarkable Court Decision and the Future of Prisons in America*. New York, NY: The New Press.

Smith, A. (2015) *Conquest: Sexual Violence and American Indian Genocide*. Durham: Duke University Press.

Smith, A., Richie, B.E. and Sudbury, J. (2006) *The Color of Violence: INCITE! Anthology*. Cambridge, MA: South End.

Spade, D. (2011) *Normal Life: Administrative Violence, Critical Trans Politics, and the Limits of Law*. Durham, NC: Duke University Press.

Stanley, E.A. and Smith, N. (eds) (2011) *Captive Genders: Trans Embodiment and the Prison Industrial Complex*, Oakland, CA: AK Press.

Story, B. (2015) *Dis-Placing the Prison: Carceral Space, Disposable Life, and Urban Struggle in Neoliberal America*, PhD Thesis, University of Toronto, Canada.

Tannenbaum, F. (1938) *Crime and the Community*. New York: Columbia University Press.

Taylor, I., Walton, P. and Young, J. (1973) *The New Criminology: For a Social Theory of Deviance*. London: Routledge & Kegan Paul.

Thuma, E. (2015) 'Lessons in Self-Defense: Gender Violence, Racial Criminalization, and Anticarceral Feminism', *Women's Studies Quarterly*, 43(3/4): 52–71.

Wacquant, L. (2009b) *Urban Outcasts: A Comparative Sociology of Advanced Marginality*. Cambridge: Polity Press.

Weber, L. and Pickering, S. (2011) *Globalization and Borders: Death at the Global Frontier*. Basingstoke: Palgrave Macmillan.

Part III

From the postmodern condition to a revitalized modernity

Chapter 17

The rise of political populism

Key issues

1   Neoliberalism in crisis
2   The global rise of populism
3   Distrust of elites
4   The alt-right
5   Leaving Europe

Introduction

As we have seen earlier in this book, neoliberalism is a policy model which transfers control of economic factors to the private sector from the public sector. Its central tenet is economic growth through increasing competition by deregulation of social, welfare, health, labour and environmental laws; opening domestic markets to foreign competition; limiting the role of the state by the privatization of state assets and the liberalization of economic policies; and increasing corporate influence and involvement in governance. This agenda of economic reform was institutionalized by the International Monetary Fund (IMF) from the 1980s and became accepted worldwide because it profited the governing elite politician–corporate nexus in all countries.

Development through neoliberalism is based on profit-at-any-cost from capital- and energy-intensive industrialization. Through economic reform, governments maintain the interests of the ultra-rich, who gradually take over public assets by restricting governance to creating and defending markets and protecting private property. Neoliberal economic growth promotes global trade, consumerism and debt. It subordinates democracy, equity, social justice and freedom and wreaks economic violence on the majority poor.

Neoliberalism also nurtures inequality. At the time of writing, the wealthiest 62 people on earth own as much wealth as the bottom half 3.5 billion, with the top 1% more wealthy than the remaining 99%. Over decades, third-world governments were encouraged to introduce neoliberal economic reform. This was done through global training and outreach programmes in World Bank institutes and reputed Western universities of thousands of central and state legislators, bureaucrats, technical specialists, journalists, teachers and civil society leaders in subjects related to economic development.

The effects of neoliberal policies have been debt crises, severe environmental degradation and crashing economies, currency collapse, rising unemployment rising food and fuel prices, and falling wages. The social ill effects have been acerbated by the imposition of 'austerity measures' of cutting subsidies for the poor and reducing public spending on health, welfare and education. Worldwide, spontaneous people's grassroots movements have opposed the displacement of populations due to mega projects and environmental degradation. Governments have viciously suppressed these. Chile was an extreme case where thousands of opponents of neoliberalism were simply liquidated.

Neoliberal reform over decades has heightened inequality in European countries, leading to the economic near collapse of the PIGS (Portugal, Italy, Greece, Spain). The consequent EU-wide political instability was to be greatly heightened by the flood of immigrants from countries hit by armed conflict triggered due to neoliberal exploitation. The UK voting 52% to leave the EU is arguably the most recent reaction to the negative impact of neoliberalism.

Neoliberalism in crisis

Martin Jacques (2016) observed that the western financial crisis of 2007–8 was the worst since 1932 but noted that its immediate repercussions were surprisingly modest. The crisis challenged the very foundations of the long-dominant neoliberal ideology, but it seemed to emerge largely unscathed. The banks were bailed out. Hardly any bankers on either side of the Atlantic were prosecuted for their crimes, while the price of their behaviour was paid by the taxpayer. Subsequent economic policy – especially in the Anglo-Saxon world – was to rely overwhelmingly on monetary policy, especially quantitative easing. But it failed. The Western economy has subsequently stagnated and it is now appropriate to refer to 'the lost decade', while there appears to no real end in sight, and that is before the COVID-19 pandemic.

Jacques asks rhetorically how neoliberalism has managed to survive virtually unscathed for so long. Although it has failed the test of the real world, bequeathing the worst economic disaster for seven decades, politically and intellectually it has remained virtually unchallenged. Parties right across the political spectrum have bought into its philosophy. They know no other way of thinking or doing. It has simply become common sense. It was, as Antonio Gramsci (1977, 1978) put it, hegemonic. But it is a hegemony that we should observe cannot survive the test of the real world.

Jacques (2016) observes that the first suspicion of the wider political consequences was evident in the turn in public opinion against the banks, bankers and business leaders. For decades, they could do no wrong: they had been praised as the role models of our age, the default troubleshooters of choice in education, health and seemingly everything else. Now their star was in steep descent, along with that of the political class. The effect of the financial crisis was to undermine faith and trust in the competence of the governing elites. It was to mark the beginnings of a wider political crisis.

Jacques observes that the causes of this political crisis go much deeper than simply the financial crisis and the virtually stillborn recovery of the following decade. They go to the heart of the neoliberal project which had embraced at its core the idea of a global free market in goods, services and capital. The Depression-era system of bank regulation was dismantled, thereby creating the conditions for the 2008 crisis. Equality was scorned, the idea of trickle-down economics lauded, government was condemned as a constraint on the market and duly downsized, immigration encouraged, regulation cut to a minimum, taxes reduced and a blind eye turned to corporate evasion.

Jacques (2016) observes that by far the most disastrous feature of the neoliberal era has been the huge growth in inequality. Moreover, until very recently, this situation has been virtually ignored. But it was to emerge extremely rapidly and has probably become the most important political issue on both sides of the Atlantic. It is also the one issue driving the political discontent now engulfing the West. Given the statistical evidence, it is astonishing that it has been disregarded for so long, and this can only be explained by the total dominance of neoliberal hegemony and its values.

Let us consider those statistics briefly. In the period between 1948 and 1972, every section of the US population experienced very similar and sizeable increases in their standard of living. Yet, between 1972 and 2013, the bottom 10% experienced falling real income, while the top 10% did far better than everyone else. In the US, the median real income for full-time male workers is now lower than it was four decades ago. Quite simply, the income of the bottom 90% of the population has stagnated for over 30 years. The situation in the UK is similar and the problem has grown significantly since the financial crisis. On average, between 65% and 70% of households in 25 high-income economies have experienced stagnant or falling real incomes between 2005 and 2014.

Jacques observes that the reasons for this stagnation are not difficult to explain. The era of hyper-globalization has been systematically stacked in favour of capital against labour. International trading agreements have been drawn up in great secrecy, with business on the inside and the unions and citizens excluded. There has been a sustained politico-legal attack on the unions, with the encouragement of large-scale immigration in both the US and Europe which has helped to undermine the bargaining power of the domestic workforce and a subsequent failure to retrain displaced workers in any meaningful way.

Thomas Piketty (2014) has shown that in the absence of countervailing pressures, capitalism naturally gravitates towards increasing inequality. In the period between 1945 and the late 1970s, Cold War competition was arguably the biggest such constraint. Since the collapse of the Soviet Union, there has been none. But, as the popular backlash grows increasingly uncontrollable, such a winner-takes-all regime seems to have become politically unsustainable.

Large sections of the population in both the US and the UK were now in revolt against their situation, as demonstrated by large-scale support for Trump and Sanders in the US and the Brexit vote in the UK. This popular revolt is often described, in a somewhat scornful and dismissive fashion, as populism. Or, as Francis Fukuyama (2018) drily observes, '"populism" is the label that political elites attach to policies supported by ordinary citizens that they don't like'. Populism is a movement against the status quo. It represents the beginnings of something new, although it is generally much clearer about what it is against than what it is for. It can be progressive or reactionary but, more usually, both.

Jacques (2016) observes that Brexit is a classic example of such populism. It has overturned a fundamental cornerstone of UK policy since the early 1970s. Although ostensibly about Europe, it is, in fact, about much more: a cry of desperation from those who feel they have lost out and been left behind, whose living standards have stagnated or worse since the 1980s, who feel dislocated by large-scale immigration over which they have no control and who face an increasingly insecure and casualized labour market. Their revolt was to paralyse the governing elite.

This wave of populism significantly marks the return of social class as a central agency in politics, both in the UK and the US. This is especially remarkable in the US. For many decades, the idea of the 'working class' was marginal to political discourse. Most Americans described themselves as middle class, a reflection of the aspirational pulse at the heart of their society. According to a Gallup poll, in 2000 only 33% of Americans called themselves working class (Saad, 2000); by 2015 the figure was 48%, almost half the population (Newport, 2015).

Brexit, too, was primarily a working-class revolt. Previously, on both sides of the Atlantic, the agency of class has been in retreat in the face of the emergence of a new range of identities and issues from gender and race to sexual orientation and the environment, all of which we have encountered in this second part of this book. The return of class, because of its sheer reach, has, nevertheless, the potential, like no other issue, to redefine the political landscape (Jacques, 2016).

But the re-emergence of class should not be confused with the labour movement. They are not synonymous: this is obvious in the US and increasingly so in the UK. Indeed, over the past half-century, there has been a growing separation between the two in Britain. The re-emergence of the working class as a political voice in Britain, most notably in the Brexit vote, can best be described as an undeveloped expression of resentment and protest, with only a very weak sense of belonging to the Labour movement.

Indeed, first, the UK Independence Party (UKIP) and, latterly, the Brexit Party, have been as important – in the form of immigration and Europe – in shaping current working-class attitudes as the Labour Party. In the US, both Trump and Sanders have given expression to the working-class revolt, the latter almost as much as the former. The working class belongs to no one: its orientation, far from predetermined, as the left has liked to think, is a function of politics.

Jacques (2016) argues that the neoliberal era is being undermined from two directions. First, if its record of economic growth has never been particularly strong, it is now dismal. The European economy is barely larger than it was on the eve of the financial crisis in 2007, the US has done better, but even its growth has been anaemic. Economists such as Larry Summers – and the New Keynesian economists (see Mankiw, 2008) – believe that the prospect for a neoliberal future is most likely one of profane stagnation.

Worse, because the recovery has been so weak and fragile, there is a widespread belief that another financial crisis may well be just around the corner. In other words, the neoliberal era has delivered the West back into the kind of crisis-ridden world that was last experienced in the 1930s. With this background, it is hardly surprising that a majority now believe their children will be worse off than they were.

Second, those who have lost out in the neoliberal era are no longer prepared to acquiesce in their fate – they are increasingly in open revolt. We are seemingly witnessing the end of the neoliberal era. It is not dead, but it is in its early death throes, just as the social-democratic era was during the 1970s (Jacques, 2016).

A sure sign of the declining influence of neoliberalism has been the rising chorus of intellectual voices raised against it. From the mid-1970s through the 1980s, the economic debate was increasingly dominated by monetarists and free marketeers. But, since the Western financial crisis, the centre of gravity of the intellectual debate has shifted profoundly. This is most obvious in the US, with economists such as Joseph Stiglitz, Paul Krugman, Dani Rodrik and Jeffrey Sachs becoming increasingly influential. Thomas Piketty's *Capital in the Twenty-First Century* has been a massive seller. His work and that of Tony Atkinson and Angus Deaton have pushed the question of inequality to the top of the political agenda. In the UK, Ha-Joon Chang, for long isolated within the economics profession, has gained a following far greater than those who think economics is a branch of mathematics (Jacques, 2016).

At the same time, some of those who were previously strong advocates of a neoliberal approach, such as Larry Summers and the *Financial Times's* Martin Wolf, have become extremely critical. The critics of neoliberalism are now in the ascendency; the neoliberals and monetarists are in retreat. In the UK, the media and political worlds are well behind with few seeming to recognize that we are at the end of an era. But old attitudes and assumptions still predominate right across the political spectrum.

Following the resignation of Ed Miliband as Labour leader following defeat in the General Election 2015, virtually no one foresaw the triumph of Jeremy Corbyn in the subsequent leadership election. The assumption had been more of the same, certainly not anyone like Corbyn. But the world had changed. The membership, especially the young who had joined the party in unprecedented numbers, wanted a complete break with New Labour. One of the reasons why the left had failed to emerge as the leader of the new mood of working-class disillusionment was that most social-democratic parties became, in varying degrees, disciples of neoliberalism and uber-globalization. The most extreme forms of this phenomenon were New Labour and the Democrats, who in the late 1990s and 2000s became its advance guard, personified by Tony Blair and Bill Clinton, triangulation and the Third Way.

David Marquand (2010) was to pertinently observe that there is no point of a social democratic party if it fails to represent the less fortunate, the underprivileged and the losers. New Labour deserted those who needed them, those who historically they were supposed to represent. It is hardly surprising that large sections had now deserted the party who had deserted them.

Jacques (2016) observes that just as the Labour Party took far too long to come to terms with the rise of Thatcherism and the birth of a new era at the end of the 1970s, it could not now grasp that the Thatcherite paradigm, which they eventually came to embrace in the form of New Labour, had finally run its course. Labour, like everyone else, is obliged to think anew. The membership in their antipathy to New Labour turned to someone who had never accepted the latter, who was the polar opposite in almost every respect.

Corbyn was not a product of the new times but a throwback to the late 1970s and early 1980s. That is both his strength and his weakness. He was uncontaminated by the New Labour legacy because he had never accepted it. But neither, it would seem, did he understand the nature of the new era. The danger was that he was to be found possessed of feet of clay in what is a highly fluid and unpredictable political environment, devoid of any certainties of almost any kind, in which Labour was to find itself dangerously divided and weakened.

Jacques (2016) observes while Labour might have been in intensive care, the condition of the Conservatives was not a great deal better. Prime Minister David Cameron was guilty of a huge and irresponsible miscalculation over Brexit and was forced to resign. The party was hopelessly divided. It had no idea in which direction to move after Brexit. The Brexiters painted an optimistic picture of turning away from the declining European market and embracing the expanding markets of the world, albeit barely mentioning by name which countries it had in mind. The new prime minister, Theresa May, appeared to have a rather outdated hostility towards China and a willingness to undo the good work of previous chancellor George Osborne, who had achieved closer links. If the government was to turn its back on China, by far the fastest-growing market in the world, where were they going to turn?

Brexit has left the country fragmented and deeply divided, with the very real prospect that Scotland might choose independence. At the same time, the Conservatives appeared to have little understanding that the neoliberal era was coming to an end.

Dramatic as events had been in the UK, they cannot compare with those in the US. Almost from nowhere, Donald Trump rose to capture the Republican nomination, confound virtually all the pundits – not least his own party – and become elected president. His message was straightforward anti-globalization. He believes that the interests of the working class have been sacrificed in favour of the big corporations that have been encouraged to invest around the world and thereby deprive domestic workers of their jobs. Furthermore, he argued that large-scale immigration had weakened the bargaining power of US workers and served to lower their wages.

Trump proposed that US corporations should be required to invest their cash reserves in the US, believed that the North American Free Trade Agreement had the effect of exporting US jobs to Mexico, accused China of stealing US jobs and, in response, imposed a 45% tariff on imports from that country. Trump favoured economic nationalism: 'Put America first'. An appeal, above all, to the white working class who, until his (and Bernie Sander's) arrival on the political scene, had been ignored and largely unrepresented since the 1980s. Given that their wages had been falling for most of the last previous forty years, it is extraordinary how their interests had been neglected by the political class.

Increasingly, the working-class had voted Republican, but the party had long been captured by the super-rich and Wall Street, whose interest in hyper-globalization, had run directly counter to those of the white working class. With the arrival of Trump, they had finally found a representative: it was the working class who won Trump the presidency.

The economic nationalist argument was a vigorously pursued by Bernie Sanders, who ran Hillary Clinton extremely close for the Democratic nomination and would probably have won but for more than 700 so-called super-delegates, who were effectively chosen by the Democratic machine and overwhelmingly supported Clinton. As in the case of the Republicans, the Democrats had long supported a neoliberal, pro-globalization strategy, notwithstanding the concerns of its trade union base. Both the Republicans and the Democrats now found themselves deeply polarized between the pro- and anti-globalizers; an entirely new development not witnessed since the shift towards neoliberalism under Reagan almost 40 years previously.

Another part of Trump's nationalist appeal – 'Make America great again' – was to be his position on foreign policy. It is his view that the pursuit of great power status by the US has squandered the resources of the nation. The alliance system is seen as unfair, with the US bearing most of the cost and its allies contributing far too little, with Japan, South Korea, and the European members of the North Atlantic Treaty Organization cited as prime examples. He thus sought to rebalance these relationships and, failing that, to exit from them.

Trump has argued that as a country in decline, the US can no longer afford to foot this kind of financial burden. Rather than being the 'world's policeman', the money should be invested at home, pointing to the dilapidated state of the country's infrastructure and this represents a major critique of the US as the world's hegemonic power, arguments which mark a radical break with the neoliberal, hyper-globalization ideology which had been the dominant orthodoxy since the early 1980s and with the foreign policy orthodoxy of most of the post-war period. But Trump is no man of the left. He is a populist of the right, thus launching racist and xenophobic attacks on Muslims and Mexicans. His appeal is to a white working class which feels it has been cheated by the big corporations, undermined by Hispanic immigration, and often resentful towards African Americans who for a long time many have viewed as their inferior. We now consider the global rise of populism further.

The global rise of populism

Michael Cox (2018) observes that the populist problem – born in the US – appears to have migrated towards Europe, where previously it did not have much of a presence and in a much more widespread form. Previous populisms were specifically national in character, while this one has assumed a more international form, but its structure is by no means exactly clear. It does, however, reflect a deep suspicion of the prevailing establishment, which in the view of most populists does not just rule in the common good but conspires against the people. And it is the people, however defined, who are the true repositories of the soul of the nation.

Populists tend in the main to be nativist and suspicious of foreigners, although this is more likely to be found on the right than the left. More often than not, they are sceptical of the facts as provided to them by the establishment press, and in most cases – and again this is truer of the right than the left – they do not much like intellectuals. Nor, in general, do they like big cities and the metropolitan types who happen to live in them.

David Goodhart (2017) argues that the fault line in Britain today – and the same could well be true in many other Western countries – is between those who come from *Somewhere*, people rooted in a specific place or community, usually a small town or in the countryside, socially conservative and often less educated, and those who come from *Anywhere*, footloose, often urban, socially liberal, university educated and who tend to feel at home nearly everywhere. But it is the '*somewheres*' – he argues – that we have to understand, for it is they after all who constitute the real basis of what is seen as the populist revolt.

Cox (2018) identifies three competing narratives to explain the surge of support for populism. The first is provided by Moises Naim (2013) who agrees that populism has to be taken seriously but argues that it has no intellectual coherence. It is merely a rhetorical 'tactic' that demagogues around the world have always used – and will continue to use – to gain power and then hold on to it. This nevertheless does not make populism any the less dangerous. Indeed, it is invariably divisive, thrives on conspiracy, finds enemies even where they do not exist, criminalizes all opposition to them, plays up external threats and more often than not insists that its critics at home are merely working for foreign governments. We would be wasting our time – he implies – by seeking some deeper cause for this particular phenomenon.

A second – more influential – view is that populism in its contemporary form is a search for meaning in what Tony Giddens (2002) had earlier termed a 'runaway world' of globalization, a world which is at least shaking up our existing ways of life, no matter where we happen to be and which is emerging in 'an anarchic, haphazard, fashion . . . . fraught with anxieties, as well as scarred by deep divisions and a feeling that we are all in the grip of forces over which we have no control' (2002: 126). Indeed, not only do we have no control, but because of the speed and depth of the changes across traditional frontiers, many citizens also feel as if the world is not just passing them by but undermining their settled notion of identity born in more stable, more settled times as well. This loss has been felt by everybody, but it has been experienced most by an older cohort of white people who simply want to turn the clock back to a time when the people in their towns looked like them, sounded like them and even had the same traditional loyalties as most of them: an age, in other words, when there were fewer immigrants and even fewer Muslims living amongst them. Globalization and socio-economic factors in this account obviously play a role, but according to this narrative at the heart of the modern populist problem is not so much economics as identity- and meaning-driven by a set of undeveloped, but nonetheless key, questions about who I am, what I am, and whether or not, I still live in my own country surrounded by people who share the same values and allegiances.

The third way of understanding populism proposes that the contemporary variant is less the result of an identity crisis and much more the result of what the Indian economist (now adviser to Indian prime minister Modi) Arvind Subramanian and Kessler (2013) have termed 'hyper-globalization'. This latest form of globalization he notes began in the 1970s, accelerated rapidly in the 1980s, took off in earnest in the 1990s, and continued to accelerate thereafter – until, that is, the crash of 2008. For years, the results of this 30-year headlong drive towards the future only seemed to be positive and beneficial. Indeed, according to the many defenders of globalization, the new economic order generated enormous wealth, drew in once previously closed economies, drove up the world's gross domestic product, encouraged real development in countries that had for years been poor and, most important of all, in terms of human welfare, helped reduce poverty worldwide. Not surprisingly, he observes, India, China and the developing countries loved this new world order. They were its beneficiaries.

But for the West, more generally, globalization has created all sorts of downside problems. Wealth became ever more concentrated in the hands of the few, as shown by Thomas Piketty (2014), while middle-class incomes have stagnated. Meanwhile, many of the working class in Western countries found themselves being driven out of work, either by jobs going elsewhere or by a rush of cheap imported goods largely coming from China. And to add to their economic woes, immigration undercut the price of their labour. Thus, what may have been great for the corporations and the consumer – not to mention the Chinese – turned into an economic tidal wave for the traditional bastions of labour.

James Montier and Philip Pilkington (2017) develop the argument further and insist that what has led to the very real crisis in the West is not just globalization in the abstract but what they more precisely term 'a broken system of economic governance' or our old friend 'neoliberalism'. Taken together, the new neoliberal order, they believe, has not only skewed the balance towards capital and away from labour, but the regime it has created has also given rise to lower inflation, lower growth rates, lower investment rates, lower productivity growth, increasing wealth and income inequality, diminished job insecurity and a seriously deflationary bias in the world economy. Moreover, instead of the 2008 economic crisis undermining this social order, it has only made things much, much, worse. Given all of this, we should not be so surprised that there has been a backlash in the form of populism. The only surprise perhaps is that it did not happen earlier.

Cox (2018) observes that one does not have to pick and choose between these various narratives. All contain some element of truth. Yet, in his view, they also exclude important parts of the story. One thing they leave out – or perhaps do not stress enough – is the enormous impact long term which the failure of communism and the collapse of the

Soviet Union has had, and still has, on the world we live in. Before 1989 and 1991, there seemed to be some kind of balance in the world: some built-in limit to the operation of the free market. But, by the 1990s, all this had been swept aside and there was now a high degree of over-confidence in the West. Anything was now possible. Even if it caused pain to some, this was a price worth paying for the general good. Anyway, there was now no serious opposition or any alternative. So one could press on regardless.

Nor did we quite figure out what it might mean for the West when massive low-wage economies like China joined the world market club. Cox observes that many economists will tell you that free trade is always a good in the long term. David Ricardo said so, Adam Smith said so, J.M. Keynes said so and even Milton Friedman said so. So it must be for the best. Moreover, if jobs were lost in the EU and the US this, we are told, has little to do with free trade and more with new labour-saving technologies. In fact, all those manufacturing jobs in Europe and the US would have had to go anyway because of technology and automation. But there is ample evidence to suggest a rather different story: that, in fact, millions of jobs have been lost in the West because of new emerging economies joining in the game. It is not merely a nationalist myth. Either way, one should not have been surprised when politicians like Trump and his populist equivalents in Europe launched their tirades against globalization and gathered in the votes.

Cox (2018) argues that populism is more than just about economics. It is very much an expression in the West of a sense of powerlessness: the powerlessness of ordinary citizens when faced with massive changes going on all around them, but, at the same time, the powerlessness of Western leaders and politicians who really do not seem to have an answer to the many challenges facing them right now. Many ordinary people might feel they have no control and express this by supporting populist movements and parties who promise to restore control to them. But in reality, it is the established political parties, the established politicians and the established structures of power which are equally powerless: powerless to stop the flow of migrants from the Middle East and Africa, powerless to control the borders of their own nation states, powerless when faced with a terrorist threat, powerless to prevent off-shoring and tax avoidance and powerless to reduce unemployment to any significant degree across most of the eurozone.

Cox (2018) observes two further significant factors. First, there was the financial crisis of 2008 which not only delivered a major blow to Western economies – the EU, in particular – but, it also undermined faith in the competence of the establishment from the bankers to the economists at the London Stock Exchange. It would now be impossible for many to ever believe the experts again. Second, the other factor was a series of major setbacks in the field of foreign policy ranging from Iraq to Libya.

The notion that public figures and professionals are basically trustworthy has been integral to the health of representative democracies. The very core of liberal democracy is the idea that a small group of people – politicians – can represent millions of others. If this system is to work, there must be a basic modicum of trust that the small group will act on behalf of the much larger one, at least some of the time. As the past decade has made clear, nothing turns voters against liberal democracy more rapidly than the appearance of corruption: the suspicion, valid or otherwise, that politicians are exploiting their power for their own private interest.

Cox (2018) observes that a modern liberal society is a complex web of trust relations, held together by reports, accounts, records and testimonies. Such systems have always faced political risks and threats. The template of modern expertise can be traced back to the second half of the seventeenth century when scientists and merchants first established techniques for recording and sharing facts and figures. These were soon adopted by governments, for purposes of tax collection and rudimentary public finance. But from the start, strict codes of conduct had to be established to ensure that officials and experts were not seeking personal gain or glory and were bound by strict norms of honesty.

But regardless of how honest parties may be in their dealings with one another, the cultural homogeneity and social intimacy of these gentlemanly networks and clubs have always been grounds for suspicion. This does not discredit the knowledge they produce. But where things get trickier is when that homogeneity starts to appear to be a political identity, with a shared set of goals. This is what is implied by the concept of 'elites': that purportedly separate domains of power – media, business, politics, law, academia – are acting in unison.

A trend of declining trust has been underway across the Western world for many years, even decades, as copious survey evidence attests. Trust, and its absence, became a preoccupation for policymakers and business leaders during the 1990s and early 2000s. They feared that shrinking trust led to higher rates of crime and less cohesive communities, producing costs that would be picked up by the state.

Cox (2018) observes that what nobody foresaw was that, when trust sinks beneath a certain point, many people may come to view the entire spectacle of politics and public life as a sham. This happens not because trust in general declines but because key public figures – notably politicians and journalists – are perceived as untrustworthy. It is those figures specifically tasked with representing society, either as elected representatives or as professional reporters, who have lost credibility.

Cox (2018) argues that to understand the crisis liberal democracy faces today – whether we identify this primarily in terms of 'populism' or 'post-truth' – it is not enough to simply bemoan the rising cynicism of the public. We need also to consider some of the reasons why trust has been withdrawn. The infrastructure of fact has been undermined in part by a combination of technology and market forces. But we must seriously consider the underlying truth of the accusations made against the establishment. Too often, the rise of populist political parties and demagogues is viewed as the source of problems facing liberal democracy rather than as a symptom. But by focusing on trust, and the failure of liberal institutions to sustain it, we get a clearer sense of why this is happening now.

Cox (2018) observes that the problem today is that – across a number of crucial areas of public life – the basic intuitions of populists have been repeatedly proved. One of the main contributors to this state of affairs has been the spread of digital technology, creating vast data trails with the latent potential to contradict public statements, and even undermine entire public institutions. Whereas it is impossible to conclusively prove that a politician is morally innocent or that a news report is undistorted, it is far easier to demonstrate the opposite. Scandals, leaks, whistleblowing and revelations of fraud all serve to confirm our worst suspicions. While trust relies on a leap of faith, distrust is supported by ever-mounting piles of evidence. And in Britain, this pile has been expanding much faster than many of us have been prepared to admit. Let us consider this distrust of elites and the rise of political populism further.

Distrust of elites

As we have seen, that confronted by the rise of populist parties and leaders, some commentators have described the crisis facing liberal democracy in largely economic terms, as a revolt among those 'left behind' by inequality and globalization. Another faction sees it primarily as the expression of cultural anxieties surrounding identity and immigration. There is some truth in both arguments, but neither gets to the heart of the trust crisis that populists exploit so ruthlessly. A crucial reason liberal democracy is in danger right now is that the basic honesty of mainstream politicians, journalists and senior officials is no longer taken for granted.

There are many explanations for Trump, Brexit and so on, but insufficient attention is paid to what populists are actually saying, which focuses relentlessly on the idea of self-serving 'elites' maintaining a status quo that primarily benefits them. On the right, Nigel Farage has accused individual civil servants of seeking to sabotage Brexit for their own private ends. On the left, Jeremy Corbyn repeatedly referred to Britain's 'rigged' economic system (Elgot, 2017). The promise to crack down on corruption and private lobbying is integral to the arguments made by figures such as Donald Trump (US), Jair Bolsonaro (Brazil) or Viktor Orbán (Hungary).

William Davies (2018) observes that one of the great political riddles of recent years is that declining trust in 'elites' is often encouraged and exploited by figures of far more dubious moral character – not to mention far greater wealth – than the technocrats and politicians being ousted. On the face of it, it would seem odd that a sense of 'elite' corruption would play into the hands of 'hucksters and blaggards' such as Donald Trump or Arron Banks. But Davies observes that the authority of these figures owes nothing to their moral character, and everything to their perceived willingness to blow the whistle on corrupt 'insiders' dominating the state and media.

Davies observes that liberals – including those who occupy 'elite' positions – may comfort themselves with the belief that these charges are ill founded or exaggerated or else that the populists offer no solutions to the failures they identify. After all, Trump has not 'drained the swamp' of Washington lobbying. But this is to miss the point of how such rhetoric works, which is to chip away at the core faith on which liberal democracy depends, namely that power is being used in ways that represent the public interest and that the facts published by the mainstream media are valid representations of reality.

Populists target various centres of power, including dominant political parties, mainstream media, big business and the institutions of the state, including the judiciary. The chilling phrase 'enemies of the people' (Graham-Harrison, 2018) has been employed by Donald Trump to describe those broadcasters and newspapers he dislikes (such as CNN and the *New York Times*) and by the *Daily Mail* to describe high court judges, following their ruling in 2016 that Brexit would require parliamentary consent. But on a deeper level, whether it is the judiciary, the media or the independent civil service that is being attacked is secondary to a more important allegation: that public life in general has become fraudulent.

One aspect of this allegation is to dispute the very possibility that a judge, reporter or expert might act in a disinterested, objective fashion. For those whose authority depends on separating their public duties from their personal feelings, having their private views or identities publicized serves as an attack on their credibility. But another aspect is to gradually blur the distinctions between different varieties of expertise and authority, with the implication that politicians, journalists, judges, regulators and officials are effectively all working together.

It is easy for rival professions to argue that they have little in common with each other and are often antagonistic. Ostensibly, these disparate centres of expertise and power hold each other in check in various ways, producing a pluralist system of checks and balances.

Twentieth-century defenders of liberal democracy, such as the American political scientist Robert Dahl, often argued that it did not matter how much power was concentrated in the hands of individual authorities, as long as no single political entity was able to monopolize power. The famous liberal democratic ideal of a 'separation of powers' – distinguishing executive, legislative and judicial branches of government – and which was so influential in the framing of the US Constitution, could persist only so long as different domains of society hold one another up to critical scrutiny.

Davies (2018) observes that one thing that these diverse professions and authorities do have in common is that they trade primarily in words and symbols. By lumping together journalists, judges, experts and politicians as a single homogeneous 'liberal elite', it is possible to treat them all as indulging in a babble of jargon, political correctness and, ultimately, lies. Their status as public servants is demolished once their claim to speak honestly is thrown into doubt. One way in which this is done is by bringing their private opinions and tastes before the public, something that social media and email render far easier. Tensions and contradictions between the public face of, say, a BBC reporter, and their private opinions and feelings, are much easier to discover in the age of Twitter.

Whether in the media, politics or academia, liberal professions suffer a vulnerability that a figure such as Donald Trump does not, in that their authority hangs on their claim to speak the truth. Oliver Hahl et al. (2018) have drawn a distinction between two types of lies. The first, 'special access lies', may be better termed 'insider lies'. This is dishonesty from those trusted to truthfully report facts, who abuse that trust by failing to state what they privately know to be true. The authors cite the example of Bill Clinton's infamous claim that he 'did not have sexual relations with that woman'.

The second, which they refer to as 'common knowledge lies', are the kinds of lies told by Donald Trump about the size of his election victory or the crowds at his inauguration, or by the Vote Leave campaign's false claims about sending '£350m a week to the EU'. These lies do not pretend to be bound by the norm of honesty in the first place, and the listener can make up their own mind what to make of them.

What Hahl et al. (2018) argue is that the rise of highly polished, professional politicians such as Tony Blair and Bill Clinton exacerbated the sense that politics is all about strategic concealment of the truth. Something that the Iraq war seemed to confirm as much as anything. Trump or Nigel Farage may have a reputation for fabricating things, but they do not – rightly or wrongly – have a reputation for concealing things, which grants them a form of credibility not available to technocrats or professional politicians.

At the same time, and even more destructively, when elected representatives come to be viewed as 'insider liars', it turns out that other professions whose job it is to report the truth – journalists, experts, officials – also suffer a slump in trust. Indeed, the distinctions between all these fact-peddlers start to look irrelevant in the eyes of those who have given up on the establishment altogether. It is this type of all-encompassing disbelief that creates the opportunity for right-wing populism in particular. Trump voters are more than twice as likely to distrust the media as those who voted for Clinton in 2016, according to the annual Edelman Trust Barometer (2018), which adds that the four countries currently suffering the most 'extreme trust losses' are Italy, Brazil, South Africa and the US.

Davies (2018) observes that it is one thing to measure public attitudes, but quite another to understand what shapes them. Alienation and disillusionment develop slowly and without any single provocation. No doubt economic stagnation and soaring inequality have played a role. But we should not discount the growing significance of scandals that appear to discredit the honesty and objectivity of 'liberal elites'. The misbehaviour of elites did not 'cause' Brexit, but it is striking, in hindsight, how little attention was paid to the accumulation of scandal and its consequences for trust in the establishment.

The 2010 edition of the annual British Social Attitudes survey included an ominous finding. Trust in politicians, already low, had suffered a fresh slump, with a majority of people saying politicians never tell the truth. But at the same time, interest in politics had mysteriously risen.

Davies (2018) asks rhetorically to whom this newly engaged section of the electorate turn if they had lost trust in 'politicians'. One answer was clearly UKIP, who were to experience their greatest electoral gains in the years which followed, to the extent of winning the most seats in the 2014 elections for the European Parliament. This electoral surge – which initially appeared to threaten the Conservative Party – was integral to the decision of David Cameron to hold a referendum on EU membership. One of the decisive (and unexpected) factors in the referendum result was the number of voters who went to the polls for the first time, specifically to vote leave.

Davies (2018) further ponders what might have prompted the combination of angry disillusionment and intensifying interest that was visible in the 2010 survey. It clearly pre-dated the toughest years of austerity. But there was one event that did more than any other to weaken trust in politicians: the members' of Parliament (MPs') expenses scandal, which blew up in May 2009 thanks to a drip-feed of revelations published by the *Daily Telegraph*.

Following as it did so soon after a disaster of world-historic proportions – the financial crisis – the full significance of the expenses scandal may have been forgotten. But its ramifications were vast. For one thing, it engulfed many of the highest reaches of power in Westminster: the Speaker of the House of Commons, the home secretary, the secretary of state for communities and local government and the chief secretary to the treasury all resigned. Not only that, but the rot appeared to have infected all parties equally, validating the feeling that politicians had more in common with each other – regardless of party loyalties – than they did with decent, ordinary people.

Davies (2018) observes that many of the issues that 'elites' deal with are complex, concerning law, regulation and economic analysis. We can all see the fallout of the financial crisis, for instance, but the precise causes are disputed and hard to fathom. By contrast, everybody understands expense claims, and everybody knows lying and exaggerating are among the most basic moral failings. Even a child understands they are wrong. This may be unfair to the hundreds of honest MPs and to the dozens whose misdemeanours fell into a murky area around the 'spirit' of the rules. But the sense of a mass stitch-up was deeply – and understandably – entrenched.

The other significant thing about the expenses scandal was the way it set a template for a decade of elite scandals – most of which also involved lies, leaks and dishonest denials. One year later, there was another leak from a vast archive of government data: in 2010, WikiLeaks released hundreds of thousands of US military field reports from Iraq and Afghanistan. With the assistance of newspapers, including the *New York Times* (US), *Der Spiegel* (Germany), the *Guardian* (UK) and *Le Monde* (France), these 'war logs' disclosed horrifying details about the conduct of US forces and revealed that the Pentagon had falsely denied knowledge of various abuses. While some politicians expressed moral revulsion with what had been exposed, the US and British governments blamed WikiLeaks for endangering their troops, and the leaker, Chelsea Manning, was jailed for espionage.

The following year, the phone-hacking scandal put the press itself under the spotlight. It was revealed that senior figures in News International and the Metropolitan Police had long been aware of the extent of phone-hacking practices and, moreover, that they lied about how much they knew. Among those implicated was the prime minister's communications director, former *News of the World* editor Andy Coulson, who was forced to resign his post and later jailed. By the end of 2011, the *News of the World* had been closed down, the Leveson inquiry was underway and the entire Murdoch media empire was shaking.

The biggest scandal of 2012 was of a different order altogether, involving unknown men manipulating a number of which very few people were aware. The number in question, the London interbank offered rate, or Libor, is meant to represent the rate at which banks are willing to loan to each other. What was surreal, in an age of complex derivatives and high-frequency trading algorithms, was that this number was calculated on the basis of estimates declared by each bank on a daily basis and accepted purely on trust. The revelation that a handful of brokers had conspired to alter Libor for private gain – with possible costs to around 250,000 UK mortgage holders, among others – may have been difficult to fully comprehend, but it gave the not unreasonable impression of an industry enriching itself in a criminal fashion at the expense of the public. Bob Diamond, the CEO of Barclays, the bank at the centre of the conspiracy, resigned in July 2012.

Towards the end of that year, the media was caught in another prolonged crisis, this time at the BBC. Horror greeted the broadcast of the ITV documentary *The Other Side of Jimmy Savile* in October 2012. How many people had known about his predatory sexual behaviour, and for how long? Why had the police abandoned earlier investigations? And why had BBC *Newsnight* dropped its own film about Savile, due to be broadcast shortly after his death in 2011? The police swiftly established Operation Yewtree to investigate historic sexual abuse allegations, while the BBC established independent commissions into what had gone wrong. But a sense lingered that neither the BBC nor the police had really wanted to know the truth of these matters for the previous 40 years.

It was not long before it was the turn of the corporate world. In September 2014, a whistle-blower revealed that Tesco had exaggerated its half-yearly profits by £250m, increasing the figure by around a third. An accounting fiddle on this scale clearly had roots at a senior managerial level. Sure enough, four senior executives were suspended the same month and three were charged with fraud two years later. A year later, it emerged that Volkswagen had systematically and deliberately tinkered with emission controls in their vehicles so as to dupe regulators in tests but then pollute liberally the rest of the time. The CEO, Martin Winterkorn, resigned.

This is by no means an exhaustive list of the scandals of the past decade, nor are they all of equal significance. But viewing them together provides a better sense of how the suspicions of populists cut through. Whether or not we continue to trust in politicians, journalists or officials, we have grown increasingly used to this pattern in which a curtain is dramatically pulled back, to reveal those who have been lying to or defrauding the public.

Davies (2018) observes that another pattern also begins to emerge. It is not just that isolated individuals are unmasked as corrupt or self-interested – something that is as old as politics – but that the establishment itself starts to appear deceitful and dubious. The distinctive scandals of the twenty-first century are a combination of some very basic and timeless moral failings – greed and dishonesty – with technologies of exposure that expose malpractice on an unprecedented scale, and with far more dramatic results.

Perhaps the most important feature of all these revelations was that they were definitely scandals, not merely failures. They involved deliberate efforts to defraud or mislead. Several involved sustained cover-ups, delaying the moment of truth for as long as possible. Several of the scandals ended with high-profile figures in prison. Jail terms satisfy some of the public demand that the 'elites' pay for their dishonesty, but they do not repair the trust that has been damaged. On the contrary, there is a risk that they affirm the cry for retribution, after which the quest for punishment is only ramped up further.

Davies (2018) observes that in addition to their conscious and deliberate nature, a second striking feature of these scandals was the ambiguous role played by the media. On one hand, the reputation of the media had taken a pummelling over the previous decade, encouraged by populists and conspiracy theorists who accuse the 'mainstream media' of being allied to professional political leaders and who now have the benefit of social media through which to spread this message.

The moral authority of newspapers may never have been high, but the grisly revelations that journalists had hacked the phone of murdered schoolgirl Milly Dowler represented a new low in the public standing of the press. The Leveson inquiry, followed soon after by the Savile revelations and Operation Yewtree, generated a sense of a media class who were adept at exposing others but equally expert at concealing the truth of their own behaviours.

On the other hand, it was newspapers and broadcasters that enabled all of this to come to light at all. The extent of phone hacking was eventually exposed by the *Guardian*, the MPs' expenses by the *Telegraph*, Jimmy Savile by ITV and the 'war logs' were reported with the aid of several newspapers around the world simultaneously.

But the media was playing a different kind of role from the one traditionally played by journalists and newspapers, with very different implications for the status of truth in society. A backlog of data and allegations had built up in secret until eventually a whistle was blown. An archive existed that the authorities refused to acknowledge until they could no longer resist the pressure to do so any longer. Journalists and whistle-blowers were instrumental in removing the pressure valve, but from that point on, truth poured out unpredictably. While such torrents are underway, there is no way of knowing how far they may spread or how long they may last.

The era of 'big data' was also the era of 'leaks'. Where traditional 'sleaze' could topple a government minister, several of the defining scandals of the past decade were on a scale so vast that they exceeded the responsibility of any individual. The Edward Snowden revelations of 2013,[1] the Panama Papers leak of 2015[2] and the HSBC files (revealing organized tax evasion)[3] all involved the release of tens of thousands or even millions of documents. Paper-based bureaucracies had never faced threats to their legitimacy on this scale.

Davies (2018) observes that the power of commissions and inquiries to make sense of so much data is not to be understated, nor is the integrity of those newspapers and whistle-blowers that helped bring misdemeanours to light. In cases such as MPs' expenses, some newspapers even invited their readers to help search these vast archives for treasure troves, like human algorithms sorting through data. But it is hard to imagine that the net effect of so many revelations was to build trust in any publicly visible institutions. On the contrary, the discovery that 'elites' have been blocking access to a mine of incriminating data is perfect fodder for conspiracy theories. In his 2010 memoir, *A Journey*, Tony Blair confessed that legislating for freedom of information was one of his biggest regrets, which gave a glimpse of how transparency is viewed from the centre of power (Cobain, 2011) .

Following the release of the war logs by Wikileaks nobody in any position of power claimed that the data were not accurate. It was, after all, the data and not a journalistic report. Nor did they offer any moral justification for what was revealed. Defence departments were left making the flimsiest of arguments: that it was better for everyone if they did not know how war was conducted. It may well be that the House of Commons was not fairly represented by the MPs' expenses scandal, that most city brokers are honest or that the VW emissions scam was a one-off within the car industry. But scandals do not work through producing fair or representative pictures of the world. They do so by exposing hidden truths and lies. Where whistle-blowing and leaking become the dominant form of truth-telling, the authority of professional truth-tellers – reporters, experts, professionals, broadcasters – is thrown into question.

Davis (2018) observes that the term 'illiberal democracy' is now frequently invoked to describe states such as Hungary under Viktor Orbán or Turkey under Recep Tayyip Erdoğan. In contrast to liberal democracy, this model of authoritarian populism targets the independence of the judiciary and the media, ostensibly on behalf of 'the people'.

Brexit was caused partly by distrust in 'liberal elites', but there is anxiety that it is also accelerating a drift towards 'illiberalism'. There is a feeling at large, albeit among outspoken Remainers, that the BBC treated the leave campaign and Brexit itself with kid gloves, for fear of provoking animosity. More worrying was the discovery by Open Democracy that the Metropolitan Police were delaying their investigation into alleged breaches of electoral law by the leave campaign due to what a spokesperson called 'political sensitivities' (Cusick and Ramsey, 2018). The risk is that key civic institutions will seek to avoid exercising scrutiny and due process, for fear of upsetting their opponents.

Davis (2018) observes that while Britain is not an 'illiberal democracy', the credibility of our elites is still in trouble, and efforts to placate their populist opponents may only make matters worse. At the more extreme end of the spectrum, the far-right activist Stephen Yaxley-Lennon (also known as Tommy Robinson) has used his celebrity and social media reach to cast doubt on the judiciary and the BBC.

Yaxley-Lennon has positioned himself as a freedom fighter, revealing 'the truth' about Muslim men accused of grooming underage girls, by violating legal rules that restrict reporting details of ongoing trials. He was found guilty of contempt of court and jailed, but this only deepened his appeal for those who believed the establishment was complicit in a cover-up and ordinary people were being deliberately duped.

The political concern here is that suspicions of this nature – that the truth is being deliberately hidden by an alliance of 'elites' – are no longer the preserve of conspiracy theorists but becoming increasingly common. The current crisis has too many causes to detail here, and it is impossible to apportion blame for a collective collapse of trust – which is as much a symptom of changes in media technologies as it is of any moral failings on the part of elites.

What is emerging now is what Michel Foucault (1980) would have called a new 'regime of truth' – a different way of organizing knowledge and trust in society. The introduction of experts and government administrators in the seventeenth century created the platform for a distinctive liberal solution to this problem, which rested on the assumption that knowledge would reside in public records, newspapers, government files and journals. But once the integrity of these people and these instruments is cast into doubt, an opportunity arises for a new class of political figures and technologies to demand trust instead.

The project that was launched over three centuries ago – of trusting elite individuals to know, report and judge things on our behalf – may not be viable in the long term, at least not in its existing form. It is tempting to indulge the fantasy that we can reverse the forces that have undermined it, or else batter them into retreat with even more facts. But this is to ignore the more fundamental ways in which the nature of trust is changing.

The main feature of the emerging regime is that truth is now assumed to reside in hidden archives of data rather than in publicly available facts. This is what is confirmed by scandals such as the MPs' expenses and the leak of the Iraq war logs and, more recently, in the #MeToo movement, which also occurred through a sudden and voluminous series of revelations, generating a crisis of trust. The truth was out there, just not in the public domain. In the age of email, social media and camera phones, it is now common sense to assume that virtually all social activity is generating raw data, which exists out there somewhere. Truth becomes like the lava below the Earth's crust, which periodically bursts through as a volcano.

Davies (2018) rhetorically asks what role is left for the traditional, analogue purveyors of facts and figures. What does it mean to 'report' the news in an age of reflexive disbelief? Newspapers have been grappling with this question for some time now. Some have decided to refashion themselves as portals to the raw data, or curators of other people's content. But it is no longer intuitively obvious to the public why they should be prepared to take the word of a journalist for something when they can witness the thing itself in digital form. There may be good answers to these questions, but they are not obvious ones.

Davies observes that a new type of heroic truth-teller has emerged in tandem with these trends. This is the individual who appears brave enough to call bullshit on the rest of the establishment, whether that be government agencies, newspapers, business, political parties or anything else. Some are whistle-blowers, others are political leaders, and others are more like conspiracy theorists or trolls. The problem is that everyone has a different heroic truth-teller, because we are all preoccupied by different bullshit. There is no political alignment between figures such as Chelsea Manning and Nigel Farage; what they share is only a willingness to defy the establishment and break consensus.

Davies observes that if a world where everyone has their own truth-tellers sounds dangerously like relativism, that is because it is, a product of the postmodern condition or the fragmentation of modernity. But the roots of this new and often unsettling 'regime of truth' do not only lie with the rise of populism or the age of big data. Elites have largely failed to understand that this crisis is about trust rather than facts, which may be why they did not detect the rapid erosion of their own credibility.

Unless liberal institutions and their defenders are willing to reckon with their own inability to sustain trust, the events of the past decade will remain opaque to them. And unless those institutions can rediscover aspects of the original liberal democratic impulse – to keep different domains of power separate and put the disinterested pursuit of knowledge before the pursuit of profit – then the present trends will only intensify, and no quantity of facts will be sufficient to resist. Power and authority will accrue to a combination of decreasingly liberal democratic states and digital platforms – interrupted only by the occasional outcry as whistles are blown and outrages exposed.

The alt-right

The controversy of the US presidential election continued to dominate the public forum not only in that country but to some extent further afield. Among the many interesting by-products of Trump's candidacy and surprise victory is the now widely talked about 'alternative right' or 'alt-right', the generally young, meme-loving conservatives whose trollish rhetoric has sparked a huge deal of debate and controversy since their rise to prominence during the election. Sources have given varying portrayals of the alt-right, some claiming them to be far-right neo-Nazi sympathizers and others arguing that they are no more than tongue-in-cheek pranksters. But the influence of the movement has continued to expand, despite lacking any central organization.

At its core, the alt-right is made up of a group of loosely aligned online communities including Breitbart, InfoWars, 4chan, and 8chan, among several others. While none of these factions shares the exact same beliefs, there are several important viewpoints linking them that may be considered to be the definitive traits of the alt-right. Thus, in general, the alt-right embraces centre-right beliefs, with added elements of nationalism, while rejecting the traditional, Protestant morals that have come to dominate mainstream conservatism, which hints at the movement having its roots in libertarianism and paleo-conservatism.[4] Support for Donald Trump – or at least the Make America Great Again objective, is also almost unanimous among alt-right members. Like Trump, the alt-right is known for being radically opposed to political correctness, which often manifests in the form of elaborate trolling operations. A notable case was the alt-right's attack on do-it-yourself (DIY) 'safe space' warehouse venues in response to the Ghost Ship warehouse fire in Oakland in 2016.[5] Following the nationwide crackdown on such locations that were in violation of the fire code, alt-right affiliated users of 4chan's politics board, '/pol/,' sought out 'safe space' venues in order to report them in hopes of having them shut down. The subsequent closure of at least four DIY venues is thought to have been influenced by / pol/. And while there is no official leadership of the alt-right, there are several notable individuals that could be cast as the most accessible and coherent voices of the group.

The most prolific of the alt-right's figureheads, and probably the closest to being a definitive spokesperson, was Milo Yiannopoules, the then 32-year-old flamboyant British conservative who served as the senior editor of Breitbart up until February 2017. He appeared to embody much of the general philosophy of the alt-right, being highly critical of social justice, multiculturalism, feminism, Islam and the deterioration of the right to privacy. In addition, his language was usually cheeky, with little regard for social sensibilities, which was to cause a great deal of controversy, including bans from popular social media platforms such as Twitter and several college campuses. Little was to be heard from him after early social media messages were discovered which appeared to show his support for paedophilia, an apparent step too far.

Similar ideologically is Alex Jones, a radio host from Austin, Texas, whose podcast and news site InfoWars was to become a staple of the alt-right community. Since 1996, Jones has made a name for himself through his libertarian outlook and accusations of conspiracy by major world governments, which include chemtrails, allegations of various politicians having New World Order affiliations and claims that the Sandy Hook School Massacre in 2012 was fabricated.[6] These alternative conservative positions preached by Jones made him a perfect fit for the alt-right, whose members share much of the same distrust for government and big business.

There are nevertheless more threatening extremist communities and entities within the alt-right which have been widely responsible for it being labelled as a racist movement by a variety of sources, including the *New York Times*, the Anti-Defamation League, and the Southern Poverty Law Center. The best example is that of Andrew Anglin, founder and owner of The Daily Stormer, an openly white nationalist news site that is self-proclaimed alt-right. Anglin and his website express views that are usually racist, anti-Semitic, and pro neo-Nazi and harbour a hostility towards social justice and liberalism that is typical of the alt-right. Similarly, members of 4chan's /pol/ are known for producing memes and other alt-right-themed content expressing extremely racist and anti-Semitic attitudes, which has also attracted criticism. Yet many other alt-right figures, including Milo Yiannopoules (who is openly gay) and Alex Jones (who is staunchly pro-Israel), have made a point to distance themselves (and the alt-right in general) from radicals such as Anglin, strongly defending the alt-right as having no core philosophical connections to any form of fascism, Nazism or racism.

The division between such sects remains generally unclear and is made even more complicated by the ambiguous means of communication favoured by the alt-right. Memes are chosen as a vehicle for conveying political ideas in a short, often sarcastic manner that, when worded cleverly enough, can be one of the simplest ways to generate support. The other side of memes, however, is that they generally fail to establish a sense of ethos for those who are not 'in' on the joke. This lack of traditional reverence for political discussion is another key characteristic of the alt-right, one born of its origins in the online cult of Anonymous.

The now-infamous hacker group Anonymous was in many ways the predecessor of the movement. Much like the alt-right, Anonymous started on 4chan and gained infamy for its outlandishly offensive opposition to political correctness. It built a massive online following through memes and pranks that would eventually create what was arguably the most monumental hacker community in history. From approximately 2005 to 2010, Anonymous embodied the collective angst and frustrations of 4chan users. Its eventual 'death' was probably just as significant to the formation of the alt-right. After years of wreaking havoc on the internet, Anonymous would change directions completely and begin fighting governments and institutions that they viewed as being corrupt, leading to the involvement in projects such as OpPayback, Occupy Wall Street, and Project Chanology. Many 4chan users were nevertheless not impressed with these efforts at rebranding the group as 'freedom fighters' and with Anonymous no longer thought of as the collective identity of 4chan, a group such as the alt-right could fill the gap.

Because the end of Anonymous was brought about by its identification with certain political dogmas, it is probable that the success of the alt-right has to do with their lack of an intelligible structure. A possible key to understanding how the alt-right uses this tactic lies in the idea of post-irony. Post-irony, a developing concept both in academia and pop culture, describes a state in which the distinction between irony and sincerity becomes obscured. /pol/'s 'official' flag is a good reference point for the alt-right and post-irony as, being modelled on the flag of Nazi Germany, it is unknown whether /pol/ intends to offend only in jest or to represent legitimate neo-Nazi interests.

The alt-right, in many ways, serves as a perfect example of post-irony: their earnest, political goals are expressed through the ironic lens of memes and trolling, which altogether create an image that is next to impossible to logically decipher. Basically, it is impossible to tell how seriously aligned with Nazism they are.

This same concept also gives the alt-right the freedom to change its aims and objectives at any given time, which has likely been responsible for the survival of the group after the fundamental goal of electing Trump to the presidency was achieved. In the same light, the alt-right, without even having a clearly defined, genuine central identity, can be interpreted not as a 'legitimate' organization at all but rather as a widespread inside joke which has hoodwinked outsiders into believing it is much more.

The attention and controversy surrounding the alt-right in itself is a clear enough sign that the internet is beginning to have an inescapable influence on the development of culture in the US, with the online alt-right now extending its influence all the way to the White House. Trump's choice of Steve Bannon for White House chief strategist, for example, was made especially controversial due to the fact that Bannon had served as executive chair of Breitbart, having strong alt-right connections. Regardless of the intentions of the alt-right whether they are ironic, sincere or some combination of the two, there is obviously some power to their message.

Leaving Europe

After three years of haggling in the UK Parliament, convulsions at the top of the government and pleas by some for Brussels to delay its exit, the UK left the EU on January 31, 2020.

The departure from the EU was sealed when the Conservative Party led by Prime Minister Boris Johnson won a resounding victory in the General Election held the previous December. Johnson now had the parliamentary majority he needed to pass legislation in early January establishing the terms of exit, a goal that had repeatedly eluded his predecessor, Theresa May. European lawmakers gave the plan their blessing later in the month.

A combination of the words Britain and exit, Brexit caught on as shorthand for the proposal that the UK change its relationship to the bloc on trade, security and migration. But the country had been debating the advantages and disadvantages of membership of a European community of nations almost from the moment the idea was first proposed. It held its first referendum on membership in what was then called the European Economic Community in 1975, less than three years after it joined. At that time, 67% of voters supported staying in the bloc. But that was not the end of what was to become a recurring debate.

In 2013, then prime minister David Cameron promised a national referendum on EU membership with the idea of settling the question once and for all. The options offered to voters were broad and vague – Remain or Leave – and Cameron was convinced that Remain would win comfortably. That turned out to be a serious miscalculation.

As Britons went to the polls on 23 June 2016, a refugee crisis had made migration a subject of political rage across Europe. Meanwhile, the Leave campaign was hit with accusations that it had relied on lies and that it had broken election laws. In the end, a withdrawal from the bloc, however ill defined, emerged with the support of 52% of voters. But the debate was not settled.

Brexit advocates had saved for another day the complex question of what should come next. Even now that Britain has settled the terms of its departure, it remained unclear what sort of relationship with the EU it wants for the future, a matter that could prove just as divisive as the debate over withdrawal.

Most voters in England and Wales supported Brexit, particularly in rural areas and smaller cities. That overcame majority support for remaining in the EU among voters in London, Scotland and Northern Ireland. Young people overwhelmingly voted against leaving, while older voters supported it.

Europe is Britain's most important export market and its biggest source of foreign investment, while membership in the bloc has helped London establish its position as a global financial centre. With some regularity, major businesses have announced that they are leaving Britain because of Brexit or have at least threatened to do so. The list of companies thinking about relocating includes Airbus, which employs 14,000 people and supports more than 100,000 other jobs. The government has projected that in 15 years, the economy of the country would be 4% to 9% smaller if Britain left the EU than if it remained. This would all depend on how it would leave (Turner, 2020).

The previous prime minister, Theresa May, had promised that Brexit would mean an end to free movement – that is the right of people from elsewhere in Europe to live and work in Britain. Working-class people who see immigration as a threat to their jobs by the importation of cheap labour viewed that as a triumph. But an end to free movement was unpopular with young – invariably middle-class – Britons hoping to study or work abroad.

Before Parliament approved Johnson's withdrawal agreement in January, just about the only clear decision it made on Brexit was to give formal notice in 2017 to quit, under Article 50 of the EU's Lisbon Treaty, a legal process setting it on a two-year path to departure. That made 29 March 2019 the formal divorce date.

But departure was delayed when it became clear that hard-line pro-Brexit Conservative lawmakers would not accept Mrs May's withdrawal deal, which they said would trap Britain in the European market. The EU agreed to push the date back to April 12. But the new deadline did not bring about any more agreement in London, and the prime minister was forced to plead yet again for more time. This time, European leaders insisted on a longer delay, and set 31 October as the date.

Boris Johnson took office in July and vowed to take Britain out of the bloc by that deadline, with or without a deal. But opposition lawmakers and rebels in his own party seized control of the Brexit process and moved to block a no-deal withdrawal, which would have meant Britain leaving without being able to cushion the blow of a sudden divorce. That forced Johnson to seek an extension something he had said he would rather be 'dead in a ditch' than do. European leaders agreed to extend the deadline by three months, to 31 January, as Britain considered its options. Ultimately, he persuaded enough opposition lawmakers to agree to an early General Election and subsequently won an 80-seat majority, the largest since Margaret Thatcher in 1987.

With 31 January marking as a symbolic milestone, at the same time, it is merely the beginning of a potentially more volatile chapter of the turbulent divorce, in which political and business leaders jostle over what sort of Brexit will come to pass. Turner (2020) observes that every path holds risks for Johnson, all the more so after an election in which he was buoyed by voters in ex-Labour heartland seats in northern and central England who now stood to suffer from trading barriers with Europe.

Among the points of contention would be the government's wish to break from European standards on labour, the environment and product safety. The more space Britain puts between its rules and those of Europe, the EU leaders have said, the more they will hamper the former access to the European market. Any restrictions of that sort would threaten British jobs, reliant as many of them are on European customers. Brexit clearly signposted the significant reality that Britain is a deeply divided country.

A deeply divided Britain

Britain is hugely divided across cultural, age and education lines, a major study of national attitudes has concluded, warning of a potential rise in far-right and anti-Islam sentiments unless politicians tackle long-standing disaffections behind the Brexit vote. The Hope Not Hate (2020) report based on six years of polling and focus groups observed a particular chasm between people living in affluent, multicultural cities and those from struggling post-industrial towns.

The study by the anti-fascism advocacy group 'sets out to understand the drivers of fear and hate' in England and, where data are available, in Wales and Scotland. It uncovers the often glaring extent of geographic divisions between people of varying attitudes, with opposition to immigration and multiculturalism correlating closely with socio-economic deprivation. It found that of the 100 areas where people were most likely to oppose immigration, all were in towns or on the outskirts of cities, with 93 of them in the Midlands or north of England. In contrast, the 100 areas most linked with what the report calls the 'confident multicultural' population were all in major cities or close to universities, with 90% of them within a few hundred metres of a university.

Another key finding is that while overall attitudes to multiculturalism are softening, the opposite is happening with Islam. It found that between 2011 and 2018, the proportion of people who believed that immigration as a whole had been good for Britain rose from 40% to 60%. On attitudes specific to Islam, the report found that while these softened between 2011 and 2016, this process then reversed, something it saw linked to the series of terror attacks in the UK in 2017 and media coverage of sexual grooming gangs in places such as Rotherham. The most recent polling by the group, of more than 10,000 people had found that 32% of people believed there were Muslim 'no-go areas' in Britain governed by Sharia law, a view endorsed by 49% of leave voters in the Brexit referendum.

An attempt to locate centres of strongly anti-Muslim or far-right sentiment – done by mapping the locations of people who signed an online petition seeking the release from prison of the anti-Islam activist Stephen Yaxley-Lennon (known as Tommy Robinson) found a strong link to the deprived towns associated with Brexit and a more general opposition to immigration. Conversely, the study concluded, areas where people feel more in control of their own lives and optimistic about their futures 'become more resilient to hateful narratives and to political manifestations of this hatred'. It found that such divisions closely correlate with the votes of people over Brexit, noting that opposition to the EU and prejudice towards Islam 'are clearly interlinked issues for many. But, it warned, departure from the EU alone is extremely unlikely to tackle the reasons why people in such poorer towns and city suburbs tend to be wary of change and hostile to immigration. In particular, it found, reducing immigration levels alone will not alleviate anxiety about new arrivals, not least since those most likely to express those views are based predominantly in areas where few immigrants actually live.

The report concluded that people in deprived communities often saw immigration as part of 'a broader story about dissatisfaction with their own lives', repeating stories from the media about immigrants supposedly receiving preferential treatment from public services.

'Immigration has become a totemic emblem for the many grievances people feel in modern Britain', said Nick Lowles, the chief executive of Hope Not Hate, in an introduction to the report. 'The strong view in many of these communities is that they have been abandoned and left to rot by the political establishment in preference to addressing the needs and wishes of new arrivals in the cities'. The only way to tackle such views would be to rebuild such neglected communities, 'equipping their young people with the skills that will enable them to compete more effectively in the modern global world and, fundamentally, giving them a sense of hope in the future'.

Another key divide, also strongly manifested in the Brexit vote, is age, with younger people found to be notably less likely to see immigration as a significant national problem or to worry about Islamist terrorism. Education was another significant division. Of people with degrees or higher qualifications, 76% believe immigration has been good for the country, against 45% of those whose schooling ended at 16. While affluent people in cities tended to be more optimistic about the future than those in deprived towns, this process was reversed when it came to one thing: Brexit. The polling found that confidence among metropolitan liberals plummeted in the wake of the referendum result. Even two years after the Brexit referendum, 71% of remain voters said they felt pessimistic for the future compared with just 35% of leave supporters.

East Marsh and Castle: a tale of contrasts

Hope Not Hate (2020) identify two geographical locations as a study in contrasts: East Marsh in Grimsby, Lincolnshire and the Castle area of Cambridge. They are, the report says, 'each one of two Englands, emerging as the most hostile and most confidently multicultural places on our heatmap'.

Grimsby, as a whole, is marked by deprivation and decline, caused by a diminished industrial base and fishing trade, as well as low skill levels. The East Marsh estate, just south of the docks, is particularly struggling and was measured in 2011 as the second-most deprived area in England and Wales, with 44% of its children and young people living in poverty. Life expectancy at birth in the area is ten years less than for the rest of Grimsby.

Interviews in the area for the report uncovered a sense of loss at the decline in fishing and the associated prosperity and worries about immigration. One interviewee complained that the immigrants were 'just coming in and taking our resources'. She added: 'I've got to wait until I'm 67 instead of retiring at 60 now to get my pension.'[7]

In contrast, the study highlights Castle as emblematic of the urban-based, university-linked areas most commonly associated with the so-called confident multiculturals, those at ease with a changing UK. A central area of Cambridge, Castle covers St John's College and the surrounding, prosperous residential area. Its levels of income, employment and adult skills are among the highest in the country. As tends to be the case for areas with fewer worries about immigration, Castle has above-average levels of black and minority ethnic residents, at 42%. The report says:

> Many of its residents are employees of Cambridge University and many more are students residing in and around the grounds of the impressive, elite colleges. The area is both pretty and prosperous, where few of its residents are dependent children or retirees. Economic concerns are uncommon in areas such as this.

Summary of main points

1 The central tenet of neoliberalism is economic growth through increasing competition by deregulation of social, welfare, health, labour and environmental laws, opening domestic markets to foreign competition, limiting the role of the state by the privatization of state assets and the liberalization of economic policies.
2 Neoliberalism nurtures inequality. The wealthiest 62 people on earth own as much wealth as the bottom half 3.5 billion, with the top 1% more wealthy than the remaining 99%.

3 Large sections of the population in both the US and the UK were now in revolt against their situation, as demonstrated by large-scale support for Trump and Sanders in the US and the Brexit vote in the UK. This popular revolt is often described as populism.

4 It can be argued that the neoliberal era is being undermined from two directions. First, its record of economic growth is now dismal. Second, those who have lost out are no longer prepared to acquiesce in their fate.

5 Populists tend in the main to be nativist and suspicious of foreigners, although this is more likely to be found on the right than the left.

6 David Goodhart (2017) argues that the fault line in Britain today is between those who come from *Somewhere* and those who come from *Anywhere*.

7 Cox (2018) observes that the problem today is that – across a number of crucial areas of public life – the basic intuitions of populists have been repeatedly proved.

8 In general, the alt-right embraces centre-right beliefs, with added elements of nationalism, while rejecting the traditional, Protestant morals that have come to dominate mainstream conservatism.

9 After three years of haggling in the UK Parliament, convulsions at the top of the government and pleas by some for Brussels to delay its exit, the UK left the EU on 31 January 2020.

10 Britain is hugely divided across cultural, age and education lines, a major study of national attitudes has concluded, warning of a potential rise in far-right and anti-Islam sentiments unless politicians tackle long-standing disaffections behind the Brexit vote.

Discussion questions

1 Discuss the ways in which neoliberalism can be said to be in crisis.
2 How would you explain populism?
3 What – according to David Goodhart – is the difference between those who come from *Somewhere* and those who come from *Anywhere*?
4 Who are the alt-right and what are their core beliefs?
5 Why is Britain allegedly a deeply divided country?

Suggested further reading

Henk Overbeek and Bastiaan van Apeldorn (eds) (2012) interrogate the condition of the neoliberal project in the wake of the global crisis and the predicted death of neoliberalism in 2007, both in terms of the regulatory structures of finance-led capitalism in Europe and North America and the impact of new centres of capitalist power on the global order. Nadia Urbinati (2019) provides a good introduction to populism and political theory.

Notes

1 Edward Joseph Snowden (born 21 June 1983) is an American whistle-blower who copied and leaked highly classified information from the National Security Agency in 2013 when he was a Central Intelligence Agency employee and subcontractor.
2 The Panama Papers were a massive leak of financial files from the database of Mossack Fonseca, the fourth-biggest offshore law firm in the world. The documents were leaked anonymously to German newspaper *Süddeutsche Zeitung*, which released them on 3 April 2016.

3 Swiss Leaks (or SwissLeaks) is the name of a journalistic investigation, released in February 2015, of a giant tax evasion scheme allegedly operated with the knowledge and encouragement of the British multinational bank HSBC via its Swiss subsidiary, HSBC Private Bank (Suisse).
4 Paleo-conservatism is a political philosophy and variety of conservatism in the US stressing Christian ethics, nationalism, paternalism, regionalism and traditionalism.
5 Oakland, California, US. On 2 December 2016, at approximately 11:20 p.m. PST, a fire broke out in a former warehouse that had been converted into an artist collective with living spaces known as Ghost Ship. Of the 80 to 100 people attending the concert, 36 were killed, the deadliest in the history of Oakland.
6 In December 2019, a judge in Austin, Texas, ordered conspiracy theorist Alex Jones to pay $100,000 (£76,000) in another court setback over the Infowars host using his show to promote falsehoods that the 2012 Sandy Hook school massacre was a hoax. Jones was sued for defamation successfully by the parents of a 6-year-old who was among the 26 people killed in the Newtown, Connecticut, attack. Jones was forced to admit during the case that he had invented the whole hoax story,
7 The retirement age for women rose from 60 to 65, in line with men, and will go up to 66 by 2020 and to 67 by 2028.

References

Alexander, M. (2010) *The New Jim Crow: Mass Incarceration in the Age of Colorblindness*. New York: The New Press.
Cobain, I. (2011) 'Mixed Results Since Blair's "Dangerous" Freedom of Information Act' Launched', *The Guardian*, September 20.
Cohen, S. (1988) Against Criminology. New Brunswick, NJ: Transaction.
Cox, M. (2018) *Understanding the Global Rise of Populism*. London: LSE Ideas.
Cuneen, C. and Tauri, J. (2015) *Indigenous Criminology*. Chicago, IL: University of Chicago Press.
Cusick, J. and Ramsey, A. (2018) *Police Still Not Investigating Leave Campaign, Citing Political Sensitivities*. London: Open Democracy.
Davies, A. (1998) 'Racialized Punishment and Prison Abolition', in J. James (ed.), *The Angela Y. Davies Reader*. Oxford: Blackwell.
Davies, W. (2018) 'Why We Stopped Trusting Elites', *The Guardian*, 29 November.
Edelman Trust Barometer (2018) *Edelman Trust Barometer*. New York: Edelman.
Elgot, J. (2017) 'Corbyn: Hammond Right to Say Labour Threatens Whole Economic System', *The Guardian*, October 13.
Foucault, M. (1980) *Power/Knowledge: Selected Interviews and Other Writings 1972–77*, edited by C. Gordon. Brighton: Harvester Press.
Fukuyama, F. (2018) 'Against Identity Politics: The New Tribalism and the Crisis of Democracy', *Foreign Affairs*, September/October.
Garland, D. (2001) The Culture of Control. Oxford: Oxford University Press.
Giddens, A. (2002) *Runaway World: How Globalisation Is Reshaping Our Lives*, 2nd ed. London: Profile Books.
Goodhart, D. (2017) *The Road to Somewhere: The Populist Revolt and the Future of Politics*. London: G. Hurst and Co.
Graham-Harrison, E. (2018) 'Enemy of the People: Trump's Phrase and Its Echoes of Totalitarianism', *The Guardian*, August 3.
Gramsci, A. (1977, 1978) *Selections from the Political Writings*. London: Lawrence & Wishart.
Hahl, O., Kim, M. and Zuckerman Sivan, E.W. (2018) 'The Authentic Appeal of the Lying Demagogue: Proclaiming the Deeper Truth about Political Illegitimacy', *American Sociological Review*, 3(1): 34–60.
Hope Not Hate (2020) *State of Hate 2020: Our Most Extensive Report of the Far Right*. London: Hope Not Hate.
Jacques, M. (2016) 'The Death of Neoliberalism and the Crisis in Western Politics', *The Guardian*, August 23.
Mankiw, G.N. (2008) 'New Keysianian Economics', in D.R. Henderson (ed.) *Concise Encyclopedia of Economics* (2nd ed.). Indianapolis: Library of Economics and Liberty.

Marquand, D. (2010) 'Why the Left is Losing the Crisis', New Statesman, 25 November.

Montier, J. and Pilkington, P. (2017) 'The Deep Causes of Secular Stagnations and the Rise of Populism', GMO White Paper, March.

Mountz, A. and Loyd, J. (2014) 'Transnational Productions of Remoteness: Building Onshore and Offshore Carceral Regimes Across Borders'. Geographica Helvetica, 69(5): 389-98.

Naim, M. (2013) The End of Power. New York: Basic Books.

Newport, F. (2015) 'Fewer Americans Identify as Middle Class in Recent Years', Gallip Inc. [Online' Available from: https://news.gallup.com/poll/1291/fewer-americans-identify-middle-class-recent-years.aspx [Accessed 1 February 2020].

Overbeek, H. and Apeldoorn, B. (eds.) (2012) Neoliberalism in Crisis. London: Palgrave Macmillan.

Piketty, T. (2014) Capital in the Twenty-First Century. Cambridge, MA: Harvard University Press.

Saad, L. (2000) 'Big Gender Gap Distinguishes Election 2000: Men Voting Overwhelmingly for Bush', Gallip Inc. [Online] Available from: https://news.gallup.com/poll/24/Big-Gender-Gap-Distinguishes-Election-2000.aspx [Accessed 1 February 2020].

Stein, D. (2014) 'Full Employment for the Future', Lateral 3. Available from: http://csalateral org/issue3/theory/stein [Accessed February 12, 2020].

Subramanian, A. and Kessler, M. (2013) 'The Hyperglobalizations of Trade and Its Future', Peterson Institute for International Economics, Working Paper Series, WP13-6, July.

Terry, C.M. (2003) The Fellas: Overcoming Prison and Addiction. Belmont, CA: Wadsworth.

Turner, M. (2020) 'UK Leaves the EU, Embarking on an Uncertain Future', New York Times, January 31.

Urbinati, N. (2019) 'Political Theory of Populism', Annual Review of Political Science, 22: 111–27.

Wilson, J.Q. and Herrnstein, R.J. (1985) Crime and Human Nature. New York: Simon and Schuster.

Chapter 18

Risk, surveillance and social control

Key issues

1   The risk society
2   The surveillance society
3   Universities, neoliberalism and new public management
4   Punishing the poor
5   Neoliberal penality

Introduction

Trust is good, control is better.

– Attributed to Vladimir Ilyich Lenin

We explored the concept of risk earlier, but in this chapter, we examine the notion further. At the same time, we consider how contemporary societies, in an era epitomized by the postmodern condition – or the fragmentation of modernity and the rise of a multiplicity of competing and invariably incompatible interest groups – are governed and populations controlled, not least in a world fundamentally underpinned by neoliberal exhortations to pursue profit at any cost, regardless of its impact on other aspects of society.

The risk society revisited

Ulrich Beck (1992) describes a paradigmatic shift from modernity to a 'second modernity' where he argues that man-made, yet unwanted and unplanned side effects of modernity challenge the very basis of its definition, producing growing societal uncertainties and thus leading to a new age where people must come to terms with the consequences of their actions. This ongoing process he calls 'reflexive modernization'. Reflexive does not mean 'reflected' or 'conscious' in this context: on the contrary, it refers to a 'boomerang' effect, where mostly unplanned results of (production) processes in modern societies backfire on these societies and force them to change – certainly not a consciously planned chain of events.

As a result of this process, society in the 'second modernity' is no longer concerned with the distribution of power and wealth, but instead with the way it handles risks. This influences the definition of societal groups as well, because problems like ecological risks, climate change and pandemics, are not distributed according to wealth, social milieus and strata. They simply impact on society as a whole. But the ability to avert risk is highly dependent on knowledge and information, and here, the mass media and investigative journalism are important because they make these risks visible.

Beck (1992) observes that the process of reflexive modernization challenges society and the individual alike. It changes the way we work, the concept of the nation state, as well as the economic basis of society. In an analysis highly compatible with the post-modern condition/fragmentation of modernity thesis, second modernity is seen to be a non-linear, anti-determinist era with competing, sometimes seemingly paradoxical developments going on simultaneously, with problematic political and social options in this process of dissolving norms and changing power structures. In such a complex, frac-tious. risk-bound social formation, the achievement and maintenance of social control is fraught with difficulty. Surveillance is thus a key component of gaining and maintaining control in such societies.

The surveillance society

The outcome of a local and global social environment founded on increasing individual-ism, growing inequality, disorder and crime has been – as we have seen – the production of very significant widespread risk. There is therefore a need to control highly diffuse, mobile, actual and potential problematic populations. Central to such strategies has been the increasing use of surveillance techniques.

Surveillance has become widespread, pervasive and a central part of our lives (Hopkins Burke, 2004). Surveillance societies are those which function, in part, because of the extensive collection, recording, storage, analysis and application of information collated on individuals and groups as they go about their lives. Retail loyalty programmes, website cookies, national identity schemes, routine health screening and no-fly lists all qualify as surveillance. Each features the routine collection of data about individuals with the specific purpose of governing, regulating, managing or influencing what they do in the future. This is surveillance.

Considering the use of surveillance enables an ethical, social and spatial critique of the information processing practices which are part of the way society is formed, governed and managed. It enables us to question and evidence its impact on the social fabric: on discrimination, trust, accountability, transparency, access to services, mobility, free-doms, community and social justice. Moreover, it enables us to engage in debates with watchdogs, businesses and journalists about the consequences of their surveillance-based activities.

Instead of considering surveillance to be the product of a single all-knowing oppressive force – the 'Big Brother' is watching us model famously depicted by George Orwell in his novel *Nineteen Eighty-Four* – we should observe that it tends to be more complex, mul-tilayered and insidious, creeping and seeping into every aspect of social life. The covert high-tech world of the spy or the all-seeing authoritarian tyrant is thus only a part of the surveillance society. Consider the many different activities in which we engage during the course of a single day which involve surveillance. As workers, performance information is collected by our employers to review performance for both positive (improving perfor-mance and productivity) and negative motives (disposing of underperforming workers).

As consumers, our transactions are monitored by financial institutions to detect fraud and our preferences are scrutinized by loyalty programmes to enable future marketing campaigns to target us. As mobile (cell) phone users our movements and communica-tions can be tracked for use by the emergency services: some people use location-based services – such as GPS – to find their way around new places. Surveillance is thus something which can confer access, entitlement and benefit as well as something which is dangerous, oppressive and discriminatory.

Wherever we find surveillance it tends to perform the same function: it enables corporations and governments to manage or govern resources, activities and populations. It works through interconnected but distributed chains of organizations, infrastructures and people and its application is aligned to different organizational strategies and purposes. How surveillance plays out in a call centre, where every minute of the working day is monitored and recorded, as compared to a military setting, where armies are using unmanned aerial vehicles (drones) to look for the enemy, is obviously very different in terms of its processes and consequences. Yet both situations feature surveillance as one of their organizing principles.

If surveillance is a normal aspect of the management and governance of modern life with so many positive uses, we might ask ourselves why so many people – not least critical criminologists – consider surveillance to be so problematic, but using surveillance to achieve aims, no matter how grand or how minuscule, bestows great power. Thus, to label a phenomenon as 'surveillant' involves acknowledging that information processing which takes place as part of governance or management is never a neutral process. Some interests will be served, while others will be marginalized. Some will receive benefits and entitlements, while others will not. Surveillance coalesces in places where power accumulates, underpinning and enhancing the activities of those who rule and govern.

The danger is that surveillance power becomes ubiquitous: embedded within systems, structures and the interests they represent. Its application becomes taken for granted and its consequences go unnoticed. As data travel silently across international boundaries, between national states and within transnational corporations, the impact of surveillance becomes even harder to identify, regulate and debate. We might think that this power, based on the oversight of activities and of personal data, is wielded fairly, responsibly and with due respect to human rights, civil liberties and the law. But wielding surveillance power can have very undesirable consequences: world leaders appeal to some greater good such as the war on terror to justify unusual surveillance tactics on everyday citizens. Sifting through consumer records to create a profitable clientele means that certain groups obtain special treatment based on their ability to pay whereas those deemed 'less valuable' are ignored. Surveillance, moreover, fosters suspicion in those who are charged with using it. It focuses on correcting the negative and therefore gives a message to those who are watched that they are not trusted to behave in the appropriate manner. It is certainly a useful tool for those seeking to gain significantly to the considerable disadvantage of the many and is thus a central component of a grossly unequal neoliberal society.

Controlling or punishing the poor, often through the use of the criminal justice system is very much a central part of the surveillance society and we will return to that crucial element later in this chapter. Surveillance is nevertheless – as observed earlier – pervasive throughout neoliberal society. As the great majority of readers of this text will be students and their tutors, it is prescient to consider the impact of neoliberalism on the higher education industry.

Universities, neoliberalism and new public management

Chris Lorenz (2012) observes that the spectacular growth in the number of students and faculty in the 1960s was immediately followed by administrative reforms aimed at managing this growth and the demands of students for democratic reform and societal relevance. But the real change has occurred since the 1980s, where the fiscal crisis of the welfare states and the resulting neoliberalism instigated by the Reagan and Thatcher administrations has made the battle against budget deficits and government spending a political priority. The neoliberal agenda has become increasingly more radical – smaller state and bigger market – attacks on the public sector through efforts to systematically reduce public expenditure by privatizing public services and introducing market incentives. At the same time, the societal relevance of the universities, demanded by critical students, was turned on its head to become economic relevance to business and industry in the knowledge society.

Lorenz (2012) observes that the neoliberal dream can be divided into four dogmas. First, *the dogma of the free market* can be expressed by a simple formula: free market = competition = best value for money = optimum efficiency for individuals as both consumers and owners of private property. The consumer is seen as an owner of private property and as a shareholder in an economy organized on a commercial basis. It is in the interests of individuals as shareholders that the market economy functions freely. It is the task of the state to remove all obstacles in the way of free markets.

Neoliberalism simultaneously shifts its focus from rights to risks: where the 'risk society', job insecurity, and 'flexibility' are the normal, present-day global condition. The globalized individual is detached from the fundamental rights which were previously central components of national citizenship, such as the right to education and welfare. All of these civil rights are now exchanged for one new right: the right to buy services in the privatized service market.

Second, *the dogma of the private company* implies that it is the job of the state to remove all obstacles to private ownership of companies, in particular former state-owned companies. All former state activities in the domains of education, social security and health care can be privatized and commodified so that they can be made efficient and profitable. In neoliberal societies, collective goods do not exist. The functioning of free markets assumes well-organized companies which function in the interest of all shareholders because optimal management results in optimal efficiency and thus in optimal shareholder value.

Third, *management dogma* makes the task of the state to remove all obstacles to efficient management. Because management equals efficiency in neoliberalism, it is Value for Money (VFM) by definition. New Public Management (NPM) is VFM.

Fourth, *consumer dogma* makes it the task of the state to remove all obstacles standing in the way of private consumers exercising their purchasing power, as well as all obstacles to market transparency. The functioning of free markets assumes the presence of well-informed consumers who have sufficient purchasing power and can make rational, individual choices to buy goods and services based on their individual preferences. The ideology of consumerism also transforms citizens into consumers. Thus, consumerist ideology provides the justification to abolish all interference with fair market relationships, including taxation. This anti-tax viewpoint is most deeply rooted in the US, but it is increasingly being heard in Europe.

Lorenz (2012) observes that fundamentally new public management is the application of these four dogmas to the domain of what used to be called the public sector. The latter is now redefined as a service sector which functions best when it operates in accordance with the principles of the free market. The neoliberal denial of any other organizational principles is nevertheless something radically new because classical liberalism had empha-sized the autonomy of the public sector (protected by law) from interference by the pri-vate sector. Market fundamentalism is thus something both new and which is at the very core of neoliberalism.

The development of new public management and the rise of entrepreneurial govern-ment in the US sought to reform the public sector by implementing serious cuts in public spending. Its arrival in Britain was marked by private-sector management techniques and strategies. Thus, in higher education, the Thatcher government introduced league tables relying on quantifiable indicators that claimed to rank institutions by the quality of their teaching and research. This policy was highly significant because it systematically reduced the grip that the academic professions had on their own autonomy. Moreover, the with-drawal of trust in its universities and processes instigated by the government forced the sector to create bureaucratic machinery and formulas to steer and manage the institutions from outside the system. The outcome was the rise of a regime of bureaucrats, inspectors, commissioners, regulators and experts which were to erode professional autonomy and initiate a move away from the disciplines, which had previously been the impenetrable fortresses of the professions.

Lorenz (2012) observes moreover that the new public management claim to be anti-bureaucratic was suspect from the outset. This should not come as a surprise because – given the evident absence of a market mechanism in the public-service sector – the prices of services in the quasi-markets created by the state must be organized according to a dif-ferent principle. Thus, in NPM quasi-markets, the open place of the market mechanism has been superseded by the notion of efficiency. And because the nebulous notion of efficiency, unlike the concept of effectiveness, is a concept entirely without substance, the essence of this discourse turns out to consist of the notion of cost-efficiency.

In practice, cost-efficiency is interpreted as, at least, the self-financing of organiza-tions, and if possible, it is expected to make them profitable. Thus, the introduction of new public management into the former public sector has revealed itself in the guise of permanent reductions in costs, that is permanent spending cuts. It is a trend evident in the typical combination of (1) a constant decrease in the level of service; (2) a constant decrease in the level and quality of employment in the former public sector, which is realized through a steady process of de-professionalization and a reduction in the number and the quality of jobs; and (3) constantly rising prices for the consumers of services such as student fees in the case of education.

Lorenz (2012) observes that the introduction of NPM is revealed in four tendencies in the case of higher education. First, there is a continuous deterioration in the staff/student ratio and ever-increasing teaching loads for faculty and continuing increases in the scale of education. Second, academic staff are transformed into a shrinking core of tenured faculty and a growing periphery of part-time, temporary teaching staff hired for one year, one semester or one course. Quite simply, there is the substitution of inflexible and expensive faculty – especially tenured, full-time professors – by flexible and cheap staff, especially untenured, part-time adjuncts, teaching assistants and symbolic profes-sors. In the US, almost two-thirds of teaching is now done by untenured faculty under increasingly deteriorating conditions, creating a class of 'scholar gypsies'. Third, teaching and research are continuously disassociated with the proportion and quantity of teaching which is ever increasing. Thus, more and more academic staff are hired only to teach tem-porarily. Fourth, tuition fees are increasing, and the duration of studies is being reduced, for instance, through the introduction of the BA/MA structure in the EU following the Bologna Declaration in 1999.[1] NPM manifests itself in an ongoing rise in the (absolute and relative) price of education and in the permanent acceleration in its regime of time for both faculty and students. Increasing student debt and decreasing faculty income are therefore direct consequences of these policies.

Greater managerial power, structural reorganization, more emphasis on marketing and business generation move towards performance-related pay and a rationalization and computerization of administrative structures are all characteristic of the new higher education organization, as is the standardization of all performances. The unstoppable rise of league tables – the ranking of citations, individual researchers, research groups, institutes and whole universities – is an integral part of this development in the direction of audit cultures and an audit society. League tables simultaneously produce winners and losers, while the policy of naming and shaming failing institutions has become an annual ritual in humiliation.

Likewise, the unstoppable rise of 'accreditation agencies' replaces professional controls by providing 'stamps of quality' to individual departments and that determine whether they 'serve the demand of the market'. Here again, market rhetoric is good, but central control is better.

Lorenz (2012) pertinently notes that the new public managerialism is remarkably reminiscent of state communism. Both are totalitarian because they leave no institutionalized room for criticism, which is always seen as subversive. The questions of whether managers really do spend the taxpayers' money more efficiently and whether they are more reliable than faculty cannot be asked. Nor may one ask whether the cost of the management controls is less than the money saved on inefficient academic personnel. The fact that there is not a shred of evidence for these two crucial assumptions makes it abundantly clear where the blind spots lie in new public management. All recent economic scandals – from Enron, WorldCom and Barings to the Lehman Brothers – happened despite constant audits, which provides us with some extra empirical food for critical thought on both management and audits.

The new public management is an organizational discourse which promotes and legitimizes the takeover of power by managers in public organizations that were previously run by professionals in accordance with their standards. Professions are defined by the following five characteristics. First, there is the mastery of specialist theoretical knowledge which the professional has to acquire through extended education and training. Second, there is autonomy and control over the work and how it is done. Third, being motivated by the interests of clients takes priority over the interests of the professional. Fourth, there is a commitment to a professional career and the objectives of the service provided by the employing organization. Professional identity is thus mainly bound to the profession and not to management aims which are geared to profit and efficiency. Five, there is a sense of commitment and collegiality in the professional group and a sense of responsibility to colleagues. The professional body operates as an internal control both for admitting people to the profession and for maintaining professional standards.

Lorenz (2012) observes that there is an inherent conflict between bureaucracy and professionalism because they operate from opposing principles and beliefs, with respect to aims, authority and loyalty. First, whereas bureaucracy expects its members to primarily promote and represent the interests of the organization, the professional presumes the interests of the client to be supreme. Second, bureaucracy sees authority as residing in legal contracts backed by legal sanctions: as utilitarian and goal-driven formal organizations, bureaucracies focus on contractual arrangements and formal structures. By contrast, professionals tend to think of authority being rooted in the expertise of the person holding the position rather than in the power of the status itself. Along these same lines, bureaucracies expect their members to comply with directives of the organization: professionals, by contrast, expect to be guided by the ethical standards of their discipline as outlined by professional associations. Because professionals develop a reference system focusing on professional colleagues, they are typically more concerned with maintaining a reputation with peers in their field than they are with pleasing organizational superiors.

Lorenz (2012) notes that the new public management regards education to be the faculty production of credit points (input) and the student consumption (output), usually in the form of standardized units called courses or modules. A module is defined in terms of a fixed quantity of time investment by both its producers and its consumers. Moreover, it is characteristically independent of its producers (professional teachers) because it has a standardized (online) form and content, formatted by commercial course management corporations like Blackboard and Pearson-eCollege. Online modules typically are no longer owned by their direct producers – the faculty – but by management. The modularization of higher education thus forms an essential station on its way to commodified instruction.

Management in practice nevertheless differs somewhat from management discourse in at least two fundamental respects. The breaking up of professions into processes may work in theory, but in practice, this discourse runs up against a number of fundamental problems on the question of the recognition of both professionals – who work under the leadership of a manager – and of the managers themselves.

The first problem is that while only quantitative criteria is used to control the quality of professional activities, this in itself creates enormous inefficiency with respect to both the job motivation and job satisfaction of those who used to be professionals. The introduction of the management model implies the abolition of qualitative professional criteria, including its own regime of time and their replacement with an entrepreneurial model of faculty subjectivity based on quantitative output criteria. The logic of this model also implies that financial incentives to enforce conformity with output criteria can ultimately be translated to individual faculty members via individualized contracts and performance-related pay. The latter is a well-known tool to de-professionalize professional groups.

The second problem is the chronic lack of understanding of the difficulties faced by managers themselves. Because the organizations that they are managing were previously organizations run on the basis of professional standards and hierarchies, managers are confronted with a structural problem of authority and legitimacy. The solution has been to apply a number of management strategies with this shift characterized by a tendency to manipulative and strategic behaviour. Moreover, because they lack professional authority, managers are inclined to treat any lack of cooperation on the shop floor as a threat to their position and as subversion. Those who dare to cast doubt on their decisions can thus count on pressure, blackmail, divide-and-conquer tactics, open humiliation and their reputation trashed.

Lorenz (2012) observes that rationally organized NPM administrations tolerate a staggering range of irrational management practices under the wide, protective, ideological umbrella of efficiency. In this respect (the lack of objective reality checks and the ensuing unconstrained power of management) organizations in the quasi-market sector under NPM and party organizations under state communism again show striking similarities.

From a psychological perspective, the growth of management has also been directly linked with the lack of professional authority and legitimacy held by managers. Because they do not receive recognition for their expertise from the professionals they are managing, they tend to surround themselves with kindred spirits, as a means of organizing some kind of professional recognition for themselves. Whatever the problem, the solution proposed is always more management, more efficiency and more control. It is no coincidence that the obsessive rhetoric about professionalization started at the same time as the new public managers made their appearance in the universities, that is to say, when for the first time in their history power over the universities was given to a group that was unprofessional in the original meaning of the word. Nor is it a coincidence that it was from that moment that academic personnel started to be treated as if they needed to acquire new professional skills. *Lifelong learning* is also used as a means to discipline the faculty itself.

Lorenz (2012) observes that the paradoxical and disastrous effect of the introduction of NPM, with its self-referential notions of accountability and quality, is that someone can be both an excellent teacher and researcher while, at the same time, be assessed as poor by the quality assurance (QA) system. This disquieting fact illustrates the head-on clash between the substantial values of academic professionalism and the bureaucratic formalism of the new management. This characteristic also explains another consequence of its introduction in the academic world: the existence of widespread cynicism and hypocrisy among faculty regarding the application of QA procedures. Most colleagues find audit exercises ludicrous but nevertheless go through the motions of complying with their imperatives lest the wrath of management is incurred.

The fundamental gulf between the professional, substantial view of quality and its formalistic perversion in management discourse can be traced back to the reduction of education to the economic. For it is not at all clear what the product is – or ought to be – in the education process. There is no product in the economic sense, and thus, there are no criteria by which to measure quality. This gap in the education discourse is filled by defining the product of education as qualification – expressed in terms of ECTS points[2] and their accumulation into diplomas. The quality of the education is then defined as the quantitative efficiency with which these qualifications are produced. This economic reduction of education is remarkable because the latter does not by any stretch of the imagination resemble the purchase of a product to satisfy a specific need. Participating in education is an ongoing, reciprocal and hierarchical process, in which student and teacher are both actively involved and in which the teacher represents professional authority. The fact that education costs money – and so in this respect resembles the purchase of products such as Coca-Cola and cornflakes – does not mean that education is an economic transaction between a buyer and seller, as the economic view of education claims.

Lorenz (2012) observes that the economic education discourse seems to have produced a new dual identity for academic staff who are transformed into both producers of a consumer good called education and sellers of the same. This dual entrepreneurial identity implies that the entire responsibility for both producing and selling education is laid on the faculty. At the same time, the management is shielded from all risky activities in the outside world: its sole and exclusive responsibility is control over the faculty. Should anything go wrong in the outside world – for instance, that the education consumers fail to turn up in sufficient numbers, or they do not behave as model consumers because they take longer to complete their studies than the official time allowed – then the faculty are always responsible and can be judged as such. Again, as in state communism, in practice, the managers are almost always right.

In the economic view, students do not pay to be taught a discipline by professionals who have proven expertise and subject knowledge based on professional criteria. Instead, students pay for the end product of education: a degree or other qualification, the investment of which will bring them profits in the labour market. Just like everything else in the economic universe, studying has been reduced to a simple exchange. The fundamental idea that a degree has cultural value because it represents a specific level of knowledge and skills according to professional criteria is completely obscured. The economic value of a degree has actually always depended on its cultural value, and the economic value is simply leeching on the cultural value. What is basically now happening in neoliberal, economic education practice is a paradoxical attempt to uncouple the economic and cultural values of the degree – and of education in general – and to retain the derivative economic value of education without leaving its cultural basis intact. The economic view of education, in other words, turns out to be a complete parasite on the professional view of education and is undermining and eroding it.

Lorenz (2012) observes that support for the new public management in higher education is based on an unholy alliance between the neoliberal political class and the managers on one side and aligned faculty and students on the other. The latter are being strongly encouraged to adopt the definition of themselves as consumers and are being asked to control the quality of their education through constant evaluations. By all appearances, a not insignificant share of students are susceptible to this consumer ideology and its associated short-term benefits. It is not entirely accidental that the grade inflation that is clearly detrimental to consumers in the long term is a well-kept secret in this discourse and is not a popular research subject in educational science.

At the same time, the scores in student satisfaction surveys show no statistical significance in relation to the effectiveness of that education, while there is invariably a negative correlation between relatively strict assessment and the enthusiasm of students to enrol for those subjects. Reaching conclusions about the quality of education from student satisfaction surveys may seem an obvious thing to do in the economic cosmos, but in the empirical world of statistics, no adequate support for it has been found.

Lorenz (2012) observes that where the logics of professionalism and of management clash – as is the case with professional and economic views on education – the outcome has been determined by the political power of neoliberalism and its use of the microphysics of managerialism. The introduction and continuation of output-based education funding represent nothing less than the continuation of neoliberal NPM control, the domination and de-skilling of a former higher education system staffed by professional and autotomized academics. But neoliberal NPM techniques in pursuit of profit does not imply the absence of surveillance of higher education institutions by higher authorities with their own interests such as governments charged with the protection of the public purse and getting best value in the interests of a neoliberal economy.

In a speech made on 1 July 2000, the universities minister, Michelle Donelan, effectively announced that the 20-year crusade to get more young people into higher education was at an end and accused universities in England of 'taking advantage' of students with dumbed-down (sic) courses which left them burdened with debt. In a significant shift in policy, the minister declared it was time to 'think again' about governmental use of higher education to boost social mobility:

> Since 2004, there has been too much focus on getting students through the door, and not enough focus on how many drop out, or how many go on to graduate jobs. Too many have been misled by the expansion of popular-sounding courses with no real demand from the labour market.
>
> Quite frankly, our young people have been taken advantage of, particularly those without a family history of going to university. Instead some have been left with the debt of an investment that didn't pay off in any sense.
>
> And too many universities have felt pressured to dumb down – either when admitting students, or in the standards of their courses. We have seen this with grade-inflation, and it has to stop.
>
> (Cited by Adams, 2020)

Adams (2020) observed that the minister's comments came as the government was to offer new policies on skills and qualifications for school-leavers in England, rebalancing away from universities and emphasizing social mobility through skilled, well-paid jobs secured through further education and apprenticeships. A white paper on further education was to be announced later in the month, along with a green paper on higher education to limit courses in which a high percentage of students drop out or where few go on to graduate-level employment. Those close to the government said the rebalancing effort brings to an end policies promoted since the late 1990s, including New Labour prime minister Tony Blair's famous pledge for half of all young people to go on to higher education. Donelan said:

> For decades we've been recruiting too many young people on to courses that do nothing to improve their life chances or help with their career goals.

Adams (2020) observes that the minister's comments appeared to repudiate her own government's guidance to the Office for Students, the higher education regulator for England. Asked about the use of contextual admissions by universities to help under-represented groups gain entry, Donelan said:

> To be frank, we don't help disadvantaged students by levelling down, we help by levelling up.

Graeme Atherton, director the National Education Opportunities Network (Neon) led the inevitable challenges to the minister and said:

> The government's own evidence still shows that going to university brings economic and social benefits for the vast majority of students – from all backgrounds, but sometimes these benefits are apparent only over the long term.
>
> It is not true that widening access work has taken advantage of young people, rather it has transformed thousands of lives over the last 20 years.

Jo Grady, general secretary of the University and College Union, rather understandably joined in the criticisms and observed that the government's obsession with graduate earnings – obviously in line with the requirements of a neoliberal economy – was a worrying signal:

> Instead of making the case for education, the minister appears to be trying to turn some students off university by saying it is expensive and substandard. Universities using contextual data to increase opportunity for students from the poorest backgrounds should be applauded.
>
> For the minister to say students have been left indebted and let down is quite remarkable when the Conservatives are responsible for increasing tuition fee debt and letting the private sector squeeze more and more money out of higher education.

Chris Hale, director of policy at Universities UK, said official data showed that a university degree gave a significant boost to career prospects, as graduates earned about £9,000 more a year than those without a degree. Yet, these claims are not supported by a report from international recruitment experts Chartered Institute of Personnel and Development which said that UK universities should be prevented from charging the maximum level of tuition fees unless they deliver better graduate outcomes.

The report *The Graduate Employment Gap: Expectations versus Reality* shows that just half (52%) of graduates secure a graduate-level job six months after they finish their course, and this figure has been inflated to 77% by including 'associate professional and technical occupations' such as dancers, choreographers, fitness instructors, youth and community workers, despite the Office for National Statistics stating that these jobs 'do not require a degree'. Lizzie Crowley, skills adviser at the CIPD, said:

> As we look ahead to the Budget next week, the Government should consider linking tuition fees to graduate destination data in order to prevent higher education institutions charging top rate fees while delivering bottom rate outcomes.
>
> This report shows that the preoccupation of successive governments with boosting graduate numbers is leading to high levels of over-qualification and potentially skills mismatches, which the OECD [Organisation for Economic Co-operation and Development] suggests undermines productivity growth. Many people in 'graduate jobs' are actually in roles that don't require degrees, and with the spiralling costs of university students need to ask themselves whether a degree path is the best route into their career.
>
> (Cited in Talint International, 2020)

Punishing the poor

Having considered the surveillance and control of previously autonomous professional middle-class groups via the new public management in the interests of neoliberal society, we now turn our attention to mechanisms to control the poorer and often 'socially excluded' groups in society invariably via the use of the criminal justice system – in this complex, risk-bound, fragmented modernity.

Loïc Wacquant rhetorically asks why it is that the prison in the twenty-first century has returned to the institutional forefront of the advanced societies, when four decades previously penological analysts were convinced that it was on the decline and perhaps terminally. In his book *Punishing the Poor* (Wacquant, 2009b) makes three arguments to resolve this historical conundrum. First, the expansion and glorification of the police, the courts and the penitentiary are a response not to *criminal* insecurity but to the *social* insecurity caused by the casualization of wage labour and the disruption of ethno-racial hierarchy. Second, we need to reconnect social and penal policies and treat them as two variants of poverty policy to grasp the new punitive politics of marginality. Third, the simultaneous and converging deployment of restrictive 'workfare' and expansive 'prison fare' partake of the forging of the neoliberal state. We next consider each of these arguments further.

Ramping up the penal state in response to social insecurity

Wacquant's first argument is that the ramping up of the penal wing of the state is a response to social insecurity, and not a reaction to crime trends. He observes that in the three decades after the peaking of the civil rights movement, the US went from being a leader in progressive justice to an apostle of 'zero tolerance' policing, architect of 'Three Strikes and You're Out,' and world champion in incarceration. But why? The conventional answer is that this stupendous expansion of punishment was driven by the rise in crime. Yet victimization at first stagnated and then decreased during this entire period. Consider this simple statistic: the US held 21 prisoners for every 10,000 'index crimes' in 1975; 30 years later, it locked up 125 prisoners for every 10,000 crimes. This means that the country had become six times more punitive, holding crime constant.

Wacquant argues that to explain this punitive turn in penal policy, we need to *break out of the crime-and-punishment box* and pay attention to the extra-penological functions of penal institutions. We then discover that, in the wake of the race riots of the 1960s, the police, courts and prison were subsequently deployed to contain the urban dislocations wrought by economic deregulation and the implosion of the ghetto as a medium of ethno-racial containment and to impose the discipline of insecure employment at the bottom of the polarizing class structure. As a result, the resurging prison has come to serve three missions that have little to do with crime control: (1) to bend the fractions of the post-industrial working class to precarious wage work, (2) to warehouse their most disruptive or superfluous elements and (3) to patrol the boundaries of the deserving citizenry while reasserting the authority of the state in the restricted domain it now assigns itself.

Wacquant observes that rates of confinement in Western Europe are comparatively modest compared to the US but adds that this must not hide two crucial facts. First, penalization takes many different forms and is not reducible to incarceration. Second, incarceration rates have shown steady and sturdy growth across Western Europe since the early 1980s: they have grown by more than one-half in France, Italy, and Belgium; nearly doubled in England and Wales, Sweden, Portugal, and Greece; and quadrupled in Spain and the Netherlands, the latter long lauded as a model of humane penality. In reality, he observes, a drift towards the penalization of urban marginality has swept through Western Europe with a lag of two decades, albeit on a smaller scale (commensurate with the makeup of the state and social space in these societies).

This drift presents three distinctive features. First, the new penal laws embraced by European governments typically 'bark' louder than they 'bite' because the texture of social and economic citizenship is more robust, human rights standards thwart excessive criminalization and judicial professionals have been able to resist penal extension from within the state apparatus. But hyping 'insecurity' and promoting crime-fighting in and around districts of dereliction to the rank of government priority, in preference to fighting unemployment in these same areas, has definitely shifted government priorities in favour of penal posturing and action.

Second, European societies endowed with a strong statist tradition are using the front end of the penal chain, the police, rather than the back end, the prison, to curb social disorders and despair in low-income districts. One example: in France, the inmate population has risen by one-third over a period of ten years, but during that same period, the number of persons arrested and held overnight for a *'garde à vue'* in a police lockup nearly tripled to approach the extravagant figure of 1 million.

Third, instead of a brutal swing from the social to the penal management of poverty as in the US, continental countries have intensified both, expanding welfare protection and police intervention simultaneously in a contradictory thrust that has both stimulated and limited the extension of the punitive mesh.

Wacquant observes that these three features define a 'Western European road' to the penalization of poverty which is not that of the US. Yet, from a longer macro-political perspective, the dominant trend is similar: a punitive revamping of public policy that weds the 'invisible hand' of the market to the 'iron fist' of the penal state.

Re-linking social and penal policy

Wacquant's second argument is that we must re-link shifts in penal and social policy, instead of isolating them from one another. The downsizing of public aid, complemented by the shift from the right to welfare to obligation of workfare (i.e. forced participation in sub-par 'gig-economy' employment as a condition of support), and the upsizing of the prison are the two sides of the same coin. Together, workfare and prison-fare effect the double regulation of poverty in the age of deepening economic inequality and diffusing social insecurity. It is his contention that *welfare and criminal justice are two modalities of public policy toward the poor,* and so they must imperatively be analysed – and reformed – together. Supervisory workfare and the neutralizing prison 'serve' the same population drawn from the same marginalized sectors of the unskilled working class. They are guided by the same philosophy of moral behaviourism and employ the same techniques of control, including stigma, surveillance, punitive restrictions, and graduated sanctions to 'correct' the conduct of their clients. In some states in the US, welfare recipients stand in line together with parolees to undergo their monthly drug tests to maintain eligibility for support. In others, parolees who fall into homelessness because they cannot find a job are returned to prison for failure to maintain a stable residence.

Nowadays, you cannot track penal policy without reckoning with social policy and vice versa. You cannot understand trends in offending without factoring in the major changes in welfare provision, public housing, foster care, and related state programmes, including the oversight of irregular migration that set the life options of the populations most susceptible to street crime (as both perpetrators and victims).

Crafting the neoliberal state

Wacquant's third argument is that the meshing of workfare and prison-fare fundamentally contributes to the making of the neoliberal state. Economists have proposed a conception of neoliberalism that equates it with the rule of the 'free market' and the coming of 'small government' and, by and large, other social scientists have adopted that conception. The problem is that it captures the ideology of neoliberalism, not its reality. The comparative sociology of actually existing neoliberalism reveals that it involves everywhere the building of an erection of a *Centaur state*, liberal at the top and paternalistic at the bottom. Then neoliberal Leviathan practices *laissez faire et laissez passer* toward corporations and the upper class, at the level of the causes of inequality. But it is fiercely interventionist and authoritarian when it comes to dealing with the destructive consequences of economic deregulation for those at the lower end of the class and status spectrum. This is because the imposition of market discipline is not a smooth, self-propelling process, it meets with recalcitrance and triggers resistance, it translates into diffusing social instability and turbulence among the lower class and it practically undermines the authority of the state. So it requires institutional apparatuses that will anchor and support it, among them an enlarged and energetic penal institution.

Wacquant argues that the linked meanness of the welfare wing and the benevolence of the penal wing under the guidance of moralism are profoundly injurious to democratic ideals. As their sights converge on the same marginal populations and districts, deterrent workfare and the nullifying prison-fare foster vastly different profiles and experiences of citizenship across the class and ethnic spectrum. Thus, they contravene the fundamental principle of equality of treatment by the state and routinely abridge the individual freedoms of the dispossessed. Moreover, they undermine the consent of the governed through the aggressive deployment of involuntary programmes stipulating personal responsibilities, just as the state is withdrawing the institutional supports necessary to shoulder these and avoiding its own social and economic charges. In short, the penalization of poverty divides citizenship along class lines, saps civic trust at the bottom and sows the degradation of republican tenets. The establishment of the new government of social insecurity wedding restrictive workfare and expansive prison-fare shows that neoliberalism is constitutively corrosive of democracy. Yet it is the result of policy choices, not a preordained necessity. Other historical paths out of the turmoil of the 1960s and the stagflation of the 1970s were open and remain open.

It is nevertheless a thesis that has attracted a lot of criticism, not least because the rigorous and expensive criminal justice interventions of the past three decades appear to be rather contrary to a cost-conscious small state favouring neoliberalism.

Neoliberal penality

Neoliberalism is said to have generated a distinctive set of penal policies which have been characterized as 'neoliberal penality', appearing in its own right (Wacquant, 2009a, 2009b) or as a key element in more complex formations such as a 'culture of control' (Garland, 2001). Typically, it is argued that neoliberal penality is characterized by three broad interlinked trends. First, the increasing use of punishment – a 'punitive turn' – especially focused on a greater use of imprisonment and longer terms of imprisonment, particularly in the pursuit of increasing individual responsibility for offending. Second, a linked denial of 'welfare' or 'therapeutic' sanctions both because these detract from responsibility and because of their cost and alleged failure to correct offenders. Third, there is a focus on penality as providing protection for citizens, sometimes understood as the 'customers' of justice and 'victims' of crime.

Pat O'Malley (2016) observes that much analysis has focused on the emergence or accentuated use of specific sanctions – also often characterized as 'neoliberal' – such as 'three strikes' legislation, home detention, electronic monitoring, naming and shaming and boot camps. Usually, these are each said to relate to different components of neoliberalism, with home detention and electronic monitoring said to reflect an 'economic register', boot camps and shaming are indicative of individual responsibility (O'Malley, 1999). A great deal of emphasis is placed on social exclusion rather than reintegration, especially with respect to an underclass conceived in neoliberal discourse as not having adapted to the new post-industrial economy and its competitive conditions. Finally, emergent risk-based practices are seen to express neoliberal economic preferences for prevention over cure, for improved cost-effectiveness, and for protecting the public (O'Malley, 1992; Garland, 2001; Reiner, 2006).

Accounts vary with respect to the extent of causal power attributed to neoliberalism. In more uncompromising accounts, such as that associated with Loïc Wacquant – outlined above – neoliberal penality appears to be a consequence of the global influence of a powerful US hegemony backed up by institutions such as the International Monetary Fund. A ruling class of state leaders, transnational CEOs and bureaucrats is seen to be a neoliberal political and economic regime, a *core element* of which is a penal politics aimed at coercively transforming – or excluding – unproductive elements of the population through 'prison-fare' or 'workfare'. (Wacquant, 2009a). In this account, neoliberal penality is not merely an effect or a specific result of neoliberalism but is a core defining feature.

Wacquant's thesis has attracted more than its share of criticism (Lacey, 2008, 2013; Valverde, 2010; O'Malley, 2014), but it does make tangible claims about the specific influence of neoliberalism on penal politics. In other accounts, neoliberalism is connected to penality as part of an interacting bundle of forces. Thus, in Garland's (2001) 'culture of control' thesis, it is connected with the emergence of risk techniques, the impact of robustly high crime rates not least on the middle classes. In Young's (1999) account it is part of a fundamental shift in the entire social formation toward social segregation and exclusion. In other views – for example O'Malley, 1992 – neoliberalism impacts on penality primarily through the shaping of risk, which in turn reshapes crime prevention, policing, sentencing and the content of sanctions. These accounts may be seen as being less dogmatic about neoliberal penality through their attribution of change to a number of factors, but, at the same time, they make it difficult to discern exactly how to untangle the specific influence of neoliberalism.

O'Malley (2016) observes that no matter whether in 'strong' or 'weak' form, the neoliberal penality thesis shares a common view that it is displacing the penal framework of 'social democracy' or 'the welfare state'. Neoliberal penal reform is depicted as undoing the assemblage that Garland (1985) referred to as the 'welfare sanction' – which had emerged around the turn of the twentieth century – and where correctional expertise challenged or undermined the punitive moralism which had characterized nineteenth-century liberalism. Penal policies were largely distanced from populist politics: they constituted a scientific approach which was held to require some insulation from the politics of vengeance that would always be expected to flow from crime victims and the 'uneducated' public.

O'Malley (2016) observes that while the neoliberal penality thesis has been highly influential and arguably a fertile ground for criminological understandings of contemporary penality, a series of interrelated questions emerge that seem not to have been systematically examined or for which answers appear problematic.

Exactly what 'is' neoliberalism?

Most criminologists are happy to refer to neoliberalism as if it were a settled, consistent and rational formation of practical policy preferences. For Wacquant, it is a specific internationalizing political programme emanating from definable US agencies and institutions. David Harvey (2005: 71), on the other hand, concludes that neoliberalism has experienced a diverse, uneven and 'chaotic' evolution that has produced a 'welter of divergent and often wildly disparate state practices' and that as a result, 'any attempt to extract some composite picture of a typical neoliberal state from this unstable and volatile historical geography would seem to be a fool's errand'. Even summary analyses – such as that of Steger and Ray (2010) – conclude that the term *neoliberalism* should be used with extreme care given that it has been associated with political leaders as different as Reagan, Blair, Keating, Pinochet, Yeltsin and so on, none of whom self-identified as neoliberals, some of whom (Keating, Blair) declared themselves opponents of neoliberalism. Likewise, they suggest that because neoliberalism has been adapted to specific environments 'it makes sense to think of our subject in the plural – *neoliberalisms* – rather than a single monolithic manifestation' (Steger and Ray, 2010: xi). From this perspective, it is argued, analyses have misrepresented neoliberalism as a coherent rationality, as a set of abstract and incompletely integrated foundational principles.

O'Malley (2016) observes that the possible implications of such insights for the neoliberal thesis seem far-reaching. If historical neoliberalism is plural and mobile, then how adequate can any account be of a neoliberal penality unless it relates to a specific political formation, affecting penal policy at a specific time and place. It would require much more careful work to be done linking such specific formations of neoliberalism to specific formations of penality in detail. Indeed, empirical examination of variability within neoliberal penality make for problems exactly on these grounds.

The US as the heartland of increased penality

In the neoliberal penality literature, the US appears as the heartland of an increased punitivism associated with the shift away from social democracy. Garland (2011) nevertheless argues that such a proposal does not stand up to scrutiny and he shows in detail – with respect to such iconic sanctions as the death penalty – that there is no 'typical' American penality. Thus, while he accepts that the period since the 1960s 'has seen the political dominance of social conservatism and neoliberalism as well as a new form of racial segregation in the build-up of mass incarceration . . . and a revival of capital punishment', he continues that it is 'a . . . complex social field – state institutions, group relations, culture, and history, operating as a changing contradictory whole – rather than any single attitude or institution that has shaped the past and the present of US capital punishment' (Garland, 2011: 182). Lacey (2013: 273) moreover notes that imprisonment rates in the US vary so much between states that it is hard to credit any notion of an 'overarching neoliberal penal state'.

Wacquant (2009a, 2009b) argues – as we have seen – that not only is the US characterized by neoliberal penality, but it is the spread of neoliberalism from that country which has necessarily resulted in the expansion of its component neoliberal penality. The image of a 'global firestorm' of punitivism is one of his more striking turns of phrase. Yet, as all criminologists would know, a burgeoning literature has been growing up precisely around the fact that treating 'western European' or Anglophone penalities as a unity with respect to a wave of punitivism is highly problematic (O'Malley, 2002; Mayer and O'Malley, 2005; Pratt, 2008a, 2008b; Newburn, 2010). While not inconsistent with the 'globalization' thesis in neoliberal penality, studies such as those of Pratt on Scandinavia suggests that resistance has been long term and quite successful. It is difficult to discern a marked trend toward neoliberal penality in countries such as Sweden.

This geopolitical 'unevenness' has led to attempts – such as that of Cavadino and Dignan (2006) – to tenuously link penalities to differences between *more or less* social democratic versus *more or* less neoliberal formations. They suggest that neoliberal political economies have high prison rates because they foster 'exclusionary cultural attitudes toward deviant and marginal citizens' (2006: 23), while social-democratic political economies, on the other hand, promote more inclusionary approaches. Lacey (2008) argues that countries with a first-past-the-post electoral system are more likely to embrace extreme penal policies because the winners are less likely to have to negotiate with coalition partners. While such revisions are important it is difficult not to notice how far we have moved from the rich and complex issues surrounding the nature of specific neoliberalisms and their 'corresponding' penalities. That is the neoliberal penality thesis – which Lacey (2013) rejects – has, in effect, been watered down to an inclusionary/exclusionary binary that it can be correlated 'globally' with such a vague index of 'penality' as rates of imprisonment.

Jamie Peck (2010) puts considerable emphasis on the fact that when models of neoliberalism are transported between countries or states, they never remain untouched. The norm is that they 'arrive' in environments where there are different social and economic problems, intellectual and social histories, institutional arrangements, existing political rationalities and so on. Inevitably, *hybridity* is the norm.

O'Malley (2016) observes that hybridity is a key characteristic even of the supposedly foundational 'neoliberal' regimes of the 1970s in the US and the UK – the Thatcher–Reagan 'axis'. While time may have distanced us from the terminology of those times, neoliberalism was not that often mentioned. Rather, the catch-all terminology was that of the 'New Right', with these supposedly foundational neoliberal regimes much more accurately understood as amalgams of neoliberals and neoconservatives. These alliances were understood to give rise to a 'volatile and contradictory' penality (O'Malley, 1999) in which a wide variety of sanctions, seemingly at odds with each other in their foundational principles and assumptions, jostled together in a continually changing penal politics. The picture became even more convoluted when it was recognized that neoliberalism could be and often is intertwined with rationalities associated with social democracy. Once we move to this more historically specific form of analysis, the more it appears that 'neoliberal penality' appears akin to the 'welfare penality' that preceded it: a highly variable, often internally inconsistent and changing array of penalities that is no more than a vague umbrella term which perhaps conceals more than it reveals.

The neoliberal penality that never was

While it may well be that there is no single starting point for neoliberalism, accounts tend to go back to a key blueprint of historical neoliberal 'theory' – that of Hayek and his followers, in which 'the state' is something to be dismantled as far as possible. Thus, Harvey (2005: 80–88) argues that the emergence of the 'nemeses' of neoliberalism – populism, nationalism and authoritarianism – arise out of the need to deal with the 'social incoherence' that is itself the product of neoliberalism's 'drive toward market freedoms and the commodification of everything'.

O'Malley (2016) observes that if Harvey is correct in his suppositions, then much of what is seen to be the 'neoliberal' characteristic of neoliberalism's 'punitive turn' has to be rethought. For Harvey, at least, the punitive turn is far from an inherent component or corollary of neoliberal political economy: it is precisely a reaction to failures in neoliberalism. Put another way, the punitive turn may have been put in place by governments that embrace neoliberal ideas in other domains, but it is quite misleading to regard it as a neoliberal penality let alone an integral part of neoliberalism itself. Here, surely, we have something that begins to approach the kind of complexity that Garland addressed in his examination of the emergence of the welfare sanction: not a simple transmission belt from fixed and abstract governmental attributes to specific penal policy, but a messy and emergent politics capable of radically transforming the plans of 'original' political framework(s).

Harvey (2005: 77–78) observes that 'neoliberal' commentators have argued that such state institutions as criminal courts, prisons and the police would become largely irrelevant with the orderly working out of neoliberal theory. In this, among others, Harvey had in mind the interventions of those such as Milton Friedman, who had advocated abandoning the War on Drugs in favour of a drug policy based on legalization and reliance on market mechanisms to drive down demand and minimize harms. Now Friedman was not just any neoliberal. Clearly his position was at odds with other US neoliberals, such as George Bush, who were advocating a highly moralized warfare on illicit drug use. More precisely, he emerged from the Chicago School of Economics, and it is this highly specific form of (self-defined) neoliberalism that is most closely associated with an 'economizing' of criminal justice to which Harvey refers. This becomes clear when we turn to another Chicago school leader Gary Becker, who has made decisive statements on matters of crime and punishment.

Becker's (1974) criminology was based on the subjectivity of the rational actor, and his analysis had a heavy emphasis on punishment rather than reform. Likewise, as would be expected, an economic register was at the forefront of all aspects of his writing. But if this makes Becker an arch-candidate as a neoliberal penologist, there is one significant problem. He did not envisage an expansion of the penal sphere, certainly not an increase in imprisonment – quite the reverse. True, he did not propose its total withering away, but his distinctive position was that prison would/should become marginal, while money should be paid where a private individual was harmed, money fines paid where the state was harmed. The difference between the two sanctions (as Bentham had argued two centuries earlier) he regards as merely procedural. Prison should be reserved only for the relative handful too dangerous to be at large or who would not pay. Surprisingly, while Foucault (2004) devoted a lecture to Becker and his criminology/penology as epitomizing 'American' neoliberalism, he failed to pay attention to Becker's writings on the fine – and in this omission, he shares much with criminologists, especially, and significantly, those concerned with neoliberal penality.

Becker – as Foucault (2004) makes clear – defines crime as any action that puts the individual at risk of legal penalty. In Foucault's (2004: 251) words, 'the crime is that which is punished by the law and that's all there is to it' and points out that this definition of crime follows from the Chicago school's distinctive focus on human capital.

All actors are imagined as seeking an income that is productive of personal satisfaction. In this way, subjects become 'entrepreneurs of themselves' (rather, say, than as producers), managing their capital – skills, education, inventiveness – to maximize satisfactions. In this way, all manner of human desires can be subjected to an economic grid of intelligibility and thus rendered governable through economic means, agencies, apparatuses and so on. It is this attempt to universalize the economic framework of governance that Foucault saw as distinguishing these 'American' neoliberals from previous liberalisms.

With respect to crime, the problem confronting Chicagoans was the dominance of individual justice. The nineteenth-century liberal reformers – especially Bentham – had initially sought to impose an economic grid on crime. However, because these reformers understood crime not as an economic issue but as a *legal* problem with penalties applied according to the moral register of law, the criminal became the problem rather than the crime. As Foucault mapped out in *Discipline and Punish* (1977), this led to the unanticipated shift from *homo economicus* to an individualized *homo criminalis* about whom information would be gathered in the form of a criminal record. As a result, the criminal was understood within a moral register and subject to an 'anthropology' of crime: individualized justice emerged from this human science of crime.

O'Malley (2016) observes that by imposing a vision imported from human capital, the Chicagoans were able to escape *homo criminalis*, and instead, 'the criminal, any person, is treated only as everyone whomsoever who invests in an action, expects a profit from it, and who accepts the risk of loss' (Foucault, 2004: 253). Now the Chicagoans could reintroduce a fully economic register of crime, for it is no longer necessary to carry out an anthropology of the criminal. Once more, the offence becomes the focus rather than the offender. At the same time, as crime appears merely as a calculated risk involved in profit-seeking activity, and no different from any other profit-seeking action, it is no longer necessary to apply a moral register. The penalty then is now set by economic register: actions that attract penal sanctions are those profit-seeking actions that inflict non-market externalities on other entrepreneurs. The price of these externalities sets the level of the penalty. Hence, for Becker, crime may now be reduced to any action or set of actions that attract a legal penalty (or premium). In this way, crime appears as a matter of capital in a market. Not only is an economic register re-established, but the field of its governance also becomes intelligible in terms of governing markets: of pricing, supply and demand – rather than of eliminating crime.

O'Malley (2016) observes that it is unfortunate that Foucault did not follow up Becker's work on the fine, precisely because its depiction as a sanction is not just that it allows compensation for harms or just that it is cheap to administer. Perhaps its most significant characteristic is that it is literally a price: a technique for pricing crime and thus governing its supply and demand. Like a price, but unlike other legal penalties, the fine may be paid by anyone – not necessarily the offender but quite possibly the offender's spouse, employer, child and so on. The focus is thus not on the offender but on the offence. In this sense, fines do not seek to punish but to govern demand through pricing. Those sufficiently determined to offend may pay this price – a money premium – all that matters to the system of penality is that the price is paid by someone and that the distribution of crime is kept below a certain 'tolerable' level. (O'Malley, 2009, 2010). The fine appears as the sanction par excellence for a (neoliberal) economization of crime and criminal justice.

It is perhaps surprising that Becker is arguing a 'neoliberal' case for fines in a country where fines are a rarely used sanction – outside of traffic fines and regulatory offences – especially if we consider fines as a primary sanction rather than an add-on to imprisonment. This has not changed since 1974. Seemingly no one heeded this eminent Nobel Prize–winning neoliberal with his eminently 'neoliberal' penality. Instead – as O'Malley (2016) observes – neoliberal penality was locking people up *en mass*, in historically unprecedented numbers – a step that Becker regarded as economically irrational. Moreover, what actually happened to fines was something rather different to anything envisaged by Becker. His 'offender pays' penality was not followed up by the displacement of prison by fines, quite the reverse. Rather, what happened in the US was the invention of prison fees, fines and other monetary costs on top of prison sentences.

O'Malley (2016) observes that certainly *post facto* we can see a 'neoliberalism' in this, of an economic rationalist sort. But this is something very different to what the Chicagoan 'neoliberal' advocated or envisaged and appears to have owed nothing to his input. It is an unanticipated emergence which, no doubt, a determined neoliberal theoretician could attribute as an effect of neoliberalism.

O'Malley (2016) observes that the new discourse of neoliberal penality facilitates the growth of the penal sphere. It makes it easier to resist government intervention in the marketplace and to embrace criminalizing any and all deviations from the market. It facilitates passing new criminal statutes and wielding the penal sanction more liberally, because that is where administration is necessary, that is where the state can legitimately act, that is the proper sphere of policing. In other words, the neoliberal vision not only goes hand-in-hand with a certain way of perceiving markets and history but also facilitates the growth of the penal sphere. By marginalizing and pushing punishment to the outskirts of the market, the neoliberal discourse fertilizes the penal sphere.

Conclusion

Mariana Valverde (2010) suggests that we should place a moratorium on the use of 'neoliberalism' in penological and criminological analyses until we are clearer about what we are saying. Nicola Lacey (2013) suggests that the need is to build 'a systematic account of how political institutions shape penality' with an aim to generate an 'institutionally concrete view of the relation of punishment to politics'. In this, she argues, we need to move on to 'causal, genealogical or other more ambitious frameworks' (2013: 278).

O'Malley (2016) nevertheless cautions us against simply disposing of 'neoliberalism' altogether in the analysis of penality because it has played a key role in understanding the emergence and transformation of new discourses and forms of punishment. We may now be in a position where this usefulness is becoming compromised: through its supersession by other more contemporary 'isms' and penalities, through its misuse in some less-than-helpful criminological scholarship, and because of the increasing sophistication of our understandings of the diagrams and programs sheltering under the umbrella of 'neoliberalism'. But this should not blind us to its past value in highlighting in broad brush strokes major changes that were occurring in penality after the 1960s. Nor should it blind us to some of the difficulties that would confront a criminology that has of yet provided no alternative 'big picture' concept to reference some major shifts in the genealogy of liberalism and penality.

Summary of main points

1   In a risk society, there is a need to control a highly diffuse, mobile, actual and potentially problematic populations. Central to such strategies has been the increasing use of surveillance techniques which have become a pervasive part of our lives (Hopkins Burke, 2004).

2   Surveillance societies are those which function, in part, because of the extensive collection, recording, storage, analysis and application of information collated on individuals and groups. It enables corporations and governments to manage or govern resources, activities and populations.

3   The societal relevance of the universities demanded by critical students has been turned on its head in neoliberal society to become economically relevant to business and industry.

4   The development of NPM and the rise of entrepreneurial government have sought to reform the public sector by implementing serious cuts in public spending and by the introduction of private-sector management techniques and strategies.

5   The withdrawal of trust in universities via processes instigated by the government forced universities to create bureaucratic machinery and formulas to steer and manage the institutions from outside the system.

6   The introduction of NPM into universities has been revealed in the guise of permanent reductions in costs and spending cuts. It is a trend evident in a constant decrease in the level of service; a constant decrease in the level and quality of employment, realized through a steady de-professionalization and reduction in the number and quality of jobs; and constantly rising prices for the consumers such as student fees.

7   Lorenz (2012) observes that new public managerialism is remarkably reminiscent of state communism. Both are totalitarian because it leaves no institutionalized room for criticism, which is always seen as subversive. It is an organizational discourse which promotes and legitimizes the takeover of power by managers in public organizations that were previously run by professionals in accordance with their standards.

8   In the now-orthodox economic view, students do not pay to be taught a discipline by professionals who have proven expertise and subject knowledge but for the end product of education: a degree or other qualification, the investment of which will bring them profits in the labour market.

9   Neoliberalism is said to have generated a distinctive set of penal policies which have been characterized as 'neoliberal penality', appearing in its own right (Wacquant, 2009a, 2009b) or as a key element in more complex formations such as a 'culture of control' (Garland, 2001).

10   Gary Becker's (1974) criminology was based on the subjectivity of the rational actor and he did not envisage an expansion of the penal sphere, certainly not an increase in imprisonment – quite the reverse.

Discussion questions

1   Explain the need for increased surveillance in risk society.
2   What were the main consequences of the application of the NPM to universities?
3   Explain the de-professionalization of university faculty and its impact.

4   How does Wacquant explain his criminalization of poverty thesis?
5   Is the neoliberal penalty thesis valid? Explain why this is – or is not – the case.

Suggested further reading

The notion of risk society in general is discussed by Beck (1992) and the significance of this analysis for controlling crime and the notion of governance with the decline of the sovereign state by Garland (1996). For an excellent discussion of 'actuarial justice' and 'risk society' as applied to criminal justice, see O'Malley (1992), Feeley and Simon (1994) and Ericson and Haggerty (1997). David Harvey (2005) thus provides an essential introduction to neoliberalism, with surveillance as the handmaiden of neoliberalism discussed and theorized at the outset of the following chapter, with Hopkins Burke (2012) providing a more comprehensive discussion. Loïc Wacquant (2009a, 2009b, 2011) provides an introduction to both the penal society thesis and the work of a fine contemporary, thought-provoking sociologist. A critique of the neoliberal penality thesis can be found in the work of O'Malley (2014, 2016) and Lacey (2008, 2013).

Notes

1   The Bologna Declaration is a pledge by 29 countries to reform the structures of their higher education systems in a convergent way. The declaration is a key document which marks a turning point in the development of European higher education.
2   ECTS stands for European Credit Transfer System. The ECTS point system indicates the workload – measured in time – that it takes to complete a specific course. ECTS points do not measure the subject level or degree of difficulty, only the workload. The ECTS system equates 60 ECTS points for one year of full-time study.

References

Adams, R. (2020) 'Minister Lambasts English Universities for Letting Down Students', *The Guardian*, July 1.
Beck, U. (1992) *Risk Society*. London: Sage.
Becker, G.S. (1974) 'Crime and Punishment: An Economic Approach', in G.S. Becker and W. Landes (eds.) *Essays in the Economics of Crime and Punishment*. New York: Columbia University Press.
Cavadino, M. and Dignan, J. (2006) *Penal Systems: A Comparative Approach*. London: Sage.
Ericson, R.V. and Haggerty, D. (1997) *Policing the Risk Society*. Oxford: Clarendon Press.
Feeley, M. and Simon, J. (1994) 'Actuarial Justice: The Emerging New Criminal Law', in D. Nelken (ed.) *The Futures of Criminology*. London: Sage.
Foucault, M. (1977) *Discipline and Punish: The Birth of the Prison*. London: Allen Lane.
Foucault, M. (2004) *The Birth of Biopolitics*. London: Palgrave Macmillan.
Garland, D. (1985) *Punishment and Welfare: A History of Penal Strategies*. Aldershot: Gower.
Garland, D. (2001) *The Culture of Control*. Oxford: Oxford University Press.
Garland, D. (2011) *Peculiar Institution. America's Death Penalty in an Age of Abolition*. Oxford: Oxford University Press.
Harvey, D. (2005) *A Brief History of Neoliberalism*. New York: Oxford University Press.
Hopkins Burke, R.D. (ed.) (2004) *'Hard Cop/Soft Cop': Dilemmas and Debates in Contemporary Policing*. Cullompton: Willan Publishing.
Hopkins Burke, R.D. (2012) *Criminal Justice Theory: An Introduction*. Abingdon, Oxon: Routledge.
Lacey, N. (2008) *The Prisoner's Dilemma: Political Economy and Punishment in Contemporary Democracies*. Cambridge: Cambridge University Press.

Lacey, N. (2013) 'Punishment, (Neo)liberalism and Social Democracy', in J. Simon and R. Sparks (eds.) *The Sage Handbook on Punishment and Society*. New York: Sage.

Lorenz, C. (2012) 'If You're So Smart, Why Are You under Surveillance? Universities, Neoliberalism, and New Public Management', *Critical Enquiry*, 3(3): 599–629.

Mayer, J. and O'Malley (2005) 'Missing the Punitive Turn? Canadian Criminal Justice 1955–2003', in J. Pratt and D. Brown *et al.* (eds.) *The New Punitiveness*. London: Sage.

Newburn, T. (2010) 'Diffusion, Differentiation and Resistance in Comparative Penality', *Criminology and Criminal Justice*, 10: 314–52.

O'Malley, P. (1992) 'Risk, Power and Crime Prevention', *Economy and Society*, 21(3): 252–75.

O'Malley, P. (1999) 'Volatile and Contradictory Punishment', *Theoretical Criminology*, 3(2): 175–96.

O'Malley, P. (2002) 'The Globalisation of Risk? Distinguishing Styles of Neo-Liberal Criminal Justice in Australia and the USA', *Criminal Justice*, 2: 205–22.

O'Malley, P. (2009) *The Currency of Justice: Fines and Damages in Consumer Societies*. London: Routledge.

O'Malley, P. (2010) 'Simulated Justice: Risk, Money and Telemetric Policing', *British Journal of Criminology*, 50: 795–7.

O'Malley, P. (2014) 'Prisons, Neoliberalism and Neo-Liberal States: Reading Loïc Wacquant and Prisons of Poverty', *Thesis Eleven*, 3: 9–96.

O'Malley, P. (2016) 'Neoliberalism, Crime and Criminal Justiuce', in *Legal Studies Research Paper 16/10*. Sydney: Sydney Law Scool, The University of Sydney.

Peck, J. (2010) *Constructions of Neoliberal Reasoning*. Oxford: Oxford University Press.

Pratt, J. (2008a) 'Scandinavian Exceptionalism in An Era of Penal Excess: Part 1', *British Journal of Criminology*, 47: 119–37.

Pratt, J. (2008b) 'Scandinavian Exceptionalism in an Era of Penal Excess: Part 2', *British Journal of Criminology*, 4: 275–92.

Reiner, R. (2006) 'Beyond Risk: A Lament for Social Democratic Criminology', in T. Newburn and P. Rock (eds.) *The Politics of Crime Control*. Oxford: Clarendon Press.

Steger, M. and Ray, J. (2010) *Neoliberalism: A Very Short Introduction*. Oxford: Oxford University Press.

Talint International (2020) *Only 52% of Graduates Get Graduate-level Jobs, CIPD Reveals*. London: Talint International.

Valverde, M. (2010) 'Comment on Loic Wacquant's "Theoretical Coda" to *Punishing the Poor*', *Theoretical Criminology*, 14: 117–120.

Wacquant, L. (2009a) *Prisons of Poverty*. Minneapolis: University of Minnesota Press.

Wacquant, L. (2009b) *Urban Outcasts: A Comparative Sociology of Advanced Marginality*. Cabridge: Polity Press.

Wacquant, L. (2011) *Deadly Symbiosis: Race and the Rise of the Penal State*. Cambridge: Polity Press.

Young, J. (1999) *The Exclusive Society: Social Exclusion, Crime and Difference in Late Modernity*. London: Sage.

Chapter 19

Ultra-realist criminology

Key issues

1   Criminological closure
2   The Influence of zemiology
3   The influence of critical realism
4   Transcendental materialism
5   Eight critiques of ultra-realist crime causation theory

Introduction

Ultra-realism is one of the first new Western criminological paradigms to emerge in the twenty-first century, and it offers a distinctive perspective on contemporary subjectivity in its socio-economic context (see Hall and Winlow, 2015; Ellis, 2015; Raymen, 2015; Smith and Raymen, 2016a, 2016b). Ultra-realists argue that criminology must return to its fundamental question and ask why it is that some individuals and groups risk harm to others as they pursue their instrumental and expressive interests rather than seek solidarity with each other. To answer this question, ultra-realism seeks to conceptualize subjectivity in ways that move beyond existing assumptions of innate selfishness, repressed goodness, social learning, flexible socio-linguistic construction or ideology as positive hegemony.

Hall and Winlow (2018) propose that if criminology wishes to retain its status as a respected social scientific discipline it must renew its efforts to dig below empirical description, normative discussions of rules and 'criminalization' and crude social-structural comparisons of relative harms to construct convincing explanations of mutating forms of crime and harm in contemporary society. To do this, it is argued that the discipline requires a new philosophical basis, theoretical framework and research programme. For, the observed twentieth-century intellectual tug of war between left-liberalism (progressivism) and right-liberalism (neoliberalism) – both in their own way hostile to traditional conservative and socialist discourses and successful in rendering them both redundant – is seen to have produced few results. The political, cultural and socio-economic body of liberalism is seen to be dying. The broad liberal project has clearly been unable to control rampant global financial capitalism or organize equitable social relations. The divisive identity politics which now dominates intellectual and political liberal worlds is seen to have failed the men and women of the multi-ethnic working class. Ultra-realists thus claim that it is the failure of the liberal left rather than the success of neoliberalism which has precipitated a dangerous drift to the right and far right across Europe and the US (Winlow *et al.*, 2017).

Leaving the well-documented intellectual failures of conservative and neoclassical criminology aside, the theoretical concepts and frameworks used by leftist criminology to explain phenomena – those which have been produced by seminal nineteenth- and twentieth-century thinkers – are seen to be founded upon the intellectual paradigms which underpin this failed 'progressive' political project. Thus, any social scientific discipline which restricts itself to this orthodox thinking is seen to risk political irrelevance in what appears to be a very difficult future (Streeck, 2016). Criminology must heed this warning – it is proposed – and begin to reconstruct its mode of explanation by rethinking the hitherto crudely polarized ontological and ethical assumptions, which underly mainstream ways of thinking about essential issues, such as authority, freedom, subjectivity, the role of collective politics and the nature and causes of harm. It must also once again open its mind to the possibility that general and wide-ranging theories of crime can be constructed, not as closed explanatory systems but as the suppliers of new concepts and hypotheses for new research programmes. Many traditional thinkers believed that these grand theories are indeed possible, whereas today liberal pluralists and postmodernists tend to assume that they are forever inadequate and blind to what they imagine to be the boundless pluralism of Western societies. Ultra-realists are happy to admit that we cannot be sure until we try harder and improve our ability to engage with and represent the real world. Even if the postmodernists are right to assume that grand theories fail to capture the inherent diversity and uncertainty of the social world, the exploratory impetus generated by the attempt to develop such theories will certainly reveal hidden experiences and knowledge and open up a space in which new perspectives, concepts and understandings can be constructed.

Criminological closure

Hall and Winlow (2018) argue that ultra-realism remains on the critical side of the fence but responds to the inadequacy of social constructionism, post-structuralism and intersectionality, which, over the past 50 years, is seen to have fragmented criminology into a matrix of closed positions – now commonly derided in broad intellectual life as 'echo chambers' – that are all resistant to criticisms of their fundamental domain assumptions. Such closure and standstill, they argue, do not require a descent into the strong idealist form of relativism but simply a separatist and defensive form of perspectivism. This does not deny the objective world or our ability to have some knowledge of it but simply resists the possibility that new or even substantially modified perspectives might have something significantly more useful to offer. Ultra-realists thus argue that criminology must summon up the courage to construct and eventually synthesize new perspectives, but this is not the standard move to replace 'privileged' perspectives with 'suppressed knowledges'. What were once 'suppressed knowledges' have already been brought to light to occupy newly 'privileged' positions in the sub-dominant liberal-progressive paradigm, which have subsequently become closed and protected from critique (see Hall and Winlow, 2015).

The current discipline is seen to be a moribund hierarchy in which 'seminal' thinkers from the past have been consecrated despite their intellectual failings and time-limited views. In the past, alternative thinkers who were an uncomfortable fit in dominant neoliberal or sub-dominant liberal-progressive perspectives were often rejected for rather nebulous and mysterious reasons, a practice which is seen to be continuing today (Hall, 2012a). In this climate, too much new theory and research, much of it put forward by younger academics to challenge existing perspectives, is either ignored, misinterpreted or distorted and reclaimed. New thinking which directly threatens underlying core assumptions and is potentially fit for purpose in the twenty-first century is constantly ignored.

Hall and Winlow (2018) argue that to move forward, criminology must escape the truncated parameters imposed on the intellectual world by dominant right-wing liberalism and sub-dominant left-wing liberalism. Both political groups are seen to limit criminological thought to their own agendas and degenerative research programmes. Post-war paradigms constructed within these parameters – such as strain theory, labelling theory, sub-cultural theory, radical feminism, risk theory and so on – are seen to be of little use to us as we try to explain the phenomena and underlying dynamic processes which constitute the advanced capitalist world. Criminologists today are observed to produce excellent and very revealing research, but the theoretical dimension of the discipline is seen to be failing to keep up with it and perform its two major functions: (1) to supply researchers with advanced concepts that can inspire new research projects and (2) provide researchers with satisfactory theoretical frameworks for their findings. This failure leaves research marooned in the superficial empirical dimension and hostage to positivism and its dominant method of mathematical testing.

The current theoretical frameworks of criminology are seen to be both separatist and stagnant because they are anchored in various traditional Western political philosophies. Each is founded on ontological and ethical assumptions about the dynamics of history, the nature of human subjectivity, the role of the state and politics in human life and the nature of harm. The assumptions taken by criminological theories from these philosophical positions are complex and varied (Hall and Winlow, 2015), but it is a complexity underpinned by a basic tripartite division in the ontology of the subject. First, there is the potentially dangerous 'beast within' which requires constant repression, guidance and discipline to function as a civilized, sociable and cooperative being. Second, there is the creative, autonomous and moral agent despoiled by repressive forms of institutionalized collective politics and moral authority. Third, there is a dialectical subject that both responds to and reproduces, either consciously or unconsciously, its material and ideological circumstances and has the potential to overturn them by means of collective politics.

Dominant conservative and neoclassical liberal frameworks accept the first ontological model of the subject, sub-dominant left-liberal frameworks rely on the second model and the third model was used by the traditional Marxist and Marxist-Freudian models, whereas traditional Freudian models were more closely related to the conservative position. These three basic ontological positions are informed at an even deeper level by their preferred models of political and social organization – traditional conservative, liberal-democratic reformist and revolutionary-transformative – which would suggest that they are little more than convenient models of subjectivity constructed to justify preferred political and socio-economic arrangements. Thus, each position automatically rejects models that contradict its basic assumptions and for ultra-realists, these convenient off-the-peg ontologies of the subject are simply inadequate. Social science in general – and criminology in particular – need to key into and contribute to the development of reflexive models of subjectivity, a task that demands the rejection of traditional models of convenience and a move to contemporary explorations of advanced thinking in cognate fields ranging from neuroscience to philosophy.

It is observed that, in the post-war period, when politics took flight from failed Leninist revolutions and repressive forms of conservative moral authority, fundamental aspects of the third position were incorporated and neutralized by the first and second positions. In this climate of political *catastrophism* (Hall, 2012a), which gave rise to *capitalist realism* (Fisher, 2009) – the ideological first principle being that no alternative to liberal-capitalism will ever be possible – the original conservative/socialist dichotomy was now curtailed in intellectual and political life.

Hall and Winlow (2018) observe that the new restricted parameters were represented by the Liberal Progressive Social Administration (LPSA) on the centre-left and the Conservative Classical Liberal Alliance (CCLA) on the centre-right. Neither position is political in any traditional sense of the word but merely a biopolitical mode of managing neoliberal capitalism and its socio-cultural consequences.

Both positions are seen to come to dominate the social sciences, commissioning empirical studies designed to maintain political parameters and discourage depth thinking (see Hall and Winlow, 2015). Because crime is an important political football – perhaps slightly less so now that the enthusiastic broadcasting of the statistical 'crime decline' has maintained a temporary calming effect – criminological research was placed under strict control. Critical thought did occasionally extend beyond these parameters, but it was never allowed to establish credibility in the mainstream discipline. However, the current drift to a right-wing politics that seems to be reaching beyond these safe parameters indicates that many people who occupy a precarious socio-economic position in the US and Europe have had enough of the ignorance and contempt the CCLA and LPSA seem to have for their real everyday experiences. They also suspect that these two political groups are concealing truths that exist outside their parameters of approved knowledge. Patience is being worn down by the chronic inability of political institutions to regulate the destructive processual and structural pressures that neoliberalism has brought to bear down on them (Winlow *et al.*, 2017). It is argued that the voluminous conceptual work of thinkers ignored or marginalized for decades by social science is now revealing itself to be far more prescient than the work of 'approved' liberal thinkers (see Winlow and Hall, 2013).

The ultra-realist project is thus based on a rejection of these narrow political and intellectual parameters. Criminologists, it is argued, must revisit the experiential realities of everyday life with a revisionist enthusiasm which rejects the confirmation bias that sustains current political orthodoxies and their associated theoretical frameworks. Researchers can therefore reject the intermediary filtering of obsolete theoretical frameworks – with their prepackaged assumptions of crime as resistance, harmless, masculine, evil or whatever – to begin the process of relocating their 'data' in the broad structures and processes of neoliberal capitalism and its attendant culture of consumerism and hyper-individualism. Moreover, in a climate of free and open enquiry, researchers will also be able to reconsider some concepts and frameworks previously rejected by the dominant conservative and sub-dominant left-liberal positions. Nevertheless, to prevent too many babies being thrown out with the bathwater, revived and reformulated extant concepts can be synthesized with new concepts in a thorough revisionist process that will allow criminological theory to renew itself and literally begin from the beginning as it revisits fundamental epistemological, ontological and ethical questions essential to theory construction.

Hall and Winlow (2018) advise us that ultra-realism does not claim to be the theory that fell to earth. It is thus partially influenced by some previous criminological schools of thought, such as victimology, feminism and left realism, all of which are seen to have attempted to make significant breaks from existing frameworks and have advocated the return to reality. But, whilst ultra-realism retains the spirit of the former, it also seeks to break away from their theoretical frameworks, which are seen to be largely restricted to intersectional power relations. Moreover, we cannot simply theorize perpetrators exclusively through the eyes of victims because the latter – even if they are intimate partners – do not necessarily have a full understanding of the contexts in which the lives of the perpetrators are located. Thus, we must look at third parties, biographies, cultures, histories and socio-economic contexts, which echoes the suggestion from the 'new criminologists' (Taylor *et al.*, 1973) to explore 'structure, culture and biography'. But, if we are to make the necessary connections, it is argued, we need to look beyond approved thinkers and frameworks to locate and apply more refined concepts.

For instance, it is observed that the more traditional radical feminist analyses are too restricted to female victimhood in domestic circumstances and, by their own admission, are theoretically unsophisticated (Heidensohn, 2012), constantly falling back on the approved explanation of violent actions as expressions of the patriarchal form of social power. The domestic violence issue is far more complex (Dutton and Nichols, 2005), and other forms of street violence even more complex (Ellis, 2015). Hall and Winlow (2018) pertinently observe that the same critique can be levelled at all standpoint positions on the criminological spectrum. Criminology, they argue, cannot simply sit back and watch approvingly as various standpoint positions choose concrete universals in their own inimitably biased and one-dimensional ways to support their own identity politics. Nor should the discipline demand that these positions immediately dissolve themselves. The way forward is seen to be free and open debate as a principle that must be established throughout the whole process of funding, research, publication and education.

Ultra-realists are also keen to apply left realism's principle of digging underneath discourse and language in the process of theory construction. Crime is not simply a social construct used by right-wing politicians to justify an authoritarian state. It is defined as an act that breaks rules, but no matter how criminal acts are defined or redefined, they often inflict harm on individuals, their environments and their fragile social systems (Reiner, 2016). There is thus a pressing need to establish an ongoing zemiological discussion at the core of the discipline, which extends beyond premature typologies and 'harm indexes' to revisit the aetiological, ontological and ethical roots of the concept (Yar, 2012). Left realism simply failed to engage with the concept of harm, relied on legal definitions of crime, produced little qualitative research, ignored subjectivity, aetiology and the concrete universal, and neglected consumer culture as a criminogenic environment. It thus left too many stones unturned at the fundamental philosophical and theoretical levels for ultra-realists to regard themselves as heirs to its legacy. But it does seek to revisit these fundamentals.

In its early stages, some ultra-realists are exploring the possibilities offered by current forms of Lacanian psychoanalysis updated by the latest neuroscientific research (Hall, 2012a; Winlow, 2014), but ultra-realism is a reflexive project and has no intention of designating this as a protected species. It does nevertheless demand that any conceptual framework that is adopted and developed must undercut failed idealist/constructivist/linguistic frameworks to deal with dynamics external to the individual and the internal and contextual materiality of subjectivity which underpins its socio-symbolic dimension.

Hall and Winlow (2018) propose that criminology must break free from the restrictive parameters imposed on its theoretical project by the cynical pragmatism of the CCLA, which dominates the governmental policy field, and the LPSA, which dominates in academia. The former, driven by a deep fear of the *barbarism of disorder*, has rejected its

traditional conservative social integration programme to pursue deterrence and incapacitation policies that have been temporarily effective but ultimately harmful. The latter,
driven by an equally deep fear of the *barbarism of order*, restricts itself to the 'avoidance of
mistreatment' (Badiou, 2001), or the maintenance of the negative liberty of the individual.
The LPSA, despite its pious proclamation of 'equality', is seen to have been extremely
circumspect about the realization of positive liberty or the politically organized conditions in which vital social, psychological and material needs can be met (Winlow *et al.*,
2015). It is seen that such narrow parameters have contributed to political failure, the
alienation of populations across Europe and the US, and the recent drift to the far right
(Winlow *et al.*, 2017). It is argued that a criminological project restricted by the systematic exclusion of what these curtailed political groups do not like – extreme phenomena,
unconscious desires, drives, pessimism, structural analyses, deep political intervention and
so on (see Hall and Winlow, 2015) – cannot remain relevant as a genuine producer and
disseminator of knowledge in our increasingly unstable future.

The influence of zemiology

Hall and Winlow (2018) observe that the term *crime* is a socio-legal construct, which has
no ontological basis and that some criminologists are now realizing that we cannot restrict
our study to acts defined as criminal. Postmodernism is seen as the last in a procession of
post-war schools of thought to lead us to an imaginary place as far from reality as possible by insisting that we focus on 'crime' as a pure linguistic-idealist act driven by the
authoritarian desire to criminalize 'otherness'. It is seen to be part of a general intellectual
flight from both reality and the practice of substantive political transformation in the wake
of the horrors Stalin and Mao inflicted on their own people (Heath and Potter, 2006;
Jacoby, 2007). A powerful wave of liberal intellectuals thus expanded and associated this
empirical fear to a general abstract fear of modernity itself, which led some influential
figures to reject truth, objectivity and universalism. The outcome was the normalization
of the principles of extreme relativism and pluralism and the celebration of the supposedly
unique norms and values of each 'subcultural' group. It is not difficult to see how this led
to the intellectual neglect of objective harm, a concept that was virtually criticized out of
existence across the social sciences from relativist and autonomist viewpoints.

   Critical criminology, arguing from a more structural viewpoint, offered a utilitarian
calculation and comparative assessment of harms, which produced the cliché that the
crimes of the powerful cause more harm than the crimes of the powerless. The pluralistic relativism of liberal-postmodern criminology and the structural relativism of critical
criminology thus diminished the impact of myriad harms experienced by a variety of
victims, and this eroded the credibility of the discipline amongst all social groups apart
from liberals educated to think in this way. This neglect, disseminated by liberal politics
and media, was particularly galling to the working classes across the US and Europe, who
thought that nobody on the left-liberal side of the fence believed them or cared about
their everyday experiences. This relativist disregard of everyday experiential harms and
their contexts of insecurity, burgeoning criminal markets and communal decline caused
by deindustrialization is seen as a catastrophic error that backfired and contributed to
what every liberal wanted to avoid – the recent drift to the far right (Winlow *et al.*, 2017).

   Hall and Winlow (2018) note that harm is usually defined as an action which leaves
whatever it impacts in a worse condition. How well legally defined 'crime' represents

real harm varies and depends on how well specific rules and laws have been constructed in relation to the incidents they attempt to represent. By developing a core–periphery model of harm (Hall, 2012a), ultra-realism has set out to establish some theoretical principles about the study of the relationships between empirical harm and definitions of crime. By developing an advanced conception of trauma (Winlow, 2014; Ellis, 2015), it also sets out to understand the genesis and reproduction of harmful 'hardened subjectivities' (Crank and Jacoby, 2015). In a defensive manoeuvre over the past few years when its credibility was waning, postmodernism, in its 'affirmative' variant, acknowledged a thin core of universally harmful crime, but more recent research into contemporary criminality reveals that this allegedly thin core is actually quite thick – at least as thick as the periphery of less harmful crimes (Hall, 2012a).

Hall and Winlow (2018) argue that typologies of harm are of limited use and the pressing need is for criminology to dig underneath orthodox interpretive theories to understand the external contexts, motivations, causes and consequences of harm and integrate our findings and understandings in a new theoretical framework. Excellent research on the various contexts of harm – personal, social, environmental and so on – is seen to be constantly forthcoming in criminology, but the establishment of such a framework is yet to happen. It is the concept of 'lack of social recognition' (Honneth, 1996), which accords with the claim of Roy Bhaskar that absence is causative, that presents us with a useful starting point. This hypothetical absence would, of course, create an ethically deregulated social context in which abuse, neglect and harm – on a variety of scales – could be practised and justified by dominant actors without guilt. Honneth (1996) claims that in the traditional Hegelian master–slave relation of imbalanced mutual interdependency such an extreme hypothetical situation was prevented because the master was compelled to grant the slave a minimal degree of recognition and rights, which, hypothetically, can be fully established only in an equal democratic society.

Ultra-realists observe that neoliberal capitalism has not progressed towards democracy and equality but towards a historically unique situation in which the master–slave relation has been virtually severed. Throughout history, the need of the master for the labour of the slave and acquiescence forced the former to at least recognize the existence, functions, opinions and partial rights of the slave. But, in advanced capitalism, where automation and outsourcing in a competitive global market are rendering so many types of labour functionally redundant, we are witnessing the end of such traditional socio–economic obligations (Winlow and Hall, 2013). This provides dominant actors in any position in the social structure with opportunities to exercise 'special liberty' (Hall, 2012a), which involves a sense of entitlement felt by individuals as they pursue business, wealth and enjoyment.

Thus, as capitalist history has unfolded, the obscene license of *special liberty* is seen to have percolated down from aristocratic and bourgeois culture to popular culture, diffusing and normalizing the sense of entitlement of the subject to risk harm to others in its attempts to gratify expressive or instrumental desires (Hall, 2012a; Horsley, 2014). It is too easy for ambitious individuals to justify doing what they think is necessary, on or beyond the boundaries of ethics and law to secure their own acquisitive or expressive interests regardless of the welfare of others. The victims and potential victims of myriad harmful practices neglected or inadequately covered by the existing legal system now have very little bargaining power in relation to their exploiters. In such a rapidly transforming socio-economic and cultural milieu, it is argued that a criminological discipline restricted to legally defined 'crime' as the object of its research and theorization simply cannot do its job.

Ultra-realists use the concept of *special liberty* in the context of the severed master–slave relation and in doing so invert Axel Honneth's (1996) direction of causality where harm is seen to be a product of social inequality. Rather, social inequality is seen to be a consequence of the willingness of ruthless individuals and groups to perpetrate multiple harms as they outcompete, dispossess and politically disempower others to the extent that the latter can be coerced into a position of permanent insecurity and exploitation. Political and economic inequality is sustained and reproduced not simply by 'mediated hegemonic naturalization', but by a culture of hardened, domineering and ruthless pseudo-pacified subjectivity which has become normalized and successful throughout the history of the capitalist project. This competitive subjectivity, driven by the libidinal energy of obscene enjoyment into the competitive spaces opened up by the historical proliferation of competitive markets, is, moreover, not unique to white upper-class males. Their wealth and power are the products of centuries of ruthless and successful accumulation, but competitive subjectivity is active throughout the social structure in a variety of pseudo-pacified micro-relations. Its ubiquitous presence and enthusiastic adoption by so many opportunistic individuals are seen to permanently postpone the establishment of the long-term human solidarity which could restart genuine cultural and political opposition. At this time, we remain confined in the advanced capitalist culture where the competitive individual measures their success relative to the downfall and subjugation of others. In this culture too many amongst the subjugated – as John Steinbeck once remarked – do not see themselves as an exploited proletariat but 'temporarily embarrassed millionaires' (Hall and Winlow, 2018).

Hall and Winlow (2018) observe that such competitive individuals dominate in all aspects of culture and politics. They do not seek solidarity or social transformation but increased security, lest some undeserving soul should steal their enjoyment of the permanent dissatisfaction which they have won to keep their desires and energetic striving alive (see McGowan, 2016). But the harms of securitization[1] equal or perhaps even outweigh the harms of street crime and white-collar crime. Such a proliferation and broad diffusion of harms and hardened yet insecure subjectivities, some of whom now look to a revived far right to solve their problems, demand that criminology revisit its fundamental assumptions with a view to placing itself on a firmer ontological platform. Simply locating domineering parties on the social axes supplied by intersectional identity politics has nevertheless proved to be inadequate, even an obstacle to the production of knowledge. In such a competitive and insecure milieu, the motivation and the ability to risk harm to others, in acts that further interests of the self, are seen not to be exclusive to any specific social group, even those who have historically achieved more success in their endeavours.

Advocates of ultra-realism argue that twenty-first-century criminology should frame its analyses of harm in a coherent critique of the whole advanced capitalist way of life – its economic logic, its competitive-individualistic culture, its hardened subjectivity and its multiple harms. Re-arranging the intersectional deckchairs – we are advised – will make little overall difference to the eventual fate of the ship. As a first step towards theoretical reconstruction, criminology must therefore look beyond the slippery socio-legal concept of crime towards the more ontologically grounded concept of harm.

The influence of critical realism

Left-realist criminology – first developed in the UK and later in the US in the 1980s – was a response to the intellectual and political failings of left idealism and the success of right realism in influencing government policy. Whereas right realism ignored the crimes of the powerful and overstated and de-contextualized the harm caused by street crime, left idealism virtually ignored the latter and passed it off as an ideological construct. Against the backdrop of the 'crime explosion' in the UK and the US in the 1980s (see Reiner, 2007) the dogmatic left–idealist stance had alienated leftist criminology from governments and the public alike. The principal message of left realism was to take the more harmful crimes seriously but to reject the assumption of the eternal propensity of the individual for 'evil' promoted by right realists and which has justified policies of repressive securitization. Left realism was heavily influenced by the successful attempt of feminism to put the individual's experiential reality of harm back on the political and intellectual agendas. Feminism nevertheless pursued a very specific agenda focused on violence against women. Left realism, despite the efforts of some – such as Currie (1985) – became bogged down in administrative pragmatism and ended up as an adjunct to ineffective 'Third-Way' politics. Despite these failings, feminism and left realism helped to stir criminology out of the social constructionist inertia of left idealism, which reduced ontology and politics to a language game and reduced sociology and criminology to a branch of media studies. Ensuring progressive momentum was reduced to changing subjectivity through language. Current political events tell us quite clearly that this has failed.

Hall and Winlow (2018) observe that a simple return to empiricism is not enough to reset the programme. If messing around with structures of language has had little effect, revealing truth – if indeed empiricism can be said to perform this function – and speaking it to power has also fallen flat. Power already knows the truth; it just does not care. The political agenda of ultra-realism is driven by the need to connect the popular will to substantive political and cultural interventions in the deep recesses of the capitalist system. Criminology is seen to have become an apologist for *capitalist realism* (Fisher, 2009), the negative ideological first principle being that there is no possible alternative. The cultural normalization of capitalist realism has not simply established the idea of 'revolution' as an impossibility in the popular imagination but even what were once regarded as standard social-democratic structural reforms (Hall and Winlow, 2013b). Of all the social scientific disciplines, criminology is now seen to be the least likely to have an input into the debate on alternative futures, even though the reduction of social hostility and multiple harms sits alongside the fight against poverty, exploitation, insecurity and oligarchic state repression as one of the more powerful motives for genuine transformation. Behind the ultra-realist wish to establish a new paradigm is the principle that the pragmatic investigation of what *can* be done must be replaced by the realistic investigation of what *must* be done to effect long-term transformation of the system in such a way as to reduce its propensity for multiple harms. Ultra-realism also seeks to avoid right–wing realism, which is seen not to be realism at all but merely the cynical pragmatism of a generalized *realpolitik*.

Ultra-realism is partially influenced by the ontological and epistemological model of critical realism. Critical realists thus locate an ontological realism below interpretation, moral agency and language in the intransitive dimension of society, what are called the 'deep system' of structures and dynamic processes, which produce very real consequences, all of which can be detected and understood as plausible tendencies and patterns, not iron laws. For instance, the crime explosion in the UK and the US during the 1980s correlated very strongly with deindustrialization, depoliticization and the diffusion of consumer culture. Critical realists argue that it is inadequate to understand meaning and action as autonomous because meaning is influenced and action is controlled and enforced in a gridlocked system of imperatives and interdependencies, a totality of system dynamics, social relations, tendencies, events and experiences. We are free to talk and act, but only in a very limited sphere, not at the deepest level where the power of politics, militarism and investment operate within the confines of the abstract logic of an accountant to decide whether whole communities – and, in some cases, whole regions or nations – are built or destroyed. It is here that we find the decisions which affect the life chances of millions.

Alongside this ontological model, critical realism also offers criminology a complex epistemological schema. There are three layers of reality and variations of our ability to know about it: (1) *empirical* – representative knowledge of events and their patterns, (2) *actual* – events and subjective experiences and (3) *real* – underlying generative mechanisms that with all likelihood cause events.

For critical realists, positivism is descriptive and correlational: it simply cannot reveal enough about the world. Interpretivism is interminably wrapped up in the subjective and cultural construction of meanings that can never be firmly established or regarded as consistently representative of the actual and the real. Thus, if we conceptualize crimes as events and their harms as subjective experiences, the first task of ultra-realist criminology is to forge feasible connections between the empirical and actual levels. Of course, because crime carries penalties, most events are concealed, which is why criminologists cannot rely on quantitative methods and need the penetrative ethnographic method practised by researchers who are capable of penetrating and revealing selected parts of the 'hidden figure' of crime. Statistics and surveys are seen to be of very limited use and too susceptible to political manipulation by governments, interest groups and both mainstream and new synoptic media.

Hall and Winlow (2018) argue that socio-economic structures and processes are not simply theoretical concepts but systems of real possibilities and constraints, which are experienced by us in our everyday lives as 'natural necessities' that allow or deny thought and action. Structures and processes are generative and degenerative mechanisms, creating and destroying our fundamental conditions of existence and causing sequences of events whose influence is so strong it can be granted a place in the causal chain. This chain links the real with the actual and the way people tend to act – in a way that often bypasses interpretive thought and stretches the boundaries of morality when alternative actions appear impossible or harmful to the self – as they experience these events. Ultra-realist criminology can thus produce knowledge of observed events and human responses, which can be linked with real systems of possibilities and constraints, and from this begin to construct a theoretical framework for future research (Hall and Winlow, 2015).

For instance, at the broadest and deepest level, the structures and dynamic processes of neoliberalism, for which market logic is the dominant organizing principle, have since the 1980s been hollowing out the vital socio-economic conditions of existence in specific locales and regions. It is a process which has impacted heavily on rates of crime, forms of crime and the growth of criminal markets. For critical realists, absence is also causative, and the specific absences found in these places – of politics, solidarity, investment, employment, hope and so on – are determined by market logic as it controls systems of real restraints and possibilities. It has simply created spaces of desperation and nihilism in which the criminogenic mentality of *special liberty* – the individual freed from social obligations and self-permitted to do what is contextually necessary to further personal interests – and its attendant harms can flourish (Hall, 2012a). Thus, the experiences of individuals as they have seen industry disappear and criminal markets proliferate in their locales are the historical concrete universals ultra-realists seek to investigate (see Winlow, 2001), and events such as the English riots of 2011 represent the recent concrete universals which connect subjectivity with the unstable service industries and post-political consumer culture of today (Treadwell *et al.*, 2013).

Transcendental materialism

Hall and Winlow (2018) argue that critical realism offers a useful framework that encourages social scientists to once again dig beneath the empirical and abstract. But its conceptualization of the relationship between nature, the individual and the social is problematic. The core concept of 'analytic dualism' separates the individual moral agent from the structures, dynamic processes, events and dominant ways of thinking and believing, which constitute the system. This fallacy of the existence of the eternal moral agent, set in opposition to the unfair socio-economic systems of history, is observed to have has hampered our thinking for decades (see Winlow *et al.*, 2015).

Transcendental materialism is seen to get down to the task of theorizing the emergence and constitution of subjectivity, rather than simply assuming it to be an eternal presence, separated from the world, to inhabit some sort of unadulterated spiritual and ethical dimension. This new philosophical realism is seen to move far beyond the crude ontology and aetiology of genetic traits offered by biological positivism and the notion of ultimate flexibility in the metaphysical realm of ideas and language proposed by transcendental idealism. The theory of the formation of the self, offered by G.H. Mead, is considered obsolete because it theorizes only the conscious self-image of the subject seen through external others, not the formative emergence of the subject through its own unconscious drives, desires, experiences and hunger for coherent symbolism. Post-structuralists, on the other hand, are seen to have taken this metaphor given by Lacan literally as an ontological reality and overestimated the flexibility of unconscious desire in relation to symbolism. Thus, he had said that the unconscious was *structured like* a language, not that it *is* a language (see Hall *et al.*, 2008).

Lacan, moreover, reminded us that absence – in this case a symbolic void, which drives the subject outwards to find the coherent symbolic order it desperately needs to appease the terror of the unknown external and internal stimuli of the Real, and move beyond the juvenile misidentifications of the Imaginary (see Johnston, 2008; Hall, 2012b) – exists as a fundamental force at the centre of the emerging subject. For Johnston (2008), humans are hard-wired for plasticity at the material level of drives and desires. Material being is naturally and automatically transcendental. Emerging subjects are thrown outwards into rigid ideological systems that pre-exist before them and have become *deaptative* in the sense that they no longer function to inform subjects and aid survival in the current environment. But whereas past ideological systems were based on *positive beliefs*, when the liberal-postmodern subject of today emerges to seek a coherent symbolic order, it encounters a system founded on the fundamental *negative belief* that nothing beyond the current system is possible. This negative belief is not reproduced solely by the dominant elite either, but also by the sub-dominant elite who have neutralized any genuine political opposition.

Hall and Winlow (2018) thus propose that the current de-aptative ideological order of symbols is based on *capitalist realism* (Fisher, 2009), the negative principle being, that we have reached the end point of economic history and that no alternative to liberal capitalism will ever be possible. Despite the descent of the neoliberal economy into localized social and environmental catastrophes observed in this book, capitalist realism decrees that any attempt to establish a new socio-economic order will inevitably and immediately degenerate into brutal totalitarianism (Žižek, 2001). The dominant ideology of the West which is shared by the liberal right and liberal left instructs us that choice and moral agency must be prohibited at the deepest level of socio-economic system dynamics. As liberal social scientists have argued for decades, Western individuals have all sorts of diverse opinions about positive phenomena in the world (Abercrombie *et al.*, 1980). Yet the vast majority now share the politically decisive negative belief that most choices are possible, except the collective choice to change the fundamental coordinates of our socio-economic mode of existence.

The accompanying consumer culture of neoliberal capitalism is seen to intensify the sense of imminent social insignificance possessed by the subject and a return to the terror of the Real (Hall *et al.*, 2008). It thus does not appease but over-stimulates the secondary form of *objectless anxiety* in the subject (Hall, 2012a), which means that the overdriven will of the subject to compete against others and incorporate itself in the social order is resolute. The capitalist imaginary functions as a powerful ideological context, shaping the desires and dreams, which energize consumer culture and accelerate the circulation of commodities, but it systematically disrupts and prevents symbolic connections with social, economic and environmental realities. Thus, the dominant negative ideology of *capitalist realism* has now reached a stage where it is the most potent causative and reproductive cultural force in all dimensions of life. It locks the individual into an active but fixated disowned engagement with the logical imperatives of the current neoliberal system.

Hall and Winlow (2018) argue that the individual still has some choice over the specific mode of engagement, but the fatalism and cynicism, which they had found in their years of research with active criminals involved in volume crime and some forms of expressive violent crime, seem to them to be rooted in extreme variants of *capitalist realism*. If capitalism is the only game in town, and not even the faintest possibility of a realistic alternative can be seen on the horizon, many individuals choose to play the game in whatever way they can. Under the conditions that exist in economically abandoned, impoverished and hopeless locales – or indeed in the top strata where regulations are lax, tempting opportunities abound and the culture of *special liberty* (see Hall, 2012a)) is normalized – the tendency towards involvement in various forms of crime and violence is ratcheted up.

Ultra-realism revisited

Hall and Winlow (2018) argue that the complacent, gentrified world of middle-class liberal media and academia could neither predict nor explain the recent seismic political events across Europe and the US, some of which are redolent of the political trajectory in 1930s Europe. Huge socio-economic problems in former manufacturing areas, and working-class subjective responses to them, had been systematically ignored or misunderstood, not only by the dominant neoliberals but also by the sub-dominant liberal left who purport to represent the interests of the disadvantaged. New research by ultra-realist criminologists (see Hall and Antonopoulos, 2016; Kotze and Temple, 2014) is exposing potentially fatal epistemological problems in the 'international crime-decline' narrative (see Hall and Winlow, 2015; Hopkins Burke, 2018, for details). The focus of the statistical industry on traditional legally defined crime and its victims has meant that this narrative is the product of ignoring harms and measuring obsolescence rather than researching the current events and subjective experiences that constitute the realm of the 'actual'. The complacency and misunderstandings that have colonized and weakened the political wing of liberalism are seen to be duplicated in its intellectual wing, with criminology being no exception. Ultra-realism instructs us to struggle free from paralysing twentieth-century paradigms and return to reality and free intellectual enquiry as a matter of political urgency.

Ultra-realism is firm in its intent to confront the worldwide zemiological environment of neoliberal capitalism full on. Parenti (2011) thus exposes the criminogenic effects of global warming, drought, flash-flooding, neoliberal economic restructuring and cheap arms dumping on the escalation of ethnic tensions, crime, corruption and violence in the tropical convergence zone (see also Wiegratz, 2016). Crank and Jacoby (2015) reveal the process of *dual exploitation* as being global warming, the mechanization of agriculture and disinvestment in the real sustainable economy, which has created huge consumer markets of desperate people on all continents needing transport, food, clothes, shelter, medical supplies and other basic goods. In various chaotic regions, proliferating criminal networks organize the supply of illicit goods and develop markets in sexual exploitation, slavery and various forms of trafficking.

If some sectors of the populations in former manufacturing regions of the old industrial world are becoming increasingly desperate, it is that much worse in the megacities of the developing world. In the 1950s there were only two cities, New York and Tokyo, with more than 10 million inhabitants. Today there are 22, and by 2025 there will probably be 30 (Crank and Jacoby, 2015). These sprawling urban areas are statistical black holes for criminologists. They are rapidly altering the fabric of human life, replacing traditional intimate, grounded human communities with vast, impersonal, fluid urban networks, socially structured by huge and increasing divisions in wealth and power. In the context of a culture of competitive individualism and *special liberty* – but in the absence of stable economies and nurturing states and social systems – these deep processes and structures at the level of the real, promote criminality and violence rather than the politics of solidarity.

Hall and Winlow (2018) observe that at the actual and empirical levels, we are witnessing the consequences of these processes right now. Anxious populations are supporting governments that promise state hardening, privatism, securitization, militarization and strict border controls. Such shifting electoral support is seen to be the product of *cultural hardening*, constituted and reproduced by intensified exclusionary sentiments, and *subjective hardening* as individuals become increasingly competitive and self-interested (Crank and Jacoby, 2015). It is observed that these cultural currents are beginning to break down the pseudo-pacification process, which means that more individuals are likely to express anger and hostile competitive urges in physical rather than sublimated symbolic forms (Hall, 2012a).

Hall and Winlow (2018) observe that these are just a few very examples of the criminogenic processes and unfolding events that ultra-realism seeks to investigate and bring to the foreground in criminology. Ultra-realists argue that criminology should encourage theory and research that can open up new or previously proscribed and obscured *parallax views* (see Žižek, 2006). By organizing ethnographic networks and encouraging researchers to generate rich and conceptually advanced qualitative data that represent different subjective experiences of individuals and localized populations, views of harmful events from multiple observational positions can be used to displace standard views. These multiple views can then be placed in broader structural and processual contexts, not to confirm existing theoretical frameworks but to overcome their inadequate ontological domain assumptions, interest-group biases and restrictive political parameters in order that we can construct replacements. A multidimensional research, theory and educational milieu is proposed, which must be built with the intention of conducting research with no intellectual restrictions, no censorship at the point of publication and none of the demarcations currently maintained by 'stand-point' interest-groups. Until we begin to do this, it is argued, we are not educating young people in the realities of today but simply affirming the soothing fantasies that reproduce the complacent, truncated politics which have quite recently been exposed as ineffective and obsolete in the troubled world of advanced capitalism.

Ultra-realism clearly provides an attractive, comprehensive and detailed account of the causal links between advanced capitalism – or neoliberalism – and contemporary criminality and wider social problems. It is highly critical of both conservative and left-liberal approaches in what ultimately is an updated economic determinist research strategy highly critical of the identity politics – identified and discussed in this book and a significant product of fragmented modernity or the postmodern condition – that are seen to be irrelevant diversions in the pursuit the real causes of the pressing woes of our society. Here lies the basis of a significant critique of ultra-realist criminology.

Eight critiques of ultra-realist crime causation theory

Wood *et al.* (2020) pertinently note that the role of political economy in shaping crime rates is nothing new, with numerous empirical studies pointing to a relationship between the two (Box, 1987; Currie, 1997, 2009). Yet, despite this robust empirical research, theoretical accounts of the relationship between political economy and crime remain underdeveloped.

Seeking to rectify this issue, ultra-realist criminology – developed by Steve Hall and Simon Winlow (2015) – has emerged as an influential critical approach, offering an abundance of concepts for examining the various relationships between political economy and crime. Key among these concepts are the intertwined theories of *the breakdown of the pseudo-pacification process* and *special liberty* (Hall, 2012a). Understood as mutually constituting processes (Hall and Wilson, 2014), these theories offer an account of 'contemporary subjectivity in its socio-economic context' (Hall and Winlow, 2018). Quite simply, each theory, in its own way, explains crime as a *direct* expression of capitalism. Thus, in the breakdown of the *pseudo-pacification process*, physical violence is understood to be a de-sublimated expression of the functional socio-symbolic competition fostered by capitalism. In the case of *special liberty*, crimes and other forms of 'positive harm' are understood to arise out of the creation of a competitive, ruthless and entitled form of subjectivity in capitalist societies (Hall, 2012a). These interlinked theories have been applied to explain a wide range of criminological and social phenomena, including that of serial murder (Hall and Wilson, 2014), workplace bullying (Lloyd, 2018), fraud (Tudor, 2019), the appeal of post-apocalyptic popular culture (Raymen, 2018) and the rise of lethal violence in the post-recession UK (Ellis, 2019).

Wood *et al.* (2020) nevertheless give voice to a series of reservations about ultra-realist crime causation theory. First, they question the ability of the breakdown of the pseudo-pacification process to account for gender-related disparities in criminal behaviour. Second, they critically consider the explanation of violence offered by ultra-realism through reference to drives, libidinal energy and sublimation, via its theory of the (breakdown of the) pseudo-pacification process. Third, they outline several reservations about special liberty, in particular, with regard to its explanation of crime as an expression of capitalist values, and its (in)compatibility with the breakdown of the pseudo-pacification process. We consider next the eight critiques offered by Wood *et al.* (2020) which can be conceptualized in the context of those three broad issues.

Issue 1: the ultra-realist explanation of the gender gap in crime

The 'gender gap', in criminal offending is one of the few indisputable 'facts' about crime (Braithwaite, 1989; Steffensmeier *et al.*, 2005). Persuasive general crime causation theories thus require a convincing explanation of why crime – and violent crime in particular – is committed overwhelmingly by men. One of the key characteristics of the ultra-realist perspective in addressing this issue has been its resistance to – as Hall and Winlow (2003a) put it – 'culturalist' crime causation theories that explain the gender gap in crime with reference to normative cultural expectations of gendered behaviour (see also Hall and Winlow, 2015). Thus, ultra-realists argue that it is fluctuations in local labour markets that are the prime explanation in gendered criminal offending.

Wood *et al.* (2020) acknowledge the importance of examining the impact of local labour markets on crime rates but observe that in ignoring the role of gender norms, the breakdown of the pseudo-pacification process theory remains unable to effectively explain why it is that women from low socio-economic status backgrounds do not commit crimes at a similar rate to men from the same background.

Ultra-realism unequivocally explains the gender gap in offending among 'working-class' individuals to be a result of the gender division of labour (Hall, 1997; Hall and Winlow, 2003a). Thus, while administrative, intellectual and related emotional forms of labour associated with women have remained relatively stable in recent years, the off-shoring and erosion of industrial manufacturing and processing jobs traditionally held by 'working-class' men explain a contemporary increase in the prevalence of crime perpetrated by men from this background (Hall and Winlow, 2004).

Critique 1: The pseudo-pacification process treats gender norms as epiphenomenal to capitalism.

Wood *et al.* (2020) observe that ultra-realism all but disregards the question of why it is that labour is gendered, regarding such arrangements as an epiphenomenon of political economy (Connell, 2002). Thus, why it is that men find service work customarily undertaken by women to be unattractive is essential to the ultra-realist pseudo-pacification process, but the issue remains unaddressed by ultra-realism. On the other hand, reasons have been unpacked in considerable detail within social reproduction feminism (Bakker, 2007), and dual-systems theory feminism (Weeks, 1998; Fraser, 2013), with one key contention being that normative expectations and patterns of gendered behaviour cannot be explained through economic 'single system' Marxian theories or 'totalizing discourses' which propose that all gender inequality is driven purely by the functional needs of the economic system (see Weeks, 1998; Fraser, 2013). This single-system gender epiphe-nomenalism is challenged by a considerable body of empirical evidence which indicates that cultural gender norms are of significant importance to understanding national varia-tions in gender divisions of labour (Pfau-Effinger, 1998).

Hall (1997: 459) nevertheless argues that 'it is much more likely that the primary force that motivates and reproduces most forms of life constituted in capital's productivist era is neither structural nor ideology, but *visceral*' (his emphasis). For Hall, the production of vis-ceral cultures was functionally central to the formation of industrial capitalism because it not only provided capitalists with a workforce able to endure the physically demanding work but also workers with the egocentrism necessary to negotiate the intense competition of the casual labour market. Thus, the fact that such visceral cultures construct physical labour as 'men's work' can be understood as a *functional* product of the specific needs of capitalism.

A further debateable association is made between physical 'hardness' and interpersonal violence. An essentialist and potentially spurious link is thus proposed between endurance, persistence, physical rigour and egocentrism, on one hand, and 'undirected aggressivity', intimidation and violence, on the other. Wood *et al.* (2020) observe that just as egocen-trism is not, arguably, a necessary condition of negotiating the casual labour market, so, too, are egocentrism and 'hardness' necessary or sufficient preconditions for aggressivity, intimidation, or violence. Hall (1997: 468–469) nevertheless sees this differently:

> 'Hard lads' are in the process of being left behind by history . . . in times of recession, [such men] are the perfect 'oily rags' for criminal (or anti-criminal) organizations; the 'psychos' and 'nutters' who will do just about anything, glorifying in their abilities to withstand physical pain and ignore danger.

Thus, according to Hall (1997) such 'visceral cultures' are becoming increasingly redun-dant as the productivist era of capitalism recedes. As a result of deindustrialization and the emergence of technologies that have reduced the need for physical 'hardness' in the industrial sector, the visceral cultures generated in industrial capitalism have been dis-carded in favour of new dispositions. But this is a contention which leaves one crucial question unanswered: Why is it that only some members of 'visceral cultures' become 'hard lads' who commit physical violence? Moreover, in bracketing the cultural norms underpinning working-class occupational identity, yet constructing a theory of pseudo-pacification that presupposes such norms, ultra-realism is arguably parasitic on the very 'culturalist' frameworks that it critiques. Thus, to explain why it is that men pursue cer-tain forms of employment and not others and, in turn, why men commit more crime than women, one must arguably turn to 'culturalist' theories capable of explaining pat-terns in social behaviour related to gender labour norms (Pfau-Effinger, 1998). How-ever, to admit to gender norms and cultural attitudes driving the gendering of different occupations, ultra-realism would have to concede that there is a coexistent cultural sphere which is partly autonomous to an economic centre. But doing so would call into ques-tion a central premise of pseudo-pacification – that labour markets are the central driving force of crime, hence the gender gap in offending can be explained with exclusive refer-ence to different labour markets.

Critique 2: The pseudo-pacification process ignores social reproduction, offering a framework that only examines crime through the lens of capitalist production and consumption.

Wood *et al.* (2020) observe that in the ultra-realist account of the pseudo-pacification process, the functional role of masculinity is explained as entirely related to production, as opposed to social reproduction. This conceptualization of the role of gender in criminal offending simply overlooks the potential for crime to emerge as a response to not only consumption and production processes but also to *breakdowns in social reproduction processes* brought about by specific political-economic arrangements. Such breakdowns include, notably, the inability of parents to engage in positive child-rearing practices as a result of the stresses of economic marginalization, marginal work, social exclusion, poverty, and a lack of adequate social support (Currie, 2009). Ultra-realism, in other words, focuses on the productive dimension of capitalism – namely, labour and consumption – to the neglect of social reproduction: 'the activities and attitudes, behaviours and emotions, and responsibilities and relationships directly involved in maintaining life, on a daily basis and intergenerationally' (Brenner and Laslett, 1991: 314). Wood *et al.* (2020) thus maintain that theories on the relationships between political economy and crime must account not only for production and consumption but also for social reproduction. They simply must move beyond 'single system' theories that explain gender relations as a product of late capitalist economic conditions to acknowledge the broader fact that gender – and other social forms of – oppression predate capitalism (Bhattacharya, 2017).

Critique 3: Ultra-realism's reason for dismissing gender norms as a factor in offending is founded on a denial of the antecedent fallacy

The ultra-realist perspective on the role gender plays in patterns of offending is neatly summarized in the following statement by Hall and Winlow (2015: 58):

> The feminist and pro-feminist assumption that violence and harm are typical products of masculine culture or 'masculinity' is based on the sort of statistical illusion that empiricists are very good at presenting to their peers and the public. Only a relatively small percentage of the male population commits serious crime or inflicts non-criminalized harms on others. Therefore, despite the inherent unreliability of statistics, although it looks likely that 80 per cent of crime/harm is committed by men, it is 80 per cent of this small percentage, not 80 per cent of the whole male population. It follows that because the majority of men do not commit crime, crime cannot be an expression of 'traditional' masculinity.

Wood *et al.* (2020) see this line of reasoning to be simply invalid. First, ultra-realists are seen to engage in the inverse error of 'denying the antecedent'. An argument that 'If A then B, Not A, therefore, not B'. Their argument thus has the following logically invalid form: If A (most men commit crime) is true, then B (crime is an expression of 'traditional' masculinity) is true. A (most men commit crime) is not true; therefore, B (crime is an expression of 'traditional' masculinity) is not true. This is nevertheless logically invalid because (a) the premise of the argument does not guarantee the truth of the conclusion and (b) we can never validly deny an antecedent to reject its consequent. In other words, it does *not* logically follow that because most men do not commit acts of interpersonal violence, particular codes of 'traditional' masculinity play no role in acts of violence committed by men. Thus, the claim that crime cannot be an expression of 'traditional' – or dominant and significantly socially reproduced forms of masculinity – cannot be valid. Second, if only a small percentage of the population socialized into special liberty commit crime, it follows that because the majority of neoliberal subjects do not commit crime, crime cannot be an expression of the neoliberal cultural current of special liberty.

Issue 2: ultra-realism's explanation of violence reduction through drives, libidinal energy and sublimation

A second set of issues relate to the Freudian-esque hydraulic model of the mind presupposed by the pseudo-pacification model. Thus, the sublimation of libidinal energy away from interpersonal aggression and into 'socio-symbolic competition' is central to the ultra-realist account of the pseudo-pacification process (Hall, 2012a, 2014a). Wood *et al.* (2020) first observe that such hydraulic conceptions of libidinal energy channelled within a 'dynamic unconscious' are repudiated by many contemporary traditions within social and cognitive psychology (O'Brien and Jureidini, 2002). Second, even if we accept the hydraulic model of the mind, the pseudo-pacification model rests upon key inconsistencies within the model itself. Thus, the pseudo-pacification process model proposes that physical, interpersonal violence and aggression are underpinned by the same 'drives' as 'socio-symbolic competition'. This is a key claim that might be problematized with scrutiny.

> Critique 4: *The pseudo-pacification process naturalizes violent drives, contradicting ultra-realism's claim that we are hardwired for plasticity.*

The first problem with the hydraulic model of drives and psychic energy described by the ultra-realist pseudo-pacification model is that it proposes that a set amount of 'libidinal' energy can be moved around, channelled or blocked but not diminished or fundamentally transformed. Hence, rather than diminishing the 'libidinal energy' that also drives interpersonal violence, capitalism instead channels the energy underpinning such drives into a different form of violence: socio-symbolic competition. This model thus presents a number of claims, each inviting contradictions into the ultra-realist account of crime.

First, the pseudo-pacification model has the unfortunate effect of naturalizing and universalizing violent 'instinctual drives' (Hall, 2012b: 367), which simply shift in their mode of expression depending on the milieu. It is a point which might appear to be an erroneous reading of the transcendental materialist focus on the plasticity of the human neurological system which is a central part of the ultra-realist theory:

> The core of the human neurological system is shot through with conflicting drives; therefore, the human being has weak 'instincts'. This means that the human being is malleable at the material level, hard-wired but only, paradoxically, for plasticity, which has been necessary for survival in multiple and changing environments.
>
> (Hall, 2014b: 154)

Wood *et al.* (2020) nevertheless observe that such assertions are fundamentally incompatible with the 'strong' instincts presupposed by the pseudo-pacification process. Thus, in explaining the pseudo-pacification process, Hall (2014b: 155) states:

> The pseudo-pacification process fundamental psychosocial drive is provided by the sublimation of the once ubiquitous physical aggression that ordered Feudal societies, and its subsequent conversion into socio-symbolic competition ordered by the signifiers of consumer culture.

Now, if this is the case, it introduces a temporal problem. For without naturalizing aggressive drives, the theory *can* explain the sublimation of interpersonal violence into socio-symbolic aggression among those living at the dawn of (neoliberal) capitalism. But it *cannot* explain the sublimation of interpersonal violence into socio-symbolic aggression among those born *into* capitalism without naturalizing aggressive drives to interpersonal violence. For if aggression channelled into socio-symbolic competition is central to the *ongoing* momentum of capitalism, and not just its *establishment* as a new socio-economic system, then this aggression cannot be attributed to the preceding feudal order, but to the constitution of humanity. And if it is the case that aggression is simply a 'weak instinct', then pseudo-pacification is the best we can hope for.

Critique 5: In presupposing a hydraulic model of the psyche, the pseudo-pacification process sets up a zero-sum game between socio-symbolic competition and physical aggression.

Wood *et al.* (2020) observe that the theory of pseudo-pacification sets up an opposition between socio-symbolic competition and physical aggression as two *distinct* and *separate* expressions such drives may take. This posits something of a zero-sum game between socio-symbolic competition and physical aggression: thus, all the psychic energy that is channelled into socio-symbolic aggression is taken away from physical aggression. The problem with this hydraulic conception of the mind becomes particularly clear when we address instances when individuals engage in interpersonal violence but remain committed to socio-symbolic competition through consumption and other capitalistic practices. Yet if we are to follow the processes proposed by ultra-realist theorists to explain the role of sublimation in the pseudo-pacification process – violent drives are channelled into socio-symbolic competition – then it should follow that the breakdown of the pseudo-pacification process should entail the de-channelling or de-sublimation of energy away from socio-symbolic competition *back* to acts of physical aggression. If not, then proponents of the perspective might admit that there are different, and at least partly autonomous mechanisms underpinning the formation of socio-symbolically competitive subjectivities and the formation of 'violent subjectivities'.

In practice, it is the theoretical premise of ultra-realism that with the breakdown of the pseudo-pacification process, individuals engage in acts of physical violence *because* of their commitment to socio-symbolic competition vis-à-vis consumerism and 'anything to get ahead' capital accumulation (Raymen, 2016). But this fundamentally contradicts the hydraulic model of the psyche used to explain the fall in violent crime as a product of the pseudo-pacification process.

Issue 3: ultra-realism's explanation of crime as an expression of capitalist values and special liberty

> *Critique 6: It is incoherent to understand special liberty and the pseudo-pacification process as mutually reinforcing processes.*

Ultra-realists have variously argued that special liberty and the pseudo-pacification process 'represent what look like mutually reinforcing processes' (Hall and Wilson, 2014: 651). Wood *et al.* (2020) disagree and argue that the theories actually work at cross-purposes, with the claims of special liberty theory contradicting the underlying presuppositions of the breakdown of the pseudo-pacification process. There is, in other words, a central contradiction at the heart of ultra-realist crime causation theory. It is thus incoherent to simultaneously argue that (a) the increasing prevalence of violence can be explained by rises in special liberty (Hall and Winlow, 2015), (b) the reduction in rates of violence can be explained by the pseudo-pacification process (Hall, 2007, 2012a) and (c) special liberty and the pseudo-pacification are mutually reinforcing processes (Hall and Wilson, 2014). If, for example, the pseudo-pacification process generates a general cultural current of special liberty, which encourages individuals to 'transcend the normative restrictions' set by this process (Hall and Wilson, 2014: 650), then it cannot alone lay claim to decreases in the incidence of violence in capitalist societies since the beginning of the twentieth century.

> *Critique 7: Ultra-realism's crime causation theory ignores the array of values, beliefs and vocabularies of motive for crime that are not an expression of capitalism.*

Wood *et al.* (2020) also query the assertion of ultra-realism that the constellation of values that together characterize special liberty, such as competitive individualism, ostentatious displays of cultural capital, hedonistic consumption, and ruthless capital accumulation are a 'general cultural current' in neoliberal societies (see Hall, 2012a; Hall and Winlow, 2015; Raymen, 2016). Certainly, this constellation of values may have driven the offending of individuals interviewed by ultra-realist criminologists (see Tudor, 2019). But it cannot be inferred from their data that such a particular constellation of values is 'general' in neoliberal societies (Hall and Winlow, 2015). Even if we were to accept that a consensus exists around the aforementioned norms and values, an additional problem remains – thus, these norms and values are far from the *only* systems of belief that might contribute to crime. Put simply, contemporary expressions of subjectivity in neoliberal societies are more varied and complex than described by the ultra-realist account. Personal and social identities pertain not only to attitudes towards consumerism – themselves varied in contemporary capitalist societies – but to a variety of personal commitments we invest in (Archer, 2000). Furthermore, there exists a variety of values, beliefs, and 'vocabularies of motive' driving crimes which are not an expression of capitalism. Compelling evidence indicates, for example, that rape myth acceptance is a strong predictor of sexual violence perpetration (Bohner *et al.*, 1998; Johnson and Beech, 2017). Similarly, convincing evidence points to the impact of 'honour cultures' in sanctioning violence by men against women (Vandello and Cohen, 2003). Now, while such social standards often intersect with economically driven factors in generating crime, they are not reducible to them, nor are the strictly economic aspects of political economy always a primary factor driving criminalized acts.

Issue 4: ultra-realism's direct expression theory of the crime–political economy nexus

Wood *et al.* (2020) make a distinction between two approaches to understanding the role of political economy in crime, which are termed 'direct expression theories' and 'indirect expression theories'. With direct expression theories, crimes are a product of (a) individuals mirroring the values of a political economy and/or (b) responding directly to the conditions of their political-economic environment. The ultra-realist theories of special liberty and the breakdown of the pseudo-pacification process are seen to correspond to these two interpretations of the role of political economy in crime causation. Thus, with the theory of special liberty (Hall, 2012a), crime is driven by a sense of entitlement to harm others fostered by neoliberalism, while in the breakdown of the pseudo-pacification process, crime is the result of individuals responding to being 'left behind' by neoliberal capitalism. The direct influence of capitalism on crime within ultra-realism theory is further signposted when Hall and Winlow (2004: 290, emphasis in the original) lament that

> [t]he pervasive acceptance that the capitalist system might not be superseded or even brought under democratic political control in the foreseeable future has, with a few notable exceptions . . . created something of a hiatus in which thought has been largely distracted from critical investigations into ways in which human beings are interfacing in more *direct* ways with the demands of consumerism and global market capitalism.

Direct expression theories propose that the impact of political economy on crime is not mediated by other structural and cultural factors. Thus, in setting out the core principles of the ultra-realist perspective, Hall (2012a: 150) bemoans that in 'liberal' criminological theory, 'everything is mediated by cultural systems and susceptible to the choices made by the autonomous sovereign ego, therefore even complex concatenations of causes and probabilistic conditions are out of bounds'. This reasoning leads to the following significant issue with ultra-realist crime causation theory.

> Critique 8: *In setting up a dichotomy between 'causative' political-economic factors and merely 'symptomological' factors, ultra-realism engages in downwards conflation, leaving it unable to explain the formation of the structures it discusses*

As we have seen, ultra-realist crime causation theories treat a variety of phenomena – including gendered power relations – as epiphenomenal to political economy; that is they are a secondary by-product which possesses no causative power. Wood *et al.* (2020) observe that this ultra-realist account of social order is characterized by what Margaret Archer (1995) has termed 'downwards conflation': understanding social activity as determined by social structures, with agency merely a product of these structures. In such theories, 'actors may be indispensable for energizing the social system . . . but it is not they whose actions give it direction by shaping structural properties' (Archer, 1995: 81).

Agency is thus explained in terms of structure, leaving perspectives that engage in this form of conflation no latitude to explain how it is that actors shape these social structures.

Archer (1995) observes numerous examples of downwards conflation within social theory, including varieties of functionalism, structuralism, economism and technological determinism. In the case of ultra-realism, downwards conflation is chiefly illustrated in the economism of the pseudo-pacification process, which understands the sublimation and stimulation of libidinal drives in terms of their *functions* for capital. Horsley (2014) therefore propose that 'pacification was – before individuals became accustomed to its codes and internalized its sensibilities – initially a functional by-product of political-economic change'. Hall (2014a: 28) similarly asserts that the pseudo-pacification process represents the 'functional stimulation and control of libidinal drives' and that 'mainstream culture and its institutions work on behalf of the pseudo-pacification process to socialise tough individual competitors willing to play by the rules' (Hall, 2015: 19).

Wood *et al.* (2020) observe that this unacknowledged economism points to a broader issue with the pseudo-pacification model, namely that it offers a rather conspiratorial interpretation of the birth of capitalism. Thus, capitalism, and the kinds of social relationships which have led to its expansion in different forms, were fully programmed at its outset by shadowy forces, rather than reproduced through the functions of industry and the widespread societal adoption of contemporary capitalist values. Ultra-realism thus understands crime to be a combination of both neoliberal values (special liberty) and the functional drives cultivated by capitalism to ensure production and consumption – the breakdown of the pseudo-pacification process. But, problematically and perhaps crucially, such theories are unable to explain why it is that certain individuals respond to political-economic conditions by offending while others do not.

Ultra-realist direct expression theories consequently offer a 'totalizing discourse' on crime that conceptualizes the economy and labour markets as the driving force behind all spheres of society (Wood, 2019). Proponents of ultra-realism might object that their position on causation has been misrepresented because they do, in fact, admit a range of causal mechanisms beyond the political economy. But Wood *et al.* (2020) argue that they have on numerous occasions, made statements which indicate the opposite: that the only structure or factor which has any causative status in understanding crime is the global political economy, specifically its economic, market-oriented aspects (Hall, 2012a; Hall and Winlow, 2015, 2016). Indeed, ultra-realism often contrasts such 'causative' political-economic factors with merely 'symptomological' factors (Hall, 2012a; Hall and Winlow, 2015, 2018). Raymen (2019) accordingly observes the always symptomological status of technology in a favourable review of Hall and Antonopoulos's (2016) book, *Fake Meds Online*:

> To focus too much upon the issue of technology and the internet would be to fall prey to much of contemporary criminology's tendency towards a spurious *symptomology* (Hall, 2012b), in which empirically observable trends such as the technologically-facilitated mutation of criminal markets are wrongly elevated to carrying a *causative* status. *Fake Meds Online* avoids this trap, skilfully situating the issue of technology and the internet in its proper sub-dominant analytical place, and instead keeps its focus fixed firmly upon the concrete causative processes of global political economy and its impact upon contemporary subjectivities.

Raymen (2019) thus makes the questionable assumption that the largest system – the dominant capitalist political–economic model – is always the most analytically important and causal mechanisms only pertain to the structures of capitalism. The assumed symptomological nature of all that is not political–economic means that ultra-realism does not inject gender, racialization, culture, technology and sexuality, with any causative power: all are mere epiphenomena animated by the contemporary political–economic order. In short, the ultra-realist counter-position of 'causative' political–economic factors against 'symptomological' factors is seen to (a) wrongly universalize what constitutes a causative and symptomological factor, (b) present a false dichotomy that omits the importance of *mediating* factors and (c) ignores the often-polygenetic nature of social phenomena (Wood *et al.*, 2020).

Sayer (1999) – a critical realist – nevertheless emphasizes that what constitutes a causative and a symptomological factor *depends on the phenomenon we are examining*. If, for example, we are examining whether predictive policing technologies perpetuate racial profiling, it makes perfect sense to focus our investigation on the issue of technology and, in particular, the production and effects of technology combined with entrenched practices of racialized policing. In investigating such a phenomenon, it would, in fact, be spurious to focus our analysis exclusively on political economy, as opposed to technology, for we cannot reduce such a technology to the political–economic values and economic motivations of its creators.

Wood *et al.* (2020) thus observe that for all the importance of examining the values inscribed into technologies by their creators, we cannot ignore the intended and unintended broader effects of technologies. The authors observe that the inability of ultra-realism to adequately address these unintended *emergent* effects calls into question whether political economy is, as its proponents argue, *invariably* the necessary 'level of abstraction' (Floridi, 2013) for examining crime and criminal justice–related generative mechanisms.

Conclusion

Wood *et al.* (2020) argue that it is essential that any theory of the relationships between political economy and crime avoids epiphenomenalism: wrongly withholding causative power from all but certain facets of the world. In the case of theories that engage in downwards conflation – such as ultra-realism – this epiphenomenalism results in sociological accounts which disregard the power of individual agency. Individual actors play no role in shaping the structural and cultural environments in which they live – they are instead mere conduits for the special liberty and socio-symbolic competition wrought through pseudo-pacification.

Moreover, such epiphenomenalism results in theories that are unable to explain the very formation and change of the structures to which they grant sole custody of causation. This issue is readily apparent when we interrogate the ultra-realist theory of the pseudo-pacification process, which is unable to identify 'what hidden hand ensures the functionality of ideological . . . state apparatuses in providing the non-material preconditions of production' (Archer, 2000: 29). Far from representing a free-floating structural and cultural edifice that determines all structures and subjectivities, capitalism is actually shaped by, and, in turn, shapes, the individuals, material structures and cultural systems it emerges from (Ferrell, 2007).

Wood *et al.* (2020) argue that to overcome the issues associated with ultra-realist direct expression theory, an indirect expression theory of crime and political economy would need to account for a diverse range of personal, cultural *and* structural emergent properties and that means evading treating key social factors, such as gender, as epiphenomenal to capitalism. They argue that the approach of Margaret Archer (1995) provides a framework for resolving not only the structure/agency conflation of ultra-realist crime causation theory but also for moving past the unhelpful 'materialist' and 'culturalist' dichotomies that characterize the perspective. Thus, as Archer (1996) emphasizes, we can treat neither structure nor culture as epiphenomena of the other. Material structures and propositional culture hold autonomous causative powers which shape one another in turn. In the final analysis, we might observe that the ultra-realist account reads like a latter-day restatement of traditional Marxist economic determinism.

Summary of main points

1   Ultra-realism offers a perspective on contemporary subjectivity in its socio-economic context which moves beyond existing assumptions of innate selfishness, repressed goodness, social learning, flexible socio-linguistic construction or ideology as positive hegemony.

2   Crime is defined by ultra-realism as an act which inflicts harm on individuals, their environments and their fragile social systems.

3   Typologies of harm are seen to be of limited use and there is a pressing need for criminology to dig underneath orthodox interpretive theories to understand the external contexts, motivations, causes and consequences of harm and integrate this into a new theoretical framework.

4   Ultra-realists use the concept of *special liberty* which is a consequence of the willingness of ruthless individuals and groups to perpetrate multiple harms as they outcompete, dispossess and politically disempower others.

5   With the *breakdown of the pseudo-pacification process*, individuals engage in acts of physical violence because of their commitment to socio-symbolic competition vis-à-vis consumerism and 'anything to get ahead' capital accumulation (Raymen, 2016).

6   Political and economic inequality is sustained and reproduced by a culture of hardened, domineering and ruthless pseudo-pacified subjectivity that has become normalized and successful throughout the history of the capitalist project.

7   Ultra-realism is partially influenced by critical realism which locates an ontological realism below interpretation, moral agency and language in the intransitive dimension of society.

8   For critical realists, positivism is simply descriptive and correlational while interpretivism is wrapped up in the subjective and cultural construction of meanings that can never be firmly established.

9   Ultra-realism can supposedly produce knowledge of observed events and human responses which can be linked with real systems of possibilities and constraints and from this begin a to build a theoretical framework for future research.

10 Wood *et al.* (2020) articulate an series of reservations about ultra-realist crime causation theory whereby they (1) question the ability of the breakdown of the pseudo-pacification process to account for gender-related disparities in criminal behaviour;

(2) critically consider the explanation of violence offered by ultra-realism through reference to drives, libidinal energy and sublimation; and (3) outline reservations about special liberty with regard to its explanation of crime as an expression of capitalist values.

Discussion questions

1 How does ultra-realism define crime?
2 Explain the concept of *special liberty* in ultra-realist criminology.
3 Explain the concept of the *breakdown of the pseudo-pacification process* in ultra-realist criminology.
4 Explain the theoretical contribution of critical realism to ultra-realist criminology?
5 Sum up briefly the main reservations about ultra-realist criminology made by Wood *et al.* (2020).

Suggested further reading

Hall and Winlow (2015) produce the essential introduction to ultra-realist criminology. Everything written by Steve Hall and Simon Winlow whether on their own or together is worth a read. All are included in the bibliography.Hall (2012a, 2012b) in particular is an essential read. Wood (2019) and Wood *et al.* (2020) provide constructive criticisms.

Note

1 Securitization is the financial practice of pooling various types of contractual debt such as residential mortgages, commercial mortgages, auto loans or credit card debt obligations (or other non-debt assets which generate receivables) and selling their related cash flows to third-party investors as securities, which may be described as bonds, pass-through securities or collaterized debit obligations). Investors are repaid from the principal and interest cash flows collected from the underlying debt and redistributed through the capital structure of the new financing. Securities backed by mortgage receivables are called mortgage-backed securities, while those backed by other types of receivables are asset-backed securities.

References

Abercrombie, N., Hill, S. and Turner, B.S. (1980) *The Dominant Ideology Thesis*. London: Allen and Unwin.
Archer, M.S. (1995) *Realist Social Theory: The Morphogenetic Approach*. Cambridge: Cambridge University Press.
Archer, M.S. (1996) *Culture and Agency: The Place of Culture in Social Theory*. Cambridge: Cambridge University Press.
Archer, M.S. (2000) *Being Human: The Problem of Agency*. Cambridge: Cambridge University.
Badiou, A. (2001) *Ethics: An Essay on the Understanding of Evil*. London: Verso.
Bakker, I. (2007) 'Social Reproduction and the Constitution of a Gendered Political Economy', *New Political Economy*, 12(4): 541–56.
Bhattacharya, T. (ed.) (2017) *Social Reproduction Theory: Remapping Class, Recentering Oppression*. London: Pluto Press.
Bohner, G., Reinhard, M.A., Rutz, S., Sturm, S., Kerschbaum, B. and Effler, D. (1998) 'Rape Myths as Neutralizing Cognitions: Evidence for a Causal Impact of Anti-Victim Attitudes on Men's Self-Reported Likelihood of Raping', *European Journal of Social Psychology*, 2(2): 257–6.

Box, S. (1987) *Recession, Crime and Punishment*. London: Macmillan.

Braithwaite, J. (1989) *Crime, Shame and Reintegration*. Cambridge: Cambridge University Press.

Brenner, J. and Laslett, B. (1991) 'Gender, Social Reproduction, and Women's Self-Organization: Considering the US Welfare State', *Gender & Society*, 5(3): 311–33.

Connell, R.W. (2002) 'On Hegemonic Masculinity and Violence: Response to Jefferson and Hall', *Theoretical Criminology*, 6(1): 89–99.

Crank, J.P. and Jacoby, L.S. (2015) *Crime, Violence and Global Warming*. New York: Routledge.

Currie, E. (1985) *Confronting Crime: An American Challenge*. New York: Pantheon Books.

Currie, E. (1997) 'Market, Crime and Community', *Theoretical Criminology*, 1(2): 147–72.

Currie, E. (2009) *The Roots of Danger: Violent Crime in Global Perspective*. New York: Prentice Hall.

Dutton, D.G. and Nichols, T.L. (2005) 'The Gender Paradigm in Domestic Violence: Research and Theory', *Aggression and Violent Behavior*, 10: 60–714.

Ellis, A. (2015) *Men, Masculinities and Violence: An Ethnographic Study*. London: Routledge.

Ellis, A. (2019) 'A De-civilizing Reversal or System Normal? Rising Lethal Violence in Post-Recession Austerity United Kingdom', *British Journal of Criminology*, 59(4): 62–7.

Ferrell, J. (2007) 'For a Ruthless Cultural Criticism of Everything Existing', *Crime Media Culture*, 3(1): 91–100.

Fisher, M. (2009) *Capitalist Realism: Is There No Alternative?* Alresford: Zero Books.

Floridi, L. (2013) *The Philosophy of Information*. Oxford: Oxford University Press.

Fraser, N. (2013) *Fortunes of Feminism*. London: Verso.

Hall, A. and Antonopoulos, G.A. (2016) *Fake Meds Online: The Internet and the Illicit Market in Pharmaceuticals*. London: Palgrave.

Hall, S. (1997) 'Visceral Cultures and Criminal Practices', *Theoretical Criminology*, 1(4): 453–7.

Hall, S. (2007) 'The Emergence and Breakdown of the Pseudo-Pacification Process', in K. Watson (ed.) *Assaulting the Past: Placing Violence in Historical Context*. Cambridge: Cambridge Scholars Press.

Hall, S. (2012a) *Theorising Crime and Deviance: A New Perspective*. London. Sage.

Hall, S. (2012b) 'The Solicitation of the Trap: On Transcendence and Transcendental Materialism in Advanced Consumer-Capitalism', *Human Studies: Special Issue on Transcendence and Transgression*, 35(3): 365–31.

Hall, S. (2014a) 'The Socioeconomic Function of Evi', *The Sociological Review*, 62(2): 13–31.

Hall, S. (2014b) 'Synopsis of Theorizing Crime and Deviance: A New Perspective 2012', *Journal of Theoretical & Philosophical Criminology*, 6(2): 145–155.

Hall, S. and Wilson, D. (2014) 'New Foundations: Pseudo-Pacification and Special Liberty as Potential Cornerstones for a Multi-Level Theory of Homicide and Serial Murder', *European Journal of Criminology*, 11(5): 635–55.

Hall, S. and Winlow, S. (2003a) 'Culture, Gender and Male Violence: A Key Problem', *Criminal Justice Matters*, 53(1): 14–15.

Hall, S. and Winlow, S. (2003b) 'Rehabilitating Leviathan: Reflections on the State, Economic Regulation and Violence Reduction', *Theoretical Criminology*, 7(2): 139–62.

Hall, S. and Winlow, S. (2004) 'Barbarians at the Gate: Crime and Violence in the Breakdown of the Pseudo-Pacification Process', in J. Ferrell, K. Hayward, W. Morrison and M. Presdee (eds.) *Cultural Criminology Unleashed*. London: Routledge-Cavendish.

Hall, S. and Winlow, S. (2015) *Revitalizing Criminological Theory: Towards a New Ultra-Realism*. London: Routledge.

Hall, S. and Winlow, S. (2018) 'Ultra Realism', *Routledge Handbook of Critical Criminology*. London: Routledge.

Hall, S., Winlow, S. and Ancrum, C. (2008) *Criminal Identities and Consumer Culture: Crime, Exclusion and the New Culture of Narcissism*. Cullompton: Willan Publishing.

Heath, J. and Potter, A. (2006) *The Rebel Sell: How Counterculture Became Consumer Culture*. London: Capstone.

Heidensohn, F. (2012) 'The Future of Feminist Criminology', *Crime, Media, Culture: Special Issue: York Deviancy Conference 2011*, (2): 123–134.

Honneth, A. (1996) *The Struggle for Recognition: The Moral Grammar of Social Conflicts*. Cambridge: Polity Press.

Hopkins Burke, R.D. (2018) *An Introduction to Criminological Theory*. 5th ed. Abingdon: Oxon.

Horsley, M. (2014) 'The "Death of Deviance" and the Stagnation of Twentieth Century Criminology' in M. Dellwing, J. Kotarba and N. Pino (eds.) *The Death and Resurrection of Deviance: Current Research and Ideas*. Basingstoke: Palgrave Macmillan.

Jacoby, R. (2007) *Picture Imperfect*. New York: Columbia University Press.

Johnston, A. (2008) *Žižek's Ontology*. Evanston, IL: Northwestern University Press.

Johnson, L.G. and Beech, A. (2017) 'Rape Myth Acceptance in Convicted Rapists: A Systematic Review of the Literature', *Aggression and Violent Behavior*, 34: 20–34.

Kotze, J. and Temple, D. (2014) 'Analyzing the Crime Decline: News from Nowhere', National Deviancy Conference, Teeside.

Lloyd, A. (2018) 'Serving Up Harm: Systemic Violence, Transitions to Adulthood and the Service Economy', in A. Boukli and J. Kotzé (eds.) *Zemiology: Reconnecting Crime and Social Harm*. London: Palgrave Macmillan.

Lloyd, A. (2019) 'Harm at Work: Bullying and Special Liberty in the Retail Sector', *Critical Criminology*: 1–15.

McGowan, T. (2016) *Capitalism and Desire: The Psychic Cost of Free Markets*. New York: Columbia University Press.

O'Brien, G. and Jureidini, J. (2002a) 'Dispensing with the Dynamic Unconscious', *Philosophy, Psychiatry, and Psychology*, 9(2): 141–53.

Parenti, C. (2011) *Tropic of Chaos: Climate Change and the New Geography of Violence*. New York: Nation.

Pfau-Effinger, B. (1998) 'Gender Cultures and the Gender Arrangement: A Theoretical Framework for Cross-National Gender Research', *Innovation: The European Journal of Social Science Research*, 11(2): 147–66.

Raymen, T. (2015) 'Designing-in Crime by Designing-Out the Social? Situational Crime Prevention and the Intensification of Harmful Subjectivities', *British Journal of Criminology*, 56(3): 497–514.

Raymen, T. (2016) 'Time to Get (Ultra) Real: The Future of Critical Criminology', *The Critical Criminologist*, 26(3): 19–23.

Raymen, T. (2018) 'Living in the End Times through Popular Culture: An Ultra-Realist Analysis of the Walking Dead as Popular Criminology', *Crime Media Culture*, 14(3): 429–47.

Raymen, T. (2019) *Book Review: Alexandra Hall and Georgios Antonopoulos (2016) Fake Meds Online: The Internet and the Transnational Market in Illicit Pharmaceuticals*. London: Palgrave Macmillan.

Reiner, R. (2007) *Law and Order: An Honest Citizen's Guide to Crime and Control*. Cambridge: Polity.

Reiner, R. (2016) *Crime: The Mystery of the Common-Sense Concept*. Cambridge: Polity.

Sayer, A. (1999) *Realism and Social Science*. London: Sage.

Smith, O. and Raymen, T. (2016a) 'Deviant Leisure: A Criminological Perspective', *Theoretical Criminology*, 22(2): 63–4.

Smith, O. and Raymen, T. (2016b) 'What's Deviance Got to Do with It? Black Friday Sales, Violence, and Hyper-Conformity', *British Journal of Criminology*, 56(2): 39–405.

Steffensmeier, D., Schwartz, J., Zhong, H. and Ackerman, J. (2005) 'Assessment of Recent Trends in Girls' Violence using Diverse Longitudial Sources: Is the Gender Gap Closing', *Criminology*, 43(2): 355.

Streeck, W. (2016) *How Will Capitalism End?* London: Verso.

Taylor, I., Walton, P. and Young, J. (1973) *The New Criminology: For a Social Theory of Deviance*. London: Routledge & Kegan Paul.

Treadwell, J., Briggs, D., Winlow, S. and Hall, S. (2013) 'Shopocalypse Now: Consumer Culture and the English Riots of 2011', *British Journal of Criminology*, 53(1): 1–17.

Tudor, K. (2019) 'Symbolic Survival and Harm: Serious Fraud and Consumer Capitalism's Perversion of the Causa Sui Project', *The British Journal of Criminology*: 1–17.

Vandello, J.A. and Cohen, D. (2003) 'Male Honor and Female Fidelity: Implicit Cultural Scripts That Perpetuate Domestic Violence', *Journal of Personality and Social Psychology*, 4(5): 997–1010.

Weeks, K. (1998) *Constituting Feminist Subjects*. Ithaca: Cornell University Press.

Wiegratz, J. (2016) *Neoliberal Moral Economy: Capitalism, Socio-Cultural Change and Fraud in Uganda.* London: Rowman and Littlefield.

Winlow, S. (2001) *Badfellas: Crime, Tradition and New Masculinities.* Oxford: Berg.

Winlow, S. (2014) 'Trauma, Guilt and the Unconscious: Some Theoretical Notes on Violent Subjectivity', *The Sociological Review,* 62(S2): 32–49.

Winlow, S. and Hall, S. (2013) *Rethinking Social Exclusion: The End of the Social?* London: Sage.

Winlow, S., Hall, S. and Treadwell, J. (2017) *The Rise of the Right: English Nationalism and the Transformation of Working-Class Politics.* Bristol: Policy Press.

Winlow, S., Hall, S., Treadwell, J. and Briggs, D. (2015) *Riots and Political Protest: Notes from the Post-Political Present.* London: Routledge.

Wood, M.A. (2019) 'What Is Realist about Ultra-Realist Criminology?', *Journal of Theoretical and Philosophical Criminology,* 11: 95–114.

Wood, M.A., Anderson, B. and Richards, I. (2020) 'Breaking Down the Pseudo-Pacification Process: Eight Critiques of Ultra-Realist Crime Causation Theory', *The British Journal of Criminology,* 60(3): 642–61.

Yar, M. (2012) 'Critical Criminology, Critical Theory and Social Harm', in S. Hall and S. Winlow (eds.) *New Directions in Criminological Theory.* London: Routledge, 52–66.

Žižek, S. (2001) *Did Somebody Say Totalitarianism?* London: Verso.

Žižek, S. (2006) *The Parallax View.* Cambridge, MA: MIT Press.

Radical moral communitarian criminology

Introduction

It has been shown in this book that 'crime' and 'criminality' are concepts understandable in the context of the nature of the socio-political system in which we live. Thus, we have seen that contemporary neoliberal society encourages and promotes attributes of competitiveness and greed as essential characteristics for success. Notions of the pursuit of the collective good, collaboration, not competition, have become relegated often to mockery in such societies. It is the premise of this chapter – indeed the book – that collaborative, more equal societies, based on cooperation rather than invariably aggressive competition, are likely to be happier societies, with far less crime and criminality. Such societies are most likely to have high levels of communitarianism.

Communitarianism is a social and political philosophy which emphasizes the importance of community in the functioning of political life, in the analysis and evaluation of political institutions, and in understanding human identity and well-being. Mainstream communitarianism arose in the 1980s as a critique of two prominent philosophical schools: first, contemporary liberalism, which seeks to protect and enhance personal autonomy and individual rights, in part, through the activity of government and, second, libertarianism, a form of liberalism (sometimes called 'classical liberalism') which aims to protect individual rights – especially the rights to liberty and property through placing strict limits on the power of government.

But the broad concept of communitarianism is nothing new with compelling communitarian elements in many modern, historical political and religious belief systems, for example in the Hebrew Bible (Old Testament), the Christian New Testament (Acts 4:32): 'Now the whole group of those who believed were of one heart and soul, and no one claimed private ownership of any possessions, but everything they owned was held in common', in the early Islamic concept of shura ('consultation'), in Confucianism, in Roman Catholic social thought (the papal encyclical *Rerum Novarum* [1891]), in one-nation conservatism ('to be attached to the subdivision, to love the little platoon we belong to in society, is the first principle . . . of public affections' – Edmund Burke) and in social democracy, especially Fabianism. Communitarian ideas have also played a significant role in public life through their incorporation into the electoral platforms and policies of Western political leaders of the late twentieth and early twenty-first centuries, including British prime minister Tony Blair, Dutch prime minister Jan Peter Balkenende, and US presidents Bill Clinton and Barack Obama.

The term *communitarian* was first used in 1841 by John Goodwyn Barmby, a leader of the British Chartist movement, who used it to refer to utopian socialists and others who experimented with unusual communal lifestyles. But it was not until the 1980s that the term gained currency through its association with the work of a small group of political philosophers – mainly in the US – who argued for the importance of the common good in opposition to contemporary liberals and libertarians, who emphasized the good for individuals, particularly including personal autonomy and individual rights. The Canadian philosopher Charles Taylor and the US political theorist Michael Sandel were among the most prominent scholars of this brand of communitarianism.

During the same period, students of East Asian politics and society used *communitarianism* to describe the social thinking within authoritarian societies such as China, Singapore and Malaysia, which extolled social obligations and the importance of the common good and accorded much less weight to autonomy and rights. Indeed, these societies viewed individuals as more or less interchangeable cells who find meaning in their contribution to the social whole rather than as free agents. In 1990, Amitai Etzioni and William Galston founded a third school, known as 'responsive' communitarianism. Its members formulated a platform based on their shared political principles, and the ideas in it were eventually elaborated in academic and popular books and periodicals, gaining thereby a measure of political currency, mainly in the West. The main thesis of responsive communitarianism – or mainstream communitarianism, as it is termed in this book – is that people face two major sources of normativity,[1] that of the common good and that of autonomy and rights, neither of which in principle, it is argued, should take precedence over the other.

Whereas the classical liberalism of the European Enlightenment can be viewed as a reaction to centuries of authoritarianism, oppressive government, overbearing communities and rigid dogma, modern communitarianism can be considered a reaction to excessive individualism, understood by communitarians as an undue emphasis on individual rights, leading people to become selfish or egocentric. Excessive individualism was discussed in an oft-cited communitarian work, *Habits of the Heart: Individualism and Commitment in American Life* (1985) by the US sociologist Robert Neelly Bellah, who observed that increasing prosperity from the 1950s onwards – among other factors – has contributed to a decline in respect for traditional authority and institutions, such as marriage, and has fostered a kind of materialistic hedonism.

The close relation between the individual and the community was discussed on a theoretical level by Sandel and Taylor – among other academics – in their criticisms of philosophical liberalism, including especially the work of US liberal theorist John Rawls and earlier that of the German Enlightenment philosopher Immanuel Kant. The core of their argument was that contemporary liberalism and libertarianism presuppose an incoherent notion of the individual as existing outside and apart from society rather than embedded within it. To the contrary, they argued, there are no generic individuals but rather only

Germans or Russians, Berliners or Muscovites or members of some other particular community. Moreover, because individual identity is partly constructed by culture and social relations, there is no coherent way of formulating individual rights or interests in abstraction from social contexts. In particular, there is no point in attempting to found a theory of justice on principles that individuals would choose in a hypothetical state of ignorance of their social, economic and historical circumstances – from behind a Rawlsian 'veil of ignorance'[2] – because such individuals cannot exist, even in principle.

Liberal scholars were to argue that this line of criticism is overstated or misconceived. Despite its emphasis on autonomy and rights, they contend, contemporary liberalism is not incompatible with the notion of a socially embedded self. Indeed, Rawls himself, in his foundational work *A Theory of Justice* (1971), recognized the importance of what he called 'social unions' and asserted that 'only in a social union is the individual complete'. Thus, according to liberals, the communitarian critique does not rebut the core of liberal theory but merely serves as a corrective to 'stronger' liberal doctrines such as libertarianism, which does embrace an atomized notion of individual identity.

The mainstream communitarian agenda

Responsive – or mainstream – communitarianism emerged as we have seen in the US during the 1980s as a response to what its advocates considered to be the limitations of liberal theory and practice. Significantly, diverse strands in social, political and moral thought, arising from very different locations on the political spectrum – such as Marxism (Ross, 2003) and traditional 'one-nation' conservatism (Scruton, 2001) – can be identified within this body of thought. The dominant themes of mainstream communitarianism are, first, the individual rights which have been vigorously promoted by traditional liberals need to be balanced with social responsibilities and, second, autonomous individual selves do not exist in isolation but are shaped by the values and culture of communities. Communitarians propose that, unless we redress the balance towards the pole of community, our society will continue to become normless, self-centred and driven by special interests and power seeking.

This critique of the one-sided emphasis on individual civil or human rights promoted by liberalism is the key defining characteristic of mainstream communitarianism, for it is observed that rights have tended to be asserted without a corresponding sense of how they can be achieved or who will pay for them. 'Rights talk' is thus seen to corrupt political discourse, inhibit genuine discussion and is consistently employed without any parallel sense of responsibilities (see Emanuel, 1991; Glendon, 1991; Etzioni, 1993, 1995a, 1995b). Mainstream communitarians do support the preservation of traditional liberal rights and their extension in non-democratic regimes – or those which practise discrimination – but crucially propose that these rights need to be located in a more balanced framework.

Communitarians argue that the one-sided emphasis on rights in liberalism is related to philosophical notions of the individual as a 'disembodied self', one who has been uprooted from their fundamental cultural meanings, community attachments and the life stories which constitute the full identities of real human beings. Dominant liberal theories of justice, as well as much of economic and political theory, presume such a self (see Etzioni, 1993). Communitarians, in contrast, shift the balance and argue that the 'I' is constituted through the 'We' in a dynamic tension. Significantly, this is not, in terms of this purist form of mainstream communitarianism, an argument for the restoration of traditional community, with high levels of mechanical solidarity, the repressive dominance of the majority or the patriarchal family, although some on the conservative fringes do take up that position. Mainstream communitarians are, in fact, critical of community institutions which are authoritarian and restrictive and which cannot bear scrutiny within a larger framework of human rights and equal opportunities, and they accept the (post)modern condition argument that we are located within a complex web of pluralistic communities – or organic solidarity – with genuine value conflicts within them and within selves.

Amitai Etzioni *et al.* (1991) outlined the basic framework of mainstream communitarianism and essentially urged that the crucial focus should be on the family and its central role in socialization. Thus, central to this perspective is the proposition that employers should provide maximum support for parents through the creation of work-time initiatives – such as the provision of crèche facilities and after-school homework clubs – and, moreover, in an analysis which is highly compatible with contemporary social control theories (see Hirschi, 1969, 1995; Hirschi and Gottfredson, 1995, 2004), we are warned against avoidable parental relationship breakdowns, to put the interests of children first:

> The fact is, given the same economic and social conditions, in poor neighbourhoods one finds decent and hardworking youngsters next to antisocial ones. Likewise, in affluent suburbs one finds antisocial youngsters right next to decent hardworking ones. The difference is often a reflection of the homes they come from.
>
> (Etzioni, 1995b: 70)

Etzioni refers to the existence of a 'parenting deficit' in contemporary Western societies, where self-gratification is considered as much a priority for many parents as ensuring that their children are properly socialized and instilled with the appropriate moral values that act as protection against involvement in criminality and antisocial behaviour. The outcome is both inevitable and disastrous:

> Juvenile delinquents do more than break their parents' hearts. They mug the elderly, hold up stores and gas stations, and prey on innocent children returning from school. They grow up to be useless, or worse, as employees, and they can drain taxpayers' resources and patience. . . . Therefore, parents have a moral responsibility to the community to invest themselves in the proper upbringing of their children, and communities – to enable parents to so dedicate themselves.
>
> (Etzioni, 1995b: 54)

In the UK, Dennis and Erdos (1992) explained the 'parenting deficit' in terms of the liberalization of sexual mores which have been endemic in Western societies since the 1960s. They observe that the illegitimate children of single parents do less well on several fronts, with young males becoming involved in criminal behaviour because of the absence of a positive male role model, while, at the same time, the whole project of creating and maintaining the skills of fatherhood is being abandoned and lost.

Mainstream communitarians essentially seek to reverse these trends and demand a revival of moral education in schools at all levels, including the values of tolerance, peaceful resolution of conflict, the superiority of democratic government, hard work and saving. They also propose that government services should be devolved to an appropriate level, with the pursuit of new kinds of public–private partnerships and the development of national and local service programmes. These ideas were to become very influential and were to filter through into the Clinton administration during the 1990s and beyond, and, in a pamphlet written shortly after he became prime minister of the UK, Tony Blair demonstrated his communitarian or 'Third Way' credentials:

> We all depend on collective goods for our independence; and all our lives are enriched – or impoverished – by the communities to which we belong. . . . A key challenge of progressive politics is to use the state as an enabling force, protecting effective communities and voluntary organisations and encouraging their growth to tackle new needs, in partnership as appropriate.
>
> (1998: 4)

The most familiar and resonant of the 'abstract slogans' used by Blair in the promotion of the importance of community was the idea that rights entail responsibilities, and this was taken from the work of Etzioni (1993). In contrast to the traditional liberal idea that members of a society may simply be entitled to unconditional benefits or services, it was now argued that the responsibility to care for each individual should be seen as resting, first and foremost, with the individuals themselves.

For Blair and his sociological guru Anthony Giddens (1998), community was invoked very deliberately as residing in *civil society*: in lived social relations and in 'common-sense' notions of our civic obligations to each other and the communities in which we live. This 'Third Way' was presented as avoiding what its proponents observed to be the full-on atomistic egotistical individualism which was demanded by the Thatcherite maxim that 'there is no such thing as society', and, on the other hand, the traditional social-democratic recourse to a strong state as the tool by which to realize the aims of social justice, most notably that of economic equality. For Blair, 'the grievous twentieth century error of the fundamentalist Left was the belief that the state could replace civil society and thereby advance freedom' (1998: 4). He thus took the view that the state has a role to play, but as a facilitator, rather than a guarantor, of a flourishing community life.

Dissenters noted that the implementation of the New Labour agenda was to take a somewhat different course with its character rather more authoritarian (and, thus, focused perhaps inevitably more on the usage of the state apparatus to deliver particular outcomes) than is suggested by the rhetorical appeal to the relatively autonomous powers of civil society to deliver progress by itself (see Driver and Martell, 1997; Jordan, 1998). Hughes (1998) thus refers to the communitarianism of Etzioni and his acolytes – and pursued enthusiastically by governments in both the US and the UK – as moral *authoritarian* communitarianism and calls for a more radical non–authoritarian variant.

Radical egalitarian communitarianism

Radical egalitarian communitarians such as Bill Jordan (1992, 1996), Elliott Currie (1993, 1996, 1997) and Jock Young (1999) focused their attention on inequality, deprivation and the free market (capitalist and neoliberal) economy as causes of crime and subsequently proposed policies to eliminate poverty, which they define as a degree of deprivation which seriously impairs the ability of individuals to participate in society. Jordan (1992) argued persuasively that, in recent years, in the UK and similar Western societies, a major deterioration in social relations had occurred: first, because of the poor being denied access to material goods and, second, their simultaneous negative experience of power simply being unjust. Following the major socio-economic transformations of the last 20 years of the twentieth century, Jordan identified the formation of two very different opposing communities of 'choice' and 'fate'. On one hand, 'communities of choice' were identified as being those where individuals and families had developed income security strategies, which were associated with comfortable 'safe', convenient, healthy and status-giving private environments. On the other hand, 'communities of fate' were those which were bound together into long-term interdependencies because of a lack of opportunities to move geographical location, gain access to good education or health care, get decently paid legitimate employment and share in the cultural enjoyments of mainstream society.

Jordan argued – and that was nearly 30 years ago – for an unconditional basic income for all citizens as one specific means of sharing out the common good in a more equitable fashion, although he acknowledged that on its own this would be no policy panacea. The provision of a basic income for all would nevertheless open up the possibility for individuals and groups to participate in their own chosen projects and commitments and, moreover, such a scheme would reduce the institutionalized traps and barriers to labour market participation which had undermined legitimate efforts by members of 'communities of fate' to rejoin mainstream society. Thus, from this unambiguous critical criminological perspective, it is observed that marginalization, inequality and exclusion provide the foundations for much crime and antisocial activity. As a consequence, the radical *egalitarian* communitarian agenda for crime prevention gives ethical priority to decisions about the redistribution of resources, which allows all members an opportunity to share adequately in the life of the community on an equal basis. This is clearly a laudable agenda, but this contribution does raise the question as to whether the state has to first 'repair' the social wounds before 'the community' can be allowed to participate in an inclusive politics of crime control and social justice. Such an agenda would appear to be clearly beyond the capacity of civil society and require some significant government intervention.

Elliott Currie (1985, 1993, 1996, 1997) made a major contribution to the radical communitarian debate on crime, disorder, the decline of communities in the US and the left-realist programme on crime prevention and argued that the most serious problem in the US is that the most disadvantaged communities are sinking into a permanent state of terror and disintegration, in a society dominated by the market and consumerism. Currie (1993) outlined the complex deprivations of life in the inner city and the failure of the state to respond humanely to the drug crisis. Instead, implementing a mass programme of incarceration and incapacitation, while at the same time introducing huge cutbacks in welfare expenditure. He argued that what characterized the 'underclass' in the US more than anything was a 'surplus of vulnerability' exacerbated by the pervasive movement towards a more deprived, more stressful, more atomized and less supportive society. Many parents in the deprived communities were overwhelmed by multiple disadvantages and were in no position to counter the effects of family crises on their children.

Currie observed that the 'triumph' of neoliberalism has created deprived communities characterized by the destruction and absence of legitimate livelihoods, significant extremes of economic inequality, the increasing withdrawal of public services, the erosion of informal/communal support networks, the spread of a materialistic and neglectful culture, the unregulated marketing of a technology of violence and a weakening of social and political alternatives:

> The policies of the seventies and eighties, then, did more than merely strip individuals of jobs and income. They created communities that lacked not only viable economic opportunities, but also hospitals, fire stations, movie theatres, stores, and neighbourhood organizations – communities without strong ties of friendship or kinship, disproportionately populated by increasingly deprived and often disorganised people locked into the bottom of a rapidly deteriorating job market. In many cities these disruptive trends were accelerated by the physical destruction left by the ghetto riots of the 1960s or by urban renewal projects and freeways that split or demolished older, more stable neighbourhoods and dispersed their residents.
>
> (Currie, 1993: 70)

Radical communitarians – like Currie – are thus arguing that behind the growth of crime is a cultural, as well as a structural transformation of poor communities, and in this regard, there are some common themes between Etzioni and the radicals. The situation has certainly not improved in the intervening years, and in some geographical locations, we can observe communities where there are three or four generations of welfare claimants with little or no experience of the legitimate labour market. The reintegration of these socially excluded groups into mainstream society was an essential and laudable New Labour strategy termed 'reintegrative tutelage' (Hopkins Burke, 1999), and while there were clearly some success stories, this was ultimately a flawed strategy scuppered not least by the unremitting ravages of neoliberalism.

Some – as we have seen elsewhere in this book – have argued that the last decades of the twentieth century saw 'welfarism' as a regime of social regulation replaced by neoliberalism in post-industrial Western societies (see Lacey, 2013), with the latter significantly responsible for the harsher penal regime of the last few decades (Cavadino and Dignan, 2006), which helped discipline and tutor a recalcitrant working-class population in the interests of a neoliberal economy (Wacquant, 2009a, 2009b, 2009c). But Houdt and Schinkel (2013) take this all a step further and pertinently observe that neoliberalism is not separate from – but actually operates in combination with – communitarianism. Thus, the emphasis on individual 'responsibility' in communitarianism is totally compatible with the notion of 'responsibilization'[3] in neoliberalism, in other words, we have a neoliberal communitarianism.

Houdt and Schinkel (2013) thus argue that neoliberal communitarianism is a strategy of governmentality,[4] one that combines the main features of neoliberal governmentality (Foucault, 2004) with those of governmental communitarianism (Delanty, 2003; Ross, 2003; Adams and Hess, 2001; Van Swaaningen, 2008). This strategy consists of a combination of the new public management and the outsourcing of responsibility to a plethora of agencies and organizations, combining scientific measurement and the treatment of social problems with the stimulation of notions of 'active citizenship' and the rational governing of community.

Houdt and Schinkel (2013) further illustrate how neoliberal and communitarian elements have combined in crime policies over the last few decades with reference to three crucial trends. First, there is 'the prioritization of crime and the intensification and pluralization of punishment' where we have seen increasing 'selective incapacitation' and 'selective rehabilitation', which involves a broader range of possible punishments, including restorative justice and a variety of tactics deployed to suppress 'risky' behaviour. Second, there is the 'actuarialization of crime', where there is a transformation from the criminal subject as causally determined, towards one as a bundle of risk factors, a focus on choice, and the discovery of inappropriate subculture as a risk factor (O'Malley, 1992; Osborne and Gaebler, 1993). Third, there is 'the institutional transformation of crime regulation' following the 1980s where penal welfarism was attacked for being 'inefficient' and 'ineffective' and which was replaced by the adoption of managerial principles and a business model to make criminal justice both more 'effective' and 'efficient'.

Hopkins Burke (2012, 2013) argues that the practitioners, professionals and experts that have implemented these neoliberal strategies are invariably unaware of their contribution to the increasingly pervasive socio-control surveillance matrix of the carceral society which is encouraged and legitimized by a depoliticized general public, ultimately but again usually unwittingly, in the interests of the market economy and neoliberalism.

Hall *et al.* (2008) – who we encountered in the previous chapter – conducted a study of the criminal patterns and criminals living on the alienated housing estates of the north-east of England, where in some cases there was no one in legitimate employment. The researchers observe – in an analysis that was central to their development of ultra-realism – that the significant economic downturn of the 1980s was more than a mere structural adjustment for those living in these communities. Rather, it was a radical shift in political economy and culture, a move to the unprecedented domination of life by the market, which was to create a large number of locales in permanent recession in both the UK and the US. Hall *et al.* observe that

> [t]he criminal markets developing in these areas now tend to operate in the relative absence of the traditional normal insulation . . . regarded as essential to the restraint of the inherently amoral and social logic that lies at the heart of the liberal-capitalist market economy.
>
> (2008: 3)

The researchers pointedly observe that, contrary to the arguments presented by some, the 1980s was not a time of vigorous progressive cultural change, at least not in those large brutalized and inherently criminogenic communities in which they conducted their research. Indeed, we might well ask ourselves whether communities are inevitably the supportive protectors and focus of transformation that they are sometimes thought and proposed to be by some in the literature.

The concept of community reconsidered

Some commentators have argued that communities can be restored and revitalized through the provision of community justice and the restorative justice mechanisms that we have encountered elsewhere in this book and, by doing so, facilitate strong bonds of social control which are perceived as being legitimate and acceptable to their members. Strang sums up this viewpoint pertinently: 'strong communities can speak to us in moral voices' and they allow 'the policing by communities rather than the policing of communities' (1995: 20). Braithwaite (1989: 100) had observed that these informal control processes such as reintegrative shaming have been significantly more effective in communitarian cultures, but, at the same time, noted that in urban, individualistic and anonymous cultures, such as those which exist in most Western towns and cities, informal control mechanisms have simply lacked potency. He ironically observes that this appeal to revive or transform community has arisen at exactly the time it appears most absent and when Durkheimian anomie or normlessness is rampant and out of control.

The whole notion of community is complex and extends well beyond the more traditional definitions based on locality – or neighbourhood – and embraces a multiplicity of groups and networks to which, it is believed, we all belong (Strang, 1995: 20). This conception does not rely upon a fixed assumption of *where* a community will be found but builds on the notion of 'communities of care' – that is the networks of obligation and respect between the individual and everyone who cares about the person the most – and these are significantly not bounded by geography (Braithwaite and Daly, 1994: 195).

These communities of care are considered more relevant to contemporary modern living in urban societies because they provide a developed notion of 'community' where membership – or social identity – is personal and does not necessarily carry any fixed or external attributes of membership. The fact that such communities do not carry any connotations of coercion or forced membership is one of the distinctive appeals of the concept (Crawford and Clear, 2003), and from this perspective, there is an assumption that people can move freely between communities if they disagree with their practices and values and/or remain within a community but dissent from the dominant moral voice that exists. But this is a significantly problematic situation: for, on one hand, these contemporary 'light' communities are held up as examples of how they can allow sufficient space for individual or minority dissent, innovation and difference, but, on the other hand, they are also seen as insufficient with regard to informal control.

Crawford and Clear (2003) note that this all raises the question of exactly what is meant by the claim to 'restore' or 'reintegrate' communities (see Van Ness and Strong, 1997; Braithwaite, 1989; Clear and Karp, 1999). The very notion of restoring communities suggests a return to some pre-existing state and appears to involve a nostalgic urge to return to a mythical age of genuine human identity, connectedness and reciprocity. It certainly does seem questionable that the concept of community constitutes a dynamic force for democratic renewal, which challenges existing inequalities of power and the differential distribution of life opportunities and pathways to crime that characterize our society.

Crawford and Clear (2003) argue that it is important that we avoid idealistic notions and confront the empirical realities of most communities. The ideal of unrestricted entry to, and exit from, communities needs to be reconciled with the existence of relations of dominance, exclusion and differential power. The reality is that many stable communities contain very high levels of mechanical solidarity and tend to resist innovation, creation and experimentation and shun diversity (Hopkins Burke and Pollock, 2004). These communities may well be able to come together for informal social control but the way these processes play out lacks inclusive qualities and offender-sensitive styles. These communities can be – and often are – pockets of intolerance and prejudice, which can be coercive and tolerant of bigotry and discriminatory behaviour. Weaker individuals – and minority groups – within such communities often experience them not as a home of connectedness and mutuality but as the foundations of inequalities, which sustain and reinforce relations of dependence – for example, with regard to gender role and the tolerance of domestic violence or child abuse. Such communities are thus often hostile to minorities, dissenters and outsiders and can tolerate and even encourage deviant and offending behaviour. Communities are hierarchical formations, which are structured on lines of power, dominance and authority and which are intrinsically exclusive – as social exclusion presupposes processes of exclusion – and many confess and define themselves around notions of 'otherness', which are potentially infused with racialized overtones.

It is the work of the French sociologist and social theorist Emile Durkheim and his observations on the moral component of the division of labour in society that provides the theoretical foundations of a 'new' liberalism but one, which at the same time, provides a legitimate social context for community, that is a political philosophy which actively promotes the rights and responsibilities of both individuals and communities but in the context of an equal division of labour. It is this latter element that deviates significantly from the mainstream communitarianism which was embraced and distorted in the UK by New Labour with its enthusiasm for a strong dictatorial central state apparatus to enforce its agenda – and provides us with the basis of a genuine radical moral communitarianism, founded on notions of consensual interdependency with others we all recognize and identify as fellow citizens and social partners and not as potential legitimate crime targets.

In developing that argument, this chapter (1) summarizes the development of the concept of individualism in Western European thought from its Christian antecedents, locating the origins of three very different conceptualizations of individualism: French, Anglo-Saxon and German; (2) outlines the influential German conception of individualism and its implications for political organization; (3) outlines the response of Durkheim to these traditions and shows how his work builds on the French conception of individualism; and (4) shows how this provides the basis of a radical moral communitarianism, which is based on a more equal division of labour in society and which, it is argued, can provide the foundation for significant reductions in crime.

The development of the concept of individualism in Western Europe

Characteristics of the development of the concept of individualism in Western Europe can be identified within the disciplines of Christian theology, politics, economics and cultural studies. We consider the contribution of each.

Individualism and Christian theology

Prior to Christianity the only individual was the rare person who was in a position to renounce worldly affairs, was self-sufficient and thus fully independent, in a society where the secular was the dominant political force. With the emergence of Christianity, we get a fundamental shift in the conception of humanity which the nineteenth-century German Protestant theologian and philosopher Ernst Troeltsch identifies as man as an individual-in-relation-to-God: where all people are equal in the presence of God but where, at the same time, the (Catholic) church emerges as a form of institutional link, a mediator, between the individual and the divine (Dumont, 1994).

It is with St Augustine (354–430 CE) that the concept of sacred kingship, where the position of monarch is considered to be identical with that of a high priest and a judge and which had been the dominant orthodoxy until that time, is replaced by the idea that the state should be completely acquiescent to a dominant church. At the same time, we can observe a subtle advance in the concept of individualism, where the state is conceived to be a collection of men united through agreement on values and common utility (see the following discussion). The church now pretends to rule, directly or indirectly, which means that the Christian individual is now committed to the world to an unprecedented degree. He or she is an individual with responsibilities and obligations via their membership of the church and this includes kings and the aristocracy. It is with John Calvin (1509–1564) and the (Protestant) Reformation that this relationship completely changes, and the individual becomes fully part of the world and individualist values are dominant without restriction or limitation (Bouwsma, 1988).

It was Martin Luther (1483–1546), whose actions as a disillusioned Catholic priest, had previously removed God from the world by rejecting the mediation institutionalised in the Catholic Church. God was now accessible to the individual consciousness. The ritualism of the Catholic Church and the justification of good works which had previously enabled the person access to heaven were now replaced within Protestant theology by the concept of justification through faith, which left the individual some margin of freedom, that is whether to believe (faith) or not to believe. This was now a matter of individual choice.

Calvin later went further than Luther and declared that the individual has complete impotence in the face of the power of God and neither good works nor faith guarantees access to heaven (Bouwsma, 1988). Now, at first sight, this appears to be an important limitation rather than a development of the notion of individualism, but Troeltsch warns us against interpreting Calvin in terms of the unfettered atomistic individualism which – as we will see later – is central to the Anglo-Saxon conception. Instead, there is the notion of the imposition of values: the identification of our will with that of God. The Puritans, who followed the lead of Calvin, believed that the Bible was God's true law and which provided a plan for living. The established church of the day described access to God as monastic and possible only within the confines of 'church authority', which was the will of God. The puritans simply stripped away the traditional trappings and formalities of Christianity which had been slowly building throughout the previous 1,500 years. Theirs was an attempt to 'purify' both the church and their lives.

It is thus with Luther, Calvin and the Protestant Reformation that we can identify the origins of a specific Germanic conception of individualism where the person expresses their individuality in relation to close identification with something greater than themselves, in this case God but later in the case of Germany, the Volk; in the case of Marxists, the proletariat; or for others, simply society, however it might be constituted (Dumont, 1986). It is thus a conception of individualism that has its origins in sixteenth-century Germany but which clearly has had considerable impact outside the frontiers of that country.

Individualism and politics

The political perspective on individualism has two useful starting points. First, there is the combination of Christian revelation and Aristotelian philosophy in Thomas Aquinas (1225–74), the medieval philosopher and theologian, where at the level of religion each person is conceptualized as a whole being, a private individual in direct relation to their creator, and on a political level where they are considered to be a member of the secular commonwealth, a part of the social body. Second, there is the theory of Natural Law which dominates in the period leading up to the French Revolution, where the idea is to establish an ideal society while starting from the individual person of nature. The device for this purpose was the idea of contract which in turn involves the combination of two elements: the first or 'social' contract introduced the relationship characterized by equality or 'fellowship' and the second or political contract introduced subjection to a ruler or a ruling agent.

Subsequently, the philosophers reduced this multiplicity of contracts to one. First, Thomas Hobbes (1588–1679) makes the social contract a contract of subjection. This occurs when individuals come together and surrender some of their individual rights and hand these over to an emergent state, a sovereign entity like the individuals now under its rule used to be and which creates laws to regulate social interactions. In this way, human life is given order and is no longer 'a war of all against all'. Second, John Locke (1632–1704) replaces the political contract by a trust. Taking the opposite view to Hobbes, he believed that individuals in a state of nature would be bound morally, by 'The Law of Nature', not to harm each other in their lives or possession. Yet, without government to defend them against those seeking to injure or enslave them, people would have no security in their rights and would live in fear. Locke thus argued that individuals would agree to form a state which would provide a 'neutral judge', acting to protect the lives, liberty and property of those who lived within it. Third, Jean-Jacques Rousseau (1712–78) suppresses the ruler altogether. The 'contract social' is the contract of association where it is assumed that one enters society at large as one enters any other voluntary association. His collectivism is most evident in his development of the concept of the 'general will', where he argues that a citizen cannot pursue his true interest by being egocentric (as in the Anglo-Saxon conception of individualism) but must instead subordinate himself to the law created by the citizenry acting as a collective.

It is with the Puritans, who founded colonies in what is now the US (New England) in the early seventeenth century, that we get an actual example of the establishment of a commonwealth developed on the basis of a contract. What the English radical collectivists, the Levellers, had unsuccessfully demanded in their 'Agreement of the People' published in 1647: the rights of man and religious freedom had been enjoyed in the American colonies since the beginning. We have here an abstract statement of the concept of the Individual as being over and above the State, which is endorsed by the French Revolution, but which is first articulated by the Puritans. These developments are closely linked to the emergence of utilitarian philosophy in Britain which is usually associated with Jeremy Bentham (1748–1832) and John Stuart Mill (1806–73) and which proposes that the correct course of action to take is the one that maximizes total benefits while, at the same time, reduces suffering or any associated negatives. It thus applies a moral foundation, and the basis of practical political solutions, to the *laissez-faire* liberal economic ideas of Adam Smith (1723–90) who influentially argued for an economic system in which transactions between private parties are free from intrusive government restrictions, tariffs and subsidies, with only enough regulations to protect property rights (Dumont, 1986). It is this notion that individuals pursuing their rational self-interest and maximizing their own gain will result in a beneficial social good for all, which provides the origins of the Anglo-Saxon conception of individualism that has become extremely influential throughout the world.

In France, for the early French socialist Henri de Saint-Simon (1760–1825) and his followers, the French Revolution, the Rights of Man and the advent of liberalism had a purely negative and destructive value, and they concluded that the time had come to *organize* society and to regenerate it. For the Saint-Simonians and this decidedly French conception of socialism, the state is conceived as an industrial association which should be hierarchical, rewards should be unequal, as performances are, but the inheritance of property should be suppressed. We have here the origins of a French secular conception of individualism where secondary groups act as intermediaries between individuals and the state. Moreover, in a society spared a Protestant Reformation, it is a conception of social organization based on the medieval Catholic Church (Dumont, 1986).

Meanwhile, in Protestant Germany, G.W.F. Hegel's (1770–81) highly influential philosophy of the state appears to be the culmination of everything that had gone before. As is the case for Hobbes and Rousseau, the conscious individual is called to recognize in the state their higher self and in the command of the state the expression of their own will and freedom. This indirect presentation of society in terms of the state leads to a kind of religion of the state. Thus, in the realm of the political, Hegel does for the German concept of individualism what Luther and Calvin had previously done in the realm of the religious.

Individualism and economics

The economic perspective on individualism arises with the reversal of the traditional idea that relations between people are more important than the relationship between people and things. The converse is now considered more important. At the same time, the champions of free trade were impatient with the mercantilist view of state intervention and there hence occurred a basic ideological change. The idea that in trade the gain of one party means inevitably a loss to the other, which was central to mercantilist thinking, is replaced with the notion that exchange is advantageous to both parties. This economic perspective which promotes the value and dominance of the free market was to become fundamental to the Anglo-Saxon conception of individualism.

Individualism and culture

At the beginning of the eighteenth-century German culture exhibits an unprecedented development which brings about a complete emancipation in relation to the French culture which had previously dominated European thought (Dumont, 1994). It is at this point that we can identify the rise of the German conception of individualism. Central to this development is Johann Gottfried Herder (1744–1803), a German philosopher and theologian, who saw in history the contrasted interplay of individual cultures each constituting a specific Volk, in which an aspect of general humanity is embodied in a unique manner. There is, from this perspective, a deep transformation in the definition of humanity; as opposed to the abstract individual, a representative of the human species, endowed with reason, humanity is what it is, in all its modes of thinking, feeling and acting, by virtue of their belonging to a given cultural community (Nisbet, 1985). In doing so, Herder provides the basis for what later will be called the 'ethnic theory' of nationalities as against the 'elective theory', in which the nation rests essentially on consensus. This is a peculiarly German conception of nationality and indeed individualism.

The social and political philosophy of Johann Gottlieb Fichte (1762–1814) is significant here. Ostensibly, Fichte sets out to be the philosopher of the French Revolution but is considered in Germany to be a precursor of pan-Germanism. His position is essentially that the German spirit is characterized by universality. The German people are destined to dominate the world, but he modifies this meaning by basing it in the identity of universality and Germanness (James, 2010). There is indeed a powerful holistic trend in German ideas where the German people as a whole have been strongly inclined to obey the dominant power. In agreement with this general background, the great majority of German intellectuals have admitted to the necessity of subordination to society. Combined with the ethnocentrism that is found universally, the valuation of 'us' as against 'others' or strangers, we have the social basis of what has been called 'pan-Germanism'. In this conception, a person is essentially a German, and through being a German is a social being. There is a devotion to the whole: 'Germans have in their blood devotion to a thing, an idea, an institution, a super-individual entity' (Troeltsch, 1925: 96). In other words, the subject subordinates their self spontaneously to the whole; they have no feeling of alienation in doing so, and therefore, all their personal qualities are given free rein in the fulfilment of their role.

On the other hand, neither the French or Anglo-Saxon traditions can see the possibility of liberty arising from that formulation, only autocracy and slavery. Troeltsch argues that this is Hegel's conception of liberty and that this is expressed, one way or another, in all the great German creations of the nineteenth century: in the Socialist Party as well as in the army. Thus, this German conception of liberty can be identified in German political movements apparently as diverse as national socialism and Marxism (Dumont, 1994). For example, in *Mein Kampf*, Hitler explains very clearly that he designed his movement as a sort of counter-copy of the Marxist and Bolshevik movement, replacing among other things, the class struggle by a race struggle. According to Pribram (1953), German nationalism, on one hand, and German socialism (i.e. Marxist socialism), on the other, rest on similar ideological formulas so that a possible shift is understandable from one to the other, or from Marxist socialism to 'national socialism'. Both German nationalism and Marxism were built on an individualist, 'nominalist' foundation, and both claim to reach a collective being (Dumont, 1994).

The origins of Durkheim's social theory

French sociologist Emile Durkheim (1858–1917) disagreed with both the German and Anglo-Saxon conceptions of the relationship between individuals and society, and he developed a social theory which embodied three main influences, but which in essence is founded on the French conception of individualism. First, there is French philosopher Charles Bernard Renouvier's (1815–1903) rationalism, his concern with morality and his attempt to reconcile determinism with the concept of human freedom and morality. Renouvier accepted that progress through mastery over nature was possible but considered this conditional on moral progress based on the mastery a person had over themselves and their actions. Essentially, he combined a concern for the dignity of the individual with a theory of social cohesion based on the person's sense of utility with and dependence on others (Verneaux, 1945). Second, there are the aforementioned French socialist leader Saint-Simon's ideas about economic institutions in industrial society and for the need of new forms of social and political organization to regulate these (Berlin, 2002). Third, there is French thinker Alfred Espinas's (1844–1922) emphasis on the superiority of the collective consciousness over the individual: his attribution of the superiority of the social over the individual, where altruism and sympathy were to predominate over egoism and find their ultimate point of focus in the national society.

Durkheim's social theory is fundamentally a reaction to Anglo–Saxon utilitarianism, German state socialism and French authoritarianism. First, in the case of French authoritarianism, he accepts Comte's argument that the increasing division of labour among occupational groups leads to social solidarity or cohesion but that, at the same time, it tends to extinguish any sense of community. Yet, where Comte looked for a solution in an increasing role for the state as a unifying force, Durkheim observed that this account had no regard for the naturally achieved solidarity of an independent system of activities, a spontaneous consensus of the parts which could not be maintained by force against the nature of things. But, for Durkheim, this rejection of authoritarianism did not mean an acceptance of the utilitarian tradition.

Second, Herbert Spencer, a part of the Anglo–Saxon utilitarian tradition, disagreed with Comte and argued that industrial societies had a natural coherence as a result of the unhindered play of individual interests. These required neither conformity to shared beliefs and norms nor state regulation and social solidarity would eventually develop in accordance with individual interests. Durkheim nonetheless took the opposite view and contended that the free play of individual interests would lead to instability, not harmony, and which would only give rise to transient relations and passing associations. Moreover, he observed that Spencer's account of contract was misleading. A contract was the product of a society, which gave it its binding force and defines the condition of its operation.

Third, from the tradition of German state socialism, Tönnies's concept of Gesellschaft was close to that of Spencer's concept of industrial society, emphasizing individual property, the 'free market', traditional beliefs superseded by freedom of thought and the isolation of individuals. Tönnies nevertheless observed the need for a strong state to safeguard interests, a form of state-regulated capitalism, which was his version of socialism. Durkheim criticized the theory of Gesellschaft as accounting for social solidarity in terms of a temporary and artificial mechanism, the imposition of the state. He subsequently reversed the dichotomy between modern and traditional societies, which had been characteristic of German thought (Hopkins Burke, 2014).

Durkheim and social solidarity

Durkheim (1933, originally 1893) argued that in more simple societies people are bound together by a mechanical form of solidarity where like are drawn to like, where we all share the same values and cultural norms. There is a common identity, the same beliefs and interests are shared, with a collective consciousness and common awareness shared by all. In more complex industrial societies people are bound together by an organic form of solidarity. Individuals are often unlike each other, perform very different roles, have different experiences, beliefs and philosophies.

Durkheim provides a crucial organic analogy between society and the human body: both need regular, stable, ongoing, functioning organs. Thus, at the centre of organic society is the continuing progress of the division of labour between groups, but with this increasing fragmentation of society, it is extremely likely that we are all believing different things. There is thus a fragmentation of the collective consciousness, which has both positive consequences, for example, where many are willing to tolerate the actions and beliefs of a plurality of diverse groups, and negative outcomes, where some are not willing to tolerate a diversity of views, with the outcome being an increased likelihood of social conflict between varied, often belligerent, factions – 'culture wars', to use the language of today.

Fundamentally, the progressive escalation in levels of organic solidarity has brought about an extensive intensification in individualism. The European Enlightenment tradition has created a much higher degree of tolerance with a greater capacity and potential for individual development, but at the same time, there are also problematic, pathological developments. First, there are spectacular increases in a new form of human existence – *egoism* – where a person is too poorly integrated into society and can make choices and pursues their material interests without regard to others, and second, a sense of *anomie* can thereupon occur, whether you are in a group or not, a sense of not belonging, where you are not subject to regulative norms. These pathological developments are often the result of rapid social change which can cut people adrift from their familiar social moorings. For example Durkheim would undoubtedly have attributed the failure of the Bolshevik Social Revolution in the years after 1917 to the widespread anomie that was the outcome of the abolition of such traditional institutions as the church and family. The message for V.I. Lenin from this perspective is clear: you can abolish the bourgeois institutions overnight if you wish, but you cannot change the collective consciousness of the people as quickly. False consciousness or not! It is a lesson that might usefully be heeded by the ultra-realists we encountered in the previous chapter.

Durkheim observed that with the rise of organic society – and the simultaneous increase in individualism – it was now possible in industrial society to believe in self-indulgence, for both the bourgeoisie and proletarian; the only check would be conflict. For if the division of labour in society is forced or unequal, some groups have more power than others, usually the product of inherited wealth or social position but in more recent years because of the great disparity in economic rewards. Durkheim considered that the division of labour works best if people are in positions where their talents are best optimized, that is an ideal division of labour where everyone is content with their position and the rewards they are receiving. But, the division of labour that people invariably experience is forced, egoistical, anomic and riddled with individual despair and conflict and this has become increasingly the case in recent years with significant economic recession and ongoing austerity.

For Durkheim, the solution to an anomic society is the creation of an ideal division of labour whereby everyone is rewarded adequately and appropriately according to their talents, but this is clearly something that is very difficult to bring about, although he did propose a threefold political project to address this situation. First, it is necessary to clarify what are reasonable and acceptable aspirations in life for all people and the appropriate rewards they should receive. Second, the isolated and egoistical individual needs to be integrated into an interactive and inclusive social network. Third, it is necessary to remove the conditions that sustain inequality. In short, the key thing is to unite individuals into a higher community to which they feel a part and belong.

Durkheim and radical moral communitarianism

It is the work of Emile Durkheim and his observations on the moral component of the division of labour in society which provides the theoretical basis of a radical moral communitarianism which actively promotes not only the rights and responsibilities of both individuals and communities *in equal measure* but also in the context of an *equal division of labour* (Hopkins Burke, 2014, 2015). It is this element which deviates significantly from the mainstream communitarianism that was embraced but distorted by governments in the UK, the US and beyond. Indeed, being used as part of a neoliberal strategy to help restructure the economy in order to benefit the capitalist classes and the affluent, increasingly super-rich, to the detriment of the poor. The radical moral communitarian agenda, in contrast, provides us with the basis of a way of life founded on notions of appropriate contributions to society (obligations and responsibilities), suitable fair rewards (rights), consensual interdependency with others who we all recognize, identify and respect as fellow citizens and social partners, not as people of no consequence to be ignored, avoided and, in criminological terms, identified as potential legitimate crime targets. It is a philosophy which promotes a fairer, more equal world, based on mutual respect between all citizens.

Radical moral communitarianism is thus a variant on the communitarian theme promoted by Etzioni and his acolytes but, which, it is argued, has come to over-emphasize responsibilities to the detriment of rights. The call is for a re-balancing of the two. Thus, individuals have rights and responsibilities, but at the same time so do communities, and it is essential to maintain a negotiated balance between the two at all levels in society.

Policy implications of radical moral communitarian criminology

Table 20.1 provides a summary of some of the basic rights which it is proposed that a citizen should enjoy, along with the simultaneous responsibilities that they ought to have

Table 20.1 Rights and responsibilities in a moral communitarian society

Rights	Responsibilities
1 The provision of an adequate income on which to live appropriate to the stage of life of the individual.	1 To play an active role in the economy – in the wider sense of the term – while fit and healthy and of working age.
2 The provision of good-quality affordable accommodation/housing of an acceptable size and proper rights of tenure.	2 Being a good neighbour and a responsible member of the community, paying rent or mortgage where appropriate, and not engaging in antisocial behaviour to the disadvantage of fellow citizens.
3 To be treated with fairness and respect by all (including criminal justice) agencies, institutions and individuals regardless of age, disability, ethnicity, gender and religion.	3 To treat others with fairness and respect regardless of age, disability, ethnicity, gender and religion.
4 The provision of good-quality free health care at the point of delivery for all citizens.	4 To maintain a reasonable standard of natural health and fitness where at all possible.
5 The provision of appropriate, high-quality education and training.	5 To fully engage and participate in education and training and behave appropriately.
6 To be protected from crime and antisocial behaviour in our communities.	6 Not to engage in crime and criminal behaviour.

in a moral communitarian society built on mutual trust and respect (Hopkins Burke and Hodgson, 2013; Hopkins Burke, 2014, 2015). It is thus proposed that policies should be introduced which recognize that people and communities have both rights and responsibilities and there should be a fine balance between them. It is a balance which will invariably require negotiation, renegotiation and an enabling political context.

An acceptable income

All citizens in a radical moral communitarianism society should have access to an acceptable level of income at all stages of their life. This is clearly commensurate with the notion of an adequate welfare benefits system and a reinforcement of the basic right that all citizens enjoy in the appropriate circumstances. It should nevertheless be the responsibility of the individual to make an active contribution to society and the economy wherever possible in some form or another, and they should certainly not refuse suitable work that becomes available. For some, this will be a controversial proposal because it is suggestive of 'workfare' schemes – widely introduced in the US – and the requirement to work to obtain benefits which has been strongly resisted in countries such as the UK, but which are currently being introduced with not little resistance. There will thus need to be well-devised strategies to get people into meaningful employment and those taking part in back-to- (or introduction-to-)work schemes should be paid a higher rate of benefit than non-participants. Moreover, while there should be an expectation that all citizens become usefully involved productively in the economy in some shape or form, there should be no hounding of the sick and disabled and the withdrawal of their benefits when they are clearly unable to work. This has clearly been the case with the recently introduced Universal Credit.

Universal Credit is a UK social security payment introduced with the supposed intention of streamlining the benefits system and to incentivize paid work. There is currently an ongoing programme being introduced to replace and combine six benefits for working-age people who have a low household income.[5] The new policy was initially announced at the Conservative Party Annual Conference 2010 by the then work and pensions secretary, Iain Duncan Smith, who said it would make the social security system fairer to both claimants and taxpayers. A key feature of the proposed new benefit was that unemployment payments would taper off as the recipient moved into work, not suddenly stop, thus avoiding a 'cliff edge' that was said to 'trap' people in unemployment.

Universal Credit was introduced by the Welfare Reform Act 2012. In the following year, the new benefit began to be rolled out gradually, initially focusing on new claimants with the least complex circumstances. There were nevertheless problems with the early strategic leadership of the project and with the information technology system on which the benefit relies. Implementation costs, initially forecast to be about £2 billion, later grew to over £12 billion. More than 3 million recipients of the six older 'legacy' benefits were expected to have transferred to the new system by 2017, but currently, the full move is not expected be completed before 2024.

One specific concern is that payments are made monthly, with a waiting period of at least five weeks before the first payment, which can particularly affect claimants of Housing Benefit and lead to rent arrears (although claimants can apply for emergency loans which are paid more promptly but which nevertheless need to be repaid via deduction from future payments of a benefit which is at best targeted at subsistence level). In May

2019 one million people were receiving less than their maximum entitlement, mainly due to overpayment of tax credits under a previous government. In September 2019, a total of 2.5 million people were receiving the benefit, 65% of which were out of work.

Food bank use has increased significantly since the commencement of Universal Credit. Delays in providing money have forced claimants to use food banks, while the benefit itself does not provide enough to cover basic living expenses. Claiming is complex and the system is hard to navigate, many claimants cannot afford internet access or obtain online assistance with claiming. Some claimants feel they cannot get enough to live on without resorting to crime. One in five claims fail because the claimant does not follow the procedure correctly and there are fears this is because it is too hard to understand. A report by the Trussell Trust says:

> Rather than acting as a service to ensure people do not face destitution, the evidence suggests that for people on the very lowest incomes . . . the poor functioning of universal credit can actually push people into a tide of bills, debts and, ultimately, lead them to a food bank. People are falling through the cracks in a system not made to hold them. What little support available is primarily offered by the third [charity] sector, whose work is laudable, but cannot be a substitute for a real, nationwide safety net.
>
> (Butler and Duncan, 2018)

The National Audit Office maintains that there is no evidence Universal Credit helps people into work, and moreover, it is unlikely to provide value for money with the system in many ways unwieldy and inefficient. There are calls for delays in implementation and for the system to be fixed before it is rolled out to millions of further claimants. Whistle-blowers maintain that the system is badly designed, broken and glitches regularly lead to hardship for claimants with one saying that design problems existed due to failure to understand what claimants need, particularly when they do not have digital skills or internet access. He said, 'We are punishing claimants for not understanding a system that is not built with them in mind' (Savage, 2018).

In October 2018, former Conservative prime minister Sir John Major warned against Universal Credit being introduced 'too soon and in the wrong circumstances'. He argued that people who faced losing out in the short term had to be protected, 'or you run into the sort of problems the Conservative Party ran into with the poll tax in the late 1980s' (BBC News, 2018). At the time of writing (July 2020) the Conservative government seems to have 'got away with it'. There is more than a suspicion that the plight of the poor and benefit claimants enjoys far from widespread concern amongst a population long desensitized by a populist media defining such people as 'workshy' and 'scroungers'. But by April 2020, there had been a huge explosion in the number of Universal Credit claimants as an outcome of the COVID-19 coronavirus and the resulting government-ordered lockdown, which made many people unable to work and without an income. Now a new huge cohort of people previously unfamiliar with the benefits system were about to experience a rude awakening to its limitations, not least the inadequate level of payments.

Many people currently excluded from employment are fit enough to make a useful contribution to society. If such employment opportunities can be created, introductory schemes will help pay for themselves by being a significant part of a restructuring of the economy and crucially part of a longer-term return to a full-employment economy. Only a few years ago, apparently the fanciful meanderings of dreamers and those accused of living in the past, full-employment policies are becoming mainstream and popular with economists and politicians across the political spectrum in different countries.

Economist Robert Pollin (2012) argues that the US – at that time faced with its highest levels of unemployment since the Great Depression – should put full employment back on the agenda, observing that such a policy would help individuals, families and significantly the economy as a whole while promoting equality and social stability. The biggest obstacle to creating a return to full employment, he argued, was the absence of a political will and the crucial opposition of neoliberals opposed to any constraint on profitability. In the UK, Tony Dolphin and Kate Lawton, 2013) have argued that by reducing levels of unemployment and inactivity among the working-age population, policies designed to increase the employment rate could help to raise the incomes of low-income households and ease the burden on the tax and benefit system. Adopting full employment as a goal would also present opportunities to address both regional inequalities and those associated with gender and disability and to enable more people access to the paid work which is vital for a sense of social identity, participation and well-being. This is a view which is gaining support across the political spectrum in the UK and becoming increasingly influential in the US (Lawrence, 2013).

Indeed, in the intervening years, there has been a significant decline in unemployment in both the US and the UK with the latter enjoying its lowest level of unemployment for 40 years. We are indeed seeing a return to full employment, and moreover, this time it has the approval of neoliberals, not least because most jobs that have been created are low paid with little or no job security, zero-hours contracts and 'self-employment' in the gig economy. Unless the individual has a particular, scarce marketable skill, they are invariably paid at one of two low pay rates – the minimum wage or the slightly higher living wage. Radical moral communitarian does not support this form of low-paid insecure employment but the provision of proper jobs with good conditions of employment. At the time of writing, such jobs are in short supply and those lucky enough to be in secure jobs increasingly seeing their conditions of employment – including pension provision – very much under attack.

Suitable accommodation

The second identified right of citizens in a radical moral communitarian society should be access to suitable good quality affordable accommodation, of an acceptable size and proper rights of tenure, with the rent paid linked to the ability to pay and reviewable periodically. There should also be an end to the stigmatization of local authority and housing association estates as 'social housing' or even worse 'sink estates'. Conservatives Greenhalgh and Moss (2009) controversially – but quite correctly – observed that social housing had become synonymous with welfare housing where both a 'dependency culture' and a 'culture of entitlement' had come to predominate. Two-thirds of social tenants of working age were found to be unemployed with only 22% in full-time employment. Fifty per cent of social housing – some 2 million homes – is located in the most deprived 20% of the country. The authors of the report observe that public-sector housing is run as a national service which fails many of the very people it was designed to help and delivers a risible return on assets. This view is not just held by Conservatives. The then Labour mayor of Newham, Sir Robin Wales, told a conference that many 'council estates have become what they were fighting in the first place – social ghettos'.

There is a clear need to deliver rebalanced mixed communities which incentivizes people into employment instead of leaving them in welfare ghettos. Good-quality housing built to decent specifications with proper sound-proofing should be made available to wider sections of society on proper long-term tenancy agreements providing that the tenants do not engage in antisocial behaviour. Hopkins Burke and Hodgson (2013) propose the rebalancing of communities so that 'respectable' people are in the majority and where it is their standards of behaviour which prevail. The researchers thus propose the provision of public-sector housing for key workers with rents dependent on income and designated accommodation provided for recognizable serving police officers and others from the 'policing family' as part of a return to the 'police house' system. This inclusive housing strategy would help rebalance and restore communities to the glory days of public-sector housing in the 1950s and 1960s when this author as a child and his family were tenants along with 56% of the population. Assistance should also be provided for young people who wish to buy their homes and who find themselves excluded from the market as incomes stagnate, go down and the price of houses forever increase, not least as the limited available supply is bought by landlords often with mortgages. 'Generation rent' we are told. If this is the case there should be a proper public sector house building programme, so families are not forced to live in substandard accommodation which profits only private landlords.

Entitlement to respect

The third identified right of all citizens should be the entitlement to be treated fairly with respect by all agencies, institutions and individuals regardless of their social position, occupation, age, disability, ethnicity, gender, religion and sexual preferences. It will be the responsibility of all individuals to reciprocate this behaviour or face appropriate sanctions. Mutual respect should be central to any moral communitarian project but will be difficult to achieve in a society epitomized by an excessively unequal division of labour and neoliberal greed. Conversely, a more equal division of labour – with more equitable pay differentials – will help provide a culture of respect for different occupational groups. not least front-line health workers who remain very poorly paid regardless of their newly acquired 'hero' status in dealing with the COVID-19 pandemic.

Good-quality health care

The fourth identified right of all citizens should be the provision of good-quality health care which means in the UK supporting and publicly funding the existing National Health Service (NHS). With the current worldwide pandemic, the importance of a properly funded NHS has never been more apparent. Clearly starved of resources by government austerity policies since 2010, the NHS has struggled to cope with the biggest health crisis since at least the 1980s' AIDS pandemic. A crucial difference between the two crises being that in the current case front line workers are themselves being sacrificed, dying in sizeable numbers for want of proper protective equipment. It has become the thing for hordes of grateful citizens on lockdown to stand outside their homes at 8 p.m. on a Thursday evening to applaud these key workers for their efforts and sacrifices. But for many, the fact that these regular 'love-ins' are led by cynical government ministers, who have been responsible for the serious underfunding of the NHS and were among loudly cheering Conservative members of Parliament when legislation to pay for wage increases for poorly paid nurses was defeated in the House of Commons in 2017.

It should nevertheless be the responsibility of all citizens to actively pursue good health and the failure to do so will involve ultimately a state health and welfare (not criminal) intervention against, for example, those with alcohol, drugs and dietary (obesity) problems. The key to this strategy is the progressive decriminalization but not the legalization of drugs which it is interesting to note is increasingly taking place in the US, which has conducted an extremely expensive (in terms of human lives lost and economic resources) war against drugs for many years and which it has shown no sign of winning. Illegal drug production, smuggling and dealing are both extremely profitable at all levels of the hierarchy of demand and supply while, at the same time, it is a major employer with well-paid involvement very much a rational choice for many excluded from the legitimate good life by the paucity of opportunity. Crime can clearly pay.

A six-year study of Britain's drug laws by leading scientists, senior police officers, academics and experts concluded that the time had come to introduce decriminalization (The Guardian, 2012). The report by the UK Drug Policy Commission, an independent advisory body, advised that possession of small quantities of controlled drugs should no longer be a criminal offence and concluded that the move would not lead to a significant increase in use. The report noted that the criminal sanctions imposed on the 42,000 people sentenced each year for possession of all drugs – and the 160,000 given cannabis warnings – should be replaced with simple civil penalties, such as a fine, attendance at a drug awareness session or a referral to a drug treatment programme. Imposing minimal sanctions on those growing cannabis for personal use could also go some way to undermining the burgeoning illicit cannabis factories controlled by organized crime.

The report observed that existing draconian drugs policies struggle to make an impact and, in some cases, may actually make the problem worse. The current UK approach is seen to be simplistic in seeing all drugs as problematic and fails to recognize that entrenched drug problems are linked to inequality and social exclusion and that the separation of drugs from alcohol and tobacco use makes it more difficult to tackle the full range of substance use. The £3bn a year spent tackling illegal drugs is not based on any evidence of what works, with much of the money wasted on policies which are not cost-effective. Even the large-scale seizures by the police often have little or no sustained impact on the supply of drugs. 'Just Say No' campaigns in schools sometimes actually lead to more young people using drugs.

Good-quality education

The fifth identified right of all citizens should be the provision of good-quality education for all and every effort should be made to ensure that standards are maintained, improved and appropriate to the skills and aptitudes of individuals with a close fit and links to employment opportunities. But not all young people take advantage of these opportunities and it is their responsibility – and crucially that of parents and carers – to ensure that they do so with appropriate sanctions taken against those who do not and/or are disruptive.

Following the post-2008 financial meltdown and the subsequent era of sustained austerity, there was to be increased calls for government to invest in education and the reason for this is self-evident. Education is an excellent investment for individuals and societies both in monetary and non-monetary interests and values. The reality is that education – and the acquisition of knowledge as a value in itself, to both the individual and community – is often lost in the pursuit of neoliberal economic goals and is one which should be prioritized by radical moral communitarianism, acting in accordance with UNESCO principles. These essentially state that education is not a privilege – to be delivered or not at the whim of the individual neoliberal state – but an essential human right to be enjoyed by all.

Education as a human right means three things. First, the right to education is legally guaranteed for all without discrimination. Second, states have the obligation to protect, respect, and fulfil the right to education. Third, there are ways to hold states accountable for violations or deprivations of the right to education. Human rights are essential to all human beings, regardless of nationality, sex, national or ethnic origin, colour, religion, language or any other status. They cannot be given or taken away.

Human rights are the foundation for freedom, justice and peace in the world. They are formally and universally recognized by all countries in the Universal Declaration on Human Rights. Since the adoption of the UDHR, many treaties have been adopted by states to reaffirm and guarantee these rights legally. International human rights law sets out the obligations of states to respect, protect and fulfil human rights for all. These obligations impose specific duties on states, regardless of their political, economic and cultural systems. All human rights are universal, indivisible, interdependent and inter-related Vienna Declaration and Programme of Action, 1993: para. 5. Equality and non-discrimination are fundamental and cross-cutting principles in international human rights law. This means that all human rights apply to everyone.

International human rights law guarantees the right to education. The UDHR, adopted in 1948, proclaims in Article 26: 'everyone has the right to education'. Since then, this right has been widely recognized and developed by a number of international normative instruments elaborated by the United Nations, including the International Covenant on Economic, Social and Cultural Rights 1996; the Convention on the Rights of the Child 1989; and the UNESCO Convention against Discrimination in Education 1996.

Both individuals and society benefit from the right to education. It is fundamental for human, social and economic development and a key element to achieving lasting peace and sustainable development. It is a powerful tool developing the full potential of everyone and ensuring human dignity and in promoting individual and collective well-being. In brief, (1) it is an empowerment right, (2) it lifts marginalized groups out of poverty, (3) it is an indispensable means of realizing other rights and (4) it contributes to the full development of the human personality (see the Committee on Economic, Social and Cultural Rights' General Comment 13 on the right to education 1999: para. 1.

The right to education encompasses both entitlements and freedoms, including (1) the right to free and compulsory primary education; (2) the right to available and accessible secondary education (including technical and vocational education and training), made progressively free; (3) the right to equal access to higher education on the basis of capacity made progressively free; (4) the right to fundamental education for those who have not received or completed primary education; (5) the right to quality education both in public and private schools; (6) the freedom of parents to choose schools for their children which are in conformity with their religious and moral convictions; (7) the freedom of individuals and bodies to establish and direct education institutions in conformity with minimum standards established by the state; and (8) the academic freedom of teachers and students.

The 4As were developed by the first UN Special Rapporteur on the right to education, Katarina Tomaševski, and adopted by the Committee on Economic, Social and Cultural Rights in its General Comment 13 on the right to education 1999: para. 6. To be a meaningful, education in all its forms and at all levels should exhibit these interrelated and essential features:

- *Available* – Education is free and there is adequate infrastructure and trained teachers able to support the delivery of education.
- *Accessible* – The education system is non-discriminatory and accessible to all, and positive steps are taken to include the most marginalized.
- *Acceptable* – The content of education is relevant, non-discriminatory and culturally appropriate and of quality; schools are safe, and teachers are professional.
- *Adaptable* – Education evolves with the changing needs of society and challenges inequalities, such as gender discrimination; education adapts to suit locally specific needs and contexts.

Violations of the right to education may occur through direct action of state parties (act of commission) or through their failure to take steps required by law (act of omission). Concrete examples are given in paragraph 59 of General Comment 13.

Whilst the vast majority of countries have ratified international treaties that recognize the full right to education, it is still denied to millions around the world due to lack of resources, capacity and political will. There are still countries that have not integrated the right to education into their national constitution or provided the legislative and administrative frameworks to ensure that the right to education is realized in practice. Most of the children and adults who do not fully enjoy the right to education belong to the most deprived and marginalized groups of society which are often left behind in national policies.

Protection from crime and antisocial behaviour

The sixth right that all citizens should enjoy – appropriately in a book which is ostensibly about crime and criminality – protection from crime and antisocial behaviour and should be able to expect appropriate adequate public-sector protection. It is thus the responsibility of citizens to not engage in criminality, but it would be clearly overly utopian to suggest that everyone will abstain and desist from criminality, not least in a neoliberal society where illegitimate opportunities abound and easily outnumber well-paid legitimate ones for many people. Those who do not accept their responsibility to society not to engage in such activities should be nonetheless targeted and dealt with efficiently and appropriately by the agencies of the criminal justice system but with the crucial recognition that our prison system is full of people who could and should be dealt with without that sanction.

The research evidence – much of it reviewed elsewhere in this book – has repeatedly shown that prisons only work in the sense that they keep people off the street for a period, while it is an extremely expensive containment strategy that very rarely does anything more than contain. Little happens during the negative experience of imprisonment that turns prisoners into better citizens by the time of their eventual release, and it is not surprising that the great majority return within a very short period of their release. Incarceration is moreover painful and damaging with those regimes built on reputations for gratuitous toughness being inherently criminogenic. Prisoners are separated from their families and social networks, they are terminally stigmatized and labelled, they are part of an inherently antisocial subculture and social norms and they lack meaningful activity and lose all autonomy. Meanwhile, some 'lifestyle offenders' – those who are actually proud of their criminality – thrive in prison. They certainly do not find prison hard and it can actually enhance their image (Travers et al., 2013).

Travers et al. (2013) argue that prisons could actually be positive experiences for the inmates and actually reduce offending with the introduction of a cognitive skills intervention which addresses the hierarchy of their needs. At the first level, there is a basic need for a safe and decent carceral environment, which gives the individual the headspace to think about a personal transformation, free from dirt, disorder, clutter and graffiti. The second level requires the development of a rehabilitative culture which is dependent on a strong staff engagement with this ethos, a willingness to participate and strong leadership skills to bring about these changes. The third level is about dealing with the very significant issues of drugs and alcohol which are central to much contemporary offending and which are closely linked to the lives of many prisoners with close links to acquisitive crimes and those involving violence. The fourth level is about changing attitudes to criminality and the researchers observe that the hard-line approach so favoured by neoliberals – notions of deterrence epitomized by 'three strikes and you're out' initiatives, 'scared straight' and boot camps for young offenders – simply do not work. Conversely, it is those initiatives with strong links to communitarianism such as restorative justice conferences which bring offenders and their victims together and help reduce crime and help to rebuild and invigorate communities. Such strategies should be central to a fully inclusive radical moral communitarian social policy agenda.

Conclusion

It is the central proposition of communitarianism that the individual rights promoted by traditional liberals need to be balanced with social responsibilities and a commitment made by the individual to the community in which they live. But we have observed how the balance between rights and responsibilities has shifted excessively and unhealthily towards the pole of community, with a much greater emphasis on the responsibilities of individuals to the detriment of their rights. Communitarianism has thus become a key component of the neoliberal project with the notion of responsibility in the former highly compatible with that of responsibilization in the latter.

A highly significant element of the neoliberal disciplinary project in both the US and the UK has been the abandonment of full-employment as a central economic strategy, but in the long term, this has been hugely problematic. First, the major neoliberal economic restructuring of the 1980s destroyed traditional income-creating manufacturing jobs in huge numbers, with the outcome being a large non-productive workless sector with growing associated social problems. Second, this situation was significantly intensified by the rapid expansion of a whole class of public-sector employees paid increasingly good salaries to look after (health and social work agencies) and control (the criminal justice system) the first sector. There was a clear, recognized need to rebalance the economy and the Coalition government which came to power in 2010 sought to address this issue by the introduction of established neoliberal techniques of huge cuts in public expenditure and concerted assaults on the living standards of increasingly more sectors of workers and the workless poor. Most public-sector workers have received on average a 18% reduction in their incomes in the intervening years with significant benefit cuts and ongoing income freezes, the workless poor have fared even worse. Food banks unknown for most of the long life of this author are now commonplace, not just for the workless but also for the low paid such as our now widely recognized heroic and deserving nurses who also find it difficult to find affordable accommodation.

Hopkins Burke (2015) proposed that these various socio-economic problems appeared to have reached a 'tipping point' where the social and economic costs of neoliberal fiscal policies had come to outweigh any benefits other than for a small group of powerful economic players. A radical moral communitarian response would be the introduction of an alternative more inclusive approach founded on notions of appropriate contributions to society (obligations and responsibilities), suitable fair rewards (rights) and consensual interdependency in the context of a fairer, more equal world, based on mutual respect between all citizens.

These identified rights and responsibilities are highly compatible and closely inter-connected. Thus, the call for a return to legitimate full-employment policies would – it was argued – lead not only to a more productive and balanced economy but also to the provision of the material and psychological preconditions of the other essential rights. The provision of good quality (invariably rented public-sector) accommodation for all those who need it is also about rebuilding communities by providing a broad mix of interrelated interdependent people from different social backgrounds within a particular geographical neighbourhood. The right to be treated with respect by all public servants and with the parallel responsibility to treat each other with respect is more achievable in a world of full employment and good-quality accommodation in proper communities where people have respect both for themselves and for others and their contribution to society. The provision of good-quality health care for all citizens with the parallel responsibility to pursue good health will be more achievable with sensible alcohol and drug policies which decriminalize and medicalize a significant social problem. The provision of good quality education and the parallel responsibility to engage with this is also far more achievable in a society with full employment and citizens with good health and is highly applicable to the right to live in a crime-free society.

The provision of proper alternative rational choices to crime and criminality will – it is argued – lead to a significant reduction in the need to treat and punish miscreants and in this rebalanced economy provide more resources for highly skilled professionals and practitioners to concentrate their expertise on the very small groups of citizens with real medical or social problems. Clearly central to a radical moral communitarian social strategy will be an enhanced role for an expertise-driven public sector both in service provision and in wealth creation.

But how could all of this be brought about? What would be the ignition factor that helped to transform our society into something fairer and morally communitarian? The problems faced by a failing world neoliberal economy have been clearly identified in this book, but following the General Election in late 2019 – and the election of a Conservative government highly committed to that worldview – the possibilities looked further away than ever. And then? Well, the novel coronavirus and a worldwide COVID-19 pandemic. Suddenly it looked as though the world would never be the same again. Cue speculation and discussion in the concluding chapter.

Summary of main points

1 Mainstream communitarianism emerged in the US during the 1980s as a response to what its advocates considered to be the limitations of liberal theory and practice.

2 The dominant themes are (1) the individual rights that have been vigorously promoted by traditional liberals need to be balanced with social responsibilities and (2) autonomous individual selves do not exist in isolation but are shaped by the values and culture of communities.

3 Communitarians thus propose that, unless we redress the balance towards the pole of community, our society will continue to become normless, self-centred and driven by special interests and power seeking.

4 Radical egalitarian communitarians focus on inequality, deprivation and the market economy as causes of crime and promote policies to eliminate poverty, which they define as a degree of deprivation which seriously impairs participation in society.

5 The whole notion of community is complex and extends well beyond the more traditional definitions based on locality – or neighbourhood – and embraces a multiplicity of groups and networks to which, it is believed, we all belong.

6 These communities of care are considered more relevant to contemporary modern living in urban societies because they provide a developed notion of 'community' whereby membership – or social identity – is personal and does not necessarily carry any fixed or external attributes of membership.

7 Durkheim observed that – with organic society – it was now possible to believe in self-indulgence – for both the bourgeoise and proletarian – the only check would be conflict.

8 Durkheim considered that the division of labour works best if people are in positions where their talents are best optimized – that is an ideal division of labour. The actual division of labour in society is nevertheless forced, egoistical, anomic and riddled with individual despair and conflict. The solution is thus the creation of an ideal division of labour.

9 It is the work of Emile Durkheim and his observations on the moral component of the division of labour in society which provides the theoretical basis of a radical moral communitarianism, which actively promotes the rights and responsibilities of both individuals and communities but in the context of an equal division of labour.

10 Policies should be introduced which recognize that people and communities have both rights and responsibilities and that there is a fine balance between them. This balance will invariably require negotiation and renegotiation.

Discussion questions

1 In what ways does communitarianism differ from traditional liberalism?

2 What is radical egalitarian communitarianism, and in what ways does it differ from the variant promoted by Etzioni?

3 Briefly outline the differences between Anglo-Saxon, French and German individualism.

4   What is an 'equal division of labour', and what are its implications for radical moral communitarianism?
5   Briefly outline the main principles of moral communitarianism.

Suggested further reading

Etzioni (1993, 1995a, 1995b) should be consulted for an introduction to the notion of communitarianism, while Dennis and Erdos (1992) discuss the 'parenting deficit' in a UK context. Jordan (1992, 1996), Currie (1993, 1996, 1997) and Young (1999) should be consulted on radical egalitarian communitarianism. Hopkins Burke and Hodgson (2013) discuss radical moral communitarianism in terms of antisocial behaviour. Hopkins Burke (2014, 2015) provides an introduction to the theoretical foundations and implications of radical moral communitarianism.

Notes

1 Normativity is the phenomenon in human societies of designating some actions or outcomes as good or desirable or permissible and others as bad or undesirable or impermissible.
2 John Rawls suggests that you imagine yourself in an original position behind a veil of ignorance. Behind this veil, you know nothing of yourself and your natural abilities, or your position in society. Behind such a veil of ignorance, all individuals are simply specified as rational, free and morally equal beings.
3 Responsibilization is a term developed in the governmentality literature to refer to the process whereby subjects are rendered individually responsible for a task which previously would have been the duty of another – usually a state agency – or would not have been recognized as a responsibility at all. The process is strongly associated with neoliberal political discourses, where it takes on the implication that the subject being responsibilization has avoided this duty or the responsibility has been taken away from them in the welfare state era and managed by an expert or government agency.
4 Governmentality is an expression originally formulated by the twentieth-century French philosopher Michel Foucault combining the terms *government* and *rationality*. Government in this sense refers to conduct, or an activity meant to shape, guide or affect the conduct of people.
5 The six benefits being replaced are income-based Employment and Support Allowance, income-based Jobseekers Allowance, Income Support, Child Tax Credit, Working Tax Credit and Housing Benefit.

References

Adams, D. and Hess, M. (2001) 'Community in Public Policy: Fad or Foundation', *Australian Journal of Public Administration*, 60(2): 13–23.
BBC News (2018) 'Major: Universal Credit Like 0s Poll Tax', October11. [Online] Available from: www.bbc.co.uk/news/uk-politics-451797 [Accessed 30 April 2020].
Bellah, R.N. (ed) (1985) *Habits of the Heart: Individualism and Commitment in American Life*. London: University of California Press.
Berlin, I. (2002) *Freedom and its Betrayal*. Princeton, NJ: Princeton University Press.
Blair, T. (1998) The Third Way: New Politics for the New Century. London: The Fabian Society.
Bouwsma, W.J. (1988) *John Calvin: A Sixteenth-Century Portrait*. New York: Oxford University Press.
Braithwaite, J. (1989) Crime, Shame and Reintegration. Cambridge: Cambridge University Press.
Braithwaite, J. and Daly, K. (1994) 'Masculinities, Violence and Communitarian Control', in T. Newburn and E.A. Stanko (eds.) Just Boys Doing Business? Men, Masculinities and Crime. London: Routledge, 19–213.

Butler, P. and Duncan, P. (2018) 'People with "Nowhere Else to Turn" Fuel Rise in Food', *The Guardian*, 24 April.

Cavadino, M. and Dignan, J. (2006) *Penal Systems: A Comparative Approach*. London: Sage.

Clear, T.R. and Karp, D.R. (1999) *The Community Justice Ideal: Preventing Crime and Achieving Justice*. Boulder, CO: Westview.

Crawford, A. and Clear, T.R. (2003) 'Community Justice: Transforming Communities through Restorative Justice?', in E. McLaughlin, R. Fergusson, G. Hughes and L. Westmarland (eds.) *Restorative Justice: Critical Issues*. London: Sage/Open University.

Currie, E. (1985) *Confronting Crime: An American Challenge*. New York: Pantheon Books.

Currie, E. (1993) *Reckoning: Drugs, the Cities and the American Future*. New York: Hill and Wang.

Currie, E. (1996) *Is America Really Winning the War on Crime and Should Britain Follow Its Example? NACRO 30th Annual Lecture*. London: NACRO.

Currie, E. (1997) 'Market, Crime and Community', *Theoretical Criminology*, 1(2): 147–72.

Delanty, G. (2003) *Community*. London: Routledge.

Dennis, N. and Erdos, G. (1992) *Families Without Fatherhood*. London: Institute for Economic Affairs.

Dolphin, T. and Lawton, K. (2013) *A Job for Everyone: What Should Full Employment Mean in 21st Century Britain?* London: Institute for Public Policy Research.

Driver, S. and Martell, L. (1997) 'New Labour's Communitarianisms', *Critical Social Policy*, 52: 27–46.

Dumont, L. (1986) *Essays on Individualism: Modern Ideology in Anthropological Perspective*. Chicago: University of Chicago Press (First published in French in 1983).

Dumont, L. (1994) *German Ideology: From France to Germany and Back*. Chicago, IL: The University of Chicago Press.

Durkheim, E. (1933 originally 1893) *The Division of Labour in Society*. Glencoe, IL: Free Press.

Emanuel, E. (1991) *The Ends of Human Life: Medical Ethics in a Liberal Polity*. Cambridge, MA: Harvard University Press.

Etzioni, A. (1993) *The Spirit of Community: The Reinvention of American Society*. New York: Touchstone.

Etzioni, A. (ed.) (1995a) *New Communitarian Thinking: Persons, Virtues, Institutions and Communities*. Charlottesville, VA: University of Virginia Press.

Etzioni, A. (1995b) *The Parenting Deficit*. London: Demos.

Etzioni, A., Glendon, M.A. and Galston, W. (1991) *The Responsive Communitarian Platform*. Washington, DC: The Communitarian Network.

Foucault, M. (2004) *The Birth of Biopolitics*. London: Palgrave Macmillan.

Giddens, A. (1998) *The Third Way: The Renewal of Social Democracy*. Cambridge: Polity Press.

Glendon, M.A. (1991) *Rights Talk: The Impoverishment of Political Discourse*. New York: Free Press.

Greenhalgh, S. and Moss, J. (2009) *Principles for Social Housing Reform*. London: Localis.

The Guardian (2012) 'Decriminalise Drug Use, Say Experts after Six-Year Study'. [Online] Accessed at: Travers, R., Wakeling, H., Mann, R.E. and Hollin, C. (2013) 'Reconviction Rates Following a Cognitive Skills Intervention', *Legal and Criminological Psychology*, 01/2013; 1: 4–65.

Hall, S., Winlow, S. and Ancrum, C. (2008) *Criminal Identities and Consumer Culture: Crime, Exclusion and the New Culture of Narcissism*. Cullompton: Willan Publishing.

Hirschi, T. (1969) *Causes of Delinquency*. Berkeley, CA: University of California Press.

Hirschi, T. (1995) 'The Family', in J.Q. Wilson and J. Petersilia (eds.) *Crime*. San Francisco, CA: ICS Press.

Hirschi, T. and Gottfredson, M. (1995) 'Control Theory and the Life Course Perspective', *Studies on Crime and Crime Prevention*, 4: 131–42.

Hirschi, T. and Gottfredson, M. (2004) 'Self Control and Crime', in R.F. Baumeister and K.D. Vohs (eds.) *Handbook of Self-Regulation, Theory and Application*. New York: Guilford.

Hopkins Burke, R.D. (1999) Youth Justice and the Fragmentation of Modernity. Scarman Centre for the Study of Public Order Occasional Paper Series, The University of Leicester.

Hopkins Burke, R.D. (2012) *Criminal Justice Theory: An Introduction*. Abingdon, Oxon: Routledge.

Hopkins Burke, R.D. (2013) 'Theorizing the Criminal Justice System: Four Models of Criminal Justice Development', *Criminal Justice Review*, September (3): 335–53.

Hopkins Burke, R.D. (2014) 'The Case for a Radical Moral Communitarianism', *British Journal of Community Justice*, 12(3): 5–1.

Hopkins Burke, R.D. (2015) 'The Case for a Radical Moral Communitarian Agenda', *British Journal of Community Justice*, 13(1): 7–23.

Hopkins Burke, R.D. and Hodgson, P. (2013) 'Responding to Repeat Anti-Social Behaviour and Moral Communitarianism', paper given to the British Society of Criminology Conference 2013, 'Criminology on Trial', University of Wolverhampton, July 1–4.

Hopkins Burke, R.D. and Pollock, E. (2004) 'A Tale of Two Anomies: Some Observations on the Contribution of (Sociological) Criminological Theory to Explaining Hate Crime Motivation', *Internet Journal of Criminology*, November.

Houdt, J.F. van and Schinkel, W. (2013) 'A Genealogy of Neoliberal Communitarianism', *Theoretical Criminology*, 17: 493–515.

Hughes, G. (1998) *Understanding Crime Prevention: Social Control, Risk and Late Modernity*. Buckingham: Open University Press.

James, D. (2010) *Fichte's Social and Political Philosophy: Property and Value*. Cambridge: Cambridge University Press.

Jordan, B. (1992) 'Basic Income and the Common Good', in P. van Parisjs (ed.) *Arguing for Basic Income*. London: Verso.

Jordan, B. (1996) *A Theory of Social Exclusion and Poverty*. Cambridge: Polity Press.

Jordan, B. (1998) 'New Labour, New Community?', *Imprints*, 3(2): 113–31.

Lacey, N. (2013) 'Punishment, (Neo)liberalism and Social Democracy', in J. Simon and R. Sparks (eds.) *The Sage Handbook on Punishment and Society*. New York: Sage.

Lawrence, M. (2013) 'Vast Majority of Wage Earners are Working Harder and for Not Much More: Trends in U.S. Work Hours and Wages over 1979–2007', *Economic Policy Institute Issue Brief No. 34*. Available from: www.epi.org/publication/ib34-trends-us-work-hours-wages-

Nisbet, H.B. (1985) *German Aesthetics and Literary Criticism: Winckelmann, Lessing, Hamann, Herder, Schiller, Goethe*. Cambridge: Cambridge University Press.

O'Malley, P. (1992) 'Risk, Power and Crime Prevention', *Economy and Society*, 21(3): 252–75.

Osborne, D. and Gaebler, T. (1993) *Reinventing Government: How the Entrepreneurial Spirit Is Transforming the Public Sector*. New York: Penguin.

Pollin, R. (2012) *Back to Full Employment*. Boston: The MIT Press.

Pribram, K. (1953) 'Patterns of Economic Reasoning', *American Economic Review*, 43(2), Supplement.

Rawls, J. (1971) *A Theory of Justice*. Cambridge, MA: Harvard University Press.

Ross, P. (2003) 'Marxism and Communitarianism', Imprints, 6(3): 215–43.

Savage, M. (2018) 'Complex Rules for Universal Credit See One in Five Claims Fail', *The Guardian*, May 12.

Scruton, R. (2001) The Meaning of Conservatism, 3rd ed. Houndmills: Palgrave.

Strang, H. (1995) 'Replacing Courts With Conferences', *Policing*, 11(3): 20.

Travers, R., Wakeling, H., Mann, R. E. and Hollin, C. (2013) 'Reconviction Rates Following a Cognitive Skills Intervention', *Legal and Criminological Psychology 01/2013*, 1: 4–65.

Troelsch, E. (1925) *The Christian Faith*. Minneapolis: Fortress Press.

Van Ness, D. and Strong, K.H. (1997) *Restoring Justice*. Cincinnati, OH: Anderson Publishing.

Van Swaaningen. R. (2008) 'Sweeping the Street: Civil Society and Community Safety in Rotterdam', in J. Shapland (ed.) *Justice, Community and Civil Society: A Contested Terrain*. Cullompton: Willan Publishing.

Verneaux, R. (1945) *L'idéalisme de Renouvier*. Paris: Vrin.

Wacquant, L. (2009a) *Prisons of Poverty*. Minneapolis: University of Minnesota Press.

Wacquant, L. (2009b) *Urban Outcasts: A Comparative Sociology of Advanced Marginality*. Cambridge: Polity Press.

Wacquant, L. (2009c) *Punishing the Poor: The Neoliberal Government of Social Insecurity*. Durham, NC: Duke University Press.

Young, J. (1999) The Exclusive Society: Social Exclusion, Crime and Difference in Late Modernity. London: Sage.

Chapter 21

Conclusion

Post-COVID-19 society

Key issues

1   100 days that shook the world
2   The experts are back in fashion
3   COVID-19 conspiracy theories
4   A turning point in history
5   Pandemic crime opportunities

The story so far . . .

Q: 'Why do you think that people commit crime?'
ME: 'Because it makes sense to them in the circumstances in which they find themselves'.

Explaining why people commit crime can be a complex matter. Much depends on how you define crime. If an act is not designated a crime – usually by the criminal law – then the person undertaking the activity cannot legitimately be called a criminal. That brings us to the issue of criminal motivation, or why it is that people commit crime? Well, there are a whole range of acts which are designated offences, and these appear to be committed by very different people. Thus, coming up with a general explanation of criminal motivation does appear to be a rather tall order, although some have tried but never with complete success.

We saw in our brief review of criminological theories in Chapter 3 – which in itself is a resume of the more extensive discussion of these issues in the companion text (Hopkins Burke, 2018) – that there are three competing but invariably compatible models for explaining criminal behaviour. First, there is the rational actor model which proposes that individuals enjoy free will and can choose to commit criminal acts, in very much the same way that they choose other activities. It is their choice. Second, the predestined actor model rejects the idea that human beings enjoy free will and, in contrast, proposes that behaviour is determined by factors over which the individual has little or no control. These factors can be internal to the person – either biological or psychological – or external. In the latter sociological case, there is something in the environment of the individual which encourages criminal behaviour. In all three variants, crime is most likely the destiny of the individual. Third, the victimized actor model proposes that it is invariably the disadvantaged and powerless in society whose activities are criminalized and targeted by an unfair criminal justice system skewed in favour of the rich and powerful. But it is important to note that this latter model excludes neither the rational actor nor predestined actor model propositions entirely from its explanatory schema. It thus crucially recognizes that although people make choices, these are invariably not in the circumstances of their choosing. Choices available are invariably seriously limited by circumstances in which the individual finds themselves, and it may well be the case that criminal enterprise provides the best available choice.

People commit crime because it makes sense to them in the circumstances in which they find themselves. There is something about the nature of the society in which we live that provides the essential criminogenic socio-economic circumstances which make criminal behaviour of some kind or another – it might be, for example, a bit of street drug dealing, burglary, theft from your employer, driving your high-performance car at excessive speeds on the motorway, domestic violence, being drunk and disorderly or designing a nice little earner of a Ponzi scheme[1] – appear an appropriate option choice in the circumstances in which you find yourself. This book identifies the two most significant macro criminogenic circumstances present in contemporary society: (1) the postmodern condition and (2) neoliberalism.

Postmodernism is, of course, at least a partial successor to modernism. The term postmodern condition is preferred in this text because it is accepted that modern societies not only continue to exist but, in many ways, also remain the dominant philosophical epoch. The postmodern condition nevertheless poses a range of challenges to modernism in an era fundamentally characterized by the fragmentation of modernity.

The principal features that best illustrate the idea of modern society can be identified in three areas. First, in the area of economics, there has been the development of a market economy which has involved the growth of production for profit, rather than immediate local use, the development of industrial technology with a considerable extension of the division of labour (where production is broken down into many separate tasks) and where wage labour has become the principal form of employment. Second, in politics, there has been the growth and unification of the centralized nation state and the extension of bureaucratic forms of administration (where most of the important decisions of government are taken by state officials rather than politicians), systematic forms of surveillance and control, the development of representative democracy and political party systems. Third, in the area of culture, there has been a challenge to local folk traditions in the name of rationality with the emphasis on scientific and technical knowledge.

The fundamental difference between modernism and postmodernism is that modernist thinking is about the search for an abstract truth of life – a grand theory, metanarrative or sacred text – that explains all and which will provide a road map for how we should design our society, live our lives and – in the case of criminology – explain why people commit crime and how we should respond; postmodern thinkers, on the other hand, believe that there is no universal truth, abstract or otherwise, merely a multiplicity of truths, each as valid as the other.

Postmodernism is thus a late twentieth-century movement characterized by broad scepticism, subjectivism or relativism; a general suspicion of reason; and an acute sensitivity to the role of ideology in asserting and maintaining political and economic power. It is essentially a reaction to the assumed certainty of scientific, or objective, efforts to explain reality that are very much a part of modernist society. Lyotard (1976) famously defines the postmodern as 'incredulity towards metanarratives', whereby metanarratives are understood as totalizing stories about history and the goals of the human race that ground and legitimize knowledges and cultural practices. A metanarrative is a narrative about narratives of historical meaning, experience or knowledge, which offers a society legitimation through the anticipated completion of a (as-yet-unrealized) master idea. For example, if only the proletariat could cast off its false consciousness and recognize its historical role as the revolutionary class then – with a bit of push and shove – communist nirvana is just around the corner. Lyotard draws our attention to the mass murder committed by twentieth-century leaders – for example Stalin, Mao and Pol Pot – who rigorously pursued variants of that idea.

One of the most distinctive characteristics of the postmodern condition is a loss of rational and social coherence in favour of cultural images, social reforms and identities marked by fragmentation, multiplicity, plurality and indeterminacy. Parts of it are wonderful and well intentioned, while others, not so much. Advantages include freedom of expression, individualism and tolerance. Disadvantages include a lack of reason and objectivity when needed, rejection of 'grand' narratives such as collectivism and welfarism and a cynical sense of irony towards society. No discourse should be prioritized. All views are equally valid. Experts and their belief in the sanctity of their scientific knowledge are a part of the problem.

Postmodernist thinkers have developed concepts like difference, repetition, trace and hyper-reality to subvert 'grand narratives', univocity of being and epistemic certainty. Postmodern philosophy questions the importance of power relationships, personalization and discourse in the 'construction' of truth and worldviews. Human nature is just a myth. There is no essence that makes us who we are. There is no self-identity, central personality or permanent soul. It is a fragmented world with a multiplicity of viewpoints where a rational modernist government appears an impossibility. The only thing seeming to hold it all altogether are the realities of living in a neoliberal society, and these are far from attractive for most people.

Neoliberalism is a specific contemporary form of free-market capitalism that has come to largely dominate global economics. It was originally referred to as 'globalization' and began with 'free-trade deals' in the last two decades of the twentieth century and the 'anti-globalization' protests at the end of that century can be seen as not very successful attempts to resist neoliberalism. It is in the main a resurgence of nineteenth-century ideas associated with laissez-faire economic liberalism and free-market capitalism.

Neoliberalism is currently used to refer to market-oriented reform policies, such as eliminating price controls, deregulating capital markets and lowering trade barriers, essentially through the reduction of state influence in the economy, especially through the use of privatization and austerity as economic measure. But – as shown in this book – neoliberalism is in crisis. It is increasingly failing to deliver the economic goods.

The central tenet of neoliberalism is economic growth through increasing competition by deregulation of social, welfare, health, labour and environmental laws, opening domestic markets to foreign competition, limiting the role of the state by the privatization of state assets and the liberalization of economic policies. But problematically, neoliberalism nurtures inequality. The wealthiest 62 people on this planet own as much wealth as the bottom half 3.5 billion, with the top 1% more wealthy than the remaining 99%. Large sections of the population in both the US and the UK have been in revolt against this situation, as demonstrated by large-scale support for Trump and Sanders in the US and the Brexit vote in the UK. It is a popular revolt often described as populism.

The neoliberal era is being undermined from two directions. First, its record of economic growth is now far from successful. Second, those who have lost out – and many have – are no longer prepared to acquiesce in their fate. Populists tend in the main to be nativist and suspicious of foreigners, but this is not universal, being more likely to be found on the political right than the left. The problem today is that – across a number of crucial areas of public life – the basic intuitions of populists have been repeatedly verified. Politicians have openly lied and cannot be trusted. At best, they have failed to deliver on their policies. Experts are no longer trusted. The nightmare of competing political discourses where that of your local conspiracy theorist is just as plausible as a government expert has become reality.

Then, after three years of haggling in the UK Parliament, convulsions at the top of the government and pleas by some for Brussels to delay its exit, the UK left the EU on 31 January 2020. It is a country hugely divided across cultural, age and education lines as is the case in the US. A major study of national attitudes warned of a potential rise in far-right and anti-Islam sentiments unless politicians tackled long-standing disaffections and social divisions behind the Brexit vote. The future looked at best challenging but mainly bleak. Then something happened . . .

100 days that changed the world

A turbulent decade had reached its final day. It was New Year's Eve 2019, and much of the world was preparing to celebrate.

Michel Safi (2020) observes that the obituaries of the past decade had focused on eruptions and waves that would shape the era ahead: Brexit, the Syrian civil war, refugee crises, social media proliferation with nationalism and populism roaring back to life. But they were written too soon.

It was not until these last hours, before the toasts and countdowns had commenced, that the most consequential development of all broke the surface. Something that was to change the world forever.

At 1:38 p.m. on 31 December, a Chinese government website announced the detection of a 'pneumonia of unknown cause' in the area surrounding the South China seafood wholesale market in Wuhan, an industrial city of 11 million people.

The outbreak was one of at least a dozen to be confirmed by the World Health Organization (WHO) that December, including cases of Ebola in West Africa, measles in the Pacific and dengue fever in Afghanistan. Outside China, its discovery was barely noticed.

Over the next 100 days, the virus would freeze international travel, extinguish economic activity and confine half of humanity to their homes, infecting more than a million people. By the middle of April, more than 75,000 would be dead.

Wednesday 1 January: Wuhan seafood market shut down

The Wuhan seafood market is ordinarily bustling, but this morning police are weaving tape between its metal frames and hustling owners to shut their blue roller doors. Workers in hazmat suits carefully take samples from surfaces and place them in sealed plastic bags.

Concerned messages are circulating on Chinese social media, fuelled by medical documents that have found their way online, warning that patients have been presenting at Wuhan hospitals with ominous symptoms.

'Sars is basically certain, don't let the nurses go out,' one message says. Another says: 'Wash your hands. Masks. Gloves'.

Authorities in Taiwan are watching with alarm. The island is already implementing health precautions: arrivals on direct flights from Wuhan are being screened for flu-like symptoms on the tarmac in Taipei before they can disembark. Within two days, Singapore and Hong Kong will be monitoring arrivals from the city at their borders.

In Wuhan, eight people accused of spreading 'rumours' about the disease are summoned to the Public Security Bureau. Another who will be reprimanded is a Wuhan ophthalmologist, Li Wenliang, for showing a group of his medical school alumni an analysis of the virus he believed was SARS.

Phrases such as 'unknown Wuhan pneumonia' and 'Wuhan seafood market' are already censored on YY, a popular livestreaming platform.

Thursday 9 January: novel coronavirus identified

The mystery disease is identified: Chinese scientists say the sick patients in Wuhan have contracted a previously undiscovered coronavirus.

Two coronaviruses, SARS and Middle Eastern Respiratory Syndrome (MERS), have already sparked pandemics this century. This new one is deadly too. Last night, a 61-year old man died in a Wuhan hospital, the first-known victim.

At this stage, the official caseload is falling. Sequencing the virus has allowed doctors to strike off patients who were thought to be infected but who, in fact, only had ordinary pneumonia. No new coronavirus cases have been announced for four days.

Later, a study will conclude that at this point the epidemic was doubling in size every week. Tomorrow, Li Wenliang, the ophthalmologist, will start to show symptoms.

Monday 13 January: Thailand reports first case

More than a week has passed since Wuhan health authorities last confirmed a case of the novel coronavirus. There has been nothing since the city began hosting an important annual meeting between state and provincial party officials.

But the virus has slipped the net. Thailand reports its first case, involving a 61-year-old Wuhan resident whose high temperature was detected by a thermal surveillance scanner in Bangkok airport.

Nervtag, committee of infectious disease specialists meets in London to discuss the virus and deems the risk to the UK to be 'very low but warrants investigation and testing'.

The Chinese government says there is not yet clear evidence of human-to-human transmission, including any signs of medical professionals becoming sick. The official message is echoed by the WHO, which issues a news release saying it is reassured of the quality of the Chinese government's response.

Epidemiologists say the news is encouraging. 'If there are no new cases in the next few days, the outbreak is over', Guan Yi, a professor of infectious diseases at the University of Hong Kong, tells the *New York Times*.

Doctors in Wuhan are seeing a different picture. Studies will later show that for more than a fortnight, hospitals in the city have been dealing with 'an exponential increase' in cases with no link to the seafood market.

Monday 20 January: human-to-human transmission confirmed

Zhong Nanshan, a trusted respiratory expert and the public face of the Chinese government response, goes on state television with bad news: two new cases of the virus have surfaced in Guangdong province among patients with no direct contact with Wuhan.

The conclusion is clear. 'We can say it is certain that it is a human-to-human transmission phenomenon', Zhong says.

Having seemed to vanish in China for more than a fortnight, the virus is now appearing across the country. On Friday night there were four new cases. By Sunday, 139. By the end of tomorrow, cases will have been confirmed in Beijing and Shanghai.

It is spreading around the world: Japan, South Korea, and the US, where yesterday a 35-year-old man who had recently returned from Wuhan presented to a clinic in Washington state with a cough and a high fever, becoming the first case in the country.

Donald Trump received his first substantive briefing on the virus two days previously, during a session where he interrupted to ask when flavoured vaping products would return to the market, according to the *Washington Post*.

Panic is growing in Wuhan. At 6 a.m., more than 100 patients with coronavirus symptoms were waiting to be seen at the city's Xiehe hospital, a worker tells the *Guardian*.

Friday 24 January: virus arrives in Europe

On the eve of the lunar new year holiday, as hundreds of millions of Chinese people are travelling to visit friends and family, Wuhan has, in effect, been sealed off. Most transport in and out of the city is suspended. More than 800 infections have been detected, and 25 people are dead.

The city is the first to experience the full glare of the outbreak: rapid increases in caseloads, hospitals under severe strain and an entire population quarantined.

The virus arrives in Europe, detected in two recent arrivals from China and a relative. The trio have had dozens of contacts and French authorities say they are racing to track down possible cases. 'You have to treat an epidemic as you treat a fire', says the French health minister, Agnès Buzyn.

Trump received his first media question about the virus while in Davos two days previously. Asked if he was concerned by a potential pandemic, he replied: 'Not at all. And we have it perfectly under control'.

Tomorrow, China's lockdown will be widened to include 56 million people. The president, Xi Jinping, will warn that the country is facing a 'grave situation'. And Liang Wudong, a physician at the Xinhua hospital in Hubei, will become the first medical professional to die.

Friday 31 January: outbreak passes milestone on Brexit Day

After nearly four years of agonizing debate in parliament and across the country, at 11 p.m., Britain formally exits the EU. But it is also a milestone day for the coronavirus: by the end of day, the outbreak will be larger than SARS. It will be confirmed to have reached the UK. Spain and Italy will detect their first cases.

Nobody has died outside China, but in China, the death toll is accelerating, now at 258, with more than 11,000 infected. The US announces it is banning foreigners who have recently been in China from entering the country.

Tuesday 4 February: first death outside China

The official case count in China passes 20,000, with 425 dead. A Wuhan resident who developed severe pneumonia last week dies in a hospital in Manila in the Philippines, the first person to succumb to the virus outside China. The Philippines bans any new arrivals from China.

The director general of the WHO says the international spread of the disease appears to be 'minimal and slow', although it could still worsen, and there is no need to unnecessarily halt trade and travel.

A London man arriving at Gatwick Airport from Shanghai tells the *Guardian* that he is alarmed at the lax approach there. He filled out a form detailing his contact information and onward travel plans but says it was ignored.

In Wuhan's central hospital, Li Wenliang's condition is worsening. His death in three days' time will trigger howls of rage and grief in the locked-down city and across China.

The former directors of a White House pandemic preparedness office disbanded in 2018 publish an opinion piece in the *Wall Street Journal*. 'Stop a US Coronavirus Outbreak Before It Starts,' the headline says.

Tomorrow the US Centers for Disease Control and Prevention will start distributing coronavirus testing kits across the country. But the devices are flawed, and over the next month, the US will carry out just over 1,200 tests, while South Korea and Germany run at least 12,000 per day.

In a few days' time, Trump will tell a rally in New Hampshire that the outbreak will soon ease. 'By April, you know, in theory, when it gets a little warmer, it miraculously goes away', he will say.

Wednesday 19 February: concerns over South Korea church

Rigorous testing and diligent contact tracing are paying off in South Korea, where just 30 cases of the virus have been recorded up to yesterday. But the 31st case, detected yesterday, is worrying authorities.

The woman, 61, belongs to a secretive megachurch and attended two services while ill. She ignored doctors' initial requests that she be tested for coronavirus, instead going to lunch at a hotel buffet. Officials determine she has had at least 1,160 risky contacts. 'After that, [the virus] just exploded', Korea's foreign minister, Kang Kyung-who, will later say.

Iran announces its first two confirmed cases, both in the holy city of Qom.

In Milan, Atalanta continue their fairy-tale run in the Champions League, defeating the Spanish club Valencia 4–1, the stadium heaving with every goal. 'Roughly a third of the population of the small town of Bergamo was present at the San Siro stadium,' a match report says. Thousands of Spaniards also made the journey to the capital of Lombardy Province for the game.

Tuesday 25 February: virus takes hold globally

Global cases have exceeded 80,000. For the first time since the outbreak was announced, cases confirmed outside China outnumber those inside. On official numbers, Beijing reached the peak of its outbreak two days ago when 150 people died.

Others are just starting their climbs. Italy recorded its first death four days ago and now has 11 fatalities. About 50,000 people across northern Italy have been under lockdown for the past four days, the first population in Europe to be quarantined.

Iran's death toll is believed to be largest outside China, with at least 12 fatalities confirmed officially and as many as 50 thought to have died in Qom alone. The disease is striking down the Islamic Republic's elites: its deputy health minister appeared on television sweating profusely as he said the virus was under control. This afternoon, Iraj Harirchi confirms he has tested positive.

As the US announces its 14th case, Trump tweets during a state visit to India: 'The coronavirus is very much under control in the USA. Stock Market starting to look very good to me!'

Friday 6 March: Italy in crisis as UK records first death

Italy's death toll has grown sixfold in six days: more than 230 Italians are dead, and caseloads are growing by more than 1,200 every day. Rome has shut schools, banned spectators from Serie A football matches and is preparing to ringfence Lombardy. 'The health system risks going into overload and we will have a problem with intensive care if an exponential crisis continues', says the prime minister, Giuseppe Conte.

A woman in her 70s becomes the first person to die from the virus in Britain, and Downing Street says the virus is now likely to spread 'in a significant way'.

Three days ago, at a press conference, Boris Johnson raised eyebrows when he said he was continuing to shake hands. 'I was at a hospital the other night where I think there were a few coronavirus patients and I shook hands with everybody', he said.

Wednesday 11 March: COVID-19 declared a pandemic

In a rare Oval Office address, Trump announces that his administration is embarking on 'the most aggressive and comprehensive effort to confront a foreign virus in modern history'.

The number of cases in the US has passed 1,000 and more than 116,000 people are infected worldwide.

Stock markets in the US and the UK are collapsing faster than at any time since the financial crash in 2008, panicked by the virus and a Saudi–Russian oil price war.

Deaths in Italy increase by 168 in a single day, the highest figure recorded anywhere. An image of an exhausted Italian nurse collapsed over her desk goes viral. The country is facing its 'darkest hour'', Prime Minister Conte says.

The WHO declares what has become obvious: COVID-19 is a pandemic.

Britain has 456 cases but is resisting the kind of mass shutdowns being implemented elsewhere in Europe. Sick and vulnerable people are being advised to stay home, but the government is leaning towards the view that the cost of totally suppressing the virus will be too high in terms of lost liberties. Allowing its spread might also 'build up some kind of herd immunity so more people are immune to this disease', Sir Patrick Vallance, England's chief scientific adviser, will later tell the BBC.

Tuesday 17 March – normal life on hold across world

European nations are sealing off their borders from each other, and the continent is sealing off from the world. 'We are at war', the French president, Emmanuel Macron, declares.

Deaths in Italy are now exceeding 450 each day and will soon outnumber those in China. Confirmed cases in Spain will double to more than 17,000 by the end of the week. Three-quarters of those who have died from the disease are European.

Every hour is bringing new developments: more cases, more deaths and more restrictions on movement. Australians overseas receive an unprecedented request to return home as soon as possible. The French are banned from riding bikes. California's 40 million residents are advised not to leave their homes.

Downing Street moves to urgently revise its strategy, including building herd immunity, after modelling lands on Boris Johnson's desk showing that it might cost half a million British lives and send the National Health Service (NHS) into meltdown.

In Burkina Faso, a former vice-president of the parliament dies from the virus, the first confirmed COVID-19 fatality in sub-Saharan Africa. By the end of the week, there will be 1,000 cases on the continent. More than 160,000 cases have been confirmed around the world.

Monday 23 March: Britain issues lockdown order

Confirmed cases around the world have exceeded 370,000, including more than 6,600 Britons. In what is one of the most-watched moments in British television history, Boris Johnson orders the closing of all non-essential businesses and urges the country: 'You must stay at home'.

Nearly 400 die in Spain, its highest daily toll so far. It will prove to be the lowest toll for at least the next fortnight.

More than 5,000 new cases are confirmed in New York, bringing the state's total to 20,000. By the end of the week, the US will have the most infections in the world.

The wave appears to be receding in China, which this week recorded its first day with no cases of domestic transmission, including in Hubei, the province where the disease first appeared.

Tomorrow India's prime minister, Narendra Modi, will urge his nation to 'forget what going out means' for the next three weeks. The lockdown order will trigger one of the largest human migrations across the subcontinent since it was partitioned in 1947, as workers try to return to their home states. It means more than 3.5 billion people around the world are now living under some form of quarantine.

Thursday 2 April: another grim milestone passed

At around 8.40 p.m. GMT, the Johns Hopkins University count of people confirmed to have COVID-19 passes 1 million, with more than 50,000 people dead. The sick include Boris Johnson, who says he is showing only minor symptoms and is still able to preside over the UK government's response.

In Hungary, the prime minister, Viktor Orbán, has been granted the power to rule by decree with no time limit.

In India, a second case is discovered in Dharavi, a vast slum area in Mumbai and one of the most densely populated places on Earth, fuelling fears that the country's outbreak may be significantly worse than the official tally of 2,069 cases.

Deaths in Spain exceed 950 in a single day, the most yet recorded. Figures show a record 6.6 million Americans filed for unemployment benefits in the previous week, in addition to the more than 3 million who did so the previous week. The US has nearly a quarter of a million cases and 6,000 deaths. Field hospitals have been set up in New York's Central Park, and refrigerated trucks are being used to store the dead. Trump warns of a 'very, very painful two weeks' ahead.

Wednesday 8 April: future course of pandemic still unknown

Boris Johnson remains in hospital, having been admitted to intensive care on Monday after his symptoms worsened.

In some of Europe's worst-hit countries, new transmissions and deaths are falling. China has recorded its first day with zero deaths and is cautiously reopening cities.

Last Saturday may have been the deadliest day so far, with more than 6,500 fatalities around the world. But with some of the poorest and most populous countries still officially relatively untouched by the virus, it is too early to say for sure.

Singapore, which was celebrated for its swift response, has introduced a strict quarantine amid signs of a possible second wave of infections. Vaccines are being fast-tracked but are unlikely to be in mass supply for at least 18 months.

Pakistan is reopening its construction sector. With a quarter of its population in poverty, the country is walking a tightrope between slowing down the virus and 'ensuring people don't die of hunger and our economy doesn't collapse', says the prime minister, Imran Khan.

A global total of more than 75,000 people are dead and 1.3 million have been infected. About 270,000 have recovered. There is no agreed-on strategy for how to return life to normal.

And that was to prove to be only the beginning. Things were to go from bad to very much worse. With no end in sight, it was patently obvious to many of us that this pandemic was having a very similar impact to a World War. At the time of writing – mid-June – it looked very unlikely this would all be over by Christmas. But one thing was certain. Experts were back in fashion.

The experts are back in fashion

John Harris (2020) observes that the arrival of the COVID-19 virus was to push the state and public sector into the foreground. The government machine suddenly looked less like an unfortunate inconvenience – which annoys people like government advisor Dominic Cummings – but more like the best means of help we have. Only weeks previously, people close to Prime Minister Boris Johnson had declared war on the civil service and the BBC. Both were now at the heart of how we were to collectively proceed. Ministers were suddenly back on the prestigious Radio 4 Today programme having previously refused to appear on political grounds. Mindful that people had actually not had enough of experts, Johnson was now at pains to be seen to be deferring to the chief medical officer and the government's chief scientific adviser. The arrival of COVID-19 seemed to mean that revolutionary plans for the state had been put on hold. Well at least for the time being, as it turned out.

Something comparable seemed to be happening in the US. The *New York Times* ran a piece of political analysis titled 'Trump Meets an Enemy That Can't Be Tweeted Away'. Writer Peter Baker (2020) said: 'COVID-19 does not respond to Mr Trump's favourite instruments of power: it cannot be cowed by Twitter posts, it cannot be shot down by drones, it cannot be overcome by party solidarity, it cannot be overpowered by campaign rally chants.' Reality, it seemed, had suddenly intruded on a presidency built on performance and manipulation, and Trump had instantly been found wanting.

There was an undeniable truth to all this regardless of political viewpoint. The US was way behind other countries on testing, and cuts made by the Trump administration to crucial branches of government now appeared extremely reckless. The kind of denial the president was still promoting only a week or so previously formed part of the same picture: with accidental echoes of the occasion when Boris Johnson in 2006 had paid humorous tribute to laissez-faire government by praising the fictional mayor from Jaws and his decision to keep his beaches open, Trump had recently been lampooned as the real thing, downplaying a mounting emergency, lest it threaten the economic success on which his re-election might depend (Baker, 2020).

Woven through this take on the position of the president is a progressive article of faith: the idea that although populists might be capable rabble-rousers, they always fall down when it comes to basic competence. Harris (2020) observes that this, clearly, was the collective rationale of the Democratic Party for the anointment of Joe Biden as their presidential candidate, seen as the walking embodiment of the idea that the best alternative to the misrule of Trump was the reassuringly dull, conventional statesmanship of yesteryear.

For a long time now, all over the world, politics and government and their surrounding discourse had increasingly amounted to a spectacle of anger, rhetoric and a supposed battle of values in which the political right – particularly its latter-day, populist incarnation – had usually been on the winning side. The story perhaps begins with George W Bush's consigliere Karl Rove and his contemptuous characterization of the then president's detractors as 'the reality-based community': its subsequent milestones including both the arrival in office of a president whose metier is outrage and provocation rather than anything material and the triumph of prejudice and romance over facts and figures epitomized by Brexit.

But as reality bites, something about coronavirus feels like it might at least have loosened the grip of these ideas. Whatever his outbursts, every day was to bring unflattering footage of Trump among scientists, officials and the representatives of big US companies and the image of an awkward, impatient man, arms folded, seemingly determined to shut out whatever wisdom might be on offer. At the same time, the BBC's *Newsnight* broadcast a characteristically nuanced view of the government's response to the virus from arch-populist former UK Independence Party (UKIP) now Brexit Party leader and serially unelectable politician, Nigel Farage, to a loud chorus of groans. His inclusion seemed not just incongruous but also silly. And therein lay a tantalizing prospect: of a political discourse that might sooner or later reconnect to the basics of government and the real world.

Europe nevertheless remained haunted by populists, predictably claiming that the virus validates everything they stand for: Matteo Salvinia (Italy), Marine Le Pen (France) and Viktor Orbán (Hungary), the latter whose national security adviser had recently claimed to see 'a certain link between coronavirus and illegal migrants'. Harris (2020) tells of being on a reporting job in Worksop, the former Nottinghamshire mining town in a local government district whose vote-share for Brexit had been nearly 70%. The huge TV in the breakfast room was blaring out a piece about COVID-19, which soon caught the attention of the staff member in charge. 'I think this is all bollocks', he said. 'You're not going to tell me it was a coincidence it started in an overpopulated country', Two 50-something men had just ordered their food and instantly joined in. 'The first thing they can do is stop all these refugees coming in', said one. Their position was stubborn disbelief, mixed with the conviction that this latest emergency would not have arrived had it not been for foreigners.

Trump had nevertheless changed his position on COVID-19. Now, as evidenced by his ban on flights from Europe, his embrace of drastic measures being framed by the kind of themes that had won him the presidency. His patter now contained the giveaway words

'America first' and 'foreign virus'. By way of mood music, senior Republicans were now talking about the pandemic as the 'Chinese coronavirus' or 'Wuhan coronavirus', and everything blurs into the ocean of conspiracy theory now swirling around online, which Trump was inevitably happy to encourage.

COVID-19 conspiracy theories

Kuper (2020) observes that every pandemic generates conspiracy theories. Thus, the coronavirus is a bioweapon created by China, or Big Pharma, or American scientists, or it is caused by 5G technology, or it does not exist, just a 'hoax' made up by the enemies of Donald Trump. Moreover, conspiracy theorists also warn that any future 'vaccines' will be a trick by governments to subjugate populations. These false beliefs will have significant consequences. They will make it harder to end this pandemic with a vaccine. They also risk making our politics even more dysfunctional. Lynas (2020) considers the ten most popular conspiracy theories relating to COVID-19.

Blaming 5G

This conspiracy theory should be easy to debunk it is biologically impossible for viruses to spread using the electromagnetic spectrum. The latter are waves/photons, while the former are biological particles composed of proteins and nucleic acids. But that is not the point. Conspiracy theories are enticing because they often link two things which at first might appear be to be correlated; in this case, the rapid rollout of 5G networks was taking place at the same time the pandemic hit. Cue a viral meme linking the two avidly promoted by anti-vaccine activists who have long been spreading fears about electromagnetic radiation, actively encouraged by the Kremlin.

It is worth repeating – as the WHO notes – viruses cannot travel on mobile networks, and COVID-19 is spreading rapidly in many countries that do not have 5G networks. Even so, this conspiracy theory – after being spread by celebrities with big social media followings – has led to cell phone towers being set on fire in the UK and elsewhere.

Bill Gates as scapegoat

Most conspiracy theories – like the viruses they resemble – constantly mutate and have several variants circulating at any one time. Many of these plots and subplots seem to involve Bill Gates, who became a new target of disinformation after gently criticizing the defunding of the WHO. According to the *New York Times*, anti-vaxxers, members of QAnon and right-wing pundits have seized on a video of a 2015 TED Talk given by Gates – where he discussed the Ebola outbreak and warned of a new pandemic – to bolster their claims he had foreknowledge of the COVID pandemic or even purposely caused it.

A recent variant of this conspiracy theory, particularly beloved by anti-vaccination activists, is the idea that COVID is part of a dastardly Gates-led plot to vaccinate the world's population. There is some truth in this, of course: vaccinating much of the world's population may well be the only way to avoid an eventual death toll in the tens of millions. But anti-vaxxers do not believe that vaccines work. Instead, some have spread the myth that Gates wants to use a vaccination programme to implant digital microchips that will somehow track and control people. The spread of misinformation has meant that

ID2020, a small non-profit organization that focuses on establishing digital IDs for poorer people around the world, has had to call in the Federal Bureau of Investigation. (Note: The Cornell Alliance for Science – the source of the information contained here – is partly funded by the Bill & Melinda Gates Foundation, and this section will undoubtedly be considered part of the conspiracy by some.)

The virus escaped from a Chinese lab

This one at least has the benefit of being plausible. It is true that the original epicentre of the epidemic, the Chinese city of Wuhan, also hosts a virology institute where researchers have been studying bat coronaviruses for a long time. One of these researchers, Shi Zhengli, a prominent virologist who spent years collecting bat dung samples in caves and was a lead expert on the earlier SARS outbreak, was sufficiently concerned about the prospect that she spent days frantically checking lab records to see if anything had gone wrong. She admits breathing a 'sigh of relief' when genetic sequencing showed that the new SARS-CoV-2 coronavirus did not match any of the viruses sampled and studied in the Wuhan Institute of Virology by her team.

But, the sheer coincidence of China's lead institute studying bat coronaviruses being in the same city as the origin of the COVID outbreak has proved too much for conspiracists to resist. The idea was seeded originally via a slick hour-long documentary produced by the *Epoch Times*, an English-language news outlet based in the US with links to the Falun Gong religious cult that has long been persecuted by the Chinese Communist Party (CCP). The *Epoch Times* insists on calling COVID 'the CCP virus' in all its coverage. The theory has now tipped into the mainstream, being reported in the *Washington Post*, the *Times* (UK) and many other outlets.

COVID was created as a biological weapon

A spicier variant is that COVID not only escaped from a lab, but it was intentionally created by Chinese scientists as a biowarfare weapon. According to Pew Research, 'nearly three-in-10' Americans believe that COVID-19 was made in a lab, either intentionally or accidentally (the former is more popular: specifically, 23% believe it was developed intentionally, with only 6% believing it was an accident).

This theory that the Chinese somehow created the virus is particularly popular on the US political right. It gained mainstream coverage thanks to US Senator Tom Cotton (Republican–Arizona) who amplified theories first aired in the *Washington Examiner* (a highly conservative media outlet) that the Wuhan Institute of Virology 'is linked to Beijing's covert bio-weapons program'.

This theory can be easily debunked now that there is unambiguous scientific evidence – thanks to genetic sequencing – that the SARS-CoV-2 virus has entirely natural origins as a zoonotic virus originating in bats. The *Examiner* has since added a correction at the top of the original piece admitting the story is probably false.

The US military imported COVID into China

The Chinese government responded to the anti-China theories with a conspiracy theory of its own that seeks to turn blame back around onto the US. This idea was spread initially by Chinese foreign ministry spokesman Zhao Lijian, who tweeted 'it's possible that the US military brought the virus to Wuhan'. These comments, according to Voice of America news, 'echoed a rumoured conspiracy, widely circulated in China, that US military personnel had brought the virus to China during their participation in the 2019 Military World Games in Wuhan last October.' For China, as the *Atlantic* reported, this conspiracy theory, and an accompanying attempt to rename COVID the 'USA virus', was a transparent 'geopolitical ploy' – useful for domestic propaganda but not widely believed internationally.

GMOs are somehow to blame

Genetically modified crops have been a target of conspiracy theorists for years, so it was hardly a surprise to see genetically modified organisms (GMOs) blamed in the early stages of the COVID pandemic. In early March, Italian attorney Francesco Billota penned a bizarre article for *Il Manifesto*, falsely claiming that GM crops cause genetic pollution that allows viruses to proliferate due to the resulting environmental 'imbalance'. Anti-GMO activists have also tried to blame modern agriculture, which is strange, since the known path of the virus into the human population – as with Ebola, HIV and many others – was through the very ancient practice of people capturing and killing wildlife.

Ironically, GMOs will almost certainly be part of any vaccine solution. If any of the ongoing 70 vaccine projects work (which is a big if), that would be pretty much the only guaranteed way the world can get out of the COVID mess. Vaccines could be based on either GM attenuated viruses or use antigens produced in GM insect cell lines or plants. If GMOs do help save the world from the curse of COVID, maybe they will stop being a dirty word.

COVID-19 does not actually exist

According to professional conspiracy theorists like David Icke and InfoWars' Alex Jones, COVID-19 does not actually exist but is a plot by the globalist elite to take away our freedoms. Early weaker versions of this theory were prevalent on the political right in the notion that the novel coronavirus would be 'no worse than flu' and later versions are now influencing anti-lockdown protests across several states in the US and beyond. Because believers increasingly refuse to observe social distancing measures, they could directly help to spread the epidemic further in their localities and increase the resulting death rate.

The pandemic is being manipulated by the 'deep state'

Some believe that a 'deep state' of the US elite is plotting to undermine the president and that Dr. Anthony Fauci, the face of the US coronavirus pandemic response, is a secret member. Fauci's expression of disbelief when the deep state was mentioned during a press briefing supposedly gave the game away.

COVID is a plot by Big Pharma

Many conspiracy theory promoters are in reality clever actors trying to sell quack products. Alex Jones, between rants about hoaxes and the New World Order, urges viewers to buy expensive miracle pills that he claims can cure all known diseases. Dr. Mercola, a quack anti-vax and anti-GMO medic who has been banned from Google due to peddling misinformation, claims that vitamins – and numerous other products he sells – can cure or prevent COVID. NaturalNews, another conspiracist site, sells all manner of pills, potions and prepper gear. These conspiracists depend for their market on getting people to believe that evidence-based (i.e. conventional) medicine does not work and is a plot by big pharmaceutical companies to make us ill. Big Pharma conspiracies are a staple of anti-vaccination narratives, so it is hardly surprising that they have transmuted into the age of the coronavirus.

COVID death rates are inflated

Another far-right meme is the idea that COVID death rates are being inflated, and therefore, there is no reason to observe lockdown regulations or other social distancing measures. Prominent in promoting this myth is Dr. Annie Bukacek, whose speech warning that COVID death certificates are being manipulated has been viewed more than a quarter of a million times on YouTube. Bukacek appears in a white lab coat and with a stethoscope around her neck, making her look like an authoritative medical source. Dig a little deeper, however, as *Rolling Stone* magazine did, and it turns out she is actually a far-right anti-vaccination and anti-abortion activist previously noted for bringing tiny plastic foetuses into the Montana state legislature. Her insistence that COVID death rates are inflated has, of course, no basis in fact. More likely the current death toll is a serious under-count.

COVID-19 conspiracies explored

The virus is the perfect generator of conspiracy theories. It is literally an invisible enemy, points out Catherine Fieschi, founder of the research group Counterpoint. She says: 'It's not very satisfying to blame the virus. Instead of a virus that you can't see, you blame a 5G tower that you can see'. She adds that blaming it on a combination of China, Huawei and 5G is 'the equivalent of one of those dreams you wouldn't take to your psychoanalyst because it's so banal' (Kuper, 2020).

Unprecedented numbers of people have been alone, a state which makes them more susceptible to conspiracy theories. They have been forced to stay at home by governments, have been losing their livelihoods and spending hours on social media, where conspiracy theories run rife, even if tech platforms have now finally tried hard to censor them. WhatsApp is as a particularly powerful vector because people tend to trust messages from friends and family. Meanwhile, when people turn on the (mainstream) news, they see distrusted politicians reciting false numbers (official statistics on deaths and infections have almost all been underestimates), flanked by scientists who cannot make up their minds. One week, the authorities say there is no problem; the next, we are all locked up. Someone who mistrusts the authorities will also mistrust their instructions to change behaviour. We saw this during the AIDS epidemic, when many South Africans and Americans who believed conspiracy theories about the virus continued having unprotected sex and did not get tested or take antiretroviral drugs.

Most epidemiologists have agreed on the best path out of this pandemic: first, tracking the virus by monitoring the locations of people through their phones, followed by later, a vaccine. But both these initiatives risk hitting a wall of mistrust. Even before the pandemic, there were well-founded fears of invasion of privacy (the characteristic business model of our time) as well as unfounded fears of vaccinations (always pushed by Russia). Trump himself linked vaccines with autism. Now conspiracy theorists were warning that a vaccine against COVID-19 fitted neatly into a government masterplan for mass surveillance or enslavement. The master puppeteer is often identified as Bill Gates. Fox News anchor Laura Ingraham quoted a tweet that said, 'Bill Gates Calls for a "Digital Certificate" to Identify Who Received Covid-19 Vaccine', adding her comment: 'Digitally tracking Americans', every move has been a dream of the globalists for years. This health crisis is the perfect vehicle for them to push this'.

In 2019, the US reported the greatest number of measles cases since 1992. According to the Centers for Disease Control and Prevention, there were 1,282 individual cases of measles in 31 states in 2019, and the majority were among people who were not vaccinated against measles. It was yet another example of how the proliferation of anti-vaccine messaging has put public health at risk, and the COVID-19 pandemic was only intensifying the spread of misinformation and conspiracy theories.

Neil Johnson is a physicist at George Washington University, where he directs the Complexity and Data Science initiative, specializing in combining 'cross-disciplinary fundamental research with data science to attack complex real-world problems'. The initiative published a study in *Nature* mapping how clusters of hate groups interconnect to spread narratives and attract new recruits (Johnson et al., 2020). They found that the key to the resilience of online hate is that the networks spread across multiple social media platforms, countries and languages.

Johnson referred to the rapidly eroding trust in health and science expertise as a 'new world war' being waged online, fuelled, in part, by distrust of 'Big Pharma' and governments but also by the proliferation of misinformation about key topics in health and science (vaccines, climate change, genetically modified organisms, to name a few). The conflict has only intensified with the COVID-19 pandemic. Following his war analogy, he decided to try to build a useful map of the online terrain to better understand how this distrust evolves. And he started with the topic of vaccines.

Johnson *et al.* (2020) analysed Facebook communities actively posting about the topic of vaccines during the 2019 measles outbreak – more than 100 million users in all – from around the world, mapping out the interconnected networks of information across cities, countries, continents and languages. They found three main groups: (1) communities that were pro-vaccine, (2) communities that were anti-vaccine and (3) communities that were neutral or undecided (groups focused on parenting, for instance).

The researchers then tracked how the various communities interacted with each other to create a detailed map of the networks:

> It's not geographic, it's to do with closeness in a social network sense – in terms of information, influence. . . . It's not whether I'm here and someone's in Australia. It's the fact that someone in Australia agrees with my slightly twisted narrative on COVID-19 and I'm getting their feed. Although my neighbour doesn't understand me, the person in Australia does.
>
> (Kuper, 2020)

The results were surprisingly counter-intuitive. While there were fewer individual people who were anti-vaccine on Facebook, there were almost three times as many anti-vax communities clustered around Facebook groups and pages. So any pro-vaccine groups seeking to counter the anti-vaccine misinformation often targeted larger communities and missed the small to medium-sized clusters growing rapidly just under their radar.

While Johnson *et al.* (2020) expected their data to show major public health organization and state-run health departments in central positions in these networks, they found just the opposite: those communities were typically fighting the misinformation war on the wrong battlefield entirely. It is similar to focusing on battling one big wildfire and missing the many different small brush fires threatening to spread out of control. In fact, 'it's even worse than that. It's almost like all the fire departments are in the other valley. They've already put out the fires there, so they're just sitting down relaxin'' (Kuper, 2020). In other words, the pro-vaccine groups were not reaching and interacting with the undecided groups nearly as effectively as the anti-vaccine communities.

With the COVID-19 pandemic, the spread of misinformation has got even worse. Johnson has attributed this disconnect in part to the lack of diverse narratives being promoted by the most reliable scientific sources. 'They're into these large blue Facebook pages that are very straightforward with their message . . . go and get a vaccine and do all the guidance that we tell you' (Kuper, 2020). In contrast, the anti-vaccine narratives are tailored to mesh well with a broad variety of Facebook groups and pages. Each one of these pages has its own flavour of distrust. For example one will be devoted to distrust of Microsoft's Bill Gates, while another will be focused on how world governments are supposedly behind a given outbreak, and still another could be a parenting group for those whose children show signs of autism and are convinced it is because of vaccines.

A good example of this type of insidious social spreading can be found in an article by Adrienne LaFrance (2020) in *The Atlantic*, where she investigates the followers of the QAnon conspiracy theory.[2] A 62-year-old New Hampshire woman named Shelly stumbled on a QAnon video while browsing YouTube for something else – 'she can't remember for what, exactly, maybe a tutorial on how to get her car windows sparkling clean'. Now she has become a true believer. The ironic twist is that she is the mother of a political-science professor at the University of Miami named Joseph Uscinski who specializes in researching conspiracy theories.

More bad news: COVID-19 misinformation was now being weaponized beyond these clusters to extreme online hate clusters (such as neo-Nazis) on other platforms. Winning the war against such malicious matter – it is argued – will require an understanding of the entire online battlefield and new approaches that do not rely on future global collaboration being achieved between social media platforms. A study by scientists at the University of Ottawa in Canada searched YouTube for the most widely viewed videos in English relating to COVID-19 (Oi-Yee and Bailey, 2020). They narrowed it down to 69 videos with more than 247 million views between them and then assessed the quality of the videos and the reliability of the information presented in each. using a system developed specifically for public health emergencies.

The majority of the videos (72.5%) presented only factual information. But 27.5% – or one in four – contained misleading or inaccurate information, such as believing pharmaceutical companies were sitting on a cure and refusing to sell it, incorrect public health recommendations, racist content and outright conspiracy theories. Those videos – which mostly came from entertainment news, network and internet news sources – accounted for about a quarter of the total views (roughly 62 million). The videos that scored the highest in terms of accuracy, quality and usefulness for the public, by contrast, did not achieve as many views.

The implications are clear: COVID-19 related misinformation is reaching more people than in past public health crises – such as the swine flu (H1N1) pandemic and outbreaks of Ebola and Zika viruses – because YouTube is becoming more of a source of health information for members of the public:

> YouTube is a powerful, untapped educational tool that should be better mobilized by health professionals. . . . Many existing marketing strategies are static, in the form of published guidelines, statistical reports, and infographics, and may not be as appealing or accessible to the general public.
>
> (Kuper, 2020)

Johnson's suggested strategy for combating misinformation is to use network mapping like the one just published for anti-vaccine sentiments to better target messages to specific groups. Because these are diverse communities, playing up the differences between them, rather than the common ground they have found in distrusting vaccines, might be one way to loosen the 'strong entanglement' between them. Exactly how this might be accomplished will require some thought, but it all starts with a map of the battlefield so that messaging efforts to combat misinformation find their way to the right targets:

> If we knew the contact network for the real world, we wouldn't have to have everybody shut indoors, because [social distancing efforts] could be precisely targeted. . . . Online, we can know the contact network. There's a chance that we can actually deal with it better than we can deal with the actual virus. I think this has always been here. It's just that now we've got a chance to actually see it online. You can't deal with what you can't see. So, I am quite hopeful.
>
> (Kuper, 2020)

The key issue would seem to be communicating with target groups in non-patronizing language which challenges the narratives they have absorbed from conspiracy theory entrepreneurs who manage to do just that. Failure to do that will be disastrous because a vaccine can be the only cure for the coronavirus. Insufficient uptake will fail to produce the crucial herd immunity.

A turning point in history

Philosoph John Gray (2020a) – presumably assuming a vaccine will become readily available and taken up in sufficient numbers – speculates that the deserted streets will fill up again, and we will leave our screen-lit burrows blinking with relief. But the world we re-enter will be inevitably different from how we imagined it in what we thought were normal times. Moreover, this will not have been a temporary rupture in an otherwise stable equilibrium: the crisis through which we are living will be a turning point in history.

Thus, the era of peak globalization will be over. An economic system that relied on worldwide production and long supply chains is morphing into one that will be less interconnected. A way of life driven by unceasing mobility is shuddering to a halt. Our lives will be more physically constrained and more virtual than they were. An even more fragmented world is coming into being but one which is more resilient.

Gray (2020a) further observes that the once formidable British state is being rapidly reinvented and on a scale not seen before. Acting with emergency powers authorized by parliament, the government has tossed economic orthodoxy to the four winds. Savaged by years of absurd austerity, the NHS – like the armed forces, police, prisons, fire service, care workers and cleaners – has its back to the wall. But, with the noble dedication of its workers, the virus will be held at bay. Our political system will survive intact. Not many countries will be so fortunate. Governments everywhere are struggling through the narrow passage between suppressing the virus and crashing the economy. Many – Gray observes – will stumble and fall.

Gray observes that in the view of the future to which progressive thinkers cling, the future is an embellished version of the recent past. No doubt this helps them preserve some semblance of sanity, but it also undermines what is now our most vital attribute: the ability to adapt and fashion different ways of life. The task ahead is to build economies and societies which are more durable, and more humanly habitable, than those that have been exposed to the anarchy of the global market.

But this does not mean a shift to small-scale localism. Human numbers are too large for local self-sufficiency to be viable, and most of humankind is not willing to return to the small, closed communities of a more distant past. But – it is argued – the hyper-globalization of the last few decades will not come back either. The virus has exposed fatal weaknesses in the economic system that was patched up after the financial crisis in 2008. Neoliberalism is supposedly finished.

Thus, with all its talk of freedom and choice, neoliberalism was, in practice, the experiment of dissolving traditional sources of social cohesion and political legitimacy and replacing them with the promise of rising material living standards. It is an experiment that seems to have run its course. Suppressing the virus has necessitated an economic shutdown which can only be temporary, but when the economy restarts, it will be in a world where governments act to curb the global market.

Gray (2020a) perceives a situation in which so many of the essential medical supplies required originate in China – or any other single country – will not be tolerated. Production in these and other sensitive areas will be re-shored as a matter of national security. The notion that a country such as Britain could phase out farming and depend on imports for food will be dismissed as the nonsense it always has been. The airline industry will shrink as people travel less. Harder borders will be an enduring feature of the global landscape. A narrow goal of economic efficiency will no longer be practicable for governments.

So Gray asks what will replace rising material living standards as the basis of society? One answer green thinkers have given is what John Stuart Mill in his *Principles of Political Economy* (1848) called a 'stationary-state economy'. Expanding production and consumption would no longer be an overriding goal, and the increase in human numbers curbed. Unlike most liberals today, Mill recognized the danger of overpopulation. A world filled with human beings, he wrote, would be one without 'flowery wastes' and wildlife. He also understood the dangers of central planning. The stationary state would be a market economy in which competition is encouraged. Technological innovation would continue, along with improvements in the art of living.

Gray (2020a) notes that this is an appealing vision but acknowledges that it is also unreal. There is no world authority to enforce an end to growth, just as there is none to fight the virus. Contrary to the progressive mantra – recently repeated by former Labour prime minister Gordon Brown – global problems do not always have global solutions. Geopolitical divisions preclude anything like world government. If one existed, existing states would compete to control it. The belief that this crisis can be solved by an unprecedented outbreak of international cooperation is magical thinking in its purest form.

Economic expansion is not indefinitely sustainable. For one thing, it can only worsen climate change and turn the planet into a garbage dump. But with highly uneven living standards, still rising human numbers and intensifying geopolitical rivalries, zero growth is also unsustainable. If the limits of growth are eventually accepted, it will be because governments make the protection of their citizens their most important objective, regardless of whether they are democratic or authoritarian states.

Gray (2020a) observes that the EU has responded to the crisis by revealing its essential weakness. Few ideas are so scorned by higher minds than sovereignty, he observes, but in practice it signifies the capacity to execute a comprehensive, coordinated and flexible emergency plan of the kind being implemented in the UK and other countries. The measures that have already been taken are larger than any implemented in the Second World War. In their most important respects, they are also the opposite of what was done then, when the British population was mobilized as never before, and unemployment fell dramatically. Today, aside from those in essential services, the workers have been demobilized. If it goes on for many months, the shutdown will demand an even larger socialization of the economy.

Whether the neoliberal structures of the EU can do anything like this is doubtful. Hitherto sacrosanct rules have been torn up by the European Central Bank's bond-buying programme and relaxing limits on state aid to industry. But the resistance to fiscal burden-sharing of northern European countries such as Germany and the Netherlands may block the way to rescuing Italy – a country too big to be crushed like Greece but possibly also too costly to save. As the Italian prime minister, Giuseppe Conte, said in March, 'If Europe does not rise to this unprecedented challenge, the whole European structure loses its *raison d'être* for the people'. The Serbian president Aleksandar Vucic has been more forthright and realistic: 'European solidarity does not exist . . . that was a fairy tale. The only country that can help us in this hard situation is the People's Republic of China. To the rest of them, thanks for nothing' (Gray, 2020a).

The fundamental flaw of the EU is that it is incapable of discharging the protective functions of a state. The breakup of the eurozone has been predicted so often that it may seem unthinkable. Yet, under the stresses they face today, the disintegration of European institutions is not unrealistic. Free movement has already been shut down. Turkish president Recep Tayyip Erdogan's recent blackmailing of the EU by threatening to allow migrants to pass through his borders, and the endgame in Syria's Idlib Province, could lead to hundreds of thousands, even millions, of refugees fleeing to Europe. Another migrant crisis in conjunction with pressure on the dysfunctional euro could prove fatal.

Gray (2020a) observes that if the EU survives, it may be as something like the Holy Roman Empire in its later years, a phantom that lingers on for generations while power is exercised elsewhere. Vitally necessary decisions are already being taken by nation states and since the political centre is no longer a leading force and with much of the left wedded to the failed European project, many governments will be dominated by the far right.

An increasing influence on the EU will come from Russia. In the struggle with the Saudis that triggered the oil price collapse in March 2020, Putin played the stronger hand. Whereas for the Saudis the fiscal break-even level – the price needed to pay for public services and keep the state solvent – is around US$80 a barrel, for Russia it may be less than half that. At the same time Putin has consolidated the position of Russia as an energy power. The Nord Stream offshore pipelines that run through the Baltics secure reliable supplies of natural gas to Europe. But they also lock Europe into dependency on Russia and enable it to use energy as a political weapon. With the fragmentation of Europe, Russia, too, looks set to expand its sphere of influence. Like China, it is stepping in to replace the faltering EU, flying in doctors and equipment to Italy.

In the US, Donald Trump has plainly considered reflating the economy more important than containing the virus. A 1929-style stock market slide and unemployment levels worse than those in the 1930s could pose an existential threat to his presidency. James Bullard, the CEO of the Federal Reserve Bank of St Louis, suggested that the American jobless rate could reach 30% – higher than in the Great Depression of the 1930s. On the other hand, with the decentralized system of government in the US; a ruinously expensive health care system and tens of millions uninsured; a colossal prison population, of which many are old and infirm; cities with sizeable numbers of homeless people; and an already-large opioid epidemic, curtailing the shutdown could mean the virus spreading uncontrollably, with devastating effects.

Unlike the British programme, Trump's US$2 trillion stimulus plan is mostly another corporate bailout. Yet, if polls are to be believed, increasing numbers of Americans approve of his handling of the epidemic. It is clearly possible that Trump could emerge from this catastrophe with the support of an American majority. But, whether or not he retains his hold on power, the position of the US in the world has changed irreversibly. What is fast unravelling is not only the hyper-globalization of recent decades but also the global order set in place at the end of the Second World War. Quite simply, the virus has hastened a process of disintegration that has been underway for many years. In his seminal *Plagues and Peoples*, the Chicago historian William H. McNeill (1976: 132) wrote:

> It is always possible that some hitherto obscure parasitic organism may escape its accustomed ecological niche and expose the dense human populations that have become so conspicuous a feature of the Earth to some fresh and perchance devastating mortality.

It is not yet known how COVID-19 escaped its niche, though there is a suspicion that the 'wet markets' of Wuhan, where wildlife is sold, may have played a role. In 1976, when McNeill's book was first published, the destruction of the habitats of exotic species was nowhere near as far advanced as it is today. As globalization has advanced, so has the risk of infectious diseases spreading. The Spanish Flu of 1918–20 became a global pandemic in a world without mass air transportation. Commenting on how plagues have been understood by historians, McNeill observed: 'For them as for others, occasional disastrous outbreaks of infectious disease remained sudden and unpredictable interruptions of the norm, essentially beyond historical explanation' (1976: 145). Many later studies have come to similar conclusions.

Yet, the notion persists that pandemics are blips rather than an integral part of history. Lying behind this is the belief that humans are no longer part of the natural world and can create an autonomous ecosystem, separate from the rest of the biosphere. COVID-19 is telling them they cannot. It is only by using science that we can defend ourselves against this pestilence. Mass antibody tests and a vaccine are crucial. But permanent changes in how we live will have to be made if we are to be less vulnerable in future.

Gray (2020a) observes that the texture of everyday life is already altered. A sense of fragility is everywhere. It is not only society that feels shaky. So, too, does the human position in the world. Viral images reveal human absence in different ways. Wild boars are roaming in the towns of northern Italy, while in Lopburi in Thailand gangs of monkeys no longer fed by tourists are fighting in the streets. Inhuman beauty and a fierce struggle for life have sprung up in cities emptied by the virus.

A number of commentators have noted that a post-apocalyptic future of the kind projected in the fiction of J.G. Ballard has become our present reality. But it is important to understand what this 'apocalypse' reveals. For Ballard, human societies were stage props that could be knocked over at any moment. Norms that seemed built into human nature vanished when you left the theatre. The most harrowing of Ballard's experiences as a child in 1940s Shanghai were not in the prison camp, where many inmates were steadfast and kindly in their treatment of others. A resourceful and venturesome boy, Ballard enjoyed much of his time there. It was when the camp collapsed – as the war drew to a close – where he witnessed the worst examples of ruthless selfishness and motiveless cruelty[3] (Gray, 2020a).

Gray (2020a) observes that the lesson he learned was that these were not world-ending events. What is commonly described as an apocalypse is the normal course of history. Many are left with lasting traumas. But the human animal is too sturdy and too versatile to be broken by these upheavals. Life goes on, if differently than before. Those who talk of this as a Ballardian moment have not noticed how human beings adjust, and even find fulfilment, in the extreme situations he portrays.

Technology will help us adapt in our present extremity. Physical mobility can be reduced by shifting many of our activities into cyberspace. Offices, schools, universities, general practitioner surgeries and other work centres are likely to change permanently. Virtual communities set up during the epidemic have enabled people to get to know one another better than they ever did before.

Gray (2020a) surmises that there will be celebrations as the pandemic recedes, but there may be no clear point when the threat of infection is over. Many people may migrate to online environments like those in Second Life, a virtual world where people meet, trade and interact in bodies and worlds of their choosing. Other adaptations, he notes, may be uncomfortable for moralists. Online pornography will likely boom, and much internet dating may consist of erotic exchanges that never end in a meeting of bodies. Augmented reality technology may be used to simulate fleshly encounters and virtual sex could soon be normalized. Whether this is a move towards the good life may not be the most useful question to ask. Cyberspace relies on an infrastructure that can be damaged or destroyed by war or natural disaster. The internet allows us to avoid the isolation that plagues have brought in the past. It cannot enable human beings to escape their mortal flesh or avoid the ironies of progress.

Gray observes that what the virus is telling us is not only that progress is reversible – a fact even bourgeois progressives seem to have grasped – but that it can be self-undermining. To take the most obvious example, globalization produced some major benefits – millions have been lifted out of poverty. This achievement is now under threat. Globalization begat the de-globalization that is now underway.

As the prospect of ever-rising living standards fades, other sources of authority and legitimacy are re-emerging. Liberal or socialist, the progressive mind detests national identity with passionate intensity. There is clearly plenty in history to show how it can be misused. But the nation state is increasingly the most powerful force driving large-scale action. Dealing with the virus requires a collective effort that will not be mobilized for the sake of universal humanity.

Altruism has limits just as much as growth. There will be examples of extraordinary selflessness before the worst of the crisis is over. In Britain, an over half-million-strong volunteer army has signed up to assist the NHS. But it would be unwise to rely on human sympathy alone to get us through. Kindness to strangers is so precious that it must be rationed.

Gray, (2020a) questions how much of their freedom people will want back when the pandemic has peaked. They show little taste for the enforced solidarity of socialism, but they may happily accept a regime of bio-surveillance for the sake of better protection of their health. Digging ourselves out of the pit will demand more state intervention not less, and of a highly inventive kind. Governments will have to do a lot more in underwriting scientific research and technological innovation. Though the state may not always be larger its influence will be pervasive, and by old-world standards more intrusive. Post-liberal government is likely to be the norm for the foreseeable future. But in the meantime, there are darker forces taking advantage of the opportunities offered by the pandemic.

Bad guys being bad

Jonathan Freedland (2020) notes that under the cover of coronavirus, all kinds of wickedness is happening. Thus, where you and I see a global health crisis, the leading authoritarians in the world, fearmongers, and populist strongmen have spotted an opportunity – and they are seizing it.

Of course, neither the political left nor the right has a monopoly on the truism that one should never let a good crisis go to waste. Plenty of progressives share that conviction (as we have seen), firm that the pandemic offers a rare chance to reset the way we organize our unequal societies, our clogged cities, our warped relationship to the natural world. But there are others – and they tend to be in power – who see this opening very differently. For them, the virus suddenly makes possible action that in normal times would exact a heavy cost. Now they can strike while the world looks the other way.

Freedland observes that for some, COVID-19 itself is the weapon of choice. Witness the emerging evidence that Bashar al-Assad in Damascus and Xi Jinping in Beijing are allowing the disease to wreak havoc among those groups whom the rulers have deemed to be unpersons, their lives unworthy of basic protection. Assad is deliberately leaving Syrians in opposition-held areas more vulnerable to the pandemic, according to Will Todman of the Center for Strategic and International Studies. As he puts it, 'COVID-19 has provided Assad a new opportunity to instrumentalize suffering' (Todman, 2020).

Meanwhile, China continues to hold 1 million Uighur Muslims in internment camps, where they contend now not only with inhuman conditions but also a coronavirus outbreak. Those camps are cramped, lack adequate sanitation and have poor medical facilities: the virus could not ask for a better breeding ground. What is more, Uighur Muslims are reportedly being forced to work as labourers, filling in for non-Muslims who are allowed to stay home and protect themselves. That, according to one observer, 'is reflective of how the [People's] Republic of China views [Uighur Muslims] as nothing but disposable commodities' (Freedland, 2020).

Elsewhere, the pandemic has allowed would-be dictators an excuse to seize yet more power. Enter Viktor Orbán of Hungary, whose response to coronavirus was immediate: he persuaded his compliant parliament to grant him the right to rule by decree. Orbán said he needed emergency powers to fight the dreaded disease, but there is no time limit on them, and they will remain in place even once the threat has passed. They include the power to jail those who 'spread false information' which has already led to a crackdown on individuals guilty of nothing more than posting criticism of the government on Facebook. Orbán has long sought to rule Hungary as an autocrat, but the pandemic has given him his chance, allowing him to brand anyone standing in his way as unwilling to help the leader fight a mortal threat.

Xi has not missed that same trick, using coronavirus to intensify his imposition of China's Orwellian 'social credit' system, whereby citizens are tracked, monitored and rated for their compliance. Now that system can include health and, thanks to the virus, much of the public ambivalence that previously existed towards it is likely to melt away. After all, runs the logic, good citizens are surely obliged to give up even more of their autonomy if it helps save lives.

Freedland (2020) wryly notes that for many of the strongmen in the world coronavirus does not even need to be an excuse. Its chief value is the global distraction it has created, allowing unprincipled rulers to make mischief when natural critics at home and abroad are preoccupied with the urgent business of life and death.

Thus, while Donald Trump got plenty of criticism for his botched handling of the virus, while everyone has been staring at the mayhem that he has been creating with one hand, the other is free to commit acts of vandalism that go all but undetected such as the steady and deliberate erosion of environmental protections. During the lockdown, Trump has eased fuel-efficiency standards for new cars, frozen rules for soot air pollution, continued to lease public property to oil and gas companies and advanced a proposal on mercury pollution from power plants that could make that easier too.

Brazilian president Jair Bolsonaro has meanwhile outstripped his mentor, Trump. Not content with mere changes to the rulebook, he has pushed aside the expert environmental agencies and sent in the military to 'protect' the Amazon rainforest. I say 'protect' because, as NBC News–reported satellite imagery has shown 'deforestation of the Amazon has soared under cover of the coronavirus'. Destruction in April was up by 64% from the same month a year ago. The images reveal an area of land equivalent to 448 football fields, stripped bare of trees – this in the place that serves as the lungs of the earth. If the world were not consumed with fighting coronavirus, there would have been an outcry. Instead, and in our distraction, those trees have fallen without making a sound.

Another Trump admirer, India's Narendra Modi, has seen the same opportunity identified by his fellow ultra-nationalists. Indian police have been using the lockdown to crack down on Muslim citizens and their leaders 'indiscriminately', according to activists. Those arrested or detained struggle to get access to a lawyer, given the restrictions on movement. Modi calculates that majority opinion will back him, as rightist Hindu politicians brand the virus a 'Muslim disease' and pro–Modi TV stations declare the nation to be facing a 'corona jihad'.

In Israel, Benjamin Netanyahu – who can claim to have been Trumpist before Trump – has been handed a political lifeline by the virus, luring part of the main opposition party into a government of national unity that will keep him in power and, he hopes, out of the dock on corruption charges. His new coalition is committed to a programme that would see Israel annex major parts of the West Bank, permanently absorbing into itself territory that should belong to a future Palestinian state, with the process starting in early July.

For now, the pandemic has been a boon to the authoritarians of the world, tyrants and bigots. It has given them what they crave most: fear and the cover of darkness. Let us now catch our breath . . . and consider the possibilities for post-pandemic 'ordinary' crime.

Pandemic crime opportunities

> Career opportunities are the ones that never knock
> The only jobs they offer are to keep you out the dock
>
> – The Clash (1977)

At the time of significant economic recession when legitimate jobs become few and far between, you can usually rely on the illegitimate market to provide new opportunities. A New Europol Report (2020) provides details of the latest crime opportunities provided by the pandemic COVID-19 in the EU.

During this unprecedented crisis, governments across Europe have been intensifying their efforts to combat the global spread of the coronavirus by enacting various measures to support public health systems, safeguard the economy and to ensure public order and safety. But a number of these measures have had a significant impact on the serious and organized crime landscape. Criminals have been quick to seize opportunities to exploit the crisis by adapting their *modi operandi* or engaging in new criminal activities. Factors that have prompted changes in crime and terrorism include the following:

- High demand for certain goods, protective gear and pharmaceutical products
- Decreased mobility and flow of people across and into the EU
- Citizens remaining at home and increasingly teleworking, relying on digital solutions
- Limitations to public life making some criminal activities less visible and displacing them to home or online settings
- Increased anxiety and fear, creating vulnerability to exploitation
- Decreased supply of certain illicit goods in the EU

Building on information provided by EU member states and in-house expertise, Europol (2020) published a situational report analysing the current developments which fall into four main crime areas.

Cybercrime

The number of cyberattacks against organizations and individuals has been significant and is expected to increase. Criminals have used the COVID-19 crisis to carry out social engineering attacks themed around the pandemic to distribute various malware packages. Cybercriminals are also likely to seek to exploit an increasing number of attack vectors as a greater number of employers have introduced telework and have thus allowed connections to their organization systems. For example the Czech Republic reported a cyberattack on Brno University Hospital which forced the institution to shut down its entire information technology network, postpone urgent surgical interventions and re-route new acute patients to a nearby hospital.

Fraud

Fraudsters have been very quick to adapt well-known fraud schemes to capitalize on the anxieties and fears of victims throughout the crisis. These have included adapted versions of telephone fraud schemes, supply scams and decontamination scams. A large number of new or adapted fraud schemes are expected as fraudsters are likely to capitalize further on the anxieties of people across Europe. For example an investigation supported by Europol focused on the transfer of €6.6 million by a company to another in Singapore to purchase alcohol gels and FFP3/2 masks. The goods have never been received.

Counterfeit and substandard goods

The sale of counterfeit health care and sanitary products, as well as personal protective equipment and counterfeit pharmaceutical products, have increased manifold since the outbreak of the crisis. There is a risk that counterfeiters will use shortages in the supply of some goods to increasingly provide counterfeit alternatives both on- and offline. For example, between 3–10 March 2020, over 34,000 counterfeit surgical masks have been seized by law enforcement authorities worldwide as part of Operation PANGEA supported by Europol.

Organized and property crime

Various types of scheme involving theft have been adapted by criminals to exploit the pandemic situation. This has included well-known scams involving the impersonation of representatives of public authorities. Commercial premises and medical facilities are expected to be increasingly targeted for organized burglaries. Despite the introduction of further quarantine measures throughout Europe, the crime threat has remained dynamic and new or adapted types of criminal activities continue to emerge during the crisis and in its aftermath. For example multiple EU member states reported on a similar *modus operandi* for theft. The perpetrators gained access to private homes by impersonating medical staff providing information material or hygiene products or conducting a 'corona test'.

Neoliberalism revisited

Then, in May 2020, the leading free-market think tanks, which had backed Margaret Thatcher's tax-cutting and privatization agenda – thus helping to introduce neoliberalism to the world and latterly sanctioning the last ten years of austerity – were to lend their support to the plans of the government for unprecedented and sustained increases in public spending.

In a shift of stance which gave Chancellor of the Exchequer Rishi Sunak political clearance to increase UK debts to levels not seen in peacetime, the Adam Smith Institute, the Centre for Policy Studies and the Institute of Economic Affairs and Policy Exchange said they endorsed public spending increases to confront the coronavirus outbreak and state-funded investment to boost the recovery. The support for widespread state intervention to rescue the economy came as Boris Johnson told backbench Tory MPs that there were no plans to impose a public-sector wage freeze or other austerity measures to bring down public spending in the crisis (Inman, 2020).

In a call to about 125 members of the 1922 Committee of backbenchers, the *Daily Telegraph* reported that the prime minister had said there was 'no question' of a return to austerity and assured them he would 'double down' on funding transport projects in the north of England.

Britain was nevertheless expected to enter a deep recession following the lockdown to prevent the spread of COVID-19. Figures from the Office for Budget Responsibility – the independent body responsible for forecasting the public finances – showed the economy suffering a 35% decline in output between April and the end of June and a rise in unemployment to at least 10%. The cost of measures such as the Treasury's furlough scheme, which had paid employers to send home more than 7 million workers, would send the public spending deficit above 15% for the year, 50% higher than the worst period following the crash in 2008 (Inman, 2020)

Left-leaning think tanks and academics had lined up to condemn plans for a return to austerity, saying it would harm the recovery, and adding that further government borrowing would be needed to secure a return to growth after the virus-induced mothballing of the economy. But Boris Johnson announced that there were no plans to impose a public-sector wage freeze or other austerity measures (Inman, 2020).

During the previous recession, most free-market think tanks had supported austerity measures imposed by the then chancellor George Osborne, arguing that the public sector deficit should be quickly reduced. This time things seemed to be different even for an austerity hawk like Warwick Lightfoot, chief economist at Policy Exchange, who said, 'I don't think anyone is arguing for a relaunch of austerity. . . . The last thing you want to do is amplify the prospects of a full-blown depression' (Inman, 2020).

Policy Exchange – founded in 2002 by Michael Gove, the Cabinet Office chief, Tory peer Francis Maude, former MP Nick Boles and businessman Archie Norman – had a loyal following in the cabinet and claimed to be behind several recent Tory policies. Lightfoot said low interest rates meant the government could borrow cheaply to invest in infrastructure to get the economy back on its feet. Matthew Lesh, head of research at the Adam Smith Institute – founded in the 1970s to promote free-market policies – said, 'Even fiscally hawkish people have less of a problem with the current increase in debt levels' (Inman, 2020).

Tom Clougherty, head of tax at the Centre for Policy Studies (CPS), said, 'I'd usually be wary of big public investment schemes in the current circumstances, though, with borrowing costs very low and little prospect of crowding out private investment, I think the pros outweigh the cons.' The CPS was founded in the 1970s to combat socialism by former MP Sir Keith Joseph, a close friend and supporter of Margaret Thatcher.

Echoing left-leaning economists, Lesh said the Bank of England should support the government with loose monetary policy, allowing it to borrow at low interest rates. Julian Jessop, an economics fellow at the Institute of Economic Affairs – a think tank founded in the 1950s with the support of free-market economist and guru Friedrich Hayek – said that he was relaxed about the debts built up during the worst of the lockdown. 'There are obvious risks that austerity will restrict growth', he said. But he was concerned that the government would harm the economy by keeping restrictions on business activity for much of the year, which would delay a bounce-back in economic growth. 'The longer the economy is kept shuttered, the greater the risk that more of the damage will be permanent, making it that much harder to pay for better public services and infrastructure in the future' (Inman, 2020).

The four think tanks continued to believe that the Treasury should examine tax-cutting measures to promote innovation and entrepreneurial activity, saying that over the longer term, Whitehall was poor at allocating funds to the economy in the most effective way.

Alex Doherty (2020) observes that from the financial crisis in 2008 until the vote for Brexit in 2016, from the rise of the alt-right to the COVID-19 pandemic, there is no way of properly grasping what has happened in our world without thinking about how neo-liberalism has informed our politics and economy. As we have seen in this book, neolib-eralism can be broadly defined as the raft of policies and overarching political ethos which had enabled governments in the late 1970s to turn away from state-directed economic planning towards an economic model which extended competitive markets into every sphere of human activity and initiated the reign of finance capital – the kind dreamed up in the City of London and Wall Street – by removing constraints on capital mobility.

Significantly, neoliberalism is not merely a policy agenda but also a moral framework which teaches individuals to conceive of themselves not as, say, wage earners but rather as risk-taking entrepreneurs who should expect to shoulder the financial risks of their participation in higher education, the credit system and deregulated labour markets. First implemented as an economic programme in the UK and the US by the Thatcher govern-ment and the Reagan administration, respectively, its principles continued to underwrite the Third-Way politics of New Labour and Clintonite Democrats. Although centre-left politicians have rejected the applicability of the term to their politics, a wealth of schol-arship produced by economists, sociologists and historians demonstrates how third-way politicians advanced the neoliberal project.

So, asks Doherty (2020) rhetorically, what is the current status of the ideology? Some are simply calling time on the neoliberal age. In the early days of the COVID-19 pan-demic, Paul Mason declared that the demands of the crisis would mean that, in short order, the political class in the UK would soon consist entirely of either 'enthusiastic' or 'reluctant socialists' – progressive state intervention was inevitably back on the agenda. But claims of this sort should be treated with caution, not least because similar predic-tions were made following the financial crisis in 2008, after the Brexit vote and after the election of Donald Trump as president of the US. And those predictions turned out to be seriously awry.

For instance, at the height of the financial crisis, the Nobel Prize–winning economist Joseph Stiglitz had announced, 'Neoliberalism . . . is dead'. Yet it soon became abundantly clear that this was premature. It is true that the crisis seemed to pose a serious threat to the veneration of markets, as governments were forced to bail out the financial sector. But, as scholars such as Philip Mirowski have shown, neoliberals have long understood that their project requires state intervention to create and maintain markets. Rather than thinking of the crisis fighting of governments in 2008 as a repudiation of market-friendly policy, it is more useful to think of it as an extreme instance of pro-business government inter-vention which aimed to maintain the long-term primacy of the market (Doherty, 2020).

On the face of it, the vote for Brexit and the election of Trump appeared to more plausibly represent a break with neoliberalism. But that diagnosis arose from a failure to understand how neoliberalism can adaptively recombine with elements of other ideolo-gies. While the Brexiteers may loathe the EU – an institution that neoliberal intellectuals had long disagreed about – they remained committed to the core of neoliberal ideology. For example the Australian points-based immigration system – so beloved by the Brexi-teers – is perfectly congruent with the neoliberal view of human beings as bundles of assets (of greater or lesser value). The educational background of the post-Brexit immigrant, their work experience and connections are in this vision redefined as forms of capital that may or may not be worth investing in – by letting them in – to secure a future return on that investment for the national economy. Points-based immigration systems, in other words, do not represent a straightforward shift away from neoliberal, free-market orthodoxy towards right-wing protectionism.

With COVID-19 – as in 2008 – politicians such as Chancellor of the Exchequer Rishi Sunak have been forced to implement policies which seem to contradict their adherence to market supremacy, but the intention is again to do so in order to swiftly return to 'normal' and wean the public off their 'addiction' to state support (Doherty, 2020). The frustrated desire of the government to curtail the furlough scheme and the clear opposition to implementing a universal basic income[4] indicate a commitment to maintaining the core of neoliberal welfare policy. This means opposing generous, non-means-tested payments, which neoliberals view as detrimental to fostering entrepreneurial activity and disciplining the workforce.

Doherty (2020) observes that more disturbingly, in the context of the pandemic and the climate crisis, the persistence of the neoliberal view of individuals as human capital raises the possibility of governments treating 'low-value' populations as disposable as in the case of old vulnerable people in care homes. Increased state intervention to protect incomes is welcome but could be used by governments to implement a kind of economic triage, with populations deemed not worth 'bailing out' excluded from state support. As Michel Feher (2019) has shown, there are milder precedents for this in welfare reforms carried out by mainstream political parties in Ireland and Portugal, which reduced benefits for younger cohorts to encourage emigration and, in the case of Portugal, to swap young, relatively poor Portuguese for wealthier retirees from abroad. In a context of ballooning national debt, where migrant populations are being treated as vectors of disease, it is not difficult to see how an exclusionary neoliberal politics that supports investment in certain populations and disinvestment in others could gain support.

None of this denies that the COVID-19 crisis poses a real threat to neoliberal orthodoxy. Physical distancing and enforced quarantine have disrupted the labour market, potentially shifting the balance of power between labour and capital in the favour of workers. Moreover, the furlough scheme has temporarily revealed the artificiality of government spending constraints. But, given the persistence and adaptability of neoliberal ideology over the past ten years, any sober assessment of the current situation needs to be attuned to the possibility of its survival – or successful mutation – as well as its possible demise.

Concluding comments

John Gray (2020b) observes that intellectual attitudes towards the state of the nation mirror those towards the coronavirus. In each case, an influential body of opinion expects a reversion to what it regards as normalcy. Thus, the pandemic will soon be defeated, or else it will fade away. With the end of lockdown, the economy will continue where it left off.

Similarly, many seem to believe that the political changes of the past four years are anomalies. The Brexit referendum, the Donald Trump's presidency, Boris Johnson's majority and the inability of the EU to achieve solidarity in face of the largest economic dislocation in its history are all seen as aberrations from the normal course of events.

Gray (2020b) observes that these expectations are not correlated with political allegiances in any simple way. Most of those who believe coronavirus is overhyped and lockdown overdone are Thatcherite Brexiteers. Those who believe the political shifts of recent years can be reversed are mostly progressive liberals and unreconciled Remainers. What these seemingly divergent groupings have in common is the faith that the order they imagine existed until a few years ago can somehow be reinstated. They recognize that things cannot be just as they used to be. But the restoration they have in mind will be 'an enhanced, re-energized, super-duper version of the old order'. Yet, this is, considered to be, a nostalgic vision, an exercise in magical thinking. Whereas the pandemic has advanced some trends and reversed others, it has also rendered some issues defunct. Debates about Brexit and the future of Western capitalism are examples. Brexit is irreversible, while 'Western capitalism' has fragmented into a variety of state capitalisms. At the same time, Britain and other Western societies find themselves without a consensus on values that can enable them to deal with the virus or shape their future.

At the time of writing – July 2020 – we are in the early phases of what has so far been a comparatively mild pandemic. But many epidemiologists believe that the virus will go on to re-emerge in successive waves, possibly in different forms, in different regions, and become endemic throughout the world. We simply do not know.

Gray (2020b) observes that there is another kind of uncertainty at work: there is nothing approaching agreement on the values that should shape policies towards the pandemic. He notes, that the spurious exactitude of quality-adjusted life years (QALYs) – which are used by the National Institute for Health and Care Excellence to evaluate whether treatments are cost-effective – conceals a host of ethical difficulties. Seen to be a rebooted version of nineteenth-century utilitarianism, QALYs multiply how much longer a patient will live after a given treatment with the future quality of their life. But what counts as quality in a human life? QALY theory may tell you a few years of life for a disabled child are worth less than longer life in a healthy productive adult. But this is not a result that squares with the intuitions of everyone. Ethics cannot be reduced to an arithmetical formula.

Gray (2020b) observes that significant numbers of people have shown they care more about other goals than bringing the pandemic under control. Some are ready to risk infection in order to promote a cause to which they are passionately committed. Yet, unfortunately, science has yet to demonstrate that the virus refrains on moral grounds from spreading in mass gatherings of protesters. Others are ready to take the risk to return to work or have a day at the beach. Growing numbers resist government advice because they insist on making their own choices about how they want to live.

Some may say this is no bad thing. People should be free to make their own judgements of risk, and act on them: that is what living a normal life means. Yet, all such arguments skim over differences in the nature of risk. Thus, if surfers choose to practise their sport in weather in which some will likely drown, that is their business. If some do die, many more will not start doing so a few weeks later as a consequence. But the risks taken when you expose yourself to the virus are multiplicative. Not only do you increase your own chances of dying, but you also greatly increase those of others. One super-spreader can infect hundreds of unknowing people. There is also a question of resources. Will those who expose themselves to a high risk of catching the virus in order to live what they consider a normal life be treated by the NHS when they fall ill?

Gray (2020b) observes that the causes of the pandemic can be found in the way we lived before it appeared. At its peak, the globalization we have identified in this book meant near-universal connectivity between economies, mass mobility of human beings and increasing population density in much of the world. Pathologists argued for years that this system was liable to epidemics of infectious disease. But they were ignored because those that occurred – such as SARS in 2002–04 – were contained. Now what they feared has happened, and some are warning of worse pandemics to come.

But progressives remain fixated on how to revive the world that engendered the present disorder. They constructed and managed that world, and it flattered their self-image as the rational vanguard of the species. It is only to be expected that they should yearn for the return of their now bankrupt authority. Yet few aspects of the contemporary scene are more laughably grotesque than defunct politicians and advisers demanding a return to the politics of competence and expertise that produced the dysfunctional euro, the ruinous Iraq War, the financial crisis of 2008 and anarchy in Libya, plus the regime of globalization that is seen to be collapsing.

Gray (2020b) observes that for many of them, this includes resisting a change that is now irresistible. Some will be clamouring to re-join the EU long after that sacred institution has passed into history. Again, many prophesy the breakup of the British state after Brexit. But once Britain has left the EU, Scottish independence ceases to be a credible option. A Scottish state outside the UK, needing to negotiate rejoining the EU at a time when oil is no longer a prize asset, a shaky banking system, no national currency and the prospect of a hard border with England, has little or no prospect of economic viability. The position of Northern Ireland is more complex, but it is not going to become part of the Republic any time soon.

Gray (2020b) observes that the most intractable difficulty the government faces is not one of its making. There is a reason – beyond that of avoiding responsibility – why ministers have gone on about 'following the science'. In Britain, only science has retained any authority. Scientists have no greater competence in questions of ethics and politics than anyone else, but there is no longer any common body of values to which political leaders can defer when trying to legitimate their policies. Values are now seen to be essentially subjective and emotive. The test of what is right, good and true has become personal feeling.

This poses a difficulty not only for governments but also protest groups. Movements of communal solidarity are currently based on the hyper-liberal premise that individuals determine their own identity and morality. But it is impossible to formulate an idea of social justice – still less embed it in society – when values have been privatized. This is also why talk of 'true conservatism' – an emerging discourse on parts of the right discontented with the Johnson government – is anachronistic and ridiculous. Intermittent and partial as it may have been, the common life of the past has gone for good. Culture war is not a passing affliction. Like the virus, it has become an endemic condition.

Gray (2020b) argues that Britain faces a grim future where no government will be able to invoke a consensus on values in support of its policies. This country is not soaked with apocalyptic religiosity as is the US, nor is it awash with guns. If opponents of protest movements take to the streets, there could be a serious threat to public order, but the problem Britain faces is subtler and deeper than suppressing lawless violence. The task is maintaining a fragile peace in the culture of fragmented modernity or the postmodern condition. Gray observes that we are going to have to learn how to live with disorder, just as we must learn to live with the virus.

Summary of main points

1   The arrival of the COVID-19 pandemic was to push the state and public sectors into the foreground. The experts were back in fashion.

2   Every pandemic generates conspiracy theories. Thus, the coronavirus is a bioweapon created by China or Big Pharma, or American scientists, or it is caused by 5G technology, or it does not exist, just a 'hoax' made up by the enemies of Donald Trump.

3   The key issue in challenging these potentially dangerous conspiracy theories would seem to be communicating with target groups in non-patronizing language.

4   Suppressing the virus necessitated an economic shutdown which can only be temporary, but when the economy restarts, it is likely to be a world where governments act to curb the global market.

5   Economic expansion is not indefinitely sustainable. It can only worsen climate change and turn the planet into a garbage dump. But with highly uneven living standards, still rising human numbers and intensifying geopolitical rivalries, zero growth is also unsustainable.

6   The notion persists that pandemics are blips rather than an integral part of history. There is a belief that humans are no longer part of the natural world and can create an autonomous ecosystem, separate from the rest of the biosphere. COVID-19 is telling them they cannot.

7   Technology will help us adapt in our present extremity. Physical mobility can be reduced by shifting many of our activities into cyberspace. Offices, schools, universities, general practitioner surgeries and other work centres are likely to change permanently.

8   At a time of significant economic recession when legitimate jobs become few and far between, you can usually rely on the illegitimate market to provide new crime opportunities. The pandemic COVID-19 has provided crime opportunities in the EU in the areas of cybercrime, fraud, counterfeit and substandard goods, organized and property crime.

9   In May 2020, the leading free-market thinktanks, which had backed Margaret Thatcher's tax-cutting and privatization agenda – thus helping to introduce neoliberalism to the world – were to lend their support to the plans of the Conservative government for unprecedented and sustained increases in public spending.

10 With COVID-19 – as in 2008 – politicians were forced to implement policies which seem to contradict their adherence to market supremacy, but it can be argued that it is again the intention to do so to swiftly return to 'normal' and wean the public off their 'addiction' to state support.

Discussion questions

1   Briefly discuss the notion that experts were now back in fashion and explain why.

2   Discuss why you think that conspiracy theories are so popular and what might be done to challenge them.

3   Discuss the possible economic implications of post-COVID-19 society.

4   Discuss the potential crime opportunities provided by the pandemic. Why might people take advantage of these?

5   Will the world be a better place after the pandemic? Explain your answer.

Suggested further reading

There are numerous books and papers on neoliberalism and its likely survival. These have been signposted throughout this book and details are included in the extensive list of references. The COVID-19 pandemic is very much happening as this book is being written. The last few chapters have indeed been written literally under lockdown. It is likely that these are early days for the crisis and exactly how it will all pan out it is unknown and a question of supposition. So, no recommended texts. You are advised to follow the media stories as they happen and to await the papers and books which are yet to be written. But they will be. I foresee future student dissertations and types of schemes involving doctoral theses and indeed the creation of legitimate career opportunities.

Notes

1 A Ponzi scheme is a form of fraud that lures investors and pays profits to earlier investors with funds from more recent investors. The scheme leads victims to believe that profits are coming from product sales or other means, and they remain unaware that other investors are the source of funds. A Ponzi scheme can maintain the illusion of a sustainable business as long as new investors contribute new funds and as long as most of the investors do not demand full repayment and still believe in the non-existent assets they are purported to own.
2 QAnon is a far-right conspiracy theory detailing a supposed secret plot by an alleged 'deep state' against President Donald Trump and his supporters.
3 While much of Ballard's fiction would prove thematically and stylistically provocative, he became best known for his relatively conventional war novel, *Empire of the Sun* (1984), a semi-autobiographical account of a young British boy's experiences in Shanghai during Japanese occupation.
4 Universal basic income is a governmental public programme for a periodic payment delivered to all on an individual basis without a means test or work requirement.

References

Baker, P. (2020) 'For Trump, Coronavirus Proves to Be an Enemy He Can't Tweet Away', *The New York Times*, March.

The Clash (1977) *Career Opportunities*. London: CBS.

Doherty, A. (2020) 'Has the Coronavirus Crisis Killed Neoliberalism? Don't Bet On It', *The Guardian*, May 15.

Feher, M. (2019) 'Disposing of the Discredited: A European Project', in W. Callison and Z. Manfredi (eds.), *Mutant Neoliberalism*. New York: Fordham University Press.

Freedland, J. (2020) 'Under Cover of Coronavirus, The World's Bad Guys Are Wreaking Havoc', *The Guardian*, 15 May.

Gray, J. (2020a) 'Why This Crisis Is a Turning Point in History', *The New Statesmen*, April 1.

Gray, J. (2020b) 'State of the Nation: Why We Are Entering a New Age of Disorder', *The New Statesmen*, July.

Harris, J. (2020) 'The Experts are Back in Fashion as Covid-19's Reality Bites', *The Guardian*, March 15.

Hopkins Burke, R.D. (2018) *An Introduction to Criminological Theory*, 6th ed. Abingdon: Oxon.

Inman, P. (2020) 'Rightwing Thinktanks Call Time on Age of Austerity', *The Guardian*, May 16.

Johnson, N., Velasquez, N., Johnson, N.J., Leahy, R., Gabriel, N., El Oud, S., Zheng, M., Manrique, P., Wuchy, S. and Lupu, Y. (2020) 'The Online Competition between Pro- and Anti-Vaccination Views', *Nature*, May 13.

Kuper, S. (2020) 'The Covid Conspiracies: A Virus That Can Only Spread', *Financial Times Magazine*, April 16.

LaFrance, A. (2020) 'The Prophecies of Q: American Conspiracy Theories Are Entering a Dangerous New Phase', *The Atlantic*, June Issue.

Lynas, M. (2020) *COVID: Top 10 Current Conspiracy Theories.* Ithaca, NY: Alliance for Science, Cornell University.

Lyotard, J.-F. (1976) The Post-Modern Condition: A Report on Knowledge. Manchester: Manchester University Press.

McNeil, W.H. (1976) *Plagues and People.* Chicago: Anchor.

Mill, J.S. (1848) *Principles of Political Economy.* London: John W. Parker.

Oi-Yee, H. and Bailey, A. (2020) 'YouTube as a Source of Information on COVID-19: A Pandemic of Misinformation?', *British Medical Journal Global Health,* 5(5): e002604

Safi, M. (2020) '100 Days That Changed the World', *The Guardian,* April.

Todman, W. (2020) *Cross-border Aid, Covid-19, and U.S. Decisions in Syria.* Washington, DC: Center for Strategic and International Studies.

Index

Note: Page numbers in *italics* refer to figures; numbers in **bold** refer to tables.

Centers for Disease Control and Prevention
(CDC) 480, 489
Centre for Policy Studies (CPS) 499, 500
Chadwick, Luke 21
Chambliss, William 358
Chang, Ha-Joon 370
chaos theory 129, 130; and constitutive
criminology 118–21
Chartist movement 22, 445
Chauvin, Derek 224, 227
Chechen rebels 241
Cheney, Dick 78
Chibnall, Steve 164
Chicago School of Economics 55–6, 410, 411
children: abuse of 37, 183, 273, 335; from
broken homes 52; and child pornography 178;
development of 51–2, 333; of incarcerated
mothers 275; removal of 199; sexual
exploitation/abuse of 156, 183; trafficking
of 178; violence against 194; see also adverse
childhood experiences (ACE); parenting
Children and Young Person's Act (1969) 27
China 102; and the coronavirus 477–80, 486–7,
497; internment camps in 496; organized
crime in 181, 182, 188; as supplier of medical
supplies 492
Chinese Triads 181, 188
Chomsky, Noam 105
Christianity: and communitarianism 444; and
individualism 453–4; liberation theology 351
Chuck D 220
citizen journalism 108
civil liberties 28–9, 123
civil rights movement 77, 347
civilizations: consciousness about 103; dialogue
among 111; differences between 103; Islamic
102, 121, 125; non-Western 103–4; Sinic 102;
Western 103–4, 121
civilizing process 30, 31, 153
Clabrian mafia 38
clash of civilizations thesis 102–5, 112; criticisms
of 104–5; and terrorism 121
Classen, Ron 146
climate apartheid 194
climate change 193–4, 302, 354, 502; see also
global warming
Clinton, Bill 80, 83, 108, 371, 378, 445, 448,
501
Clinton, Hillary 372
closed-circuit television cameras (CCTV) 153,
166, 179
Clougherty, Tom 500
club cultures 184–6
club goods 161
Cobbe, Frances Power 307
cognitive learning theories 53–4

cognitive science 109
Cohen, Albert 57, 64, 282
Cohen, Carl 314
Cohen, Stanley 64, 122
Cold War 102, 105, 235, 245
Coleridge, Stephen 308
collectivism 476; English radical 455
colonial rule 202–4
colonialism 212; settler 193, 194
Colquhoun, Patrick 21
Colston, Edward 228
communication: alternative methods of 169; mass
167; technologies of 166
communitarianism 444–5; in East Asian
politics and society 445; governmental 450;
mainstream 445–8, 470; mainstream agenda
446–8; moral authoritarian 448; neoliberal
450; and neoliberalism 468; radical egalitarian
448–51, 470; radical moral 9, 111; and
religious belief 444–5; responsive 445–8
communities: of care 452, 470; of choice 449;
and the concept of community 451–3, 470; of
fate 449; virtual 495
community justice 451
Complexity and Data Science initiative 489
computer crime 30; hacking 137, 152, 178;
sabotage 178
conflict: climate-induced 194; core-state 103;
fault-line 103; inter-civilizational 103; political
198; racial 213
conflict resolution 121
Conflict Tactics Scale 270
conflict theories 65–6, 260
Connell, Bob/Raewin 191, 205, 276
consequentialism 311
conservatism 77; neo- 77–9; paleo- 384, 391n4;
traditional 446
Conservative Classical Liberal Alliance (CCLA)
419, 420
Conservative Party 386, 461, 462
conspiracy theories 381, 383
constables 29
constitutive criminological theory 127
constitutive criminology 117–18, 137; and chaos
theory 118–21; policy implications of 129; and
postmodernism 130; and the war on terror
121–7
constructionism 329–30; social 125, 242, 327,
329, 331, 342, 417
consumer capitalism 5, 109, 111
consumer culture 160–1, 427
consumer society 25–6
consumerism 434, 435
Conte, Giuseppe 493
control theory 62, 271; see also social control
theories

securitization 423; subjective 160; typologies
of 422, 439n3
Harris, John 310, 483
Harrison, Ruth 310
Hartley, John 106
Harvey, David 408, 410
hate crime legislation 288
hate crimes 32, 178, 179, 283, 289, 293
hate speech 264
Hayek, Friedrich 73, 409, 500
Hayward, Keith 155, 170
healing 143
health care: as right 464–5, 469; universal 142
heavies 151
hedonic realism 159
hedonism 445
Hegel, G.W.F. 456
Heinzen, Karl 236
Henry, Emile 236
Henry, Stuart 117–18, 121, 125, 127, 129
Herder, Johann Gottfried 456
herd immunity 481
Hersh, Seymour 252
Hess, Rudolf 309
hijacking 241
Hill, Anita 262
Himmlers, Heinrich 309
hip-hop 230; and critical race theory 219–21,
230; criticism of 221; culture 216–19
Hirschi, Travis 61–2
Hitler, Adolf 250, 309
HIV-AIDS 32, 319, 464
Hobbes, Thomas 96, 455
Hobbs, Dick 182
Hollande, François 107
home detention 407
homelessness 75, 405; criminalization of 352
homosexuality 280, 331; official views of 280–91;
as sexual deviance 282; see also LGBTQ
movement; queer criminology
honour cultures 435
Hope Not Hate report 388, 389
Horton, Richard 339
house arrest 124
housing as right 463–4, 469
Howard, Michael 80, 81
humanism 17
human rights 112, 123, 124, 203, 466; and
abolitionism 349, 360; and surveillance 395;
and the war on terror 126
Human Rights Act (1998) 124
humiliation 151
Hunt Saboteurs Association 310, 311
Huntington, Samuel P. 102–3
Hussein, Saddam 106, 246, 250–1
hybridity 409

hypoglycaemia 48, 326
hypotheses 328–9

Ice Cube 220
Ice-T 218
Icke, David 487
iconoclasm 236
ID2020 486
identity: British 125–6; cultural 111; gender 262,
277, 279–80, 281; group 156; Islamic 125;
multi-ethnic 169; national 126, 495; negative
238; neo-tribal 185; post-neo-liberal 204;
professional 398; religious 103; social 237;
white 193
identity politics 76–7, 416, 429
identity theft 37, 178
ideoscapes 186
illegal downloading 178
illegal drug trade 34–5, 37, 145, 178, 199, 465;
in the EU 182; see also drug trafficking; war
on drugs
illegal drug use 34–5, 48–9, 53–4, 58, 137,
152, 184; and club cultures 184, 186; see also
substance abuse
illegal dumping 178
illegal file sharing 178
illegal goods and services 181–2, 184
illegal street racing 155
Ill Treatment of Horses and Cattle Bill 306
immigration 179, 501–502; backlash against 195
immigration crime 178, 183
imperialism 354
imprisonment see incarceration
incarceration: alternatives to 143; opposition to
121; in the US 404; in Western Europe 404–5;
of women 275; see also mass incarceration
incel movement 289–92
inclusion, and peacemaking criminology 139–40
income, right to acceptable 461–3, 468–9
indentured labour 38, 199
Independent Commission on International
Development Issues 192
India 497
indigenous populations 143; blamed for
crime 199–200; dispute resolution in 203;
expropriation of 194, 199; marginalization of
193; restorative justice among 206
individualism 214, 236, 428, 453; Anglo-Saxon
453, 455, 456, 457; atomistic 448, 454; and
Christian theology 453–4; and culture 456–7;
and economics 456; egotistical 448; excessive
445; French 453, 457; German 453, 454, 457;
and politics 454–6
industrialization 191, 200; capital-intensive 367;
energy-intensive 367; of farming 309; Western
192